OXFORD STUDIES IN ANCIENT DOCUMENTS

General Editors

Alison Cooley   Andrew Meadows

OXFORD STUDIES IN ANCIENT DOCUMENTS

This innovative series offers unique perspectives on the political, cultural, social, and economic history of the ancient world. Volumes include new editions and commentaries on ancient documents, interdisciplinary explorations of inscriptions and papyri, and thematic volumes that explore the boundaries of ancient documentary studies and offer new approaches to imaging, decipherment, and interpretation.

The Material Dynamics of Festivals in the Graeco-Roman East

Edited by
ZAHRA NEWBY

OXFORD
UNIVERSITY PRESS

Great Clarendon Street, Oxford, OX2 6DP,
United Kingdom

Oxford University Press is a department of the University of Oxford.
It furthers the University's objective of excellence in research, scholarship,
and education by publishing worldwide. Oxford is a registered trade mark of
Oxford University Press in the UK and in certain other countries

© Oxford University Press 2023

The moral rights of the authors have been asserted

All rights reserved. No part of this publication may be reproduced, stored in
a retrieval system, or transmitted, in any form or by any means, without the
prior permission in writing of Oxford University Press, or as expressly permitted
by law, by licence or under terms agreed with the appropriate reprographics
rights organization. Enquiries concerning reproduction outside the scope of the
above should be sent to the Rights Department, Oxford University Press, at the
address above

You must not circulate this work in any other form
and you must impose this same condition on any acquirer

Published in the United States of America by Oxford University Press
198 Madison Avenue, New York, NY 10016, United States of America

British Library Cataloguing in Publication Data
Data available

Library of Congress Control Number: 2023939083

ISBN 978–0–19–286879–4

DOI: 10.1093/oso/9780192868794.001.0001

Printed and bound by
CPI Group (UK) Ltd, Croydon, CR0 4YY

Links to third party websites are provided by Oxford in good faith and
for information only. Oxford disclaims any responsibility for the materials
contained in any third party website referenced in this work.

Preface

The idea for this volume arose from the project, *Materiality and Meaning in Greek Festival Culture of the Roman Imperial Period*, funded by a Leverhulme Trust Research Project Grant held at the University of Warwick (2017–21), with PI Zahra Newby and Researchers Dario Calomino and Naomi Carless Unwin. For funding the research for our chapters in this volume, we are all most grateful to the Leverhulme Trust.

The aims of the Leverhulme Trust project were to explore the active roles played by material culture in creating the meanings which festivals had for their participants and spectators, and to interrogate the patterns of commemoration which we find in the material culture. In order to share our findings with other scholars working on related topics, we held a panel entitled 'The spatial and material dimensions of ancient festival culture' (Proposer: Naomi Carless Unwin, Chair: Dario Calomino) at the FIEC/Classical Association joint conference held in London in July 2019. During the panel, papers were presented by Mairi Gkikaki, Zahra Newby, Sebastian Scharff, and Christina Williamson. The chapters included in this volume are expanded versions of those papers while the chapters by Dario Calomino and Naomi Carless Unwin emerge from their research on the Leverhulme project. Angelos Chaniotis was unable to attend the FIEC conference, but generously offered a paper for inclusion in the volume, while Rocío Gordillo Hervás and Paul Grigsby were also invited to contribute to the volume, given their research interests in ancient festivals.

Thus, the volume draws together both early career and established scholars from Europe and the US to interrogate the material dynamics of ancient festivals. We were particularly keen to draw on the insights of related research projects elsewhere, including the 'Connected Contests' project led by Onno van Nijf and Christina Williamson at Groningen, and the 'Token Communities' ERC grant hosted at Warwick (PI Clare Rowan) on which Mairi Gkikaki was a researcher.

Specific thanks and credits can be found in the relevant chapters, but I would like here to acknowledge a few wider debts. The Department of Classics and Ancient History at the University of Warwick has provided an excellent home for this research, and I have learnt much from my colleagues. I am particularly grateful to Dario Calomino and Naomi Carless Unwin for making our joint research such an enjoyable and stimulating process, and for their company on trips to Turkey and Greece. For acting as advisors on the Leverhulme Trust project and generously sharing their advice and comments, I am also grateful to Kevin

Butcher, Alison Cooley, and Marguerite Spoerri Butcher. Abigail Graham, Suzanne Frey-Kupper, Clare Rowan, and Michael Scott have all contributed to the thinking which lies behind this volume in various ways, and I thank them all. For their helpful comments on drafts of the volume, I am also particularly grateful to Alison Cooley, Jaś Elsner, and the anonymous readers for the press, whose comments led to the structure offered here. My thanks also go to all the contributors to the volume for their patience during the process of publication, as well as to Jacqui Butler for her help with preparation of the manuscript. For seeing the volume into press, I would also like to thank Charlotte Loveridge, Jamie Mortimer, and the wider production team at Oxford University Press.

LEVERHULME TRUST

Contents

List of Figures	ix
Abbreviations	xxiii
Contributors	xxvii

1. Introduction: The Material Worlds of Ancient Festivals — 1
   Zahra Newby

2. Establishing a Channel of Communication: Roman Emperors and the Self-Presentation of Greek Athletes in the Roman East — 26
   Sebastian Scharff

3. Agonistic Legislation in Hadrian's Time — 51
   Rocío Gordillo Hervás

4. Greek Festival Culture and 'Political' Games at Nikaia in Bithynia — 69
   Dario Calomino

5. Tokens from Roman Imperial Athens: The Power of Cultural Memory — 95
   Mairi Gkikaki

6. Festivals and the Performance of Community and Status in the Theatres at Hierapolis and Perge — 137
   Zahra Newby

7. An Epigraphic Stage: Inscriptions and the Moulding of Festival Space at Aphrodisias — 179
   Naomi Carless Unwin

8. The Artists of Dionysos and the Festivals of Boiotia — 214
   Paul Grigsby

9. Sacred Circles: Enclosed Sanctuaries and Their Festival Communities in the Hellenistic World — 250
   Christina G. Williamson

10. The Materiality of Light in Religious Celebrations and Rituals in the Roman East — 289
    Angelos Chaniotis

11. Conclusions and Future Directions — 322
    Zahra Newby

Index — 335

List of Figures

2.1. Three letters of the emperor Hadrian to the Dionysiac artists, *stele* found at Alexandria Troas, detail of the first twenty-seven lines of the first letter: the first six lines appear in larger letters. 34
Photograph: Forschungsstelle Asia Minor im Seminar für Alte Geschichte, Westfälische Wilhelms-Universität Münster, by permission of Elmar Schwertheim.

3.1. Proposed order of festivals following Hadrian's reform, as proposed in Gordillo Hervás (2017). 62

4.1. AE: Commodus, Nikaia AD 180–92 (*RGMG* I.3, 302 = *RPC* IV online 6045). BNF.945 (25 mm, 6.98 g). 76
Photograph: https://gallica.bnf.fr/ark:/12148/btv1b8556118k.

4.2. AE: Commodus, Nikaia AD 180–92 (*RGMG* I.3, 303 = *RPC* IV online 6046). BNF.947 (33 mm, 25.37 g). 76
Photograph: https://gallica.bnf.fr/ark:/12148/btv1b8556118k.

4.3. AE: Elagabalus, Nikomedia AD 218–22 (*RGMG* I.3, 278–9 = *RPC* VI online 3354). Rudolf Künker Auction 273, 14 March 2016, lot 853 (29 mm, 14.17 g); Lübke & Wiedemann KG, Leonberg. 79
Photograph by permission of Fritz Rudolf Künker GmbH & Co. KG, Osnabrück; www.kuenker.com.

4.4. AE: Valerian, Gallienus, and Valerian II, Nikomedia AD 256–8 (*RGMG* I.3, 409). NAC Auction 100, 29 May 2017, lot 1201 (26 mm, 11.78 g). 80
Photograph by permission of Arturo Russo, Numismatica Ars Classica, London.

4.5. AE: Valerian, Gallienus, and Valerian II, Nikomedia AD 256–8 (*RGMG* I.3, 413). CNG Auction 97, 17 September 2014, lot 471 (28 mm, 12.50 g). 80
Photograph by permission of Classical Numismatic Group, LLC.

4.6. AE: Valerian, Gallienus, and Valerian II, Nikaia AD 256–8 (*RGMG* I.3, 822–4). BM.1961,0301.102 (26 mm, 9.95 g). 81
Photograph: Calomino, by permission of the British Museum.

4.7. AE: Valerian, Nikaia AD 253–60 (*RGMG* I/3, 815), BM.1979,0101.1383 = *SNG von Aulock* 719 (25 mm, 7.64 g). 81
Photograph: Calomino, by permission of the British Museum.

4.8. AE: Gallienus, Nikomedia AD 253–60 (*SNG von Aulock* 7138), BM.1979,0101.1453 (25 mm, 7.96 g). 81
Photograph: Calomino, by permission of the British Museum.

4.9. AE: Valerian, Nikaia AD 253–60 (*RGMG* I/3, 808), BNF.1203 (25 mm, 8.15 g). 81
Photograph: https://gallica.bnf.fr/ark:/12148/btv1b8555658h.

4.10. AE: Julia Domna, Nikaia AD 202–7 (unpublished, cf. *RGMG* I.3, 491: Caracalla for Geta). FLK 957 (27 mm, 10.78). 85
Photograph by permission of Frank L. Kovacs.

4.11. AE: Caracalla, Nikaia AD 202–7 (*SNG von Aulock* 7040). FLK 961 (formerly UBS Gold and Numismatics 83, September 2009, lot 278 = Auctiones Basel, November 1974, lot 127: 36 mm, 28.85 g). 85
Photograph by permission of Frank L. Kovacs.

4.12. AE: Julia Domna, Nikaia AD 202–7 (unpublished; cf. *RGMG* I/3, 485 of Caracalla). Gorny & Mosch Auction 236, March 2016, lot 329 (33 mm, 26.65 g). 86
Photograph: B. Seifert/Lübke & Wiedemann, Leonberg.

4.13. AE: Caracalla, Byzantion AD 209–11 (Schönert-Geiss, *Byzantion* 1535). SMM (41 mm, 37.53 g). 87
Photograph: https://www.corpus-nummorum.eu/coins/762, by permission of Kay Ehling.

4.14. AE: Caracalla and Geta, Perinthos AD 205–9 (Schönert-Geiss, *Perinthos* 629). CNG Triton VI, 14 January 2003, lot 553 (38 mm, 24.68 g). 87
Photograph by permission of Classical Numismatic Group, LLC.

4.15. AE: Septimius Severus, Nikaia AD 202–7 (unpublished; cf. *RGMG* I/3, 397 of Julia Domna). Gorny & Mosch Auction 224, 13 October 2014, lot 360 (26.26 g). 88
Photograph: B. Seifert/Lübke & Wiedemann, Leonberg.

4.16. AE: Geta, Nikaia AD 202–7 (unpublished; cf. *RGMG* I/3, 355 of Septimius Severus). BNF.1966.453 (32 mm, 25.47 g). 88
Photograph: https://gallica.bnf.fr/ark:/12148/btv1b103118971.

4.17. AE: Geta, Nikaia AD 202–7 (*RGMG* I/3, 523). KHM.GR15649 (34 mm, 26.99 g). 89
Photograph by permission of Klaus Vondrovec.

4.18. AE: Geta, Nikaia AD 202–7 (*RGMG* I/3, 524). KHM.GR15650 (27 mm, 10.57 g). 89
Photograph by permission of Klaus Vondrovec.

4.19. AE: Septimius Severus, Nikaia AD 202–7 (*RGMG* I/3, 355). KHM.GR15606 (Slg. Tiepolo) = Calomino 2016 p. 144, fig. 64 (33 mm, 24.82 g). 90
Photograph by permission of Klaus Vondrovec.

5.1. Lead token, Numismatic Museum at Athens. Diameter 20 mm, presented here at 2:1 scale. On the left Artemis Ephesia standing frontal, on the right Hermes standing turned left holding ears of wheat in right hand and a bunch of grapes in left hand, around edge inscr. ΠΑ ΝΕΛΛΗ ΝΙ ΩΝ; Postolacca (1868), 378 no. 195, image after *Monumenti Inediti Pubblicati dall' Instituto di Corrispondenza Archeologica* 8 (1864–8), pl. LII. 98

5.2. Lead token, Numismatic Museum at Athens. Diameter 16 mm, presented here at 2:1 scale. Ship's prow right, star above, inscr. ΠΑΝΑ below;

Postolacca (1866), 352 no. 231, image after *Monumenti Inediti Pubblicati dall' Instituto di Corrispondenza Archeologica* 8 (1864–8), pl. XXXII. 99

5.3. General plan of the Agora in the second century AD with the findspots of the tokens of the Stoa of Attalos added. Courtesy of the American School of Classical Studies at Athens: Agora Excavations (PD 2671, image 2002.01.2671). 103

5.4. AE Hemidrachm, 23 mm, 10.73 g, presented here at 2:1 scale. Athena bust right: nude Theseus advancing left, brandishing club with his right hand, carrying cloak around his left arm, about to hit Minotaur, falling left, inscr. *AΘHNAIΩN*. Copenhagen 343. 107
Photograph used under CC-BY-SA. Nationalmuseet/photographer Sean Weston.

5.5. AE Hemidrachm, 25 mm, 10.85 g, presented here at 2:1 scale. Athena bust right: Themistokles standing on galley, l., wearing military dress, holding wreath and trophy; (galley with helmsman;) on ram, serpent; on prow, owl; (in water, dolphin), inscr. *AΘH*. BNF 1082. https://rpc.ashmus.ox.ac.uk/coin/198492, photograph used courtesy of BnF/Gallica. 108

5.6. Pheidias' Athena Parthenos with left hand resting on grounded spear and grounded shield. Holding small, winged Nike in right hand. Small owl perching on short column to the goddess' right flank. Border of dots. Inscribed in two columns: *ΓEP[OY]CIAC*. Cast of a uniface, lead token, 25 mm, presented here at 2:1 scale. 115
Photograph: the American School of Classical Studies Archives 2012.55.110. Courtesy of The Trustees of the American School of Classical Studies at Athens.

6.1. Copy of the *porta regia* relief of the theatre at Hierapolis, with inscriptions inked in. 141
Photograph: Newby, by permission of the Missione Archeologica Italiana a Hierapolis.

6.2. Detail of *porta regia* central panel. Hierapolis Museum. 143
Photograph: Newby, by permission of the Missione Archeologica Italiana a Hierapolis.

6.3. Relief from the balustrade of the orchestra of the theatre at Hierapolis. Hierapolis Museum. 143
Photograph: Newby, by permission of the Missione Archeologica Italiana a Hierapolis.

6.4. Coin from Hierapolis, Elagabalus on obverse, Apollo on reverse. Berlin. Münzkabinett, Staatliche Museen zu Berlin, 18223774.2. 144
Photographs by Lutz-Jürgen Lübke (Lübke und Wiedemann).

6.5. Detail of *Agonothetes*. Hierapolis Museum. 148
Photograph: Newby, by permission of the Missione Archeologica Italiana a Hierapolis.

6.6. Interior of right projection: Andreia, Synodos, Dadouchos, and Dolichos. 150
Photograph: Newby, by permission of the Missione Archeologica Italiana a Hierapolis.

xii LIST OF FIGURES

6.7. Relief showing Apollo as victor pouring a libation. Podium frieze. 152
 Photograph: Newby, by permission of the Missione Archeologica
 Italiana a Hierapolis.

6.8. *Synthusia* scene, interior of left projection. 155
 Photograph: Newby, by permission of the Missione Archeologica
 Italiana a Hierapolis.

6.9. Scene on outer face of right projection: *Synthusia*. 155
 Photograph: Newby, by permission of the Missione Archeologica
 Italiana a Hierapolis.

6.10. Reverse of a coin from Ephesos celebrating *Synthusia*. BM 1970,0909.79. 156
 Photograph: D. Calomino, by permission of the British Museum.

6.11. Relief panel of the podium of the *scenae frons*, showing worship of Artemis
 Ephesia. 158
 Photograph: Newby, by permission of the Missione Archeologica
 Italiana a Hierapolis.

6.12. Relief from the *porta regia* of the theatre at Perge. 160
 Photograph: N. Hannestad, arachne.dainst.org/entity/3122297.

6.13. Reverse of a coin minted by Perge showing the Tyche of Perge holding
 out the statuette of Artemis Pergaia; Caracalla shown on the obverse.
 BM 1979, 0101. 2385. 161
 Photograph: D. Calomino by permission of the British Museum.

6.14. Detail of *porta regia* relief, right side. 163
 Photograph: N. Hannestad, arachne.dainst.org/entity/3122297; detail.

6.15. Graffito from column on Tacitus Street, *I.Perge* 313. 166
 Photograph: S. Şahin by permission of N. Eda Akyürek Şahin.

6.16. Pentheus scene from podium frieze at Perge. Slab immediately to left of
 central *porta regia*. 168
 Photograph: Newby, by permission of Sedef Çokay Kepçe.

7.1. Aerial view of theatre. 180
 Photograph: New York University Excavations at Aphrodisias.

7.2. View of the theatre, facing east/south east. 184
 Photograph: New York University Excavations at Aphrodisias (N. Carless Unwin).

7.3. View of stage front, with Doric entablature and the dedication of Zoilos. 184
 Photograph: New York University Excavations at Aphrodisias (N. Carless Unwin).

7.4. Molossos dedication panel. 187
 Photograph: C. Roueché.

7.5. Doric entablature showing relative location of the Zoilos dedication
 and the honorific texts above. 192
 Photograph: New York University Excavations at Aphrodisias (N. Carless Unwin).

7.6. Statue and base of the boxer Kandidianos. Inv. 1967-287, 1967-28. 195
 Photograph: New York University Excavations at Aphrodisias (R. Wilkins).

7.7.	Statue and base of the boxer Piseas. Inv. 1970-508-511. Photograph: New York University Excavations at Aphrodisias (R. Wilkins).	196
7.8.	Archive Wall. Photograph: C. Roueché.	198
7.9.	Graffito of a gladiator. Photograph: C. Roueché.	204
7.10.	Muses list from the stage. Photograph: C. Roueché.	205
8.1.	Map of Central Greece, with sites mentioned in the chapter. Adapted from Corinth Archaeological Data and Basemaps by James Herbst [https://www.ascsa.edu.gr/excavations/ancient-corinth/digital-corinth/maps-gis-data-and-archaeological-data-for-corinth-and-greece] licensed under a Creative Commons Attribution-ShareAlike 4.0 International License.	216
8.2.	Altar to the Muses, once the site of Hagia Trias, looking west towards portico and theatre. Photograph: Grigsby.	226
8.3.	The sanctuary of Apollo Ptoios at modern Perdikovrysi, near Akraiphia. Photograph: Grigsby.	230
8.4.	*Stele* recording Romaia *c.* second century BC—*SEG* 54.516. Archaeological Museum of Thebes. Photograph: Grigsby, by permission of Museum of Thebes.	234
8.5.	Church of Agios Georgios, Akraiphia. Photograph: Grigsby.	242
9.1.	Festival sites in the post-classical period.	257
9.2.	Enclosed sanctuaries discussed in the text.	259
9.3.	Plan of Labraunda, after Henry (2017), figs 2, 15.	261
9.4.	Side-by-side comparison of the shrines of Zeus Soter at Megalopolis and Zeus at Dodona, after Emme (2013), 445 Taf. 57 (Megalopolis) and Gruben (1986), 113 Abb. 107 (Dodona).	262
9.5.	The Sanctuary of Meter Theon, after Conze and Schatzmann (1911), Taf. I.	264
9.6.	The Sanctuary of Asklepios on Kos, after Interdonato (2016), 171 fig. 10.1.	265
9.7.	The Sanctuary of Artemis Leukophryena and the Hellenistic *agora* of Magnesia on the Maeander, after Hammerschmied (2018), 99 fig. 2.	268
9.8.	The theoric network of Magnesia, based on *I.Magnesia* 17-87.	270
9.9.	Plan of the sanctuary complex of Hekate at Lagina by the first century BC, after Gider (2012), 274 fig. 1.	272
9.10.	The theoric network of Lagina, based on *I.Stratonikeia* 508.	274
9.11.	Plan of the *temenos* of Men Askaenos, after Mitchell and Waelkens (1998), 40 fig. 6.	276

10.1. Clay lamp from Egypt (*c.* AD 150–250), decorated with a relief of Serapis with a staff in one hand and a wreath in the other; a lamb is at his feet. 3.9 × 9.4 × 6.7 cm. 298
Photograph: Artokolo/Alamy Stock Photo, Image ID: 2B0E2D0.

10.2. Bronze lamp associated with the cult of Theos Hypsistos (imperial period). Of unknown provenance, in the antiquities marker. *Antike Kunst und Fossilien. Auktion 6.6.2000, Palais Dorotheum, Wien*, 105 no. 256. 299
Photograph: Norbert Franken (cf. Franken (2002), 380–1 fig. 9).

10.3. Column with holes, possibly for the suspension of a lamp (imperial period). Aphrodisias, Place of Palms, north portico. 301
Photograph: Chaniotis.

10.4. Column with holes, possibly for the suspension of a lamp (imperial period). Laodikeia on the Lykos, colonnaded street. 302
Photograph: Chaniotis.

10.5. The cult cave of Zeus on Mount Ida (Idaion Antron). 307
Photograph: Efi Sapouna-Sakellaraki.

Appendix of Token Types in Chapter 5

1. Three masks on altars, inscription in two lines ΘΕΟΦΟΡΟΥ ΜΕΝΗ; the whole in dotted circle 20 mm in diameter. Uniface, lead token, 27 mm. Ancient Agora of Athens Museum IL1313. Ephorate of Antiquities of Athens City, Ancient Agora, ASCSA: Agora Excavations. © Hellenic Ministry of Culture and Sports-Hellenic Organization of Cultural Resources Development (H.O.C.RE.D.). Published: Crosby (1964), 122 L329 pl. 30. https://coins.warwick.ac.uk/token-specimens/id/agorail1313.

2-1. Crested Corinthian helmet right; two stars below; in field right an owl. Countermark of cock and lizard or mouse lower left. Lead token, 24 mm. Ancient Agora of Athens Museum IL1119 Ephorate of Antiquities of Athens City, Ancient Agora, ASCSA: Agora Excavations. © Hellenic Ministry of Culture and Sports-Hellenic Organization of Cultural Resources Development (H.O.C.RE.D.). Published: Crosby (1964), 122 L28. https://coins.warwick.ac.uk/token-specimens/id/agorail1119.

2-2. Side a: Bull standing left; in field lower left uncertain small object; above star or single letter. Side b: Crested Corinthian helmet right; two stars below; in field right an owl. Lead token, 20 mm. Ancient Agora of Athens Museum IL1238. Ephorate of Antiquities of Athens City, Ancient Agora, ASCSA: Agora Excavations. © Hellenic Ministry of Culture and Sports-Hellenic Organization of Cultural Resources Development (H.O.C.RE.D.). Published: Crosby 1964, 121 L324 pl. 30. https://agora.ascsa.net/research?v=list&q=IL1238.

3. Asklepios seated left, two countermarks of stork and lizard. Uniface, lead token, 23 mm. Ancient Agora of Athens Museum IL1110. Ephorate of Antiquities of Athens City, Ancient Agora, ASCSA: Agora Excavations. © Hellenic Ministry of Culture and Sports-Hellenic Organization of Cultural Resources Development (H.O.C.RE.D.). Published: Crosby (1964), 117 L299 pl. 30. https://coins.warwick.ac.uk/token-specimens/id/agorail1110.

4. Asklepios and Hygieia facing each other with small figure of Telesphoros in between. Letters (no longer visible) around edge from left to right, ΕΥΤΥΧΗΣ. Countermark, probably of cock and lizard. Uniface, lead token, 31 mm. Ancient Agora of Athens Museum IL384. Ephorate of Antiquities of Athens City, Ancient Agora, ASCSA: Agora Excavations. © Hellenic Ministry of Culture and Sports-Hellenic Organization of Cultural Resources Development (H.O.C.RE.D.). Published: Crosby (1964), 117 L300 pl. 20. https://coins.warwick.ac.uk/token-specimens/id/agorail384.

5-1. Side a: Athena moving to her left with shield on left arm; olive tree to her right; in front lower right a snake; the whole in dotted circle 19 mm in diameter. It is overstruck with a stamp of Herakles and tripod (14-2). Side b: Standing draped figure facing left with right arm outstretched; wheel at lower left; in field right, snake, star, and traces of wing or second figure. Lead token, 23 mm. Ancient Agora of Athens Museum IL1109. Ephorate of Antiquities of Athens City, Ancient Agora, ASCSA: Agora Excavations. © Hellenic Ministry of Culture and Sports-Hellenic Organization of Cultural Resources Development (H.O.C.RE.D.). Published: Crosby (1964), 117 L301 pl. 30.

xvi   APPENDIX OF TOKEN TYPES IN CHAPTER 5

6. Athena at right with spear in left hand, Nike approaching from left with wreath; the whole in border of dots 18 mm in diameter. Two countermarks probably of cock and lizard or mouse. Lead token, 25 mm. Ancient Agora of Athens Museum IL1202. Ephorate of Antiquities of Athens City, Ancient Agora, ASCSA: Agora Excavations. © Hellenic Ministry of Culture and Sports-Hellenic Organization of Cultural Resources Development (H.O.C.RE.D.). Published: Crosby (1964), 118 L304 pl. 30. https://agora.ascsa.net/research?v=list&q=IL1202.

7-1. Athena bust in high crested attic helmet; the whole in dotted circle 17–18 mm in diameter. Two countermarks of snail and rabbit. Uniface, lead token, 22–25mm. Ancient Agora of Athens Museum IL1116. Ephorate of Antiquities of Athens City, Ancient Agora, ASCSA: Agora Excavations. © Hellenic Ministry of Culture and Sports-Hellenic Organization of Cultural Resources Development (H.O.C.RE.D.). Published: Crosby (1964), 118 L306 pl. 30. https://coins.warwick.ac.uk/token-specimens/id/agorail1116.

7-2. Side a: Athena bust in high crested attic helmet; the whole in dotted circle 17–18 mm in diameter. Side b: Theseus at right, raising sword above his head, the Minotaur falling to left, star in field, the whole in dotted circle 17 mm in diameter. Lead token, 20 mm. Ancient Agora of Athens Museum IL1326. Ephorate of Antiquities of Athens City, Ancient Agora, ASCSA: Agora Excavations. © Hellenic Ministry of Culture and Sports-Hellenic Organization of Cultural Resources Development (H.O.C.RE.D.). Published: Crosby (1964), 118 L305 pl. 30. https://coins.warwick.ac.uk/token-specimens/id/agorail1326.

8. Side a: Bust of Athena in crested Corinthian helmet; in field a star; lower right prow of ship, the whole in doted circle 14 mm in diameter. Side b: Bust of Poseidon right, in field right trident with dolphin entwined around it, the whole in dotted circle 16 mm in diameter. Lead token, 22 mm. Ancient Agora of Athens Museum IL396. Ephorate of Antiquities of Athens City, Ancient Agora, ASCSA: Agora Excavations. © Hellenic Ministry of Culture and Sports-Hellenic Organization of Cultural Resources Development (H.O.C.RE.D.). Published: Crosby (1964), 118 L307 pl. 30. https://coins.warwick.ac.uk/token-specimens/id/agorail396.

9-1. Side a: Head of Athena right in crested Corinthian helmet; the whole in border of dots 17 mm in diameter. Side b: Bull standing left; in field lower left uncertain small object; above star or single letter. Lead token 18–20 mm. Ancient Agora of Athens Museum IL1333. Ephorate of Antiquities of Athens City, Ancient Agora, ASCSA: Agora Excavations. © Hellenic Ministry of Culture and Sports-Hellenic Organization of Cultural Resources Development (H.O.C.RE.D.). Published: Crosby (1964), 118 L309 pl. 30. https://agora.ascsa.net/research?v=list&q=IL1333.

9-2. Side a: Head of Athena right in crested Corinthian helmet; the whole in dotted circle 17 mm in diameter. Side b: Tyche, draped, standing, facing, head left, modius on head, cornucopiae in left hand, rudder in right hand; in field right, palm branch; lower left uncertain object; the whole in dotted circle 14 mm in diameter. Lead token, 28 mm. Ancient Agora of Athens Museum IL554. Ephorate of Antiquities of Athens City, Ancient Agora, ASCSA: Agora Excavations. © Hellenic Ministry of Culture and Sports-Hellenic Organization of Cultural Resources Development (H.O.C.RE.D.).Published: Crosby (1964), 118 L308. https://coins.warwick.ac.uk/token-specimens/id/agorail554.

APPENDIX OF TOKEN TYPES IN CHAPTER 5   xvii

10-1. Helios in spread quadriga; whip in right hand, reins in left; the whole in dotted circle 15 mm in diameter. Uniface, lead token, 22 mm. Ancient Agora of Athens Museum IL409. Ephorate of Antiquities of Athens City, Ancient Agora, ASCSA: Agora Excavations. © Hellenic Ministry of Culture and Sports-Hellenic Organization of Cultural Resources Development (H.O.C.RE.D.). Published: Crosby (1964), 119 L311. https://coins.warwick.ac.uk/token-specimens/id/agorail409.

10-2. Side a: Helios in spread quadriga; whip in right hand, reins in left; the whole in dotted circle 15 mm in diameter. Side b: Selene/Luna in biga drawn by bulls, left; small wings or scarf on shoulder, torch in right hand, reins in left; in field three stars, one above, two below; the whole in dotted circle 16 mm in diameter. Lead token, 21 mm. Ancient Agora of Athens Museum IL523. Ephorate of Antiquities of Athens City, Ancient Agora, ASCSA: Agora Excavations. © Hellenic Ministry of Culture and Sports-Hellenic Organization of Cultural Resources Development (H.O.C.RE.D.). Published: Crosby (1964), 119 L312 pl. 30. https://coins.warwick.ac.uk/token-specimens/id/agorail523.

11. Side a: Helios bust rayed; protom of horse in field lower left, palm branch in field right; the whole in dotted circle 12 mm in diameter. Side b: Uncertain representation. Lead token, 19 mm. Ancient Agora of Athens Museum IL1323. Ephorate of Antiquities of Athens City, Ancient Agora, ASCSA: Agora Excavations. © Hellenic Ministry of Culture and Sports-Hellenic Organization of Cultural Resources Development (H.O.C.RE.D.). Published: Crosby (1964) 119 L313 pl. 30. https://coins.warwick.ac.uk/token-specimens/id/agorail1323.

12. Male, bearded head right, the whole in dotted circle. Uniface, lead token, depicted in gravure, published: Mylonas (1901), 121 no. 7 pl. 7.

13. Side a: Head of Hephaistos left with close fitting pointed cap; tongs in field left, hammer (?) in field right; the whole in dotted circle 16 mm in diameter. Side b: Themistokles facing front standing on small ship right; uncertain object in left hand; two dolphins (?) below ship. Lead token, 21 mm. Ancient Agora of Athens Museum IL1118. Ephorate of Antiquities of Athens City, Ancient Agora, ASCSA: Agora Excavations. © Hellenic Ministry of Culture and Sports-Hellenic Organization of Cultural Resources Development (H.O.C.RE.D.). Published: Crosby (1964), 119 L314 pl. 30. https://coins.warwick.ac.uk/token-specimens/id/agorail1118.

14-1. Herakles, laureate (?) seated left on rock, facing a tripod, from which a snake arises; uncertain object in right hand; the whole in dotted circle 17 mm in diameter. Uniface lead token, 24 mm. Ancient Agora of Athens Museum IL1090. Ephorate of Antiquities of Athens City, Ancient Agora, ASCSA: Agora Excavations. © Hellenic Ministry of Culture and Sports-Hellenic Organization of Cultural Resources Development (H.O.C.RE.D.) Published: Crosby (1964), 119 L315. https://agora.ascsa.net/research?v=list&q=IL1090.

14-2. Herakles, laureate (?) seated left on rock, facing a tripod, from which a snake arises; uncertain object in right hand; the whole in dotted circle 17 mm in diameter, with countermark of cock and lizard at 12 o'clock approximately. Uniface lead token, 25 mm. Ancient Agora of Athens Museum IL1249. Ephorate of Antiquities of Athens City, Ancient Agora, ASCSA: Agora Excavations. © Hellenic Ministry of Culture and Sports-Hellenic Organization of Cultural Resources Development

(H.O.C.RE.D.) Published: Crosby (1964), 119 L315. https://agora.ascsa.net/research?v=list&q=IL1249.

14-3. Side a: Herakles, laureate (?) seated left on rock, facing a tripod, from which a snake arises; uncertain object in right hand; the whole in dotted circle 17 mm in diameter. Side b: Bust of youth left with long face and flat back of the head, probably a portrait of Commodus, club in field behind; the whole in dotted circle 17 mm in diameter. Lead token, 21 mm. Ancient Agora of Athens Museum IL1244. Ephorate of Antiquities of Athens City, Ancient Agora, ASCSA: Agora Excavations. © Hellenic Ministry of Culture and Sports-Hellenic Organization of Cultural Resources Development (H.O.C.RE.D.) Published: Crosby (1964), 119 L315 https://coins.warwick.ac.uk/token-specimens/id/agorail1244.

14-4. Face a: Herakles, laureate (?) seated left on rock, facing a tripod, from which a snake arises; uncertain object in right hand; the whole in dotted circle 17 mm in diameter. Face b: Three countermarks: cock holding a lizard by the tail, snail and rabbit, a plump pitcher or an owl. Lead tokens, 25 mm (for IL1322) and 22 mm (for IL584). Ancient Agora of Athens Museum, IL1322 is depicted for face a and Agora Museum IL584 for face b. Ephorate of Antiquities of Athens City, Ancient Agora, ASCSA: Agora Excavations. © Hellenic Ministry of Culture and Sports-Hellenic Organization of Cultural Resources Development (H.O.C.RE.D.) Published: Crosby (1964), 120 L317 pl. 30.

15-1. Bust of Minotaur, head left. Countermark of stork and lizard. Uniface, lead token, 20 mm. Ancient Agora of Athens Museum IL1329. Ephorate of Antiquities of Athens City, Ancient Agora, ASCSA: Agora Excavations. © Hellenic Ministry of Culture and Sports-Hellenic Organization of Cultural Resources Development (H.O.C.RE.D.) Published: Crosby (1964), 122 L327. https://agora.ascsa.net/research?v=list&q=IL1329.

15-2. Side a: Bearded Herakles head right, club in field behind; the whole in border of dots 15 mm in diameter. Side b: Bust of Minotaur, half left; in field at either side a star; the whole in border of dots 15 mm in diameter. Ancient Agora of Athens Museum IL501. Ephorate of Antiquities of Athens City, Ancient Agora, ASCSA: Agora Excavations. © Hellenic Ministry of Culture and Sports-Hellenic Organization of Cultural Resources Development (H.O.C.RE.D.) Published: Crosby (1964), 120 L318 pl. 30. https://coins.warwick.ac.uk/token-specimens/id/agorail501.

16-1. Dionysos seated right on throne, staff in left hand, uncertain object in right. In field left, kantharos and crescent; lower right, thyrsus or cluster of graphes. Letters around edge from left to right: *IEPAC ΓEPOYCIAC* (not legible on this specimen), in exergue right to left *ΚΛΩ* (not legible on this specimen; a countermark of cock at approx. 7 o'clock. Uniface, lead token, 23 mm. Ancient Agora of Athens Museum IL1111. Ephorate of Antiquities of Athens City, Ancient Agora, ASCSA: Agora Excavations. © Hellenic Ministry of Culture and Sports-Hellenic Organization of Cultural Resources Development (H.O.C.RE.D.) Published: Crosby (1964), 118 L310 pl. 30. https://agora.ascsa.net/research?v=list&q=IL1111.

16-2. Dionysos seated right on throne, staff in left hand, uncertain object in right. In field left, kantharos and crescent; lower right, thyrsus or cluster. Letters around edge from left to right: *IEPAC ΓEPOYCIAC* (only the lower part of the letters visible on this specimen), in exergue right to left *KΛΩ*; a countermark of cock holding a lizard or mouse at approx. 7 o'clock. Uniface, lead token, 25 mm. Ancient Agora of Athens Museum IL1112. Ephorate of Antiquities of Athens City, Ancient Agora, ASCSA: Agora Excavations. © Hellenic Ministry of Culture and Sports-Hellenic Organization of Cultural Resources Development (H.O.C.RE.D.) Published: Crosby (1964), 118 L310 pl. 30. https://agora.ascsa.net/research?v=list&q=IL1112.

16-2. Dionysos seated right on throne, staff in left hand, uncertain object in right. In field left, kantharos and crescent; lower right, thyrsus or cluster. Letters around edge from left to right: *IEPAC ΓEPOYCIAC*, in exergue right to left *KΛΩ*; a countermark of cock at approx. 2 o'clock and a countermark of cock holding a lizard or mouse at approx. 7 o'clock. Uniface, lead token, 29 mm. Ancient Agora of Athens Museum IL1113. Ephorate of Antiquities of Athens City, Ancient Agora, ASCSA: Agora Excavations. © Hellenic Ministry of Culture and Sports-Hellenic Organization of Cultural Resources Development (H.O.C.RE.D.) Published: Crosby (1964), 118 L310 pl. 30. https://coins.warwick.ac.uk/token-specimens/id/agoraiI1113.

17-1. Side a: Zeus seated left on throne, Nike in right hand, staff in left; in field right thunderbolt, left star, crescent below throne; the whole in dotted circle 17 mm in diameter. Side b: Nude Nike in biga drawn to left by horses, whip in right hand; in field upper right star; wavy ground line; the whole in dotted circle 16 mm in diameter. Lead token, 21 mm. Ancient Agora of Athens Museum IL1107. Ephorate of Antiquities of Athens City, Ancient Agora, ASCSA: Agora Excavations. © Hellenic Ministry of Culture and Sports-Hellenic Organization of Cultural Resources Development (H.O.C.RE.D.) Published: Crosby (1964), 121 L323 pl. 30. https://coins.warwick.ac.uk/token-specimens/id/agoraiI1107.

18-1a. Serapis standing, semi-draped, wearing modius, head left, right arm raised, staff in left hand; in field right crested serpent, left scrolls; a countermark of stork and lizard at approx. 6 o'clock. Uniface, lead token, 18–22 mm. Ancient Agora of Athens Museum IL1342. Ephorate of Antiquities of Athens City, Ancient Agora, ASCSA: Agora Excavations. © Hellenic Ministry of Culture and Sports-Hellenic Organization of Cultural Resources Development (H.O.C.RE.D.)Published: Crosby (1964), 120 L319. https://agora.ascsa.net/research?v=list&q=IL1342.

18-1b. Side a: Serapis standing, semi-draped, wearing modius, head left, right arm raised, staff in left hand; in field right crested serpent, left scrolls. Side b: countermark of stork (?) and lizard in centre of face b. Lead token, 22 mm. Ancient Agora of Athens Museum IL1106. Ephorate of Antiquities of Athens City, Ancient Agora, ASCSA: Agora Excavations. © Hellenic Ministry of Culture and Sports-Hellenic Organization of Cultural Resources Development (H.O.C.RE.D.) Published: Crosby (1964), 120 L319. https://agora.ascsa.net/research?v=list&q=IL1106.

18-1c. Serapis standing, semi-draped, wearing modius, head left, right arm raised, staff in left hand; in field right crested serpent, left scrolls; a countermark of stork (?) and lizard at approx. 6 o'clock and another countermark of stork and lizard at approx. 3 o'clock. Uniface, lead token, 21 mm. Ancient Agora of Athens Museum IL1252.

Ephorate of Antiquities of Athens City, Ancient Agora, ASCSA: Agora Excavations. © Hellenic Ministry of Culture and Sports-Hellenic Organization of Cultural Resources Development (H.O.C.RE.D.). Published: Crosby (1964), 120 L319. https://agora.ascsa.net/research?v=list&q=IL1252.

18-2a. Side a: Serapis standing, semi-draped, wearing modius, head left, right arm raised, staff in left hand; in field right crested serpent, left scrolls. Side b: Bearded Triton with fish-tail legs, dolphin on outstretched right hand, trident in left; around edge letters: *ΠΟCEI*; the whole in dotted circle 15 mm in diameter. Lead token, 21 mm. Ancient Agora of Athens Museum IL1103. Ephorate of Antiquities of Athens City, Ancient Agora, ASCSA: Agora Excavations. © Hellenic Ministry of Culture and Sports-Hellenic Organization of Cultural Resources Development (H.O.C.RE.D.). Published: Crosby (1964), 120 L320 pl. 30. https://agora.ascsa.net/research?v=list&q=IL1103.

18-2b. Side a: Serapis standing, semi-draped, wearing modius, head left, right arm raised, staff in left hand; in field right crested serpent, left scrolls. Side b: Bearded Triton with fish-tail legs, dolphin on outstretched right hand, trident in left; around edge letters: *ΠΟCEI*; the whole in dotted circle 15 mm in diameter; a countermark of cock and mouse at approx. 6 o'clock. Lead token, 18–22 mm. Ancient Agora of Athens Museum IL1104. © Hellenic Ministry of Culture and Sports-Hellenic Organization of Cultural Resources Development (H.O.C.RE.D.). Published: Crosby (1964), 120 L320 pl. 30. https://agora.ascsa.net/research?v=list&q=IL1104.

18-2c. Side a: Serapis standing, semi-draped, wearing modius, head left, right arm raised, staff in left hand; in field right crested serpent, left scrolls; a countermark of cock and mouse at approx. 6 o'clock and another countermark (illegible) at 3 o'clock. Side b: Bearded Triton with fish-tail legs, dolphin on outstretched right hand, trident in left; around edge letters: *ΠΟCEI*; the whole in dotted circle 15 mm in diameter; a countermark of cock and mouse at approx. 6 o'clock. Lead token, depicted in gravure, published: Mylonas (1901), 121 no. 13 pl. 7.

18-3. Side a: Serapis standing, semi-draped, wearing modius, head left, right arm raised, staff in left hand; in field right crested serpent, left scrolls. Side b: Five petalled rosette; countermark of cock/stork and lizard. Lead token 25 mm. Ancient Agora of Athens Museum IL429. © Hellenic Ministry of Culture and Sports-Hellenic Organization of Cultural Resources Development (H.O.C.RE.D.). Published: Crosby (1964), 121 L321 pl. 30 https://coins.warwick.ac.uk/token-specimens/id/agorail429.

19. Side a: Tyche draped, standing, facing, head left, cornucopiae in left hand, rudder in right hand; in field right, palm branch; lower left uncertain object; the whole in dotted circle 14 mm in diameter. Side b: Alexander the Great head left. Lead token, 17 mm. Ancient Agora of Athens Museum IL539. © Hellenic Ministry of Culture and Sports-Hellenic Organization of Cultural Resources Development (H.O.C.RE.D.). Published: Crosby (1964), 121 L322 pl. 30. https://agora.ascsa.net/research?v=list&q=IL539.

20. Eagle standing left, head turned back, wreath (?) in beak; in field right filleted boukranion; left star; lower left branch. Uniface, lead token, 19 mm. Ancient Agora of Athens Museum IL1092. © Hellenic Ministry of Culture and Sports-Hellenic

Organization of Cultural Resources Development (H.O.C.RE.D.). Published: Crosby (1964), 121-2 L325 pl. 30. https://coins.warwick.ac.uk/token-specimens/id/agorail1092.

21. Lion's head with open mouth right. Inscription around edge in front of head *ΛΗΜΝΙΟ*; The whole in dotted circle 14 mm in diameter; countermark of cock and mouse at approx. 1 o'clock. Uniface, lead token, 18 mm. Ancient Agora of Athens Museum IL1317. © Hellenic Ministry of Culture and Sports-Hellenic Organization of Cultural Resources Development (H.O.C.RE.D.). Published: Crosby (1964), 122 L326 pl. 30. https://agora.ascsa.net/research?v=list&q=IL1317.

22. Group of symbols: at bottom dolphin swimming right with poppy head at right; ear of wheat at left; at upper right a kantharos with bird standing right in cup; star at top; the whole in dotted circle 17 mm in diameter. Uniface, lead token, 21-3 mm. Ancient Agora of Athens Museum IL1114. © Hellenic Ministry of Culture and Sports-Hellenic Organization of Cultural Resources Development (H.O.C.RE.D.). Published: Crosby (1964), 122 L330 pl. 30. https://agora.ascsa.net/research?v=list&q=IL1114.

Abbreviations

Agora XV	B. D. Meritt and J. S. Traill. *The Athenian Agora*, XV. *Inscriptions. The Athenian Councillors.* Princeton, 1974.
BCH	*Bulletin de Correspondance Hellénique. Paris.*
BE	*Bulletin épigraphique* in *Revue des études grecques*. Paris, 1888–.
BGU	*Aegyptische Urkunden aud den Koniglichen (later Staatlichen) Museen zu Berlin, Greischische Urkunden.* Berlin.
BMC	P. Gardner, B. V. Head, G. F. Hill, R. S. Poole, and W. Wroth. *Catalogue of Greek Coins. The British Museum Collection.* London, 1873–1927.
BNF	Bibliothèque Nationale de France. Cabinet des Médailles.
BM	British Museum.
CGRN	J.-M. Carbon, S. Peels, and V. Pirenne-Delforge. *A Collection of Greek Ritual Norms (CGRN)*, University of Liège, 2017–. http://cgrn.ulg.ac.be/.
CID	*Corpus des inscriptions de Delphes.* Paris, 1977–.
CIG	*Corpus inscriptionum Graecarum.* Berlin, 1828–77.
CIL	*Corpus inscriptionum Latinarum.* Berlin, 1863–.
CNG	Classical Numismatic Group.
Corinth VIII 3	J. H. Kent. *Corinth*, VIII.3. *The Inscriptions 1926–1950.* Princeton, 1966.
Ebert, *Sieger*	J. Ebert. *Griechische Epigramme auf Sieger an gymnischen und hippischen Agonen.* Berlin, 1972.
F.Delphes III	*Fouilles de Delphes*, III. *Épigraphie.* Paris, 1909–85.
FGrH	F. Jacoby. *Die Fragmente der griechischen Historiker.* Berlin, 1923–.
FLK	Frank L. Kovacs Collection.
Franke-Nollé	P. R. Franke and M. K. Nollé. *Die Homonoia-Münzen Kleinasiens und der thrakischen Randgebiete.* Saarbrücker, 1997.
Frg. Rose	V. Rose. *Aristotelis qui ferebantur librorum fragmenta.* Leipzig, 1886.
I.Prusias	W. Ameling. *Die Inschriften von Prusias ad Hypium* (Inschriften griechischer Städte aus Kleinasien 27). Bonn, 1985.
I.Aphrodisias 2007	J. Reynolds, C. Roueché, and G. Bodard (eds). *Inscriptions of Aphrodisias.* 2007. https://insaph.kcl.ac.uk/insaph/iaph2007/
I.Aphrodisias and Rome	J. Reynolds. *Aphrodisias and Rome.* London, 1982.
I.Aphrodisias Late Ant.[2]	C. Roueché. *Aphrodisias in Late Antiquity. The Late Roman and Byzantine Inscriptions.* Revised second edition, 2004. https://insaph.kcl.ac.uk/ala2004.
I.Aphrodisias Performers	C. Roueché. *Performers and Partisans at Aphrodisias in the Roman and Late Roman Periods: A Study Based on Inscriptions from the Current Excavations at Aphrodisias in Caria.* London, 1993.

I.Cos Segre   M. Segre. *Iscrizioni di Cos*, I–III. Rome, 1993.
I.Cret.   M. Guarducci. *Inscriptiones Creticae*, I–IV. Rome, 1950–3.
I.Délos   F. Durrbach. *Inscriptions de Délos*. Paris, 1926–37.
I.Delphinion   Milet, I 3. *Das Delphinion in Milet*. Berlin, 1914.
I.Didyma   A. Rehm. *Didyma*, II. *Die Inschriften*, ed. R. Harder. Berlin, 1958.
I.Eleusis   K. Clinton. *Eleusis. The Inscriptions on Stone. Documents of the Sanctuary of the Two Goddesses and Public Documents of the Deme*, I A, I B, II. Athens, 2005–8.
I.Ephesos   H. Wankel and R. Merkelbach, et al. *Die Inschriften von Ephesos*, I–VII (Inschriften griechischer Städte aus Kleinasien 11–17). Bonn, 1979–84.
I.Ilion   P. Frisch. *Die Inschriften von Ilion* (Inschriften griechischer Städte aus Kleinasien 3). Bonn, 1975.
I.Kalchedon   R. Merkelbach. *Die Inschriften von Kalchedon*, ed. with help from F. K. Dörner and S. Şahin (Inschriften griechischer Städte aus Kleinasien 20). Bonn, 1980.
I.Labraunda   J. Crampa. *Labraunda. Swedish Excavations and Researches*, III, 1/2. *Greek Inscriptions I–II*. Lund, 1969–72.
I.Laodikeia Lykos   T. Corsten. *Die Inschriften von Laodikeia am Lykos*, I (Inschriften griechischer Städte aus Kleinasien 49). Bonn, 1997.
I.Leukopetra   P. M. Petsas et al. *Inscriptions du sanctuaire de la Mère des Dieux autochthone de Leukopetra (Macédoine)*. Athens, 2000.
I.Magnesia   O. Kern. *Die Inschriften von Magnesia am Maeander*. Berlin, 1900.
I.Milet   Milet, VI. *Inschriften von Milet*, 1–3. Berlin, 1997–2006.
I.Mus.Iznik   S. Şahin. *Katalog der antiken Inschriften des Museums von Iznik (Nikaia)*, I–II, 1–3. Inschriften griechischer Städte aus Kleinasien 9-10.1-3. Bonn, 1979–87.
I.Mylasa   W. Blümel. *Die Inschriften von Mylasa*, I–II. Inschriften griechischer Städte aus Kleinasien 34–5. Bonn, 1987–8.
I.Olympia   W. Dittenberger and K. Purgold. *Die Inschriften von Olympia*. Berlin, 1896.
I.Olympia Suppl.   P. Siewert and H. Taeuber. *Neue Inschriften von Olympia. Die ab 1896 veröffentlichten Texte* (Tyche Sonderband 7). Vienna, 2013.
I.Oropos   B. C. Petrakos. Οἱ ἐπιγραφὲς τοῦ Ὠρωποῦ. Athens, 1997.
I.Pergamon   M. Fraenkel. *Altertümer von Pergamon*, VIII. *Die Inschriften von Pergamon*, 1–2. Berlin, 1890–5.
I.Pergamon Asklepieion C. Habicht. *Altertümer von Pergamon*, VIII. 3. *Die Inschriften des Asklepieions*. Berlin, 1969.
I.Perge   S. Şahin. *Die Inschriften von Perge*. Inschriften griechischer Städte aus Kleinasien 54, 61. Bonn, 1999, 2004.
I.Sardis   W. H. Buckler and D. M. Robinson. *Sardis*, VII. *Greek and Latin Inscriptions*. Leiden, 1932.
I.Sestos   J. Krauss. *Die Inschriften von Sestos und der thrakischen Chersones*. Inschriften griechischer Städte aus Kleinasien 19. Bonn, 1980.

I.Sinope	D. H. French. *The Inscriptions of Sinope*, I. Inschriften griechischer Städte aus Kleinasien 64. Bonn, 2004.
I.Smyrna	G. Petzl. *Die Inschriften von Smyrna*, I-II 1/2. Inschriften griechischer Städte aus Kleinasien 23-24 1/2. Bonn, 1982-90.
I.Stratonikeia	M. Ç. Şahin. *Die Inschriften von Stratonikeia*, I-II, 1/2. Inschriften griechischer Städte aus Kleinasien 21-22 1/2, 68. Bonn, 1981-2010.
I.Thespies	P. Roesch. *Les inscriptions de Thespies*. Electronic second edition. Lyon, 2009. https://www.hisoma.mom.fr/production-scientifique/les-inscriptions-de-thespies.
I.Tralleis	F. B. Poljakos. *Die Inschriften von Tralleis und Nysa*, I. *Die Inschriften von Tralleis*. Inschriften griechischer Städte aus Kleinasien 36.1. Bonn, 1989.
IAG	L. Moretti. *Iscrizioni agonistiche greche*. Rome, 1953.
IG	*Inscriptiones Graecae*. Berlin, 1873-.
IG Napoli	E. Miranda. *Iscrizioni greche d'Italia, Napoli*. 2 vols. Rome, 1990-5.
IGBulg	*Inscriptiones Graecae in Bulgaria repertae*. Sofia, 1956-97.
IGLS	Inscriptions grecques et latines de la Syrie. Paris, 1929-.
IGR	*Inscriptiones graecae ad res romanas pertinentes*. Paris, 1906-27.
IGUR	L. Moretti. *Inscriptiones Graecae Urbis Romae*. Rome, 1968-90.
ILS	H. Dessau. *Inscriptiones Latinae selectae*. Berlin, 1892-1916.
IMT	M. Barth and J. Stauber. *Inschriften Mysia und Troas*. Munich, 1993.
KHM	Kunsthistorisches Museum Vienna.
LBW	P. Le Bas and W. H. Waddington. *Voyage archéologique en Grèce et en Asie Mineure, fait par ordre du gouvernement français pendant les années 1843 et 1844*, III. *Inscriptions grecques et latines*. Paris, 1870.
LSJ	H. G. Liddell and R. Scott. *A Greek-English Lexicon*. Revised by H. S. Jones. Oxford, 1996.
MAMA	*Monumenta Asiae Minoris Antiqua*, I-XI. London, 1928-2013.
Mionnet IV	T. Mionnet. *Description de Médailles antiques grecques et romaines*, IV. Paris, 1809.
Moretti, *Olympionikai*	L. Moretti. *Olympionikai. I vincitori negli antichi agoni olimpici*. Rome, 1957.
NAC	Numismatica Ars Classica, London.
OGIS	W. Dittenberger. *Orientis graeci inscriptiones selectae*. Leipzig, 1903-5.
PAA	J. S. Trail. *Persons of Ancient Athens*. Vols. 1-23. Toronto. 1994-2021.
PIR	*Prosopographica Imperii Romani*.
POxy	*The Oxyrhynchus Papyri*.
POxy Hels	H. Zilliacus et al. *Fifty Oxyrhynchus Papyri*. Helsinki, 1979.
RGMG	E. Babelon, T. Reinach, and W. H. Waddington. *Recueil Général des monnaies grecques d'Asie Mineure*. Paris, 1910-25.
RIC	H. Mattingly et al. *The Roman Imperial Coinage*, I-X. London, 1923-94.

Robert, OMS	L. Robert. *Opera minora selecta*, I–VII. Amsterdam, 1969–90.
RPC	A. Burnett, M. Amandry, et al. *Roman Provincial Coinage*, I–X. London and Paris, 1992–.
Schönert-Geiss, *Byzantion*	E. Schönert-Geiss. *Die Münzprägung von Byzantion*. Berlin, 1972.
Schönert-Geiss, *Perinthos*	E. Schönert-Geiss. *Die Münzprägung von Perinthos*. Berlin, 1965.
SEG	*Supplementum Epigraphicum Graecum*. Leiden, 1923–.
SMM	Staatliche Münzsammlung, Munich.
SNG Fitzwilliam	*Sylloge Nummorum Graecorum. Fitzwilliam Museum, Part 7. Asia Minor: Lycia–Cappadocia*. London, 1967.
SNG Levante	*Sylloge Nummorum Graecorum. Switzerland. The Levante Collection*, I. *Cilicia*. Berne, 1986.
SNG Paris	Sylloge Nummorum Graecorum. France, Cabinet des Médailles, Bibliothéque Nationale. Paris, 1993–2001.
SNG von Aulock	*Sylloge Nummorum Graecorum. Deutchland, Sammlung v. Aulock*. 18 vols. Berlin, 1957–68.
Sydenham	E. Sydenham. *The Coinage of Caesarea in Cappadocia*, with supplement by A. Malloy. New York, 1968.
Syll.³	W. Dittenberger. *Sylloge inscriptionum graecarum*. 3rd edition. Leipzig, 1915–24.
TAM	*Tituli Asiae Minoris*. Vindobonae, 1901–.

Contributors

Dario Calomino is Associate Professor of Numismatics in the Department of Cultures and Civilisations at Verona University. Since 2012 he has been a member of the *Roman Provincial Coinage* research team. From 2012–17 he worked at the British Museum Department of Coins and Medals as British Academy Newton Research Fellow (2012–13) and Project Curator (2014–17). From 2017–20 he was Research Fellow on the Leverhulme Trust-funded project *Materiality and Meaning in Greek Festival Culture of the Roman Imperial Period*, based at the University of Warwick. He is currently the PI of the ERC funded research project RESP, *The Roman Emperor Seen from the Provinces* (2021–6). Publications include *Defacing the Past. Damnation and Desecration in Imperial Rome* (2016), *Studies in Ancient Coinage in Honour of Andrew Burnett* (2015, with Roger Bland), and *Nicopolis d'Epiro. Nuovi studi sulla zecca monetale* (2011).

Naomi Carless Unwin was Research Fellow on the Leverhulme Trust-funded project *Materiality and Meaning in Greek Festival Culture of the Roman Imperial Period*, based at the University of Warwick (2017–21). She specializes in the history and cultures of Asia Minor, with a particular interest in the insights offered by epigraphy. Her first book, *Caria and Crete in Antiquity: Cultural Interaction between Anatolia and the Aegean*, was published in 2017.

Angelos Chaniotis is Professor of Ancient History and Classics at the Institute for Advanced Study in Princeton. His research is dedicated to emotion, historical memory, religion, and society in the Hellenistic world and the Roman East. He has edited three collective volumes on the history of emotions in the Greek world (*Unveiling Emotions* I–III, 2012–21) and a collective volume on the history of the night (*La nuit. Imaginaire et réalités nocturnes dans le monde gréco-romain*, 2018). His most recent book is *Age of Conquests: The Greek World from Alexander to Hadrian* (2018).

Mairi Gkikaki is an honorary research fellow at the Department of Classics and Ancient History, University of Warwick, where she has been a Marie Skłodowska-Curie Research Fellow (2018-2021) and a team member of the ERC-funded project 'Token Communities in the Ancient Mediterranean' (2016-2018). Her first book *Die weiblichen Frisuren auf den Münzen und in der Großplastick der Klassichen und Hellenistischen Zeit* was published in 2014. She is co-editor of the volume *Tokens: Culture, Connections, Communities* (2019) and sole editor of the volume *Tokens in Classical Athens and Beyond* (2023). Her monograph *Symbola. Athenian Tokens from Classical to Roman Times* is planned to be published in 2024.

Rocío Gordillo Hervás is a Lecturer at the University Pablo de Olavide (Spain) and completed her research doctorate at the Università degli Studi di Firenze. Her research focuses on the impact of Roman rule on Greek territories during imperial times. She is author of the monograph *La construcción religiosa de la Hélade Imperial: El Panhelenion* (2012) and has published a number of articles and book chapters relating to ancient festivals. She is the main researcher together with Elena Muñiz Grijalvo of the project *Celebrations of the Empire from the Provinces* hosted by the University Pablo de Olavide and financed by the Ministerio de Ciencia e Innovación, Goberment of Spain.

Paul Grigsby is a Research Fellow in Outreach and Impact in the Department of Classics and Ancient History where he runs the Warwick Classics Network. His PhD focused on the agonistic festivals in Boiotia and their role in the development of Boiotian identity.

Zahra Newby is Professor of Classics and Ancient History at the University of Warwick. Her research focuses on how Greek culture was experienced and adapted in the period of the Roman empire, explored through the lens of material culture. She has published books and articles on ancient athletics, festivals, and mythology in Roman art, including a monograph on *Greek Athletics in the Roman World: Victory and Virtue* (2005). She was Principal Investigator of the Leverhulme Trust-funded project *Materiality and Meaning in Greek Festival Culture of the Roman Imperial Period* (2017–21).

Sebastian Scharff earned his PhD from Münster University in September 2013 and received his *venia legendi* at Mannheim University in November 2019. He has published extensively on ancient athletics including a co-edited volume on *Athletics in the Hellenistic World* (Steiner 2016) and a forthcoming monograph on *Hellenistic Athletes. Agonistic Cultures and Self-Presentation* (2023). In 2016, he was awarded a fellowship at the Center for Hellenic Studies, and he raised a research grant with Gerda Henkel Stiftung for a project on Posidippus' Hippika in 2017.

Christina G. Williamson is Associate Professor of Ancient History at the University of Groningen. She is author of *Urban Rituals in Sacred Landscapes in Hellenistic Asia Minor* (2021) and is co-directing the NWO (Dutch Research Council) project *Connecting the Greeks. Multi-scalar Festival Networks in the Hellenistic World*, within which she also conducts her own project, *Deep-mapping Sanctuaries*, in which she considers sanctuaries as network hubs of complex interactions.

1
Introduction

The Material Worlds of Ancient Festivals

Zahra Newby

1.1. The dynamics of material culture in festivals of the Greek East

By the second and third centuries AD, festivals were thriving across the eastern Mediterranean. The 'agonistic explosion' famously described by Louis Robert included festivals both big and small, ranging in their geographical scope, funders, and participants.[1] Much of our knowledge of these festivals, and their associated processions, rituals, banquets, and competitions, comes from material culture.[2] Festivals could be celebrated on civic coinage, as well as in public or private art, while detailed decrees outlining the proper procedures for particular festivals are preserved in the form of monumental inscriptions.[3] Victorious performers were commemorated through honorific statues, whose inscribed bases often provide copious details about their careers.[4]

All of this evidence allows us to draw a picture of a vibrant and thriving festival culture, through which cities celebrated their religious traditions, honoured the emperor, and placed themselves within a wider Mediterranean community of shared values and traditions. Yet each of these pieces of material evidence is also the result of a conscious act, of what to record, and where and how to record it, with varying patterns discernible across different areas, and in different media. The aim of this volume is to draw attention to the choices made in a variety of different forms of material culture relating to festivals in the eastern Mediterranean and to unpick the ways in which they encode or forge particular social relationships

---

[1] 'Explosion agonistique': Robert (1984), 38 with critique by Nollé (2012).
[2] Chaniotis (2011b), 27 notes that the phrase *pompe kai thusia kai agon* (procession, sacrifice, and contest) can be used in place of *heorte* (festival). The bibliography on festivals is extensive and only a selection is given here: Hornblower and Morgan (2007); Wilson (2007a); Rüpke (2008); Hermary and Jaeger (2011); esp. Chaniotis (2011b); Brandt and Iddeng (2012a); on processions, Connolly (2011); Chaniotis (2013); Carless Unwin (2020); on banquets, Stavrianopoulou (2009).
[3] The bibliography on coinage is given below, n. 27. On art, see Dunbabin (2016). A discussion of the epigraphy of imperial Greek festivals will be provided by Carless Unwin (forthcoming).
[4] See Moretti (1953) and (1957); König (2005), 125–32, including references to the numerous works by Louis Robert, many included in Robert (1969–90); now also Mouratidis (2020) and (2021).

and power structures, as well as creating senses of community or communication between different groups. Thus the volume is shaped by an interest and belief in the agency of material culture: the idea that material culture is both created by humans, to serve individual or collective desires or objectives, and also exerts its own influence back onto those who use or view this material, shaping the ways in which they understand themselves and the meaning of their actions.[5] It suggests that the ancient experience of civic festivals was, in large part, created through material culture, which helped to fix ephemeral events into public memory, to present particular views of their significance for the wider community, and to frame the experience of participants.

Material culture, and especially epigraphy, has been central to the scholarship on festivals and their development in the Hellenistic and Roman periods.[6] Wolfgang Leschhorn suggested that at least five hundred different *agones* (contests/festivals) are attested in Roman inscriptions and coins, while detailed studies, such as Michael Wörrle's discussion of the foundation of the Demostheneia festival at Oinoanda during the reign of Hadrian, have illuminated our understanding of the roles played by donors, cities, and the emperor and details of programmes and prizes.[7] New discoveries, such as the letters of the emperor Hadrian to the Dionysiac Artists, found at Alexandria Troas, continue to increase our understanding of the integral role played by the Roman emperor in this newly expanded festival culture.[8] Yet this material takes a number of forms, including decrees, imperial letters, and honorific inscriptions, which all have their own norms and dynamics influencing their form and content.[9] In part, this volume takes up the challenge posed by an earlier volume in this series, Peter Wilson's edited volume, *The Greek Theatre and Festivals: Documentary Studies* (2007), in which Wilson argues the need to approach festivals from the 'bottom up':

> [T]here remains a real need to energise the study of the documentary base of the Greek theatre—and the same is true of the performance culture of Greek festivals more broadly—"from the ground up". This volume is a first step in such a project.[10]

---

[5] On agency, see Gell (1998); on applying these ideas to classical art, see Osborne and Tanner (2007); Bielfeldt (2014); Gaifmann and Platt (2018); on the entanglement of humans and objects, see Hodder (2012).

[6] On the development of festivals, see König (2009); Pleket (2014); van Nijf and Williamson (2015), (2016); and the Connected Contests project at Groningen: connectedcontests.org, last accessed 8 September 2022. On the political importance of festivals in the Hellenistic and Roman periods, see Chaniotis (1995) and van Nijf (2012). On festivals in late antiquity, see Graf (2015) and Remijsen (2015). Earlier on Greek athletics and festivals in the Roman world, see König (2005) and Newby (2005); on the development of guilds, see Le Guen (2001) and Aneziri (2003).

[7] Leschhorn (1998); Wörrle (1988), with review by Mitchell (1990). For studies of festivals in individual cities, see e.g. Roueché (1993); Lehner (2005).

[8] See Petzl and Schwertheim (2006) and discussions in Chapters 2 and 3 below.

[9] This variety is echoed in the inscriptions regulating ritual matters, previously referred to as 'Greek sacred laws'; see Sokolowski (1955), (1962), (1969); and Lupu (2005), 1–8, with Parker (2004); Harris (2015); and the project *Collection of Greek Ritual Norms*: cgrn.ulg.ac.be/, last accessed 8 September 2022.

[10] Wilson (2007b), 3. See also now, for theatrical festivals, Csapo and Wilson (2019).

The papers collected there drew on a range of materials, particularly epigraphic, to look in detail at the workings of festivals and theatres in specific contexts. In his chapter William Slater draws particular attention to the multiplicity of the epigraphic evidence for ancient festivals and the difficulties of drawing firm, overarching conclusions, noting '[t]hey are all inconveniently different'.[11] Such studies warn us of the complexities involved in extrapolating common patterns from individual texts. While some common features do emerge, we also need to think about how such texts and monuments worked within their own contexts, as responses to particular local concerns or circumstances.

Indeed, ever since Ramsay MacMullen's seminal 1982 article, it has been widely accepted that setting up inscriptions was a deliberate act, the history of which can be traced as a habit, or culture.[12] While inscriptions in both the West and East of the Roman empire seem to peak in the second and early third centuries AD, and subsequently decline, recent discussions have underlined the complexities in the picture, and the difficulties in drawing common patterns across different areas or indeed types of materials.[13] These observations are important for our understanding of the epigraphic material relating to festivals, as for other areas. An absence of evidence of a particular kind need not be taken as evidence that a particular festival or ritual itself was absent. In particular, John Bodel notes the variety of epigraphic cultures which existed in the Greek East, commenting in particular on the prolific epigraphy of Lycian Oinoanda, which includes the important text recording the establishment of a festival by the local notable, C. Iulius Demosthenes.[14] Oinoanda seems to have had a taste for lengthy inscriptions, and the challenge for the historian is to decide how typical such texts are, how much they are influenced by prevailing epigraphic norms, and what they do not tell us, as well as what they do.[15]

As well as recognizing patterns in the commissioning of inscriptions, there has also been a growing interest in the ways in which they were experienced and displayed, recognizing the monumentality of inscriptions, and their roles as visual monuments, as well as texts, interacting with the wider locations in which they were set up. Important work for the West has been done by Alison Cooley, while Abigail Graham has identified the importance of thinking about the visibility of inscriptions in the East, with particular focus on Aphrodisias and Ephesos.[16] When considering how such documents function, we need to consider not only

---

[11] Slater (2007), 24.
[12] MacMullen (1982); also Meyer (1990). Woolf (1996), 30–4 argues for a focus on epigraphic cultures; see also Cooley (2000) (on the epigraphic landscape) and Cooley (2012), 1–325.
[13] MacMullen (1986), 236 noted that the decline in inscriptions in Lydia is gentler than in the Roman West (cf. MacMullen (1982), 243). See esp. Nawotka (2021) for new discussions of the epigraphic cultures of the eastern Mediterranean.
[14] Bodel (2001b), 14; see Wörrle (1988) on Demosthenes' inscription.
[15] For general comments on the problems of using inscriptions as historical evidence, see Bodel (2001a), esp. Bodel (2001b), 34 and 46–7 on epigraphic bias and Rives (2001) on civic and religious life.
[16] Cooley (2000), (2012); Graham (2013), (2019).

their content, but also the viewing context, and the occasions on which they would have been viewed and experienced. Henner von Hesberg's discussion of the publication of documents in the Greek East establishes the importance in Asia Minor of structures such as temples, stoas, and theatres as spaces for the public inscription of civic documents.[17] The display of these texts in spaces which were used for public ceremonies, such as honours or banquets, helped to define the aura of the space, and set up a close connection between the inscribed text and the building's social, civic, or religious character.[18] The recent edited volume by Andrej Petrovic, Ivana Petrovic, and Edmund Thomas also explores the range of ways in which the physicality of inscribed text can be approached and interrogated.[19] Joseph Day's chapter on the spatial dynamics of archaic Greek epigram draws on Michael Scott's work on spatial dynamics; both show the ways that monuments act in relation to one another and can set up conversations of collaboration or competition.[20]

Another key source of information on festivals is provided by civic coinage, which shows both similarities with and some notable differences from the shape of the epigraphic material. Just as epigraphic cultures vary, so too we can see changing patterns in the production of civic coinages (the bronze coinages minted by the cities of the eastern Roman provinces), and in the iconographies chosen to appear on coins.[21] The motivations lying behind the production and appearance of coins is the focus of the 2005 edited volume on *Coinage and Identity in the Roman Provinces*, arguing that coins can be seen as expressions of civic identities.[22] Volker Heuchert's chapter discusses the shape of the evidence and the factors which influenced civic coin production. While the evidence suggests an increase in the number of cities minting coins between the first century AD and the Antonine period, especially in Asia Minor, peaking in the Severan period before declining in the mid-third century AD, overall quantities of coinage are harder to estimate.[23] Production practices, such as the use of travelling workshops to produce dies might also have affected the production of specific iconographies, especially for the imperial images which usually appear on the obverses, though the combination of shared obverses with very specific reverse images show that coins could be tailored to the expression of particular civic identities.[24] The

---

[17] von Hesberg (2009). [18] von Hesberg (2009), 31–2.
[19] Petrovic, Petrovic, and Thomas (2019); see also Eastmond (2015); Angliker and Bultrighini (2023).
[20] Scott (2010); J. W. Day (2019). On co-operation and competition, see J. W. Day (2019), 75, drawing from Ma (2013), 113.
[21] The volumes and website of the Roman Provincial Coinages project are a central resource here, adding greatly to our understanding of the patterns of these coinages: rpc.ashmus.ox.ac.uk, last accessed 5 June 2023.
[22] Howgego, Heuchert, and Burnett (2005).
[23] Heuchert (2005) 33–4. His map 3.2.2 details the cities minting coins in western Asia Minor in the Antonine period. For further discussion of the difficulties of estimating overall production, see the debate between Leschhorn (1981) and Johnston (1984).
[24] Heuchert (2005), 43–4; see Kraft (1972), and comments by Robert (1975), 188–92; now also Watson (2020).

themes which appear on civic coinages also show overlaps with other arenas in which identities were expressed. The key importance of religious traditions, civic gods, and local mythologies can be seen on coins as well as in rhetoric, literature, and other visual art.[25]

Yet there are also some interesting differences in explicit references to festivals between inscriptions and coins. While we have some lengthy texts relating to the organization of festivals from the earlier Roman period (from Gytheion under Tiberius, and Oinoanda under Hadrian), the most popular period for references to festivals on coins is the period after AD 180.[26] Dario Calomino's forthcoming study of the material reveals the varying patterns of minting and iconographic choices in mainland Greece and Asia Minor, suggesting that the cities of mainland Greece were more likely to use traditional iconographies to represent their festivals, and included some references to festivals on coinage even in the first century AD, whereas those in Asia Minor mostly featured festivals on coins in the second and third centuries, and were more likely to innovate in the iconographies chosen to represent these.[27] Even when we know that a particular festival was being celebrated in a city at a particular period, the decision to commemorate it in coinage may only appear later.[28]

Unlike the occasional coinages minted in the Hellenistic period in the name of gods or religious associations, which appear to have been minted for use in transactions at particular festivals, these coinages were minted in the name of individual cities, and sit alongside their regular output; they thus need to be seen in the light of the self-representation of these individual cities and not only within the economic activity of a particular festival (though they may on occasions have fulfilled a role here too).[29] The choice to mint coins celebrating festivals at a particular time often seems to be prompted as part of a city's strategies of self-representation and positioning of itself within the local region.[30] The increase in references to festivals on coins at the end of the second and during the third centuries AD has also been associated in part with the presence of imperial troops, and the desire for emperors to show favour to the cities which were supporting their eastern campaigns.[31] Thus, a complex web of factors might have influenced particular cities to commemorate their festivals in numismatic form,

---

[25] See Howgego (2005) for a review of all themes (esp. 17 on overlaps with other media) and Price (2005) on mythological traditions, also discussed in Newby (2003).

[26] Klose (2005), 130–3; Nollé (2012).

[27] Calomino (forthcoming), chs 1 and 4. For earlier discussions, see Karl (1975); Harl (1987), 63–70; Leschhorn (1998); Klose (2005).

[28] e.g. Nikopolis, whose Aktia festival was refounded by Augustus, but only appears on coins from the reign of Trajan: e.g. *RPC* III 486, 489.

[29] On the earlier 'festival coinages', see Psoma (2008) and (2009).

[30] See here Chapter 4 on Nikaia and Nikomedia. Compare also the rivalry between Perge and Side in Pamphylia: Nollé (1993) and Calomino in Newby and Calomino (2022), 48–52. A similar pattern is found in references to Perge's neokorate status which does not appear on coins until the third century: Burrell (2004), 175–80.

[31] See esp. Ziegler (1985); also Klose (2005), 130–3.

while others chose to focus on other themes. As with inscriptions, each group of images or references needs to be seen in its own context, with nuanced attention to the sorts of festivals which are being advertised, by whom and to whom.

A common feature uniting the production of coins and inscriptions, and the organization of festivals, is the role played by the elites. While coins assert a communal civic identity, it is undoubtably one framed and formulated by the elites, who were in control of the production of coinage.[32] Inscriptions too largely record the activities and priorities of the elite, who also exercised control over civic institutions such as the *boule*. The extent to which other parts of the population bought into these concerns, and the image of civic identities or priorities which they presented, is difficult to ascertain and must surely have varied depending on personal experiences. As discussed later, we might see some assertions of the importance of civic cult as a response to the rise of other forms of religiosity; yet on the whole I tend to agree with Christopher Howgego that coins may have helped to spread and fix ideas about certain communal identities which were broadly accepted by others within the society.[33] At the same time, the involvement of civic elites, many of whom were Roman citizens, also helped to ensure that the self-representation of the city, its cults and traditions, went hand in hand with loyalty to the Roman emperor.[34]

There remain questions, though, about the audiences for these assertions of status and identity. While coins can travel, the evidence of hoards and of finds from excavations seems to suggest that most bronze civic coinage circulated locally, with some rare exceptions.[35] Inscriptions were also set up in well-frequented places around cities. While the messages presented often declare the international outlook of a city, and its connections with the imperial family, we might wonder whether these statements of prestige were also speaking to the city's own citizens, reasserting their sense of themselves, as well as attempting to persuade external audiences.

1.2. The material frameworks for the experience of festivals: continuity and change

In addition to epigraphy and coinage, and the interests and relationships they encode, this volume also looks at the role played by other aspects of material culture in creating the experience of ancient festivals. This includes the role

---

[32] Heuchert (2005), 40–4; Howgego (2005), 16–17; see also Butcher (2005) on Syria and Watson (2020) on Asia Minor.
[33] Howgego (2005), 16–18.
[34] Weiss (2005), 68. On the importance of the Roman emperor, see esp. Price (1984).
[35] T. B. Jones (1963), 313–23; Heuchert (2005) 31; on coins with countermarks travelling along major routes, see Howgego (1985), 32–50.

played by particular spaces and their architectural arrangement and decoration, as well as more portable objects, such as tokens or lamps. There are a number of ways in which we can explore the role played by material culture in the creation of festival experiences, drawing on the growing interest in scholarship of considering the roles played by both space and material artefacts in human activities, the so-called 'spatial' and 'material' turns.[36] Since the influential work of Henri Lefebvre and Pierre Bourdieu in the 1970s, which established the importance of considering how the interaction of space and human activity both reflects and generates social hierarchies, scholars of the classical world have increasingly turned their focus to the ways that human engagement with spaces and landscapes helped to generate meaning, particularly in the construction and expression of senses of identity and the creation of communal memories.[37]

Within the study of Greek religion, earlier work on the roles played by sanctuaries in relation to the *polis* has been complemented more recently by a focus on the ways in which such spaces helped to frame particular ritual activities, and on experiential accounts of rituals which consider how religious experience was intrinsically material.[38] This interest can be coupled with the question of continuity and change in religious rituals and experience.[39] Thus while we can see that changing political systems in the post-classical period effected ritual change, appeals to ancestral custom also played a crucial role, and in many cases the two went hand in hand, with new rituals represented as the restoration of proper ancestral practices.[40] Ritual practice and experience was also affected by the architectural development of ritual spaces.[41] Volumes such as Bonna Wescoat and Robert Ousterhout's *Architecture of the Sacred* and Wiebke Friese and Troels Myrup Kristensen's *Excavating Sacred Pilgrimage*, through their focus on the interaction of ritual and space, have established the central role played by spatial frameworks in engendering and accommodating sacred engagement with the divine.[42] A good example is the growing use of monumental staircases in sanctuaries

---

[36] On the spatial turn, see esp. Warf and Arias (2009).

[37] Lefebvre (1974); Bourdieu (1977). The literature is extensive. For a review and bibliography, see Scott (2013), 1–10, 170–1. On space and memory, see Nora (1984–92); Alcock (2002); Gangloff (2013); Galinsky and Lapatin (2015); Mortensen and Poulsen (2017).

[38] The bibliography relating to Greek religion and sanctuaries is extensive and here I refer only to works I have found particularly useful in framing this project. Sanctuaries: Marinatos and Hägg (1993); Alcock and Osborne (1994); de Polignac (1995) (first published in French in 1984); space and experience: Cole (2004); Scott (2010) and (2013), 45–76; Mylonopoulos (2011); Moser and Feldman (2014). For further bibliographies, see Østby (1993) and Raja and Rüpke (2015).

[39] See esp. Stavrianopoulou (2006); Hekster, Schmidt-Hofner, and Witschel (2009); Chaniotis (2011a), partly linked with the Ritual Dynamics project at the University of Heidelberg, 2002–13: ritualdynamik.de, last accessed 8 September 2022; also Alston, van Nijf, and Williamson (2013). On the relationship between changes in content and form in Greek festivals, see Brandt and Iddeng (2012b), 3–5; Brandt (2012).

[40] On change in festivals, see Chaniotis (2011b), 40–3.   [41] Mylonopoulos (2008).

[42] Wescoat and Ousterhout (2012); Friese and Kristensen (2017); see esp. Elsner (2012) for some of the methodological problems. For changes to Hellenistic sanctuaries, see Melfi and Bobou (2016).

and along sacred ways. As Mary Hollinshead has shown, steps formally orchestrated the roles of spectator and participants, helping to create a sense of spectacle and reinforce the power structures on display.[43] The enclosure of space could also directly affect the experience of those participating in particular rituals, so that even if the rituals themselves had not changed, the ways they were perceived may have done so.[44]

For the study of festivals, where many of the activities took place within cities as well as sanctuaries, we can also broaden our focus to consider the ways that the monumental landscape of the city would have been energized in times of festivals to create particular memories and meanings. Work on the idea of mediation and pre-mediation has asserted the importance of expectation and prior experience, and its commemoration in physical form, in shaping communal understandings of events and in framing cultural memories.[45] In the ancient world, monuments erected in key spaces within a cityscape helped to formulate specific identities for a city, and to encode particular structures of power, pointing both to the past, and to the present.[46] These senses of religious, cultural, and political identities could be further reinforced during festivals by the processions and rituals which took place within the city. The ways in which movement through cityscapes helped to engender meaning has received attention in a number of recent studies, with a particular focus on Rome.[47] These approaches can help us to explore festivals in the Greek East too. Festival processions passed through many central spaces of the city and the decoration of those spaces would have taken on additional resonances when seen in the context of religious processions. Rogers's discussion of the procession funded by Salutaris at Ephesos draws attention to the ways in which the different images carried in the procession picked up on aspects of the urban landscape through which they passed; together, the interaction of procession and cityscape helped to formulate a particular historical and mythical identity for the city, embedding the imperial presence into civic traditions.[48] Permanent monumental imagery resonated with ephemeral rituals and spectacles to create a lasting image of the religious traditions which lay at the heart of civic identities.[49] The material records and spaces of ancient festivals thus sit at the intersection of past and present: festivals are embedded in a past; through rituals, aetiological myths and processions they tie the participants to that past, but also continually re-experience this in the present and use it to serve contemporary needs and identities.

---

[43] Hollinshead (2012) and (2015).
[44] On the effect of walls on ritual experience, see Scott (2022); Williamson, Chapter 9 below.
[45] Erll and Rigney (2009), developing Halbwachs's work on collective memory: Halbswachs (1950).
[46] See e.g. Dickenson and van Nijf (2013); Ma (2013); on late antiquity, J. Day et al. (2016).
[47] Östenberg, Malmberg, and Bjørnebye (2015); Popkin (2016); Latham (2016).
[48] Rogers (1991), 80–126; cf. also Scherrer (2008) on the development of Ephesos as a festive landscape connected with the imperial cult.
[49] See Newby in Newby and Calomino (2022), 41–8 on Perge.

A further aspect of portable material culture also deserves a mention here. A number of theorists have shown the ways in which objects can act as social agents, entangling humans in particular sorts of relationships or acting as extensions of the human body.[50] Objects can be used to look at the interconnections between cultures, but they also actively helped to forge those connections, and to define what they meant—objects are not just witnesses but active producers of connectivity and conversation between different social groups.[51] Within ancient festivals, objects and images played a variety of functions, from the cult statues which were the recipients of ritual action, to the images of gods, emperors, and other bodies carried in processions, making those entities physically present in the rituals which concerned them.[52] Some objects, such as tokens or coins distributed in acts of public munificence, created relationships between different social groups, while others, such as the keys and baskets frequently carried as part of the ritual procession, may have played both a functional and a symbolic role.[53]

1.3. Cities, emperors, and the elite: the social frameworks of civic festivals

While earlier scholarship on Greek religion and the *polis* often painted a picture of decline in the Hellenistic and Roman periods, more recent studies have shown the continued vitality of both civic religion and the post-classical *polis* in these periods.[54] At the same time, scholars of Greek religion have challenged the dominance in scholarship of a *polis*-centred model of religion, arguing that it only offers us a partial understanding into ancient religiosity.[55] This has led to an increased interest in personal religion, and in aspects such as magic, the role of charismatic individuals and mystery cults.[56] As studies of the Hellenistic and Roman city show, civic cults also continued to play a defining role within public life, providing the festivals which helped to structure the civic calendar, as well as the priesthoods which civic elites held as part of their ostentatious commitment to their civic communities.[57] They offered an important framework and focus for

---

[50] See e.g. Gell (1998); Brown (2001); Hodder (2012); Bielfeldt (2014); Gaifmann and Platt (2018).
[51] See Versluys (2014); Pitts and Versluys (2015).
[52] On cult statues, see Gordon (1979); Elsner (1996); Gaifmann (2006); Platt (2011). On statues in processions, Gebhard (1996); Edelmann (2008).
[53] See Rogers (1991), 39–79 on distributions; and Gkikaki, Chapter 5 below on tokens. Carless Unwin (2020) discusses references to the bearers of ritual objects in epigraphic texts.
[54] van Nijf and Alston (2011); Alston, van Nijf, and Williamson (2013); Dickenson and van Nijf (2013). For an overview of continuity and change in Hellenistic religion, see Mikalson (2006).
[55] Woolf (1997); Kindt (2012), esp. 12–35 on the model of *polis* religion. For a key discussion of this see Sourvinou-Inwood (1990).
[56] e.g. Kindt (2012); Rüpke and Woolf (2013).
[57] van Nijf, Alston, and Williamson (2013), 4–10. On priesthoods, see further below. On festivals as part of civic life, see Graf (2015), 11–60.

identity for their civic communities, bringing together different segments of society, while also reinforcing social hierarchies. Yet at the same time, we can also see the visibility of civic cults, priesthoods, and festivals, both in the literary and material record and in the lived reality of cities, as the result of efforts by civic elites to continually assert the communal importance of such rituals, and themselves, as the key officiants, in response or opposition to alternative forms of identity or religiosity which were also available.[58]

Indeed, civic elites played a central role in the functioning of cults and festivals. It is mostly members of the elite that we find taking on roles as priests or priestesses, sometimes for life. In his influential chapters in Mary Beard and John North's *Pagan Priests*, Richard Gordon argued that the ubiquitous imagery of the emperor as a sacrificer in Roman art and on coins provided a model for the provincial aristocracy, who combined roles as priests with ones as *euergetai*.[59] He cites the example of Kleanax, son of Sarapion from Kyme, who is acclaimed in an inscription from the reign of Augustus as the priest of Dionysos Pandamos: he celebrated the mysteries of the city, paying all the expenses of the festival, provided a yearly feast to members of the community in the sanctuary of Dionysos, as well as another to the priests, victors in the sacred games, and magistrates, and also paid for sacrifices and feasts as part of an imperial festival.[60] Numerous other examples could be attested; thus, as Onno van Nijf has shown, the honorific inscriptions of Roman Termessos place particular importance on priesthoods, athletic victories, and family lineage, painting a picture of a tightly controlled civic elite where a number of influential families monopolized civic priesthoods as well as providing the most prominent exemplars of sporting success at civic *agones*, many of which were themselves the result of elite benefaction.[61] Members of the elite were prominent throughout festivals at all stages of the action, from funding through to organization and participation.[62]

As *euergetai*, elite individuals could fund complete festivals, setting up new foundations, such as the Demostheneia at Oinoanda.[63] They could also act as *agonothetai* for existing festivals, sometimes paying for specific aspects, such as sacrifices, feasts, or processions, from their own funds.[64] In many cases too, when imperial permission was required, they may have used their skills as ambassadors

---

[58] See Woolf (1997); also Chaniotis (2003) for discussion of the motivations of the elite and the arguments they used.

[59] Gordon (1990a) and (1990b).

[60] SEG 32, 1243; Gordon (1990a), 226–31, also discussing the third-century AD Menodora from Sillyon. On benefactions of feasts in the Roman period, see Stavrianopoulou (2009).

[61] van Nijf (2011), esp. 225–8. On the festivals of Termessos, see Heberdey (1923), (1929).

[62] The range of individuals who performed at festivals in the musical or athletic contests probably encompassed a wider social range than those who served as priests, *agonothetai*, or benefactors, but here too numerous elite individuals are still attested, see Pleket (2014) for discussion.

[63] See Wörrle (1988), 151–82; on foundations, see also Laum (1914); Rogers (1991), 39–74; Zuiderhoek (2009), 86–109, 165–6.

[64] Wörrle (1988), 183–209.

to achieve this. A good example is Epameinondas of Akraiphia in Boiotia, who in the mid-first century AD organized the festival of Hermes and Herakles in the gymnasium, and also spent considerable amounts of money reviving the Ptoia festival with ancestral dances and accompanying feasts, processions, and contests.[65] It is easy to see these acts as assertions of or bids for status and power, and in many cases they may have been. Yet, as Angelos Chaniotis has noted, while the epigraphic evidence tells us what these individuals did, it does not tell us why, or how successful new initiatives ultimately were.[66] Thus Damas of Miletos' insistence on celebrating the ancestral banquets for the *molpoi* and *kosmoi* in connection with the cult of Apollo at Didyma in the mid-first century AD may well have been primarily provoked by his own personal piety; while the action was approved by the city, we cannot tell whether the celebration of these banquets actually outlived Damas himself.[67]

Much also rests on restoration and interpretation. We cannot always know for certain whether particular choices recorded in inscriptions were in opposition to or concordance with public opinion. The letter written by Antoninus Pius to Ephesos, endorsing the desire of P. Vedius Antoninus to construct public buildings in his home city (the very *bouleuterion* in which the letter was inscribed, as well as a bath-gymnasium complex), rather than spending his money on immediate pleasures, such as spectacles and distributions, is often taken as a rebuke to the city, which is assumed to have preferred the latter. Yet a different reconstruction of a single letter undermines this, suggesting that the city too had recognized Vedius' contribution.[68] Elsewhere, we find the money traditionally reserved to fund banquets being redirected to pay for an aqueduct instead; while Chaniotis draws attention to the city's participation in this request, Graf associates it instead with the donor's self-interest.[69] A similar redirection of funds had been authorized by Hadrian in the city of Aphrodisias, though in his letter to the Dionysiac Artists he himself prohibits the diversion of public funds meant for festivals towards the construction of buildings.[70]

Scholars have sought to make sense of these choices, seeing an imperial preference for Greek games over Roman-style *munera*, or debating the varying merits of buildings versus festivals for elite display and memorialization.[71] Yet we might

---

[65] *IG* VII 2711, 2712; for discussions, see Kantiréa (2007), 208–13; Graf (2011) and (2015), 18–24; on the feasts, Stavrianopoulou (2009), 161–5; also Grigsby below, Section 8.3.4.
[66] Chaniotis (2003). [67] *I.Delphinion* 134; discussed by Chaniotis (2003), 179–84.
[68] *I.Ephesos* 1471, compare Kalinowski (2002) and Kokkinia (2003), esp. 203–5, offering a different reading of l. 12; at l. 16 the emperor speaks vaguely of shows and distributions but it is not entirely clear what θέαι refers to, and the third element is lost; the restoration as τὰ τῶ[ν ἀγώνων θέματα], the prizes of games, is plausible but unproven; Kokkinia (2012), 114–15 suggests there might instead have been a reference to *munera* here.
[69] Malay (1999), 115, no. 127; Chaniotis (2003), 180; cf. Graf (2015), 39–40.
[70] *SEG* 50, 1096, see Reynolds (2000) and Coleman (2008); Petzl and Schwertheim (2006), ll. 8–13 with C. P. Jones (2007), 153, discussed by Kokkinia (2012), 107–10.
[71] See esp. Kokkinia (2012) and Ng (2015); also Graf (2015), 36–40.

be wrong to look for sustained preferences on the part of either emperors or elites. Imperial rescripts addressed the problem immediately at hand, and might have been ad hoc solutions rather than sustained coherent strategies, while circumstances and needs on the ground and their own preferences and histories could have influenced the choices of individual benefactors.[72] Such episodes give a glimpse into the competing priorities of different groups at particular times, yet I do not think we necessarily need to see buildings or festivals as pitched in strict opposition to one another. As can be seen in numerous examples, those who paid for festivals often provided public buildings too, and many of these structures would have played an important role during festivals.[73] Returning to P. Vedius Antoninus, his father and grandfather had previously both served as *gymnasiarch*, *asiarch*, and *panegyriarch* in Ephesos, roles which required them to organize the Ephesia and imperial cult festivals, and the family seems to have had links with the guilds of food and sacred wine workers who had their base close to Vedius III's gymnasium.[74] The construction of this bath-gymnasium complex thus consolidated a family tradition of supporting and facilitating festival activities, since it must have helped to accommodate those preparing for athletic contests in the nearby stadium. It may even have hosted ceremonies of crowning in its lavishly decorated marble room.[75] The *bouleuterion* too, while serving a civic function in hosting meetings of the *boule*, could also have acted as an *odeion*, a venue for musical performances.[76] While Antoninus Pius' letter puts shows and buildings in opposition to one another, as fleeting pleasures versus lasting monuments, they could also be seen as complementary, the one facilitating the other.[77]

1.4. Outline of the volume

The chapters collected here explore the material dynamics of festivals in a variety of ways, focusing both on the social relationships and senses of identity which are encoded and created through material culture, and on the ways that material culture helped to construct particular meanings for festivals in the Graeco-Roman

---

[72] Given the extensiveness of imperial correspondence, vividly portrayed in Millar (1992), some contradictions might be expected, even for emperors like Hadrian who seem to have had a consistent policy towards the East; see Boatwright (2000).

[73] See e.g. Opramoas of Rhodiapolis who funded festivals as well as buildings: Ng (2015), 103–5; the documents are collected in Kokkinia (2000).

[74] *I.Ephesos* 728; see Kalinowski (2002), 125–31, esp. 130 arguing that the two Vedii Antonini named here are Vedius I and II.

[75] See the convincing discussion of Burrell (2006), esp. 444–6, 460–2. She rightly rejects the idea that such spaces were predominantly for the imperial cult, noting the lack of firm evidence. On the decoration of the space, see also Newby (2005), 235–44.

[76] On musical contests as part of the city's festivals, see Lehner (2005), 137, 149, 205–6.

[77] See also Zuiderhoek (2009), 86–92 linking together the donation of festivals, oil, and bath-gymnasia complexes.

East. They speak in different ways to the themes and questions outlined in this introduction, and we have not sought to impose any common methodology or theoretical framework. The majority of the chapters focus on the Roman imperial period, although the broader focus taken in Chapters 8, 9, and 10 also sets this within the development of festivals and sacred space from the Hellenistic period onwards. Together, then, the chapters reveal both continuity and change in the festival culture of the post-classical period; while the authority of the emperor is a pervasive theme in the material from the imperial period, we also see the enduring importance of other groups, such as the guild of the Dionysiac artists, and the local elites.

We start with the figure of the Roman emperor, whose symbolic presence within the imperial festival circuit is explored in Chapters 2 to 4. In Chapter 2 Sebastian Scharff sets the scene by focusing on the role played by the emperor within festivals, and in particular in the material self-representation of successful athletes. He shows that an emperor could be present at the games in a variety of forms. He could attend physically as contestant, *agonothetes*, or spectator. Yet even when physically absent, the emperor was symbolically present in the form of statues, the nomenclature of festivals, and through his inscribed letters and edicts. Having established the dominant role played by the emperor, Scharff considers the ways in which material testimonies, in the form of athletic victory inscriptions, embody and reflect this change. This shows how the claims made by victorious athletes took on a wider and wider geographical scope with successful athletes claiming to be the first of a particular area to achieve their victory. While home cities remained important, athletes also boasted of the additional citizenships they had acquired and, where possible, of their proximity to imperial power. We see here how athletes responded to imperial power, and how the dynamics of athletic self-representation changed in conversation and competition with other inscriptions of the same type.

In Chapter 3 Rocío Gordillo Hervás further explores the ubiquitous symbolic presence of the emperor through discussion of the letters of Hadrian which were found at Alexandria Troas. Analysis of the text establishes that it was highly likely that similar *stelai* were put on display in other cities, including both those whose games were part of Hadrian's reorganization of the festival circuit, and others who introduced new games whose timing would be compatible with the new festival calendar. This chapter shows the profound impact the emperor had not only on the visual landscape of festival venues, but also on the very ordering of time; through inscribed copies of this decree, the emperor's central place in agonistic life was asserted and made manifest to all, while the decision to erect a copy of the decree in Alexandria Troas also suggests that the city was using this opportunity to draw attention to its own specific cults and festivals.

Chapters 4 and 5 turn from inscriptions to portable objects, looking at the insights provided by coinage and tokens. In Chapter 4 we see again the central importance held by the imperial family, but this time from the perspective of the individual cities who sought to advertise their closeness to imperial power through the designs chosen for civic coinage. Dario Calomino explores the references made to festivals celebrating the imperial family on the coinage of Nikaia, in particular in relation to its rivalry with the neighbouring city of Nikomedia. While Nikaia employed an innovative iconography on its coins to assert the importance of its festivals, and used them to assert links with the imperial family, Nikomedia chose instead to celebrate its neokorate status. Both cities chose the imagery which could most effectively prove their claims to importance; at Nikaia this includes imagery evoking the rituals which took place during the festivals, such as the honouring of the imperial image, again underlining the ways that the imperial presence was felt during festivals, even when the emperor himself was physically absent.

In Chapter 5 we move from Asia Minor to Greece, specifically Athens, looking at the collection of lead tokens found in the Agora and their likely use in the context of ephebic and civic festivals. While the preceding chapters focus on the imperial family as an important reference point, here Mairi Gkikaki underlines instead the enduring importance of the past and Athens' mythological and religious traditions for the city's sense of self. Through images of important civic gods as well as figures from myth and history, such as Theseus, Herakles, and Themistokles, Gkikaki argues that tokens helped to create festival communities, binding together those participating through appeal to a shared set of cultural memories. At the same time, the adoption of some of these figures as ancestors by wealthy Athenian families also suggests that the tokens could have asserted claims to prominence by particular individuals. The circulation of tokens thus bound together elites, ephebes, officials, and participants, drawing them into a common shared festival culture, which hearkened back to Athens' historical and religious past but also helped to reinforce social hierarchies in the present—all in a manner consistent with the imperial vision of what Athens should be.

The following three chapters turn to the theatre, and musical festivals more generally. Chapters 6 and 7 both discuss the visual display of theatres in Asia Minor, with a focus on iconography in Chapter 6 and epigraphy in Chapter 7. Theatres played a key role during the celebration of festivals, acting as a stage not just for theatrical and other performances, but also for civic rituals, processions, and spectacles. In her discussion of the decoration of the theatres at Hierapolis and Perge in Chapter 6, Zahra Newby explores the ways in which this set forth a normative view, defining the intended social meanings of civic festivals and the roles played by different individuals, groups, and communities within these two cities in the early third century. While the imperial family remains important here, the chief recipients of the festivals celebrated at Hierapolis and Perge are clearly the patron gods of the communities, Apollo and Artemis Pergaia, placing ancestral religious cults at the heart of civic identity.

In Chapter 7 Naomi Carless Unwin discusses the theatre at Aphrodisias as a space for epigraphic display, noting the ways in which different groups were made present here in both inscribed and sculpted form. While the previous chapter focused on a key moment in the early Severan period, this chapter takes a diachronic approach, looking at the development of the epigraphic landscape of the theatre from the late first century BC through to the fourth century AD. Carless Unwin shows how inscribing practices here helped to create specific memories and identities for the city and her citizens, through reference to important benefactors, civic political history, and the more unofficial records of those using the space, either as spectators or performers.

The next three chapters take a wider view, moving back in time to look at the expansion of the festival circuit in the Hellenistic period and at both continuity and change as we move into the Roman period. Chapter 8 picks up on the discussion in Chapter 3 of the role played by the Artists of Dionysos in the imperial festival circuit and on Carless Unwin's discussion of performers in the theatre at Aphrodisias in Chapter 7, but moves back in time to focus on the Hellenistic period and the festivals of Boiotia. Paul Grigsby shows how inscriptions assert the role played by the guild of Artists of Dionysos in the organization of festivals in Boiotia, helping to promote a new kind of festival culture, centred around a reputation for musical performance. As we move into the Roman period however, their influence seems to wane, replaced by that of individual members of the local aristocracy, who proudly assert the use of their wealth to promote and revive ancestral festivals.

Chapter 9 turns to the spatial framing of festivals, with a focus on the development of sanctuary architecture across the Hellenistic period, setting this within the context of the expansion in Panhellenic festivals. While others have associated the peristyle with increasing social hierarchy and exclusion, Christina Williamson argues that the increasing enclosure of sanctuary spaces would have helped to intensify the sense of community within the space, emphasizing inclusion rather than exclusion, and spreading ideas among different members of the *oikoumene*. Chapter 10 turns from the effects of space on ritual participants to that of light and darkness. Angelos Chaniotis looks at the material dimensions of nocturnal celebrations in the Hellenistic and imperial periods. The production of artificial light through lamps and torches in nocturnal rituals seems to have played an increasingly important role in festivals, contributing to the emotional effect of the rituals on their participants. Both Chapters 9 and 10 thus turn our focus from the competitions and processions which were integral to festivals, but often took place outside sanctuaries within civic spaces, to a focus on the material framing of religious rituals, through architecture and artificial light. Williamson and Chaniotis suggest that these aspects can intensify the experience of rituals, heightening the emotional engagement of ritual participants and creating a shared emotional community.

The final concluding chapter helps to draw together the insights of the individual chapters and to outline some areas for future research. Throughout all the chapters we see how different forms of material culture—both permanent and fixed features such as monumental inscriptions and architectural space, as well as portable objects such as coins and tokens—help to express the chosen identities of cities, individuals, and prominent groups, and to forge communities and relationships within the context of festivals. Discussion of different groups spans a number of chapters: both Gordillo Hervás and Grigsby discuss guilds and cities, Scharff discusses athletic victors, Calomino, Scharff, and Gordillo Hervás discuss the importance of the emperors, while elites feature in a number of different papers, with Newby and Carless Unwin considering how the interactions between different groups are manifested within the space of the theatre. While some chapters focus on the material dynamics within an individual city (e.g. Gkikaki for Athens), others show the importance of the wider *oikoumene* in which festival culture developed, in both the Hellenistic (Williamson) and Roman (Newby) worlds. The creation of particular civic and regional traditions relating to the past and festival culture is shown through the chapters by Grigsby and Gkikaki, while the power of material culture to create particular sorts of 'emotional communities' is revealed through the discussions of Williamson, Chaniotis, and Gkikaki.[78] While we discuss a range of different spaces here, including sanctuaries, civic spaces, and theatres, objects also have the power to link together these *loci* of festival activities, either through their portability, or by echoing texts and images set up elsewhere. Across the chapters, we are prompted to think about who defines the meaning of specific festivals, to interrogate the complex negotiations between different groups which helped to construct festival culture in the Greek East, and to recognize the integral role played by material culture in expressing and embedding specific meanings in the wider cityscape and the minds of participants or spectators.

Works Cited

Alcock, S. E. (2002) *Archaeologies of the Greek Past. Landscape, Monuments, and Memories*. Cambridge.

Alcock, S. E. and Osborne, R. (eds) (1994) *Placing the Gods. Sanctuaries and Sacred Space in Ancient Greece*. Oxford.

Alston, R., van Nijf, O., and Williamson, C. (eds) (2013) *Cults, Creeds and Identities in the Greek City after the Classical Age*. Leuven.

---

[78] On the idea of emotional communities, see Rosenwein (2006); though the individual chapters explore this in a variety of different ways.

Aneziri, S. (2003) *Die Vereine der dionysischen Techniten im Kontext der hellenistischen Gesellschaft. Untersuchungen zur Geschichte, Organisation und Wirkung der hellenistischen Technitenvereine.* Stuttgart.

Angliker, E. and Bultrighini, I. (eds) (2023) *New Approaches to the Materiality of Text in the Ancient Mediterranean. From Monuments and Buildings to Small Portable Objects.* Turnhout.

Beard, M. and North, J. (eds) (1990) *Pagan Priests: Religion and Power in the Ancient World.* London.

Bielfeldt, R. (ed.) (2014) *Ding und Mensch in der Antike: Gegenwert und Vergegenwärtigung.* Heidelberg.

Boatwright, M. T. (2000) *Hadrian and the Cities of the Roman Empire.* Princeton.

Bodel, J. (ed.) (2001a) *Epigraphic Evidence: Ancient History from Inscriptions.* London.

Bodel, J. (2001b) 'Epigraphy and the ancient historian', in J. Bodel (ed.), *Epigraphic Evidence: Ancient History from Inscriptions.* London, 1–56.

Bourdieu, P. (1977) *Outline of a Theory of Practice.* Trans. R. Nice. Cambridge.

Brandt, J. R. (2012) 'Content and form: some considerations on Greek festivals and archaeology', in J. R. Brandt and J. W. Iddeng (eds), *Greek and Roman Festivals: Content, Meaning, and Practice.* Oxford, 139–98.

Brandt, J. R. and Iddeng, J. W. (eds) (2012a) *Greek and Roman Festivals: Content, Meaning, and Practice.* Oxford.

Brandt, J. R. and Iddeng, J. W. (2012b) 'Introduction: some concepts of ancient festivals', in J. R. Brandt and J. W. Iddeng (eds), *Greek and Roman Festivals: Content, Meaning, and Practice.* Oxford, 1–10.

Brown, B. (2001) 'Thing theory', *Critical Enquiry* 28.1: 1–22.

Burrell, B. (2004) *Neokoroi: Greek Cities and Roman Emperors.* Leiden and Boston.

Burrell, B. (2006) 'False fronts: separating the aedicular facade from the imperial cult in Roman Asia Minor', *American Journal of Archaeology* 110.3: 437–69.

Butcher, K. (2005) 'Information, legitimation, or self-legitimation? Popular and elite designs on the coin types of Syria', in C. Howgego, V. Heuchert, and A. Burnett (eds), *Coinage and Identity in the Roman Provinces.* Oxford, 143–56.

Calomino, D. (forthcoming) *Pride, Profit and Prestige. Greek Festival Culture and Civic Coinage in the Roman East.* Cambridge.

Carless Unwin, N. (2020) 'Basket-bearers and gold-wearers: epigraphic insights into the material dimensions of processional roles in the Greek East', *Kernos* 33: 89–125.

Carless Unwin, N. (Forthcoming) *Inscribing Festival Culture in the Graeco-Roman East.* Cambridge.

Chaniotis, A. (1995) 'Sich selbst feiern? Städtische Feste des Hellenismus im Spannungsfeld der Religion und Politik', in P. Zanker and M. Wörrle (eds), *Stadtbild und Bürgerbild im Hellenismus.* Munich, 147–72.

Chaniotis, A. (2003) 'Negotiating religion in the cities of the eastern Roman Empire', *Kernos* 16: 177–90.

Chaniotis, A. (ed.) (2011a) *Ritual Dynamics in the Ancient Mediterranean. Agency, Emotion, Gender, Representation*. Habes 49. Stuttgart.

Chaniotis, A. (2011b) 'Greek festivals and contests; definition and general characteristics', in A. Hermary and B. Jaeger (eds), *Thesaurus Cultus et Rituum Antiquorum (ThesCRA)*. Vol. VII: *Festivals and Contexts*. Los Angeles, 4–43.

Chaniotis, A. (2013) 'Processions in Hellenistic cities: contemporary discourses and ritual dynamics', in R. Alston, O. M. van Nijf, and C. Williamson (eds), *Cults, Creeds and Identities in the Greek City after the Classical Age*. Leuven, 21–47.

Cole, S. G. (2004) *Landscapes, Gender and Ritual Space. The Ancient Greek Experience*. Berkeley.

Coleman, K. M. (2008) 'Exchanging gladiators for an aqueduct at Aphrodisias (*SEG* 50.1096)', *Acta Classica* 51: 31–46.

Coleman, K. and Nelis-Clément, J. (eds) (2012), *L'Organisation des Spectacles dans le Monde Romaine*. Fondation Hardt, Entretiens sur l'antiquité classique 58. Geneva.

Connolly, J. B. (2011) 'Ritual movement through Greek sacred space: towards an archaeology of performance', in A. Chaniotis (ed.), *Ritual Dynamics in the Ancient Mediterranean. Agency, Emotion, Gender, Representation*. Habes 49. Stuttgart, 313–46.

Cooley, A. E. (ed.) (2000) *The Epigraphic Landscape of Roman Italy*. Bulletin of Classical Studies Supplement 73. London.

Cooley, A. E. (2012) *The Cambridge Manual of Latin Epigraphy*. Cambridge.

Csapo, E. and Wilson, P. (2019) *A Social and Economic History of the Theatre to 300 BC. Vol. 2: Theatre beyond Athens: Documents with Translation and Commentary*. Cambridge.

Day, J. W. (2019) 'The "spatial dynamics" of archaic and classical Greek epigram: conversations among locations, monuments, texts, and viewer-readers', in A. Petrovic, I. Petrovic, and E. Thomas (eds), *The Materiality of Text: Placement, Perception and Presence of Inscribed Texts in Classical Antiquity*. Leiden and Boston, 73–104.

Day, J., Hakola, R., Kahlos, M., and Tervahauta, U. (eds) (2016) *Spaces in Late Antiquity. Cultural, Theological and Archaeological Perspectives*. Abingdon and New York.

Dickenson, C. P. and van Nijf, O. M. (eds) (2013) *Public Space in the Post-Classical City*. Leuven.

Dunbabin, K. M. D. (2016) *Theatre and Spectacle in the Art of the Roman Empire*. Ithaca.

Eastmond, A. (ed.) (2015) *Viewing Inscriptions in the Late Antique and Medieval World*. Cambridge.

Edelmann, B. (2008) 'Pompa und Bild im Kaiserkult des römischen Ostens', in J. Rüpke (ed.), *Festrituale in der römischen Kaiserzeit*. Tübingen, 153–67.

Elsner, J. (1996) 'Image and ritual: reflections on the religious appreciation of classical art', *Classical Quarterly* 46.2: 515–31.

Elsner, J. (2012) 'Material culture and ritual: state of the question', in B. D. Wescoat and R. G. Ousterhout (eds), *Architecture of the Sacred. Space, Ritual and Experience from Classical Greece to Byzantium*. Cambridge, 1–26.

Erll, A. and Rigney, A. (eds) (2009) *Mediation, Remediation, and the Dynamics of Cultural Memory*. Berlin and Boston.

Friese, W. and Kristensen, T. M. (eds) (2017) *Excavating Pilgrimage. Archaeological Approaches to Sacred Travel and Movement in the Ancient World*. Abingdon and New York.

Gaifmann, M. (2006) 'Statue, cult and reproduction', *Art History* 29.2: 258–79.

Gaifmann, M. and Platt, V. (2018) 'Introduction: from Grecian urn to embodied object', *Art History* 41.3 (special edition): 402–19.

Galinsky, K. and Lapatin, K. (eds) (2015) *Cultural Memories in the Roman Empire*. Los Angeles.

Gangloff, A. (ed.) (2013) *Lieux de mémoire en orient grec à l'époque impériale*. Bern and Oxford.

Gebhard, E. R. (1996) 'The theatre and the city', in W. J. Slater (ed.), *Roman Theater and Society*. Ann Arbor, 113–27.

Gell, A. (1998) *Art and Agency. An Anthropological Theory*. Oxford.

Gordon, R. (1979) 'The real and the imaginary: production and religion in the Graeco-Roman world', *Art History* 2.1: 5–34.

Gordon, R. (1990a) 'The veil of power: emperors, sacrificers and benefactors', in M. Beard and J. North (eds), *Pagan Priests: Religion and Power in the Ancient World*. London, 201–34.

Gordon, R. (1990b) 'Religion in the Roman empire: the civic compromise and its limits', in M. Beard and J. North (eds), *Pagan Priests: Religion and Power in the Ancient World*. London, 235–55.

Graf, F. (2011) 'Ritual restoration and innovation in the Greek cities of the Roman Imperium', in A. Chaniotis (ed.), *Ritual Dynamics in the Ancient Mediterranean: Agency, Emotion, Gender, Representation*. Habes 49. Stuttgart, 105–17.

Graf, F. (2015) *Roman Festivals in the Greek East: From the Early Empire to the Middle Byzantine Era*. Cambridge.

Graham, A. (2013) 'The word is not enough. A new methodology for assessing monumental inscriptions: a case study in Ephesus', *American Journal of Archaeology* 117: 388–412.

Graham, A. (2019) 'Re-appraising the value of same-text relationships: a study of "duplicate" inscriptions in the monumental landscape at Aphrodisias', in A. Petrovic, I. Petrovic, and E. Thomas (eds), *The Materiality of Text: Placement, Perception and Presence of Inscribed Texts in Classical Antiquity*. Leiden and Boston, 275–302.

Halbwachs, M. (1950) *La mémoire collective*. Paris.

Harl, K. W. (1987) *Civic Coins and Civic Politics in the Roman East A.D. 180–275*. Berkeley and London.

Harris, E. M. (2015) 'Towards a typology of Greek regulations about religious matters: a legal approach', *Kernos* 28: 53–83.

Heberdey, R. (1923) 'Gymnische und andere Agone in Termessus Pisidiae', in W. H. Buckler and W. M. Calder (eds), *Anatolian Studies Presented to Sir William Mitchell Ramsay*. Manchester, 195–206.

Heberdey, R. (1929) *Termessische Studien*. Vienna.

Hekster, O., Schmidt-Hofner, S., and Witschel, C. (eds) (2009) *Ritual Dynamics and Religious Change in the Roman Empire*. Leiden and Boston.

Hermary, A. and Jaeger, B. (eds) (2011) *Thesaurus Cultus et Rituum Antiquorum (ThesCRA)*. Vol. VII: *Festivals and Contexts*. Los Angeles.

Von Hesberg, H. (2009) 'Archäologische Charakteristika der Inschriftenträger staatlicher Urkunden: einige Beispeile', in R. Haensch (ed.), *Selbstdarstellung und Kommunikation. Die Veröffentlichung staatlicher Urkunden auf Stein und Bronze in der römischen Welt*. Vestigia 61. Munich, 19–56.

Heuchert, V. (2005) 'The chronological development of Roman provincial coin iconography', in C. Howgego, V. Heuchert, and A. Burnett (eds), *Coinage and Identity in the Roman Provinces*. Oxford, 29–56.

Hodder, I. (2012) *Entangled. An Archaeology of the Relationships between Humans and Things*. Malden, MA.

Hollinshead, M. B. (2012) 'Monumental steps and the shaping of ceremony', in B. D. Wescoat and R. G. Ousterhout (eds), *Architecture of the Sacred. Space, Ritual and Experience from Classical Greece to Byzantium*. Cambridge, 27–65.

Hollinshead, M. B. (2015) *Shaping Ceremony. Monumental Steps and Greek Architecture*. Madison, WI.

Hornblower, S. and Morgan. C. (eds) (2007) *Pindar's Poetry, Patrons and Festivals: From Archaic Greece to the Roman Empire*. Oxford and New York.

Howgego, C. (1985) *Greek Imperial Countermarks: Studies in the Provincial Coinage of the Roman Empire*. London.

Howgego, C. (2005) 'Coinage and identity in the Roman provinces', in C. Howgego, V. Heuchert, and A. Burnett (eds), *Coinage and Identity in the Roman Provinces*. Oxford, 1–17.

Howgego, C., Heuchert, V., and Burnett, A. (eds) (2005) *Coinage and Identity in the Roman Provinces*. Oxford.

Johnston, A. (1984) 'Greek imperial statistics: a commentary', *Revue Numismatique* 26: 240–57.

Jones, C. P. (2007) 'Three new letters of the emperor Hadrian', *Zeitschrift für Papyrologie und Epigraphik* 161: 145–56.

Jones, T. B. (1963) 'A numismatic riddle: the so-called Greek Imperials', *Proceedings of the American Philosophical Society* 107: 308–47.

Kalinowski, A. (2002) 'The Vedii Antonini: aspects of patronage and benefaction in second-century Ephesos', *Phoenix* 56: 109–49.

Kantiréa, M. (2007) *Les dieux et les dieux Augustes: le culte impérial en Grèce sous les Julio-Claudiens e les Flaviens*. Athens.

Karl, H. (1975) 'Numismatische Beiträge zum Festwesen der kleinasiatischen und nordgriechischen Städte im 2./3. Jahrhundert'. Diss. Saarbrücken.

Kindt, J. (2012) *Rethinking Greek Religion*. Cambridge.

Klose, D. O. W. (2005) 'Festivals and games in the cities of the East during the Roman empire', in C. Howgego, V. Heuchert, and A. Burnett (eds), *Coinage and Identity in the Roman Provinces*. Oxford, 125–33.

Kokkinia, C. (2000) *Die Opramoas-Inschrift von Rhodiapolis: Euergetismus und soziale Elite in Lykien*. Bonn.

Kokkinia, C. (2003) 'Letters of Roman authorities on local dignitaries: the case of Vedius Antoninus', *Zeitschrift für Papyrologie und Epigraphik* 142: 197–213.

Kokkinia, C. (2012) 'Games vs. buildings as euergetic choices', in K. Coleman and J. Nelis-Clément (eds), *L'Organisation des Spectacles dans le Monde Romaine*. Fondation Hardt, Entretiens sur l'antiquité classique 58. Geneva, 97–130.

König, J. (2005) *Athletics and Literature in the Roman Empire*. Cambridge.

König, J. (2009) 'Games and festivals', in G. Boys-Stones, B. Graziosi, and P. Vasunia (eds), *Oxford Handbook of Hellenic Studies*. Oxford.

Kraft, K. (1972) *Das System der kaiserzeitlichen Münzprägung in Kleinasien. Materialien und Entwürfe*. Berlin.

Latham, J. A. (2016) *Performance, Memory, and Processions in Ancient Rome. The Pompa Circensis from the Late Republic to Late Antiquity*. New York.

Laum, B. (1914) *Stiftungen in der griechischen und römischen Antike: ein Beitrag zur antiken Kulturgeschichte*. 2 vols. Leipzig.

Le Guen, B. (2001) *Les Associations de Technites Dionysiaques à l'époque Hellénistique*. Nancy: Association pour la diffusion de la recherche sur l'antiquité.

Lefebvre, H. (1974) *La production de l'espace*. Paris.

Lehner, M. F. (2005) 'Die Agonistik im Ephesos der römischen Kaiserzeit'. PhD thesis, Ludwig-Maximilians-Universität, Munich.

Leschhorn, W. (1981) 'Le monnayage impérial d'Asie Mineure et la statistique', *PACT* 5: 252–66.

Leschhorn, W. (1998) 'Die Verbreitung von Agonen in den östlichen Provinzen des römischen Reiches', in W. Orth (ed.), Colloquium 'Agonistik in der römischen Kaiserzeit', *Stadion* 24.1: 31–58.

Lupu, E. (2005) *Greek Sacred Law. A Collection of New Documents*. Leiden and Boston.

Ma, J. (2013) *Statues and Cities: Honorific Portraits and Civic Identity in the Hellenistic World*. Cambridge.

MacMullen, R. (1982) 'The epigraphic habit in the Roman empire', *American Journal of Philology* 103.3: 233–46.

MacMullen, R. (1986) 'Frequency of inscriptions in Roman Lydia', *Zeitschrift für Papyrologie und Epigraphik* 65: 237–8.

Malay, H. (1999) *Researches in Lydia, Mysia and Aiolis*. Vienna.

Marinatos, N. and Hägg, R. (eds) (1993) *Greek Sanctuaries. New Approaches.* Abingdon and New York.

Melfi, M. and Bobou, O. (eds) (2016) *Hellenistic Sanctuaries: Between Greece and Rome.* Oxford.

Meyer, E. (1990) 'Explaining the epigraphic habit in the Roman empire: the evidence of epitaphs', *Journal of Roman Studies* 80: 74–96.

Mikalson, J. D. (2006) 'Greek religion: continuity and change in the Hellenistic period', in G. Bugh (ed.), *The Cambridge Companion to the Hellenistic World.* Cambridge, 208–22.

Millar, F. (1992) *The Emperor in the Roman World. 31 BC–AD 337.* 2nd edition. London.

Mitchell, S. (1990) 'Festivals, games and civic life in Roman Asia Minor', *Journal of Roman Studies* 80: 183–93.

Moretti, L. (1953) *Iscrizioni agonistiche greche.* Rome.

Moretti, L. (1957) *Olympionikai: i vincitori negli antichi agoni olimpici.* Rome.

Mortensen, E. and Poulsen, B. (eds) (2017) *Cityscapes and Monuments of Western Asia Minor: Memories and Identities.* Oxford.

Moser, C. and Feldman, C. (eds) (2014) *Locating the Sacred: Theoretical Approaches to the Emplacement of Religion.* Oxford and Oakville.

Mouratidis, G. (2020) 'Athlete and *polis*: the relationship between athletes and cities in the epigraphic record of the Late Hellenistic and Imperial periods', PhD thesis, University of St Andrews.

Mouratidis, G. (2021) 'Athletes, citizenships and Hellenic identity during the imperial period', *Klio* 103.2: 675–703.

Mylonopoulos, J. (2008) 'The Dynamics of Ritual Space in the Hellenistic and Roman East', *Kernos* 21: 49–79.

Mylonopoulos, J. (2011) 'Das griechische Heiligtum als räumlicher Kontext antiker Feste und Agone', in A. Hermary and B. Jaeger (eds), *Thesaurus Cultus et Rituum Antiquorum (ThesCRA).* Vol. VII: *Festivals and Contexts.* Los Angeles, 43–78.

Nawotka, K. (ed.) (2021) *Epigraphic Culture in the Eastern Mediterranean in Antiquity.* Abingdon and New York.

Newby, Z. (2003) 'Art and identity in Asia Minor', in S. Scott and J. Webster (eds), *Roman Imperialism and Provincial Art.* Cambridge, 192–213.

Newby, Z. (2005) *Greek Athletics in the Roman World: Victory and Virtue.* Oxford.

Newby, Z. and Calomino, D. (2022) 'The materiality of Greek festivals in the Roman East: the view from Perge', *Asia Minor* 2: 41–54.

Ng, D. (2015) 'Commemoration and élite benefaction of buildings and spectacles in the Roman world', *Journal of Roman Studies* 105: 101–23.

van Nijf, O. M. (2011) 'Public space and the political culture of Roman Termessos', in O. M. van Nijf and R. Alston (eds), *Political Culture in the Greek City after the Classical Age.* Leuven, 215–42.

van Nijf, O. M. (2012) 'Political games', in K. Coleman and J. Nelis-Clément (eds), *L'Organisation des Spectacles dans le Monde Romaine*. Fondation Hardt, Entretiens sur l'antiquité classique 58. Geneva, 47–95.

van Nijf, O. M. and Alston, R. (eds) (2011) *Political Culture in the Greek City after the Classical Age*. Leuven.

van Nijf, O. M., Alston, R., and Williamson, C. G. (2013) 'Introduction: the Greek city and its religions after the classical age', in R. Alston, O. M. van Nijf, and C. Williamson (eds), *Cults, Creeds and Identities in the Greek City after the Classical Age*. Leuven, 1–20.

van Nijf, O. M. and Williamson, C. G. (2015) 'Re-inventing traditions: connecting contests in the Hellenistic and Roman world', in D. Boschung, A. W. Busch, and M. J. Verluys (eds), *Reinventing 'The Invention of Tradition'? Indigenous Pasts and the Roman Present*. Paderborn, 95–111.

van Nijf, O. M. and Williamson, C. G. (2016) 'Connecting the Greeks: festival networks in the Hellenistic world', in C. Mann, S. Remijsen, and S. Scharff (eds), *Athletics in the Hellenistic World*. Stuttgart, 43–71.

Nollé, J. (1993) 'Die feindlichen Schwestern: Betrachtungen zur Rivalität der pamphylischen Städte', in D. Gerhard and G. Rehrenböck (eds), *Die epigraphische und altertumskundliche Erforschung Kleinasiens: Kleinasiatische Kommission der Österreichischen Akademie der Wissenschaften. Akten des Symposiums vom 23. bis 25. Oktober 1990*. Denkschriften der philosophisch-historischen Klasse 236. Vienna, 297–317.

Nollé, J. (2012) 'Stadtprägungen des Ostens und die 'Explosion agonistique', in K. Coleman and J. Nelis-Clément (eds), *L'Organisation des Spectacles dans le Monde Romaine*. Fondation Hardt, Entretiens sur l'antiquité classique 58. Geneva, 1–45.

Nora, P. (1984–92) *Les Lieux de mémoire*. 3 vols. Paris.

Osborne, R. and Tanner, J. (eds) (2007) *Art's Agency and Art History*. Malden, MA.

Østby, E. (1993) 'Twenty-five years on research on Greek sanctuaries: a bibliography', in N. Marinatos and R. Hägg (eds), *Greek Sanctuaries. New Approaches*. Abingdon and New York, 192–227.

Östenberg, I., Malmberg, S., and Bjørnebye, J. (eds) (2015) *The Moving City: Processions, Passages and Promenades in Ancient Rome*. London.

Parker, R. (2004) 'What are Greek sacred laws?', in E. M. Harris and L. Rubinstein (eds), *The Law and the Courts in Ancient Greece*. London: 57–70.

Petrovic, A., Petrovic, I., and Thomas, E. (eds) (2019) *The Materiality of Text: Placement, Perception and Presence of Inscribed Texts in Classical Antiquity*. Leiden and Boston.

Petzl, G. and Schwertheim, E. (2006) *Hadrian und die dionysischen Künstler: drei in Alexandria Troas neugefundene Briefe des Kaisers an die Künstler-Vereinigung*. Bonn.

Pitts, M. and Versluys, M. J. (eds) (2015) *Globalisation and the Roman World: World History, Connectivity and Material Culture*. Cambridge.

Platt, V. (2011) *Facing the Gods. Epiphany and Representation in Graeco-Roman Art, Literature and Religion*. Cambridge.

Pleket, H. W. (2014) 'On the sociology of ancient sport', in T. F. Scanlon (ed.), *Sport in the Greek and Roman Worlds. Vol. 2: Greek Athletic Identities and Roman Sports and Spectacles*. Oxford, 29–81.

de Polignac, F. (1995) *Cults, Territory and the Origins of the Greek City-State*. Trans. J. Lloyd. Chicago.

Popkin, M. (2016) *The Architecture of the Roman Triumph: Monuments, Memory and Identity*. New York.

Price, S. R. F. (1984) *Rituals and Power: The Roman Imperial Cult in Asia Minor*. Cambridge.

Price, S. R. F. (2005) 'Local mythologies in the Greek East', in C. Howgego, V. Heuchert, and A. Burnett (eds), *Coinage and Identity in the Roman Provinces*. Oxford, 115–24.

Psoma, S. (2008) '*Panegyris* coinages', *American Journal of Numismatics* 20: 227–55.

Psoma, S. (2009) 'Profitable networks: coinages, *panegyris* and Dionysiac artists', in I. Malkin, C. Constantakopoulou, and K. Panagopoulou (eds), *Greek and Roman Networks in the Mediterranean*. Abingdon, 230–48.

Raja, R. and Rüpke, J. (eds) (2015) *A Companion to the Archaeology of Religion in the Ancient World*. Chichester.

Remijsen, S. (2015) *The End of Greek Athletics in Late Antiquity*. Cambridge.

Reynolds, J. (2000) 'New letters from Hadrian to Aphrodisias: trials, taxes, gladiators and an aqueduct', *Journal of Roman Archaeology* 13: 5–20.

Rives, J. (2001) 'Civic and religious life', in J. Bodel (ed.), *Epigraphic Evidence: Ancient History from Inscriptions*. London, 118–36.

Robert, L. (1984) 'Discours d'ouverture', *Praktika of the Eighth International Congress of Greek and Latin Epigraphy*. Athens, I: 35–45.

Robert, L. (1969–90) *Opera Minora Selecta*. Amsterdam. 7 volumes.

Robert, L. (1975) 'Nonnos et les monnaies d'Akmonie de Phrygie', *Journal des Savants* 1975: 153–92. Reprinted in L. Robert, *Opera Minora Selecta* VII: 185–224.

Rogers, G. M. (1991) *The Sacred Identity of Ephesos: Foundation Myths of a Roman City*. London.

Rosenwein, B. H. (2006) *Emotional Communities in the Early Middle Ages*. Ithaca.

Roueché, C. (1993) *Performers and Partisans at Aphrodisias in the Roman and Late Roman Periods: A Study Based on Inscriptions from the Current Excavations at Aphrodisias in Caria*. With Appendix IV by Nathalie de Chaisemartin. London.

Rüpke, J. (ed.) (2008) *Festrituale in der römischen Kaiserzeit*. Tübingen.

Rüpke, J. and Woolf, G. (eds) (2013) *Religious Dimensions of the Self in the Second Century CE*. Tübingen.

Scherrer, P. (2008) 'Die Stadt als Festplatz: das Beispiel der ephesischen Bauprogramme rund um die Kaiserneokorien Domitians und Hadrians', in J. Rüpke (ed.), *Festrituale in der römischen Kaiserzeit*. Tübingen, 35–65.

Scott, M. (2010) *Delphi and Olympia: The Spatial Politics of Panhellenism in the Archaic and Classical Periods*. Cambridge and New York.

Scott, M. (2013) *Space and Society in the Greek and Roman Worlds*. Cambridge.

Scott, M. (2022) 'Walls and the ancient Greek ritual experience: the sanctuary of Demeter and Kore at Eleusis', in E. Eidinow, A. Geertz, and J. North (eds), *Cognitive Approaches to Ancient Religious Experience. Ancient Religion and Cognition*. Cambridge, 193–217.

Slater, W. (2007) 'Deconstructing festivals', in P. Wilson (ed.), *The Greek Theatre and Festivals: Documentary Studies*. Oxford, 21–47.

Sokolowki, F. (1955) *Lois sacrées de l'Asie Mineure*. Paris.

Sokolowski, F. (1962) *Lois sacrées des cites grecques. Supplement*. Paris.

Sokolowski, F. (1969) *Lois sacrées des cites grecques*. Paris.

Sourvinou-Inwood, C. (1990) 'What is polis religion?', in O. Murray and S. Price (eds), *The Greek City from Homer to Alexander*. Oxford, 295–322.

Stavrianopoulou, E. (ed.) (2006) *Ritual and Communication in the Graeco-Roman World*. Liège.

Stavrianopoulou, E. (2009) 'Die Bewirtung des Volkes: öffentlichen Speisungen in der römischen Kaiserzeit', in O. Hekster, S. Schmidt-Hofner, and C. Witschel (eds), *Ritual Dynamics and Religious Change in the Roman Empire*. Leiden and Boston, 159–83.

Versluys, M. J. (2014) 'Understanding objects in motion: an archaeological dialogue on Romanization', *Archaeological Dialogues* 21.1: 1–20.

Warf, B. and Arias, S. (eds) (2009) *The Spatial Turn: Interdisciplinary Perspectives*. London and New York.

Watson, G. (2020) *Connections, Communities, and Coinage: The System of Coin Production in Southern Asia Minor, AD 218–276*. New York.

Weiss, P. (2005) 'The cities and their money', in C. Howgego, V. Heuchert, and A. Burnett (eds), *Coinage and Identity in the Roman Provinces*. Oxford, 57–68.

Wescoat, B. D. and Ousterhout, R. G. (eds) (2012) *Architecture of the Sacred: Space, Ritual and Experience from Classical Greece to Byzantium*. Cambridge.

Wilson, P. (2007a) *The Greek Theatre and Festivals: Documentary Studies*. Oxford.

Wilson, P. (2007b) 'Introduction: from the ground up', in P. Wilson (ed.), *The Greek Theatre and Festivals: Documentary Studies*. Oxford, 1–17.

Woolf, G. (1996) 'Monumental writing and the expansion of Roman society in the early empire', *Journal of Roman Studies* 86: 22–39.

Woolf, G. (1997) 'Polis-religion and its alternatives in the Roman provinces', in H. Cancik and J. Rüpke (eds), *Römische Reichsreligion und Provinzialreligion*. Tübingen: 71–84.

Wörrle, M. (1988) *Stadt und Fest im kaiserzeitlichen Kleinasien: Studien zu einer agonistichen Stuftung aud Oinoanda*. Munich.

Ziegler, R. (1985) *Städtisches Prestige und kaiserleitliche Politik: Studien zum Festwesen in Ostkilikien im 2. und 3. Jahrhundert n. Chr.* Dusseldorf.

Zuiderhoek, A. (2009) *The Politics of Munificence in the Roman Empire: Citizens, Elites and Benefactors in Asia Minor*. Cambridge.

2
Establishing a Channel of Communication
Roman Emperors and the Self-Presentation of Greek Athletes in the Roman East

Sebastian Scharff

2.1. Introduction

In an honorific decree from Karian Aphrodisias dating to the AD 160s,[1] the personal relationship between an athlete and the emperor is emphasized in a remarkable way. The passage reads as follows:

[ἀ]νελέσθαι εὐτυχῶς τοσούτους ἀγῶ|[ν]ας καὶ δοξάσαι καθ᾽ ἕκαστον ἀγῶνα τὴν | [λ]αμπροτάτην πατρίδα αὐτοῦ κηρύγμα|[σ]ιν καὶ στεφάνοις, μάλιστα δὲ καὶ ἐπὶ | [θ]εοῦ Ἀντωνείνου, ὡς οὐ μόνον στε[φαν|ω]θῆναι ταῖς ἐκείνου χειρσὶν, ἀλλὰ καὶ | [τει]μαῖς ἐξαιρέτοις τειμηθῆναι, (…).

he (i.e. Aelius Aurelius Menandros) has won with good fortune so many contests and has brought honour at each contest to his splendid homeland by proclamations and crowns and especially also in the time of the divine Antoninus, so that he was not only crowned at his hands, but also honoured with particular honours (…).[2]

What is striking about the way this Aphrodisian athlete is presented here is that he is said to have received at least one of his crowns directly from the hands of the emperor (ταῖς ἐκείνου χειρσίν),[3] an honour the athlete and his hometown were obviously especially proud of. Clearly, being close to the emperor is understood as a positive quality here. At first glance, such a statement may not come as a total

---

[1] All translations if not explicitly otherwise stated are my own.
[2] *I.Aphrodisias* 2007, 12.920, I a, ll. 14–20 (Aphrodisias, AD 138–69; transl. C. Roueché). The cited passage is part of a statue base bearing honours for the successful pancratiast Aelius Aurelius Menandros from Aphrodisias. The statue base is inscribed on three faces (a, b, c) and includes two inscriptions (i, ii), one put up by the Athletic Guild (i), the other by the Council and the People of Aphrodisias (ii); see also *CIG* 2811b (a), 2810b (b), *LBW* 1620a (i), 1620b (ii), *IAG* 72 (ii), and *MAMA* VIII 421.
[3] Heinemann (2014), 242.

surprise; and yet, it is far from self-evident that such a logic does automatically apply in the agonistic discourse since victor inscriptions focus very much on the personal achievements of the athlete. In fact, the emphasis on a close relationship with the emperor had the potential to diminish the personal achievements of the victor and thus the grandeur of the success due to the notion of potential favouritism. This is why a second-century pancratiast from Alexandria explicitly emphasized that he had won his athletic victories 'not by imperial favour' (μήτε κατὰ χάριν βασιλικήν).[4] Highlighting a closeness to the emperor (as in the case of Menandros from Aphrodisias) could at times be understood as being contrary to the logic of agonistic self-presentation.

The fact that Menandros' emphasis on being close to the emperor is not automatically in line with the logic of the genre makes his case all the more appealing and calls for a new analysis of the relationship between Roman emperors and Greek athletes.[5] I will tackle this relationship from the point of view of the athletes. By focusing on the question of what role Roman emperors played in the material evidence of athletic self-presentation, I will also analyse if, how, and why the agonistic discourse changed from the Hellenistic to the Roman imperial period.

To better understand the way in which the athletes' self-presentation worked in the imperial period—and especially the role the emperors played in it—we first have to take a look at the emperors' point of view. Therefore, this chapter starts with an analysis of how Roman emperors of roughly the first three centuries AD used athletic festivals as a means of establishing a channel of communication with the people of the Greek-speaking parts of the empire, looking at the manners in which emperors were present at these festivals (2.2), and how they intervened in the agonistic circuit (2.3). In a last section (2.4), then, we will take the athletes' perspective and analyse in detail how agonistic self-presentation changed in imperial times and what part material culture (i.e. victor inscriptions) played in this process.

---

[4] *IG* XIV 1102, l. 14 (= *IGUR* I 240; *IAG* 79; cf. *SEG* 55, 1061; Rome, c. AD 200; transl. S. Miller (2004a), no. 153). Note that the victor, the famous pancratiast Marcus Aurelius Asklepiades, also openly refers to the fact that he dropped out of his career at the age of 25 due to the 'jealousy and envy of his competitors' (διὰ τοὺς συνβάντας μοι κινδύνους καὶ φθό|νους). Clearly this was a different φθόνος from the one earlier athletes had experienced. Just think of the case of the Athenian aristocrat Megakles whose epinician by Pindar explicitly references the envy of his fellow citizens—not the φθόνος of his competitors (Pindar, *Pythian Odes* 7, ll. 18–19; cf. Mann (2001), 297–8). On Asklepiades' career, see also *IG* XIV 1103 (*IGUR* I 241), *IG* XIV 1104, and *IGUR* I 250, for further details, Moretti (1953), 230–5; Harris (1962), 19–20; and König (2005), 3 n. 3.

[5] The current state of research with regard to the relationship of Roman emperors and Greek athletes is represented by a splendid article written by Pleket (2010) (see also van Nijf (1999), 181 and 186–8; König (2005), 225–35 [with a focus on literary evidence, esp. Sallustius] and Gouw 2009). Pleket has shown that most emperors saw themselves as protectors of the athletes' interests and privileges, but also cared for Roman tax income and the budget of Greek cities. For single emperors and their approach to Greek athletics, see Langenfeld (1975) and Spawforth (2012), esp. 86 and 162 (for Augustus); Zoumbaki (2007) (Tiberius); Kennell (1988) (Nero); Spawforth (2007) (Domitian); and Heinemann (2014) (Nero and Domitian).

2.2. The emperor at the games. Direct (and indirect) presence of emperors at Greek festivals

There were primarily two ways for a Roman emperor to show his presence at an athletic contest. The first possibility included actual participation: the emperor could actively engage in equestrian competitions as the owner of the horses. Another way was simply to be present at a festival, but not to compete himself. For the first possibility, a long tradition of Greek sole rulers existed since the sixth century BC who participated in the Olympic games and other contests and made good use of their successes in their self-presentation.[6] Since the second century BC, some non-Greek royalty also won victories in Greek horse races,[7] and Roman horse owners did the same since the first century BC.[8]

Despite the fact that we know of victories won by Roman emperors, they did not play an important part in the self-representation of those emperors, but were rather recorded by other parties: Tiberius succeeded at the Olympic games (probably of the year 20 BC) and gained another victory at the Erotideia Rhomaia of Thespiai,[9] Germanicus achieved an Olympic crown in AD 17,[10] and Domitian won at the Sebasta of AD 82,[11] yet all of these victories are known to us only from Greek inscriptions set up at the place of victory and are not attested in any Roman source.[12] This state of the evidence, however, is not surprising, given the fact that the Romans certainly had a rather ambivalent approach to Greek athletics in general. As Christian Mann has convincingly argued, 'the exclusion of Greek athletics from Roman culture in discourse went hand in hand (…) with inclusion

---

[6] On the victories of Sicilian tyrants, Mann (2001), 236–91 and (2013); for victorious kings and queens of the Hellenistic age, see Mann (2018); Scharff (forthcoming).

[7] The Numidian prince Mastanabal son of Masinissa, for instance, won the two-horse chariot race for colts at the Panathenaic games of 158/7 BC (*IG* II² 2316, col. II, ll. 42–4; for the date, Tracy and Habicht (1991), 232), and Mithridates VI Eupator succeeded in four horse races in an anonymous *agon* in Chios (Evangelidis (1927–8), no. 12, ll. 8–15; cf. Robert (1935); van Bremen (2007), 368–9).

[8] Publius Licinius son of Publius, for instance, won five (!) equestrian victories including both four-horse chariot races (for adult horses and for colts) at one and the same iteration of the Basileia of Lebadeia (*SEG* 3, 367 [= Manieri (2009), *Leb*. 12], ll. 16–17 and 20–7). His victories clearly represent the most splendid agonistic successes of a Roman horse owner in the Hellenistic period (on the date of the victory: Gossage (1975) [65–60 BC] and Müller (2014), 126–9 [40 and 30 BC]). Another successful Roman horse owner of the Hellenistic period was Caius Octavius Pollio, who won the single horse race at the Rhomaia of Xanthos in the late 70s or 60s BC (*SEG* 28, 1246 [= Robert (1978)], ll. 40–2; on the date of the inscription, see now Schuler and Zimmermann (2012), 582–97.

[9] For the year 20 BC as the date of Tiberius' Olympic success (*I.Olympia* 218), see Zoumbaki (2007) (accepted by Spawforth (2012), 164). Moretti, *Olympionikai* no. 738 tentatively dated the victory to the year 4 BC and rightly insisted that it was at least prior to AD 4 ('certo anteriore al 4 d. Cr., quando egli [sc. Tiberius] assunse il gentilizio di Augusto'); similarly Kaplan (1990), 223–6 who put the Olympic victory into the time of Tiberius' Rhodian exile and suggested AD 1 as a possibility. Tiberius' victory at the Erotidaia Rhomaia is attested in a Thespian victor list dating between 6 BC and AD 2 (*I.Thespies* 188, ll. 76–7 [*SEG* 44, 420]).

[10] *I.Olympia* 221; date: Moretti, *Olympionikai*, no. 750.

[11] Miranda De Martino (2017a), col. I, ll. 7–8 (with fig. 1): συνωρίδι τελεία | Αὐτοκράτωρ Δομιτιαν(ὸς) Καῖσαρ.

[12] Cf. Mann (2014). On the special case of Nero's agonistic tour across Greece which is attested in Roman sources, Kennell (1988).

in practice'.[13] While a lot of dismissive statements on Greek athletics authored by Roman sources have come down to us,[14] such utterances do not represent the overall picture of Roman attitudes towards Greek-style contests; in particular the *plebs urbana* showed great interest in the public performance of Greek games.[15]

Several emperors gladly yielded to this demand and established *certamina Graeca* in Rome and Italy: the first *princeps* set the pace and founded both the *Ludi pro valetudine Caesaris*[16] in Rome in 28 BC and the Sebasta[17] of Naples in 2 BC. In the provinces, he re-established the Aktia of Nikopolis and raised their status remarkably to that of a crown game, which even became part of the new *periodos* of the imperial age.[18] All these measures were part of what Antony Spawforth has called the 'Augustan cultural revolution'.[19] Nero, Domitian, and Antoninus Pius followed this agenda and established, with varying degrees of success, the Neronia (in AD 60),[20] Capitolia (in AD 86),[21] and Eusebeia of Puteoli (in AD 142) respectively.[22] In the third century AD, Caracalla tried to introduce the Antoninia Pythia as a permanent festival in AD 214,[23] Gordian III an *agon Minervae* (for Athena Promachos) in AD 242,[24] and Aurelian an *agon Solis* (or Helieia in Greek)[25] in AD 274. Additionally, 'one-off contests'[26] were organized from time to time to celebrate a military victory, such as the Epinikia of Marcus Aurelius and Commodus.[27]

But all these activities of Roman emperors who established Greek contests were not only intended to satisfy the demands of the Roman *plebs*, as can easily be seen by the geographical distribution of these festivals which were not only held in

---

[13] Mann (2014), 173.

[14] It may suffice here to refer to Martial, *Epigrams* 14.49, CIL XIII 1668, II (= ILS 212), l. 15 (from Claudius' speech for the admittance of Gauls to the Senate of AD 48), and Pliny, *Epistles* 4.22.7 where an *agon* in Vienna is compared to an infectious disease (*agona..., qui mores Viennensium infecerat*) and to quote Pliny, *Epistles* 10.40.2 verbatim: *gymnasiis indulgent Graeculi*—'Those little Greeks are really hooked on their gymnasia' (the latter dictum is ascribed to the emperor Trajan).

[15] According to Tacitus, *Annals* 14.21, the Roman populace actually 'demanded' such contests 'from the magistrates' (*populo efflagitandi Graeca certamina a magistratibus*) and Horace, *Epistles* 2.186 includes the telling notice that the people called for 'a bear and for boxers' (*aut ursum aut pugiles*) during a play.

[16] Cassius Dio, *Roman History* 51.19.2; cf. Caldelli (1993), 21–4; Newby (2005), 27.

[17] Newby (2005), 31–3; Miranda De Martino (2007), (2010), (2013), (2017a), (2018).

[18] On the re-foundation of the Aktia, Lämmer (1986–7); Pavlogiannis and Albanidis (2007); Wacker (2017), 65–8, and (2018), esp. 16–17.

[19] Spawforth (2012), 1.

[20] The Neroneia were only repeated once in AD 65 (on the logic of the unusual five-year interval, convincingly Heinemann (2014), 224–36; for the Neroneia, cf. Kaplan (1990) 327–9; Champlin (2003), 37–43) and did not survive Nero's *damnatio memoriae*.

[21] Caldelli (1993); Rieger (1999). On Greek games in Rome in general, Wallner (2002).

[22] On the Eusebeia, Caldelli (1993), 43–5; for the evidence on other games in Italy (e.g. the Eleusinia of Tarentum), Remijsen (2015), 132.

[23] Strasser (2004). [24] Wallner (2004); Remijsen (2015), 132–3.

[25] Remijsen (2015), 133 (with n. 22). [26] Remijsen (2015), 132.

[27] There also were Herakleia Epinikia under Trajan (*IAG* 68 = *IG* XIV 747, l. 13, Naples, c. AD 110), but it is not entirely clear, whether they were held in Rome (as optimistically stated by Heinemann (2014), 223) or elsewhere; Moretti (1953), 187–8 and Robert (1970), 11 remain uncertain in this matter. On Epinikia in the eastern provinces of the empire, see now Blanco-Pérez (2018).

Rome, but also in Greece (Aktia) and Italy (Sebasta, Eusebeia). As a consequence, it is plausible to assume that these contests served to connect the emperor not only with the spectators of the games, but also with the people who competed in them, that is the athletes who mainly came from the Greek-speaking provinces of the empire. In this sense, festivals in the West like the Capitolia, the short-lived Neroneia, the Sebasta, and the Eusebeia provided the emperor with the opportunity to establish a channel of communication with Greek citizens from the East.

This can be seen very clearly for the Capitolia[28] and now also for the Sebasta, especially during Domitian's reign: at both festivals, the victor lists were dominated by Greek athletes from Asia Minor and Egypt, an observation which is strongly supported by the new evidence from Piazza Nicola Amore in Naples.[29] What is more, Titus and Domitian are also attested as *agonothetai* of the Sebasta of the years AD 70–8 (Titus) and probably AD 74–90 (Domitian).[30] Domitian's approach to athletics included, as we have seen, the foundation of a periodic contest in Rome, actual participation in chariot races at the Sebasta,[31] and the fulfilment of the duty of an *agonothetes* in the same festival. It is likely that it was informed by a desire to relate to the population of the empire in line with the Flavian policy of 'integrating the Greeks into the imperial elite'.[32]

We can observe the same policy with regard to Domitian's predecessor Titus who not only served as an *agonothetes* in Naples,[33] but also personally supported the famous boxer Melankomas who appeared to be his lover.[34] No doubt, imperial favour was always crucial for social advancement in the imperial period,

---

[28] Heinemann (2014), 236–43.

[29] The newly discovered inscriptions refer to the Sebasta of the years AD 74 to 84. The material consisting of 855 little pieces (Miranda De Martino (2013), 521), some of which are blank, is very fragmentary and obviously one has to await the final publication to draw sustainable conclusions. Yet the already published lists of the years AD 82 (Miranda De Martino (2017a)) and AD 86 (Miranda De Martino (2018)) alone demonstrate that the events which were open to foreign competitors were dominated by professional Greek athletes from the East: the athletic victors of AD 86, for instance, hailed from cities like Alexandria (eight different victors), Myra, Xanthos, Tralleis, Aphrodisias, Adana, Tyana, Tarsos, and Sardis (Miranda De Martino (2018), no. 4). Four years earlier, in addition to multiple victors from Alexandria the successful athletes came from Ephesos (twice), Prusa, Tralleis, Kyzikos, Tarsos, Xanthos, Nikopolis, Samos, and Smyrna (Miranda De Martino (2017a), 257–8). On the origin of these victors, see also Miranda De Martino (2014), 1182–3.

[30] Miranda De Martino (2014), 1170. It is interesting to note that the same is true for several Roman senators as well (Miranda De Martino (2010), 418–20). For Titus, Themistius, *Oration* 10, 139a–b,

[31] It is interesting to note that even Nero's extravagant engagement in the agonistic world which included, according to our sources, the emperor falling off a ten-horse chariot in Olympia did not bring an end to the active participation of Roman emperors in Greek horse races. On Nero's agonistic tour as a 'PR debacle' (van Nijf (1999), 187), see Alcock (1994).

[32] Chaniotis (2018), 253. Since Domitian admitted at least eight senators from Asia Minor to the senate, it may not come as a surprise that he was 'enormously popular in the eastern provinces': Chaniotis (2018), 254.

[33] Themistius, *Oration* 10, 139a–b; Miranda De Martino (2014), 1170.

[34] Themistius, *Oration* 10, 139; on Melankomas, Dio Chrysostom, *Orations* 28, 29. According to Miranda De Martino (2013), 531–5, Melankomas whose very existence has been questioned by older research, now appears as [Μελα]γχόμας from Alexandria in the new victor lists from Piazza Nicola Amore.

in the agonistic sphere as well as in other fields,[35] but under the Flavians (and subsequently during the Nerva-Antonine dynasty)[36] an active policy was expedited by the emperors that aimed at integrating the Greeks into the political elite of the empire: the people from the provinces (at least from those in the East) had become the fourth relevant status group of the empire on which the acceptance of an emperor now largely depended.[37]

In addition to serving as *agonothetes* or participating in horse races, an emperor could also simply show his presence at an athletic festival as a spectator,[38] whether this was in Rome or on his travels, as is best attested for Hadrian.[39] There can be no doubt that the status of a contest was enhanced by the imperial presence. The crucial point with regard to our research question, however, is whether this presence had an impact on the agonistic discourse, that is the way successful athletes presented their victories to their fellow citizens.[40] We will return to this question later.

For now, it is important to note that there were also a lot of opportunities for an emperor to be present at an athletic contest without actually attending: invited by the cities through rituals and artworks, he could be indirectly present at the games and festivals. Indirect presence was achieved, for instance, by the ever-present statues and busts of emperors.[41] Provincials like the wealthy Roman knight and Ephesian citizen C. Vibius Salutaris were eager to provide the funds. In AD 104, Salutaris sponsored one golden statue of Artemis and twenty-eight silver statues some of which represented the emperor Trajan and his wife Plotina, but also the Roman senate and the Roman people.[42] Yet, there was also a more subtle way to create indirect presence that had initially more to do with the

---

[35] Chaniotis (2018), 301–2.

[36] It was under the adoptive emperors (starting with Trajan and continued by Hadrian) that also mainland Greeks were admitted to the senate, Herodes Atticus being the first Greek to become ordinary consul in AD 143 (Chaniotis (2018), 255).

[37] According to a model developed by Flaig (2019), the imperial monarchy has to be understood as an 'acceptance system'. In order to gain acceptance, the emperor had to concede his favour separately to the three most important status groups of the empire: the senate, the Praetorian Guard, and the *plebs urbana*. This model has been very influential in the German academic discourse with good reason. Yet it has also been noted long since that 'others (i.e. other groups) may be added' (Bang (2013), 432). For the people of the provinces as a fourth group, see now e.g. Deeg (2019), 239–44.

[38] Augustus, for instance, is reported as having still been present at the Sebasta of AD 14, shortly before his death (Suetonius, *Lives of the Caesars, Divus Augustus* 98.5; Velleius Paterculus, *Compendium of Roman History*, 2.123.1; Cassius Dio, *Roman History* 56.29.2). Claudius was a spectator in AD 42 (Suetonius, *Lives of the Caesars, Divus Claudius* 11.2; Cassius Dio, *History* 60.6.1–2).

[39] On Hadrian's travels, Halfmann (1986); Birley (1997), 77–92, 113–41, 151–88, 203–78.

[40] In the traditional forms of athletic self-presentation, nearness to a sole ruler, be it an archaic tyrant or a Hellenistic king, does not appear as a regular feature. Athletic self-presentation of the late archaic, classical, and Hellenistic periods focused very much on the personal achievements of the victor. It goes without saying that victorious courtiers sometimes behaved differently (e.g. Kallikrates of Samos who ascribed his Pythian victory to the Ptolemaic dynasty: Poseidippos, *Epigram* 74, ll. 13–14).

[41] On images of the emperors in theatres, see Gebhard (1996); Edelmann (2008), 157–65; for the Severan family at the theatre in Hierapolis, Newby, Chapter 6, this volume. On the ways the emperors are made present in coinage, Calomino, Chapter 4, this volume.

[42] *I.Ephesos* 27; cf. Gebhard (1996), 121–3; Chaniotis (2018), 378.

organizing communities than with the emperor himself who alone more or less became the object of the ostentatious admiration expressed by the respective cities, when they named a contest after him.[43] Cities aimed at outdoing each other by accumulating imperial games. The city of Tarsos in Cilicia, for instance, organized Hadriania Olympia, Kommodeia Olympia,[44] and Augusteia Aktia.[45] Yet the emperor had to be included in the equation, since it is not very probable that such designation happened very often without explicit imperial approval.[46] Sometimes contests even included performances in praise of a current (or previous) *princeps* like the *enkomion eis ton Theon Titon* at the Sebasta.[47] In addition to indirect imperial presence in the name of a discipline, even age-classes bore the name of emperors, as the events *klaudianes kriseos* at the Sebasta demonstrate.[48]

To sum up, some Roman emperors of the first three centuries AD actively engaged in agonistic competition, several founded more or less successfully athletic festivals, others served at least as *agonothetai* or were simply present at Greek contests from time to time. At most games, however, their presence was an indirect one, but through the materiality of statues, busts, and inscriptions imperial presence (and Roman rule) was nevertheless felt during the absence of the emperor. In any case, there can be no doubt that athletic festivals and contests were among 'the various forms of communication' that 'acquainted the population with the ruler of the empire'.[49]

2.3. The emperor and the games. Imperial intervention in the agonistic circuit

Beyond the direct or indirect presence of Roman emperors at Greek games, there was a 'confusing variety of different ways' in which emperors influenced the agonistic culture.[50] Undoubtedly, the degree of imperial involvement in athletics was 'remarkable'—as Jason König already stated one year prior to the publication of

---

[43] For an overview on festivals named after an emperor, see the list in Pleket (2010), 200–1; for a survey of emperors and festivals in Asia Minor in general, see Mitchell (1993).

[44] These games were later renamed Severeia Olympia, which under Caracalla were known as the Severeia Antoneia Olympia (van Nijf (1999), 181).

[45] Ziegler (1985), 32. For the numismatic evidence on festivals in the East of the empire, see Klose (2005) and the case study of Calomino, Chapter 4, this volume.

[46] For a similar observation with regard to Roman festivals (in general) in the East, Graf (2015), 315: 'The festivals did not create the empire; but they helped to hold it together by suggesting a unity well beyond the administrative structures that always could be debated, changed, or rejected'. Graf emphasizes that emperors between Nero and Caracalla realized the potential of festivals for the imperial ideology and the unity of the empire. He argues that the dissemination and adoption of Roman festivals must not simply be considered a bottom-up or top-down movement, but an amalgamation of both developments.

[47] In one of these performances the emperor Domitian himself won another victory in addition to his equestrian success: Miranda De Martino (2017b), 237.

[48] Miranda De Martino (2014), no. 3, col. II, l. 9.   [49] Chaniotis (2018), 264.

[50] König (2005), 225.

the three Hadrianic letters from Alexandria Troas which now constitute our most important piece of evidence of such an involvement.[51]

The Hadrianic letters are addressed to the association of 'wandering musicians and actors around Dionysos' and date to the year AD 134. They mainly respond to a petition filed by the association that asked for the establishment of a new 'circuit' of high-level games with fixed dates that would enable the performers to participate in contests as frequently as possible. Hadrian happily used this opportunity to integrate his own newly founded games into the existing Greek agonistic landscape:[52] the games in his honour celebrated at Athens, the Hadrianeia, were only preceded in his new calendar by the most prestigious Olympic and Isthmian games while the Panhellenia celebrating his political project of the Panhellenion appear at the very end of the four-year cycle. Hadrian integrated both games into his *nea periodos* in order to make sure that the Athenian organizers of the contests would be able to attract the best athletes and performers possible (and by this help increase the status of the contest). In other words: he cared about 'his' Athenian games and actively translated this idea into public policy. No doubt Hadrian's establishment of a new circuit of games is active policy-making, and it is not sufficiently characterized by Fergus Millar's model of 'petition and response'. It rather seems to follow the logic of 'order and obey', as argued by Clifford Ando in a forthcoming article.[53] The language of the letters is telling in this regard: κελεύω ('I command') is the first finite verb form in the entire inscription,[54] and the second letter is similarly presented as a decision of the emperor making a *taxis* ('order').[55]

We see the agency of material culture very clearly here: in order to attract everybody's attention, Hadrian's imperial titulature and the proud addressee are written in larger letters than the rest of the inscription (Fig. 2.1). The first line of the title especially sticks out since the letters are still larger than the rest of the prescript.[56] There also is a long *vacat* in line 7 strongly emphasizing the word χαίρειν. Thus the layout of the inscription highlighted that this was not any type of imperial document but a letter. No doubt Hadrian ruled 'by dispatching letters',[57] and this ruling had an impact even on games not mentioned in his new circuit

---

[51] König (2005), 225; Petzl and Schwertheim (2006); in addition to the remarks in *SEG* 56, 1359, see esp. Slater (2008). The literature on this inscription has now become something of an industry unto itself. See e.g. Gouw (2008); Schmidt (2009); Sänger-Böhm (2010); Le Guen (2010); Strasser (2010–12); Gordillo Hervás (2011); Shear (2012); Fündling (2014); Strasser (2016); and Gordillo Hervás, Chapter 3, this volume.

[52] Or 'market', as Pleket (2010), 181, and (2014), 364 calls it. Hadrian clearly cared for the agonistic landscape of the empire. Even a newly founded and privately sponsored local contest like the Demostheneia of Oinoanda (Wörrle (1988)) had 'imperial fingerprints all over it' (van Nijf (1999), 187).

[53] Ando (forthcoming).

[54] Petzl and Schwertheim (2006), l. 8: Τοὺς ἀγῶνας πάντας ἄγεσθαι κελεύω (...); κελεύω is used again in l. 53. Note also the wording at the end of the letter (l. 55): ὡς ἐγὼ διέταξα.

[55] Petzl and Schwertheim (2006), l. 60: Ὡς ἔδοξέ μοι τετάχθαι τοὺς ἀγῶνας, (...); cf. l. 84: οἱ ἀγῶνες οἱ διατεταγμένοι.

[56] The *editio princeps* gives 0.023 m for l. 2 and 0.016 m for ll. 3–7: Petzl and Schwertheim (2006), 7.

[57] Cortés-Copete (2017), 107 borrowing the words from Aristides, *Oration* 26.33: πᾶσαν ἄγειν τὴν οἰκουμένην δι' ἐπιστολῶν.

Fig. 2.1 Three letters of the emperor Hadrian to the Dionysiac artists, *stele* found at Alexandria Troas, detail of the first twenty-seven lines of the first letter: the first six lines appear in larger letters.

Photograph: Forschungsstelle Asia Minor im Seminar für Alte Geschichte, Westfälische Wilhelms-Universität Münster, by permission of Elmar Schwertheim.

because there were periods of time in this calendar which seem to have been deliberately left free for other contests to be filled in so that the cities of the empire could adjust the dates of their own festivals accordingly.[58] This does not come as a surprise in a period that saw the development of regional circuits and, according to Wolfgang Leschhorn, at least five hundred different athletic festivals across the empire.[59] Unquestionably, the games mentioned in Hadrian's second letter only constituted the tip of an enormous iceberg formed by Greek contests in the Graeco-Roman world.

Hadrian's new circuit clearly had a large impact on the festival calendars of the cities of the empire,[60] yet it affected the lives and careers of the people who had asked for such a new calendar even more: the performers and athletes.[61] The new

---

[58] Petzl and Schwertheim (2006), 85; Pleket (2010), 182.

[59] Leschhorn (1998), see also Leschhorn (2004). Among those festivals were no less than twenty different 'Olympic games' (Pleket (2010), 182). A prosperous city like Ephesos alone even organized up to ten athletic festivals a year (Pleket (2010), 181). The local agonistic culture of Ephesos in the imperial period has been intensively studied including three dissertations focusing on this topic alone (Lämmer (1967); Brunet (1998); Lehner (2004); cf. also Engelmann (1998); on the building activities in connection with the festivals, see Scherrer (2008), 53; on regional circuits, Strasser (2004–5), 438, Remijsen (2010), 196, and Gouw (2009), 33–56).

[60] On this aspect, Gordillo Hervás, Chapter 3, this volume.

[61] Technically the letters are exclusively addressed to the association of the performers, but it is very clear from the remaining text that the athletes are included in all important provisos of the letters, most evidently in the fact that Hadrian's new circuit began with the Olympic games as an 'ancient and most venerable of the Greek contests' (ll. 61–2: ἀρχαῖος ὁ ἀγὼν οὗτος καὶ ἐνδοξότατος τῶν γε | Ἑλληνικῶν) in which, however, the performers with the exception of some heralds and trumpeters did not compete; cf. also l. 48: ἀθληταῖς καὶ μουσικοῖς; l. 82: ἐν τῷ θεάτρῳ καὶ τῷ σταδίῳ.

circuit influenced the way successful athletes presented their victories to their fellow citizens; in other words: it had an impact on the agonistic discourse. In a victor inscription from Athens that celebrates the athletic achievements of a certain Markos Tyllios [...] it is explicitly stated that this boxer succeeded as 'the first and only pugilist of all times who won in order Panhellenia, Olympia, Isthmia, Hadrianeia, Rome (i.e. Capitolia)'.[62] Although this cannot be understood as self-presentation in its literal sense—it is an epitaph and the athlete already dead—, the monument and its inscription do reflect the perspective of the athlete's family that may not have been so different from the boxer's own view.[63] In any case, the order presented in the inscription is precisely the new *taxis* Hadrian had established—and the composer of the text was very proud of this fact.

Hadrian's new agonistic calendar is a very good example of how a Roman emperor could implement a general policy by means of dispatching letters.[64] The publication clause which is to be found at the end of the second letter is revealing in this respect: it is explicitly stated that the 'cities where the (newly) arranged contests take place and the associations' ought to set up *stelai* 'in their sanctuaries'.[65] We can safely assume that the text of the inscription was not only published in Alexandria Troas, but throughout the empire. This way Roman rule was implemented by means of agonistic inscriptions. The letters—in their material, inscribed form—had an agency and they clearly had an impact on athletes and cities alike.[66]

---

[62] IG II² 3163 (SEG 33, 177), ll. 3–6: μόνος | καὶ πρῶτος τῶν ἀπ' αἰῶνος πυκτῶν | νεικήσας κατὰ τὸ ἑξῆς Πανελλήνια, | Ὀλύμπια, Ἴσθμια, Ἁδριάνεια, Ῥώμη[ν]. Rome clearly means the Capitolia here. See for this inscription, already Robert (1930), 36–8.

[63] IG II² 3163, ll. 27–8: Μᾶρκος Τύλλιος Εὐτύχης ο[ὑ]ν τῷ [υ]ἱῷ καὶ | ἀδελφῷ ἐποίει. According to the inscription, Markos Tyllios hailed from Apameia in Bithynia, was naturalized in Athens, Corinth, and Smyrna (IG II² 3163, ll. 1–3), won thirty-five additional victories in games that offered money-prizes (ll. 24–5), and died abroad at the age of 32 years and three months (ll. 25–6).

[64] The letters from Alexandria Troas are not the only case in which Hadrian addresses agonistic competition by means of imperial letters. In another letter dating to the same year, precisely to 5 May AD 134 (Oliver (1989), no. 86), the emperor takes care of matters concerning the association of athletes. We also know of an edict of the same emperor that is partly preserved in three Egyptian papyri of the third century AD (Frisch (1986), no. 1, ll. 3–4; no. 3, ll. 4–6; no. 4, ll. 1–3) and that stipulates privileges for the performers. This is why Chaniotis (2018), 262 explicitly refers to Hadrian (in a line with Vespasian and Trajan) among the emperors of the first and second centuries AD who 'also implemented general policies' in addition to simply answering and reacting to problems and petitions.

[65] Petzl and Schwertheim (2006), ll. 83–4: ταυτά μου τὰ γράμματα ἐν στήλλαις ἀναγραψάτωσαν αἱ πόλεις, παρ' αἷς | οἱ ἀγῶνες οἱ διατεταγμένοι ἄγονται, αἱ δὲ σύνοδοι ἐν τοῖς ἱεροῖς τοῖς ἑαυτῶν.

[66] In addition to what we have already seen for the Hadrianic letters from Alexandria Troas, the agency of epigraphic culture with regard to Greek athletics can also be seen on a much smaller scale. For Pisidian Termessos (Pleket (2010), 184), for instance, it is very clear that athletic victors, even if 'only' successful in gymnasion contests and local Termessian games, published their victor inscriptions at the most 'prestigious locations in the city' (Pleket (2010), 184). On Termessos' local dossier of agonistic inscriptions (TAM III.1, 141–213), van Nijf (1999), 191 ('There was no escape: wherever you went in Termessus, you were confronted with the powerful image of the victorious youth'); van Nijf (2000); and van Nijf (2011) (for local identity in Termessos, van Nijf (2010)). On a somewhat smaller scale such dossiers are also known from the Lycian cities of Balboura (SEG 38, 1446–8, 1459; 41, 1343–54), Oinoanda (SEG 44, 1165–1201), and Patara (Schuler and Zimmermann (2012), nos. 4–5; Lepke (2015)).

2.4. Athletes and their victories. The agency of material culture in imperial athletics

But how did all this imperial engagement in athletics affect the way in which successful Greek athletes presented their victories to a public audience? Angelos Chaniotis has recently argued for a 'long Hellenistic Age' that also includes 'the first 150 years of the Imperial period',[67] since, in his view, the most important societal, economic, religious and cultural trends of the Hellenistic age just continued into the imperial age.[68] This is a landmark study, and Chaniotis is certainly right that the chronological caesura of 30 BC is, generally speaking, a more important turning point in political than in cultural history. Yet this is not necessarily true for all fields of cultural history in equal measure. With regard to athletics there are good reasons to assume that the year 30 BC constituted a turning point, both with regard to the practical experience of sport and in the way in which athletic victories were advertised by successful competitors.[69]

It is true that not everything changed in terms of athletics with the emergence of Roman emperorship. For instance, the framework of Greek athletics with its 'classical' set of the most important disciplines, its festival culture and its local facilities for athletic training (the *gymnasia*) persisted.[70] What is more, the *polis* not only remained 'the point of reference against which any political entity should be measured',[71] it also remained the basic unit of athletic representation. The hometown of the athlete continued to be the most important point of reference in victor epigrams, which still represented the most characteristic genre for athletic self-presentation in the imperial period.[72] It was still the hometown of the victor for which the term *patris*, expressing a rather emotional connection to one's state of origin, was reserved. A successful boy-pancratiast of the first century AD even had the composer of his Olympic victor epigram invent a somewhat sophisticated term for the praise of his hometown Ephesos which is called Ἰωνογενής in the inscription.[73]

---

[67] Chaniotis (2018), 1–2 (and elsewhere). [68] Chaniotis (2018), 3 (and elsewhere).
[69] Of course, chronological caesuras are seldom valid in an absolute sense and there certainly also were continuities in the agonistic field. However, my argument in what follows is that there are good reasons to emphasize the changes rather than the continuities between Hellenistic and imperial-time athletics.
[70] On the 'local infrastructure' of athletics in Roman Asia Minor, see Pleket (1998).
[71] Chaniotis (2018), 124.
[72] On this aspect and the epigraphic record for athletes in the imperial age in general, see Mouratidis (2020).
[73] Ebert (1972), no. 76, A, ll. 5–6 (= *I.Olympia* 225, B, ll. 10–11): Εἰρηναῖος ἐμοὶ γενέτης, ξένε, τοὔνομ᾽ Ἀρίστων, | πατρὶς Ἰωνογενὴς ἀμφοτέρων Ἔφεσος.—'Eirenaios is my father, stranger, Ariston my name; Ephesos having Ion as her ancestor is home for both of us.' Ariston who probably held Roman citizenship won his Olympic victory in AD 49, as an additional prose inscription informs us (*I Olympia* 225, A, l. 4). On Ἰωνογενής as a *hapax legomenon*, see Ebert (1972), 228. Ephesos is again referred to as *patris* in a second epigram on the same stone praising the same victory (Ebert (1972), no. 76, B, l. 10 [= *I.Olympia* 225, C, l. 23]). The composer of the poem, Ti. Claudius Thessalos from Kos, proudly signed the stone and even referred to his own agonistic victories as a performer: Τιβερίου Κλαυδίου Θεσσαλοῦ Κῴου πλειστονείκου (*I.Olympia* 225, C, l. 24).

Yet, the fact that the *polis* took pride of place in the agonistic discourse holds true for all epochs of ancient athletics in the same way. So in this regard the turning point of 336 BC is in no way stronger than that of 30 BC. And the same is true for the framework of Greek athletics: whereas the overall structure of Greek athletics remained steady from the emergence of the *periodos* and of the *gymnasion* in the sixth century BC until the fourth century AD, we can observe important changes between the epochs inside this structure.[74] In the Hellenistic period, for instance, powerful kings became important players in the field of athletics.[75] They participated in equestrian contests, the most important of which they dominated in the third century BC, and they sponsored hopeful young athletes. They also established games like the Ptolemaia and even introduced a completely new category of contests, the iso-games (i.e. isolympic, iso-pythian, etc.).[76] On the other hand, local athletic festivals thrived in the third and second centuries BC and often tried to raise their status to that of more prestigious crown games. Also, social advancement through athletics seems to have increased in this period. Undoubtedly, athletics reflected political and social change in the Hellenistic age. This is why it is promising to use athletics as a lens through which to explore the impact of the most dramatic political change at the beginning of the imperial period, that is the emergence of Roman emperorship, as well. I cannot help but wonder: what was imperial about athletics in the imperial period?

The best starting point for such an approach is to look at the self-presentation of victorious athletes and horse owners. By means of agonistic inscriptions in verse or prose, these successful competitors showed how they wanted their victories to be understood. This is the closest we come to gaining insight into the athletes' own perspective.

An in-depth analysis of the surviving inscriptions reveals at least four characteristic elements.[77] The first change in athletic self-presentation set in already at the beginning of the imperial period. We may call it the expansion of the frame of reference. Starting with the late first century BC, agonistic victors were no longer just 'the first and only' of a *polis* or region who won a particular victory,[78] they began to think in larger categories and now became 'the first of the inhabited earth' (πρῶτος τῶν ἀπὸ τῆς οἰκουμένης),[79] 'the first of all people' (πρῶτος ἀνθρώπων)[80]

---

[74] On the question of what is Hellenistic about Hellenistic athletics, see the second chapter of my forthcoming monograph on the self-presentation of Hellenistic athletes (Scharff (forthcoming)).

[75] Mann (2018). [76] Mann (2018), 466–73 (with further references).

[77] For what follows, I have studied in detail—yet not limited myself to—the material collected by Moretti (1953) in *IAG* and Ebert (1972).

[78] On the *protos (kai monos)*-formula which athletes used for setting themselves apart, Ebert (1972), 19, 22, 24, 106–7. One of the earliest uses of this formula in agonistic self-presentation is to be found in the famous Damonon-inscription from late fifth- or early fourth-century BC Sparta (*IAG* 16 = *IG* V 1, 213; cf. now Christesen (2019)).

[79] *IAG* 62. Note that the association of athletes even carried the word *oikoumenikos* in its name (Pleket (2010), 202).

[80] *IAG* 66–8; *I.Smyrna* 661; *I.Ephesos* 4114; *F.Delphes* III, 1, 547.

or 'the first and only of all times' (πρῶτος καὶ μόνος τῶν ἀπὸ αἰῶνος).[81] The Alexandrian 'heavy weight' T. Flavius Archibios even used the term πρῶτος ἀνθρώπων eight times in his victor inscription to set himself apart by emphasizing that he had achieved certain combinations of victories as 'the first of all people'.[82] This change goes hand in hand with a general increase in the use of titles or records in athletic self-presentation.[83] Or, as Onno van Nijf put it, athletes now portrayed themselves 'as cultural agents whose job it was to represent an oecumenical, or global, cultural policy'.[84]

Secondly, starting from the late first century BC, victors did not hesitate to mention their double, triple, quadruple etc. citizenships as well as their multiple council memberships in their agonistic prose inscriptions.[85] A famous athlete like the pancratiast M. Aurelius Demostratos Damas from Sardis listed no fewer than fifteen cities where he was naturalized.[86] The Sinopean herald Valerius Eclectus proudly referred to six different council memberships and explicitly stated that he had even more.[87] By this, the victors' exclusive connection with their hometowns was at least in part suspended in the agonistic discourse.

The third characteristic resulted from this practice: it became very important in the agonistic discourse of the second and third centuries AD to showcase the victor's status as being part of an empire-wide aristocracy ('Reichsaristokratie'). This can be seen very clearly in an Olympic victor epigram of the (early) third century AD. The short poem reads as follows:

---

[81] Examples include *IAG* 69–72, 76, 84, 90. See also Newby (2021).

[82] *IAG* 68, ll. 12, 16–17, 19, 22–3, 26, 30.

[83] It is true, the use of such titles already set in in the Hellenistic age, when records like (the first, second etc.) 'successor of Heracles' (for someone who succeeded in both the Olympic wrestling and pankration contest of one and the same year; cf. Miller (2004b), 204–5), *triastes* (a 'triple winner' in running events), and especially *periodonikes* (*IAG* 46, Olympia, *c*.180 BC, is the earliest epigraphic attestation, see Remijsen (2011), 99; Remijsen (2015), 28–9 and 35) emerged in athletic self-presentation. Yet in the imperial period the number and frequency of the use of these titles which now also included *paradoxos* (*IAG* 72–3, 76, 78, 80, 83, 89), *paradoxonikes* (e.g. *IAG* 68), and *pleistonikes* (e.g. *IAG* 72, 83; *IG* V 1, 553) clearly increased to a great extent (Wallner (2001), Miller (2004b), 205–6; Remijsen (2015), 119–21). On titles and records in Greek athletics in general, still Tod (1949).

[84] van Nijf (2006), 234.

[85] Multiple citizenships: *IAG* 63, 65–72, 74, 76–7, 79–80, 83–5, 89–90; *I.Smyrna* 661 (the listed examples date from AD 45 to the 250s); multiple council memberships: *I.Olympia Suppl.* 33 (*SEG* 17, 203); *I.Smyrna* 661; *IAG* 79–80, 82, 90 (*IAG* 79 dates to *c*. AD 200). On the multiple citizenships, see now also Mouratidis (2021), 675–86 (with table 1) with a slightly different interpretation.

[86] *IAG* 84, A, ll. 1–6 (Sardis, AD 212–7); on Damas' career, Strasser (2003).

[87] *IAG* 90 (= *IG* II² 3169–70), ll. 2–6 (Athens, *c*. AD 253–7: of Eclectus' four known Olympic victories that date to the years AD 245, 253, 257, and 261 [Moretti, *Olympionikai* 934, 938–40] two are listed in this inscription): after naming Sinope, Delphi, Elis, Sardis, Perge, and Nikaia, the list is interrupted in l. 6 by the reference to other unnamed citizenships and council memberships (καὶ ἄλλων πολ|λῶν πόλεων πολείτης καὶ βουλευτής) four of which (i.e. Smyrna, Philadelphia, Hierapolis, Tripolis) are added in his Olympic victor inscription which has also survived (*I.Olympia* 243 and *SEG* 17, 203 [cf. *SEG* 26, 479]) and in which even nine honorary council memberships are listed. The practice of the Athenian inscription to present just a selection could be called 'Abbruchsformel', a term Ebert (1972), 18 (again 68 and 243) has coined for comparable cases in which successful athletes refrain from listing all the minor victories they had won in addition to their most important ones.

Ἵππῳ νικήσαντα Θεόπροπον ἔστεφε Πῖσα,
εὐπατρίδην Ῥόδιον, συνκλητικῶν γενετῆρα.

After his victory with his horse, Pisa crowned Theopropos, the noble-born Rhodian and father of senators.[88]

Although the athlete's father is always mentioned in victor epigrams, the focus is usually not on hailing from a good family.[89] What mattered in the agonistic discourse was the personal *arete* of the victor, not the family he stemmed from. It is striking how different the focus is in this epigram: Theopropos was especially proud of being a *eupatrides*.[90] He even boasted about what his sons had achieved in the field of empire-wide politics, information whose appearance in the poem cannot be explained by the conventions of the genre of agonistic epigrams.[91] Unquestionably, it was of great importance for the family that Theopropos' sons had become Roman senators.[92] Yet, the information was not really relevant in the agonistic discourse. Such political achievements, however, mattered for other athletic families as well: it was in the same century that the 'holy association of athletes around Heracles' honoured one of his members, a certain Claudius Rufus Apollonios, not only for being a two-times *periodonikes*, but also for hailing from a 'family of *consulares*' (*γένους ὑπατικῶν*).[93] A victor in the local Meleagreia from Balboura was praised for having won in a wrestling contest. But before his athletic victory is mentioned, it is stated that he was 'a man of first rank in the city, kinsman of League officials of the Nation, his father a League Official'.[94] To put it in a nutshell, the political and the agonistic discourse had become intertwined since at least the second half of the second century AD. Make no mistake, agonistic poetry (epinicians as well as victor epigrams) had never just reflected an innocent desire to remember past events, but was political poetry in ancient Greece.[95] Yet, political achievements did not matter in this discourse. It was rather the other way round: agonistic victories enhanced the 'symbolic capital' and by this the political standing of an athlete among his peers and in his local community. From the

---

[88] Ebert (1972), no. 80 (= *I.Olympia* 239).

[89] Exceptions can be found in the agonistic representation of royal dynasties of the Hellenistic period like the Ptolemies and the Attalids (see Scharff (forthcoming), ch. 5).

[90] Ebert (1972), no. 80, l. 2. With regard to similar tendencies in agonistic inscriptions from Termessos, van Nijf (1999), 192 speaks of the presentation of victory as 'a birthright'.

[91] Victor epigrams usually included the name and father's name of the victor, his hometown, the place of victory as well as the event and age class in which the athlete had been successful (Ebert (1972), 9–25; Köhnken (2007), 295–6).

[92] A parallel can be found in an inscription set up by an *alytarches* in Olympia in the same century (*I.Olympia* 240 [Olympia, AD 245?]) who proudly referred to the fact that he was related to senators and *consulares* (cf. Ebert (1972), 247).

[93] *IGUR* I 244 (= *IG* XIV 1107), ll. 12–13 (Rome, *c.* AD 200–50).

[94] *SEG* 41, 1345 (Balboura, AD 170–80; trans. O. van Nijf); cf. van Nijf (1999), 192.

[95] See Mann and Scharff (2020), 169–75.

second century AD onwards, then, political accomplishments became part of athletic self-presentation.

The same aspect can be seen very clearly in a dossier of inscriptions praising the political and athletic achievements of a certain Gaius Perilius Alexandros from third-century Thyateira in Asia Minor.[96] Alexandros won victory as a pancratiast in a local contest, the Great Asklepeia,[97] and also served as an ambassador to the emperor Elagabalus who is emphatically addressed as τὸν κύριον ἡμῶν in one of the inscriptions.[98] On his diplomatic mission, Alexandros achieved the establishment of a sacred, eiselastic, *isopythios*, and ecumenical contest for his hometown.[99] It is striking that he is praised for this deed as 'undefeated ambassador' (ἄλειπτον πρεσβευτήν).[100] By this 'a well-known agonistic surplus-value term' is transferred to the political discourse.[101] So the amalgamation of both fields also worked the other way round.

What is more important, however, is that Alexandros' case is also indicative of the fourth main characteristic of athletic self-presentation in the imperial period: proximity to power. It is true that some victorious courtiers of archaic tyrants and Hellenistic kings had already expressed their nearness to a sole-ruler in their agonistic poetry in the past, but these were clearly exceptional cases of people who owed their entire career to the favour of their royal patron. In contrast, a detailed analysis of agonistic inscriptions of the imperial period reveals that the Roman emperors as the most important monarchs of the time now became a factor in athletic self-presentation on a much larger scale. In Alexandros' case, his embassy to Elagabalus, the athlete's major moment of fame, was commemorated in a different inscription than his athletic victory.[102]

In other cases, we do not find such a separation of the fields of athletics and politics: in about AD 60, Tiberius Claudius Patrobios, a wrestler from Antioch's glamourous suburb Daphne and 'favorito di Nerone',[103] directly referred to the emperor in his victor inscription.[104] The successful pancratiast P. Aelius Aristomachos from Magnesia on the Maeander proudly mentioned the fact that

---

[96] *TAM* V.2, 1017–20 (Thyateira, AD 218–22).   [97] *TAM* V.2, 1017.
[98] *TAM* V.2, 1018, l. 3.
[99] *TAM* V.2, 1018, ll. 6–9. Although the 'new' contest was probably rather 'a rebranding and (...) upgrading of the local Hadrianeia' (Papakonstantinou (2019), 145–6) which are mentioned in another inscription from Thyateira (*TAM* V.2, 1022, l. 1), the embassy has recently been called '[t]he highlight of his (i.e. Alexandros') public career' (Papakonstantinou (2019), 145) with good reason.
[100] *TAM* V.2, 1019, ll. 9–10.   [101] Papakonstantinou (2019), 146.
[102] Athletic victory: *TAM* V.2, 1017; embassy: *TAM* V.2, 1018. Yet both deeds somewhat come together in *TAM* V.2, 1019, in which Alexandros is praised as μόνον καὶ πρῶτον | τῶν ἀπ' αἰῶνος ἀθλη|τῶν (ll. 4–6) on the one hand, and as ἄλειπτον πρε|σβευτήν (ll. 9–10) on the other.
[103] Moretti (1953), 174.
[104] *IAG* 65 = *IGUR* I 249, ll. 11–12 (Rome, c. AD 60). Although clearly a favourite of Nero, this athlete is not to be identified with the Patrobios who was one of the favourite freedmen of Nero (Cassius Dio, *Roman History* 63.3; Pliny, *Natural History*, 35.165; Suetonius, *Lives of the Caesars, Nero*, 45.1), because the athlete, successful already in his youth as a *pais* and *ageneios* (ll. 9–10), cannot have been a *libertus*, as Moretti (1953), 175 convincingly argues.

'he was often sent as an ambassador to the *autokratores*', the emperor Hadrian and his adoptive son L. Ceionius Commodus.[105] Aristomachos also refers to the fact that his family received Roman citizenship directly from the emperor (ὑπὸ θεοῦ Ἀδριανοῦ).[106] By the time the inscription was set up, Hadrian was obviously already dead. Yet, the athlete's personal relationship to him still mattered greatly. Of equal importance was the proximity to Roman emperors for the famous 'heavy weight' Marcus Aurelius Demostratos Damas who highlighted in his victor inscription that he had received a priesthood and especially thirteen different *xystarchiai* directly from the emperors Septimius Severus and Caracalla,[107] a motif that occurs again at the end of the inscription, where it is extended by the mention of 'many other and great honours' gained from these emperors.[108] Damas had already held personal relations with Marcus Aurelius and Commodus from whom he had received citizenship, as is also explicitly stated by the inscription.[109] Finally, the successful runner and pentathlete Demetrios emphasized directly at the beginning of his victor inscription that he had received his *xystarchiai* for life by the emperors.[110]

Of all the athletes we know, the closest relationship to an emperor was upheld by the undefeated boxer Melankomas. According to Themistius, he was the lover of the emperor Titus.[111] Dio Chrysostom did not only commemorate Melankomas' fame, he even invented a new genre of agonistic praise for him with his two 'epinician orations'. However, the orations do not constitute athletic self-presentation.[112] One is a funeral address on the deceased pugilist who was so famous for his beauty and his characteristic boxing style, while the other includes a dialogue with a former competitor's trainer, also held post mortem. Both are typical literary artefacts of the Second Sophistic.[113] Therefore, we simply do not know how Melankomas

---

[105] IAG 71 (= I.Magnesia 180-1), ll. 21-2 (Magnesia on the Maeander, c. AD 140): πρεσβεύσας τε πολλά|κις πρὸς τοὺς αὐτοκράτορας. The inscription even refers to the places where Aristomachos was sent (ll. 23-4): εἴς τε τὴν βασιλίδα Ῥώμην καὶ εἰς | Παννονίαν (…). On the accompanying epigram, Ebert (1972), no. 78.

[106] IAG 71, l. 17.

[107] IAG 84 (= SEG 53, 1355), A, ll. 18-22 (Sardis, AD 212-17): αἰτησάμενος καὶ τυχὼν παρὰ τ[ῶν κυ|ρ]ίων ἡμῶν θειοτάτων Αὐτοκρατόρ[ων] | Σεουήρου καὶ Ἀντωνίνου τήν τε ἀρ[χιερ|ω]σύνην καὶ τὰς ξυσταρχίας εἰς τή[ν τῶν] | παίδων διαδοχήν· The *xystarchiai* were even transferable onto Damas' sons who also were distinguished athletes. On Damas' *xystarchiai*, Strasser (2003), 264. Xystarchs had the duty to supervise contests in a given city or region, cf. Pleket (2010), 188 and (2012), 104-6.

[108] The inscription consists of three parts. At the end of part C it reads (IAG 84, C, ll. 28-32): καὶ ὑπὸ θεοῦ Σεουήρου καὶ τοῦ κυ|ρίου ἡμῶν θειοτάτου Αὐτοκράτο|ρος Ἀντωνίνου ἄλλαις τε πολ|λαῖς καὶ μεγάλαις τειμαῖς κα[ὶ] | ξυσταρχίαις.

[109] IAG 84, C, ll. 11-13: τειμηθεὶς ὑπὸ θεοῦ Μάρκου | καὶ θεοῦ Κομμόδου πολει|[τ]είᾳ μὲν Ἀλεξανδρέων ἰθ[α|γ]ενεῖ.

[110] IAG 86 (= SEG 12, 512), ll. 2-3; Anazarbos, AD 198-211 (SEG 12, 512) or after AD 229 (Moretti (1953), 253): τειμηθεὶς ὑπὸ τῶν κυρίων Αὐτοκρατόρων | ξυσταρχίαις διὰ βίου.

[111] Themistius, Oration 10, 139; cf. Chaniotis (2018), 302, 327.

[112] Dio Chrysostom, Oration 28, 29. On both orations, König (2005), 97-157.

[113] For instance in the way that they rather speak about the athlete's virtues like endurance, temperance, and self-control than on his athletic victories; but probably also in the way they speak about beauty 'with an ingenuity which constantly verges on absurd humour but which nevertheless need not detract from these texts' commemoratory power' (König (2005)| 156).

wanted his victories to be praised. What we do know, however, is that he is a very good example of the fact that '[a]cquaintance with an emperor was the single most important factor in achieving social advancement' in the imperial period.[114]

Athletes were usually part of the provincial elites, and it was exactly these elites that were responsible for law and order and for safe-keeping Roman tax income.[115] The emperors thus had a keen interest in establishing and maintaining good relations with these elites, especially those from rich provinces. So the emperors made sure that athletes were committed to them. One way was to bring them to Rome temporarily after their athletic career as high officials in the association of athletes who had their headquarters in the city.[116] This was a very promising way of keeping open the channel of communication with the provincials. The athletes, on the other hand, highly appreciated this imperial favour and proudly referred to it in their self-presentation.[117]

Of course, the Greek cities also profited from good relations between emperors and athletes. The Spartan athlete P. Aelius Damokratidas, for instance, who held a high position in the emperor cult of his city was honoured by the *polis* for being a 'friend of the emperor and of his hometown'.[118] Note that he is praised in that order. It is interesting to observe that of all the athletic victories this athlete won only one is singled out in the inscription: Damokratidas is called 'the best of the Greeks' (ἄριστος Ἑλλήνων) which meant that he had succeeded in the race in armour (*hoplites*) at the Eleutheria of Plataea,[119] a contest once established to commemorate the Greek victory over the Persians in 479 BC and now called Eleutheria Kaisareia in Damokratidas' life time.[120] In this victory, both came together: the athlete in his traditional role as representative of his hometown and the athlete in his new persona as imperial agent.[121]

---

[114] Chaniotis (2018) 301.   [115] Pleket (2010), 190 and 196.

[116] The originally two empire-wide associations of athletes which had merged into one association of 'wandering athletes and victors in sacred crown games' in the mid-second century AD (Caldelli (1992)) had its headquarters in Rome near the imperial baths and, as Pleket (2010), 188 emphasized, '[a] top-official of that association—invariably a prominent ex-athlete—was at the same time director of those Baths.'

[117] Like multiple citizenships and council memberships, eminent positions as officials in the associations of athletes and performers were always mentioned in agonistic inscriptions since the second century AD at the latest: see e.g. *IAG* 68, 71, 77–9, 82, 84, 86.

[118] *IG* V.1, 553, ll. 5–6 (Sparta, late second century AD); cf. Pleket (2010), 202. On the connection of imperial cult and athletics, see Herz (2016); for Lycia, Reitzenstein (2016).

[119] *IG* V.1, 553, l. 9. On this title, van Nijf (2005); on Damokratides, Pleket (2010), 202–3.

[120] On this contest, Jung (forthcoming).

[121] Note that it had been Sparta which took the leading role among the Greeks in the battle of Plataea. Plataea was, at least in Sparta, always remembered as a Spartan victory (Jung (2006), 225–383). This actually is an 'authentic Greek identity oriented toward the glorious past', as Pleket (2010), 202 has put it. We should also note that this happened in a period whose literature was deeply oriented towards the past. On athletics in the Second Sophistic and especially the role of athletics in elite education, see van Nijf (2001) and (2003).

2.5. Concluding remarks

To sum up, let us return to the two athletes mentioned at the beginning. There can be no doubt that it was Menandros' approach that became characteristic for athletes of the imperial period. When the opportunity arose, the chance to make the emperor a point of reference was seldom missed in agonistic inscriptions.[122] Only in cases where a very successful athlete like Asklepiades was accused by his competitors of having won merely due to the emperor's favour, was a connection to the emperor explicitly omitted or even flatly denied. It is an important finding and not self-evident that nearness to power mattered in the athletic self-presentation of the imperial period, because this may be, at first sight, contrary to the logic of agonistic praise. What successful athletes of this age emphasized in their self-presentation is different from the agonistic discourse of the Hellenistic period. As we have seen, characteristics now included the general expansion of the frame of reference which became much larger in the imperial period, a claim of being part of an empire-wide aristocracy also expressed through the multiple citizenships and council memberships of the athletes, the amalgamation of the agonistic and the political discourse, and finally the proximity to power which athletes were now keen to address in their agonistic self-presentation.[123]

To put it in a nutshell, the way athletes of the imperial period wanted their victories to be understood clearly changed in comparison to their predecessors. Athletes were now part of an empire that was composed of almost the entire inhabited earth. Their self-presentation is indicative of this aspect.

From the point of view of the emperors, ruling over such an empire meant that they had to create strategies of an imagined omnipresence. Undoubtedly, athletic festivals constituted a perfect (though definitely not the only) occasion to do so. Consequently, it was at games that athletes were confronted with an infinite number of imperial busts, statues, and inscriptions in whose materiality the grandeur

---

[122] This is one of the reasons why I do not think that the Greeks only changed one ruler for another. No Hellenistic king has ever been publicly honoured by his subjects as γῆς καὶ θαλάσσης δεσπότης ('complete master over land and sea'), with a term that was usually used to describe the rule of a master over his slaves and thus characterized the largest possible difference between a ruler and his subjects. Although the term seems to have still been problematic by the time of Antoninus Pius (SEG 53, 1463, Hierapolis, c. AD 138–61; cf. Haake (2017), 196), it is already attested under Hadrian (Paribeni and Romanelli (1914), no. 128, Iotape, AD 117–38) and certainly became rampant from the AD 190s. By this time, Septimius Severus was even called μέγιστος γῆς καὶ θαλάσσης δεσπότης (CIG 3883i, Dokimeion, AD 199–211).

[123] These were certainly not the only, but just the most important changes in the self-presentation of victorious athletes of the imperial period. Others included the fact that female competitors in athletic events could now be praised for their victories (IAG 63, Delphi, c. AD 45; erected by the father of three girls from Tralleis), as successful female horse owners had been since the early fourth century BC; or that athletes could be celebrated for simply having participated in renowned contests in an honourable manner (SEG 41, 1351; SEG 44, 1191, Oinoanda, AD 207; I.Didyma 194, ll. 5–12, Didyma, first half of the second century AD). For a long time in history, the latter statement would have constituted a serious offense to any dedicated Greek athlete.

and imagined ubiquity of the emperor manifested itself. Therefore, new elements of athletic self-presentation in the imperial period as the claim of being part of an empire-wide aristocracy and the emphasis on the proximity to power may have resulted from the repeated confrontation with this omnipresent figure that appeared larger than life. Creating imperial presence during absence was a strategy based on materiality, and it was this materiality of busts, inscriptions and the like which had an impact on the self-portrayal of victorious athletes.

Works Cited

Alcock, S. E. (1994) 'Nero at play? The emperor's Grecian Odyssey', in J. Elsner and J. Masters (eds), *Reflections of Nero: Culture, History, and Representation*. Chapel Hill, NC, 98–111.

Ando, C. (forthcoming) 'Petition and response, order and obey: contemporary models of Roman government', in M. Jursa and S. Prochazka (eds), *Governing Ancient Empires. Proceedings of the 3rd to 5th International Conferences of the Research Network Imperium and Officium*. Vienna.

Bang, P. F. (2013) 'The Roman empire II: the Monarchy', in P. F. Bang and W. Scheidel (eds), *The Oxford Handbook of the State in the Ancient Near East and Mediterranean*. Oxford, 412–74.

Birley, A. R. (1997) *Hadrian. The Restless Emperor*. London and New York.

Blanco-Pérez, A. (2018) '*EPINIKIA*: celebrating Roman victory in the eastern provinces of the empire', *Tyche* 33: 9–41.

van Bremen, R. (2007) 'The entire house is full of crowns. Hellenistic *agōnes* and the commemoration of victory', in S. Hornblower and C. Morgan (eds), *Pindar's Poetry, Patrons and Festivals. From Archaic Greece to the Roman Empire*. Oxford, 345–75.

Brunet, S. (1998) 'Greek Athletes in the Roman World: The Evidence from Ephesos'. PhD thesis, University of Texas at Austin.

Caldelli, M. L. (1992) '*Curia athletarum, iera xystike synodos* e organizzazione delle terme a Roma', *Zeitschrift für Papyrologie und Epigraphik* 93: 75–87.

Caldelli, M. L. (1993) *L'Agon Capitolinus. Storia e protagonisti dall' istituzione domizianea al IV secolo*. Rome.

Champlin, E. (2003) *Nero*. Cambridge.

Chaniotis, A., (2018) *Age of Conquests. The Greek World from Alexander to Hadrian*. Cambridge, MA.

Christesen, P. (2019) *A New Reading of the Damonon Stele. Histos* Supplement 10. https://histos.org/documents/SV10.ChristesenDamononStele.pdf.

Cortés-Copete, J. M. (2017) 'Governing by dispatching letters: the Hadrianic chancellery', in L. Rosillo-López (ed.), *Political Communication in the Roman World*. Leiden and Boston, 107–36.

Deeg, P. (2019) *Der Kaiser und die Katastrophe. Untersuchungen zum Umgang mit Umweltkatastrophen im Prinzipat (31 n. Chr. bis 192 n. Chr.)*. Stuttgart.

Ebert, J. (1972) *Griechische Epigramme auf Sieger an gymnischen und hippischen Agonen*. Berlin.

Edelmann, B. (2008) 'Pompa und Bild im Kaiserkult des römischen Ostens', in J. Rüpke (ed.), *Festrituale in der römischen Kaiserzeit*. Tübingen, 153–67.

Engelmann, E. (1998) 'Zur Agonistik in Ephesos', *Stadion* 24: 101–8.

Evangelidis, D. (1927–8) 'Ἐπιγραφαὶ ἐκ Χίου', *Ἀρχαιολογικὸν Δελτίον* 1: 23–33.

Flaig, E. (2019) *Den Kaiser herausfordern. Die Usurpation im Römischen Reich*. 2nd edition. Frankfurt.

Frisch, P. (1986) *Zehn agonistische Papyri*. Opladen.

Fündling, J. (2014) 'Vom Wettkampfreglement zur sozialen Grenzziehung durch ritualisierte Gewalt–Überlegungen zu Hadrians erstem Brief aus Alexandreia Troas', in K. Harter-Uibopuu and T. Kruse (eds), *Sport und Recht in der Antike*. Vienna, 217–47.

Gebhard, E. R. (1996) 'The theatre and the city', in W. J. Slater (ed.), *Roman Theatre and Society*. Ann Arbor, 113–28.

Gordillo Hervás, R. (2011) 'La organización adrianea de los certámenes panhelénicos', in J. M. Cortés Copete, R. Gordillo Hervás, and E. Muñiz Grijalvo (eds), *Grecia ante los imperios: V Reunión de historiadores del mundo griego*. Seville, 335–43.

Gossage, A. G. (1975) 'The comparative chronology of inscriptions relating to Boiotian festivals in the first half of the first century BC', *Annual of the British School at Athens* 70: 115–34.

Gouw, P. (2008) 'Hadrian and the calendar of Greek agonistic festivals. A new proposal for the third year of the Olympic cycle', *Zeitschrift für Papyrologie und Epigraphik* 165: 96–104.

Gouw, P. (2009) *Griekse atleten in de Romeinse Keizertijd (31 v.Chr.–400 n.Chr.)*. Amsterdam.

Graf, F. (2015) *Roman Festivals in the Imperial Greek East: From the Early Empire to the Middle Byzantine Era*. Oxford.

Haake, M. (2017) 'Image-Politik. Antoninus Pius, "Greeks under Rome" und das kaiserliche Image zwischen Erwartungshaltungen und Selbstdarstellung—skizzenhaft exemplarische Überlegungen', in C. Michels and P. F. Mittag (eds), *Jenseits des Narrativs. Antoninus Pius in den nicht-literarischen Quellen*. Stuttgart, 195–213.

Halfmann, H. (1986) *Itinera principum. Geschichte und Typologie der Kaiserreisen im Römischen Reich*. Stuttgart.

Harris, H. A. (1962) 'Notes on three athletic inscriptions', *Journal of Hellenic Studies* 82: 19–24.

Heinemann, A. (2014) 'Sportsfreunde: Nero und Domitian als Begründer griechischer Agone in Rom', in S. Bönisch-Meyer et al. (eds), *Nero und Domitian. Mediale Diskurse der Herrscherrepräsentation im Vergleich*. Tübingen, 217–64.

Herz, P. (2016) 'Die Agonistik und der Kaiserkult', in A. Kolb and M. Vitale (eds), *Kaiserkult in den Provinzen des Römischen Reiches. Organisation, Kommunikation und Repräsentation*. Berlin and Boston, 123–31.

Jung, M. (2006) *Marathon und Plataiai. Zwei Perserschlachten als 'lieux de mémoire' im antiken Griechenland*. Göttingen.

Jung, M. (forthcoming) 'Die Eleutherien von Plataiai', in S. Scharff (ed.), *Beyond the Big Four. Local Games in Ancient Greek Athletic Culture*. Münster.

Kaplan, M. (1990) *Greeks and the Imperial Court, from Tiberius to Nero*. New York.

Kennell, N. M. (1988) 'ΝΕΡΩΝ ΠΕΡΙΟΔΟΝΙΚΗΣ', *American Journal of Philology* 109: 239–51.

Klose, D. O. W. (2005) 'Festivals and games in the cities of the East during the Roman empire', in C. Howgego, V. Heuchert, and A. Brunett (eds), *Coinage and Identity in the Roman Provinces*. Oxford, 125–33.

Köhnken, A. (2007) 'Epinician epigram', in P. Bing and J. S. Blass (eds), *Brill's Companion to Hellenistic Epigram*. Boston and Leiden, 295–312.

König, J. (2005) *Athletics and Literature in the Roman Empire*. Cambridge.

Lämmer, M. (1967) *Olympien und Hadrianeen im antiken Ephesos*. Cologne.

Lämmer, M. (1986–7) 'Die Aktischen Spiele von Nikopolis', *Stadion* 12–13: 27–38.

Langenfeld, H. (1975) 'Die Politik des Augustus und die griechische Agonistik', in E. Lefèvre (ed.), Monumentum Chiloniense. *Studien zur augusteischen Zeit. Kieler Festschrift für Erich Burck zum 70. Geburtstag*. Amsterdam, 228–59.

Le Guen, B. (2010) 'Hadrien, l'Empereur philhellène, et la vie agnostique de son temps. À propos d'un livre récent: *Hadrian und die dionysischen Künstler. Drei in Alexandreia Troas neugefundene Briefe des Kaisers an die Künstler-Vereinigung*', *Nikephoros* 23: 205–39.

Lehner, M. (2004) 'Die Agonistik im Ephesos der römischen Kaiserzeit'. Dissertation. Munich.

Lepke, A. (2015) 'Neue agonistische Inschriften aus Patara', *Zeitschrift für Papyrologie und Epigraphik* 194: 135–57.

Leschhorn, W. (1998) 'Die Verbreitung von Agonen in den östlichen Provinzen des römischen Reiches', *Stadion* 24: 31–57.

Leschhorn, W. (2004) 'Sport und Spiele im Münzbild der römischen Kaiserzeit', in M. Gutgesell and A. V. Siebert (eds), *Olympia. Geld und Sport in der Antike*. Hanover, 55–68.

Manieri, A. (2009) *Agoni poetico-musicali nella Grecia antica*, Vol. I: *Beozia*. Pisa and Rome.

Mann, C. (2001) *Athlet und Polis im archaischen und frühklassischen Griechenland*. Göttingen.

Mann, C. (2013) 'The victorious tyrant: Hieron of Syracuse in the epinicia of Pindar and Bacchylides', in N. Luraghi (ed.), *The Splendors and Miseries of Ruling Alone. Encounters with Monarchy from Archaic Greece to the Hellenistic Mediterranean*. Stuttgart, 25–48.

Mann, C. (2014) 'Greek sport and Roman identity: the *certamina athletarum* at Rome', in T. F. Scanlon (ed.), *Sport in the Greek and Roman Worlds*, Vol. II: *Greek Athletic Identities and Roman Sports and Spectacle*. Oxford, 151–81. (= Mann, C. (2002). 'Griechischer Sport und römische Identität: die *certamina athletarum* in Rom', *Nikephoros* 15: 125–58).

Mann, C. (2018) 'Könige, Poleis und Athleten in hellenistischer Zeit', *Klio* 100: 447–79.

Mann, C., and Scharff, S. (2020) 'Horse races and chariot races in ancient Greece: struggling for eternal glory', *International Journal of the History of Sport* 37: 163–82.

Miller, S. G. (2004a) *Arete. Greek Sports from Ancient Sources*. 3rd edition. Berkeley.

Miller, S. G. (2004b) *Ancient Greek Athletics*. New Haven and London.

Miranda De Martino, E. (2007) 'Neapolis e gli imperatori', *Oebalus* 2: 203–15.

Miranda De Martino, E. (2010) 'Consoli e altri elementi di datazione nei cataloghi agonistici di *Neapolis*', in M. Silvestrini (ed.), *Le tribù Romane, Atti della XVI Rencontre sur l'Épigraphie, Bari 8–10 ottobre 2009*. Bari, 417–22.

Miranda De Martino, E. (2013) 'Ritratti di campioni dai *Sebastà* di Napoli', *Mediterraneo Antico* 16: 519–36.

Miranda De Martino, E. (2014) 'Les *Sebasta* de Naples à l'époque de Domitien. Témoignages épigraphiques', *Comptes rendus de l'Académie des inscriptions et belles-lettres* 3: 1165–88.

Miranda De Martino, E. (2017a) 'I *Sebasta* dell' 82 d.C.: restauro delle lastre e aggiornamenti', *Historika* 7: 253–69.

Miranda De Martino, E. (2017b) 'La propaganda imperiale e i concorsi isolimpici di Neapolis', in C. Capaldi and C. Gasperri (eds), *Complessi monumentali e arredo scultoreo nella Regio I Latium et Campania*. Naples, 235–41.

Miranda De Martino, E. (2018) 'I vincitori dei *Sebastà* nell'anno 86 d.C.', in F. Camia, L. Del Monaco, and M. Nocita (eds), *Munus Laetitiae. Studi miscellanei offerti a Maria Letizia Lazzarini, II*. Rome, 267–86.

Mitchell, S. (1993) *Anatolia. Land, Men and Gods in Asia Minor*, Vol. I: *The Celts in Anatolia and the Impact of Roman Rule*. Oxford.

Moretti, L. (1953) *Iscrizioni agonistiche greche*. Rome.

Mouratidis, G. (2020) 'Athlete and *Polis*. The relationship between athletes and cities in the epigraphic record of the Late Hellenistic and Imperial periods'. PhD thesis, University of St Andrews.

Mouratidis, G. E. (2021) 'Athletes, citizenships and Hellenic identity during the imperial period', *Klio* 103.2: 675–703.

Müller, C. (2014) 'A *Koinon* after 146? Reflections on the political and institutional situation of Boeotia in the late Hellenistic period', in N. Papazarkadas (ed.), *The Epigraphy and History of Boeotia. New Finds, New Prospects*. Boston and Leiden, 119–46.

Newby, Z. (2005) *Greek Athletics in the Roman World: Victory and Virtue*. Oxford.

Newby, Z. (2021) 'Greek festivals in the Roman era', in A. Futrell and T. F. Scanlon (eds), *Sport and Spectacle in the Ancient World*. Oxford, 168–81.

van Nijf, O. M. (1999) 'Athletics, festivals and Greek identity in the Roman East', *Proceedings of the Cambridge Philological Society* 45: 176–200.

van Nijf, O. M. (2000) 'Inscriptions and civic memory in the Roman East', *Bulletin of the Institute of Classical Studies* 75: 21–36.

van Nijf, O. M. (2001) 'Local heroes: athletics, festivals and elite self-fashioning in the Roman East', in S. Goldhill (ed.), *Being Greek under Rome: Cultural Identity, the Second Sophistic and the Development of Empire*. Cambridge, 306–44.

van Nijf, O. M. (2003) 'Athletics and *paideia*: festivals and physical education in the world of the Second Sophistic', in B. E. Borg (ed.), *Paideia. The World of the Second Sophistic*. Berlin, 203–28.

van Nijf, O. M. (2005) '*Aristos Hellenôn*. Succès sportif et identité grecque dans la Grèce romaine', *Mètis* 3: 271–94.

van Nijf, O. M. (2006) 'Global players: athletes and performers in the Hellenistic and Roman world', *Hephaistion* 24: 225–34.

van Nijf, O. M. (2010) 'Being Termessian. Local knowledge and identity politics in a Pisidian city', in T. Whitmarsh (ed.), *Local Knowledge and Microidentities in the Imperial Greek World*. Cambridge, 163–88.

van Nijf, O. M. (2011) 'Public space and political culture in Roman Termessos', in O. M. van Nijf and R. Alston (eds), *Political Culture in the Greek City after the Classical Age*. Leuven, 215–42.

Oliver, J. H. (1989) *Greek Constitutions of Early Roman Emperors from Inscriptions and Papyri*. Philadelphia.

Papakonstantinou, Z. (2019) *Sport and Identity in Ancient Greece*. London and New York.

Paribeni, R. and Romanelli, P. (1914) 'Studii e ricerche archeologiche nell' Anatolia Meridionale', *Monumenti antichi* 23: 5–274.

Pavlogiannis, O. and Albanidis, E. (2007) 'Τα Άκτια της Νικόπολης. Νέες προσεγγίσεις', in K. Zachos (ed.), Νικόπολις Β. Πρακτικά του Δευτέρου Διεθνούς για τη Νικόπολη (11.–15. Sept. 2002). Preveza, 57–76.

Petzl, G. and Schwertheim, E. (2006) *Hadrian und die dionysischen Künstler. Drei in Alexandria Troas neugefundene Briefe des Kaisers an die Künstler; mit Beiträgen von Gudrun Heedemann, Emmanuel Hübner und Sebastian Scharff*. Bonn.

Pleket, H. W. (1998) 'Mass-sport and local infrastructure in the Greek cities of Roman Asia Minor', *Stadion* 24: 151–72.

Pleket, H. W. (2010) 'Roman emperors and Greek athletes', *Nikephoros* 23: 175–203.

Pleket, H. W. (2012) 'An agonistic inscription from Sardis', *Zeitschrift für Papyrologie und Epigraphik* 181: 102–7.

Pleket, H. W. (2014) 'Sport in Hellenistic and Roman Asia Minor', in P. Christesen and D. G. Kyle (eds), *A Companion to Sport and Spectacle in Greek and Roman Antiquity*. Malden, MA, Oxford, and Chichester, 364–76.

Reitzenstein, D. (2016) 'Agonistik und Kaiserkult in Lykien', in A. Kolb and M. Vitale (eds), *Kaiserkult in den Provinzen des Römischen Reiches. Organisation, Kommunikation und Repräsentation*. Berlin and Boston, 133–58.

Remijsen, S. (2010) '*Pammachon*, a new sport', *Bulletin of the American Society of Papyrologists* 47: 185–204.

Remijsen, S. (2011) 'The so-called "crown-games". Terminology and historical context of the ancient categories for agones', *Zeitschrift für Papyrologie und Epigraphik* 177: 97–109.

Remijsen, S. (2015) *The End of Greek Athletics in Late Antiquity*. Cambridge.

Rieger, B. (1999) 'Die Capitolia des Kaisers Domitian', *Nikephoros* 12: 171–203.

Robert, L. (1930) 'Études d'épigraphie grecque', *Revue de philologie* 24: 36–8 (= Robert, *OMS* II: 1136–8).

Robert, L. (1935), 'Sur des inscriptions de Chios IV–VI', *Bulletin de correspondance hellénique* 59: 459–65 (= Robert, *OMS* I: 518–24).

Robert, L. (1970), 'Deux concours grecs à Rome', *Comptes rendus de l'Académie des inscriptions et belles-lettres* 114: 6–27.

Robert, L. (1978) 'Catalogue agonistique des Romaia de Xanthos', *RA* 277–90 (= Robert, *OMS* VII: 681–94).

Sänger-Böhm, K. (2010) 'Die *syntaxeis* und *tele ta epi tais taiphais* in der Hadriansinschrift aus Alexandria Troas: Eine papyrologische Bestandsaufnahme', *Zeitschrift für Papyrologie und Epigraphik* 175: 167–70.

Scharff, S. (forthcoming). *Hellenistic Athletes. Agonistic Cultures and Self-Presentation*. Cambridge.

Scherrer, P. (2008) 'Die Stadt als Festplatz: Das Beispiel der ephesischen Bauprogramme rund um die Kaiserneokorien Domitians und Hadrians', in J. Rüpke (ed.), *Festrituale in der römischen Kaiserzeit*. Tübingen, 35–66.

Schmidt, S. (2009) 'Zum Treffen in Neapel und den Panhellenia in der Hadriansinschrift aus Alexandria Troas', *Zeitschrift für Papyrologie und Epigraphik* 170: 109–12.

Schuler, C. and Zimmermann, K. (2012) 'Neue Inschriften aus Patara I: Zur Elite der Stadt in Hellenismus und früher Kaiserzeit', *Chiron* 42: 567–626.

Shear, J. L. (2012) 'Hadrian, the Panathenaia, and the Athenian calendar', *Zeitschrift für Papyrologie und Epigraphik* 180: 159–72.

Slater, W. J. (2008) 'Hadrian's letters to the athletes and Dionysiac artists concerning arrangements for the "circuit" of games (Rev. of Petzl and Schwertheim 2006)', *Journal of Roman Archaeology* 21: 610–20.

Spawforth, A. J. S. (2007) 'Kapetoleia Olympia: Roman emperors and Greek agones', in S. Hornblower and C. Morgan (eds), *Pindar's Poetry, Patrons, and Festivals. From Archaic Greece to the Roman Empire*. Oxford, 377–90.

Spawforth, A. J. S. (2012) *Greece and the Augustan Cultural Revolution*. Cambridge.

Strasser, J.-Y. (2003) 'La carrière du pancratiaste Markos Aurèlios Démostratos Damas', *Bulletin de Correspondance Hellénique* 127: 251–99.

Strasser, J.-Y. (2004) 'Les Antôninia Pythia de Rome', *Nikephoros* 17: 181–220.

Strasser, J.-Y. (2004–5) 'Les Olympia d'Alexandre et le pancratiaste M. Aur. Asklepiades', *Bulletin de Correspondance Hellénique* 128-9: 421–68.

Strasser, J.-Y. (2010–12) '"Qu'on fouette les concurrents...": à propos des lettres d'Hadrien retrouvées à Alexandrie de Troade', *Revue des Études Grecques* 123: 585–622.

Strasser, J.-Y. (2016) 'Hadrien et le calendrier des concours (*SEG*, 56, 1359, II)', *Hermes* 144: 352–75.

Tod, M. N. (1949) 'Greek-record keeping and record-breaking', *Classical Quaterly* 43: 105–12.

Tracy, S. and Habicht, C. (1991) 'New and old Panathenaic victor lists', *Hesperia* 60: 187–236.

Wacker, C. (2017) 'The ancient games of Aktion. An ethnical festival turns into a Panhellenic mega-event equal to the Olympics', *Journal of Olympic History* 25: 62–9.

Wacker, C. (2018) 'Die Spiele von Aktion—vom ethnischen Kultfest zum panhellenischen Megaevent', in J. Court and A. Müller (eds), *Jahrbuch 2017 der Deutschen Gesellschaft für Geschichte der Sportwissenschaft e.V.* Berlin, 9–34.

Wallner, C. (2001) 'M. Ulpius Heliodoros und T. Flavius Archibios. Beobachtungen zu ihren Ehreninschriften (IG IV 591; I. Napoli I,51)', *Nikephoros* 14: 91–108.

Wallner, C. (2002) 'Zu griechischen Agonen in Rom während der Kaiserzeit', *Stadion* 28: 1–11.

Wallner, C. (2004) 'Der Agon Minervae: eine Dokumentation', *Tyche* 19: 223–35.

Wörrle, M. (1988) *Stadt und Fest im kaiserzeitlichen Kleinasien. Studien zu einer agonistischen Stiftung aus Oinoanda.* Munich.

Ziegler, R. (1985) *Städtisches Prestige und kaiserzeitliche Politik. Studien zum Festwesen in Ostkilikien im 2. und 3. Jahrhundert n. Chr.* Düsseldorf.

Zoumbaki, S. B. (2007) 'Tiberius und die Städte des griechischen Ostens: Ostpolitik und hellenisches Kulturleben eines künftigen Kaisers', in Y. Perrin (ed.), *Neronia, VII: Rome, l'Italie et la Grèce: hellénisme et philhellénisme au premier siècle ap. J.-C., Actes du VIIe Colloque international de la SIEN (Athènes, 21–23 octobre 2004).* Brussels, 158–69.

3
Agonistic Legislation in Hadrian's Time

Rocío Gordillo Hervás

3.1. Introduction

As Louis Robert has rightly pointed out, during the Roman empire games of Greek typology experienced an exceptional increase, mainly due to the number of such celebrations that were held in Greece and Asia Minor.[1] Since the classical era the Olympic games of Pisa, the Pythian games of Delphi, the Isthmian games of Corinth, and the Nemean games of Argos formed the *periodos* (circuit), that is, the four Panhellenic *agones* (games) that the athletes regarded as the most prestigious to win. With the passage of time, to these four games other lesser ones were added, the name and typology of which are known to us thanks to the victory lists of the athletes who took part in them.[2] One of the highest peaks in the creation of *agones ex novo* can observed during the reign of Emperor Hadrian (AD 117–38), with the organization of at least twenty-one games dedicated to the emperor, to which we ought to add the new ones established by the emperor himself in order to commemorate the death of Antinous.[3]

The large number of games made it necessary for the emperor to organize and regulate them by means of a calendar. A *stele* from Alexandria Troas displays three letters by Hadrian, where he establishes the new rules that should govern the competitions and draws up a new calendar of games according to a four-year cycle. In the letters, the emperor ordered that the text should be inscribed onto *stelai* (plaques) in those places where games were held. As Sebastian Scharff has

---

This chapter was funded by the European Union 'NextGenerationEU' recovery plan 'Recuperación, Transformación y Resilencia' by the Spanish Ministerio de Universidades, within the framework of the 'Recualificación del profesorado universitario funcionario o contratado' grants for recalibrating the Spanish university system 2021–3, by the Pablo de Olavide University, Seville. It has been written with the support of the Research Project '*Discursos del Imperio romano: Palabras y rituales que construyeron el Imperio*' (PGC2018-096500-B-C31).

[1] Robert, *OMS* 6, 712. See also: Harris (1964), 226; Pleket (1975); Müller (1995); Leschhorn (1998), 31–57.
[2] The inscriptions mention ἀγῶνες ἱεροὶ καὶ στεφανῖται (sacred crown games), ἀγῶνες ἱεροὶ (καὶ) εἰσελαστικοί (sacred triumphal entry games), and ἀγῶνες θεματικοί (money games): Pausanias, *Description of Greece* 8.48.2–3; Lucian, *Anarcharsis* 9–14. Looy (1992); Klose (2005), 127; Remijsen (2011); Pleket (1975); Pleket (2014a), 61 n. 140; Pleket (2014b); Spawforth (1989); van Nijf (2001), 310; Slater (2013); Mann (2018).
[3] Gordillo Hervás (2018). See also: Lammer (1967); Le Glay (1976); Boatwright (2000), 99.

shown in the previous chapter, the emperors exerted a significant effect on imperial festival culture, intervening in various ways. Copies of Hadrian's letters would have become part of the landscape of the agonistic enclosures and symbolize the emperor's presence during the competitions. The physical carving of the imperial regulation in these public places also reveals the active role of material culture in carrying out the emperor's authority. The objective of this chapter is to analyse the impact and diffusion of the new regulations established by Hadrian in the territories where games were organized, focusing on three main issues: the work carried out by the synods of athletes and artists in the transmission of the imperial provisions, the presence of the new imperial regulation both in the centres that were included in the calendar and in those which were not, and the impact of the calendar after Hadrian's death on the cities that established new games, such as Puteoli and Aphrodisias.

3.2. The letters at Alexandria Troas and the role of the synod

Hadrian's effort is known to us thanks to the archaeological work of the 'Forschungsstelle Asia Minor im Seminar für Alte Geschichte der Universität Münster', which in 2003 found in the city of Alexandria Troas, located in northwestern Turkey in the current province of Çanakkale, a marble *stele* that had inscribed on it the text of three official letters signed by Hadrian (see Fig. 2.1, previous chapter). This *stele* was located near a structure that has been identified as a Roman-era temple, probably meant for imperial worship.[4] The three letters are dated between AD 133 and 134 and are addressed to the συνόδῳ θυμελικῇ περιπολιστικῇ τῶν περὶ τὸν Διόνυσον τεχνειτῶν ἱερονεικῶν στεφανειτῶν ('the traveling musical union of artists associated with Dionysos and victorious in sacred and crowned contests').[5] They describe in detail a major reorganization of the entire system of *agones* which were held across the Roman empire.

In the first letter Hadrian outlines the regulations to be followed within the organization of all the games that were to be celebrated across the empire. He gives clear instructions for the proper funding of the festivals, among other things stating that the public money allocated for the games could not be used for other purposes, even the purchase of food or the construction of essential infrastructure. The letter also regulates the contributions to be received by the *xystarchs* (officials of the xystic synod)[6] and the exemption from liturgies and taxes due to the members of the synod. The letter also provides detailed instructions for the delivery of the prizes to the winners, an important clarification since in some

---

[4] First edited by Petzl and Schwertheim (2006). On the Alexandria Troas letters see Jones (2007); Gouw (2008); Haensch (2008); Slater (2008); Guerber (2009); Schmidt (2009); Le Guen (2010); Strasser (2010); Gordillo Hervás (2011); Shear (2012); Strasser (2016); Gordillo Hervás (2017).
[5] Petzl and Schwertheim (2006), ll. 5–6. Translation from Jones (2007), 153.
[6] Fauconnier (2018), 180–4.

cases the *agonothetes* (the official in charge of the games) illegally appropriated part or all of the money or prizes that were meant for the athletes. It also specifies the kind of punishment to be administered to athletes who had committed some infraction.[7]

In the second letter, Hadrian presents an exhaustive calendar for the major agonistic games over a four-year cycle that begins with the Olympics games, described as 'the ancient and certainly the most prestigious of the Greek ones',[8] and ends with the newly established Panhellenia games of Athens. Hadrian's agonistic calendar included the most important games of the Roman empire. Among them were the games of the *archaia periodos* (Olympia, Pythia, Nemea, and Isthmia) together with the great Roman games of Nikopolis, Rome, and Neapolis.[9] These major games were joined by many city-games which granted a privileged status to their own cities.[10] The third and last letter is the shortest of all. In it the emperor allows for a banquet offered to the winners to be carried out, but only in those cities where it had already been organized previously.[11]

The letters of Alexandria Troas are not mere epistles in which Hadrian addresses a synod of artists in order to answer or advise them on a particular issue, but a proper edict with ecumenical impact that emanates directly from the emperor. As also noted by Sebastian Scharff in the previous chapter, the very language that Hadrian adopts when addressing the synods and elucidating his new mandate represents an argument in favour of Hadrian's personal authorship in the elaboration of the agonistic legislation. Throughout the letters, the emperor employs the first person ('I order', 'I allow', 'I decide'...) when conveying the new regulation.[12]

The first letter shows what kind of importance the emperor places on the need to disseminate his new mandate and the means by which such dissemination should be carried out. In two separate passages of the first letter, it is stated that the rules of the games must be written up before the competitions begin so that none of the participants (spectators, artists and athletes or organizers) can justify their behaviour through pleading ignorance of the rules. Lines 53–4 state:

τοὺς νόμους τοὺς τῶν ἀγώνων καθ' ἑκάστην πανήγυριν προγεγράφθαι | κελεύω, ὡς μὴ ὑπὸ ἀγνοίας πράττοιτό τι τῶν ἀπειρημένων.

I order that the rules of the contests be written up at the time of each festival, so that nothing that has been forbidden be done out of ignorance.[13]

---

[7] Petzl and Schwertheim (2006), ll. 1–56.
[8] Petzl and Schwertheim (2006), ll. 61–2. Translation from Jones (2007), 155.
[9] Pleket (2014b), 103.   [10] Petzl and Schwertheim (2006), ll. 57–84.
[11] Petzl and Schwertheim (2006), ll. 85–8.
[12] Cortés Copete (2019), 120. Petzl and Schwertheim (2006), ll. 8, 9, 16, 52, 55, 60.
[13] Petzl and Schwertheim (2006), ll. 53–4. Translation from Jones (2007), 155.

In the second passage Hadrian gives permission to the synod to carve the letter on *stelai*. Lines 55–6 state that:

> τοῦ δὲ γείνεσθαι ταῦτα πάντα, ὡς ἐγὼ διέταξα, ἐπιμελήσονται παρ' ἑκάστοις οὗτοι ἔθνους ἡγού<με>νοι· συνχωρῶ | δὲ ὑμεῖν, ἔνθα ἂν βούλησθε, καὶ στήλλαις ἐνγράψαι αὐτά, ὡς πᾶσιν εἴη γνώριμα.

> The governors of the province shall ensure in each place that all this is done as I have arranged, but I permit you also to inscribe them on *stelai* wherever you wish, so that they may be known to everyone.[14]

The first letter from Alexandria Troas states that the rules set by Hadrian had to be made public (προγράφω) for everybody participating in the games to be aware of them before the games were held. In the second passage quoted above, the emperor authorizes the synod to erect *stelai* in order to publicize the regulation. The verb employed here is ἐνγράφω, which specifically indicates the act of inscribing, and is also found within a decree by Hadrian on the sale of fish in Eleusis, where the emperor goes as far as to specify where the *stele* ought to be erected, that is, 'in the Piraeus in front of the Deigma'.[15] Although no archaeological evidence has been found to prove this conclusively, it is very likely that copies of this regulation were part of the architectural landscape of the venues where the games were held. *Stelai* similar to that of Alexandria Troas would be located in strategic places of maximum visibility so that they were seen, and even consulted if necessary by all the participants to the games. The importance of spreading the new imperial instructions is also underlined in lines 83–4 of Alexandria Troas' second letter:

> ταῦτά μου τὰ γράμματα ἐν στήλλαις ἀναγραψάτωσαν αἱ πόλεις, παρ' αἷς | οἱ ἀγῶνες οἱ διατεταγμένοι ἄγονται, αἱ δὲ σύνοδοι ἐν τοῖς ἱεροῖς τοῖς ἑαυτῶν.

> This letter of mine is to be set up on *stelai* by the cities in which the contests that have been set in order are held, and by the unions in their own sanctuaries.[16]

In this case, the emperor does not 'allow', but commands the cities whose games have been included in the new agonistic calendar, as well as the synods, to inscribe the text on *stelai* for its proper dissemination. The task of the agonistic associations as the entities responsible for the transmission of edicts and imperial provisions is supported by other epigraphic evidence. A marble *stele* found in the vicinity of the theatre of Dionysos at Athens was inscribed on both sides with responses sent by the emperor to various queries posed by the synod of musicians

---

[14] Petzl and Schwertheim (2006), ll. 55–6. Translation from Jones (2007), 155.
[15] Translation from Oliver (1989), no. 77.
[16] Petzl and Schwertheim (2006), ll. 83–4. Translation from Jones (2007), 156.

of Dionysos Choreios (συνόδῳ τῶν περὶ τὸν Χορεῖον τεχνειτῶν μουσικῶν).[17] This kind of evidence makes it likely that the synod would have had at their headquarters in Athens a copy of the emperor's three letters that have been found in the *stele* of Alexandria Troas, detailing the new calendar and rules of the games. During Hadrian's time, Athens also hosted the '[society] of Dionysiac artists [---] at Athens, [of sacred and] crowned victors' which the emperor addresses, probably regarding the creation of a new musical synod that could well be the aforementioned synod of musicians of Dionysos Choreios.[18] There is also evidence of other synods in Asia that may have had copies of Hadrian's letters, such as in the city of Sardis, where there are remains of an edict by Hadrian addressed to the artists of Dionysos concerning pentaeteric games (the identity of which is left unspecified due to the poor state of conservation of the inscription).[19] Agonistic synods were also found in the Egyptian territory, where a collection of three *papyri* has been discovered which includes an edict by Hadrian addressing the union of artists (συνόδῳ τῶν τεχνιτῶν) and listing a series of privileges for its members, such as exemption from military service or immunity from the payment of public liturgies.[20]

It is hard to establish with certainty whether there were a large number of synods spread throughout all the cities where games were being held, or some kind of central synod that was responsible for controlling and organizing the games of all the empire, although the existence of a *thymelic* synod in Rome can be traced back to the Julio-Claudian period,[21] and its centralizing function is supported by an inscription from Nysa in Karia dated to the year AD 141.[22] In the inscription, Publius Aelius Pompeianus Paion of Side states that Aelius Alkibiades was granted a series of honours, including the erection of statues and images, by the 'game-conquering and crown-winning worldwide performers associated with Dionysos and emperor Caesar T. Aelius Hadrian Antoninus Augustus Pius and the fellow-contestants whom they met during the quinquennial contests of the great Ephesian games' because of his many *euergesiai*.[23] And so that everyone would be aware of the work of Pompeianus, 'a copy of the decrees will be sent out to his brilliant fatherland, the city of Nysa [....] Copies of the inscription will be sent by an embassy to the greatest emperors and to the synod in Rome'.[24] This reinforces the hypothesis of a centralizing function by the synod of Rome, and therefore it would not be unlikely that the said synod kept a copy of the text of Hadrian's letters and took responsibility for sending copies of it to

---

[17] *IG* II² 1105 = *SEG* 30, 86. On the possible association of Antinous with Dionysos Choreios: *IG* III 280; Geagan (1972), 133–60; Oliver (1989), nos. 98–108.
[18] The name of the organization can be found at Oliver (1989), no. 97. See also Daux (1966), 731.
[19] *CIG* 3455 = *IGR* IV 1517.   [20] A: *POxy*, 2476; B: *BGU*, 1074; C: *POxy Hels.* 25.
[21] See also Jory (1970).
[22] Clerc (1885), 125; *BE* 1924, 355; *SEG* 4, 418; Harland (2014), no. 144.
[23] All the translations of the Nysa inscription are from Harland (2014), 353–4.
[24] Harland (2014), no. 144, ll. 59–60, 66–8.

the other synods of the empire so that they would be inscribed and placed in the most visible spots.

Although the letters from Alexandria Troas were addressed to the synod of the *technitai*, it is very likely that a copy would also have been sent to the athletes' synod, given that they are constantly mentioned in the letters and that the new imperial dispositions affect them directly.[25] During Hadrian's time, the athletes' synod underwent a substantial reform aimed at centralizing all the documentation related to the administration of the games. An inscription on a marble base found in the city of Rome relates a letter from the emperor Hadrian to the 'Athletic Guild of the Athletes Devoted to Herakles'.[26] In the letter the emperor grants the synod a space for the construction of a building for storing the association's archive, and permission to make modifications to their own statutes. The base belongs to a statue dedicated to M. Ulpius Domesticus, a Roman citizen from Ephesos, who was the recognized ambassador of the athletes and a *pankratiast* who had obtained privileges for the synod from the emperor.[27] It can be thus hypothesized that the new imperial dispositions would be sent to this organization in order for it to disseminate them for their implementation.

As mentioned above, it is likely that copies of Hadrian's letters were present in the venues where games were held. Sanctuaries typically hold a large amount of epigraphic material that includes the new imperial mandates and decrees emanating from the synods. On the southern wall of the Acropolis of Sardis a decree by the synod of performers of Dionysos was found, in which the emperor Hadrian is referred to as new Dionysos.[28] A decree found in the city of Ankara and dated to 3 December AD 128 could also have been located in a sanctuary. The text refers to the 'world-wide performers (*technitai*) gathered around Dionysos and emperor Trajan Hadrian Augustus Caesar, new Dionysos, namely, those who are crowned sacred victors, fellow-contestants, and registered members of the sacred theatrical synod'.[29] It is signed by Hadrian and Trebius Sergianus,[30] and celebrates Ulpius Aelius Pompeianus for his *euergesia* within the organization of the first *mystikos agon* of Ankara.[31]

On the walls of the temple of Apollo in Delphi there are several inscriptions that reproduce the correspondence between the emperor and the city of Delphi.[32] In one of them the emperor addresses the issue of the winners of the games held at Pylae, one of the two centres of the Delphic Amphictyony, being awarded a

---

[25] Fauconnier (2018), 111–15. See also Fauconnier (2020).
[26] Translation from Oliver (1989), no. 86.
[27] *IG* XIV 1110 = *IGUR* I 238; *IG* V1 669; *I.Ephesos* IV, 1089; 1155. See also: *IG* XIV 1052. These benefits though will not be granted till Antoninus Pius' time: *IGUR* 236. See also Pleket (1973); Caldelli (1992).
[28] *I.Sardis* 13. Due to the poor state of conservation it is impossible to ascertain the exact content.
[29] Translation by Harland (2014), no. 212. [30] Governor of Galatia: *PIR*² T 325.
[31] Petzl and Schwertheim (2006), 30–1. See also Gordillo Hervás (2018).
[32] Weir (2004), 168–73.

crown equal to the one given to the winners of the sacred contests at Delphi. To solve this conflict, the emperor decreed that only the winners in the Pythian games at Delphi were allowed to wear the crown of the victors in the sacred games.[33] The decrees emanating from the synods and the emperor may have been part of the landscape of agonistic venues also in the western part of the Roman empire. An example of this is the decree from Nemausus dated to Hadrian's time and written in Latin and Greek, in which the synod of artists bestows a series of honours to T. Iulius Dolabella for his help with the games at Naples.[34] Taking into account everything that has been mentioned, it could be hypothesized that the agonistic venues included by the emperor Hadrian in his new calendar would have hosted a copy of the three letters found in Alexandria Troas.

On the other hand, it is quite possible that cities where games were held which were not included in the calendar also had *stelai* inscribed with Hadrian's letters, and the very *stele* found in Alexandria Troas is proof of that. Even though this city is not included in Hadrian's calendar, it provides the only copy known of today of the three letters written by the emperor. Although J.-Y. Strasser hypothesizes that a sanctuary of the synod was located in Alexandria Troas, there is no hard evidence of its existence, and an alternative explanation for the presence of this *stele* can be looked for within the restoration of the city-games.[35] According to epigraphic evidence, since the second century BC the city held the Smintheia, games that were surely connected with the cult of Apollo Smintheus ('lord of mice'), which was widely spread throughout the territory of the Troad.[36] In the inscription of the athlete Aurelius Hygianos from Smintheion from the second half of the second century AD it is stated that he won the *pankration* and the *pale* in the Smintheia Pauleia (Σμίνθια Παύλεια) games of Alexandria Troas.[37] This brings us to the issue concerning the modifications that the name of some of the traditional *agones* could undergo during imperial times. The most widespread practice was to introduce the imperial cult into the cities' own traditional festivals. This method was the simplest of all since the only change made were to the titulature of the *agones* by adding to them the name of the emperor, and to the programme by the introduction of contests meant to honour the imperial figure.[38] In the case of

---

[33] *F.Delphes* III, IV 302; Oliver (1989), no. 75; Strauch (1996), 202–3; Rousset (2002), no. 43; Lefèvre et al. (2002), no. 152. See also: Cortés Copete (1999), 100–1; Sánchez (2001), 452; Lozano Gómez and Gordillo Hervás (2015).

[34] *CIG* III 6786 = *IG* XIV 2495 = *IGR* I 17 = *CIL* XII 3232 = *ILS* 5082 = *SEG* 47, 1527.4 = *SEG* 57, 985; Caldelli (1997), 413, no. 1.

[35] Strasser (2010), 592.

[36] On Apollo Smintheus see: Homer, *Iliad* 1.39; Ovid, *Metamorphoses* 12.585. See also Smith (1870), Smintheus. On the inscriptions related to the Smintheia of Alexandria Troas see: *SEG* 16, 733; *SEG* 46, 422, ll. 6–7. Alexandria Troas organized also the Pythian games in the third century AD: *F.Delphes* III, I 550, l. 29; Robert (1939), 247.

[37] *IMT* 552; Robert, *OMS* 1, 630–2; Farrington (2012), no. 1204.

[38] For example, *I.Thespies* IV 177: μεγάλων Τραϊανήν Ἁδριανήνων Σεβαστήων Μουσήω[ν] (Great Trajanean Hadrianean Augustan Musean games); Des Courtils and Laroche (2002); Baker and Thériault (2014), 100: Letoa Traianeia Hadrianeia Antoneia.

Alexandria Troas, the epithet Pauleia could refer to the *euergesia* of Paullus Fabius Maximus, proconsul of Asia under Augustus, who signed an edict addressed to the Koinon of Asia in which a series of initiatives to honour the reigning emperor were established.[39] Among them, the reform of the calendar of the province stands out, which was meant to have the New Year start on the day of Augustus' birth (23 September).[40]

During the second century AD a series of architectural reforms were carried out in the city of Alexandria Troas that could be related to the interest of the city in promoting the Smintheia Pauleia games. Among such initiatives was the aqueduct of Herodes Atticus.[41] The aqueduct probably ended in a monumental *nymphaeum*, also dated in the same period. The Alexandrian *nymphaeum* is a semicircular building of the 'sigma formed *nymphaea*' typology, with seven semicircular *exedrae* meant to hold statues of which nothing remains.[42] It is also during the second century AD that Alexandria Troas began to place on its coins the iconography of Apollo Smintheus: on the reverse of the coins from Antoninus Pius to Trebonianus Gallus the god is usually represented standing on a column, with a quiver on his shoulder, holding a *patera* and a bow, and encircled by the legend COL(onia) AUG(usta) TROA(d).[43]

Therefore, while the city of Alexandria Troas was not included in Hadrian's new calendar, the city had its own Smintheia games dedicated to its traditional divinity, which might have been restored in the first century BC thanks to the *euergesia* of Paullus Fabius Maximus and probably in the second century AD with the help of Herodes Atticus. The finding of the *stele* inscribed with Hadrian's three letters attests to the diffusion of the ecumenical regulation that all the games of the empire had to comply to. In this way, we can assume that in all the places where *agones* were held, there should be at least one copy of it. The fact that Alexandria Troas included on the *stele* not only the letter setting out the rules which affected all festivals, but also Hadrian's reorganization of the circuit of games, of which the games of Alexandria Troas were not a part, could suggest an attempt by the city to elevate itself to the same level of the games that were part of Hadrian's new system. Likewise, the fact that the city had Hadrian's new calendar on display would imply that the Smintheia Pauleia were not simple city-games but were open to all the synod athletes who wanted to participate. The inscriptions do

---

[39] Robert (1939), 247.   [40] *OGIS* 458; *SEG* 4, 492; Samuel (1972), 174–6; Stern (2012), 274–9.

[41] Philostratus, *Lives of the Sophists* 548. On Herodes Atticus see Schultess (1904); Graindor (1930); Ameling (1983); Tobin (1997); Galli (2002); Skenteri (2005); Pomeroy (2007).

[42] Öztaner (1999). Herodes Atticus was also responsible for the nymphaeum at Olympia: Walker (1979), 182–96; Ameling (1983), 112–30; Bol (1984); Arafat (1996), 37–8; Tobin (1997), 315–22.

[43] *RPC* IV.2 141, 3155, 9194, 3168, 8951, 9193, 150, 9190, 11288, 149, 11287, 196, 9200. *RPC* VI 4040, 4041, 4043, 4042. *RPC* VII.1 2.1, 2.2. *RPC* IX 400, 403, 440. For the same iconography but with Apollo Smintheus with a tripod beside him: *RPC* IV.2 9202, 153, 174, 1194, 11063, 3011, 175, 151, 10900, 3156, 176, 192. *RPC* VI 3948, 3955, 3957, 3960, 3968, 3974, 4001, 4003, 4000, 4002, 4039, 4053, 4073. *RPC* IX: 410, 411, 472. Apollo Smintheus and his temple: *RPC* IV.2 9699, 3172, 24, 3158, 3984, 4026, 4027, 4037. *RPC* VI 3984, 4026, 4027, 4028, 4029, 4037, 5067, 4068, 4071, 4086.

not provide the exact date on which the games were held, but it is likely that they were scheduled to fit into Hadrian's calendar so that the athletes could attend the Alexandrian games between more prestigious contests.

3.3. Hadrian's impact on the festival calendar

As a result of the imperial establishment of the new agonistic calendar, the *agones* were distributed over a period of four years beginning with the Olympic games of Pisa and ending with the Panhellenia games, the new *agones* held in Athens to commemorate the creation of the Panhellenion assembly.[44] Hadrian's idea was to establish a calendar which would include all the main games of the empire without any overlaps in time, so that the participants could attend all of them and also have enough time to travel between their places of celebration:

γενήσονται δὲ οἱ ἀγωνισταὶ ἐπὶ πάντας | τούς τε νῦν ὑπ' ἐμοῦ τεταγμένους ἀγῶνας Κ . . . . διὰ τὸ | μηδένα ἀξιῶσαι ΠΑΡϹΛΙΟΙ περὶ αὐτῶν τοὺς πλείστους, ἐὰν πρῶτον μὲν | πᾶσαι πανταχοῦ πανηγύρεις ἐπὶ τεσσαράκοντα ἡμέρας ἄγωνται (καὶ διατετάχθω | τοῦτο), εἶτα δὲ μὴ κατατρείβωντα<ι> μετὰ τοὺς ἀγῶνας τὰ θέματα ΛΠΛ|ΤΟΥΝΤΟΥΣ.

The contestants will get both to all the contests now set in order by me and to... since nobody saw fit to... the majority concerning them [?] provided, first, that all festivals everywhere are held for forty days (and let this be laid down), and then that they (i.e. the contestants) are not worn down demanding the prize-moneys after the contests.[45]

One of the main characteristics of the athletic calendar is its extremely exhaustive and precise character when it comes to indicating the time when some of the celebrations had to start. In the case of the games of the western part of the empire, the calendar expressly indicates the time at which they should start according to the Julian year. For example, 'the contest in Tarentum shall be held next to the Hadrianeia in the month of January, with the celebration of the contests in Naples after the Capitolia, as it has been accomplished up to now'.[46] The dates that appear

---

[44] The celebration of the first Panhellenia was in AD 137. See Wörrle (1992), 337–49: Αὐτοκράτορι Καίσαρ[ι] | Τ. Αἰλίωι Ἁδριανῶι Ἀν|τωνείνωι Σεβαστῶι | Εὐσεβεῖ καὶ Θεῶι Ἁδρι|ανῶι Πανελληνίωι καὶ θεαῖς Ἐλευσεινί|αις καὶ Ἀθηνᾶι Πολιά|δι καὶ Ποσειδῶνι καὶ Ἀμφιτρείτηι - Εὐρυ|κλῆς - ἐπὶ - τῆς - σλδ΄ - Ὀ|λυμπιάδος - Πανελ|ληνιάδι - ϛ΄. On the Panhellenion see Spawforth and Walker (1985) and (1986); Gordillo Hervás (2012); Corcella, Monaco, and Nuzzo (2013); Monaco (2018).

[45] Petzl and Schwertheim (2006), ll. 78–82. Translation from Jones (2007), 156. In this analysis of the text, Jones 2007: 152, integrates Κ[αί]... at line 79 and emendates ἀπα(ι)τοῦντες at ll. 81-2.

[46] Petzl and Schwertheim (2006), ll. 63–4.

in Hadrian's calendar correspond to the days in which the games of Rome and Naples were previously held, so that no change had to be made to them.

However, a problem arose when two games would overlap according to the traditional calendar. An example of this is what occurred with Athens' Panathenaic games and the Delphi Pythian games which, according to the traditional calendar, were both to be held during the third Olympic year. The main day of the Panathenaia was 28 Hekatombaion (July-August) and for the Pythian 7 Boukatios (August-September). According to Hadrian's new calendar, the games of the Asian Koinon were inserted between the Panathenaic and the Pythian games, with a total duration, between holidays and trips, of 141 days. Therefore, it would be impossible to maintain the traditional calendar of the festivities and consequently it would be necessary to reorganize the games. Scholarship is split between two hypotheses on how this problem was solved: the Pythian games were kept by Hadrian on the 7 Boukatios of the third Olympic year, with the Panathenaic games being moved to the spring of the second Olympic year; or the Panathenaic games stayed on 28 Hecatombaion of the third Olympic year and the Pythian games had to be moved to the fourth Olympic year.[47] I consider the second hypothesis to be more likely since, in the calendar, Emperor Hadrian expressly states that the Panathenaic games must be held on the same date they had been always held.[48] The case of Delphi is different, especially considering how the aforementioned inscriptions on the temple of Apollo show that Pylae had begun to promote its victors. As seen above, the emperor Hadrian arranged that if an athlete had managed to win only the games at Pylae he had to be deprived of his victory, but if he had been victorious in Delphi, then he had to be crowned according to tradition.[49] The letters sent by Hadrian to the city of Delphi show that the Pythian games had lost part of the prestige they had during the classical era. It could be safely hypothesized that at the time of the creation of the new agonistic calendar, the emperor favoured the games of Asia over the Pythian games, relegating the last games to the fourth Olympic year.[50] Issues such as the ones undergone by the Pythian games underline the importance of the dissemination of Hadrian's new calendar across the provinces of the empire.

Hadrian's focus on the need to disseminate the new calendar would make it likely that there be a copy in all agonistic venues, at least in those that were included in the calendar, but also in other cities of the empire, mainly those of

---

[47] About the options see Petzl and Schwertheim (2006); Gouw (2008); Strasser (2010); Shear (2012).

[48] About the problem see Gordillo Hervás (2017). Petzl and Schwertheim (2006), ll. 66-7. Translation from Jones (2007), 155: 'after the Nemea [shall be] the Panathenaia, so that the contest is completed on the same (day) by the Attic calendar as it ended up to now'.

[49] F.Delphes III, IV 302, Col. II. ll. 6-8. On Hadrian's letter, see Cortés Copete (1999); Sánchez (2001), 452; Weir (2004), 169; Lozano Gómez and Gordillo Hervás (2015).

[50] On this problem and other consequences of the distribution of the games see Gordillo Hervás (2017).

Hellenic tradition. The games were not only attended by athletes, but also by a very large audience. Because of this, the cities had to provide the necessary information to their citizens so that they would be aware of the new calendar according to which the most important games of the Roman empire were organized. As stated by Sebastian Scharff the emperor could 'be present at an athletic contest without actually attending'.[51] The presence of a *stele* reproducing the emperor's letters would therefore become an essential component of the landscape of the sanctuaries, and an invaluable tool for setting the presence of the emperor within the agonistic precincts as the games' tutelary figure.

The calendar served as a guide to the cities to be able to know the place and the time in which the athletes would be active within the empire, and thus schedule the most appropriate time for holding their *ex novo* games (see Fig. 3.1 for a proposed order of festivals following this reform). In the first place, they could hold their games when other *agones* were not celebrated, and therefore athletes would be able to attend. Secondly, it would be easier to ensure the participation of the athletes if they were competing in games located close to the games being organized. These two elements were taken into account when the Eusebeia games were created. These *agones* were meant to commemorate the death of Emperor Hadrian that occurred in AD 138, and they were first held in the Italian city of Puteoli in AD 142.[52] The games took place during the first and second Olympic years when athletes were competing in western *agones* such as the games of Tarentum, the Capitoline games of Rome, the Sebastan games of Neapolis and the Actian games of Nikopolis. The list of games of the athletes help us to further pinpoint the time when the Eusebeia were held, since before the establishment of the Eusebeia the western games were always listed in the same order, Capitoline–Sebastan games–Actian games. However, starting from the second century AD, in lists of competitions the winners of the Eusebeia begin to appear between the Capitoline and the Sebastan games.[53]

In the eastern part of the empire, the *ex novo* games were established according to the same criteria mentioned above. An example of this is found in the letters of M. Ulpius Appuleius Eurykles, high-priest of Asia, addressed to the citizens of Aphrodisias and dated around AD 180–9. They provide a series of guidelines for the good organization of new games in Aphrodisias, including the amount of money that the winners should get and of course the most convenient time when the *Lysimacheia* games ought to be held:

---

[51] See Scharff, Chapter 2, this volume.

[52] *Scriptores Historiae Augustae, Hadrian* 27, 3–4. The first celebration of the Eusebeia can be dated by reason of the base of a statue dedicated to Antoninus Pius which shows him being bestowed with the fifth *tribunicia potestas*: *CIL* 515 = Strasser (2000) 362.

[53] Strasser (2000), 363. See *IAG* 76; *IG* II² 3169/70; *IG* VII 49; *F.Delphes* III. I 89 and 555; *I.Magnesia* 192; *TAM* II 587; Caldelli (1993) no. 57.

1st Year (133–134 AD)	
Game	Place
Olympic	Olympia
Isthmian games	Isthmia
Hadrianeia	Athens
Games of Tarentum	Taranto
Capitoline Games	Rome

2nd Year (134–135 AD)	
Game	Place
Sebastan Games	Naples
Actian Games	Nicopolis
Games of Patras	Patras
Heraea and Nemeia	Argos

3rd Year (135–136 AD)	
Game	Place
Panathenaia	Athens
Koina of Asia	Smyrna
Koina of Asia	Pergamon
Hadrianeia	Ephesos

4th Year (136–137 AD)	
Game	Place
Pythian games	Delphi
Caesareos Isthmia	Corinth
Games of Mantinea	Mantinea
Olympieia	Athens
Hadrianeia	Smyrna
Olympieia Balbilleia	Ephesos
Panhellenia	Athens

Fig. 3.1 Proposed order of festivals following Hadrian's reform, as proposed in Gordillo Hervás (2017).

προθεσμία δὲ εἰς τὸν ἑ-
ξῆς χρόνον καὶ τὴν ἐπιοῦσαν τετραετηρίδα {Σ} ἔσται χρ<ό>[νος]
ὁ ἀπὸ [Βαρ]<β>ιλλήων τῶν Ἐφέσῳ [ἀγομένων] πρὸς [? Κοινὰ] Ἀσίας
[? ἔρρωσθε] leaf

The appointed time for the following period and the next four-yearly celebration will be the time after the Barbilleia at Ephesus up to [? the Koina] of Asia. [? Farewell][54]

---

[54] *I.Aphrodisias Performers* 50, ll. 21–3. CIG 2741 = OGIS 509 B = *I.Aphrodisias and Rome* 57 = SEG 32, 1097; BE 1983, 392.

According to Charlotte Roueché the *Lysimacheia* were held for the first time between September AD 180 and August AD 181.[55] Eurykles uses Hadrian's calendar of games in order to narrow down the temporal range in which the Lysimacheia were to be celebrated. In the inscription Eurykles mentions two specific Asian games as temporal markers: the Balbilleia (or Barbilleia depending on the sources), and the games of the *koinon* of Asia. Therefore, the city of Aphrodisias could have celebrated the *Lysimacheia* in any date occurring within the two and half years of time between the Balbilleia held in the fourth year and the games of the Koinon of Asia held in the third year of the following cycle.

This letter by M. Ulpius Appuleis Eurykles is not the only one that provides us with information on the timing of the games of the city of Aphrodisias. Concerning the new *Kallicrateia* another inscription states:

τῇ τοῦ ἀγῶνος χρείᾳ εὐτρεπίζειν καὶ δη[νάρια...c.24...]
καὶ τὰ ἆθλα καὶ τὰ ἀγωνίσματα ἀκολούθως [τῇ τοῦ τελευτήσαντος γνώμῃ· ἀγω]-
νοθετήσει δὲ τὸν πρῶτον ἀγῶνα Φλάβιος Εὐ[—...c.18...ἐκ τοῦ]-
των δὲ ὁ ἀπὸ τῶν Καλλικράτου τοῦ Διοτείμου [ἀγὼν ἐπιτελεσθήσεται τοῦ ἐπί]-
οντος ἔτους <π>ερὶ μῆνα ἕκτον πρὸ τῆς εἰς Ῥώμην [ἀποδημήσεως ἀγωνίστων·

to prepare them for the requirements of the contest and? denarii [...] and the prizes and the competitions in accordance with [? the intention of the deceased;] the president of the first contest will be Flavius Eu[- ?...? after] these the contest from the (bequest) of Callikrates son of Diotimus [will be celebrated in the coming] year, in the sixth month, before the [departure of the synod] for Rome.[56]

Assuming that the reconstruction is correct, the text states that the games must be held before the synod leaves for Rome. According to L. Robert, the synod would be nothing more than the group of athletes who, after the celebration of the Aphrodisian games, would move to Rome in order to compete in the Capitoline games.[57] Therefore, if the *Kallicrateia* were linked to the games in Rome, they would have been held in AD 182, the year in which the Capitoline games were held.[58]

The inscriptions of Aphrodisias and the creation of the new games in honour of Hadrian suggest that the games established *ex novo* were scheduled according to the Hadrian's new calendar, thus reinforcing the hypothesis of the presence of a copy of the second letter even in those cities that had not been included in the calendar.

---

[55] Roueché (1993), 168.
[56] Trans. Roueché (1993), 167, no. 51, ll. 1-5; *I.Aphrodisias 2007*, 15.330 = *I.Aphrodisias and Rome* 59.
[57] Robert, *OMS* II, 1130-1.   [58] Roueché (1993), 168.

3.4. Conclusion

Despite being the only extant copy of Hadrian's new agonistic calendar, the *stele* of Alexandria Troas carries far-reaching implications not only in terms of the dissemination of Hadrian's mandate but also of the presence of the imperial text within the agonistic venues, both in those cities that were part of the new calendar and in the ones which were not included in it. To this end, the synods of the athletes and of the *technitai* would have played an important role in the transmission of the new regulation and calendar to the cities where agonistic celebrations were held. The three letters of Emperor Hadrian inscribed in the *stele* of Alexandria Troas clearly state how new dispositions should be announced. In the first letter the emperor establishes a new regulation that would encompass all agonistic competitions. The second letter organizes the main games held across the Roman empire in a four-year circuit. Hadrian clearly orders that the new regulations must be inscribed on *stelai* to be set in the appropriate places, and that a copy of the calendar must be present in the sacred precincts that have been included in the calendar.

A more thorough analysis of Alexandria Troas' letters shows that the level of dissemination went beyond the agonistic sanctuaries included in the calendar. It is very possible that cities not included in the calendar but where games were nevertheless held also had a *stele*, or at least some kind of copy of Hadrian's letters. The *stele* found in Alexandria Troas is proof of this since this city was not part of the Hadrianic calendar. It is also likely that cities that organized *agones ex novo* possessed a copy of Hadrian's edict to programme the most appropriate moment for holding their games and maximize the participation of those athletes who were competing in other games taking place in the vicinity of the city. This fact can be observed at least in two cases, namely the new Eusebeia games organized by Puteoli in honour of Hadrian, and the games of the Asian city of Aphrodisias. If these two cities can be considered as exemplary cases, this would mean that the impact of Hadrian's new calendar went beyond the organizational level, and potentially affected the landscape of the agonistic venues where the festivals were held across the whole empire.

Works Cited

Ameling, W. (1983) *Herodes Atticus*. Hildesheim and New York.

Arafat, K. W. (1996) *Pausanias' Greece. Ancient Artists and Roman Rulers*. Cambridge.

Baker, P., Thériault, G. (2014) 'La vie agonistique xanthienne: nouvel apport épigraphique (première partie)', *Revue des Études Grecques* 127.1: 97–118.

Boatwright, M. T. (2000) *Hadrian and the Cities of the Roman Empire*. Princeton, NJ, Oxford.

Bol, R. (1984) *Das Statuenprogramm des Herodes-Atticus-Nymphäums in Olympia*. Olympische Forchschungen 15. Berlin.

Caldelli, M. L. (1992) 'Curia athletarum, iera xystike synodos e organizzazione delle terme a Roma', *Zeitschrift für Papyrologie und Epigraphik* 93: 75-87.

Caldelli, M. L. (1993) *L'agon capitolinus. Storia e protagonisti dall'istituzione domizianea al IV secolo*. Rome.

Caldelli, M. L. (1997) *Gli agoni alla greca nelle regioni occidentali di la Gallia Narbonensis*. Rome.

Clerc, M. (1885) 'Inscription de Nysa', *Bulletin de Correspondance Hellénique* 9: 124-31.

Corcella, A., Monaco, M. C., and Nuzzo, E. (2013) 'Ancora su Pausania I 18,9, la cd. Biblioteca di Hadrian ed il Panellenio', *Annuario della Scuola Archeologica di Atene* 91, Serie III.13: 111-56.

Cortés Copete, J. M. (1999) 'El fracaso del primer proyecto panhelénico de Adriano', *Dialogues d'Histoire Ancienne* 25.2: 91-112.

Cortés Copete, J. M. (2019) 'Koinoi nomoi: Hadrian and the harmonization of local laws', in O. Hekster and K. Verboven (eds), *Proceedings of the Thirteenth Workshop of the International Network Impact of Empire (Gent, June 21-24, 2017)*. Leiden and Boston, 105-21.

Daux, G. (1966) 'Chronique des fouilles et découvertes archéologiques en Grèce en 1965', *Bulletin de Correspondance Hellénique* 90: 715-1019.

Des Courtils, J. and Laroche, D. (2002) 'Xanthos et le Létôon. Rapport sur la campagne de 2001', *Anatolia Antiqua* 10.1: 297-333.

Farrington, A. (2012) *Isthmionikai: A Catalogue of Isthmian Victors*. Hildesheim.

Fauconnier, B. (2018) 'Ecumenical Synods: The Associations of Athletes and Artists in Roman Empire'. Unpublished PhD thesis, Universiteit van Amsterdam.

Fauconnier, B. (2020) 'The emperor and the ecumenical synods of competitors', *Latomus* 79.3: 647-60.

Galli, M. (2002) *Die Lebenswelt eines sophisten: Untersuchungen zu den Bauten und Stiftungen des Herodes Atticus*. Mainz am Rhein.

Geagan, D. J. (1972) 'Hadrian and the Athenian Dionysiac Technitai', *Transactions and Proceedings of the American Philological Association* 103: 133-60.

Gordillo Hervás R. (2011) 'La organización adrianea de los certámenes panhelénicos', in J. M. Cortés Copete, R. Gordillo Hervás, and E. Muñiz Grijalvo (eds), *Grecia ante los imperios: V Reunión de historiadores del mundo griego*. Seville, 335-43.

Gordillo Hervás, R. (2012) *La construcción religiosa de la Hélade imperial: el Panhelenion*. Firenze.

Gordillo Hervás, R. (2017) 'Adriano y el calendario imperial de juegos atléticos: propuesta sobre el tercer y cuarto año del ciclo olímpico'. *Gerión* 35.1: 119-42.

Gordillo Hervás, R. (2018) 'Competing for the emperor: games and festivals in honour of Hadrian', in R. Gordillo Hervás, J. López Benítez, and J. M. Cortés Copete (eds), *Deis Gratias: Diversidad Religiosa y Política Imperial en el Siglo II d.C.* ARYS 16. Madrid, 177–205.

Gouw, P. (2008) 'Hadrian and the calendar of Greek agonistic festivals. A new proposal for the third year of the Olympic cycle', *Zeitschrift für Papyrologie und Epigraphik* 165: 96–104.

Graindor, P. (1930) *Un milliardaire Antique. Hérodes Atticus et sa famille.* Le Caire.

Guerber, E. (2009) *Les Cités grecques dans l'Empire romain. Les privilèges et les titres des cités de l'Orient hellénophone d'Octave Auguste à Dioclétien.* Rennes.

Haensch, R. (2008) 'Des empereurs et des gouverneurs debordes', *Cahiers du Centre Gustave Glotz* 19: 177–86.

Harland, P. A. (2014) *Greco-Roman Associations II, North Coast of the Black Sea, Asia Minor. Texts, Translations, and Commentary.* Berlin.

Harris, H. A. (1964) *Greek Athletes and Athletics.* London.

Jones, C. P. (2007) 'Three New Letters of the Emperor Hadrian', *Zeitschrift für Papyrologie und Epigraphik* 161: 145–56.

Jory, E. J. (1970) 'Associations of Actors in Rome', *Hermes* 98.2: 224–53.

Klose, D. O. A. (2005) 'Festivals and games in the cities of the East during the Roman Empire', in C. Howgego, V. Heuchert, and A. Burnett (eds), *Coinage and Identity in the Roman Provinces.* Oxford, 125–33.

Lammer, M. (1967) 'Olympien und Hadrianeen im antiken Ephesos'. Unpublished PhD thesis, Cologne.

Le Glay, M. (1976) 'Hadrien et l'Asklepieion de Pergamo', *Bulletin de Correspondance Hellénique* 100.1: 347–72.

Le Guen, B. (2010) 'Hadrien, l'Empereur philhellène, et la vie agonistique de son temps. À propos d'un livre récent: Hadrian und die dionysischen Künstler. Drei in Alexandria Troas neugefundene Briefe des Kaisers und die Künstler-Vereinigung', *Nikephoros* 23: 205–39.

Lefèvre, F. et al. (2002) *Corpus des inscriptions de Delphes.* Tome IV: *Documents Amphictioniques.* Paris.

Leschhorn, W. (1998) 'Die Verbreitung von Agonen in den östlichen Provinzen des römischen Reiches', in W. Orth (ed.), *Colloquium 'Agonistik in der römischen Kaiserzeit'*, *Stadion* 24.1: 31–58.

Looy, H. (1992) 'Les couronnes valent plus que les prix', in D. Vanhove (ed.), *Le sport dans la Grece Antique. Du jeu à la competition.* Brussels: 125–9.

Lozano Gómez, F. and Gordillo Hervás, R. (2015) 'A dialogue on power: emperor worship in the Delphic Amphictyony', in J. M. Cortés Copete, E. Muñiz Grijalvo, and F. Lozano Gómez (eds), *Ruling the Greek World: Approaches to the Roman Empire in the East.* Stuttgart, 127–46.

Mann, C. (2018) 'Cash and crowns: a network approach to Greek athletic prizes', in M. Canevaro, A. Erskine, B. D. Gray, and J. Ober (eds), *Ancient Greek History and Contemporary Social Science*. Edinburgh, 293–312.

Monaco, M. C. (2018) 'Το Πανελλήνιον—Il Panhellenion—The Panhellenion', in M. Lagogianni-Georgakarakos and E. Papi (eds), *HADRIANVS—ΑΔΡΙΑΝΟΣ, Ο Αδριανός, η Αθήνα και τα Γυμνάσια—Adriano, Atene e i Ginnasi—Hadrian, Athens and the Gymnasia*. Athens, 52–3.

Müller, S. (1995) *Das Volk der Athleten. Untersuchungen zur Ideologie und Kritik des Sport in der griechisch-römischen Antike*. Trier.

van Nijf, O. (2001) 'Athletics, festivals and elite self-fashioning', in S. Goldhill (ed.), *Being Greek under Rome: Cultural Identity, the Second Sophistic and the Development of Empire*. Cambridge: 306–34.

Oliver, J. (1989) *Greek Constitutions of Early Roman Emperors from Inscriptions and Papyri*. Philadelphia.

Öztaner, S. H. (1999) 'The Nymphaeum at Alexandria Troas', in E. Schwertheim (ed.), *Die Troas. Neue Forschungen III*. Asia Minor Studien 33. Bonn: 27–36.

Petzl, G. and Schwertheim, E. (2006) *Hadrian und die dionysischen Künstler. Drei in Alexandria Troas neugefundene Briefe des Kaisers und die Künstler Vereinigung*. Bonn.

Pleket, H. W. (1973) 'Some aspects of the history of the athletic guilds', *Zeitschrift für Papyrologie und Epigraphik* 10: 197–227.

Pleket, H. W. (1975) 'Games, prizes, athletes and ideology. Some aspects of sport in the Greco-Roman world', *Stadion: internationale Zeitschrift für Geschichte des Sports* 1.1: 49–89.

Pleket, H. W. (2014a) 'On the sociology of ancient sport', in T. F. Scanlon (ed.), *Sport in the Greek and Roman Worlds*, Vol. 2: *Greek Athletic Identities and Roman Sports and Spectacle*. Oxford: 29–82.

Pleket, H. W. (2014b) 'Inscriptions as evidence for Greek sport', in P. Christesen and D. G. Kyle (eds), *A Companion to Sport and Spectacle in Greek and Roman Antiquity*. Chichester: 98–111.

Pomeroy, S. B. (2007) *The Murder of Regilla: A Case of Domestic Violence in Antiquity*. Cambridge, MA and London.

Remijsen, S. (2011) 'The so-called "crown-games": terminology and historical context of the ancient categories for agones', *Zeitschrift für Papyrologie und Epigraphik* 177: 97–109.

Robert, L. (1939) 'Inscriptions grecques d'Asie Mineure', in W. Moir Calder and J. Keil (eds), *Anatolian Studies presented to William Hepburn Buckler*. Manchester, 227–48.

Roueché, C. (1993) *Performers and Partisans at Aphrodisias in the Roman and Late Roman Periods: A Study Based on Inscriptions from the Current Excavations at Aphrodisias in Caria*. London.

Rousset, D. (2002) *Le territoire de Delphes et la terre d'Apollon*. Paris.

Samuel, A. E. (1972) *Greek and Roman Chronology. Calendars and Years in Classical Antiquity*. Munich.

Sánchez, P. (2001) *L'Amphictionie des Pyles et de Delphes*. Stuttgart.

Schmidt, S. (2009) 'Zum Treffen in Neapel und den Panhellenia in der Hadriansinschrift aus Alexandria Troas', *Zeitschrift für Papyrologie und Epigraphik* 170: 109–12.

Schultess, C. (1904) *Herodes Atticus*. Hamburg.

Shear, J. L. (2012) 'Hadrian, the Panathenaia, and the Athenian calendar', *Zeitschrift für Papyrologie und Epigraphik* 180: 159–72.

Skenteri, F. (2005) *Herodes Atticus Reflected in Occasional Poetry of Antonine Athens*. Lund.

Slater, W. (2008) 'Hadrian's letter to the athletes and Dionysiac Artists concerning arrangements for the circuit of games', *Journal of Roman Archaeology* 21: 610–20.

Slater, W. (2013) 'The victor's return, and the categories of Games', in P. Martzavou and N. Papazarkadas (eds), *Epigraphical Approaches to the Post-Classical Polis: Fourth Century BC to Second Century AD*. Oxford, 139–64.

Smith, W. (1870) *Dictionary of Greek and Roman Biography and Mythology*. London.

Spawforth, A. J. (1989) 'Agonistic festivals in Roman Greece', in S. Walker and A. Cameron (eds), *The Greek Renaissance in the Roman Empire*. Papers from the Tenth British Museum Classical Colloquium, Bulletin Supplement, 55. London: 193–7.

Spawforth, A. J. and Walker, S. (1985) 'The world of the Panhellenion I: Athens and Eleusis', *Journal of Roman Studies* 75: 78–104.

Spawforth, A. J. and Walker, S. (1986) 'The world of the Panhellenion II: three Dorian cities', *Journal of Roman Studies* 76: 88–105.

Stern, S. (2012) *Calendars in Antiquity. Empires, States and Societies*. Oxford.

Strasser, J.-Y. (2000) 'Les Concours grecs d'Octave Auguste aux invasions barbares du 3ème siècle. Recherches sur la date et la pèriodicité des concours sacrés'. Unpublished PhD thesis, Université Paris X Nanterre.

Strasser, J.-Y. (2010) '"Qu'on fouette les concurrents…": à propos des lettres d'Hadrien retrouvées à Alexandrie de Troade', *Revue des Études Grecques* 123.2: 582–622.

Strasser, J.-Y. (2016) 'Hadrien et le calendrier des concours (SEG 56, 1359, II)', *Hermes* 144(3): 352–73.

Strauch, D. (1996) *Römische Politik und griechische Tradition. Die Umgestaltung Nordwest Griechenlands unter römischer Herrschaft*. Munich.

Tobin, J. (1997) *Herodes Attikos and the City of Athens. Patronage and Conflict under the Antonines*. Amsterdam.

Walker, S. (1979) *The Architectural Development of Roman Nymphaea in Greece*. London.

Weir, R. (2004) *Roman Delphi and Its Pythian Games*. Oxford.

Wörrle, M. 1992. 'Neue Inschriftenfunde aus Aizanoi I. Eine Bruckenweihung des Eurykles', *Chiron* 22: 337–49.

4
Greek Festival Culture and 'Political' Games at Nikaia in Bithynia

Dario Calomino

4.1. Introduction

Agonistic festivals had a central role in the civic life of the eastern Roman provinces as communal events of great social and cultural significance. Our perception of festival lived experience relies essentially on the vast evidence of individual achievements of performers, organizers, and donors recorded on stone inscriptions.[1] Other than being just an opportunity for personal success and contribution to the community's life, though, festivals were also a unique showcase for the cities. Attracting athletes, performers, and spectators from across the Mediterranean, they were a profitable business and a major source of prestige for the hosting communities, enhancing their international visibility and reputation, which affected their relationships with other communities on a regional and a provincial scale. The material dimension of this reality has survived primarily in the monumental buildings and public spaces that shaped the civic landscape of festival contests and ceremonies. The magnitude and pomp of spectacle buildings and their decorative programmes were a public display of the city's rank and wealth, which foreign envoys, performers, and visitors would come to admire. The imagery of the games and of religious ceremonies revived the community's mythical past and most rooted traditions: figurative reliefs decorating theatres and other public

---

This paper results from my research on Roman provincial coinage and Greek festival culture, which is part of the Warwick University Leverhulme Research Project 'Materiality and Meaning in Greek Festival Culture of the Roman Imperial Period' led by Zahra Newby, to whom I owe my deepest gratitude. For the use of images in this contribution, I would also like to thank the following museum curators and auction houses: A. Dowler, British Museum Department of Coins and Medals (BM); F. Duyrat, Paris Bibliothèque nationale de France (BNF); K. Ehling, Münich Staatliche Museen (SMM); K. Vondrovec, Vienna Kunsthistorisches Museum (KHM); David Guest, Classical Numismatic Group LLC, London; Georg Morawietz, Gorny & Mosch Giessener Münzhandlung GmbH, Munich; Arturo Russo, Numismatica Ars Classica, London; Alexandra Elflein, Fritz Rudolf Künker GmbH & co. KG, Osnabrück. Last but not least, very special thanks to Frank L. Kovacs for giving me access to his unique collection of 'festival coins' (FLK).

[1] van Nijf (2001), 310.

venues of festival celebrations were a means to assert the community's identity and boast about its achievements.[2]

The involvement of the imperial family was a key factor in this interplay.[3] The endorsement of local festivals by the emperor was a vital element in the negotiation of power relations between Rome and the provincial communities. Also, the fact that festivals were increasingly linked to the emperor's worship meant that the bestowal of a νεωκορία could come with annexed imperial festivals:[4] both were privileges of the highest rank for which rival communities were in constant competition. Very little remains of the visual culture of festivals on civic monuments, especially the images celebrating the emperor in association with the games.[5] Local coinage is the only surviving source that fills this gap. The extraordinary variety of images featured on the reverse of civic issues reflected the imagery designed to celebrate and advertise festivals on a monumental scale. Alongside the plethora of honorary titles used in coin legends, they document how the imagery of festivals was embedded into the visual language of local rivalries. This contribution will focus on coinage to discuss the example of Nikaia in Bithynia and its antagonism with Nikomedia: the parallel between the messages conveyed by the two rivals on their issues shows that local games were not only a manifestation of civic identity but were also used as a source of political propaganda.

4.2. Nikaia and Nikomedia

The history of Roman Nikaia, founded as Antigoneia on the shores of Lake Ascanius (modern İznik) and renamed by Lysimachus after his victory over Antigonus in 301 BC,[6] is usually hard to disentangle from that of its counterpart Nikomedia: the two communities were divided by a long-standing rivalry over the leadership of Bithynia. The perception of this conflict in antiquity can be appreciated in the well-known oration 38 written by Dio Chrysostom in the Flavian period, which invited the Nikomedians to enjoy the benefits of concord instead of pointlessly quarrelling with their neighbours.[7] In the eyes of the Bithynian orator their dispute was essentially an empty 'battle of names' (περὶ τῶν ὀνομάτων μάχη),

---

[2] Newby (2003) and (2005), 247–71; Di Napoli (2015), 260–93; Newby and Carless-Unwin, this volume, Chapters 6 and 7.

[3] See contributions by Scharff and Gordillo Hervás in this volume on the impact of members of the imperial family, Chapters 2 and 3.

[4] For an overview, see Merkelbach (1978), 289; Mitchell (1993), 219–25. However, Burrell (2004), 335–41 has shown that not every provincial temple for the imperial cult was necessarily associated with imperial festivals.

[5] The only exception is the Severan frieze of the *scaenae frons* in the theatre of Hierapolis in Phrygia; cf. Newby (2005), 249–51; Di Napoli (2015), 270–2 and 280–3, with previous bibliography.

[6] Strabo, *Geography* 12.565.

[7] Dio Chrysostom, *Oration* 38, esp. 22–3, 32–6 and 41–3; on the rivalry between the two communities see also Herodian, *History of the Empire*, 3, 2, 9.

which hinged on the exclusive right to be regarded as μητρόπολις (literally 'mothertown' but essentially used as capital city) and πρώτη Βιθυνίας (first city of Bithynia).[8] What Dio's testimony fails to document is the broader political context of this clash. Even though the major events that determined the changing fortunes of Nikaia and Nikomedia unfolded towards the end of the second century, his account overlooks a fundamental aspect of their rivalry that was already crucial from the Augustan age and at the time when he was writing: the role played by Rome. Dio sees Roman authority as a moral rather than as an actual political arbiter, to whom the quarrels between provincial cities were nothing but 'subject of ridicule'.[9] In fact, the conflict between Nikomedia and Nikaia was more than a local affair: it was a matter of international diplomacy in which the position of Rome and the imperial family did tip the scales. Imperial acknowledgement of their hierarchy in the provincial ranking was a key factor, hence the rival cities' constant efforts to win the favours of the central authority.[10]

The modern perception of this phenomenon is much closer to its real dimension, especially due to the masterful study by Louis Robert on this topic.[11] His historic reconstruction of the clash of titles between Nikaia and Nikomedia, famously described as a matter of glory and hatred ('la gloire et la haine'), is based on the material evidence of coin legends and inscriptions. Robert's analysis is critical to our understanding of how the cities' behaviours could be influenced by the decisions of the central authority. One key element of the dispute omitted by Dio Chrysostom that was central in Robert's dossier is the bestowal of *neokoroi* titles, a privilege entirely depending on the city's relationship with the imperial family and on imperial approval. More recent scholarship has discussed the role and prominence of imperial cult in this rivalry relying extensively on Robert's work.[12] While nothing substantially new has emerged from archaeological finds and excavations to enhance our understanding of this topic, a closer analysis of the images on civic coins, with a specific focus on the significance of the imagery of imperial festivals, can bring us a deeper understanding of this conflict.[13]

Civic coinage is still the richest and most informative historical source on the religious, mythical and cultural traditions of Nikomedia and especially of Nikaia,

---

[8] Dio Chrysostom, *Oration* 38.26 points out that there was no economic interest associated with being the first city of Bithynia: it would not entail territorial expansion at the expense of other cities and the appropriation of their fiscal revenues.
[9] Méthy (1994), 184–6.
[10] Dio Chrysostom, *Oration* 38.38. This may be also a consequence of the loosely negative attitude of Dio towards Roman rule; cf. Jones (1978), 124–31.
[11] Robert (1977a).
[12] See especially Sheppard (1984), 163–73 and the comprehensive analysis of Burrell (2004), 147–65. See also more general works by Bekker-Nielsen (2008), 47–8; Madsen (2009), 51–3.
[13] A recent article by Weiss (2021) has given new insights based on the epigraphic evidence from market weights and he has also reconsidered the use of mythical genealogy on the coins of Nikaia as part of local propaganda against Nikomedia.

whose production was much larger.[14] Since Robert, coinage has been used essentially as an epigraphic source to complement the record of honorific titles mentioned in inscriptions on stone, whereas coin imagery has remained largely unexplored. Other studies on civic rivalry in the eastern provinces, such as between Tarsus and Anazarbus in Cilicia and between Perge and Side in Pamphylia, have combined epigraphic sources and coinage, also focusing on coin imagery, to show how their competing claims to primacy involved the number of their *neokoroi* temples as well as their imperial festivals.[15] This chapter will focus on coin designs and the role played in this clash by the celebration of civic festivals in Bithynia, to see how imperial favour and ideology interacted with local rivalries. In comparison to the analysis of inscriptions and coin legends, which yield a largely specular picture of give-and-take between the two contenders over the same honorific titles, a more in-depth analysis of coin imagery shows that the visual language designed to claim leadership at Nikaia was very different from that of Nikomedia.

Hundreds of cities in the imperial provinces advertised their festivals on civic coins, especially between the end of the second century and the third century.[16] Coin legends promoting the games were often used by the local administrations as an opportunity to magnify the reputation of their communities, especially when games were upgraded to Panhellenic rank (Olympic, Pythian, Actian) to gain international appeal, sometimes boasting worldwide outreach as *oikoumenikoi* (international).[17] The very title of 'first of the province', which sometimes featured on coins too, was indeed associated with the privilege of leading the common procession of cities taking part in provincial festivals ($\pi\rho o\pi o\mu\pi\epsilon i\alpha$).[18] The imagery of the games (both on coins and in decorative arts, such as architectural reliefs and domestic mosaics) normally drew upon a very small range of subjects, reflecting the appeal of the principal attractions of the agonistic world: athletes and prizes.[19] However, coin designs also increasingly emphasized imperial endorsement of civic festivals, which became largely associated with the rituals and practice of imperial glorification and worship.[20] For the celebration of imperial festivals the fairly standardised 'agonistic' visual language of coinage could be diversified and

---

[14] The standard reference for the coinage of Nikaia is still *RGMG* I.3: pp. 394–511, alongside Weiser (1983). On the coinage of Nikomedia, see *RGMG* I.3: pp. 512–72 and Corsten (1996). In the absence of a modern study on these mints, which allows for a quantification of the dies produced, a rough estimate on their volume of output can be based on the number of issues catalogued in *RGMG* I.3, which include specimens in the main public collections and some from trade: in the period from Augustus to Gallienus, Nikomedia has 281 issues while Nikaia has 624.

[15] On the Cilician cities see Ziegler (1985). On the Pamphylian cities see Nollé (1993) and Calomino's section in Newby and Calomino (2022), 48–52. On the Pontic cities, see Dalaison (2014).

[16] For an overview of the use and spread of coinages advertising games and festivals in the provinces, see esp. Klose and Stumpf (1996); Leschhorn (1998); Klose (2005). A more comprehensive discussion on these issues will be published in Calomino (forthcoming).

[17] Cf. Klose (2005), 126.   [18] Dio Chrysostom, *Oration* 38.38.

[19] Cf. Klose and Stumpf (1996); Klose (2005), 128–30; Calomino (forthcoming). See more broadly also Dunbabin (2010) and (2016).

[20] On this aspect, see Price (1984), 101–32; Ziegler (1985), 67–123.

sometimes reinvented, reflecting the political strategies of civic elites. This is particularly the case with the visual narrative of the struggle between Nikaia and Nikomedia, especially for the unusual outcomes that it generated on Nikaian coinage, reflecting the way in which festival culture was interpreted in the local media in the key moments of their rivalry.

As we learn from Cassius Dio, in the Augustan age Nikaia 'had been honoured above all the others' in Bithynia (προετετίμηντο, like Ephesos in Asia).[21] Indeed it was called 'ἡ μητρόπολις' by Strabo:[22] this probably means that the city served as capital of the province, overcoming Nikomedia, which had been the capital in the Hellenistic period. This hierarchy seems to have lasted only for a very short period, though, as Nikomedia took the lead under the Julio-Claudians and held it for most of the second and third centuries.[23] Surprisingly, even though we do not lack first hand imperial sources on the political history of Bithynia,[24] there is still uncertainty on whether Nikaia was designated as the capital of Bithynia instead of Nikomedia and when.[25] Under the Flavians, while Nikaia shared the leadership of Bithynia with Nikomedia, the latter was the only metropolis in the province.[26] The Hadrianic inscription of the Lefke Gate of Nikaia lists a number of major honours—first city of Bithynia and Pontus and metropolis by imperial and senatorial decision,[27] which suggests that Nikaia thrived in the second century. However, the main reason for Nikomedia's glory—and Nikaia's resentment—was the privilege of hosting a provincial temple of the imperial cult, which Nikomedia enjoyed almost by royal prerogative as the metropolis of the Bithynian Koinon since the Hellenistic period.[28] Conversely, Nikaia was never 'properly' a *neokoros*: in the Lefke Gate inscription the city was regarded as *neokoros* of the Augusti (νεωκόρος τῶν Σεβαστῶν),[29] which was not quite the same as hosting a temple dedicated to one emperor in particular.[30] Unlike Nikaia, Nikomedia could also boast of the dedication of further *neokoroi* temples (two under Commodus, three under Elagabalus), which were advertised in a timely fashion on its coins. On top of that, Nikaia was punished by Septimius Severus for siding with Pescennius Niger in May AD 194, having all its privileges and titles revoked.[31] Still, Nikaia seems to have promptly regained imperial favour as it was accorded permission

---

[21] Cassius Dio, *Roman History* 51.20.6. Cf. Millar (1964), 8.   [22] Strabo, *Geography* 12.4.7.
[23] Cf. Robert (1977a), 2 n. 4; Sheppard (1984), 163–4.
[24] Besides Pliny the Younger, who was provincial governor, our main source is the native Bithynian consul Cassius Dio. For an overview see Madsen (2009), also discussing Dio Chrysostom and Arrian (esp. 103–26).
[25] Haensch (1997), 282–90. See especially Wesch-Klein (2008), 272, opting for Nikaia, and recently Baz (2013), 263–4, opting for Nikomedia.
[26] Dio Chrysostom, *Oration* 38.39.
[27] *I.Mus.Iznik* I, 29–30. Surprisingly, none of these titles were advertised on civic coins in this period.
[28] Burrell (2004), 147.   [29] Burrell (2004), 164–5.   [30] Cf. Robert (1977a), 35.
[31] Cassius Dio, *Roman History* 75.8.3. For a thorough historical reconstruction, see Robert (1977a), 22–5; Bekker-Nielsen (2008), 147–50.

to host sacred Severan festivals to honour Caracalla and Geta. From the later Severan period up until the age of Gallienus, the bronze coinage of Nikaia was by far the largest and most regular in the province, yielding an image of continuous prosperity. The city's steady productivity was a sign of financial wealth that could also be viewed as a way of enhancing its reputation to counterbalance the gap in rank with Nikomedia. Above all, the coinage of this period was an opportunity for the Nikaian minting workshop to expand considerably its repertoire of imagery, which may reflect a broader process of renovation and diversification in the language of visual communication on public media. This marks a substantial difference from the 'communication strategy' adopted at Nikomedia, as seen through the lens of coinage.

4.3. Games for the empire

Festivals and games were an additional source of discord between Nikaia and Nikomedia. The κοινὰ Βειθυνίας, connected to the imperial cult, were the highest in rank: they were hosted mainly by Nikomedia, although instances are known in which provincial festivals were held at Nikaia, too.[32] When Cassius Dio describes the establishment of sacred games at Pergamon, in conjunction with the dedication of the first provincial temple to Roma and Augustus in Asia, he makes no mention of analogous contests being held at Nikomedia for the cult of Augustus in Bithynia:[33] the first imperial games of the Bithynian *Koinon* might have been established later, perhaps in the Neronian period.[34] One well-known passage of Dio Chrysostom's 38th oration mentions that the Nikaians and the Nikomedians worshipped the same gods and, in most cases, celebrated the same festivals too (τὰς ἑορτὰς πλείστας ὁμοίως ἄγετε).[35] This may refer to the festivals of the *Koinon* themselves, even if Nikomedia was the principal seat, or perhaps also to the ones honouring the emperor and his family, which were held in both cities. The epigraphic evidence on the festivals held at Nikomedia and Nikaia is not very large, and festivals never featured on civic coinages until the end of the second

---

[32] See *IGUR* I 249; *I.Sinope* 105; *I.Tralleis* 135. On the ones hosted by Nikomedia, see Bosch (1935), 232 n. 103.

[33] Cf. Burrell (2004), 151. This is also the passage in which Nikaia is said to have hosted a temple of the divine Julius and Roma where Roman citizens were first allowed to worship a deified ruler (Cassius Dio, *Roman History* 51.20.6-7).

[34] Burrell (2004), 335.

[35] Dio Chrysostom, *Oration* 38.22, 46. Dio does not regard festivals as a bone of contention between the two cities but as an element of shared cultural background. However, this may also allude to the fact that both communities participated in each other's games. The sending of delegates and envoys to attend another city's festivals (Price (1984), 127-8) was probably a major opportunity for self-promotion in which rivalry and tensions would come to surface.

century.³⁶ Afterwards, as in most of the provincial cities of the eastern half of the empire, it became fashionable to advertise local festivals on coins, but the two Bithynian communities did it in very different ways.

The turning point in this process was the reign of Commodus, during which the visual language used by the two communities on their civic coinages began to diverge in accordance with their different political priorities. While Nikomedian coins focused on celebrating the community's role as provincial warden of the imperial cult, Nikaian coins placed greater emphasis on the city's games, not only to counterbalance the international reputation of their rivals, but also to show allegiance to the imperial family. A meaningful aspect of the promotion of Nikaia's festivals is indeed that it always had a prominent 'imperial' character, while there were essentially no references to any of the traditional Panhellenic games until the last civic issues struck in the reign of Valerian and Gallienus.³⁷ The coinage of Commodus saw the genesis of a new visual programme at Nikaia using festival culture to connect the community to the emperor, which coincided with the lowest point in the relations between Commodus and Nikomedia, causing the capital to lose most of its privileges. According to Cassius Dio, the most influential imperial *libertus* (freedman) before Cleander was one Saoterus from Nikomedia, who managed to obtain permission for his hometown to celebrate games and erect a temple to the emperor in AD 180–2.³⁸ So, when Saoterus was put to death by Cleander, the city lost both its second *neokoria* and the annexed festivals.³⁹ It is in this context that Nikaia began to adopt 'agonistic' designs expressly to celebrate the fact that new festivals had been established to praise the emperor: the Kommodeia.⁴⁰ This meant not only introducing a new theme into the civic mint's iconographic repertoire, but in some cases also creating a whole new visual language to honour the emperor.

The main strand of designs focused on the showcase of agonistic prizes, as on most of the civic coins advertising local festivals across the provinces.⁴¹ Under Commodus, Nikaian coins also began to feature depictions of athletes,⁴² yet to become another popular subject in the third century in other regions (especially in Thrace and Pisidia), which suggests that the Bithynian workshop was among

---

³⁶ A comprehensive collection of sources can be found in Erol-Özdizbay (2011). On the festivals of Nikaia, see in particular Bosch (1950).
³⁷ Before the age of Valerian only one issue of Maximinus Thrax mentioned festivals not clearly associated with the imperial cult: the Asklepeia games (see below). There is no evidence that the Augousteia Pythia mentioned in an agonistic inscription dedicated to Gaius Perelios Alexandros from Thyateira (*TAM* V.2, 1019) were held at Nikaia, as suggested in Farrington (2012), 79, no. 2.63 and 169 n. 663.
³⁸ Cassius Dio, *Roman History* 73.12.2.   ³⁹ Cf. Robert (1977a), 34; Burrell (2004), 153.
⁴⁰ See Robert (1977a), 32–3. Nikaia was the only provincial city that advertised Kommodeia games on its coins in the emperor's lifetime alongside Miletus, where they were named ΔΙΔΥΜΕΙΑ ΚΟΜΟΔΕΙΑ; cf. *SNG von Aulock* 2109.
⁴¹ Cf. *RGMG* I.3, 304–16.   ⁴² *RGMG* I.3, 317–19.

the first ones to develop and experiment with new iconographic patterns.[43] The legends accompanying these designs read either *IEPOC AΓΩN* or *KOMOΔEIA NIKAIEΩN*, acknowledging the privilege to host sacred and imperial games. Another category of issues mentioning the games shows the legend *KOMOΔEIA* within a tetrastyle temple, possibly implying that it was devoted to the imperial cult (Fig. 4.1).[44] It seems no coincidence that this brand-new imagery was introduced at Nikaia in the time when Nikomedia had lost its privilege to host the provincial cult of Commodus and to advertise it on its coins. The centrality of the emperor in the Nikaian festivals, though, was better emphasised by another extraordinary design: a sculptural bust of Commodus resting between two crowns on a prize-table, which is inscribed with a word (no longer legible) possibly referring to the Kommodeia, too (Fig. 4.2).[45] This imagery may have been designed at Nikaia specifically for the local festivals, because it remained unparalleled in the provinces. It almost certainly refers to public ceremonies involving the presentation of sacred images of the emperor to the audience, which was part of the rituals associated with the emperor's worship.

Given the size of the bust depicted on these coins, which conforms to the portable format of private and public portraits, it falls within the category of sacred icons of members of the imperial family that used to be held in local temples for worship and then brought out and carried in processions across the city on

Fig. 4.1 AE: Commodus, Nikaia AD 180–92 (*RGMG* I.3, 302 = *RPC* IV 6045). BNF.945 (25 mm, 6.98 g).

Photograph: https://gallica.bnf.fr/ark:/12148/btv1b8556118k.

Fig. 4.2 AE: Commodus, Nikaia AD 180–92 (*RGMG* I.3, 303 = *RPC* IV 6046). BNF.947 (33 mm, 25.37 g).

Photograph: https://gallica.bnf.fr/ark:/12148/btv1b8556118k.

---

[43] These include the depiction of a fine group scene with three nude male figures preparing to perform in the contests; *RGMG* I.3, 320. This is probably the earliest example of a coin iconography that may have been inspired by a well-defined visual model, perhaps a painting, which started to be copied on coins of other cities a few decades later, such as Byzantion (Schönert-Geiss, *Byzantion* 1564) and Ancyra (cf. *BMC Galatia* 22) under Caracalla and Aphrodisias under Gordian III (*RPC* VII 625).

[44] *RGMG* I.3, 302.

[45] *RGMG* I.3, 303. This coin type is extremely rare—currently only one specimen is known.

special occasions—liturgical and festive days. Textual evidence of this practice can be found especially at Athens, Ephesos, Oinoanda, and in Egypt.[46] These icons were mainly in metal rather than stone, especially gold or silver;[47] they were carried by special officers such as σεβαστοφόροι and/or σεβαστοφάντες.[48] During festivals there usually was a public ceremony in which the sacred images were displayed before the crowd assembled in the theatre,[49] and the Nikaian issue of Commodus may have immortalised that very moment. If so, this design implicitly connects to the one mentioned above that shows a tetrastyle temple, which may be devoted to the imperial cult, constructing a cohesive visual narrative of the festival ceremonies across the civic coinage. A possible parallel for the iconography adopted on this Commodus issue can be found on certain coins of Caracalla struck at Side in Pamphylia and at Tarsus in Cilicia. On the coins of Side, the bust of Caracalla, very similar in size to the one displayed at Nikaia, was held in one hand by Athena, the city's protecting goddess.[50] On the issues of Tarsus, the bust was held by Herakles and Perseus together, as the two progenitors of the community,[51] or by Apollo Patroos.[52] Many of the Tarsus issues for Caracalla, including these two, were associated with the provincial festivals hosted by the Cilician capital, named Antoniniana after him, in which he served as honorary *demiourgos* presiding over the games.[53] So the design featuring an imperial image being presented by the local gods to the community was also probably an echo of festival ceremonies. The main difference between the imagery used in southern Asia Minor for Caracalla and the one designed at Nikaia for Commodus is that the representation of Commodus' bust on Nikaian coins was not an allegorical scene framed within a mythical setting to signify the emperor's godhead;[54] instead, it was a snapshot of a key moment in the festival ceremony that involved the display of the imperial bust on a prize table, a realistic picture showing real objects.

---

[46] Cf. Robert (1977b), 101 and, more broadly, (1960), 322; Price (1984), 189–91. The best evidence comes from Ephesos, where the procession of statues of the gods and emperors was thoroughly described in Vibius Salutaris' foundation of civic festivals: Rogers (1991), 80–126.

[47] Cf. Fejfer (2008), 239–41.

[48] Chaniotis (2009), 21–3. Cf. Strubbe (2006), 116–19, challenging the idea that this task was assigned to the *sebastophantes* only during imperial mysteries, as suggested by Price, rather than in any processions involving the emperor's worship. The *sebastophantes*, archpriest and ambassador of the city C. Cassius Chrestus (*I.Mus.Iznik* I 116) is named in the pre-Hadrianic inscription of the Lefke Gate at Nikaia: he dedicated a statue group to the Flavian family on top of its entrance under the proconsulship of M. Plancius Varus (*I.Mus.Iznik* I 25–8); cf. Bekker-Nielsen (2008), 112–14. See also Madsen (2009), 90–6 for similar examples from Bithynia.

[49] Price (1984), 110–11; Gebhard (1996).

[50] *SNG Paris* 816. The presence of a small ship in the exergue may refer to the arrival of the imperial portrait by sea to the harbour, before it was carried in procession into town; cf. Nollé (1987), 105. Alternatively, the galley may have simply commemorated an imperial visit to Side.

[51] *SNG Paris* 1539, *SNG Levante* 1069.   [52] *SNG Paris* 1534, *SNG Fitzwilliam* 5332.

[53] Ziegler (1985), 79–85.

[54] See Calomino (2020a), 170–3 for a more in-depth discussion based on comparisons with other examples.

The Severan age marked a second period of fierce rivalry between Nikaia and Nikomedia, which is also reflected in the way in which festivals were used to cement the communities' ties with the imperial family. This time the Nikaians were at a disadvantage after the punishment inflicted by Septimius at the end of the civil war (AD 193), while Nikomedia's second neokorate was being restored at the same time. Nevertheless, in response to the Augousteia Severeia (or Severeia Megala) celebrated at Nikomedia, the Nikaians established their own Severeia Philadelpheia Megala games to honour Caracalla and Geta (see below, 4.4).[55] Again, coinage was a much more prominent instrument of local self-promotion at Nikaia than at Nikomedia: the greater emphasis placed on festivals at Nikaia was probably a way of contrasting the Nikomedians' assertions of provincial supremacy based on their multiple *neokoros* titles. The Nikaian workshop minted coins advertising the civic festivals almost uninterruptedly until the cessation of its activity at the end of Gallienus' reign. Only under Elagabalus was this pattern temporarily abandoned, precisely when Nikomedia chose to celebrate the bestowal of its third neokorate on coins with a strong emphasis on its associated games. Elagabalus was wintering at Nikomedia at the end of AD 218, so the city might have had a privileged relation with the emperor by then.[56] Nikaia's decision to omit any reference to its own games in this period could be interpreted as a way of deliberately avoiding a comparison with their rivals, who were in a much stronger position.

The games advertised at Nikomedia under Elagabalus were always labelled either Demetria or, sometimes, Pythia,[57] and only once Demetria Antonia (Fig. 4.3),[58] showing that the city's patron deity had priority over the emperor in the sacred celebrations.[59] This reflects another substantial difference with Nikaia, where festivals always had a marked political character in relation to the current emperor and his attitude towards the community. Severeia Augousteia festivals were still advertised on the coins of Maximinus Thrax and Philip,[60] and only on one occasion did they mention some otherwise unattested Asklepeia games.[61] It is necessary to wait until the joint reign of Valerian and Gallienus to find the name of Panhellenic contests on Nikaia's coins, the Pythian games.[62] Coins featuring

---

[55] Bekker-Nielsen (2008), 150–1.   [56] Cf. Burrell (2004), 156–7.
[57] *RGMG* I.3, 278–9, 283.   [58] *RGMG* I.3, 281–2.
[59] The third neokorate granted by Elagabalus is probably an example of 'cult-sharing' between the emperor and the city's goddess, Demeter; Burrell (2004), 157.
[60] *RGMG* I.3, 659 (Maximinus), 717 (Gordian III), 731 (Philip), 776 and *RPC* IX 285–6 (Gallus). It must be pointed out, though, that only a very minor proportion of the civic issues produced in the post-Severan period featured agonistic designs.
[61] *RGMG* I.3, 660. A dedication to Klaudios Ioulianos Asklepiodotos, ἀγωνοθέτην τοῦ Σωτῆρος Ἀσκληπιοῦ under Elagabalus, which was found at Prusias ad Hypium (*I.Prusias* 12), may indeed refer to the Asklepeia mentioned on Maximinus coins, although festivals in honour of Asclepius are also attested at Nikomedia in the second century AD (*IG Napoli* I 47).
[62] Weiser's assumption that Valerian visited Bithynia in 256 on the occasion of the Nikaian games (Weiser (1983), 75–6) cannot be proved.

Fig. 4.3 AE: Elagabalus, Nikomedia AD 218–22 (*RGMG* I.3, 278–9 = *RPC* VI 3354). Rudolf Künker Auction 273, 14 March 2016, lot 853 (29 mm, 14.17 g); Lübke & Wiedemann KG, Leonberg.
Photograph by permission of Fritz Rudolf Künker GmbH & Co. KG, Osnabrück; www.kuenker.com.

agonistic designs mentioned either ΙΕΡΟΣ ΑΓΩΝ ΠΥΘΙΑ ΝΙΚΑΙΕΩΝ (the sacred Pythian games of the Nikaians)[63] or unspecified ΑΓΩΝΕΣ ΙΕΡΟΙ ΝΙΚΑΙΕΩΝ (sacred games of the Nikaians).[64]

For the first time under Valerian and Gallienus agonistic issues also named festivals dedicated to a god: Dionysus was honoured as the city's mythical progenitor in the Dionysia,[65] which are otherwise unattested in the epigraphic records. On coins the Dionysia were always advertised in association with festivals dedicated to Valerian and Gallienus (and named after them), as ΔΙΟΝ(ΥΣΙΑ) ΠΥΘ(ΙΑ) ΟΥΑΛΕ ΓΑΛΛΗ (sic) ΝΙΚΑΙΕΩΝ (Dionysia Pythia Valeriana Galliena of the Nikaians),[66] in line with the Nikaian tradition of emphasizing the political relevance of their games. Once again, the parallel with the contemporary coinage of Nikomedia is compelling. This time, though, the joint reign of Valerian and Gallienus witnessed a specular use of agonistic designs between Nikaia and Nikomedia to celebrate their festivals. For the first time in this battle of images, instead of introducing new graphic options to overcome their opponent, the two Bithynian workshops seem to have almost copied each other, adopting exactly the same visual language. This is particularly apparent in the issues on which both cities chose an unusual obverse design combining the busts of the three reigning emperors, Valerian, Gallienus, and Valerian II. The tripartite pattern characterizing these obverses features on the reverses, too, where both civic coinages displayed three focal elements. On Nikomedian coins these were the three *neokoroi* temples devoted to the imperial cult (Fig. 4.4), a privilege restored nearly thirty years after its abrogation due to the *damnatio memoriae* of Elagabalus. The ΤΡΙΣ ΝΕΩΚΟΡΩΝ (thrice *neokoros*) inscription announcing this new civic achievement also featured on other issues showing three prize crowns on the reverse (Fig. 4.5), implying that the sacred festivals accorded by the emperors were as many as the *neokoroi* temples.

Again, this was a level of recognition that the Nikaians had no means to match, so they had to find a new way of emphasizing their own games, both to defend their reputation and to reinstate their connection to the imperial family.

---

[63] *RGMG* I.3, 812 (Gallienus). [64] *RGMG* I.3, 813–14 (Gallienus).
[65] Dionysos was the progenitor of the community, Herakles the mythical founder; Dio Chrysostom, *Oration* 39, 8. Cf. also Robert (1977a), 8–12.
[66] *RGMG* I.3, 815–16 (Gallienus).

Fig. 4.4 AE: Valerian, Gallienus, and Valerian II, Nikomedia AD 256–8 (*RGMG* I.3, 409). NAC Auction 100, 29 May 2017, lot 1201 (26 mm, 11.78 g).

Photograph by permission of Arturo Russo, Numismatica Ars Classica, London.

Fig. 4.5 AE: Valerian, Gallienus, and Valerian II, Nikomedia AD 256–8 (*RGMG* I.3, 413). CNG Auction 97, 17 September 2014, lot 471 (28 mm, 12.50 g).

Photograph by permission of Classical Numismatic Group, LLC.

Three prize crowns were also depicted on the Nikaian coins of this period and were accompanied by much more engaging or informative inscriptions. While the games celebrated at Nikomedia remained unspecified (and they are not known from other sources), the names of the Nikaian festivals were spelled out in length, so that all together they would read: Severeia Pythia Dionysia Augousteia Valeriana and Galliena.[67] It is not clear whether each crown stood for a distinct agonistic contest or whether the names were only added to enhance the scope of the old Severeia.[68] Either way it would appear that what really mattered was to equal, at both propagandistic and visual level, the triple degree of recognition that Nikomedia had achieved, even at the cost of introducing new festivals. The reverse legends on some other issues featuring the prize crowns boldly proclaimed the Nikaians *ΜΕΓΙCΤΩΝ ΑΡΙCΤΩΝ* (the greatest and the best), without naming the games (Fig. 4.6).[69] Similarly hyperbolic legends had been used before on the Severan coins of Tarsus in its clash with Anazarbos over the leadership of Cilicia, except that the superlatives were abbreviated as A M($εγίστη$) K($αλλίστη$) (first, the greatest and most beautiful), probably to save room.[70] The overflow of festival names on Nikaian coins resulted instead in a *horror vacui* visual effect, with legends running on the edges and the legs of the prize table to fit into the flan (Fig. 4.7). The ultimate step in the use of mirrored coin designs between Nikomedia and Nikaia was the representation of the city personification on the issues of both communities: the goddess holds three miniaturized temples at Nikomedia (Fig. 4.8) and three prize crowns at Nikaia (Fig. 4.9). The result is another iconographic stretch:

---

[67] *RGMG* I.3, 810–16; 851–5 (Gallienus).
[68] The Severeia are mentioned explicitly on one issue of Salonina: *RGMG* I.3, 863–7. On the mismatch between the number of festivals celebrated in the provincial cities and that of prize crowns featured on their coins, see Klose (2005), 127.
[69] *RGMG* I.3, 822–4 (all three emperors); 846–8 (Gallienus). Cf. Weiss (2021), 158–9.
[70] Cf. Burrell (2004), 215.

Fig. 4.6 AE: Valerian, Gallienus, and Valerian II, Nikaia AD 256–8 (*RGMG* I.3, 822–4). BM.1961,0301.102 (26 mm, 9.95 g).

Photograph: Calomino, by permission of the British Museum.

Fig. 4.7 AE: Valerian, Nikaia AD 253–60 (*RGMG* I/3, 815), BM.1979,0101.1383 = *SNG von Aulock* 719 (25 mm, 7.64 g).

Photograph: Calomino, by permission of the British Museum.

Fig. 4.8 AE: Gallienus, Nikomedia AD 253–60 (*SNG von Aulock* 7138), BM.1979,0101.1453 (25 mm, 7.96 g).

Photograph: Calomino, by permission of the British Museum.

Fig. 4.9 AE: Valerian, Nikaia AD 253–60 (*RGMG* I/3, 808), BNF.1203 (25 mm, 8.15 g).

Photograph: https://gallica.bnf.fr/ark:/12148/btv1b8555658h.

since only two objects can be held in the goddess' hands, the third one (a temple or a crown) has to balance on her head.

4.4. The Severan Philadelpheia

The harsh punishment inflicted by Septimius Severus on Nikaia in the aftermath of Niger's defeat could have compromised the relations between the community and the imperial family.[71] Yet, the coinage of this period yields a different view, reflecting an apparently idyllic atmosphere of peace and reconciliation. The centrality of the glorification of the Severan family in the city's imagery was more than just an

---

[71] Birley (1988), 141–2.

emphatic campaign of flattery: it looks like a programmatic effort to use civic coinage to echo and magnify the Severan dynastic policy.

The celebration of festivals in honour of the Severan family was the centrepiece of this programme and deserves a more focused discussion. Unlike many other Severeia established in the cities of the Balkans and of Asia Minor, the Nikaian games had a manifest political scope signified by the epithet ΦΙΛΑΔΕΛΦΕΙΑ, 'fraternity festivals', and further enhanced by the imagery adopted on the coins. Some issues featured their full name as 'The Great Severan Philadelpheia, Sacred Games of the Nikaians' (CEOYHEPEIA ΦΙΛΑΔΕΛΦΕΙΑ ΤΑ ΜΕΓΑΛΑ ΝΙΚΑΙΕΩΝ ΙΕΡΟC ΑΓΩΝ).[72] The message of brotherhood that they conveyed was literally intended as a proclamation of concord between Caracalla and Geta.[73] A number of elements in the representation of the two young emperors allow for a rough approximation of the chronology of these issues, but the exact circumstances in which these coins were minted, as well as the dating of the festivals, are uncertain.

One possible celebratory occasion was the co-optation of Caracalla and Geta as co-rulers in AD 198, but a number of clues suggests in fact a later date. The young princes featured as Augustus and Caesar respectively, and Geta was always named Publius rather than Lucius in the obverse legends, which sets the *terminus post quem* in around AD 199–200. On the other hand, these series stopped definitely before AD 209, because none of the issues featuring Geta as Augustus advertised the festivals.[74] Interestingly, Plautilla was also commemorated on certain Nikaian coins but they neither mentioned the festivals nor her marriage with Caracalla. This could be an indication that the Severeia issues do not belong in the period AD 202–5 preceding her *damnatio memoriae*. As a possible parallel, we find that at Caesarea in Cappadocia, one of the very few other cities that hosted Philadelpheia festivals, a ΙΕΡΟC CEOYHPIOC ΦΙΛΑΔΕΛΦΙΟC *agon* was advertised on coins of Septimius, Caracalla, and Geta struck in years 13 and 14 of the local era, which is AD 205–7.[75] If this is the period in which the Severan festivals were held at Nikaia too, after the fall of Plautianus and the repudiation of Plautilla by Caracalla,

---

[72] *RGMG* I.3, 356 (Septimius Severus); 526 (Geta).

[73] The reverse legend on a rare issue of Septimius Severus at Sardis includes a largely illegible word that has been tentatively integrated as [ΦΙΛΑΔΕΛ]ΦΕΙΑ (Mionnet IV, 128, 729; cf. Karl (1975), 131–2), but it is in fact EYCEBEIA.

[74] Both these issues as well as one showing Caracalla and Geta shaking each other's hands and the unique legend ΕΙC ΑΙΩΝΑ ΤΟΙC ΚΥΡΙΟΙC ΝΙΚΑΙΕΩΝ ('to our lords for eternity'; *SNG von Aulock* 590) cannot date after 209, as suggested in Harl (1987), 41–2. It is not possible to determine whether this singular 'acclamation-coin' is also associated with the Philadelpheia games or with another special event—Burnett has suggested that acclamation issues for the Severans in Pontus and Bithynia cities may refer to an otherwise unattested Parthian campaign of Caracalla in 207; Burnett (2016), esp. 89–90.

[75] Cf. Sydenham 435a (Septimius Severus), 491–2 (Caracalla) and 502 (Geta). Note that the 'homonoia' issues of Smyrna and Caesarea of this period advertising agonistic festivals in the name of Septimius and Domna (featuring the Mount *Argaios* between two agonistic urns in year 14 of Caesarea's era) did not mention the Philadelpheia (Franke-Nollé F10).

it would explain why Plautilla was never celebrated in association with the games on the civic coinage. However, it is also possible that the coinage in her name was produced at the same time as the issues commemorating the festivals but was not linked to them, as could be assumed on the basis of die analysis. Some issues of Julia Domna and Plautilla showed the female personification of *Homonoia* and the legend *OMONOIA NIKAIEΩN* on their reverses.[76] Die-links show that the *OMONOIA* issues of Julia Domna were indeed struck approximately at the same time as the *ΦΙΛΑΔΕΛΦΕΙΑ* issues in her name,[77] so the coins of Plautilla featuring the same reverse type may belong in the same group, which means that all the other issues advertising the games were probably struck before she fell into disgrace.[78] So it is possible that the festivals were held before AD 205,[79] but it is probably safer to date them loosely to AD 202–7.[80]

Nevertheless, even though *homonoia* would be perfectly suitable to promote the brotherhood of Caracalla and Geta in connection with Philadelpheia festivals, it seems in fact that the concord featured on Plautilla coins had nothing to do with them. This hypothesis fits well into the scenario outlined by Robert, whereby Nikaia obtained Septimius Severus' forgiveness a few years after the end of the civil war thanks to the intercession of Caracalla and, especially, of Plautilla.[81] A statue erected by the community to honour the young Augusta bears a dedicatory inscription showing that the titles lost by the city had been restored. This is probably the *homonoia* that the coins of Plautilla were advertising, the one between Rome and Nikaia rather than between Caracalla and Geta.[82] Both Severeia festivals of Nikomedia and Nikaia had a prominent political significance, but while in the former case they were the result of Septimius' gratitude to Nikomedia for its loyalty during the war, in the latter they were established specifically to celebrate the joint rule of Caracalla and Geta at least a decade later, when Nikaia had

---

[76] *RGMG* I.3, 382 (Julia Domna), p. 461, no. 496 (Plautilla).

[77] The same obverse die was used in combination with reverses of Julia Domna's issues featuring *Homonoia* (cf. *BMC* 66) and the *dextrarum iunctio* between Caracalla and Geta (BM.1961,0301.93, unpublished).

[78] It is also possible that the coins of Plautilla were struck in AD 202, soon after her wedding with Caracalla, before the games were held. In this scenario, the same obverse die portraying Julia Domna would have been used on coins featuring *Homonoia* and then reused on those featuring the Philadelpheia festivals sometime later; this is entirely possible but less likely, and it cannot be verified in the absence of a complete die-study.

[79] Cassius Dio, *Roman History* 76.15.3, says that Septimius Severus visited Nikaia while Plautianus was still alive: an imperial visit before AD 205 could have coincided with Severan festivals held on that occasion.

[80] This chronology is compatible also with the minting of silver provincial issues (*cistophoroi*) of the Severan family in around AD 200–2, which were probably struck by the Nikaian workshop too, as suggested by the same engraving style of the imperial portraits; cf. Calomino (2020b).

[81] Robert (1977a), 25–6; Burrell (2004), 165. Birley believed that Cassius Dio also played a crucial role in regaining imperial favour for his hometown; cf. Birley (1988), 142.

[82] In the dedication to Plautilla, whose name was erased after her *damnatio memoriae*, Nikaia boasted, among numerous honours, to be 'loyal friend and ally to the Roman people and home to the House of the Emperors from the time of our ancestors' (φίλη καὶ σύμμαχος, πιστὴ τῷ δήμῳ τῷ Ῥωμαίων καὶ ἐκ προγόνων οἰκεία τῷ οἴκῳ τῶν Αὐτοκρατόρων); *I.Mus.Iznik* I, 59.

regained the favours of the emperor.[83] The peculiar character of the Nikaian festivals of this period can also be appreciated against the broader picture of the Philadelpheia introduced in other provincial communities: with the exception of the games held at Eumeneia and Philadelphia under Valerian and Gallienus, they were indeed a Severan brand.[84]

Another provincial city where the Severan Philadelpheia are well documented is Perinthos in Thrace. Coin legends claim that it was the first city that hosted festivals honouring the Severan family (ΣΕΒΗΡΕΙΑ ΠΡΩΤΑ ΠΕΡΙΝΘΙΩΝ)[85] and Philadelpheia games were advertised in connection with its Aktian and Pythian contests probably from the early reign of Septimius (ΑΚΤΙΑ ΠΥΘΙΑ ΦΙΛΑΔΕΛΦΕΙΑ ΠΕΡΙΝΘΙΩΝ ΝΕΩΚΟΡΩΝ).[86] As in Nikaia, so also at Perinthos the games were essentially built around the brotherhood between Caracalla and Geta. The fact that the joint rule of the Severan princes was emphatically promoted by two of the most prominent cities lying on either sides of the Propontis may be not irrelevant. A passage in Herodian describes the arrangements made by the two brothers in the aftermath of Septimius' death to split the territories of the empire in separate areas of control. Caracalla was to take Europe, having his headquarters at Byzantion on the Thracian side, while Geta was to take control of Asia, choosing Chalcedon in Bithynia as his base of operations.[87] While it is natural to think of the cities on the Propontis as strategic operating centres, one can see why two major provincial political centres such as Perinthos for Thrace and Nikaia for Bithynia would serve better as the seats of the imperial festivals. Even if the plan of dividing the empire in two may have been never actually implemented because of Julia Domna's opposition,[88] the separation of areas of influence between the two brothers might have already been in place from the years immediately preceding Geta's promotion to the rank of Augustus (AD 209), when the games were established at Perinthos and Nikaia: perhaps an attempt to mask the incipient conflict with a public manifestation of dynastic unity.

The visual commemoration of the Philadelpheia at Nikaia, though, stood out as another example of the civic workshop's creativity and communication skills. A series of new designs were introduced that inventively combined the celebration

---

[83] The name 'Philadelpheia' was dropped after this initial period and the games featured simply as the 'Σεβήρεια ἐν Νεικέᾳ'. Cf. IGR IV 1761 = TAM V.3, 1506, also mentioning Philadelpheia games at Philadelphia in Lydia. Even though the epithet may be loosely referring to the city's name, it seems to have been added in the Severan period, hence in honour of Caracalla and Geta, and then dropped, as in Nikaia, supposedly after the *damnatio memoriae* of Geta; cf. Buckler (1917), 89.

[84] On the use of the name 'Philadelpheia' at Philadelphia under Valerian, cf. TAM V.3, 1511. On the issues of Eumeneia, see Robert (1970), 164.

[85] Cf. Schönert-Geiss, Perinthos 457, 476. The foundation of the festivals, as well as the concession of the title of *neokoros* to Perinthos, may be connected to one of the emperor's visits to the city, as clearly indicated on an issue showing Septimius standing on the imperial galley labelled ΕΠΙΔΗΜΙΑ Β CEYHPOY: 'second arrival of Severus'; Schönert-Geiss, Perinthos 461.

[86] Cf. Schönert-Geiss, Perinthos 627–30. [87] Herodian, *History of the Empire* 4.3.5–7.

[88] Herodian, *History of the Empire* 4.3.9.

of the games with the glorification of the imperial family, in which the agonistic elements featured almost as props to provide the setup for a Severan political ceremony. While the conventional agonistic imagery was used on some issues—a prize crown with two palm branches,[89] an athlete crowning himself,[90] a laurel wreath enclosing the name of the festivals,[91] the symbolism of the games was connected to the representation of Caracalla and Geta on the others. A series of issues presented the two emperors as patrons of the festivals, adapting Roman iconography of the imperial family to the local context. On some coins either Caracalla or Geta stand wearing a toga and holding an eagle-tipped sceptre in one hand and a prize crown in the other (Fig. 4.10).[92] Another issue shows an emperor, possibly Caracalla, wearing the same garments, also holding a sceptre and a prize crown while driving a chariot (Fig. 4.11). The presence of a prize crown in both depictions connects the traditional imagery of imperial authority and triumph with the establishment of imperial games at Nikaia.

Fig. 4.10 AE: Julia Domna, Nikaia AD 202–7 (unpublished, cf. *RGMG* I.3, 491: Caracalla for Geta). FLK 957 (27 mm, 10.78).
Photograph by permission of Frank L. Kovacs.

Fig. 4.11 AE: Caracalla, Nikaia AD 202–7 (*SNG von Aulock* 7040). FLK 961 (formerly UBS Gold and Numismatics 83, September 2009, lot 278 = Auctiones Basel, November 1974, lot 127: 36 mm, 28.85 g).
Photograph by permission of Frank L. Kovacs.

---

[89] *RGMG* I.3, 357–8 (Septimius Severus).
[90] *RGMG* I.3, 359 (Septimius Severus), p. 485, no. 487 (Caracalla).
[91] *RGMG* I.3, 395 (Julia Domna), 527 (Geta).
[92] The reverse legend on Caracalla coins is: ΑΝΤΩΝΙΝΟΝ ΑΥΤΟΥC ΝΙΚΑΙΕΙC; on Geta's coins it is: ΓΕΤΑΝ ΚΑΙCΑΡΑ ΝΙΚΑΙΕΙC; cf. *RGMG* I.3, 491 (Caracalla for Geta) and *SNG Fitzwilliam* 4112 (Julia Domna for Geta).

Moreover, the bipartition of power between Caracalla and Geta, one of the key-themes of the Severan propaganda of this period, became a distinctive visual pattern on these series, too. This is manifest especially in the choice of adopting the *dextrarum iunctio* (joining of hands) another Roman iconographic tradition. The depiction of the two emperors standing together and shaking hands probably evoked the imagery designed to celebrate the joint-rule of Marcus Aurelius and Lucius Verus fifty years before,[93] as a sign of continuity with the Antonine dynasty. Interestingly, though, on Severan coins minted in Rome this imagery was not adopted until AD 209, when both Caracalla and Geta were *Augusti*, so after its introduction in the provinces.[94] At Nikaia the scene of clasping hands between the emperors was revisited and transposed into a well-defined visual context, the Severan festivals, in which a prize-table replaced the altar that sometimes featured between them (Fig. 4.12).[95] This imagery was designed at Nikaia and, again, reprised at Byzantion—although, as in Rome, only after AD 209, on issues signed by Aelius Capitolinus that showed a prize crown between Caracalla and Geta (Fig. 4.13).[96] The coins from Byzantion did not involve Philadelpheia games but Antoneina Sebasta dedicated to Caracalla,[97] whose prominence in the local festivals might confirm his territorial leadership on this side of the Bosporus.

Similar iconographic patterns can be also seen on the coins advertising the Philadelpheia at Perinthos, but in a different political situation. Among the several issues on which the local Aktian and Pythian games were advertised, only few featured the Philadelpheia, too. One showed a prize table on the reverse and the busts of Caracalla and Geta facing each other on the obverse (Fig. 4.14).[98] The Philadelpheia were also mentioned on a series of large medallions of Septimius Severus showing either two *neokoroi* temples facing each other[99] or the labours of

Fig. 4.12 AE: Julia Domna, Nikaia AD 202–7 (unpublished; cf. *RGMG* I/3, 485 of Caracalla). Gorny & Mosch Auction 236, March 2016, lot 329 (33 mm, 26.65 g).

Photograph: B. Seifert/Lübke & Wiedemann, Leonberg.

---

[93] Cf. Heuchert (2005), 53–4.

[94] *RIC* IV.1 255, 330. Other Severan coin types that adopted a similar design were introduced earlier in Septimius' reign: Caracalla and Geta standing and holding a Victory together (*RIC* IV.1 255, AD 202–10); Caracalla and Plautilla standing and clasping hands (*RIC* IV.1 124a, 361–2).

[95] *RGMG* I.3, 485–6 (Caracalla).   [96] Schönert-Geiss, *Byzantion* 536–7.

[97] Schönert-Geiss, *Byzantion* 1547, 1564, and especially Schönert-Geiss, *Byzantion* 1550 (signed by Aelius Capitolinus).

[98] Schönert-Geiss, *Perinthos* 628–30.   [99] Schönert-Geiss, *Perinthos* 518–19.

Fig. 4.13 AE: Caracalla, Byzantion AD 209–11 (Schönert-Geiss, *Byzantion* 1535). SMM (41 mm, 37.53 g).
Photograph: https://www.corpus-nummorum.eu/coins/762, by permission of Kay Ehling.

Fig. 4.14 AE: Caracalla and Geta, Perinthos AD 205–9 (Schönert-Geiss, *Perinthos* 629). CNG Triton VI, 14 January 2003, lot 553 (38 mm, 24.68 g).
Photograph by permission of Classical Numismatic Group, LLC.

Heracles.[100] This possibly means that the festivals were dedicated to both the god and the emperor, whose cult had been incorporated into the civic pantheon. Later, still after AD 209, the Philadelpheia were commemorated again at Perinthos in association with the *dextrarum iunctio* design, but exclusively on coins of Geta Augustus.[101] None of the numerous issues of Caracalla (both during Septimius Severus' reign and as the sole emperor) made any reference to the much anticipated *philadelpheia* between him and his brother, confirming that these were entirely politicised celebrations. This example also shows how ideological messages conveyed on civic coins could be diversified and tailored to match the political profile of each member of the imperial family.

---

[100] Schönert-Geiss, *Perinthos* 520–7.
[101] Schönert-Geiss, *Perinthos* 640–1. Accordingly, the series featuring Hercules' labours and mentioning the Philadelpheia in their legends were also issued in the name of Geta (Schönert-Geiss, *Perinthos* 661–7), but not of Caracalla.

Furthermore, at Nikaia the bipolarity of power in the Severan family was also communicated through the representation of the draped busts of Caracalla and Geta facing each other on the reverse (Fig. 4.15).[102] In this case it is possible that the design adopted on local coins celebrating the Severan festivals was inspired by reverse types used on imperial *aurei* between AD 202 and 204. They glorified the young princes on the occasion of Caracalla's wedding with Plautilla and of the Saecular Games in Rome.[103] What made the imagery designed at Nikaia unique was the reinterpretation of the Severan dynastic motif within the context of the civic games and related rituals. In the representation of the Philadelpheia the portraits of Caracalla and Geta featured also as sculptural busts placed on a prize table, on either sides of a crown, as part of the paraphernalia used during festival ceremonies. On one issue they are seen in profile, facing each other just like their 'numismatic' portraits (Fig. 4.16).[104] Another version of this design depicted two portable busts with undefined facial features, almost as generic liturgical tools on a ceremonial altar (Fig. 4.17).[105] As on the coins of Commodus (see Fig. 4.2 above), the sacred icons of the emperor featured among the elements that characterised the liturgies of the imperial cult in festive days, unveiling some of the non-agonistic aspects of these ceremonies. At the same time, though, this imagery also suggests that the two key moments of the festivals, the public display

Fig. 4.15 AE: Septimius Severus, Nikaia AD 202–7 (unpublished; cf. *RGMG* I/3, 397 of Julia Domna). Gorny & Mosch Auction 224, 13 October 2014, lot 360 (26.26 g).

Photograph: B. Seifert/Lübke & Wiedemann, Leonberg.

Fig. 4.16 AE: Geta, Nikaia AD 202–7 (unpublished; cf. *RGMG* I/3, 355 of Septimius Severus). BNF.1966.453 (32 mm, 25.47 g).

Photograph: https://gallica.bnf.fr/ark:/12148/btv1b103118971.

---

[102] This reverse was used on both coins of Septimius Severus (unpublished) and of Julia Domna (*RGMG* I.3, 397).
[103] *RIC* IV.1 155a, 174, 540.
[104] *RGMG* I.3, 355 (Septimius Severus); cf. also BNF 1966.453 (Geta, unpublished).
[105] *RGMG* I.3, 523.

Fig. 4.17 AE: Geta, Nikaia AD 202–7 (*RGMG* I/3, 523). KHM.GR15649 (34 mm, 26.99 g).
Photograph by permission of Klaus Vondrovec.

Fig. 4.18 AE: Geta, Nikaia AD 202–7 (*RGMG* I/3, 524). KHM.GR15650 (27 mm, 10.57 g).
Photograph by permission of Klaus Vondrovec.

of the agonistic prizes and the collective worship of the imperial images, were not necessarily separate, but could be fully intertwined as parts of the same ritual practice. In this perspective, the use of coin designs alternating the busts of Caracalla and Geta and two traditional agonistic crowns on the same prize table (Fig. 4.18)[106] seems to imply that prizes and imperial icons were almost interchangeable elements of the same public ceremony: worshipping the imperial family was an honour for the members of the community comparable to a victory in the games for the athletes.

The presence of sacred images of Caracalla and Geta on the Philadelpheia series evoked again the ritual procession of imperial portraits in festival ceremonies across the city. This imagery reiterated the political significance of these celebrations and the message of devotion and allegiance to the imperial family that the community of Nikaia was committed to communicate and pass on to posterity. The fact that these designs had not only a strong visual impact but also a powerful ideological significance is documented by an extraordinary episode of defacement carried out on a number of specimens of this particular Nikaian issue. All the known coins of Septimius Severus that feature a prize table holding the busts of Caracalla and Geta on the reverse have the image of Geta erased (Fig. 4.19).[107] This was the result of *damnatio memoriae* passed on Geta after his elimination ordered by Caracalla (possibly already by the end of AD 211). This phenomenon is extensively documented on inscriptions across the empire and on bronze civic coins minted in a number of Asia Minor cities, probably in

---

[106] *RGMG* I.3, 524.
[107] Cf. specimens held in London (*BMC* 63), Vienna (GR15606), and Berlin (B23660); cf. Harl (1987), 151 pl. 12; Calomino (2016), 143–4.

4.19 AE: Septimius Severus, Nikaia AD 202–7 (*RGMG* I/3, 355). KHM.GR15606 (Slg. Tiepolo) = Calomino 2016 p. 144, fig. 64 (33 mm, 24.82 g). Photograph by permission of Klaus Vondrovec.

anticipation of Caracalla's visit in AD 214–15. Interestingly, of all the coins issued in the name of Geta in this region of the empire, only the ones showing him and Caracalla together (or with Septimius Severus) were targeted, in order to dissociate the memory of the disgraced emperor from that of the current ruler. The fact that the process of obliteration of Geta's image from coins was implemented on a more or less systematic basis (varying from one city to another) only in the half of the empire that fell under his control, seems to confirm the geopolitical organization of the Mediterranean in the aftermath of Septimius' death.[108] Nikaia was the only Bithynian city whose coins were affected by this process (even though only a very minor proportion of the Severan coinage): this confirms that the community had both strong connections with the imperial family and probably a role in the imperial strategy in this region of the empire. We can see this episode as the ultimate symbolical act of the Severan Philadelpheia at Nikaia: it confirms the political significance attached to these festivals in the first place and the ideological impact that they had even afterwards, also by means of the visual media designed to advertise them.

4.5. Concluding remarks

This chapter has discussed how the analysis of civic coinage can help us reconstruct the visual and material culture of a community in the eastern Roman Empire, such as Nikaia in Bithynia, not only from a diachronic perspective, but also in relation to their neighbours' choices. Nikaia, probably one of the most prolific civic mints under the empire in the second and the third centuries AD, is a compelling case study because its long-standing rivalry with Nikomedia was a constant stimulus for the Nikaians to think of new communication strategies to upstage their opponents. The habit of vying for honorific titles, so vividly described by contemporary authors, pushed the community to engage continuously with the central authority to gain its favour at the expense of its rival. As is widely documented by inscriptions and coin legends, the greatest honour that could be bestowed

---

[108] Cf. Calomino (2016), 130–48.

upon a community was the permission to host a provincial temple for the imperial cult. This chapter has shown how the Nikaians, who, unlike the Nikomedians, could never boast a *neokoros* title, tried to counterbalance the gap in rank with their rivals by emphasising the prominence of their imperial festivals. Indeed, these offered fertile ground to experiment and raise the bar of competition, becoming the ideal platform to combine local and international policy. By focusing on the numismatic imagery of Greek festivals, this study has reviewed the subsequent stages of visual confrontation between Nikaia and Nikomedia, from the reign of Commodus to that of Valerian and Gallienus, to shed light on the different strategies adopted by each mint over the decades. The comparison between the image repertoires of the two cities shows that the Nikaian workshop was much more inventive than that of their neighbours, and was especially keen to think of customised iconographies that connected the world of festivals with the rituals and tropes of the emperor's worship. This holds particularly true during the reign of Commodus, when Nikaia introduced a brand new set of agonistic designs linked to the Kommodeia games, and in the early reign of Septimius Severus, when the civic imagery revolved around the Philadelpheia games in honour of Caracalla and Geta. This festival in particular was entirely permeated with ideological values that echoed contemporary imperial propaganda. Altogether, the various examples of festival-related themes discussed in this chapter shed light on how the visual language of civic coinage was designed to convey messages of great political relevance for the community, in which Greek festival culture played a central part.

Works Cited

Baz, F. (2013) 'Considerations for the administration of the province Pontus et Bithynia during the imperial period', *Cedrus* 1: 261–4.

Bekker-Nielsen, T. (2008) *Urban Life and Local Politics in Roman Bithynia: The Small World of Dion Chrysostomos*. Aarhus.

Birley, A. (1988) *Septimius Severus. The African Emperor*. London.

Bosch, C. (1935) *Die kleinasiatische Münzen der römischen Kaiserzeit. Teil II. Einzeluntersuchungen, Band 1: Bithynien*. Stuttgart.

Bosch, C. (1950) 'Die Festspiele von Nikaia', *Jahrbuch für Kleinasiatische Forschung* 1.1: 80–99.

Buckler W. H. (1917) 'Lydian records', *Journal of Hellenic Studies* 37: 88–115.

Burnett, A. (2016) 'Zela, acclamations, Caracalla—and Parthia?', *Bulletin of the Institute of Classical Studies* 59: 72–110.

Burrell, B. (2004) *Neokoroi: Greek Cities and Roman Emperors*. Leiden and Boston.

Calomino, D. (2016) *Defacing the Past. Damnation and Desecration in Imperial Rome.* London.

Calomino, D. (2020a) 'Caracalla and the divine: emperor worship and representation in the visual culture of Roman Asia Minor', *Anatolian Studies* 70: 153-79.

Calomino, D. (2020b) 'Severan cistophoroi: mint and interpretation', *Numismatic Chronicle* 180: 143-56.

Calomino, D. (forthcoming) *Pride, Profit and Prestige. Civic Coinage and Greek Festival Culture in the Roman East.*

Chaniotis, A. (2009) 'The dynamics of rituals in the Roman Empire', in O. Hekster, S. Schmidt-Hofner, and C. Witscheld (eds), *Ritual Dynamics and Religious Change in the Roman Empire. Proceedings of the Eighth Workshop of the International Network Impact of Empire (Heidelberg, July 5-7, 2007).* Leiden, 3-29.

Corsten, T. (1996) *Katalog der bithynischen Münzen der Sammlung des Instituts für Altertumskunde der Universität zu Köln, Band 2.* Opladen.

Dalaison, J. (2014) 'Civic pride and local identities: the Pontic cities and their coinage in the Roman period', in T. Bekker-Nielsen (ed.), *Space, Place and Identity in Northern Anatolia.* Stuttgart, 125-56.

Di Napoli, V. (2015) 'Figured reliefs from the theatres of Roman Asia Minor', *Logeion* 5: 260-93.

Dunbabin, K. M. D. (2010) 'The prize table: crowns, wreaths and moneybags in Roman art', in B. Le Guen (ed.), *L'Argent dans les Concours du Monde Grec. Actes du Colloque International Saint Denis et Paris 5-6 Décembre 2008.* Saint Denis, 301-46.

Dunbabin, K. M. (2016) *Theater and Spectacle in the Art of the Roman Empire.* Ithaca.

Erol-Özdizbay, A. (2011) 'Roma İmparatorluk Dönemi'nde Pontus-Bithynia Eyaleti'nde Agon'lar ve Agonistik Sikkeler"' [Agons and Agonistic Coins in the Province of Pontus-Bithynia during the Roman Imperial Period]. Unpublished PhD dissertation. Istanbul.

Farrington, A. (2012) *Isthmionikai. A Catalogue of Isthmian Victors.* Hildesheim.

Fejfer, J. (2008) *Roman Portraits in Context.* New York.

Gebhard, E. R. (1996) 'The theatre and the city', in W. J. Slater (ed.), *Roman Theatre and Society.* Ann Arbor, 113-28.

Haensch, R. (1997) *Capita Provinciarum. Statthaltersitze und Provinzialverwaltung in der römischen Kaiserzeit.* Mainz am Rhein.

Harl, K. (1987) *Civic Coins and Civic Politics in the Roman East. 180-275 A.D.* Berkeley.

Heuchert, V. (2005) 'The chronological development of Roman provincial coin iconography' in C. Howgego, V. Heuchert, and A. Burnett (eds), *Coinage and Identity in the Roman Provinces.* Oxford, 29-56.

Jones, C. P. (1978) *The Roman World of Dio Chrysostom.* Cambridge, MA.

Karl, H. (1975) 'Numismatische Beiträge zum Festwesen der Kleinasiatischen und Nordgriechischen Städte im 2./3/Jahrhundert'. PhD Dissertation. Saarland.

Klose, D. A. (2005) 'Festivals and games in the cities of the East during the Roman empire', in C. Howgego, V. Heuchert, and A. Burnett (eds), *Coinage and Identity in the Roman Provinces*. Oxford, 125–33.

Klose, D. O. A. and Stumpf, G. (1996) *Sport, Spiele, Sieg. Münzen und Gemmen der Antike*. Munich.

Leschhorn, W. (1998) 'Die Verbreitung von Agonen in den östlichen Provinzen des römischen Reiches', in W. Orth (ed.), *Colloquium 'Agonistik in der römischen Kaiserzeit, Stadion* 24(1): 31–58.

Madsen, J. M. (2009) *Eager to Be Roman. Greek Response to Roman Rule in Pontus and Bitnynia*. London.

Merkelbach, R. (1978) 'Der Rangstreit der Städte Asiens und die Rede des Aelius Aristides über die Eintracht', *Zeitschrift für Papyrologie und Epigraphik* 32: 287–96.

Méthy, N. (1994) 'Dion Chrysostome et la domination romaine', *L'Antiquité Classique* 63: 173–92.

Millar, F. (1964) *A Study of Cassius Dio*. Oxford.

Mitchell, S. (1993) 'The Greek city in the Roman world: the case of Pontus and Bithynia', in. A. G. Kalogeropulu (ed.), *Proceedings of the VIIIth International Congress of Greek and Latin Epigraphy, Athens 1982*. Athens, 120–33.

Newby, Z. (2003) 'Art and identity in Asia Minor', in S. Scott and J. Webster (eds), *Roman Imperialism and Provincial Art*. Cambridge, 192–214.

Newby, Z. (2005) *Greek Athletics in the Roman World. Victory and Virtue*. Oxford.

Newby, Z. and Calomino, D. (2022) 'The materiality of Greek festivals in the Roman East. The view from Perge', *Asia Minor* 2: 41–54.

van Nijf, O.M. (2001) 'Local heroes: athletics, festivals and elite self-fashioning in the Roman East', in S. Goldhill (ed.), *Being Greek under Rome*. Cambridge, 306–34.

Nollé, J. (1987) 'Epigraphische und Numismatische Notizen 3', *Epigraphica Anatolica* 10: 104–5.

Nollé, J. (1993) 'Die feindlichen Schwestern—Betrachtungen zur Rivalität der pamphylischen Städte', in D. Gerhard and G. Rehrenböck (eds), *Die epigraphische und altertumskundliche Erforschung Kleinasiens: Hundert Jahre kleinasiatische Kommission der Österr. Akad. Wiss. Akten des Symposiums vom 23. bis 25. Oktober 1990*. Vienna, 297–317.

Price, S. (1984) *Rituals and Power. The Roman Imperial Cult in Asia Minor*. Cambridge.

Robert, L. (1960) 'Recherches épigraphiques', *Revue des Études Anciennes* 62.3–4: 276–361.

Robert, L. (1970) *Études anatoliennes: recherches sur les inscriptions grecques de l'Asie Mineure*. Paris.

Robert, L. (1977a) 'La titulature de Nicée et de Nicomédie: la gloire et la haine', *Harvard Studies in Classical Philology* 81: 1–39.

Robert, L. (1977b) 'Documents d'Asie Mineure', *Bulletin de Correspondence Hellenique* 101: 43–132.

Rogers, G. M. (1991) *The Sacred Identity of Ephesos*. London and New York.

Sheppard, A. R. R. (1984) 'Dio Chrysostom: the Bithynian years', *L'Antiquité Classique* 53: 157–73.

Strubbe, J. H. M. (2006) 'The imperial cult at Pessinous', in L. de Blois, P. Funke, and J. Hahn (eds), *The Impact of Imperial Rome on Religions, Ritual and Religious Life in the Roman Empire*. Leiden, 115–21.

Weiser, W. (1983) *Katalog der bithynischen Münzen der Sammlung des Instituts für Altertumskunde der Universität zu Köln, Band 1, Nikaia*. Opladen.

Weiss, P. (2021) '"Mia san mia". Konträre Konzepte der Selbstdarstellung von Nikomedeia und Nikaia in den M13(edien der Marktgewichte und Münzen', in A. Lichtenberger, T. Sare Agtürk, and E. Winter (eds), *Imperial Residence and Site of Councils: The Metropolitan Region of Nicaea/Nicomedia*. Bonn, 147–62.

Wesch-Klein, G. (2008) *Provincia. Okkupation und Verwaltung der Provinzen des Imperium Romanum von der Inbesitznahme Siziliens bis auf Diokletian*. Berlin.

Ziegler, R. (1985) *Städtisches Prestige und kaiserzeitliche Politik*. Düsseldorf.

5
Tokens from Roman Imperial Athens
The Power of Cultural Memory

Mairi Gkikaki

5.1. Introduction

In this chapter I will discuss the tokens discovered in Athens within the destruction layers which resulted from the Herulian sack of the city in AD 267. The destruction inflicted by the Heruli was an event of major importance which meant the abrupt and premature end to many of the city's ancient institutions. Civic coinage and the issue of tokens were both suspended. Nevertheless, enough material has been preserved in the debris to allow us an understanding of the dynamics of festivals in the period before the sack as well as of the role played by portable objects, tokens in particular. In this chapter, I will argue by means of meaningful comparisons that token imagery aimed at reclaiming the city's glorious past. Starting from the notion that tokens recovered from the destruction debris in or in the vicinity of the Stoa of Attalos relate to festivals of Roman imperial Athens, I argue that the memories of Athens' glorious past, which were activated by the tokens' imagery, defined Athenian identity against the backdrop of the Roman empire. The power of memories of Athenian history were the central node for the operation of festival communities. In these festival communities

---

This contribution arises from the 'Token Communities in the Ancient Mediterranean' research project, funded by the European Research Council (ERC) under the European Union's Horizon 2020 research and innovation programme under grant agreement no. 678042. For enabling access to the material I would like to thank John McK. Camp II, director of the American School of Classical Studies excavations at the Athenian Agora and Sylvie Dumont (registrar). The coins illustrations in the Appendix of Token Types are used courtesy of the Ephorate of Antiquities of Athens City, protocol number 17585/23-9-2016 and 11-10-2016. A particular debt of gratitude is owed to Professor Zahra Newby for her kind invitation to participate at the Panel 'The Spatial and Material Dimensions of Ancient Festival Culture' at the FIEC/CA (15th Congress of the Fédération Internationale des Associations d'Études Classiques and the Classical Association annual conference) in London 2019 and publish my paper in the present volume. I have benefitted from the very generous criticism and valuable commentary of earlier drafts from John H. Kroll (University of Texas at Austin) and Zahra Newby (Warwick) and I thank them a lot. Special thanks go to Clare Rowan (Warwick) for her continuous support and encouragement. I would also like to thank Aikaterini Peppa (École Française d'Athénes) for assistance in bibliographic research. Finally, I would like to thank the anonymous reviewers

Mairi Gkikaki, *Tokens from Roman Imperial Athens: The Power of Cultural Memory* In: *The Material Dynamics of Festivals in the Graeco-Roman East.* Edited by: Zahra Newby, Oxford University Press. © Oxford University Press 2023.
DOI: 10.1093/oso/9780192868794.003.0005

Greeks and Romans, civic elite and citizenry came in contact by using a symbology (the tokens' imagery) which could appeal to the pursuits of all participants and participating groups.

The previous chapter in this volume by Dario Calomino has shown the ways in which the imagery of coins could assert civic claims to authority and honour aimed at rival cities and at the same time evoke the prestige of imperial endorsement. Here, instead, I will focus on how a similar type of object, festival tokens, acted within the city of Athens on the occasion of festivals to set up connections to the city's prestigious past, and also to establish links between participating groups: the civic elite and the citizenry, the sacred *gerousia* and the ephebes. With these tokens the city and the festival communities—the community formed *ad hoc* by the participants—celebrated what they conceived as Athenian cultural identity. The imagery of tokens—divinities and heroes both from myth and from recorded Athenian history—placed an emphasis on the cultural memory of their festival community. Hereby the festival communities, obviously mixed in their ethnic origin, as we will see below, by exchanging and distributing lead festival tokens, propagated images from the city's glorious past and shaped their own Athenian cultural identity against the challenges set by the changing environment of the Roman empire.[1]

With Karl Galinsky's and Susan Alcock's works on Roman Greece, scholarship attempts to explain phenomena of human behaviour as the consequence of how memories of the past were perceived, managed and exploited.[2] In the case of tokens, their imagery and their function in festivals can only be explained if scholars ask what people chose to remember and why. In this chapter I will discuss in detail the tokens found in the Stoa of Attalos and in its immediate vicinity. My analysis seeks to reconsider tokens against the backdrop of society and politics in Roman imperial Athens, and to interpret the messages they conveyed in regards to the celebration of Athenian cultural identity and the formation of festival communities.

5.2. Tokens from Ancient Athens and their historiography

The present chapter focuses on the festival tokens of Roman date excavated in and around the Stoa of Attalos. Nevertheless, the discussion of older scholarship on the connections of Athenian tokens to festivals of the Roman period in the city helps to set these finds into the relevant scholarly context. Athens is the city of

---

[1] It is widely recognized that the past and how it was remembered was one of the most important parameters for the way groups and individuals shaped their cultural identity in the Graeco-Roman world; cf. Madsen (2017), lxxxi. Instructive discussions by Alcock (2002); Spawforth (2012); Galinsky and Lapatin (2016).

[2] Alcock (2002); Galinsky and Lapatin (2016).

tokens *par excellence*. In Athens tokens were known by the name of *symbola*.³ The use and circulation of *symbola* in Athens became gradually known to scholars in the course of the nineteenth century, when hundreds of them were being picked up from the muddy streets of the capital of the newly founded Greek state.

Several different functions have been proposed for the Athenian tokens; their use in festivals is just one of these. Achilleus Postolakas, Albert Dumont, and Arthur Engel, the pioneers of the study of Athenian tokens in the nineteenth century, were the first to arrange the material according to its possible functions and related tokens to festivals on account of the inscriptions and the images they carry.⁴ In the twentieth century, Margaret Crosby focused on the tokens which were excavated in the Stoa of Attalos and its immediate vicinity and argued that they formed one coherent group which was connected to festivals. Hereby, she offered evidence for the dating of the tokens of Stoa of Attalos to the years preceding the Herulian destruction.⁵ A previous study by the current author focused on another case study from the years preceding the Herulian destruction, a hoard of tokens found on the Agoraios Kolonos, and argued that these were gift distributions initiated by the civic elite, who yearned for the preservation of status and prestige.⁶

Neither Postolakas, Dumont, nor Engel had made any distinctions between classical or Hellenistic tokens on one hand and Roman period Athenian tokens on the other. This is not surprising given the state of knowledge of their time and the lack of excavation finds. The classification of Athenian tokens to historical periods is Crosby's achievement, as a result of the exploitation of excavation evidence.⁷ Retrospectively, the chronological classification is easily applied to the types presented by Postolakas, Dumont, and Engel. What follows is a detailed review of the views of the above-mentioned scholars on the connections of tokens to festivals.

The earliest instance when Athenian tokens were placed in the context of festivals was with Achilleus Postolakas's seminal papers. Postolakas published two catalogues of lead tokens from the collections of the Athens Numismatic Museum—284 in 1866 and 809 pieces in 1868—followed by a commentary.⁸ The great majority of these tokens were deprived of provenance information, as it is typical of museum pieces, and just a handful of them were accompanied by generic information referring to Athens, Piraeus, or some places of central Greece. Postolakas commented extensively on the token type featuring on the

---

³ Literary sources from Athens where the term *symbolon* means token: Plato, *Symposium* 191d; Aristophanes, *Assembly Women* 289–98; *Wealth* 277–8, Demosthenes, *Oration* 18.210; *Athenaion Politeia* 65.2, 68.2, and 68.2; *IG* II² 1749 (= *Agora* XV, 38).

⁴ Postolacca (1866) and (1868) (*sic*; these two publications authored as Postolacca); Dumont (1870); Engel (1884).

⁵ Crosby (1964), 69–146. ⁶ Gkikaki (2019).

⁷ Crosby (1964), 83–5 and see the chronological arrangement of Crosby's catalogue (1964), 86–122.

⁸ Postolacca (1866), (1868). Achilleus Postolakas was director of the Numismatic Museum in Athens from 1856 to 1887. For these two papers he signed as Achille Postolacca.

right Hermes/Mercury and on the left a frontal standing figure which looks like Artemis Ephesia. Around the edge the type is inscribed ΠΑΝΕΛΛΗΝΙΩΝ (PANHELLENION) (Fig. 5.1). He attributed the token to the festival of the Panhellenia which was founded by Hadrian and sought convincing interpretations for the image of Artemis Ephesia.[9] Furthermore, Postolakas interpreted the legend PEN (ΠΕΝ) as the abbreviation of Pentaeteris ($\pi\epsilon\nu\tau\alpha\epsilon\tau\eta\rho\acute{\iota}s$), a term referring to major festivals which took place every four years or—in other words—'on the fifth year' ($\pi\epsilon\nu\tau\epsilon$- = five).[10] Postolakas related the PEN tokens with the Great Panathenaia, which also took place 'on the fifth year'. For this Postolakas drew on another token type with a ship's prow, a star in the field above and the legend PANA (ΠΑΝΑ, an obvious abbreviation for Panathenaia) (Fig. 5.2).[11] Postolakas's interpretation was commented upon by Albert Dumont, who two years later published in Paris his dissertation and dedicated a whole chapter to Athenian festival tokens under the title *De Tesseris Agonisticis*. Dumont argued that the PEN tokens bear types related to festivals and considered the legend rather as an abbreviation of *Pentathlon* (i.e. the contest of the five exercises).[12] However, it now seems likely that these tokens date from the fourth century BC, perhaps related to the Great Dionysia festival.[13]

Otto Benndorf explored new dimensions with an influential paper published in 1875. Benndorf was well acquainted with the pieces published by Postolakas as

Fig. 5.1 Lead token, Numismatic Museum at Athens. Diameter 20 mm, presented here at 2:1 scale. On the left Artemis Ephesia standing frontal, on the right Hermes standing turned left holding ears of wheat in right hand and a bunch of grapes in left hand, around edge inscr. ΠΑ ΝΕΛΛΗ ΝΙ ΩΝ; Postolacca (1868), 378 no. 195, image after *Monumenti Inediti Pubblicati dall' Instituto di Corrispondenza Archeologica* 8 (1864–8), pl. LII.

---

[9] Postolacca (1868), 306–7 (comment on no. 195). Note that the legend ΠΑΝΕΛΛΗΝΙΩΝ is found also on Athenian civic coins of the second and third centuries AD; cf. Shear (1936), 304 fig. 26, nos. 8–12.

[10] Postolacca (1868), 304–5 (comment on nos. 76–8, 373, 660, 751). But in inscriptions the Panathenaia are never referred to as Pentaeteris.

[11] Postolacca (1866), 352 no. 231 (nos. 232–5 are of the same type but they are not depicted); Postolacca (1868), 304–5.

[12] Dumont (1870), 79–84.

[13] Dating: Davidson and Thompson (1943), 106 no. 5 with fig. on 107; it is not known for how long into the Hellenistic period they may have continued (cf. Crosby (1964), 106, L209 pl. 27). A list of the different types found with the legend PEN was compiled by Svoronos (1900), 334–6 nos. 181–228, suggesting a reference to the Council of Five Hundred. See Gkikaki (2021) for interpretation of PEN as an abbreviation of *Pentedrachmia*, a term attested in the literary sources for the money distributions for attending the Great Dionysia in the fourth century BC.

Fig. 5.2 Lead token, Numismatic Museum at Athens. Diameter 16 mm, presented here at 2:1 scale. Ship's prow right, star above, inscr. *ΠΑΝΑ* below; Postolacca (1866), 352 no. 231, image after *Monumenti Inediti Pubblicati dall' Instituto di Corrispondenza Archeologica* 8 (1864–8), pl. XXXII.

well as with Dumont's views. Benndorf's paper was very modern by the standards of his time. He placed the discussion of Athenian tokens into the broader context of *tesserae* (tokens) known from Rome and from various other parts of the Roman world. Additionally, by drawing on literary sources and not just on the tokens' iconography or the legends they carry, he focused on the possible uses tokens might have had in Athens and in the main Athenian institutions: the law courts, the Assembly, and the Council. Therefore, the paper is structured with sub-headings such as 'Tokens for the remuneration of the Assembly participants, the Councillors and the Jurors' and 'Tokens for the Theorikon'.

Benndorf starts from the premise that the state money distributions for attending festivals, known under the names *theorikon* and *diobelia* (meaning a sum of two obols), were realized and carried out by the means of tokens.[14] In consistency with this view, Benndorf selected among the types presented by Postolakas the ones with legends relating to the Roman emperors (*ΚΑΙΣΑΡ*, *CEBAC*, and *CEBACTOY*) and attributed them to the festivals of the imperial cult. Furthermore, tokens with legends and iconography relevant to the patron goddess Athena and the Panathenaia (the type with the ship's prow and the legend PANA and various types showing Athena Parthenos) were attributed to the Panathenaia. Finally, the rich iconography relating to Dionysos and Dionysos' cult (different types of theatre masks and other Dionysiac paraphernalia such as the *thyrsos* and *kantharos*) was considered by Benndorf as appropriate for distributions at the Great Dionysia.[15]

Benndorf drew useful parallels between Athenian *symbola* and Roman *tesserae* and formulated the theory that Athenian tokens were used for distributions in the course of festivals and as tickets providing access to festivals. Nevertheless, Benndorf's analysis presents a weak point: the issue of chronology was not seriously addressed. Based on the most up-to-date state of knowledge, *theorikon* and *diobelia* are institutions of the fourth century BC and the Hellenistic period.[16] On the contrary, most of the types discussed by Benndorf are of the Roman imperial period, based on the similarities between these pieces and the types from Roman Athens excavated in the Agora. Although Postolakas, Dumont, and Benndorf

---

[14] Benndorf (1875), 605.   [15] Benndorf (1875), 605–11.
[16] De Ste. Croix (1964), 190–2; Valmin (1965), 177–82; Ruschenbusch (1979), 303–8; Wilson (2008), 91–6.

could not possibly have known that they discussed tokens of the Roman period, nevertheless these three scholars have succeeded in enshrining Athenian tokens in the realm of festivals. And this connection has proven not without a good basis.

In 1964, Margaret Crosby published the tokens excavated in the Athenian Agora as part 2 of the Athenian Agora excavations, Vol. X. Crosby had access to all the material, impressive in size and variety, which was excavated in the Agora from the 1930s to her own days. Crosby adopted Benndorf's method of attributing imagery and legends to possible functions. By exploiting the inscriptions on tokens of Roman period Athens she confirmed the attributions to festivals made by earlier scholarship.[17] She ascertained that tokens of the Roman period found in Athens were used either as *tesserae* in the ever more frequent distributions made not only by the emperors and officials but also by private citizens or else as entrance tickets to the many games and festivals.[18]

Based on the excavation data of the Athenian Agora, Crosby arranged the material in five groups/sections of chronological significance. Of these five sections, the first three are dedicated to the late classical and the Hellenistic periods. Section IV presents tokens from the time between Augustus (from the later part of the first century BC) and the sack of Athens by the Heruli (AD 267).[19] Section V is also dedicated to the Roman imperial period but presents a case study. This is the assemblage of tokens which stands apart from the rest of the finds in the Agora. First, because they were found in the Herulian debris and therefore there is a solid *terminus ante quem* for these: the destruction of the city by the Heruli in AD 267. Although they were found in three groups, they form a coherent assemblage. Workmanship, types, and shared countermarks prove that the three groups are not only contemporary but that they were issued by the same authority. Furthermore, they are related to a significant architectural landmark of the Agora, the Stoa of Attalos, because they were found either in the Stoa or in its immediate vicinity. Finally, and most significantly, Crosby argued that they had the same function: they were issued as entrance tickets to festivals in third century AD Athens.[20] It is these three groups of tokens which form the focus of this chapter.

A little more than half a century later the present author examined a hoard of ninety pieces from the south slope of the hill of Agoraios Kolonos in the Agora, which had only summarily been presented by Crosby. This was a very coherent lot because the majority of the specimens shared the same type, a Hermes bust, and were all uniformly countermarked by a dolphin punch. The imagery on tokens meaningfully expressed the desire of the local elite to use their past to achieve prestige in the present. The centuries-old Athenian aristocracy used the distribution of tokens as a means to propagate their exclusive ancestry from gods

---

[17] Crosby (1964), 82–3 comments on the tokens inscribed ΠΑΝΑ, ΣΩΤΗΡ, and ΘΕΟΦΟΡΟΥΜΕΝΗ.
[18] Crosby (1964), 78.   [19] Crosby (1964), 109–15, L242–L298.
[20] Crosby (1964), 115–22, L299–L331.

and heroes and to reassert their hereditary right to social power and access to the venerable priesthoods of the city. Distribution and circulation of tokens and the propagation of the images they carried may have reached out to the citizenry, shaped moods and opinions, defined the interactions between citizenry and elite, and re-established the status of the later.[21]

Building on the insights of that study, the aim of this chapter is to clarify some particularly interesting aspects in Margaret Crosby's dense section V, the tokens from the Stoa of Attalos, and to offer scholarship with a fresh perspective on an old find. I argue that the key for the interpretation of the tokens from the Stoa of Attalos is their imagery. The images of tokens can be seen, in some cases, to relate directly to particular festivals, but also to act collectively, to celebrate memories from the glorious Athenian past. These memories were appropriated and exploited by the participating groups to celebrate Athenian cultural identity. This cultural identity offered the common ground for the conduct of the festivals and constituted the commonly accepted ideological framework for the creation of the festival communities.

5.3. The tokens from the Stoa of Attalos

The tokens from the Stoa of Attalos will be the focus of the rest of the chapter. The sheer size of the find calls for particular attention. As outlined in the Appendix of Token Types in Table 5.1 and presented subsequently as illustrations, there exist twenty-two token types. They result from the thirty-three different stamps which are either single struck (uniface token type) or have two different stamps struck on both sides (two-sided token types). Uniface are the token types: 1, 2-1, 3, 4, 6, 10-1, 12, 14-1, 14-2, 15-1, 16-1, 16-2, 16-3, 17-1, 18-1a, 18-1b, 18-1c, 20, 21, 22. Others bear designs on both faces: 2-2, 5-1, 7-1, 7-2, 8, 9-1, 9-2, 10-2, 11, 13, 14-3, 14-4, 15-2, 18-2a, 18-2b, 18-2c, 18-3, 19. In two cases it is clear that the two faces are not contemporary but that at some later point a design was placed on one side, while the design on the other face had faded from use. On 9-2 the Athena head was struck after Tyche had faded away, while on 18-3 the rosette was placed after the Serapis design on the other face had already become worn. On 5-1 'Herakles and Tripod' was struck above 'Athena and olive tree', while the 'goddess with wheel' (probably Demeter) on the other side, which may have been contemporary to 'Athena and olive tree' had already become worn and almost illegible. On 5-3 (= 22-3 on Table 5.1) the stamp 'group of symbols' is much fresher that the 'Athena and olive tree' of the other side. Crosby notes that Triton is fresher than Serapis, and thinks that the former was placed later (18-2a, 18-2b, 18-2c).[22]

---

[21] Gkikaki (2019), 127–43.   [22] Crosby (1964), 121 (commentary under L320).

Therefore, tokens were used, distributed and brought back for longer periods of time. Some of the designs, notably 'Athena and olive tree,' Tyche, and Serapis may be considerably earlier, perhaps even a generation earlier than the rest. The different types amount to 475 specimens. Some of the types are represented with more specimens than others, due to accidents of preservation. They form over half of the total of 900 pieces, which come from the entire area of the Athenian Agora, dating over seven centuries, from the early fourth century BC up to AD 267.[23]

Three groups of finds constitute the tokens assemblage at the Stoa of Attalos. These three groups—one from the shop floors in the Stoa of Attalos, one from the trench dug into the floor of the interior colonnade and the third consisting of the tokens found scattered in front of the Stoa of Attalos—all belong together (Fig. 5.3). Specimens of the same designs and the same types are found shared among the three find spots, as shown by Table 5.1.[24] In total, they can be considered as one coherent lot, hereafter named simply as 'the tokens from the Stoa of Attalos'. A hundred and fifty specimens (distributed over fourteen token types) came to light in 1898, in the course of excavations conducted by the Archaiologiki Etaireia.[25] They were found resting in piles on the floors of the fourth and fifth rooms of the Stoa, when numbered from the south (the second column of Table 5.1). These were published by Kyriakos D. Mylonas in *Archaiologiki Ephemeris* in 1901. The fourteen types were depicted within the gravure which accompanied the article.[26] To the 'Mylonas find' two more lots were added: In the 1930s 262 tokens (distributed over twenty-nine token types) were excavated by the archaeologists of the American School of Classical Studies and were found scattered in late Roman levels in the area immediately in front and to the south of the Stoa of Attalos (the sections/areas O–P 7–8, O7, N–P 7–13, Q–R 12–15; cf. the relevant columns of Table 5.1).[27] In the 1950s, while the restoration of the Stoa of Attalos was underway, 213 examples (twenty-three types) were recovered from a trench dug already in antiquity below the floor level towards the north end of the Stoa of Attalos (the second column of Table 5.1). The purpose of the trench may have been to investigate the robustness of the foundation in the process of building the late Roman fortification wall.[28] The trench contained debris—chiefly architectural remains—as

---

[23] Crosby (1964), 76 states that 'some nine hundred tokens sufficiently well preserved' have been excavated in the Athenian Agora. The large number of the tokens of the Stoa of Attalos is easily explained when one considers the size and the abruptness of the destruction inflicted to the Agora by the Heruli. The author has studied approximately sixty more lead tokens which have been excavated in the Athenian Agora after Crosby's time.

[24] Individual specimens have been found in some proximity from the Stoa of Attalos as is again shown by the table.

[25] Archaiologiki Etaireia (Archaeological Society in English) is an independent learned society, in a position to assist the State in its work of protecting, improving and studying Greek antiquities. For more see: www.archetai.gr, last accessed 8 September 2022.

[26] Mylonas (1901), 119–22, pl. 7.

[27] A few specimens have been found even further: F–H 16–17 South of Square, O15 East Stoa, N12 Middle Stoa Terrace; cf. the relevant columns of Table 5.1.

[28] Deposit Q 7:3 of the Agora.

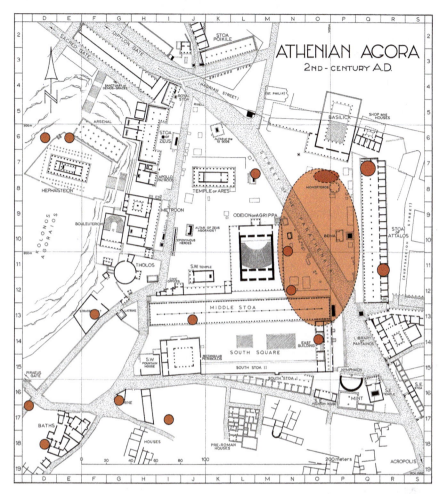

Fig. 5.3 General plan of the Agora in the second century AD with the findspots of the tokens of the Stoa of Attalos added. Courtesy of the American School of Classical Studies at Athens: Agora Excavations (PD 2671, image 2002.01.2671).

a result of clean-up operations after the Herulian destruction of the city in AD 267. The circumstances are corroborated by the hundred and five coins deposited in the trench. More than half of them date from the reigns of Valerian (AD 253–60) and Gallienus (AD 260–8).[29]

Of the thirty-three designs, Crosby pointed out that one displays three masks and is inscribed *Theophoroumene* ('The girl possessed by the god'), a name known as title of a Menander's play. This is a clear indication of its specific use as giving entrance to a performance of that play. By analogy, therefore, she argued that the

---

[29] Crosby (1964), 115–16 and 138.

rest were also used as tickets of admission for various games and festivals.[30] Sebastiana Nervegna expressed serious scepticism on the use of tokens as access tickets to theatre performances in general as well as for a revival of Menander's *Theophoroumene* in particular.[31] Nevertheless, the scantiness of evidence or even the total absence of literary testimonies does not necessarily mean that tokens could not have been distributed as tickets for theatre performances. On the contrary, the 'Theophoroumene' token may be this missing piece of material evidence.

Furthermore, Crosby argued that the tokens from the Stoa of Attalos were tickets for festivals of the ephebes. She based her argument on the images of gods and heroes which can be associated with festivals and games, which were particularly celebrated by the ephebes, an argument discussed further below. Additionally, Crosby sought an explanation for the countermarks which appear on many of the tokens. Most of the specimens are countermarked by the same punch, which is suggestive of their having been issued by the same authority. The countermarking may signify that they were returned to their source where they were stamped to be used in recurring events. According to Crosby again, the persistence of the finds in the Stoa of Attalos and in its immediate vicinity proves that this was the focal point, with tokens being distributed from the Stoa or brought back to the Stoa for re-stamping before another use; or that they were collected at the Stoa for admission to its upper colonnade, which offered an advantageous view over the square of the *Agora* at the time of one of the festivals.[32]

Most of the designs depict gods: Athena, Asklepios and his family, Helios, Hephaistos, Herakles, Nike (alone or as companion to Athena or Zeus), Selene, Serapis, Tyche, and Zeus. In juxtaposition, on late classical and Hellenistic Athenian tokens gods are a rare occurrence. The gods on imperial Athenian tokens either relate to Athenian cults or directly to the city and its emblems. The crested helmet with the owl next to it (2-1, 2-2) and the image of Athena and the olive tree (5-1, 5-2) stand for the latter case.[33] Athena is represented by at least five different stamps: full-figure with an olive tree next to her (5-1, 5-2, 5-3) or accompanied by Nike (6), or just by the goddess' bust in two different styles (7-1, 7-2, 8) or the goddess' head (9-1, 9-2). Asklepios is found both alone seated on a throne (3) and also with his family, in a divine assembly, composed of Asklepios, Hygieia, and Telesphoros (4). Gods are found in company with minor gods, who complement them. So, Athena is depicted in the company of Nike (6), while the Nike in a chariot on face b acts as the counterpart of Zeus on face a (17-1 and 17-2). More 'modern gods', who made their first appearance in the early Hellenistic period or later are represented by the designs of Tyche (9-2 and 19),

---

[30] Crosby (1964), 116 and 122, L329.
[31] Nervegna (2013), 191 n. 215. I thank Eric Csapo for this reference.
[32] Thompson and Wycherley (1972), 107.
[33] Here and below the numbers correspond to the type numbers shown in the Appendix of Token Types on Table 5.1 and subsequently illustrated.

Serapis (18-1a, 18-1b, 18-1c, 18-2a, 18-2b, 18-3) and Helios (Helios bust 11, Helios in quadriga 10-1, 10-2). The designs of gods seated exhibit a type of iconography which is well rooted in the classical period. These are Asklepios (3), Dionysos (16-1, 16-2), and Zeus (17-1, 17-2), whose designs preserve the traits of classical statuary in miniature.

Another trend observed is that international as well as Athenian coin types have acted as sources of inspiration. The eagle with a wreath in its beak, Helios in a two-horse chariot, Selene in a two-horse chariot, and the head of Alexander the Great neither represent Athenian cults nor are they related to the city. Instead, they are taken from contemporary coin types. Helios in spread four-horse chariot can be compared to a similar type from the coinage of Aurelian and Probus.[34] Selene (Latin Luna) in a two-horse chariot is attested on coins of Caracalla.[35] The Eagle copies closely a type of denarii of the late second and early first centuries BC.[36] Alexander the Great is modelled after the contemporary roman provincial coinage of Macedonia and Asia Minor.[37] Themistokles on a galley, Theseus and the Minotaur, Athena and olive tree are likewise inspired by coins, this time by contemporary coin types of imperial Athens. The affinity to the civic coinage will be further explained below.

Herakles has been noted as a figure deriving from the city's cults. Three distinct designs with Herakles are found stamped on the tokens of the Stoa of Attalos. The Herakles head (15-2) follows a schema known from the classical period. The youthful bust shows Commodus (14-3) in the guise of Herakles. Finally, the youthful Herakles (5-2, 14-1, 14-2, 14-3, 14-4) seated on a rock and facing a tripod is meaningfully inspired by models of the high classical period which are revived for the design of this token. This design is found either on uniface tokens (14-1, 14-2, 14-4) or it is paired with the bust of youthful Herakles only (14-3). The lion's head, inscribed with a personal name, could be interpreted as a personal badge (21). Finally, the group of symbols (22) arranged on the token's flan constitute a challenge. Neither their meaning nor the source of inspiration is clear.

The uniface tokens are emphatically countermarked, sometimes with more than two countermarks. There exist three different countermarks with a bird. The stork (with its long legs) can be securely identified in just a few cases: on the specimens depicted here Asklepios (3), on the bust of Minotaur (15-1), as well as on Serapis (18-1a, 18-1b, and 18-1c). On the contrary, on types 16-1 (Dionysos seated on throne) and 18-1c (Serapis) the depicted lacks the very long legs and a

---

[34] http://numismatics.org/ocre/results?q=Aurelian+Sol+quadriga and http://numismatics.org/ocre/results?q=Probus+Sol+quadriga, last accessed 26 April 2022. Both these coinages are later than AD 268.

[35] http://numismatics.org/ocre/results?q=Luna+Caracalla and http://numismatics.org/ocre/results?q=Salonina+Luna, last accessed 26 April 2022.

[36] Here are two examples: http://numismatics.org/crro/id/rrc-314.1a and http://numismatics.org/crro/id/rrc-398.1, last accessed 20 March 2022.

[37] Mondello (2023).

cock is a more likely identification. In fact, it could be a cock, who had captured a small animal. This may be a lizard as was interpreted by Crosby or a mouse, as interpreted by Mylonas. The group of the two animals is more clearly shown by the countermark on the illustrated specimen of the type 18-2b.[38] This simple cock is differentiated from the cock which has captured a small animal by the flamboyant tail (on 'Asklepios with Hygieia and Telesphoros' 4; on 'Herakles and Tripod' 14-2).[39] 'Herakles with tripod' can feature on its side b up to three different countermarks—'cock and lizard', 'snail and rabbit', and a third stamp which features something round, either an 'owl' or a 'pitcher' (14-4).

None of the countermarks on the specimens with Asklepios, Hygieia, and Telesphoros (Type 4 on Table 5.1) is clear enough to provide a judgement. Two countermarks with the design of snail and rabbit are found also on the type 7-1 (Athena in neoclassical style). Therefore, the same countermark could be applied twice on the same specimen.

There is some consistency preserved in the placement of countermarks. This is evident for the types of Dionysos (16-1 and 16-2) and Serapis (18-1a and 18-1c). Both Dionysos and Serapis are uniface types. They bear two countermarks, one struck at approximately 6 o'clock (16-1 and 18-1a) and the other struck at approximately 3 o'clock (16-2 and 18-1c). Therefore, multiple countermarks stand for successive stages, i.e. they were countermarked for a second time after the first, probably for attendance at recurring events.

5.4. Tokens in the festivals of Roman Athens

The shared designs on the reverses and the common countermarks make it quite probable that the tokens from the Stoa of Attalos were all issued by the same authority. These are signs of a coherent programme of production which makes a civic purpose very probable. Not only were the tokens issued by the same authority, but they featured an almost official character. Crosby noted that many of the designs are closely linked to coins but not with the purpose to counterfeit money. The coarse, chunky, lead pieces could not possibly have passed as coins. A probable explanation for the conscious copying of coin types is the need to ascribe to tokens a semi-official character and to emulate procedures inherent in the most official aspects of public life. Particular value was assigned to tokens by the

---

[38] Mylonas (1901), 121-2 nos. 3, 6, 7, 9, 11 has interpreted all the countermarks with a bird as a representation of a cock, while Crosby (1964), 117 L300, 118 L304, and L310 suggested for the same countermarks the image of a stork with a lizard in its beak. The present author suggests that in fact there exist three different designs as detailed in the text above.

[39] This punch of the simple cock was discerned by Mylonas (1901), 120 no. 3, but obviously not observed by Crosby (1964), 117 under L300, 119 (under L315). Dionysos seated is countermarked by the cock with lizard/mouse in beak as well as by the simple cock (16-2).

meaningful association to coins. Those using the tokens were reminded that these tokens have an 'acquired' value. This value was created either by the issuers or by the end recipients or by both. By referring to coins, tokens created 'trust' in the issuing authority. At the same time the message of the exchange—for a service, a material good, or for money—could be effortlessly conveyed because of the familiarity of the designs.[40]

This undeniable affinity of the tokens of the Stoa of Attalos to contemporary coin imagery calls for particular attention. Coins and tokens bear considerable similarities to one another. The mass reproduction of the images they carried impregnated the minds of the recipients, exercised influence, and evoked the power associated with the issuers. Coins and tokens were mass media in motion and they easily propagated their messages because the images they carried became inevitably ubiquitous. These ubiquitous images were commonly shared and hereby were appropriated by everyone, they became everyone's possession and they ultimately became part of the collective unconscious, were very much standardized, familiar and immediately recognizable.[41]

By adopting coin imagery, the issuers of tokens carefully chose the ubiquitous, familiar images, which were now more emphatically reiterated in the world of festivals. What is more important is that the particular coin imagery—the models for the token iconography—were already loaded with meaning. This was first acknowledged by Josephine P. Shear.[42] 'Theseus slaying the Minotaur'[43] and

Fig. 5.4 AE Hemidrachm, 23 mm, 10.73 g, presented here at 2:1 scale. Athena bust right: nude Theseus advancing left, brandishing club with his right hand, carrying cloak around his left arm, about to hit Minotaur, falling left, inscr. *AΘHNAIΩN*. Copenhagen 343.
Photograph used under CC-BY-SA. Nationalmuseet/photographer Sean Weston.

---

[40] Crisà, Gkikaki, and Rowan (2019), 4–6.   [41] Rowan (2020), 247–74.
[42] Shear (1936), 296–316.
[43] Athenian provincial coins with Theseus slaying the Minotaur: https://rpc.ashmus.ox.ac.uk/search/browse?q=Athens+Theseus+Minotaur, last accessed 20 March 2022.

Fig. 5.5 AE Hemidrachm, 25 mm, 10.85 g, presented here at 2:1 scale. Athena bust right: Themistokles standing on galley, l., wearing military dress, holding wreath and trophy; (galley with helmsman;) on ram, serpent; on prow, owl; (in water, dolphin), inscr. *AΘH*. BNF 1082. https://rpc.ashmus.ox.ac.uk/coin/198492, photograph used courtesy of BnF/Gallica.

'Themistokles standing on a galley'[44] are found on Athenian bronze *hemidrachms* of the second and the third centuries AD (Figs 5.4 and 5.5). Along with several other types they refer to heroes from myth as well as to recorded Athenian history and they relate to festivals and games of Roman imperial Athens.[45] 'Theseus slaying the Minotaur' has been associated with the Theseia, a festival which was celebrated by the ephebes with particular pomp in Roman Athens based on the testimony of inscriptions.[46] Theseus was elaborated as the *par excellence* role model of the ephebes, as exemplified by the discourse of an ephebe in AD 184/5 under Commodus' reign.[47] The *peri alkes* contest of the ephebes—contest of strength—implies a competition between two divisions of ephebes: The ones standing under Theseus' patronage were called *Thesiadae*.[48] Theseus was therefore a central figure for the Athenian *Ephebeia*.[49]

The tokens from the Stoa of Attalos were probably issued by a common authority due to shared designs and countermarks and were distinguished by their quasi-official character. To the question, who this authority may be, there is a plausible

---

[44] Athenian provincial coins with 'Themistokles on galley': https://rpc.ashmus.ox.ac.uk/search/browse?q=Athens+Themistokles, last accessed 20 March 2022.

[45] Shear (1936), 285–327.

[46] *IG* II² 2298, 2299; Graindor (1922), 205–7; Graindor (1927), 127; cf. Follet and Peppas-Delmousou (2000), 11–17.

[47] *IG* II² 2291A + 1125; Follet and Peppas-Delmousou (2000), 11–17.

[48] *IG* II² 2119, ll. 237–62; Newby (2005), 198.

[49] Festivals and imagery alike were not altogether alien to Hadrian's association to Theseus, as exemplified by the inscriptions on Hadrian's Arch in Athens. *IG* II² 5185; Lagogianni-Georgakarakos and Papi (2018), 72.

answer provided by the tokens themselves. On one of the types from the Stoa of Attalos the inscription reads 'of the sacred *gerousia*' (*ΙΕΡΑC ΓΕΡΟΥCΙΑC*) around the edge from left to right, with the name 'Klo[dios]' (*ΚΛΩ[ΔΙΟΣ]*) in the exergue (types 16-1 and 16-2). The legends can plausibly be restored to read 'of the sacred *gerousia*, [Archon] Klodios'. Therefore, *Klodios*, probably presiding magistrate of the sacred *gerousia* of the Athenians, was responsible for the issue.[50]

The sacred *gerousia* was established in Athens between AD 175 and AD 176 by Marcus Aurelius and Commodus under the official pretext of a response to an Athenian embassy but in reality on Marcus Aurelius' initiative while he was visiting Athens in AD 176; it was meant to rearrange the financing of certain festivals.[51] This is a useful *terminus post quem* for the dating of the '*gerousia* tokens'. There is a series of imperial letters preserved from the first years of the consolidation of the new institution, the years between AD 176 and AD 184. The first of these letters begins with an enigmatic reference to purchases 'for the *synhedrion* of the *gerousia*' by the emperors in order to supply free distributions. This may well refer to distributions for festivals. It is evident from the letters that the *gerousia* was concerned with the administration of the imperial cult and the Panathenaic festival, which since Hadrian's time had the status of a '*hieros agon*' or sacred game.[52] The letters accord to the *gerousia* the revenues of certain estates from which to draw the capital for the upkeeping of the festivals.[53] Although only the type with the enthroned Dionysos bears the legend 'of the sacred *gerousia*', it is highly probable that all the tokens from the Stoa of Attalos were issued by the sacred *gerousia*, on account of the *gerousia*'s special role in connection to festivals and the semi-official character of the tokens' iconography.

Based on the great number of tokens with imagery connected to festivals and their having been heavily countermarked, Crosby inferred that the Stoa of Attalos served as the 'office' from where tokens were distributed, then brought back to the Stoa to be re-stamped or to be countermarked. Crosby's argument can be exploited even further, suggesting that the Stoa of Attalos may have been the seat of the *gerousia*. The honorific decrees for Ulpius Eubiotus Leurus issued by the *gerousia* stipulate their setting up 'in the *synhedrion* of the sacred *gerousia*'.[54] Fragments of the decrees have been excavated in the Agora but not *in situ*. If tokens for the festivals of the ephebes were distributed by the *gerousia*, then the *gerousia* would have administered at least some aspects of the festivals of the ephebes. Although ephebic lists and ephebic honorific decrees have been excavated in the vicinity of the Church of Hagios Demetrios Katephores, to the east of the Roman Agora, the finds at the Stoa of Attalos indicate that the administration of the festivals of the ephebes and at least a part of the festival performances

---

[50] Crosby (1964), 118–19, L310.   [51] Oliver (1941), 28–38.
[52] Spawforth and Walker (1985), 90–1.   [53] Oliver (1941), 108–22 nos. 24–6.
[54] Oliver (1941), 1, 7, 128 no. 31 fragment b ll. 13–14.

would have taken place in the Agora.[55] All this suggests intense activity with the 'sacred *gerousia*' regulating participation in the festival and distributing admission tickets and probably also gifts. The possibility that the Stoa of Attalos was the seat of the sacred *gerousia* and focal point of the festival tokens distribution, does not contradict one possible practicality: tokens may have been collected for admission to its upper colonnade at the time of the festivals for festivities or for offering a premium view over the Agora square and a particularly privileged view on the Panathenaic Way crossing the Agora square from the NW to the SE (see Fig. 5.3).[56]

5.5. Tokens and their meaning in the contexts of festivals

Crosby argued that many of the designs should be related to the festivals and games celebrated by the ephebes. In particular, she related the following to specific festivals: Athena either in portrait (7-1, 7-2, 8, 9-1, 9-2) or in full figure (5-1, 5-2, 5-3, 6) to the Athenaia and the Panathenaia; Asklepios, seated (3) or in the company of his family (4) to the Asklepeia, Minotaur alone (15-1 and 15-2), Theseus slaying the Minotaur (7-2),or the bull as long as it stand for the Marathonian Bull (2b, 9-1) to the Theseia; Nike accompanying Zeus (17-1 and 17-2) to the Epinikia and two designs with Commodus in the guise of Herakles (the youthful bust 14-3 and Herakles resting with tripod, cf. 14-1, 14-2, 14-4) to the Commodeia. Crosby draws on the apparent affinity of the designs listed to the third century AD festival programme of the ephebes, which has come down to us by the means of inscriptions. The ephebes formed an aristocratic club focused on athletics, open to wealthy members of the international elite of the time who were eager to train themselves intellectually and militarily according to the values of classical Athens.[57] There are numerous 'matches' between the festivals suggested by the imagery and the festivals listed on one particular inscription, which cannot be ascribed to coincidence. The programme of the ephebes' annual celebrations, ten games, are listed in the ephebic inscription *IG* II² 2245 dated either to AD 262/3 or AD 266/7 with some forming part of the imperial cult and others relating to traditional civic cults.[58] By sequence of reference these are the Germanikeia, Antinoeia at Eleusis, Asklepeia, Antoneia, Antinoeia in the city, Epinikia, Athenaia, Hadrianeia, a second Epinikia, and the Theseia.[59]

While the images of Athena may also have a wider relevance as symbols of the city, the fact that the majority of the designs pertain to festivals suggests that here

---

[55] Ephebic decrees of Hellenistic Athens have been excavated in the Agora: Perrin-Saminadayar (2007), 34–46 nos. T1–T22 (with the exception of T2 (pp. 34–5)). Ephebic decrees of Roman Athens have been excavated in the area of the church St. Demetrius Katephores: Wiemer (2011), 529–31 nos. 1–9.

[56] Crosby (1964), 116–17 for all the conclusions; see also under L298.

[57] Wiemer (2011), 487–538.   [58] *SEG* 18, 57; 62, 86.   [59] Crosby (1964), 116–17.

too Athena is associated with the Panathenaia festival. Each token type may have served as ticket for a specific festival and therefore the designs were adapted to this purpose. Corroborating evidence is found with the design of Herakles and tripod which is either found on uniface tokens (14-1, 14-2, 14-4) or is solely paired with the youthful bust of Commodus in the guise of Herakles (14-3).[60]

Earlier in this chapter it was noted that token iconography borrows heavily from contemporary coin iconography. Theseus slaying the Minotaur and Themistokles holding trophy on a galley are designs shared by coins and tokens. The image repertory of second and third centuries AD Athenian coinage is particularly rich. Perhaps, the image repertory of tokens was equally rich but the historical circumstances were a hindrance for their preservation.[61] The systematic survey of coin types proves that all of them can be explained as references to festivals of Roman imperial Athens celebrated by the ephebes with particular pomp. The long list includes the festivals of Theseia, Panathenaia, Asklepieia, and festivals of the imperial cult which were signalled as the festivals connected with the tokens from the Stoa of Attalos. The triumph over the Persians was also celebrated by the ephebes and Themistokles was also one of the role models of the Athenian *ephebeia*. Although the literary evidence is fragmentary, Zahra Newby has provided strong evidence that the naval contest referred to in the sources had developed into mock naval battles conducted by the ephebes, in which they could distinguish themselves.[62] In fact the design chosen for coins with Themistokles and the transfer of this design on tokens provides additional evidence for the naval battles of the ephebes.

Besides Theseus, Herakles—also present on coin and tokens—was the other significant role model of the Athenian *jeunesse dorée*.[63] At the *peri alkes* contest of the ephebes the division standing under Herakles' patronage and rivalling with *Thesiadae* were called *Herakleidae*.[64] Although an exact parallel for Herakles between coins and tokens has not been observed between the two categories, *Herakles Farnese* was struck on Athenian civic coinage of the second and third centuries AD.[65] Very eloquently, the image of Herakles Farnese framed by training ephebes is standing in the midst of the pediment relief crowning an

---

[60] Note that on type 5-1 the design of Herakles resting with tripod was probably struck when the goddess with wheel (Demeter? or Nemesis?) on the other face had faded away and was not visible. Therefore, the type 5-1 counts for a uniface type.

[61] As far as a similar category, the coins of the imperial period Athens, all the hoards discovered so far date from the Herulian sack of the city in AD 267; cf. Kroll (1997), 62

[62] Newby (2017), 87–8. Cf. *IG* II² 2087 of AD 163/4: Newby (2005), 181–2 figs 6.6 and 6.7; *IG* II² 2130 of AD 192/3: Newby (2005), 183 fig. 6.8; *IG* II² 2208 of AD 212/13: Newby (2005), 176 fig. 6.4. The earliest references to *naumachia* in inscriptions are *IG* II² 1996 and 1997 from the reign of Domitian: Newby (2017), 90.

[63] Follet and Peppas-Delmousou (2000), 16–17.

[64] *IG* II² 2119, ll. 237–62; Newby (2005), 198.

[65] Shear (1936), 313 fig. 20; Kroll (1993), 179, 365.

ephebic inscription.[66] A votive relief set up by an official of the ephebes commemorating an ephebic victory in Eleusis also shows the hero reclining in a posture very similar to the one found on tokens (cf. 14-1, 14-2, 14-3, 14-4) and is indicative of the god's relevance to the *ephebeia* and ephebic festivals.[67] The bust of the robust young man on Athenian tokens was also designed to create associations between Commodus and Herakles and relates to the Commodeia festival which in Athens is attested only as a festival of the ephebes.[68] The designs exploit in a subtle way this simile of Commodus to Herakles without the explicit reference to the ruler (the token lacks inscription and there are no imperial insignia).[69]

Shared references on coins and tokens to Theseus, Themistokles, and Herakles evoke the importance of these figures for the institution of the *ephebeia*. Theseus, Themistokles, and Herakles were brought alive in the ephebic festivals. This emphatic reprise of these heroes on coins and tokens suggests the conscious desire to relate to the legendary traditions of the city, to revive them by the means of the performances and the festivals of the ephebes and finally to commemorate the splendid past of Athens. The designs celebrated Athenian identity, expressed civic pride, and glorified the city's unique and brilliant past.

5.6. Tokens and elite self-representation

Although the designs related to the city's glorious past, associated legends, heroes, and festivals and expressed national pride, which was clearly important in Roman Athens, the same designs propagated on tokens also served the self-representation and the glorification of the elite clans of Athens. Divinities, heroes, and glorious personalities were tied into the self-representation of particular elite families.

This has already been observed for coins and can be applied also to the imagery on tokens. The 'Theseus slaying the Minotaur' design offers itself for this dual reading. John H. Kroll observed that the Theseus known from Athenian imperial half drachms is associated with half drachms which bear Miltiades erecting a trophy. In a similar way the Themistokles design known from half drachms is

---

[66] Athens, National Museum 1470 (a part of it is in the Ashmolean Museum, Oxford): *IG* II² 2130, dated to AD 192/3; Newby (2005), 182–3 fig. 6.8.

[67] Ashmolean Museum, Oxford: IG, II² 3012 dated to the mid-second century AD; Newby (2005), fig. 6.14

[68] *SEG* 46, 19bis and 46, 2268. Cf. Crosby (1964), 117 under L288 and 120 under L316.

[69] The emperors were seemingly moderate in many ways. One of the imperial letters regarding the establishment of the sacred *gerousia* (Oliver (1941), 4, 116 under no. 24: Letter II, ll. 32–7) preserves the offer on the part of the *gerousia* to make gold or silver images of them and their consorts and the emperors' reply that they would prefer it if the elders made the portraits of bronze, preferably busts of uniform and moderate size that could easily be transported on the occasion of festivals.

associated with drachms which bear a design showing Poseidon's and Athena's rivalry over the city.[70] The two constellations betray respectively connections to the ancestry and the self-representation of two powerful clans of Roman imperial Athens. One was the Claudii of Marathon with Herodes Atticus the most prominent of them, who took pride in having as its ancestors both Miltiades, the victorious general at the Battle of Marathon and Cimon, who brought back Theseus' bones to Athens.[71] The other was the clan of the Claudii of Melite, who traditionally held the priesthood of Poseidon-Erechtheus and counted Themistokles among its noble ancestors, and who was with all probability responsible for the issue of the drachms.[72]

That the Theseus and Themistokles designs may have had the same meaning when it comes to tokens from the Stoa of Attalos should not seem unlikely. It is the function of distribution which relates the two categories, coins and tokens. John H. Kroll, who discussed the imagery of these Athenian coins, put forward the hypothesis that the two clans may have financed the issues of these coins to be distributed upon holding high offices in the city. The coin designs were motivated by the rivalry between the clans, rivalry for prestige and power in the city, and for gaining the favour of the citizenry.[73] Tokens with the badges of the competing clans would have fuelled the rivalry for a specific period and would conform to the sentiments of national pride later. Therefore, the images are multivalent and their meanings reveal themselves through multiple resonances. One string—the elite self-representation—does not cancel or exclude the other—the desire to link with the city's glorious past. On the contrary, divinities, heroes, and memories of the legendary events and their exploitation by different agents in Roman imperial Athens, and in particular, the *gerousia*, the ephebes, and the elite clans harmonize with each other to create a well-orchestrated ensemble. There is a reciprocal interplay of memories of the glorious past which are activated by these various different agents, with the purpose of asserting Athenian identity against the challenges set by the Roman empire, and also as a way of obtaining imperial attention.

5.7. Athenian heritage, ephebes, and the *gerousia*

Two different types with the legend 'of the sacred *gerousia*' have survived to us. One of them has already been mentioned. It was found among the tokens from

---

[70] Kroll (1997), 61–9 pl. III, 6–7. For the types: Kroll (1993), 129 no. 174 pl. 16, and 142 no. 261 pl. 18 (Poseidon and Athena) and 144 nos. 278–9 pll. 18–19 (Themistokles on galley).

[71] For Herodes Atticus' clan and ancestry: Graindor (1930), 1–17; Ameling (1983), I:3–14 and II:36–64; Ameling (2013), 176–9.

[72] Davies (1971), 219–20; Clinton (1974), 50–7. That the Claudii of Melite counted Themistokles among their ancestors is evidenced by the naming of several of its members as Themistokles and a female member as Themistokleia; cf. *IG* II² 3679, dated to AD 240: Clinton (2004), 55.

[73] Kroll (1997), 63–4, 66.

the Stoa of Attalos (16-1 and 16-2). The type depicts the upright figure of Dionysos, enthroned and bearded, and is especially striking for the visual expression of venerability and its eloquent archaism. The god is seated to the right with a staff in his left hand and some other unidentified object (*kantharos*?) in his right. A crescent and a *kantharos*—Dionysos' typical drinking cup—are shown in the field left and a cluster of grapes or a *thyrsus*—Dionysian staff—in the field right. The enthroned figure is probably a copy in miniature of the gold-ivory cult statue of the god by the hand of Alkamenes which was housed in Dionysos Eleuthereus' sanctuary on the south slope of the Acropolis.[74]

The image is, like most of the tokens from the Stoa of Attalos, a very close copy drawn from contemporary coinage, this time from Athenian civic coinage. On the coins the god is seated before an altar, which is not shown on tokens. As far as the coins are concerned, the suggestion has already been put forward that the design is symbolic of a major Athenian festival, the Greater or City Dionysia.[75] The Dionysos tokens too may well have played a role in the Greater Dionysia, which in Roman imperial Athens were celebrated with particular pomp with a procession of the ephebes, according to Pausanias.[76] Therefore, this token type may be counted among the ones for the festivals of the ephebes.

The other type is known by just one specimen excavated along with a hundred bronze coins dating from the Hellenistic to the Ottoman period to the south of the Odeion of Herodes Atticus in a Roman imperial-period context.[77] The specimen—known from black and white photos of the cast—depicts Athena Parthenos and is inscribed ΓΕΡΟΥΣΙΑΣ (Fig. 5.6). It is the gold-ivory colossal work by the hand of Pheidias, as testified by the figure of Nike that the Goddess is supporting with her right hand. Beneath and right next to Athena's right flank there is an owl on a tree (or column or altar), an eloquent reference to the sanctuary and the Acropolis.

The antiquarian approach in the style of the images highlights the pursuits and aspirations of the elite elders who formed the *gerousia*. In both cases—Alkamenes' Dionysos and Pheidias' Athena Parthenos—the detailed depiction of cult statues which at the time would have been almost seven centuries old and especially the enthroned figure of Dionysos place a particular ambiguity in the foreground, which takes shape in the minds of the beholders: should the design be understood as the old and venerable cult statue or as the image of the god in truth? The perception of the image for the beholders of the tokens would have been more contextual than iconographic. It is not just a question of the composition or the

---

[74] Pausanias, *Description of Greece* 1.20.3; Travlos (1971), 537.   [75] Shear (1936), 306–7.
[76] Pausanias, *Description of Greece* 1.20.3, 1.29.2.
[77] Crosby (1964), 109 under L244; Stevens (1961), 5–6 pl. 1e. The coins remain unpublished until today, see the comment in Oikonomidou (1992–3), 63–77. The excavation was conducted by Ioannès Mèliadès—director of the Acropolis Ephorate—in the late 1950s when construction works in the Dionysiou Aeropageitou street were underway. The coins and the only lead token were taken to the Numismatic Museum: Varoucha (1957), 498. The lead token with the image of the Athena Parthenos in the Berlin Coin cabinet does not bear the legend ΓΕΡΟΥΣΙΑΣ but the legend ΑΘΗ: Sallet (1883), right depiction on p. 152.

Fig. 5.6 Pheidias' Athena Parthenos with left hand resting on grounded spear and grounded shield. Holding small, winged Nike in right hand. Small owl perching on short column to the goddess' right flank. Border of dots. Inscribed in two columns: ΓΕΡ[ΟΥ]CIAC. Cast of a uniface, lead token, 25 mm, presented here at 2:1 scale.

Photograph: the American School of Classical Studies Archives 2012.55.110. Courtesy of The Trustees of the American School of Classical Studies at Athens.

attributes that the figures are carrying, but it was the framing of the figure with additional symbols, the rendering of the location, the exact placement of the statue, its insertion into local traditions and rituals, as well as its historical frame that delivered the decisive clues for understanding the figure.[78] The meaningful abolition of distinction between image and divine prototype, cult statue and 'real' god, puts an emphasis on the location and on the sacred topography. The festival topography was mediated by circulating tokens either through commemorative mechanisms—a reference to the gods presiding over festivals—or because this is the sanctuary to which the tokens enabled the access.[79]

When the findspot is taken into consideration, it is likely that the 'Athena Parthenos' token enabled entrance either to the Odeion of Herodes Atticus or to the Acropolis sanctuary. Issuers and users of tokens interact with the gods—both during encounters with naturalistic images of the gods as well as with the gods as active agents shaping the religious experience. The above described procedures enable the re-definition of the identity of the 'token-holders' as members of the same community, linked to each other either by relating to the same set of classical landmark-monuments, ones highly cherished in Roman imperial period, or by experiencing enchanted encounters with the divinity in festival locations as defined by the designs on the tokens.

The sense of festival space is evident on another type set of tokens excavated in and around the Stoa of Attalos. The type features a tritons: bearded figure with fish-tail legs holding a dolphin in right hand and a trident in the left (18-2a, 18-2b, 18-2c).[80] The creature refers to the three tritons and through the tritons to Poseidon on the Parthenon's west pediment. The tritons formed pairs with three

---

[78] Mylonopoulos (2015), 1–19.

[79] The ambiguity surrounding the experience of the divine through the autopsy of cult statues and the experience of divinity transcended through material images especially at the time of the Second Sophistic: Platt (2011), 260–6.

[80] Crosby (1964), 120–1 L320. Crosby discusses and rejects the identification with Tritons and thinks that it is Poseidon. But the remarkable similarity with the fish-tail legs of the Tritons on the

giants supporting the open colonnade of the north side of the Odeion of Agrippa. The tritons and the giants as sculptural decoration of the Odeion connected meaningfully to the Parthenon and classical heritage in general.[81] The open space at the heart of the Agora—the administrative centre of the democratic *polis*—was taken up at the time of Augustus by the Odeion, the cultural building, which was intended for plays and musical performances—an emblematic transformation for the Agora. But in the second century AD, according to Philostratus, who describes three different meetings with students attending the lectures of a visiting sophist, the Odeion also served as a lecture hall for the city's youth.[82]

This 'move' from the landmarks of classical Athens—Alkamenes' Dionysos and Pheidias' Athena Parthenos—to a landmark of contemporary Athens—the tritons of the façade of the Odeion of Agrippa, a building which exemplified the cultural and educational centre that imperial Athens was, emphasizes that Athens' civic pride and identity could lie as much in the present as in the past. The tritons of the Odeion of Agrippa constitute 'commemorative choices of the elite' and a conscious attempt to enshrine the more recent past and almost contemporary monuments into the city's social memory.[83]

Besides the legends THEOPHOROUMENE (*ΘΕΟΦΟΡΟΥΜΕΝΗ*) and 'of the sacred *gerousia*' (*ΙΕΡΑΣ ΓΕΡΟΥΣΙΑΣ*), the only other legends found on the tokens from the Stoa of Attalos are personal names. On type 16, the letters under the groundline (in the exergue) on which Dionysos' throne rests read KLO (*ΚΛΩ*). As noted above, Crosby thought that this might be restored to read KLODIOS (*ΚΛΩ[ΔΙΟΣ]*). Therefore, the inscription would read 'the magistrate of the sacred *gerousia*, Klodios' (*ΙΕΡΑΣ ΓΕΡΟΥΣΙΑΣ [ΑΡΧΩΝ] ΚΛΩΔΙΟΣ*).[84] The name suggests that the man had probably Roman roots and that he was concerned to associate himself with the sacred *gerousia*, the festival of Greater Dionysia, the actions which formed part of the festival and ultimately with the glorious past of the city and Athenian cultural tradition.

The three other names preserved on the tokens are equally interesting in terms of the associations they enable. The lion's head type (21) bears the name LEMNIOS or LEMNIOU (*ΛΗΜΝΙΟ*). In three different inscriptions from Sicily and Magna Graecia this is the name of a freedman.[85] In Athens there is an ephebe named Lemnios, son of Hermeios mentioned in an ephebes list of AD 145/6.[86]

---

north side of the Odeion of Agrippa speaks for itself. Poseidon with fish-tail legs would have been very unusual.

[81] Thompson (1950), 103–9; Thompson and Wycherley (1972), 111–13.
[82] Philostratos, *Lives of the Sophists* 2.5 (571); 2.8 (579).
[83] Alcock (2002), 87–99, quote at p. 18.   [84] Cf. discussion above.
[85] SEG 52, 894 (inscription known from a manuscript copy); IG XIV 904 (undated); SEG 52, 988 (fourth century AD).
[86] IG II² 2055, l. 16.

The name is also mentioned once in Euboia.[87] The token type with Asklepios and his family (4) was inscribed around edge from left to right Eutyches (*ΕΥΤΥΧΗΣ*, barely legible at Crosby's time). Eutyches was a common name in Roman imperial Athens and is found on lists of ephebes' names.[88] Beyond Athens the name is popular in Roman imperial Macedonia,[89] and Asia Minor,[90] also as a slave.[91] Lemnios and Eutyches may have been non-Athenians living in Athens. The legend of the triton design (18) reads POSEI (*ΠΟΣΕΙ*), probably abbreviation for the personal name Poseidonios (*ΠΟΣΕΙΔΩΝΙΟΣ*). Crosby suggested that the image of triton, associated with Poseidon, functioned as a pun for the person's name. Several ephebes and *bouleutai* (Council members) of the second and third centuries AD with the name Poseidonios are attested.[92]

These few names preserved on the festival tokens reveal that persons of multiple ethnicities took an active role in the festivals of Roman imperial Athens. The different groups involved in the festivals were extremely diverse, comprising ephebes, the *gerousia*, the elite, and the citizenry, including both Athenians and non-Athenians. Nevertheless, they all claimed Athens' venerable past. Communities of Roman citizens from across the empire came together in Athens, in particular on the occasion of festivals, and they valued the memories of past exploits in Athenian mythology and recorded history—the deeds of Theseus and Herakles, Themistokles' triumph over the Persians—and celebrated the emblems of classical Athens such as Alkamenes' Dionysos and Pheidias' Parthenos. The reclaiming of the past for the purposes of the present was not the initiative of the Athenians alone but was a multilateral concern. Athenian cultural memory was a collective memory and it materialized on the images carried by coins and tokens. It is this selective memory, selective because the groups involved chose what to remember and what not to, that motivated behaviours and practices.[93] Athenian cults and festivals were the preferred venue where sacred continuity was exercised, links with the heroes of the city's mythology and past were asserted and the past was re-lived for the sake of the present, while at the same time it served as the focal point for the cultural contact of groups with diverse ethnic and social background.

Research on the festivals of Roman imperial Athens and the roles played by tokens inevitably focuses on the elite. The effect is a top-down view for cultural

---

[87] In a fourth-century BC inscription from Eretria (*IG* XII.9 191 B, 28). This Lemnios originates from Styra (Euboia).

[88] *IG* II² 2192 dated to c. AD 200; *IG* II² 2243 dated to after AD 243/4; *IG* II² 2245 dated to AD 262/3 or AD 266/7.

[89] *IG* X.2 1 809; *IG* X.2 1 534; *SEG* 29, 590; 48, 854.

[90] *SEG* 30, 1354 (Miletos); 38, 1354 (Aspendos).

[91] *SEG* 55, 1488 dated to the second century AD.

[92] *PAA* 14, nos. 785410, 785420, 785450, 785490 (ephebes) and nos. 785425, 785430, 785470 (*bouleutai*).

[93] Alcock (2002), 1–35 on the importance of memory management/manipulation as the incentive for human behaviours.

practices and memory policies: it was the elite who set the tone and the masses followed. Nevertheless, the diverse origin of the few inscribed names on tokens reveals that the imagery reflected a broad consensus. The power of the images on the tokens lies in their intricacy and multi-valency. They appealed to the pursuits of the elders of the *gerousia* and the ephebes, to the wealthy benefactors of the elite, and to the citizenry for sacred continuity in the upkeeping of cultural traditions against the changing face of the Roman empire. The shared memories of the past developed to shared festival experience for the participating groups. The participating groups—although diverse upon their inception—functioned as a homogenous festival community with well-defined roles including parades, actions which imitated the glorious deeds of the pasts, adoration of the venerable cult statues, marshalling the festivals, and managing the tokens' distribution.

The multivalence of the tokens' imagery—offering memories of Athenian past glories, cultural identity for the city and the festivals' participants, role models for the youth, media for elite self-representation—is closely linked to ambiguity: The same image may be the emblem of an influential clan, or the role model of the ephebes or even count among the symbols of Athenian cultural identity. This ambiguity was particularly valuable because it enabled the confluence of attitudes and the harmonious functioning of the festival community.

5.8. Tokens' distribution, value, and euergetism

The individuals' names carried by the second and third centuries AD Athenian tokens find their closest parallel in Ephesos. Of the approximately 269 known token types of Roman Ephesos published recently on a catalogue by Gülbay and Kireç, seven of them bear names.[94] Four of those token types have been identified with persons belonging to the highest echelons of the Ephesian society mentioned in the contemporary epigraphic record.[95] They are therefore dated securely to the period of the high Roman empire and in particular the second and early third centuries AD. What the four persons had in common was that they were involved in the imperial cult, they came from families of the elite with influential connections, and they held high administrative offices involving personal expense and particular prestige. While holding their term of office, they sponsored festivals and instigated distributions of gifts. The tokens with their names are tangible evidence of these procedures.[96] Members of the elite in the great urban centres during the high Roman empire engaged increasingly in acts of euergetism. Euergetism or else the systematic and regular distribution of gifts to the citizen body can be considered as a social system which entertained needs and demands on both ends:

---

[94] Gülbay and Kireç (2008), 148–52 nos. 225, 226, 230, 231, 233, 234, 235.
[95] Gülbay and Kireç (2008), 148–52 nos. 225, 230, 233, 235.   [96] Kuhn (2014), 137–40.

recipients and benefactors. Besides the obvious profits for the former, benefactors demonstrated the rightfulness to hold and preserve their position in the highest echelons of society. The motives were of idealistic nature: the establishment and justification of grandiosity, the strive for posterity, the yearning for honours and recognition by the community.[97]

That tokens were the medium for the fulfilment of the purposes of euergetism is only inferential and based on a series of plausible assumptions.[98] Nevertheless, the imagery—as exemplified by the illustrious figures of Theseus and Themistokles— glorified elite families and strengthened their efforts to maintain their status and prestige. This noble ancestry was no less a paradigm for the elite members to act on the model of their forefathers than for the community to continue to attribute honours to the same clans in exchange for benefactions. In an earlier study the author has argued that distributions by the means of tokens with imagery advertising noble ancestry were brought about as a consequence of the never-before experienced circumstances in a changing world and in particular the granting of Roman Citizenship in AD 212 with the *Constitutio Antoniniana*.[99]

The tokens from the Stoa of Attalos reveal behaviour patterns of the social communities having access to tokens and as a result to gifts, privileges, and preferential relationships between citizen groups and the upper class. Distribution and access to tokens encoded specific behaviours, analogous to rituals.[100] Aspects of these rituals are evidenced by the means of countermarks. There are just five different punches across the thirty-two different token types in the Stoa of Attalos. Margaret Crosby considered the homogeneity of the countermarks and the careful and regular application on the token round as evidence for attributing the issues to the same authority.[101] In an analogous case, the hoard excavated in the 'house' on the hill of Agoraios Kolonos in the Athenian Agora, all the specimens bear the countermark of a dolphin. The sign of the sea creature has been tentatively associated with the authority responsible for the issue and distribution of the tokens. This may have been a member of the influential clan of the Claudii of Melite who in second and third centuries AD held the hereditary priesthood of Poseidon-Erechtheus.[102]

The application of countermarks could have only reinforced the social hierarchy. In analogy to the dolphin countermark, the countermarks applied on the tokens of the Stoa of Attalos could also stand for the badge of prestigious clans or even the personal sign of individual members of the elite, who in their official capacity as members of the *gerousia* may have been responsible for the issue and

---

[97] Zuiderhoek (2011), 192–4.
[98] As stated by John H. Kroll in the key-note address at the Workshop 'Tokens: The Athenian Legacy to the Modern World', December 2019 (Kroll 2019). For the roles played by tokens in the Roman world in general, including gift distribution: Regling (1934), cols 851–4; Crosby (1964), 176.
[99] Gkikaki (2019), 136–7.   [100] Crisà, Gkikaki, and Rowan (2019), 6–7.
[101] Crosby (1964), 116 with n. 6.   [102] Gkikaki (2019), 135–6.

distribution of tokens and the hosting of the festivals related to the tokens. The 'cock/stork holding a small animal by the tail' refers to ideas of power and dominance while the countermark 'snail and rabbit' has a moralistic character. The types are symbolic and bear similarities to heraldry of the mediaeval and modern period. In terms of function the repetition of the same countermark referred to successive validations for recurring events.[103] Contemporary inscriptions from Athens as well as cities of Asia Minor, including the '*Salutaris* endowment' have the distributions carried out among well-defined subgroups, which stand out from the whole citizen body and can be regarded as privileged.[104] The distribution of tokens enabled the creation of communities by the almost natural procedures of inclusion and exclusion. Athenian inscriptions of the time of the high Roman Empire can bring us closer to the phenomenon of euergetism and its practicalities. An honorific inscription of *c.* AD 100 informs us that some Athenian magistrates made distributions of money and grain. Distributions of a *medimnos* of grain and fifteen (Athenian bronze?) *drachmai* were made when assuming the office of the Eponymos Archon and of two *denarii* when assuming the office of the Herald of the Boule and the Demos.[105]

Around AD 120, Tiberius Claudius Atticus, Herodes Atticus' father, while serving as treasurer of the *prytaneis*, assumed the expenses for his tribe's *prytany* sacrifices and set up an endowment in an effort to relieve his tribe from the financial burden.[106] At some point later Tiberius Claudius Atticus set up endowments in perpetuity for the other tribes as well.[107] The *Eleusinian Endowment* was set up by Flavius Xenion of Gortyn, *archon* of the Panhellenion in AD 165–9, and had the approbation of the Roman authorities.[108] The text stipulates money distributions from interests accrued over the years from a capital investment. The distributions were to be made on the occasion of the Mysteries and continue in perpetuity. The beneficiaries were the members of the Areopagus, Eleusinian dignitaries—priests and priestesses—as well as priests and priestesses of other Athenian cults. The endowment itself has been set up by a wealthy benefactor coming from outside Athens, but who had been adlected to the priestly clan of the Eumolpids, the ones who traditionally held the hierophancy. Flavius Xenion's descendants came to

---

[103] Crosby (1964), 116.
[104] Such is the case for the recipients from the Salutaris endowment dated to AD 104: *I.Ephesos* 1a, 27 ll. 220–332; Rogers (1991a), 39–79. The *ekklesiastai* and the *sitometroumenoi* mentioned in a number of cities in Asia Minor: Zuiderhoek (2011), 191 with references. General remarks in Rogers (1991a), 39–40. Cf. below in the text the discussion for the Eleusinian Endowment *IG* II² 1092 and for Tiberius Claudius Atticus' endowment which covered the Athenian tribe, of which he was a member.
[105] *IG* II² 3546, ll. 14 and 16; Geagan (1967), 6; Kroll (1997), 63–4 with n. 16.
[106] *IG* II² 1073+1074, ll. 12ff.; Oliver (1949), 299–308; Geagan (1967), 99.
[107] The endowments are reflected in *IG* II² 3597a–e.
[108] The text is preserved carved on stone and was excavated in the sanctuary of Eleusis. *IG* II² 1092; *SEG* 12, 95; *SEG* 15, 107; Oliver (1952); *I.Eleusis* 489. The text was inscribed shortly after 170, when the Eleusinian sanctuary was raided by the Costoboci.

domicile in Athens and were granted the Athenian citizenship, probably owing to this endowment.[109]

Klodios, the *archon* of the *gerousia* named on the Dionysos tokens, was in all probability the sponsor of a distribution. The naming could be indicative of a contribution of money out of the *archon*'s personal fortune. Klodios is probably related to Ulpius Eubiotus Leurus, as has been detailed by Margaret Crosby.[110] The text particularly stresses that Eubiotus acted on a voluntarily basis out of his own good will. Eubiotus is showered with exceptional honours reflecting his benefactions, most prominent among them the *agonothesia* of the Panathenaia.[111]

Outside Athens, in contemporary Asia Minor, members of the civic elite similarly set up endowments which aimed at maintaining festivals in perpetuity and involved the distribution of money and gifts.[112] The foundation set up by Salutaris in Ephesos in AD 104 provided for a civic lottery followed by distributions with a large number of Ephesian citizens as beneficiaries. The foundation provided also for a frequently recurring parade of temple officials and ephebes escorting statues representing the mythical and historical past of Ephesos featuring Artemis' nativity myth and the imperial cult. The benefactor was C. Vibius Salutaris, a Roman equestrian. As in the case of the Eleusinian endowment the distributions occurred on the occasion of a major civic festival, which in Ephesos was no other than Artemis' Mysteries. The impressive details of the endowment provide an idea of the largess, the grandiosity and the significance of the foundation, especially when we consider that the text was inscribed on the wall of the theatre of Ephesos. The year's interest of 1,935 denarii was to be distributed to specific designated groups of citizens: members of the tribes, the *boule*, the *gerousia*, and the ephebes. The distributions were meant to privilege some groups, especially the ephebes, over others, and at the same time imposed on them a series of obligations, integrated in a system of exchange.[113]

Euergetism could therefore be seen as the locus, where multiple tendencies converge. Tokens and the imagery they carried should be acknowledged as one of the few surviving direct testimonies on euergetism. Euergetism by providing money, facilities, and other amenities was the institution which channelled the expression of communal cultural identity.[114]

---

[109] Follet (1976), 127; Spawforth and Walker (1985), 101.
[110] Crosby (1964), 119 under L310.   [111] Oliver (1941), 125–42 nos. 31–2.
[112] *I.Ephesos* 1a, 27 with fragments 28–37; Rogers (1991a), *passim*.
[113] Rogers (1991a), 136–51.
[114] Research has attempted to seek interpretative models for the phaenomenon of euergetism. Veyne (1990) has particularly stressed the motives of the individual benefactors, who were competing for honours, privileges, and the favours of the people. Gauthier (1985) placed euergetism in its social dimensions and thought of the phaenomenon as a system of government over the passive and disinterested masses of the Roman empire. More nuanced interpretations were offered by their critics. Rogers (1991b, 99–100) considered euergetism as the outcome of 'negotiating' procedures bridging the benefactor's will and the beneficiaries' needs and demands. Zuiderhoek (2011, 185–95), following

5.9. Conclusion: token imagery or 'imagining Athens' in the third century AD

From the previous discussion, then, it seems likely that the tokens excavated in the Stoa of Attalos enabled entrance to Athenian festivals and/or were exchanged for gifts and privileges on festive occasions in the second and third centuries AD. The imagery offered itself to multiple readings and successfully threw a bridge across aspects which are at first sight fundamentally different: communal ideals for the citizens and individual aspirations for the elite, collective spirit and personal excellence, and the Roman vision of classical culture and the striving toward defining Athenian identity.

Such expressions of the community's self-imagination along with the benefactors' self-interests coexist on the imagery of the Athenian tokens. Each time points of observance alternate constantly from the 'Roman' standpoint to the local focus and highlight the extent to which the aura of the classical past enchanted those entering the 'realm' of Athenian cultural achievements. The 'Theseus slaying the Minotaur' tokens, the imagery on the tokens of the Theseia festival, could potentially be viewed against the backdrop of the festival's manifold narratives and the multiple symbolisms of Theseus' figure.[115] He emerges as the most political figure of Athenian history, as the sheer embodiment of communal identity. He is here remembered and his life story is re-mediated as representation and justification for the high status of the elite. Simultaneously, Theseus is re-invented and re-discovered in order to celebrate the very recent history and success story of Hadrian's reign. Hadrian had after all also acted as a unifier, unifying the entire Greek world of the eastern Mediterranean and assigning Athens with the supremacy as the seat and centre of the league of Greek cities, the so-called Panhellenion, its members convening in Athens and playing important role in the organization of festivals, as seen previously in the case of the Eleusinian endowment.[116] The document IG II² 2291A prescribes that with the conclusion of the festival of the Theseia, the ephebes convened.[117] Why was all this so important? Because—quoting the very last lines—'by emulating the heroic deeds and by competing among ourselves in prowess, we become worthy of Theseus and worthy of our officer, the officer of the ephebes'.[118] Tracing the officers of the ephebes in the epigraphic record of Athens demonstrates the brilliant *cursus honorum* of these exceptional leading figures of the Athenian elite.[119]

Rogers, recognized the parameters of the historical circumstances, the multi-cultural environment, and political instability.

[115] IG II² 2291A; Follet and Peppas-Delmousou (2000), 11–17.
[116] Spawforth and Walker (1985), 78–104.   [117] Wiemer (2011), 487–538.
[118] IG II² 2291A; Follet and Peppas-Delmousou (2000), 11–17.
[119] Wiemer (2011), 500–10 with bibliography.

Similarly, Themistokles encapsulates collective imagination and elite self-representation by advertising the elite's adherence to civic memory and traditions. Civic memories collide with Roman attitudes of exploiting the Greek past to celebrate the achievements of imperial Athens. Theseus and Themistokles qualify the relevant coins and tokens of Roman imperial Athens for distributions on the occasion of festivals. Research over recent years has demonstrated that the Theseus and the Themistokles design belong to a broader repertory of emblems of prominent clans, the members of which financed public endeavours and distributed gifts. According to an abundant epigraphical record, clans of the Athenian elite, conscious of their family traditions, and aspiring to distinction, traced at that time their lineage back to personalities of the classical age. Themistokles, Miltiades, and Pericles and even Alexander the Great are ancestries meticulously recorded in honorific decrees.[120]

Classical monuments—Alkamenes' Dionysos and Pheidias' Parthenos—and contemporary landmarks—the tritons of the Odeion of Agrippa—on tokens of Roman imperial Athens would have invited hosts and participants not only for festive and religious experience but for social interactions. Athens' symbolic capital is meticulously exploited and elaborated so that memories of the past glory activated the mobilization of powers. Not only was elite status asserted but Athenian identity was also celebrated and established in the changing world of the Roman imperial period and the eastern Mediterranean.

The designs on the tokens are open to multiple readings, offering images from the glorious past of Greece, symbols of Athenian cultural identity, the ancestors of Athenian prestigious clans, and the role-models of the ephebes, and appealed equally to Greeks and non-Greeks. Hereby tokens expressed a pan-Athenian ideology transcended in a pan-imperial ideology. They were the tickets for the festivals which functioned as the hub for the cultural exchange of Greeks and Romans. Both ancestral figures as well as landmarks and monuments invited the attendees to experience civic identity, historic traditions, and above all community cohesion. Designs on tokens were chosen with great care so as to satisfy the pursuits of groups—elite and clients, Athenian and Romans—which at first sight seem incompatible. The success story of the city's classical past, the commemoration of victories, the high cultural achievements as embodied by magnificent cult statues, and the renaissance promised by Augustus cultivated a common consciousness by successfully enabling participation and promoting group cohesion. The incongruities helped the city define its particularities through bilateral procedures: not only did the elite claim distinction but the elite was thanked and commemorated, not only did Rome impose imperial ideals but the emperor was glorified in return.

---

[120] Clinton (2004), 39–57.

Appendix of Token Types

Table 5.1 Token types and numbers found in different findspots. The type numbers correlate with those shown on plates 1-2.

Type Number	Shop floors	O-P 7-8	N-P 7-13	H 11-12	O15	N12	Q 7:3
1. Three masks, inscr. THEOPHOROUMENE	6 Mylonas no.1						6 Crosby L329
2-1. Helmet, countermark		1 in O7 Crosby L32					
2-2. Helmet: Bull	9 Mylonas no. 2	3 Crosby L324					
3. Asklepios, two countermarks		5 Crosby L299					
4. Asklepios, Hygieia and Telesphoros, inscr. *EYTYXHΣ*, countermarked	8 Mylonas no. 3	6 Crosby L300					3 Crosby L300
5-1. Athena and olive tree: Demeter with serpent car not quite clear representation [Side A is overstruck with a stamp of Herakles and tripod. both sides are overstruck. The design of Athena and olive tree is the earlier stamp]		4 Crosby L301					
5-2. Athena and olive tree: Herakles and Tripod							1 Crosby L302
5-3. Athena and olive tree: Group of Symbols =22-3 below			8 Crosby L303				3 Crosby L303
6. Athena and Nike, two countermarks	1 Mylonas no. 6					1 Crosby L304	
7-1. Athena bust of Neoclassical style, two countermarks		5 Crosby L306	8 Crosby L306				14 Crosby L306

Description				
7-2. Athena bust of Neoclassical style: Theseus und Minotaur		1 Crosby L305		2 Crosby L305
8. Athena bust of Roman style: Poseidon bust		18 Crosby L309		3 Crosby L309
9-1. Athena head: Bull + one from SW Area B22 and from central part of Square J13	6 Crosby L307			14 Crosby L307
9-2. Athena head, countermarked: Tyche		1 in P 9-10 Crosby L308	1 in Q-R 12-15 Crosby L308	
10-1. Helios in quadriga + one from Agoraios Kolonos + one from SW area D 16	8 Crosby L311			7 Crosby L311
10-2. Helios in quadriga: Selene/Luna in biga. + one from Kolonos Agoraios E 6, +one from central part of square M-O 9-11, + one from SW area B-C 16-17.	20 Mylonas no. 5	12 Crosby L312		2 Crosby L312
11. Helios bust: Uncertain representation	2 in O7 Crosby L313			2 Crosby L313
12. Male, bearded head right, the whole in dotted circle, countermarked	2 Mylonas no. 7			
13. Hephaistos head: Themistokles on galley	1 Mylonas no. 8		2 Crosby L314	
14-1. Herakles and Tripod + one from SW Area D 18		21 Crosby L315		72 Crosby L315
14-2. Herakles and Tripod, countermarked + one from Kolonos Agoraios D 6		12 Crosby L315		18 Crosby L315

Continued

Table 5.1 *Continued*

14-3. Herakles and Tripod: Commodus in the guise of Herakles +one from deposit F 13: 2		2 Crosby L316	
14-4. Herakles and Tripod: Three countermarks		1 Crosby L317	8 Crosby L317
15-1. Bust of Minotaur, countermarked	7 Crosby L318		2 Crosby L327
15-2. Bust of Minotaur: Herakles head	1 in O 7 Crosby L310	1 Crosby L327	4 Crosby L318
16-1. Dionysos seated, inscr. *IEPAC ΓEPOYCIAC*, countermark			
16-2. Dionysos seated, inscr. *IEPAC ΓEPOYCIAC*, two countermarks	5 Mylonas no. 9	5 Crosby L310	3 Crosby L310
17-1. Zeus seated: Nike in biga +one from South of Square F-H 16-17	11 Mylonas no. 10	18 Crosby L323	4 Crosby L323
17-2. Zeus seated, countermarked: Nike in biga			2 Crosby L323
18-1a. Serapis with one countermark at bottom			1 Crosby L319
18-1b. Serapis with one countermark at centre of back		2 Crosby L319	1 Crosby L319
18-1c. Serapis with two countermarks on front		3 Crosby L319	
18-2a. Serapis: Triton, inscr. *ΠΟΣΕΙ*	10 Mylonas no. 12	2 in O 7 Crosby L320	
18-2b. Serapis: Triton, inscr. *ΠΟΣΕΙ*, countermark + six from South of Square I 17, K-N 6-9		64 Crosby L320	14 Crosby L320

18-2c. Serapis with two countermarks: Triton, ΠΟΣΕΙ, countermark	44 Mylonas no. 13			
18-3. Serapis: Rosette, countermark		9 Crosby L321		1 Crosby L321
19. Tyche: Alexander the Great head left. For Tyche see also 9-2 in this table Crosby L308	1 Mylonas no. 4		12 Crosby L322	
20. Eagle.			15 Crosby L325	5 Crosby L325
21. Lion's head, inscr. ΛΗΜΝΙΟ, countermarked			3 Crosby L326	
22-1. Group of symbols, countermarked		9 Crosby L330		1 Crosby L330
22-2. Group of symbols: uncertain representation				1 Crosby L331
22-3. Group of symbols: Athena and olive = 5-3 on this table				

Key to the findspots:

Q7: 3 = Deposit Q 7: 3 trench dug below the floor level against the foundations of the piers for the columns near the north end

O-P 7–8 = In front of the Stoa

O7 = In front of and to the South of the Stoa

N–P 7–13 = In front of the Stoa

Q–R 12–15 = South of Stoa

F–H 16–17 = South of Square

H 11-12 = West side of Square

O15 = East Stoa

N12 = Middle Stoa Terrace

Continued

Table 5.1 Continued

Key to the bibliography abbreviations used in the table

Mylonas = Mylonas (1901). Number denotes the catalogue number in Mylonas' publication.

Crosby = Crosby (1964). 'L' denotes the catalogue number in Crosby's publication

Key to the designs

1. Three masks, inscr. ΘΕΟΦΟΡΟΥΜΕΝΗ = Three masks on pedestals, inscr. ΘΕΟΦΟΡΟΥΜΕΝΗ

2. Helmet = Crested, corinthian helmet right, two stars below, in field right an owl.

Bull = Bull standing left, in field lower left uncertain small object, above star or single letter.

3. Asklepios = Asklepios seated on stool, leaning on serpent staff. In field left: tree-trunk and crescent moon, right: five stars, to left of head: uncertain object; the whole in dotted circle 17 mm in diameter.

4 Asklepios, Hygieia and Telesphoros = Asklepios and Hygieia facing with small figure of Telesphoros between. In field right, palm branch; snake beside Asklepios' right leg; uncertain object in field above. Around edge left to right inscribed ΕΥΤΥΧΗΣ at Crosby's time no longer legible.

5. Athena and olive tree = Athena moving to her left with shield on left arm; olive tree to her right; in field lower right a snake. Very similar to Athenian Imperial coins Crosby L301, cf. Svoronos (1923–6), pl. 84, 36–9, pl. 87, 26. The design is overstruck with a stamp of Herakles and Tripod.

Demeter with serpent car = Standing draped figure facing left with right arm outstretched; wheel at lower left; in field right: snake, star and trances of wing or second figure. For representations of Demeter with serpent car on Athenian Imperial coins, see Svoronos (1923–6), pl. 94, 19-26. Alternatively, the stamp could depict Nemesis, cf. Svoronos (1900), 338–9 no. 251 pl. IV, 8.

6. Athena and Nike = Athena at right with spear in left hand, Nike approaching from left with wreath; the whole in dotted circle 18 mm in diameter.

7. Athena bust in Neoclassical style = Athena bust in a high crested Attic helmet with the triple tuft; the whole in dotted circle 17–18 mm in diameter. The design is found also on Athenian Imperial coins.

Theseus und Minotaur = Theseus at right with sword above his head, the minotaur falling to left; star in field; the whole in dotted circle 17 mm in diameter. It is found on Athenian Imperial coins. The combination of Athena bust: Theseus und Minotaur is found on Svoronos (1923–6), pl. 96, 17.

8. Athena bust of Roman style = Athena bust in crested Corinthian helmet; in field, a star; lower right, prow of ship; the whole in dotted circle 14 mm in diameter.

Poseidon bust = Poseidon bust right.

9. Athena head = Head of Athena right in crested Corinthian helmet; the whole in dotted circle 17 mm in diameter.

Tyche = Tyche standing, facing, head left, modius on head, cornucopiae in left hand, rudder in right hand; in field right, palm branch; lower left uncertain object; the whole in dotted circle 14 mm in diameter

10. Helios in quadriga = Helios in spread quadriga; whip in right hand, reins in left. Border of dots 15 mm in diameter. The same design is used as reverse on coins of Aurelian and Probus, which are later than the assumed *terminus ante quem* AD 267.

Selene/Luna in biga = Selene/Luna in biga, drawn by bulls, left; small wings or scarf on shoulder, torch in right hand, reins in left; in field three stars, one above, two below; the whole in dotted circle 16 mm in diameter. The same design is found also on coins of Caracalla and Salonina.

11. Helios bust = Male bust left, rayed; protome of horse in field lower left; palm branch in field right; the whole in dotted circle 12 mm in diameter.

12. Male, bearded head right, the whole in dotted circle = This is a type known only from Mylonas (1901), no. 7 sketch. The head seems to be laureate. It has not been possible to identify with a type excavated in the Agora and published by Crosby.

13. Hephaistos head = Hephaistos head left, bearded with close fitting pointed cap; tongs in field left, hammer in field right; the whole in dotted circle 16 mm in diameter.

Themistokles on galley = Themistokles holding a trophy, standing on a galley. The same design is found on Athenian Imperial coins, cf. Svoronos (1923–6), pl. 97, 10-11.

14. Herakles and Tripod = Young Herakles, laureate, seated left on a rock facing a tripod, from which a snake arises; uncertain object in right hand; the whole in dotted circle 17 mm in diameter.

Commodus in the guise of Herakles = Bust of youth left; club in the field behind. The long face and the relatively flat back of the head are acknowledged as portrait features of Commodus. It may represent Commodus in the guise of Herakles.

15. Bust of Minotaur = Bust of Minotaur, half left; in field at either side a star; the whole in dotted circle 15 mm in diameter.

Herakles head = Bearded head right, club in field behind; the whole in dotted circle 15 mm in diameter.

16. Dionysos seated = Dionysos seated right on throne, staff in left hand, kantharos in right. In field left, kantharos and crescent; lower right, thyrsus. Letters are edge from left to right *ΙΕΡΑϹ ΓΕΡΟΥϹΙΑϹ*, in exergue, right to left *ΚΛΑ*; the whole in dotted circle 22 mm in diameter.

17. Zeus seated = Zeus seated left on throne, Nike in right hand, staff in left; in field right, thunderbolt, left star, crescent below throne; the whole in dotted circle 17 mm in diameter.

Nike in biga = Nike as a winged nude figure in biga drawn to left by two horse, whip in right hand; in field upper right star; wavy ground line; the whole in dotted circle 16 mm in diameter.

18. Serapis = Serapis standing, semi-draped, wearing modius, head left, right arm raised, staff in left hand; in field right crested serpent, in field left scrolls.

Triton = Triton as a bearded figure with fish-tail legs, dolphin on outstretched right hand, trident in left. Around figure left to right *ΠΟΣΕΙ*; the whole in dotted circle 15 mm in diameter.

Rosette = Five petalled rosette.

19. Alexander the Great head left = Alexander the Great, beardless, head flung back with flowing, flame like locks.

20. Eagle = Eagle standing left, head turned back, wreath? in beak. In field right, filleted boukranion; left, star; lower left, branch; the whole in dotted circle 15 mm in diameter.

21. Lion's head = Lion's head with open mouth, right. Inscription around edge in front of head *ΛΗΜΝΙΟ*; the whole in dotted circle 14 mm in diameter.

22. Group of symbols = at bottom dolphin swimming right, with poppy head at right; ear of wheat at left; at upper right a kantharos with bird ? standing right, in cup; star at top; the whole in dotted circle 17 mm in diameter.

TOKENS FROM ROMAN IMPERIAL ATHENS 131

Works Cited

Alcock, S. E. (2002) *Archaeologies of the Greek Past: Landscape, Monuments and Memories.* Cambridge.

Ameling, W. (1983) *Herodes Atticus. Subsidia Epigraphica 11.* 2 vols. *I. Biographie. II. Inschriftenkatalog.* Hildesheim, Zurich, and New York.

Ameling, W. (2013) 'Marathon, Herodes Atticus, and the Second Sophistic', in K. Buraselis and E. Koulakiotis (eds), *Marathon the Day After: Symposium Proceedings, Delphi 2-4 July 2010.* European Cultural Centre of Delphi. Delphi, 167–83.

Benndorf, O. (1875) 'Beiträge zur Kenntnis des Attischen Theaters', *Zeitschrift für die Österreichischen Gymnasien* 26: 1–29, 83–92, 579–618 with plate of drawings after p. 730.

Clinton, K. (1974) *The Sacred Officials of the Eleusinian Mysteries. Transactions of the American Philological Society* 64.3. Philadelphia.

Clinton, K. (2004) 'A family of Eumolpidai and Kerykes descended from Pericles', *Hesperia* 73: 39–57.

Crisà, A., Gkikaki, M., and Rowan, C. (eds) (2019) *Tokens. Cultures, Connections, Communities.* Royal Numismatic Society Special Publication No. 57. London.

Crosby M. (1964) 'Lead and clay tokens. Part II', in M. Lang and M. Crosby (eds), *The Athenian Agora X: Weights, Measures and Tokens.* Princeton, 69–146.

Davidson, G. and Thompson, D. B. (1943) *Small Objects from the Pnyx,* Vol. 1. *Hesperia Supplements* 7. Baltimore.

Davies, J. K. (1971) *Athenian Propertied Families 600–300 BC.* Oxford.

De Ste. Croix, G. E. M. (1964), 'Review of Theorika. A study of monetary distributions to the Athenian citizenry during the fifth and fourth centuries BC by James J. Buchanan', *Classical Review* 14: 190–2.

Dumont, A. (1870) *De Plumbeis apud Graecos Tesseris.* Paris.

Duval, Y. (2000) *Romanité et cité chrétienne: permanences et mutations, intégration et exclusion du Ier au VIe siècle; mélanges en l'honneur d'Yvette Duval.* Paris.

Engel, A. (1884) 'Choix de tessères grecques en plomb tirées des collections Athéniennes', *Bulletin de correspondance hellénique* 8: 1–21.

Follet, S. (1976) *Athènes au IIe et au IIIe siècle av. J.-C.: Études Chronologiques et Prosopographiques.* Paris.

Follet, S. and Peppas-Delmousou, D. (2000) 'La légende de Thésée sous l'empereur Commode d'après le discours d'un éphèbe athénien (IG II², 2291A et 1125, completes)', in Y. Duval (ed.), *Romanité et cité chrétienne: permanences et mutations, intégration et exclusion du Ier au VIe siècle; mélanges en l'honneur d'Yvette Duval.* Paris, 11–17.

Galinsky, K. and Lapatin, K. (eds) (2016) *Cultural Memories in the Roman Empire.* Los Angeles.

Gauthier, P. (1985) *Les cités grecques et leurs bienfaiteurs.* Athens.

Geagan, D. (1967) *The Athenian Constitution after Sulla. Hesperia* Supplements, Vol. 12. Princeton.

Gkikaki, M. (2019) 'Tokens in the Athenian Agora in the third century AD: advertising prestige and civic identity in Roman Athens', in Crisà et al. (2019), 127–43.

Gkikaki, M. (2021) 'Tokens for festivals in Hellenistic Athens', in A. Crisà (ed.), *Tokens, Value and Identity: Exploring Monetiform Objects in Antiquity and the Middle Ages*. Travaux du Cercle d' Études Numismatiques 22. Brussels, 55–74.

Gkikaki, M. (ed.) (2023) *Tokens in Classical Athens and Beyond*. Liverpool.

Graindor, P. (1922) 'Études sur l'ephébie attique sous l'Empire', *Musée Belge* 26: 165–228.

Graindor, P. (1927) *Athènes sous Auguste*. Le Caire.

Graindor, P. (1930) *Un milliardaire antique, Hérode Atticus et sa famille*. Cairo.

Gülbay, O. and Kireç, H. 2008. *Efes Kurşun Tesseraelari. Ephesian Lead Tesserae*. Istanbul.

Kroll, J. H. (with contributions by A. S. Walker) (1993) *The Athenian Agora XXVI: The Greek Coins*. Princeton.

Kroll, J. H. (1997) 'The Athenian imperials: results of recent study', in J. Nollé, B. Overbeck, and P. Weiss (eds), *Internationales Kolloquium zur Kaiserzeitlichen Münzprägung Kleinasiens, 27–30 April 1994 in der Staatlichen Münzsammlung*. Munich, 61–9.

Kroll, J. H. (2019) 'The corpus of Athenian tokens': 150 years of expansion and study from Postolakas to the present', keynote address delivered on 16th December 2019 at the Workshop 'Tokens: The Athenian Legacy to the Modern World': https://www.blod.gr/events/workshop-tokens-the-athenian-legacy-to-modern-world/, last accessed 15 August 2020.

Kuhn, C. (2014) 'Prosopographical notes on four lead tesserae from Roman Ephesos', *Zeitschrift für Papyrologie und Epigraphik* 190: 137–40.

Lagogianni-Georgakarakos, M. and Papi, E. (2018) *HADRIANVS. Hadrian and Athens. Conversing with an Ideal World. Exhibition Catalogue: 28/11/2017-31/12/2018*. Athens.

Lang, M. and Crosby, M. (1964) *The Athenian Agora X: Weights, Measures and Tokens*. Princeton.

Madsen, J. M. (2017) 'Empire and cultural memory: review of K. Galinsky and K. Lapatin (eds) *Cultural Memories in the Roman Empire*. Los Angeles: J. Paul Getty Museum, 2016', *Histos* 11: lxxxi–lxxxvi.

Mondello, C. (2023) 'Alexander the Great on lead: notes on some tokens from Roman imperial Athens', in M. Gkikaki (ed.), *Tokens in Classical Athens and Beyond*. Liverpool, 205–34.

Mylonas, K. D. (1901) 'Ἀττικά Μολύβδινα Σύμβολα', *Archaiologikē ephēmeris* (1901), 119–22.

Mylonopoulos, J. (2015) *Divine Images and Human Imaginations in Ancient Greece and Rome*. Leiden.

Nervegna, S. (2013) *Menander in Antiquity: The Contexts of Reception*. Cambridge.

Newby, Z. (2005) *Greek Athletics in the Roman World. Victory and Virtue.* Oxford.

Newby, Z. (2017) 'Performing the past: Salamis, naval contests and the Athenian Ephebeia', in T. M. Dijkstra, I. N. Kuin, M. Moser, and D. Weidgenannt (eds), *Strategies of Remembering in Greece under Rome* (100 BC–100 AD). Leiden, 83–95.

Nollé, J., Overbeck, B., and Weiss, P. (1997) *Internationales Kolloquium zur Kaiserzeitlichen Münzprägung Kleinasiens, 27–30 April 1994 in der Staatlichen Münzsammlung.* Munich.

Oikonomidou, M. (1992–3) 'Νομίσματα από την Ακρόπολη', *Chronika Aisthitikis* 31-2: 63–77.

Oliver, J. H. (1941). *The Sacred Gerousia.* Hesperia Supplements Vol. 6. Baltimore.

Oliver, J. H. (1949) 'Patrons providing financial aid to the tribes of Roman Athens', *American Journal of Philology* 70: 299–308.

Oliver, J. H. (1952) 'The Eleusinian endowment', *Hesperia* 21: 381–99.

Perrin-Saminadayar, E. (2007) *Éducation, culture et société à Athènes: les acteurs de la vie culturelle athénienne, 229-88: un tout petit monde.* Paris.

Platt, V. (2011). *Facing the Gods. Epiphany and Representation in Graeco-Roman Art, Literature and Religion.* Cambridge.

Postolacca, A. (1866) 'Medaglie Inediti del Nazionale Museo Numismatico di Atene', *Annali dell' Instituto di Corrispondenza Archeologica* 38: 339–56 with illustrations (drawings) in *Monumenti Inediti Pubblicati dall' Instituto di Corrispondenza Archeologica* 8 (1864–1868), pl. XXXII.

Postolacca, A. (1868) 'Piombi inediti del Nazionale Museo Numismatico di Atene', *Annali dell'Instituto di Corrispondenza Archeologica* 40: 268–316 with illustrations (drawings) *Monumenti Inediti Pubblicati dall'Instituto di Corrispondenza Archeologica* 8 (1864–8), tav. di aggiunti K and pl. LII.

Regling, K. (1934) Pauly-Wissowa's Real Enyklopädie vol. V A.1 s.v. tessera: cols 851–4. Stuttgart.

Rogers, G. M. (1991a) *The Sacred Identity of Ephesos: Foundation Myths of a Roman City.* London and New York.

Rogers, G. M. (1991b) 'Demosthenes of Oenoanda and models of euergetism', *JRS* 81: 91–100.

Rowan, C. (2020) 'The imperial image in media of mechanical reproduction. The tokens of Rome', in A. Russell and M. Hellström (eds), *The Social Dynamics of Imperial Ideology Formation in the Roman Empire.* Cambridge, 247–74.

Ruschenbusch, E. (1979) 'Die Einfuhrung des Theorikon', *Zeitschrift für Papyrologie und Epigraphik* 36: 303–8.

Sallet, A. v. (1883) 'Nachbildungen der Pallas des Phidias auf Munzen', *Zeitschrift für Numismatik* 10: 152–5.

Shear, J. P. (1936) 'Athenian imperial coinage', *Hesperia* 5: 285–332.

Stevens, G. P. (1961) 'Concerning the Parthenos', *Hesperia* 30: 1–7.

Spawforth, A. J. (2012) *Greece and the Augustan Cultural Revolution.* Cambridge.

Spawforth, A. J. and Walker, S. (1985) 'The World of the Panhellenion. I. Athens and Eleusis', *Journal of Roman Studies* 75: 78-104.

Svoronos, I. N. (1900) 'Περί των Εισιτηρίων των Αρχαίων, Μέρος Δ', Τα Μολύβδινα Σύμβολα', *Journal international d'archéologie numismatique* 3: 319-43, pll. I-IV.

Svoronos, J. N. (1923-6) *Trésor de la numismatique grecque ancienne: Les Monnaies d'Athènes*. Munich.

Thompson, H. A. (1950) 'The Odeion in the Athenian Agora', *Hesperia* 19: 31-141.

Thompson, H. A. and Wycherley R. E. (1972) *The Athenian Agora XIV: The History, Shape and Uses of an Ancient City Centre*. Princeton.

Travlos, I. (1971) *Pictorial Dictionary of Ancient Athens*. London.

Valmin, N. (1965) 'Diobelia und Theorikon', *Opuscula Atheniensia* 6: 171-206.

van Nijf, O. M. and Alshton, R. (2011) *Political Culture in the Greek City after the Classical Age*. Leuven.

Varoucha, E. (1957) 'Musée Numismatique. II. Monnaies provenant des fouilles', *Bulletin de correspondance hellénique* 81: 498-9.

Veyne, P. (1990) *Bread and Circuses: Historical Sociology and Political Pluralism*. Engl. trans. B. Pearce. London.

Wiemer, H.-U. (2011) 'Von der Bürgerschule zum aristokratischen Klub? Die athenische Ephebie in der römischen Kaiserzeit', *Chiron* 41: 487-538.

Wilson, P. (2008) 'Costing the Dionysia', in M. Revermann and P. Wilson (eds), *Performance, Iconography, Reception. Studies in Honor of Oliver Taplin*. Oxford and New York, 88-127.

Zuiderhoek, A. (2011) 'Oligarchs and benefactors. elite demography and euergetism in the Roman East of the Roman empire', in O. M. van Nijf and R. Alston (eds), *Political Culture in the Greek City after the Classical Age*. Leuven, 185-95.

6
Festivals and the Performance of Community and Status in the Theatres at Hierapolis and Perge

Zahra Newby

6.1. Introduction

In the early third century AD, the city of Hierapolis in Phrygia decided to refurbish their theatre. Dedicating it to Apollo Archegetes, the other gods of the *patria* (homeland) and the Severan imperial family, they constructed a new *scaenae frons* (stage building), ornately decorated with mythological friezes and free-standing statuary.[1] At the heart of the decoration, prominently placed above the *porta regia*, was a scene celebrating Hierapolis' chief civic festival (Fig. 6.1). An oversized prize crown sits on a table, flanked by personifications of Hierapolis and *Agonothesia* (presidency of the games) on one side, and by the imperial family on the other. At roughly the same time, the city of Perge in Pamphylia also constructed a theatre, decorating the lower storey of the *scaenae frons* with Dionysiac reliefs and placing a scene of procession above the *porta regia*. Here a series of male figures leading bulls converge on the central figure of the Tyche of the city, seated next to a lit altar and holding out the statuette of Artemis Pergaia (below, Fig. 6.12). In both cities, the decision was made to celebrate and visualize moments of a civic festival at the very centre of the decoration of the *scaenae frons*—in one, by showing a sacrificial procession towards the patron goddess; in

---

I am most grateful to Francesco D'Andria and Kadir Ozel for facilitating access to the theatre at Hierapolis in April 2018 and to Tullia Ritti for her helpful responses to various queries. For permission to publish photographs I extend my thanks to Francesco D'Andria, Sedef Çokay Kepçe; Nalan Eda Akyurek Sahin, Karsten Dahmen, and the British Museum. My colleagues at Warwick have offered numerous thoughts and insights: thanks especially to Kevin Butcher, Alison Cooley, Eric Csapo, Clare Rowan, Marguerite Spoerri Butcher, and my project colleagues, Dario Calomino and Naomi Carless Unwin. I have benefitted greatly from the responses of audiences at the British School at Rome and the Universities of Helsinki and Groningen to earlier versions of this chapter, and from the comments of the external reviewers.

[1] Ritti (2007), 407–9 reaffirms a date of AD 206–7 for the initial dedication; Ismaelli (2017), 411–13 suggests the second storey was completed under Caracalla.

the other through a more symbolic representation of the different agents and elements of the festival as a whole.² At the same time, cities across Asia Minor were celebrating their civic festivals on coin issues.³ We can see both the coins and the theatre reliefs as an attempt to celebrate and advertise religious cults and traditions, drawing attention to the specific local manifestations of a festival culture which was thriving across the Greek east.⁴ In this chapter I want to look more closely at the ways in which this imagery communicated the function and social meaning of festivals, how it constructed a framework within which festival events took place, giving meaning to them and reflecting back onto the audience and viewers the social hierarchies, roles, and communities which were re-enacted during the course of these festivals.

In doing so, I will draw on two different bodies of theory. The first is performance theory, especially as articulated within the field of anthropology.⁵ Within this, the term 'cultural performance' has been coined to describe occasions on which 'as a culture or society we reflect upon and define ourselves', encompassing not only staged performances such as plays or concerts, but also ritual ceremonies and festivals.⁶ Performance theory draws attention to the ways in which individuals play out particular social roles, and also the ways that cultural performances, such as theatre, ritual, or festival, can act to mediate the tensions and fractures existing within a society, what anthropologist Victor Turner has termed 'social drama'.⁷ Performance theory encompasses a nexus of different ideas and approaches, but what is useful for my purposes here is the ways in which it associates repeated public actions and activities, such as those which we find in civic festivals, with underlying social hierarchies and roles, seeing these 'performances' as acts of communication between different groups of a society, in which hierarchies and roles are created, reasserted, and, sometimes, challenged.

These insights can be profitably applied to the ancient world. Indeed, Rasmus Brandt and Jon Iddeng read festivals as 'orchestrated cultural performances' in which:

> power relations are manifested, popular feelings are modulated, the behaviour of the participants is orchestrated, different types of 'liminality' are expressed and so on. Within this structure, the performers and spectators (and among the

---

² Detailed bibliographies follow below.
³ Leschhorn (1998); Klose (2005). Calomino (forthcoming) will offer a comprehensive re-evaluation of these coinages.
⁴ On the context see Robert (1984); Mitchell (1990).
⁵ For an overall introduction to performance theory, which encompasses a range of different disciplinary approaches, see Shepherd (2016), esp. 42–6 on the ideas discussed here.
⁶ MacAloon (1984b), quote at p. 1; cf. Singer (1972).
⁷ Turner (1984) summarizes his theory of 'social drama', which was explored in a number of earlier works, e.g. Turner (1975), 23–59. See also Shepherd (2016), 43–6.

spectators themselves) are involved in ongoing *communication* by way of symbols of identity and meaning.[8]

Civic religion was closely tied to the interests of the civic elite, whose members usually occupied roles as priests, *agonothetai* (officials who presided over festivals) and other civic magistrates.[9] Arjan Zuiderhoek's reading of euergetism in Roman Asia Minor identifies it as a political strategy to justify financial inequality and avert social tension through the celebration of shared cultural values.[10] Exploring the popularity of festivals as a form of euergetism, he suggests that this is because festivals allowed for 'the collective celebration of a sense of civic unity'.[11] At the same time, this civic unity was premised on a hierarchical model, made manifest especially through the groups which formed part of civic processions.[12] Within festivals, all different members of the community, and indeed visitors from outside, had a specific role to play, whether as presiding officials leading particular rituals, as sacred envoys from elsewhere, as performers, or as spectators. My aim here is to explore how these different roles were expressed and presented within the visual programmes of these two theatres.

As scholars such as Elizabeth Gebhard and Angelos Chaniotis have shown, theatres were a crucial stage not only for the theatrical performances which took place as part of festivals, but also for other forms of social rituals and performances, such as processions, libations, and public honours.[13] If we see the activities which occurred as forms of 'cultural performances', actions that help to reiterate and construct social hierarchies and civic cohesion, my aim is to see what role is played by the physical environment within which they occur. Thus, the second theoretical frame employed here is that of the 'spatial turn', the idea that the environments in which actions take place are not just the product of human agency, but also have an agency of their own, helping to frame, constrain, and construct human behaviour.[14]

The importance of space as constraining and constructing human action in the ancient world has received increased attention of late, with various studies looking at the ways in which interactions with the divine were influenced by the spatial contexts in which they took place, or how the shape and decoration of the city affected social interactions.[15] A key theme is the way in which human movement

---

[8] Brandt and Iddeng (2012b), 4, italics in original. Bouvrie (2011) and (2012) offer detailed readings of ancient festivals from this approach. Cf. Turner and Turner (1982); MacAloon (1984a).
[9] Gordon (1990).   [10] Zuiderhoek (2009).
[11] Zuiderhoek (2009), 86.   [12] Zuiderhoek (2009), 95–8. Cf. Chaniotis (1995), (2013).
[13] Gebhard (1996); Chaniotis (2007). Cf. van Nijf (2013), 323–33 on the importance of festivals and the theatre in the creation of the 'social imaginary'. More widely on the social roles played by theatres, also Gybas (2018).
[14] Lefebvre (1974) is a key text; further see Warf and Arias (2009), esp. Soja (2009). On the application to ancient history, see Scott (2014). On the agency of objects and images see Gell (1998); Osborne and Tanner (2007).
[15] e.g. Moser and Feldman (2014); Dickenson and van Nijf (2013). See further above, Introduction, 1.2.

through space, and the interaction between space, architecture, objects, and people helps to generate multiple meanings and experiences, articulating identities, or shaping particular sorts of collective memories.[16] My aim is to interrogate the imagery of these two theatres from this perspective, looking at the ways in which they constructed meanings for the activities which took place there, and focusing particularly on their figural decoration. This is but one reading of two complex decorative contexts, and does not claim to be the only way to read the imagery.[17] In other contexts or depending on who was viewing, other messages might instead have come to the fore. But when the theatres were being used for festivals—both as a location for festival processions to pass through and as a place for audiences to watch festival rituals and performances—this imagery would have taken on new resonances as an assertion of which aspects of the festival were deemed most important (in the eyes of the decision makers), for these particular communities.[18] Outside of festival occasions, the imagery would also create a visual memory of festival events, giving ephemeral acts a permanent presence in the civic record, which looks backwards to past events and forwards to their next iteration.

In other words, my aim is to read the imagery not as a straightforward reflection or celebration of events, but rather to see it as playing an active part in the construction of what festivals meant to particular communities and individuals. The messages these images assert can be seen as a form of communication. This might have been with others within the city, asserting the importance of the different roles which particular members or groups of the citizen body fulfilled, or with neighbours—either asserting priority, in rivalry with others, or reaching out to connect, through shared practices and traditions.

6.2. Defining festival culture at Hierapolis

Festivals involved a variety of different participants at different stages of the action, performers, officials, and sacred envoys amongst them, and they all find their place in the imagery of the theatre at Hierapolis. The decorative programme of the theatre incorporates a number of different features, including inscriptions, relief friezes, and free-standing statuary, in addition to the columns and marble

---

[16] On identities see e.g. Day et al. (2016). On movement, see Östenberg, Malmberg, and Bjørnebye (2015), esp. Leander Touati (2015); also Connolly (2011) and on Rome, Popkin (2016) and Latham (2016).
 For theoretical perspectives on the ways that visual media provide frameworks for shaping experience and memory, see Erll and Rigney (2009).
[17] For other discussions of theatre decoration see De Bernardi Ferrero (1966–74); Sturgeon (1977); 124–9; Özren (1996); Pellino (2005); Di Napoli (2013), (2015); also Newby (2003).
[18] See Gybas (2018), 138–45 on the theatre in the context of festivals.

veneer which is now mostly lost.[19] The longest frieze runs along the projecting podia of the first order and depicts the births, lives, and worship of the gods Apollo and Artemis; each occupying one half of the stage.[20] Further mythological scenes appear elsewhere: paired scenes of the Rape of Persephone and Demeter in her chariot seem to have been placed above the far left and right doorways of the *scaenae frons*, while scenes of Dionysiac processions were positioned on the interior of the *analemmata* which close the sides of the upper cavea.[21]

Another relief is prominently positioned above the central *porta regia* of the *scaenae frons* (Fig. 6.1). Here the architectural flow of projecting *aediculae* topped with curved and triangular *tympani* is broken in favour of a receding u-shaped frieze which presents a series of figures. This break in the architectural pattern and the static nature of the figures focalizes our attention on the central scene and its messages, which are asserted through both the iconography and the use of

Fig. 6.1 Copy of the *porta regia* relief of the theatre at Hierapolis, with inscriptions inked in.
Photograph: Newby, by permission of the Missione Archeologica Italiana a Hierapolis.

---

[19] To date the decorative elements have mostly been published separately: see Ritti (1985) and D'Andria and Ritti (1985) on the friezes, Bejor (1991) on the sculpture, with overviews in De Bernardi Ferrero, Ciotta, and Pensabene (2007) and Sobrà and Masino (2010). Marco Galli is currently working on a complete reassessment of the decorative programme: for initial publications see Galli (2016) and (2022).
[20] D'Andria and Ritti (1985); Galli (2022), 75–80.
[21] Unpublished. See Sobrà and Masino (2010), 396–7 and 402–3; Galli (2022), 71–4.

labelling inscriptions on the architrave or the background of the relief.[22] The relief is well known, with a number of detailed publications.[23] Here, I wish to draw particular attention to the ways in which it represents the city's festivals, and acts as a lynchpin, drawing together other messages of the theatre's decorative programme.

At the heart of this relief is a scene proclaiming the importance of Hierapolis' civic festivals (Fig. 6.2). The oversized prize crown lying on a table signifies this immediately. As Katherine Dunbabin has shown, such crowns become a key visual symbol of festivals from the late second century AD, appearing across a range of different media, such as reliefs, coins, and mosaics.[24] Often, they bear an inscription, naming the festival which they connote. Here, however, no inscription is present, despite the numerous inscriptions elsewhere on the frieze. The prize table is flanked to the viewer's left by a personification of Hierapolis. She was originally holding a statuette of Apollo in her left hand, extended towards the prize crown, as can be seen by comparison with the central figure on a relief slab from the orchestra of the theatre (Fig. 6.3).[25] This juxtaposition of god and prize table is repeated on the reverse of coins minted under Septimius Severus, though there the god is full-size.[26] Next to Hierapolis is another female personification, this time *Agonothesia*, the presidency of the games, standing next to an amphora of the type which often appears on coins, usually associated with the drawing of lots to determine pairs of contestants.[27] Beyond her sits a male figure, leaning against a tripod. His label is lost, but he has clear visual similarities with the figure on the reverse of a coin minted by Hierapolis under Elagabalus (Fig. 6.4).[28] On both, a figure turns back towards a tripod, while raising his right hand to his head, as if to crown himself. On the coin a prize crown sits atop the tripod, while on the relief it looks as though the figure of *Agonothesia* also originally extended her hand to proffer a crown to the figure's head, and that he held a palm in his left hand, the top of which can be seen above his head.[29] These attributes suggest that he was characterised as a victor in the festival, perhaps to be identified either with the god Apollo himself (as the figure is usually identified on the coin), or a personification of the games.[30] Taken together with the reclining river god in front of

---

[22] The recent anastylosis shows that these were clearly visible from the cavea and legible to those standing on the stage.

[23] Especially Ritti (1985), 59–77; Chuvin (1987); di Napoli (2002); briefer discussions in Newby (2005), 249–52 and Dunbabin (2016), 27–9.

[24] Dunbabin (2010); see also Rumscheid (2000).   [25] Ritti (1985), 61–2.

[26] *SNG von Aulock* 8381, 8382.   [27] Gaebler (1929).

[28] https://rpc.ashmus.ox.ac.uk/coins/6/5424, last accessed 5 June 2023.

[29] Ritti (1985), 60–1 notes the crown and palm but not the gesture of *Agonothesia*.

[30] Ritti (1985), 61 (Apollo or Agon); Chuvin (1987), 102 (founding hero); di Napoli (2002), 392–3 (personification of the Pythia festival).

Fig. 6.2 Detail of *porta regia* central panel. Hierapolis Museum.
Photograph: Newby, by permission of the Missione Archeologica Italiana a Hierapolis.

Fig. 6.3 Relief from the balustrade of the orchestra of the theatre at Hierapolis. Hierapolis Museum.
Photograph: Newby, by permission of the Missione Archeologica Italiana a Hierapolis.

Fig. 6.4 Coin from Hierapolis, Elagabalus on obverse, Apollo on reverse. Berlin. Münzkabinett, Staatliche Museen zu Berlin, 18223774.2.
Photographs by Lutz-Jürgen Lübke (Lübke und Wiedemann).

the prize table, this collection of figures presents a clear celebration of a festival held in Hierapolis' locality and associated with the god Apollo.

It is widely and convincingly argued that the festival celebrated here is Hierapolis' chief festival in honour of Apollo, the Apolloneia Pythia.[31] This festival seems to have been raised to sacred and oikoumenical status around this period, most likely during the co-emperorship of Septimius Severus and Caracalla. Two inscriptions from Tralleis, in honour respectively of a fluteplayer and an athlete, refer to the iso-pythian Apolloneia in Hierapolis among other prestigious games and are dated around the turn of the second to third centuries.[32] Elsewhere, the games appear as the Apolloneia Pythia or sometimes simply as Pythia.[33] The full title, though, seems to be the megala oikoumenika Apolloneia Pythia, which appears on an honorific inscription discovered in the *agora* at Hierapolis and, without the designation 'oikoumenika', on the honorific base for C. Mem[m]ius Eutychos who, among many other duties, served as *alytarch* of the festival, responsible for keeping order.[34] However, it is significant that the crown on the theatre relief is not inscribed, in contrast to the usual practice elsewhere.[35] The prominent placement of the imperial family to the right of the prize table

---

[31] For discussions of Hierapolis' festivals see von Papen (1907); Ritti (1985), 57–103; Ritti (2017), 168–86.
[32] Blümel and Malay (1993), nos. 4 and 5; *SEG* 43, 731 and 732.
[33] e.g. *IG* II² 3169/70, l. 29, for a herald from Sinope.
[34] Ritti (2017), 175, 515–18; Memmius' base is *SEG* 53, 1464, also discussed in Ritti (2008).
[35] Note that a prize crown with the legend Apol[lonei]a Pythia appears on a ceiling coffer from the Temple of Apollo at Hierapolis (Ritti (2017), 175, fig. 38; Ismaelli (2017), 180, fig. 286), and the same legend has also been restored on crowns shown on reverses of coins with Septimius Severus and the young Caracalla: *SNG von Aulock* 8381, 8382; see Chuvin (1987), 102 and n. 19.

suggests that the elevation of the festival by Septimius Severus is being celebrated here. Yet by omitting the name of the festival, the iconography also encompasses and embraces Hierapolis' festival culture more broadly, allowing it also to include any new festivals instituted in the future.[36]

Evidence of the festival comes from scattered references in victory inscriptions, and a couple of legends on coins or reliefs.[37] We lack a detailed inscribed decree, such as those which describe with great precision the festivals at Oinoanda or Gytheion, or the procession funded by Salutaris at Ephesos.[38] While such an inscription might have originally existed, the figural decoration of the theatre can in part be seen as fulfilling a similar role, asserting the important elements of the festival to the audience who would assemble here.[39]

In the *porta regia* relief the imperial family are shown overseeing the festival, indicating the wider structures of power within which civic festival culture could flourish (see Fig. 6.1). Septimius sits enthroned and flanked by his sons, while a flying Nike crowns him. To the right of the figure of Geta (later defaced), stands Julia Domna, veiled and extending a patera in a gesture of libation. While Septimius Severus seems to share in the victory which the games bring, and symbolically presides over them, his wife participates in the action, her gesture signifying that even the imperial family recognizes the sanctity of Apollo.[40] Next to Julia Domna stands the figure of Tyche, labelled above and identified by a cornucopia; while to the far right a seated figure with armour is most plausibly identified as Roma.[41] This figure acts as a pendant to the figure of Tyche, and might also suggest that the world which these games inhabited is one governed and secured by Rome's military presence.

If we consider the social and symbolic hierarchies which were embedded in civic festival culture, the top place was occupied by two entities—the emperor and the divine. Festivals were dedicated to the gods cherished by a particular community, but could also encompass the imperial family. As we have seen in Calomino's chapter, some festivals were set up primarily in honour of the imperial family, sometimes in connection with a grant of neokorate status, while others were dedicated to a particular civic deity, but often also encompassed the emperor

---

[36] e.g. perhaps also a festival instituted as part of Hierapolis' acquisition of neokorate status, redated by Ritti (2003) to the sole reign of Caracalla, who appears along with Julia Domna as recipient of a secondary dedication of the theatre: Ritti (2017), 514–15.

[37] See n. 31 above.   [38] Wörrle (1988); *SEG* 11, 923; Rogers (1991).

[39] It should be noted that Hierapolis also had another theatre, Scardozzi (2012), and the respective use of each is unknown, though the imagery displayed here as well as the proximity to the Temple of Apollo make it very likely that festival gatherings and performances took place here.

[40] This theme of figures participating in ritual reappears elsewhere, e.g. in the theatre at Sabratha where Septimius Severus himself is shown sacrificing: Caputo (1959), 19.

[41] Ritti (1985), 63; Chuvin (1987), 102–3; Di Napoli (2002), 386–9, though some queries still remain.

in their names and rituals.⁴² The emperor played a crucial role in authorizing festivals, and especially in granting the much coveted eiselastic status, which raised a civic festival to the top tier of international and sacred contests, bringing valuable pensions to those who secured victories.⁴³ In festivals founded by private donation, such as the Demostheneia at Oinoanda, the emperor could also be consulted and incorporated in imagery and rituals, even when the main deity celebrated was a civic god.⁴⁴ Festivals allowed cities and individuals to demonstrate jointly their piety to their civic deity as well as their loyalty to the imperial house.

If we move outward from the *porta regia* relief, we can see how that dual focus was explored at Hierapolis. The dedicatory inscription proudly declared that the city dedicated the theatre to Apollo Archegetes, the other civic gods, and the Severan imperial family. The inscription was carved in large letters along the architrave of the first storey of the *scaenae frons*. While the inscription runs from left to right, those parts which run along the fronts of the aedicula are particularly prominent and easy to read. From left to right, the first three aedicula carry the names of Severus and M. Aurelius Antoneinos (Caracalla), Julia Domna, Mother of the Camps, and the city of Hierapolis. The placement is not exact—the last two letters of Antoneinos and the first three of Hierapolis spill over onto the curved architraves to either side—but nevertheless this placement reinforces the sense of a reciprocal relationship between the city and the imperial family.⁴⁵ Geta, whose inscription and image were later to be erased, already seems to have been sidelined in the carving of the inscription, which relegated him to the less-visible recess between the first and second aediculae.

Apollo's name featured at the start of the inscription and would not have been easily visible to the audience.⁴⁶ In figural form, however, he dominated the theatre's display. While only present as a statuette in the *porta regia* relief, full-scale statues and relief depictions of the god in various different guises reappeared throughout the rest of the decoration. The free-standing sculptural display of the *scaenae frons* seems primarily to have featured the gods. A family group of Apollo, Leto, and Artemis showed Apollo in the iconography of Apollo Kitharoidos, similar to his portrayal in the cult statuette, and on the frieze depicting his life which

---

⁴² For discussions see Price (1984), 101–32; Boatwright (2000), 94–104; Burrell (2004), 335–41. On imperial rituals as part of festivals, see especially Gebhard (1996) and Chapters 2 and 4 by Scharff and Calomino in this volume.

⁴³ Slater (2013), also Gordillo Hervás, Chapter 3 above.

⁴⁴ Wörrle (1988), 172–82; Mitchell (1990).

⁴⁵ For full details of the inscription and its layout see Ritti (2017), 498–506 with figs. 4-19. On the importance of thinking of Greek civic inscriptions as visual communications, see especially Haensch (2009); Graham (2013); Petrovic, Petrovic, and Thomas (2019).

⁴⁶ This part of the inscription is now lost, but known from earlier copies: Ritti (1985), 108.

decorated the podia below, while Artemis appeared in her typical Graeco-Roman guise of huntress.[47] Elsewhere, however, Apollo also appeared as Apollo Kareios and Apollo Lairbenos, linking to the other manifestations in which the god was worshipped in Hierapolis and the region.[48] On the frieze which ran along the bottom of the *scaenae frons* the life and cult of Apollo are told at length on the right half of the stage, complementing the depictions of his sister, Artemis, on the left. The importance of Apollo for Hierapolis is also underlined by the tribal inscriptions incised onto the seats of the lower cavea.[49] These also date to the Severan refurbishment and allocated spaces for each of the city's tribes, with the 'first tribe Apollonias' uniquely given the whole central cuneus, behind the honorific exedra. The names of the tribes reflect the city's long history, reaching back to the Seleucid and Attalid periods through the names Seleukis, Antiochis, Laodikis, and Attalis, as well as to its more recent history under Rome (Romais and Tiberiane). When seated in their tribes, the citizens thus embodied civic history from the foundation up to the Roman present, with Apollo dominating that identity, at the very heart of the theatre.[50]

The visual imagery also expands the dedicatory inscription's reference to other civic gods. A seated statue of Hades/Plouto, worshipped in the nearby Ploutonion, was probably placed above the leftmost door of the *scaenae frons*.[51] Nearby lay a frieze depicting the Rape of Persephone, while Demeter in her serpent chariot appeared in the corresponding frieze on the right of the stage.[52] The goddess Persephone also features in the free-standing sculptural decoration of the stage, as shown by Marco Galli, who identifies the two colossal female statues which flanked the *porta regia* as representations of Demeter and Kore-Persephone, the latter shown holding a torch.[53] Thus the theatre's decoration makes reference not only to Apollo as patron god of the community, but also to the cult of Plouto and Persephone, which was accommodated nearby in the Ploutonion shrine which attracted a certain amount of fame in the Roman period.[54]

---

[47] Bejor (1991), nos. 2, 4, and 5.

[48] Bejor (1991), no. 3 (statue of Apollo Kareios). In the busts which decorate the pediments of the aedicula, Apollo appears three times, in Graeco-Roman guise and with the attributes of Apollo Lairbenos and Kareios: Sobrà and Masino (2010), 391, fig. 18; Sobrà (2012), 196. On these cults see Ritti, Şimşek, and Yıldız (2000) and Ceylan and Ritti (1997).

[49] Kolb (1974), esp. 262–3; Kolb (1990). On the dating of the seats see Sobrà and Massino (2010), 382 n. 39.

[50] Cf. Galli (2016), 210.   [51] Bejor (1991), no. 1.

[52] Sobrà and Masino (2010), 395–9, fig. 24. A local personification with tall crown reclines at the left of the Demeter panel, situating the actions within the local territory.

[53] Galli (2016).

[54] Strabo, *Geography* 13.4.14; see further D'Andria (2013) and (2017). Note also the presence of the figure of Daidouchos or Daidouchia (torch-bearer/torch-bearing) on the *porta regia* frieze which Ritti (1985), 69–70 links with the cult of Demeter, discussed further below.

6.2.1. Officials and performers

While the gods and the imperial family both sit at the heart of Hierapolis' theatre display and her festival culture they each have different resonances. The imperial family plays a crucial role as overseers and guarantors, while the gods are placed here as the recipients of cult. Other important individuals within festivals were the officials who oversaw them, and the human participants in competitions and rituals. All of these are also celebrated and asserted on the *porta regia* frieze, on the two side panels which flank and protrude from the central relief. Prominently positioned at the front of the left panel is the labelled figure of the *agonothetes*, the magistrate whose role it was to oversee the overall running of a festival. He is dressed in the traditional elite dress of tunic and himation and wears on his head a crown with four busts, most likely representing the four members of the Severan family (Fig. 6.5).[55] His hair is brushed forwards with long sideburns extending down towards his chin, similar to the style favoured by Caracalla in the first decade of the third century. This gives the face the appearance of individuality, and may have been designed to allude to a particular individual who took on the role of *agonothetes* in the first iteration of the newly augmented Apolloneia Pythia.[56] The label, however, simply identifies the figures as [ΑΓΩΝΟ]ΘΕΤΗΣ, indicating that the role endures past any one individual, though viewers at the time the theatre was dedicated might have seen a particular resemblance.

Fig. 6.5 Detail of *Agonothetes*. Hierapolis Museum.
Photograph: Newby, by permission of the Missione Archeologica Italiana a Hierapolis.

---

[55] *SEG* 35, 1376; Ritti (1985), 66.
[56] Di Napoli (2002), 381–3, suggesting that the female figure next to him may have been his wife.

It is likely that the festival's actual *agonothetes* would have sat opposite this image, in the honorific exedra at the centre of the cavea. The Demostheneia inscription from Oinoanda expressly states that the *agonothetes* of the new festival should process in company with other magistrates, wearing a purple robe and gold crown, and take a front seat at meetings of the assembly and council as well as at the shows.[57] At Oinoanda the golden crown is one paid for by the donor of the festival, Demosthenes himself, and carries an image of the civic god Apollo and the emperor Hadrian. The presence of the emperor on the crowns at Oinoanda and Hierapolis shows that bust crowns should not necessarily be read as identifying their bearer as a priest of the emperor, but rather as an *agonothetes*.[58] The imperial bust could be included in crowns worn by *agonothetai* of other festivals, and the busts of gods as well as emperors could also appear on these crowns. The identity of the female figure who stands next to the *agonothetes* is uncertain, but she too may have represented a human participant in the festival, perhaps a priestess.[59]

In addition to the *agonothetes*, the *porta regia* frieze includes figures of performers and participants who would also have had real-life equivalents in the human participants who processed into the theatre in times of festival. On the outer side of the left-side panel we find the trumpeter, [ΣΑ]ΛΠΙ | ΚΤΗ[Σ].[60] Contests for heralds and trumpeters usually came first in an ancient festival, the winners then given the task of announcing all subsequent victors.[61] This figure is immediately followed by a naked boy, labelled above as ΠΥΘΙΚΟΣ, 'Pythian', and accompanied by a male figure whose hand is raised, perhaps in acclamation. He may be an umpire, presiding magistrate, or herald.[62] A naked athlete appears further to the right, crowning himself. Two other athletes appear elsewhere on the relief; a figure labelled above as *ANH*[*P*] (adult man) on the front of the right-hand projection, and another athlete shown crowning himself of the outside of the same block. They probably represent the different age groups into which athletes were divided, the Pythian boy reminding us also that the festival was isopythios, equal in status to the Pythian games.[63]

A further reference to athletic competition is provided by the fragmentary figure shown at the far right of the right-hand panel (Fig. 6.6). This figure is badly preserved but seems to have been a male naked figure, labelled above as

---

[57] Wörrle (1988), 10, ll. 56–9.
[58] See Rumscheid (2000); Riccardi (2007), esp. 381–2.
[59] See Di Napoli (2002), 383; Chuvin (1987), 100–1 sees her as the embodiment of the *boule* or council.
[60] *SEG* 35, 1376. Ritti (1985), pl. 3a.   [61] Crowther (1994).
[62] Ritti (1985), 65 suggests an auletes, flute player, but more recently favours Di Napoli's suggest that he is the alytarch of the games, responsible for keeping order: Di Napoli (2002), 381 n. 6; Ritti (2008), 293 n. 45, based on the presence of a fragmentary label beginning with alpha: *SEG* 35, 1376.
[63] As in the Tralleis inscription, *SEG* 43, 731; on the age groups see Chuvin (1987), 99–100; also Di Napoli (2002), 381 n. 12.

Fig. 6.6 Interior of right projection: Andreia, Synodos, Dadouchos, and Dolichos.
Photograph: Newby, by permission of the Missione Archeologica Italiana a Hierapolis.

[Δ]ΟΛΙΧΟΣ, a reference to the long race.[64] This figure embodies the race itself, rather than a contestant in it. Immediately to the viewer's left is another figure, dressed in a long garment and labelled above as ΔΑΔΟΥ[... Ritti restored this as reading either Da(i)douchos or Da(i)douchia (torch-bearer/the act of torch-bearing), and sees it as a reference to the role of the torchbearer in religious processions.[65] The figure's dress makes an allusion to ritual and processions most likely, though it is also possible that (like the neighbouring figure of Dolichos) it stands as an allusion instead to a torch-race which occurred as part of the festival itself.[66]

As well as symbolically identifying different contests and age groups in the games, the reliefs also work to encapsulate in stone the ephemeral moments of the festival. The trumpeter's duty was to call for silence and to signal the start of races, while the herald would call together the contestants, and subsequently annouce the names of the victors.[67] Here the figure of the trumpeter may echo the real figure who called the audience to attention, while the victorious figures who

---

[64] Chuvin (1987), 103 cites Pausanias 10.7.5 noting that the Delphians first added this contest for boys to the athletic schedule of the original Pythian games.
[65] SEG 33, 1377; Ritti (1985), 69–70.
[66] Chuvin (1987) 103 favours a ritual association over one with the torch race.
[67] Crowther (1994), 146–7; cf. Heliodorus, *Aethiopika* 4.3, a novelistic retelling of the torch race at the Pythia in Delphi, where both trumpeter and herald appear.

appear alongside evoke the proclamations of victories which had occured during the games.⁶⁸ Visual imagery evokes ephemeral, aural events, and fixes their memory into the cityscape.

While victorious athletes represent the physical contests which took place at the festival, with the exception of the trumpeter, musical events are represented collectively through a personification of the synod, the Guild of the Artists of Dionysos. This figure appears on the right-hand panel flanking the centre scene, in the company of the figures *Andreia* (courage), *Dadouchos* (?), and *Dolichos* (Fig. 6.6, second figure from left).⁶⁹ She is shown as a tall female figure dressed in a high belted chiton and himation. Her right arm is mostly lost but seems to have raised a wreath to her head, the remains of which are still visible. In her left hand she carries a theatrical mask, with the remains of a lyre beneath. The inscription above labels her as ΣΥΝΟΔΟΣ, synod or guild. Guilds of both athletes and musicians existed in the ancient world, so it is the iconography which identifies this personification as standing especially for the guild of the Artists of Dionysos, which represented musical contestants in sacred festivals.⁷⁰ The attributes which the figure holds link both to musical and theatrical contests, while her stance and dress are also reminiscent of the figure of Apollo Kitharoidos, who appears on the mythological friezes below, and in whose honour the festival is held. Her upstretched right arm and crown also identify her as a victor. While this single figure condenses into one all the different musical and dramatic events which could take place in ancient festivals, the decoration elsewhere expands this into the various different artistic genres. Thus in the mythological frieze below, the reliefs in honour of Apollo close at the far right with a scene of the nine Muses, led by Apollo Kitharoidos himself.⁷¹

Indeed, the podium reliefs in honour of Apollo also include a number of other scenes which echo the events which took place as part of his festival. Apollo is repeatedly shown as a victor and contestant in various athletic and musical contests—he appears as a child victor receiving a palm, as a youthful wrestler, and playing the lyre and being rewarded for his victory, in his contest with Marsyas.⁷² While all the scenes can be read as part of a mythological narrative, honouring and recounting Apollo's deeds, they also take on an extra resonance when seen in the context of the festival advertised so prominently above. Apollo appears as a divine prototype for the various competitors who will participate in his own festival, an idea summed up in the image on the front of the podium

---

[68] On the question of whether some athletic events took place here see Gybas (2018), 123–5.
[69] Ritti (1985), 68–70; Di Napoli (2002), 389–90.
[70] On the Artists of Dionysos see especially Le Guen (2001) and Aneziri (2003), both focused on the Hellenistic period; also Grigsby in Chapter 8 below. The discovery of Hadrian's letters to the Artists of Dionysos at Alexandria Troas have added to our understanding of their role in the imperial period: Petzl and Schwertheim (2006); Jones (2007); Slater (2008); Strasser (2010); Gordillo Hervás, Chapter 3 above.
[71] D'Andria and Ritti (1985), 80–92; Ap V, pll. 23–7.
[72] D'Andria and Ritti (1985), 29–31, Ap Ic; 33–6, IIa–b; 49–56, Ap IIIa, IIIc; pll. 10, 12, 16, 17.

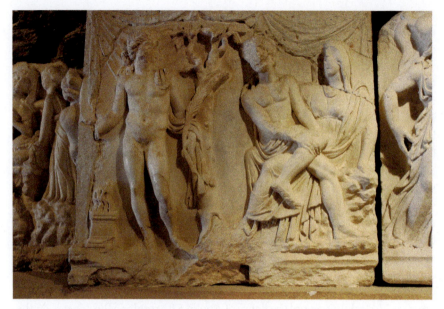

Fig. 6.7 Relief showing Apollo as victor pouring a libation. Podium frieze.
Photograph: Newby, by permission of the Missione Archeologica Italiana a Hierapolis.

which flanks the central doorway, where he appears naked except for a chlamys, holding a palm of victory in his left hand while pouring a libation onto a lit altar with his right (Fig. 6.7).[73]

The single figure of *Synodos* in the *porta regia* frieze is thus expanded in the mythological friezes to encompass a whole range of musical contests, as well as athletic pursuits. Yet within her own frieze she also acts to symbolize the body of the synod as a whole. The synod was also represented in the theatre at Hierapolis in inscribed form, as one of the bodies dedicating honorific statues to a poet and a comic actor. Here it is described as the 'sacred synod of sacred and crowned victors from the inhabited world (*oikoumene*)'.[74] The figure of *Synodos* on the *porta regia* frieze could evoke both this synod of sacred victors as a body, and also those individuals honoured by it, such as the actor and poet whose statue bases were found in the vicinity. A seated statue of a poet, holding a dramatic mask, was also found in the theatre and might have represented either a contemporary playwright or a figure from the past.[75]

---

[73] D'Andria and Ritti (1985), 35–6, Ap IIb.
[74] Ritti (1985), 96, nos. 10 and 11 and (2017), 166–7. The fullest title for the synodos is in no. 11, in honour of M. Julius Sophron. On this man's identity as a comic actor rather than playwright see Jones (1987), 208.
[75] Bejor (1991), 31–4, nos. 17 and 41 notes that the type was also used for portraits of Menander and suggests that the statue is earlier, reused in the Severan display, perhaps with a pendant image on the right.

The personification of *Synodos* on the *porta regia* relief thus takes on broader resonances when seen in the wider visual context of the theatre. As well as finding echoes in the rest of the sculptural display, this figure may also have had a living referent on the ground, amongst those assembled within the theatre. At Ephesos, an addition to the text of the Salutaris inscription shows that the sacred victors of the city were allocated specific seats next to a statue of *Homonoia* (concord) in the theatre.[76] A similar allocation of reserved seats might also have occurred at Hierapolis, allowing the living representatives of the artistic and athletic synods to find their place beneath imagery celebrating their participation in the festival. Outside festival time, the images of these personifications would stand as a crystallized reminder and enduring symbolic presence of the festival and its participants.

Art replaces the absent bodies of these participants. Work on funerary art has drawn attention to the ways in which images attempt to replace the dead, providing a permanent form to substitute for the mortal body.[77] Divine images too, work to make the invisible present and approachable to their living worshippers.[78] Here, sculpted forms stand in for and memorialise their human referents outside festival time, and set up a direct correlation with them during the course of a festival.

6.2.2. *Synthutai*—joint sacrificers

As we have seen, the viewer could move out from the images of athletes, the trumpeter, and the Synod on the *porta relief* frieze to see the wider allusions to both athletic and artistic competition in the mythological reliefs; both would also have had living referents in the bodies of those who assembled here at times of festival. A similar process can also be seen for the other major theme of the *porta regia* frieze, that of *synthusia* or joint sacrifice.

As Ian Rutherford has shown, a key role was played in ancient festivals by the official sacred observers which other states sent to participate in the rituals, usually bringing a sacrificial offering.[79] With the introduction of new Panhellenic festivals during the Hellenistic period, an even more extensive festival circuit developed in which recognition of one's festival by other cities was a key point of prestige.[80] While in the earlier period the term *theoroi* is most commonly used to refer to these external participants, by the Roman period they are usually referred to as *synthutai* and the activity as *synthusia*, common sacrifice.[81] Even local festivals, such as the Demostheneia at Oinoanda, could involve the participation of

---

[76] Rogers (1991), 180, ll. 470–7.
[77] Belting (2011) is a key text; see also Elsner (2018); Squire (2018); Newby (2019).
[78] Platt (2011); see also Gaifmann (2006) on the functions which replicated cult images could fulfil.
[79] Rutherford (2013).
[80] Parker (2004); van Nijf and Williamson (2015); Williamson, Chapter 9 below.
[81] Rutherford (2013), 68–9.

neighbouring communities.⁸² For an international festival, the reach ought to go wider, though how far it stretched in reality must have depended on the importance of the city and festival. A series of statue bases set up at Aphrodisias in the mid-third century commemorated the participation of a number of local cities in sacrifices at a sacred games there, including Hierapolis, while the bases for statues of various cities discovered in the theatre at Ephesos have also been linked with the visits of these cities to celebrate and approve Ephesos' third *neokoria* (presidency of the provincial imperial cult).⁸³ Civic coinages could also celebrate the joint sacrifices which took place at festivals, usually through the imagery of a figure bringing a sacrificial offering, sometimes presented to the Tyche of the city.⁸⁴

In the theatre at Hierapolis, the international ritual reach of her festival is celebrated three times in the theatre decoration, including two scenes on the *porta regia* reliefs: on the inside of the left projecting panel, and on the outside of the right projection. On the left panel the scene is flanked by two figures whose inscriptions are now uncertain, they may represent personifications of civic groups—the *gerousia* to the left, and *demos* to the right (Fig. 6.8).⁸⁵ Between them two female figures appear; a label above the left-hand one can be restored as [ΣΥΝ]ΘΥΣΙΑ; while the following part of the architrave reads ΟΙΚΟΥΜΕΝḢ (inhabited world).⁸⁶ These personifications of *Synthusia* and *Oikoumene* stand over the figure of a fallen bull, clearly a sacrificial offering. *Oikoumene*'s figure carries the traces of a tall turreted crown; she extends her right hand towards a patera held by *Synthusia*, who in turn puts her arm around *Oikoumene*'s shoulders, conveying visually the unity which this act of joint sacrifice embodies.

The second scene of *Synthusia* appears on the back of the right projection, next to a scene of a draped male crowning a naked athlete (Fig. 6.9). A male figure with a bare chest and wearing a long himation brings a bull towards a lit altar. In his left hand he holds a double-headed axe. A label above identifies this scene as ΣΥΝΘΥΣΙ[Α], joint sacrifice.⁸⁷ A further reference to *synthusia* appears on the relief built into the parapet, also discussed above (Fig. 6.3). This shows three female figures in similar dress, all wearing diadems and turreted crowns. The one to far right holds a cornucopia and has the upper part of a reclining male figure visible at her feet, most likely a river god; her iconography identifies her as

---

⁸² Wörrle (1988), l. 85; 198–201.

⁸³ Aphrodisias: *I.Aphrodisias 2007*, 12.924–30; Roueché (1981), 118–20. Ephesos: *I.Ephesos* 2053–6; Robert (1982), 233; Weiss (1991), 362.

⁸⁴ e.g. BM 1970,0909.79 from Ephesos discussed further below; also *RPC* IX 1115 from Perge (without legend ΣΥΝΘΥΣΙΑ). On the coins of Anazarbus, the receiving city does not appear: e.g. https://rpc.ashmus.ox.ac.uk/coins/6/7446, last accessed 5 June 2023.

⁸⁵ See Chuvin (1987), 100–1 who also identifies the female figure on the front of the projection as the *Boule*; by contrast Ritti (1985), 67–8 identified the male figure to far right as *Aion* (Time).

⁸⁶ Alternatively, it is possible that the inscription originally read *synthusia oikoumenes*, 'joint sacrifice of the inhabited world', labelling the scene as a whole, rather than each individual figure, as on some coins from Anazarbus (see above, n. 84): Ritti (1985), 67; *SEG* 35, 1376.

⁸⁷ *SEG* 35, 1377.

FESTIVALS AND THE PERFORMANCE OF COMMUNITY 155

Fig. 6.8 *Synthusia* scene, interior of left projection.
Photograph: Newby, by permission of the Missione Archeologica Italiana a Hierapolis.

Fig. 6.9 Scene on outer face of right projection: *Synthusia*.
Photograph: Newby, by permission of the Missione Archeologica Italiana a Hierapolis.

the Tyche of Hierapolis. With her right hand Tyche crowns the central figure, who carries a statuette of Apollo in her left hand, while pouring a libation with her right. She also seems to embody the city of Hierapolis, on comparison with the named figure in the central frieze. To the left, another female figure brings a bull towards the lit altar, and offers a *patera* to partake in the libation above the lit altar. Ritti identified her as *Oikoumene* on comparison with the left-hand panel relief discussed above.[88] Iconographically, the closest comparison is with an Ephesian coin celebrating *synthusia* where a female figure brings a bull towards the seated Tyche of Ephesos, who holds out the statuette of Artemis Ephesia (Fig. 6.10).[89] Whether we identify the figure as *Oikoumene* or the personification of *Synthusia* does not perhaps matter much. She can be both simultaneously. What she does seem to evoke very clearly is the idea of other cities coming to join Hierapolis in her celebration of Apollo, bringing with them sacrificial animals and libations. The sacred festival at which this ritual takes place is clearly proclaimed through the large prize crown, hovering between the two left-hand figures. This panel thus encapsulates in a single image a number of the themes of the central *porta regia* frieze, condensing into one image the idea of Hierapolis honouring her patron god and being joined by her neighbours in doing so, in the context of a prestigious festival. While two of the images represent this act at a symbolic level, carried out by personifications of the bodies of the city and the *Oikoumene* (Figs 6.3 and 6.8), the third may be more descriptive, echoing the real acts of sacrifice which occurred during the festival (Fig. 6.9).

We do not have secure references for which cities sent envoys to the festival at Hierapolis, but it is possible to see some glimpses of the reach of the festival through victory inscriptions. An athlete buried in Hierapolis appears to have

Fig. 6.10 Reverse of a coin from Ephesos celebrating *Synthusia*. BM 1970,0909.79.

Photograph: D. Calomino, by permission of the British Museum.

---

[88] Ritti (1985), 76, noting that De Bernardi also suggested Asia.
[89] Hecht (1968), 28, no. 4; pl. 8.4; https://rpc.ashmus.ox.ac.uk/coins/4/1127, last accessed 5 June 2023.

come from Magnesia ad Sipylum; his sarcophagus celebrates victories in the Apolloneia Pythia and Olympia festivals as well as in a festival named after Commodus.[90] Other victors in the Apolloneia at Hierapolis are attested at Ephesos and Philadelphia in Lydia, while Hierapolis appears amongst the cities celebrated as sharing in festivals at Aphrodisias, and might reasonably have expected Aphrodisias to reciprocate.[91] Links with Magnesia and Ephesos are also suggested through the mythological scenes depicted on the lower podia of the *scaenae frons*, which include a number of episodes with particular local relevance. The myth of Marsyas was located in Phrygia, with the city of Apamea even claiming to be able to show the tree to which Marsyas had been tied, while the myth of Niobe, shown in the corresponding position on the left half of the stage, reaches out to Lydia, a region with which Hierapolis was also linked though the shared cult of Apollo Kareios.[92] At Magnesia ad Sipylum the myth of Niobe was embedded into the topography of the city, where a rock formation was identified as the petrified figure of the grief-stricken Niobe.[93]

These mythological references to local traditions can be seen as part of a conversation with representatives from those regions—they assert that Hierapolis sees herself as part of the wider region, and shows pride and respect for these local traditions; in doing so they also reach out, inviting those communities to join in the celebration of Apollo at Hierapolis, the god who played such an important part in the myths depicted here.[94] We can see them as a compliment to those performers and envoys who came to the theatre, a way of embracing them within a shared festival culture, at the heart of which Hierapolis places herself. This sense of reciprocity can also be seen, I think, in the reliefs celebrating Artemis. As has been noted before, it is significant that the form in which Artemis appears in the cultic scenes is as Artemis Ephesia, the famous civic deity of powerful Ephesos.[95] To the far left of the stage we see scenes of religious procession and sacrifice in honour of Artemis Ephesia.[96] These include scenes of sacrificial attendants leading bulls, as well as figures carrying laden baskets. The culmination of the procession appears on the front of the left-most podium (Fig. 6.11): in the

---

[90] Pennacchietti (1966–7), 309–10, no. 29; *BE* 1971, 649. See Ritti (1985), 79–80, n. 44 and (2017), 175–6, locating the Pythia and Olympia festivals at Hierapolis while the Commodeia festival may be that held at Laodikeia, as in *I.Laodikeia Lykos* 59.

[91] Ritti (2017), 175–6, 179–80. Ephesos: *I.Ephesos* 7, 2, 3911. Philadelphia: *IGR* IV, 1645 and 1761, the latter for an athlete from Kibyra; the origin of the athlete honoured in 1645 is not recorded. Aphrodisias: *I.Aphrodisias 2007*, 12.925. As Carless Unwin notes in the following chapter, 7.5, there was also a *topos* inscription for the Hierapolitans in the tetrastoon at Aphrodisias: *I.Aphrodisias 2007*, 12.402.

[92] Marsyas: Strabo 12.8.15; Pausanias 10.30.9; Pliny, *Natural History* 16.240. Coins of Apamea show Marsyas, e.g. *RPC* III, 2585; https://rpc.ashmus.ox.ac.uk/coins/6/5692, last accessed 5 June 2023. Cult of Apollo Kareios: Ceylan and Ritti (1997), 64.

[93] Pausanias 1.21.3. Generally on *lieux de mémoire* in the imperial Greek East see Gangloff (2013).

[94] On the resonance of the mythological reliefs see especially D'Andria and Ritti (1985), 181–4; Newby (2003); Di Napoli (2013), 280–2.

[95] D'Andria and Ritti (1985), 160–5; Newby (2003), 197–8.

[96] D'Andria and Ritti (1985), 143–65.

Fig. 6.11 Relief panel of the podium of the *scenae frons*, showing worship of Artemis Ephesia.
Photograph: Newby, by permission of the Missione Archeologica Italiana a Hierapolis.

centre the sacrificial attendant lifts back his axe to bring it down on the bull, accompanied by two woman playing double flutes. A further woman appears at the left, probably originally bearing an offering dish, while to the right a male figure, holding a scroll in his left hand, pours a libation over a lit altar.[97] Further right, a woman approaches the statue of Artemis Ephesia set within a shrine.

These scenes proclaim the importance of Artemis Ephesia, and the sacrificial offerings made to her. Rather than seeing them only as generic presentations of religious activity, they may also have been designed to have a more specific resonance, prompting recollection of Hierapolis' own participation in the rites of Artemis during common sacrifices held at Ephesos. The scrolls held by figures offering libations can be read as a sign that they are acting in an official capacity, fulfilling a ritual duty on behalf of their community.[98] Thus we could read them as representatives of the community of Hierapolis, showing the city as *synthutes* in

---

[97] Note that the woman who pours a libation over the altar next to the goddess' statue on the first frieze panel, D'Andria and Ritti (1985), 146–7, Ar IVb, also holds a scroll.

[98] For officials with scrolls in sacrificial contexts see Ryberg (1955), 102–3, fig. 51; the emperor can also be shown thus: figs 75a and b (Arch of the Argentarii, Rome). A coin of Perge shows a figure passing a scroll to the Tyche of the city with the legend *ΥΟΩΤΑ*, 'vota' or 'vows'; Peter Weiss interprets it as referring to the imperial decree authorising a neokorate festival and reads the coins as celebrating the participation of the wider community in the associated vows: *SNG von Aulock* 4736 and 4754; Weiss (1991), 364, 373–5.

the festivals in honour of Artemis. While there is no explicit testimony proving that representative from Hierapolis attended the festivals of Ephesos, minting of coinage celebrating *Homonoia*, concord, between the two cities from the period of Marcus Aurelius onwards makes it very likely that they would have attended.[99] The reliefs celebrate cultic rites in honour of Artemis, and call for a similar response to Apollo. Just as Artemis receives sacrifice and ritual offerings as her due at Ephesos, with Hierapolis a likely participant in these, so too now Apollo is to welcome in worshippers from the surrounding cities to join in the common sacrifices to him.[100]

The imagery of bulls being led in sacrifice, both here and in the *synthusia* scenes on the *porta regia*, also evoke the real scenes of sacrificial procession which took place during the festival itself and the envoys who brought their offerings to Hierapolis. At Oinoanda the decree for the Demostheneia prescribes that 'the sacrifices which are sent by other cities, these too should also be escorted in procession through the theatre and announced at the time that they are sent'.[101] If a similar process was followed at Hierapolis, a direct link would be created between the imagery on the reliefs and the actual events taking place in the theatre on festival days; again the visual image also acts as a permanent stand-in for these ephemeral events, urging future envoys to continue to play their role in the joint sacrifices and asserting Hierapolis' position at the heart of a joined up ritual community. Whether or not all her neighbours did, indeed, participate, is unknown, but the visual message sets up a strong expectation that joint cult lies at the heart of festivals, and urges Hierapolis' neighbours to respond to its call.

Together, the *porta regia* frieze asserts the importance of Hierapolis' festivals and her cult of Apollo, and the involvement in this of officials, performers, civic bodies, and sacred envoys. These messages spread out into the rest of the sculptural decoration, to embrace the free-standing sculpture, and the relief decoration, where the god can be seen as offering a divine model for the rituals and performances which take place in his honour.[102] The frieze works at a number of different levels—while some figures evoke their human counterparts present in the theatre, other concepts and groups are instead visualized through personifications. These single figures act to represent the collective groups who play a role in celebrating the festival. Other figures such as *Dolichos* suggest particular events which occured as part of the festival while *Andreia* might allude to another

[99] e.g. https://rpc.ashmus.ox.ac.uk/coins/4/2017; https://rpc.ashmus.ox.ac.uk/coins/6/5895, last accessed 5 June 2023.
[100] Alternatively, as Marguerite Spoerri Butcher has suggested to me, it is possible that the scenes refer to a cult of Artemis Ephesia at Hierapolis, in which case the scrolls may suggest ritual instructions.
[101] Wörrle (1988), l. 85, trans. Mitchell (1990), 185–6.
[102] Cf. Gaifmann (2018), 117–28 on the meanings of deities participating in ritual acts, with reference to libations.

contest, such as the *euandria* contests attested elsewhere, or more broadly suggest the qualities which athletic performance inculcates in the population.[103] We cannot discern all the meanings this imagery would have had for a local audience, steeped in the activities of the festival, yet we can see how it acts to frame and structure these, asserting the importance of the different elements, and calling on spectators to see themselves as part of a community, unified in the worship of Apollo, and each playing their particular role.

6.3. Civic roles in festivals at Perge

Like Hierapolis, Perge's theatre had a prominent frieze running above the *porta regia*, here depicting a scene of sacrificial procession. Recent work on the theatre suggests that it was built in two main phases.[104] A first phase of decoration in the late Antonine to early Severan period saw the erection of a two-storey *scaenae frons*; the plinths of the lower storey were decorated with a Dionysiac frieze and a frieze was placed on the architrave above the *porta regia* which Güler Ateş dates to the early-third century AD (Fig. 6.12).[105] Later, in the mid-Severan period, the centauromachy and gigantomachy friezes were added to the plinths of the second and third storeys.[106] Further changes to the orchestra probably date to the reign of the emperor Tacitus (AD 275–6).[107] As at Hierapolis, the central *porta regia* frieze proudly celebrates the city and its religious culture. While a number of

Fig. 6.12 Relief from the *porta regia* of the theatre at Perge.
Photograph: N. Hannestad, arachne.dainst.org/entity/3122297.

---

[103] For *euandria* contests elsewhere see *IG II*² 2311, l. 71 (Panathenaia at Athens) and *I.Sestos* 1, l. 84; further see Crowther (1985), 186–8.
[104] Öztürk (2009), esp. 89–94; see also Atik in Inan et al. (2000), 321 contra the first-century date earlier proposed by Şahin (1996), 116 and (1999), 62–4, n. 49. Preliminary publication in Inan et al. (2000).
[105] Dionysiac frieze: Inan in Inan et al. (2000), 322–30; also Alanyalı (2009); *porta regia* frieze: Ateş in Inan et al. (2000), 331–6.
[106] Alanyalı (2012).   [107] Öztürk (2009), 92–3.

Fig. 6.13 Reverse of a coin minted by Perge showing the Tyche of Perge holding out the statuette of Artemis Pergaia; Caracalla shown on the obverse. BM 1979, 0101. 2385.

Photograph: D. Calomino by permission of the British Museum.

scholars have noted the role which the theatre would have played in Perge's festivals, the significance of the frieze in this context has not received much discussion and it has been linked instead to local euergetism and perhaps the dedication ritual of the theatre itself.[108] In contrast, I argue that it should be seen as promoting the city's major festival, working analogously to the imagery at Hierapolis, though with different individual resonances.

The centre of the frieze is dominated by a seated female figure with walled crown and cornucopia, clearly identifiable as the Tyche of Perge. In her right hand she holds out the cult statue of Artemis Pergaia, a distinctive local form of the goddess well attested in coinage and other imagery. A similar image appears on a coin with Caracalla on the obverse, where Tyche looks directly at the image she holds out before her (Fig. 6.13).[109] In the theatre she appears frontally, to draw attention to her and indicate that she, along with the cult statue she holds, is the focus of religious procession. Other more detailed representations of the goddess Artemis Pergaia also appeared on two pilasters of the theatre, indicating her importance within its iconographical programme.[110] Unusually, on the *porta regia* relief Tyche wears a veil over her turreted crown. This helps to assimilate her to the goddess she holds, who also wears a veil over her polos crown, further cementing the link between city and goddess.

The cult of Artemis Pergaia had a long history in the city and surrounding regions.[111] Strabo tells us that the sanctuary was near the city, on a high place, and that a yearly festival (*panegyris*) was celebrated there.[112] The sanctuary still seems

---

[108] Theatre and festivals: Öztürk (2009), 19–20; Alanyalı (2012), 167–9; Gybas (2018), 44–52, 138–45. On the frieze see Ateş in Inan et al. (2000), 331–6, esp. 334 on its significance, generally followed by di Napoli (2015), 270, 278–80 though she also notes the overlap with the Demostheneia inscriptions at 280.

[109] c.f. *SNG von Aulock* 4675; also noted by Ateş in Inan et al. (2000), 333 as providing chronological comparanda. Note a similar reverse on a coin with Septimius Severus on the obverse: *SNG Paris* 423.

[110] Ateş in Inan et al. (2000), 333. The better preserved is Antalya Museum, inv. A-3796.

[111] Onurkan (1969–70); Fleischer (1973), 233–54; MacKay (1990), 2048–82.

[112] Strabo, *Geography* 14.4.2.

to have been popular in the second century AD, when it is the site for one of the anecdotes recalled in Polemo's *Physiognomy*.[113] Evidence from coins and inscriptions suggests that the cult had a wide geographical scope, being worshipped in Attaleia and a number of cities in nearby Pisidia, as well as much further afield.[114] The location of the temple is still unknown. Iyilik Belen hill, close to the theatre to the south-west of the city is one plausible candidate, being the findspot for several inscriptions relating to the cult, while other evidence suggests that it might have been located on the Acropolis to the north of the city.[115]

The relief shows the Tyche of Perge and the cult statuette as the focal point for a procession converging from both sides. From either side approach three male figures, each bringing a bull. These are clearly to be sacrificial victims, as the small flaming altar beneath the cult image attests. The flanking panels show more bulls along with draped male figures and sacrificial attendants. There is a careful delineation of status in the figures on the relief. The figures on the central panel are all dressed in the elite Greek civic uniform of tunic, himation and sandals, and wear twisted fillets on their heads.[116] As Ateş noted, different generations of men are represented on these reliefs. The figures closest to the centre are mature, bearded males; behind them come mature but beardless males, followed by more youthful figures whom Ateş identifies as ephebes. She suggested that they might represent three generations of the same family, perhaps the notable Plancii family whose donations to the city from the first century onwards were extensive, including the lavish gateway complex funded by Plancia Magna.[117] Ateş suggests that the scene represents the dedication of the theatre, which she attributes to the Plancii family. However, this remains speculative since the link between an inscription naming a dedication by M. Plancius Rutilius and the theatre is now widely rejected.[118]

Yet it is worth considering in more detail the faces of those involved in the procession, as a key to the meaning of the scene. Ateş discusses the faces on the two sides of the relief as if they are equivalent, but in fact there are important differences in the details. On the left half we find a series of generic faces, representing three different ages: a beardless youth to the left, a youthful figure with long sideburns in the middle, and a mature male with full beard at the right. All have the same generic curly hair, and the differences in beard seem designed to represent them as different age groups rather than as specific individuals. The situation on the right side is rather different, however (Fig. 6.14). Here, the first figure with his curly hair and full beard is a close match to the corresponding figure on the

---

[113] Polemo, *Physiognomy* B53 (ch. 68), trans. Hoyland (2007), 457; Robert (1948).
[114] MacKay (1990), 2061–6.
[115] Iyilik Belen: *I.Perge* 10, a temple inventory; Pace (1923–4), 402–12; 443–4. Acropolis: Martini (2010), 56–61, 78–81. Further see Öztürk (2009), 19–20; Alanyalı (2012), 43–5.
[116] Dress: Smith (1998), 65–6. [117] Ateş in Inan et al. (2000), 334–5.
[118] *I.Perge* 49, on which see Inan et al. (2000), 298 n. 35 (Öztürk) and 299 n. 40 (Atik); also Öztürk (2009), 90–1. There is, however, circumstantial evidence suggesting a link between the Plancii and diffusion of Artemis Pergaia's cult: Mitchell (1974), 34 n. 42; Jones (1976).

Fig. 6.14 Detail of *porta regia* relief, right side.
Photograph: N. Hannestad, arachne.dainst.org/entity/3122297; detail.

other side of Tyche. However, the two figures next to him have much more individualized features. The middle one has wavy rather than curled hair, represented using the chisel rather than the drill, and is clean shaven, while the outer one has a beardless, boyish face and wears his hair brushed forwards in the Julio-Claudian style. These two figures do seem much more individualized than the rest and perhaps were intended to represent prominent youths in the local community.

All six of the figures can be clearly grouped into three separate age categories; mature men closest to the centre, followed by youths on the cusp of adulthood and then more boyish figures. There is a very clear sense here of the involvement of different age groups. Inscriptions detailing the running of festivals show that individual magistrates and representatives of specific groups played an important role in civic processions. The decree outlining the procedures for the Hadrianic-period Demosthenaia festival at Oinoanda sets out in detail the order of the procession and the number of bulls each group must contribute to the common sacrifice:

Πομπεύσ[ου]]σι δὲ διὰ τοῦ θεάτρου καὶ συνθύσουσι ἐν ταῖς τ[ῆς παν]ηγύρεως ἡμέραις, καθὼς ἂν ὁ ἀγωνοθέτης δι᾿ ἀπολόγου ἑκάστην συνθυσίαν τάξῃ, αὐτὸς ὁ ἀγω-|νοθέτης βοῦν α', ὁ πολειτικὸς ἱερεὺς Σεβαστῶ[ν καὶ ἡ ἱ]έρεια Σεβαστῶν βοῦν α', ὁ ἱερεὺς τοῦ Διὸς βοῦν α',...

The following will process through the theatre and will sacrifice together during the days of the festival, according to the way the *agonothetes* gives written instructions for each communal sacrifice: The *agonothetes* himself, one bull; the civic priest of the emperors and the priestess of the emperors, one bull; the priest of Zeus, one bull, etc.[119]

In this inscription we are explicitly told that the procession will go through the theatre, and the number of bulls each group or individual is to bring is strictly laid out, with a number of different magistrates referred to. These are predominantly adult males, including later the *ephebarch*, leader of the ephebes. Elsewhere, however, different age groups also seem to have been on prominent display in

---

[119] Wörrle (1988), ll. 68–80, trans. Mitchell (1990), 185–6.

festival processions. Ephebes often acted as official escorts for processions, as we see in the Salutaris decree at Ephesos where they escort the procession from the Magnesian gate into the theatre and again from the theatre to the Koressian gate, and they could also bring sacrificial victims in their own right, as we see from the ephebic inscriptions of Athens.[120] At Gytheion in Sparta, the different groups which make up the procession are also carefully outlined:

πομπευόντων τῶν τε ἐφήβων καὶ τῶν νέων πάντων καὶ τῶν ἄλλων πολειτῶν ἐστεμμένων δάφν[ης] | στεφάνοις καὶ λευκὰ ἀμπεχομέν<ω>ν.

with the ephebes and young men and other citizens processing wearing garlands of bay leaves, and in white clothing.[121]

The Perge relief seems to combine these two elements. While the pairing of one figure with one bull reflects the division of sacrificial gifts among different magistracies, as outlined at Oinoanda, the different generations on show reflect the dividing up of religious processions into different age groups. Inscriptional evidence suggests that at Perge, as at many other cities, the citizen body included a number of separate groupings. A late Hellenistic inscription attests to the presence of the *ephebeia* in the city, while imperial inscriptions refer to a gymnasiarch of the *paides*, *neoi*, and *geraioi* (boys, young men, and old men).[122] The figures bringing bulls in this relief are best interpreted, then, as representatives of these different age groups. While the mature figures could be magistrates or priests, the boys and youths could have stood as representatives of the ephebes and *neoi*, as at Gytheion.[123] The portrait features on the faces of the two figures to the right may reflect the important role individual ephebes or *neoi* had performed in the procession. Evidence celebrating the *ephebeia* at Athens from a similar period shows very clearly how the sons of particular wealthy or elite families could take over individual ephebic magistracies and their financial commitments, and it is very possible that at Perge too a prominent ephebe took on the responsibility of funding an offering expected from the ephebes.[124]

In reality, it seems likely that the animals would actually have been led by slaves or other sacrificial attendants, as indeed they appear on the side panels of the *porta*

---

[120] Rogers (1991), 154, ll. 49–51. Cf. also Athens where they escorted the sacred objects to Eleusis, participating in sacrifices and libations along the way: *IG* II² 1078, esp. l. 29; cf. *IG* II² 2090, l. 9.

[121] *SEG* 11, 923, ll. 26–7, trans. Sherk (1988), no. 32, slightly modified. At Gytheion the men are accompanied by sacred maidens and adult women.

[122] *I.Perge* 14, fr. 1, ll. 24–6 mentions the ephebes and perhaps, if correctly restored, the *neoi*. Gymnasiarch: *I.Perge* 56.

[123] It seems less likely here that they represent envoys from other cities, in contrast to the scene of *synthusia* at Hierapolis.

[124] Cf. *IG* II² 2130, ll. 57–63 and 87–93 where one Publius Aelius Pheidimos of Pallene paid the various festival expenses. For further discussion see Newby (2005), 168–201 and (2017); Perrin-Saminadayar (2004); Wiemer (2011).

regia reliefs, rather than directly by the magistrates who paid for them. What matters for the running of the Demostheneia was the close linkage between the various groups and the number of victims they offer. Here too, a close correlation between the sacrificer and the victim is conveyed through the pairing of one man with one animal. This is not a naturalistic representation of a real procession, but a symbolic representation which shows how the procession encompasses the whole male population of the city. Rather than seeing it as a record of the theatre's dedication, as Ateş suggests, the parallels with festival texts strongly suggest that this relief celebrates Perge's festival in honour of her chief civic deity.

Indeed, it is possible that this scene reflects and memorializes the ephemeral processions which took place within the theatre. As we have seen, processions of sacrificial animals could go through theatres, and while blood sacrifice would occur in the sanctuary, other rites such as the burning of incense could take place in the theatre.[125] We know from the Salutaris inscription that statuettes of the goddess Artemis Ephesia were carried into the theatre at Ephesos, and placed on bases set along the *diazoma* of the theatre.[126] Here too the statuette held out by Tyche could refer to a real statuette of the goddess carried in procession during her festival. Evidence for the festival itself is patchy, though the penteric Artemiseia Vespasianeia attested at the end of the first century AD was probably primarily in honour of the goddess and the *asylia* (right of asylum) of her sanctuary.[127] Peter Weiss has suggested that the Asylia Pythia, attested later in the third century under Valerian, was most likely an upgrading of a pre-existing festival to Artemis.[128] While the epigraphic and numismatic evidence does not explicitly name a festival of Artemis at the start of the third century, it seems very likely that a festival in honour of Artemis and the *asylia* of her sanctuary would have continued unbroken throughout this period, known at different times as the Artemiseia Vespasianeia and the Asylia Pythia.

Indeed, the graffiti which were inscribed later on columns along the so-called Tacitus street to the north of the *agora* of Perge clearly link scenes of procession with religious festivals.[129] The graffiti share a similar iconography, presenting large rounded prize crowns with inscribed legends, held up by one or two Nike figures. The majority celebrate the festival founded under the emperor Tacitus in association with his grant of metropolitan status to the city, the Takiteios Metropoleitios

---

[125] As at Gytheion: Gebhard (1996), 118.   [126] Rogers (1991), 80–126.
[127] The festival is attested in *I.Perge* 60, 61, 63. There is debate over when *asylia* was reconfirmed (Rigsby (1996), 449–52; Jones (1999), 13–17; Şahin (1999), 72–84 re *I.Perge* 58) but the fact that the arch dedicated to Domitian included a statue to Artemis Pergaia as Saviour and Inviolate and statues of the divinized Vespasian and Titus (*I.Perge* 56, III. 1) favours Şahin's linkage of the asylum grant with this festival. The Kaisereia festival, also attested slightly earlier in *I.Perge* 42–5, is more likely to be the festival associated with the grant of neokorate status. On *neokoria* here see also Burrell (2004), 175–80.
[128] Weiss (1991), esp. 363–75, partly on the link with the graffito, discussed below.
[129] *I.Perge* nos. 313, 333–7. See Langner (2001), nos. 1178, 1179, 1198, 1199 though note that the drawings there are not exact copies, especially for the frieze on *I.Perge* 313 = Langner (2001), no. 1199.

Isokapetolios, but one celebrates the Asyleia Pythia *agon*.[130] In the register immediately above the inscription a rough depiction of the temple of Artemis Pergaia with its distinctive cult image inside is shown flanked on either sides by stick figures—a single standing figure to the right, and a figure with an animal to the left, probably a bull being led to sacrifice (Fig. 6.15).[131] On another graffito too, this time commemorating the 'Takiteios Metropoliteios Isokapetolios', the band which runs between the second and third lines of the inscription shows a central

Fig. 6.15 Graffito from column on Tacitus Street, *I.Perge* 313.
Photograph: S. Şahin by permission of N. Eda Akyürek Şahin.

---

[130] *I.Perge* nos. 333–7, 313. On the games see Weiss (1991).

[131] *I.Perge* no. 313. The depiction of the temple and cult statue is very close to that shown on coins, e.g. *RPC* IX 1121, from the reign of Trebonius Gallus.

house-like shape flanked by a series of figures in procession. This should be interpreted as a schematic representation of the cult statue of Artemis in her temple, since it shares the same peaked shape as the statue on the Pythia graffito and as shown on Pergaian coinage.[132] Both graffiti show cultic activity to the patron goddess (sacrifice in one, procession in the other) to affirm the importance of particular festivals. As we have already seen, the iconography of a bull being brought before a Tyche holding a civic cult statue also appears elsewhere, explicitly in the context of the joint sacrifice which was such an important part of festivals.

I suggest, then, that we should see the *porta regia* relief of the theatre as commemorating Perge's festival culture through visualization of the sacrificial processions which played such a key role as part of ancient festivals, making the piety of the community clearly visible to all. While at Hierapolis sacrifice is but one part of the festival in honour of Apollo, here it dominates, though as at Hierapolis we can also expand outwards from this central image, to see other resonances to festive activities in the rest of the decoration. Thus the processions of dancing and musical figures which adorn Artemis' cult statuette on the pilasters also allude to the cultic acts with which she was celebrated.[133] In the Dionysiac frieze, too, figures of basket-carriers or individuals engaged in sacrifice and libation evoke the events of festival, while the mythological event of Pentheus' death also looks like a staged performance, with the enthroned god watching on from the right (Fig. 6.16).[134] As at Hierapolis these events staged at a divine or mythological level echo and model the real events which occurred here, in the human realm.

References to festivals can also be seen in the civic coinage of Perge at this time. As already mentioned, the scene of Tyche holding out the statuette of Artemis Pergaia appears on coins with Caracalla and Septimius Severus on the obverse; while other Severan period coins also show imagery associated with the games, such as Nike carrying a wreath and palm, as well as the cult image of the goddess.[135] Nike also appears in the theatre's decoration, on the side of one of the pilasters carrying the image of Artemis Pergaia.[136] While the Severan-period coins do not name a festival, taken together with the theatre relief they suggest a desire to assert and commemorate Perge's civic goddess and her cult at this period. On both coins and the relief, the Tyche of Perge holds out the cult deity proudly, demanding recognition of her divinity. In the theatre that recognition comes in the sculpted form of sacrifice and procession, along with the real processions and

---

[132] Contra Şahin who follows Bean in identifying it as an altar: *I.Perge* 333.
[133] Onurkan (1969–70), 292–3; Fleischer (1973), 233–5; also MacKay (1990), 2077.
[134] Alanyalı (2009), 175; Dionysos add. 20. Basket-carriers: slab XX N; sacrifice and libations: slabs X S; XVII S; Pentheus: XXVI and XXVII N. The frieze is mostly repeated in mirror image on the other side of the stage, with a few differences.
[135] Tyche: *SNG von Aulock* 4675; *SNG Paris* 423; Nike: *SNG Paris* 433 (Julia Domna); 446 (Caracalla bearded); Artemis Pergaia in Temple: *SNG Paris* 422, sharing an obverse die with 423.
[136] Inan et al. (2000), 303–6 and fig. 24 (Atik).

Fig. 6.16 Pentheus scene from podium frieze at Perge. Slab immediately to left of central *porta regia*.
Photograph: Newby, by permission of Sedef Çokay Kepçe.

performances which would have taken place here under the eyes of the city and in the symbolic presence of the goddess.

6.4. Conclusions

In his anthropological analysis of public events, *Models and Mirrors*, Don Handelmann distinguished between events that seek to effect transformation (models), and those which present the lived-in world (mirrors).[137] The latter category offers up an ideal and didactic version of society, authored by those in charge:

> The elites, who here embody the state, hold up a highly polished mirror of great clarity to the nation, and the nation sees an incisive vision of itself stand forth ....Public events like this say, 'Look, this is how things should be, this is the proper, ideal pattern of social life'.[138]

---

[137] He also has a third category, those events which re-present the world through refraction: Handelman (1998), 22–62; for application to Greek festivals see Bouvrie (2011) and (2012).
[138] Handelman (1998), 44, commenting on Soviet ceremonies and quoting Skorupski (1976), 164 at end.

While Handelman's 'models' have transformation at the heart of them, events which 'mirror' or 'present the lived-in world' provide normative examples of proper conduct. Discussing the tercentenary celebrations of Yankee City in Massachusetts in the 1930s, which included a procession defining the city's history, Handelman draws a distinction between the debate and discussion which occurred during the preparatory stages of the event, and the event itself, in which this history is presented as the only possible history of the city:

> Displayed as 'fact' and truism, the thematic contents of the procession demonstrated a determinate sense of certainty and consistency.[139]

The reliefs at Hierapolis and Perge similarly present a normative mirror of what their festivals mean for their societies. The differences between them give an insight into the different possibilities, and both should be seen as the result of a conscious choice taken by the elites of their cities, as to what they wanted their festivals to mean.[140] At Perge the stress is on the involvement of the citizen body, embodied in the three different age categories, while at Hierapolis the imagery expands further to embrace the wider world. Part of this might reflect reality—that Hierapolis possessed an international festival elevated to Pythian status, while Perge, at this point, probably did not. Yet, it also seems likely that the different senses of self at Perge and Hierapolis may have been reflected here—Hierapolis keen to reach out to the wider world, Perge content to assert her civic identity and status within a more local area. Rivalries with neighbouring cities might also have played a part: Hierapolis with Laodikea, which also boasted two theatres; Perge with Side.[141] Motivations at individual and civic levels lay behind these programmes, and often they cannot be fully unpicked. Yet in both cases it is communal religious worship and festival celebrations which sit in pride of place at the centre of the decorative programme, offering messages which can be seen as further elaborated in the rest of the sculptural decoration and which must also have been brought to life through interaction with verbal elements, such as encomiastic orations or acclamations.[142]

A key theme to consider is whose vision of the city it is that we receive. At Hierapolis, the dedicatory inscription asserts that it is the city which has paid for

---

[139] Handelman (1998), 45.
[140] Handelman (1998), 44–5 also notes the dominance of elites within both the Soviet and American events he uses as examples. Other cities may also have used reliefs similarly, see esp. reliefs from the theatre at Miletos, which Spoerri Butcher also situates within a festive context (work in progress).
[141] Laodikeia: Şimşek and Sezgin (2012); Perge and Side: Nollé (1993), 310–13; Ng (2016), 242–5; Calomino in Newby and Calomino (2022), 48–52.
[142] An epigram in honour of the city is inscribed on the diazoma at Hierapolis: Ritti (1985), 114, no. 1 while acclamations honouring the city and particular individuals were later inscribed at Perge: I.Perge 338–42. See further Newby in Newby and Calomino (2022), 42–8.

the construction of the *scaenae frons*.¹⁴³ Yet what is the 'city' here, other than a group of elite citizens tasked with implementing and funding the council's decision?¹⁴⁴ The formulation of Hierapolis' civic identity, then, is itself an elite product, and we might pause to wonder to what extent the populace as a whole, gathered here to enjoy the spectacles of the festival, accepted or challenged this view of civic society.¹⁴⁵ They might have seen their role reflected instead in some of the more light-hearted scenes of revelry which appear within the Dionysiac procession at Perge, and in the reliefs positioned on the *analemmata* which close the sides of the upper cavea at Hierapolis. Festivity, eating, and drinking were a key attraction of festivals, and might have offered a respite from the toil of the everyday for non-elite citizens. The imagery can thus be seen as offering a role also for them, celebrating their enjoyment as a key part of the festival process. In reality, however, even this opportunity for excess was kept within limits by the whip-bearers charged with keeping discipline at public festivals.¹⁴⁶ While the visual imagery does not give space to these, inscriptional evidence attests to their presence, highlighting the fact that these representations of festival activities are very much an ideal, didactic view of the meanings of festivals. Through interaction with the ephemeral events which took place both within and outside the theatre, they acted to generate meaning and create a particular memory of their city's religious culture which helped both to form civic identity and to cement social roles and hierarchies.

Works Cited

Alanyalı, H. S. (2009) 'Dionysos', *LIMC Supplement 1*: 174–5.

Alanyalı, H. S. (2012) *Der Kentauromachie- und der Gigantomachiefries im Theater von Perge*. Vienna.

Aneziri, S. (2003) *Die Vereine der dionysischen Techniten im Kontext der hellenistischen Gesellschaft. Untersuchungen zur Geschichte, Organisation und Wirkung der hellenistischen Technitenvereine*. Stuttgart.

Attanasio, D. and Pensabene, P. (2002) 'I marmi del teatro di Hierapolis', in D. de Bernardi Ferrero (ed.), *Saggi in Onore di Paolo Verzone. Hierapolis Scavi e Ricerche IV*. Rome, 69–85.

Bejor. G. (1991) *Hierapolis. Scavi e Ricerche III. Le statue*. Rome.

---

[143] On the purple dyers' contribution, recorded in smaller letters, see Attanasio and Pensabene (2002), 69–85.
[144] D'Andria and Ritti (1985), 184–6 suggest that the sophist Antipater might have been involved.
[145] Cf. Woolf (2010), 194 on the difficulties of accessing the views of non-elites.
[146] Wörrle (1988), 10, ll. 63–4; 219–20; cf. *I.Perge* 47, 49, 193.

Belting, H. (2011) *An Anthropology of Images: Picture, Medium, Body*. Trans. T. Dunlap. Princeton and Oxford.

Blümel, W. and Malay, H. (1993) 'Inscriptions from Aydın Museum', *Epigraphica Anatolica* 21: 129–40.

Boatwright, M. T. (2000) *Hadrian and the Cities of the Roman Empire*. Princeton.

Bouvrie, S. des (2011) 'The Attic ritual theatre and the "socially unquestionable" in the tragic genre', in Chaniotis (2011), 139–78.

Bouvrie, S. des (2012) 'Greek festivals and the ritual process. An inquiry into the Olympia-cum-Heraia and the Great Dionysia', in Brandt and Iddeng (2012a), 53–93.

Brandt, J. R. and Iddeng, J. W. (eds) (2012a) *Greek and Roman Festivals: Content, Meaning, and Practice*. Oxford.

Brandt, J. R. and Iddeng, J. W. (2012b) 'Introduction. Some concepts of ancient festivals', in Brandt and Iddeng (2012a), 1–10.

Burrell, B. (2004) *Neokoroi. Greek Cities and Roman Emperors*. Leiden and Boston.

Calomino, D. (forthcoming) *Pride, Profit and Prestige. Civic Coinage and Greek Festival Culture in the Roman East*.

Caputo, G. (1959) *Il teatro romana di Sabratha e l'architettura teatrale Africana*. Rome.

Ceylan, A. and Ritti, T. (1997) 'A new dedication to Apollo Kareios', *Epigraphica Anatolica* 28: 57–67.

Chaniotis, A. (1995) 'Sich selbst feiern? Städtische Feste des Hellenismus im Spannungsfeld von Religion und Politik', in M. Wörrle and P. Zanker (eds), *Stadtbild und Bürgerbild im Hellenismus*. Munich, 147–63.

Chaniotis, A. (2007) 'Theatre rituals', in P. Wilson (ed.), *The Greek Theatre and Festivals. Documentary Studies*. Oxford, 48–66.

Chaniotis, A. (ed) (2011) *Ritual Dynamics in the Ancient Mediterranean. Agency, Emotion, Gender, Representation*. Habes 49. Stuttgart.

Chaniotis, A. (2013) 'Processions in Hellenistic cities. Contemporary discourses and ritual dynamics', in R. Alston, O. M. van Nijf, and C. G. Williamson (eds), *Cults, Creeds and Identities in the Greek City after the Classical Age*. Leuven, Paris, and Walpole, MA, 21–47.

Chuvin, P. (1987) 'Observations sur les reliefs du théatre de Hierapolis. Thèmes agonistiques et lègendes locales', *Revue Archéologique* 1987 1: 97–108.

Connolly, J. B. (2011) 'Ritual movement through Greek sacred space: towards an archaeology of performance', in Chaniotis (2011), 313–46.

Crowther, N. B. (1985) 'Male "beauty" contests in Greece: the Euandria and Euexia', *L'antiquité Classique* 54: 285–91.

Crowther, N. B. (1994) 'The role of heralds and trumpeters at Greek athletic festivals', *Nikephoros* 7: 135–55.

D'Andria, F. (2013) 'Il Ploutonion a Hierapolis di Frigia', *Istanbuler Mitteilungen* 63: 157–217.

D'Andria, F. (2017) 'Nature and cult in the Ploutonion of Hierapolis before and after the colony', in Şimşek, C. and D'Andria, F. (eds), *Landscape and History in the Lykos Valley. Laodikeia and Hierapolis in Phrygia*. Newcastle upon Tyne, 207–40.

D'Andria, F. and Ritti, T. (1985) *Hierapolis Scavi e Ricerche II. Le sculture del teatro. I rilievi con i cicli di Apollo e Artemide*. Rome.

Day, J., Hakola, R., Kahlos, M., and Tervahauta, U. (eds) (2016) *Spaces in Late Antiquity: Cultural, Theological and Archaeological Perspectives*. Abingdon and New York.

De Bernardi Ferrero, D. (1966–74) *Teatri classici in Asia Minore, I–IV*. Rome.

De Bernardi Ferrero, D., Ciotta, G., and Pensabene, P. (eds) (2007) *Il teatro di Hierapolis di Frigia. Restauro, architettura ed epigrafia*. Genova.

Di Napoli, V. (2002) 'Il fregio a tema agonistico del teatro di Hierapolis' *Annuario della Scuola archeologica di Atene* 80: 379–401.

Di Napoli, V. (2013) *Teatri della Grecia Romana: Forma, Decorazione, Funzioni. La Provincia d'Acaia (Meletemata 67)*. Paris.

Di Napoli, V. (2015) 'Figured reliefs from the theatres of Roman Asia Minor', *Logeion. A Journal of Ancient Theatre* 5: 260–93.

Dickenson, C. P. and van Nijf, O. (eds) (2013) *Public Space in the Post-classical City: Proceedings of a One Day Colloquium Held at Fransum, 23rd July 2007*. Leuven.

Dunbabin, K. M. D. (2010) 'The prize table: crowns, wreaths, and moneybags in Roman art', in Le Guen, B. (ed), *L'argent dan les concours du monde grec*. Paris, 301–45.

Dunbabin, K. M. D. (2016) *Theatre and Spectacle in the Art of the Roman Empire*. Ithaca and London.

Elsner, J. (2018) 'The embodied object: recensions of the dead on Roman sarcophagi', *Art History* 41.3: 546–65.

Erll, A. and Rigney, A. (eds) (2009) *Mediation, Remediation and the Dynamics of Cultural Memory*. Berlin and New York.

Fleischer, R. (1973) *Artemis von Ephesos und verwandte Kultstatuen aus Anatolien und Syren*. Leiden.

Gaebler, H. (1929) 'Die Losurne in der Agonistik', *Zeitschrift für Numismatik* 39: 271–312.

Gaifmann, M. (2006) 'Statue, cult and reproduction', *Art History* 29.2: 258–79.

Gaifmann, M. (2018) *The Art of Libation in Classical Athens*. New Haven and London.

Galli, M. (2016) 'Le statue di Demetra e Kore-Persephone nel teatro di Hierapolis', *Istanbuler Mitteilungen* 66: 161–224.

Galli, M. (2022) 'Sculpture in context: new research on the theatre at Hierapolis in Phrygia', *Asia Minor* 2: 67–92.

Gangloff, A. (ed.) (2013) *Lieux de mémoire en Orient grec à l'époque impériale*. Echo [Université de Lausanne. Institut d'archéologie et d'histoire ancienne] 9. Bern and Oxford.

Gebhard, E. R. (1996) 'The theatre and the city', in W. Slater (ed.), *Roman Theatre and Society*. Ann Arbor, 113–27.

Gell, A. (1998) *Art and Agency. An Anthropological Theory*. Oxford.

Gordon, R. (1990) 'The veil of power: emperors, sacrificers and benefactors', in M. Beard and J. North (eds), *Pagan Priests: Religion and Power in the Ancient World*. London, 201–34.

Graham, A. (2013) 'The word is not enough. A new methodology for assessing monumental inscriptions: a case study in Ephesos', *American Journal of Archaeology* 117: 388–412.

Gybas, M. (2018) *Das Theater in der Stadt und die Stadt im Theater: urbanistischer Kontext und Funktionen von Theatern im kaiserzeitlichen Kleinasien*. Hamburg.

Haensch, R. (ed.) (2009) *Selbstdarstellung und Kommunikation. Die Veröffentlichung staatlicher Urkunden auf Stein und Bronze in der römischen Welt*. Munich.

Handelman, D. (1998) *Models and Mirrors. Towards an Anthropology of Public Events*. 2nd edition. New York and Oxford.

Hecht, R. C. (1968) 'Some greek imperial coins in my collection', *Numismatic Chronicle* 8: 27–45.

Hoyland, R. (2007) 'A new edition and translation of the Leiden Polemon', in S. Swain (ed.), *Seeing the Face, Seeing the Soul. Polemon' Physiognomy from Classical Antiquity to Medieval Islam*. Oxford, 329–463.

İnan, J., Atik, N., Öztürk, A., Alanyalı, H. S., and Ateş, G. (2000) 'Vorbericht über die Untersuchungen an der Fassade des Theaters von Perge', *Archäologischer Anzeiger: Beoblatt zum Jahrbuch des deutschen archäologischen Instituts* 2000: 285–340.

Ismaelli, T. (2017) *Hierapolis di Frigia X. Il Tempio A nel Sanctuario di Apollo. Architettura, Decorazione e Contesto*. Istanbul.

Jones, C. P. (1976) 'The Plancii of Perge and Diana Planciana', *Harvard Studies in Classical Philology* 80: 231–7.

Jones, C. P. (1987) 'Sophron the comoedus', *Classical Quarterly* 37: 208–12.

Jones, C. P. (1999) 'Old and new in the inscriptions of Perge', *Epigraphica Anatolica* 31: 8–17.

Jones, C. P. (2007) 'Three new letters of the emperor Hadrian', *Zeitschrift für Papyrologie und Epigraphik* 161: 151–62.

Klose, D. O. A. (2005) 'Festivals and games in the cities of the East during the Roman empire', in C. Howgego, V. Heuchert, and A. Burnett (eds), *Coinage and Identity in the Roman Provinces*. Oxford, 125–33.

Kolb, F. (1974) 'Zur Geschichte der Stadt Hierapolis in Phrygien: Die Phyleninschriften im Theater', *Zeitschrift für Papyrologie und Epigraphik* 15: 255–70.

Kolb, F. (1990) 'Bemerkungen zu einer fragmentarisch erhaltenen Phyleninschrift im Theater von Hierapolis/Phrygien', *Zeitschrift für Papyrologie und Epigraphik* 81: 203–6.

Langner, M. (2001) *Antike Graffitizeichnungen: Motive, Gestaltung und Bedeutung*. Wiesbaden.

Latham, J. A. (2016) *Performance, Memory, and Processions in Ancient Rome. The Pompa Circensis from the Late Republic to Late Antiquity*. New York.

Le Guen, B. (2001) *Les Associations de Technites Dionysiaques à l'époque Hellénistique*. Nancy.

Leander Touati, A.-M. (2015) 'Monuments and images of the moving city', in Östenberg, Malmberg, and Bjørnebye (2015), 203–24.

Lefebvre, H. (1974) *La production de l'espace*. Paris.

Leschhorn, W. (1998) 'Die Verbreitung von Agonen in den östlichen Provinzen des römischen Reiches', *Stadion* 24.1: 31–57.

MacAloon, J. J. (ed.) (1984a) *Rite, Drama, Festival, Spectacle: Rehearsals towards a Theory of Cultural Performance*. Philadelphia.

MacAloon, J. J. (1984b) 'Introduction: cultural performances, culture theory', in MacAloon (1984a), 1–15.

MacKay, T. S. (1990) 'The major sanctuaries of Pamphylia and Cilicia', *Aufstieg und Niedergang der römischen Welt* II. 18, 3: 2045–129.

Martini, W. (2010), *Die Akropolis von Perge in Pamphylien vom Siedlungsplatz zur Akropolis*. Sitzungsberichte der Wissenschaftlichen Gesellschaft an der Johann Wolfgang Goethe-Universität Frankfurt am Main 48.1. Stuttgart.

Masino, F., Mighetto, P. and Sobrà, G. (eds) (2012) *Restoration and Management of Ancient Theatres in Turkey. Methods, Research, Results*. Galatina.

Mitchell, S. (1974) 'The Plancii in Asia Minor', *Journal of Roman Studies* 64: 27–39.

Mitchell, S. (1990) 'Festivals, games and civic life in Roman Asia Minor', *Journal of Roman Studies* 80: 183–93.

Moser, C. and Feldman, C. (eds) (2014) *Locating the Sacred. Theoretical Approaches to the Emplacement of Religion*. Oxford.

Newby, Z. (2003) 'Art and identity in Asia Minor', in S. Scott and J. Webster (eds), *Roman Imperialism and Provincial Art*. Cambridge, 192–213.

Newby, Z. (2005) *Greek Athletics in the Roman World. Victory and Virtue*. Oxford.

Newby, Z. (2017) 'Performing the past: Salamis, naval contests and the Athenian Ephebeia', in T. M. Dijkstra, I. N. I. Kuin, M. Moser, and D. Weidgennant (eds), *Strategies of Remembrance in Greece under Rome (100 BC–100 AD)*. Leiden, 83–95.

Newby, Z. (2019) 'The Grottarossa doll and her mistress: hope and consolation in a Roman tomb', in Z. Newby and R. E. Toulson (eds), *The Materiality of Mourning: Cross-Disciplinary Perspectives*. London and New York, 77–102.

Newby, Z. and Calomino, D. (2022) 'The materiality of Greek festivals in the Roman East. The view from Perge', *Asia Minor* 2: 41–54.

Ng, D. (2016) 'Making an artful case: public sculptural programmes as instruments of civic rivalry in imperial Perge and Pamphylia', *Istanbuler Mitteilungen* 66: 225–55.

van Nijf, O. (2013) 'Ceremonies, athletics and the city: some remarks on the social imaginary of the Greek city of the Hellenistic period', in E. Stavrianopoulou (ed.), *Shifting Social Imaginaries in the Hellenistic Period. Narrations, Practices, and Images*. Leiden and Boston, 311–38.

van Nijf, O. and Williamson, C. (2015) 'Re-inventing traditions. Connecting contests in the Hellenistic and Roman worlds', in D. Boschung, A. Busch, and M. J. Versluys (eds), *Reinventing 'The Invention of Tradition'? Indigenous Pasts and the Roman Present* Morphomata 32. Paderborn, 95–111.

Nollé, J. (1993) 'Die feindlichen Schwestern—Betrachtungen zur Rivalität der pamphylischen Städte', in G. Dobesch and G. Rehrenböck (eds), *Die epigraphische und altertumskundliche Erforschung Kleinasiens: hundert Jahre Kleinasiatische Kommission der Österreichischen Akademie der Wissenschaften*. Vienna, 297–317.

Onurkan, S. (1969–70) 'Artemis Pergaia', *Istanbuler Mitteilungen* 19–20: 289–98.

Osborne, R. and Tanner, J. (eds) (2007) *Art's Agency and Art History*. Malden, MA and Oxford.

Östenberg, I., Malmberg, S., and Bjørnebye, J. (eds) (2015) *The Moving City. Processions, Passages and Promenades in Ancient Rome*. London and New York.

Özren, A. Can (1996), 'Die Skulpturenausstattung kaiserzeitlicher Theater in der Provinz Asia, am Beispiel der Theater in Aphrodisias, Ephesos und Hierapolis', *Thetis* 3: 99–128.

Öztürk, A. (2009) *Die Architektur der scaenae frons des Theaters in Perge*. Berlin and New York.

Pace. B. (1923–4) 'Ricerche nella regione di Conia, Adalia e Scalanova', *Annuario della Scuola Archeologica di Atene* 617: 343–452.

von Papen, F. G. (1907) 'Die Spielen von Hierapolis', *Zeitschrift für Numismatik* 26: 161–82.

Parker, R. (2004) 'New "panhellenic" festivals in Hellenistic Greece', in R. Schlesier and U. Zellmann (eds), *Mobility and Travel in the Mediterranean from Antiquity to the Middle Ages*. Münster, 9–22.

Pellino, G. (2005) 'Considerazioni sull'assetto decorativo di alcuni teatri d'età imperiale in Asia Minore', *Orizzonti* 6: 49–78.

Pennacchietti, F. A. (1966–7) 'Nuove iscrizioni di Hierapolis Frigia', *Atti della Accademia delle scienze di Torino* II. 101: 287–322.

Perrin-Saminadayar, E. (2004) 'L'éphébie attique de la crise mithridatique à Hadrien: miroir de la société athénienne?' in S. Follet (ed.), *L'Hellénisme d'époque romaine. Nouveaus documents, nouvelles approches (Ier s. a.C—IIIe. s. p. C.)*. Paris, 87–103.

Petrovic, A., Petrovic, I., and Thomas, E. (eds) (2019). *The Materiality of Text—Placement, Perception, and Presence of Inscribed Tests in Classical Antiquity*. Leiden.

Petzl, G. and Schwertheim, E. (2006) *Hadrian und die dionysischen Künstler. Drei in Alexandria Troas neugefundene Briefe des Kaisers und die Künstler Vereinigung*. Bonn.

Platt, V. (2011) *Facing the Gods: Epiphany and Representation in Graeco-Roman Art, Literature and Religion*. Cambridge.

Popkin, M. (2016) *The Architecture of the Roman Triumph: Monuments, Memory, and Identity*. Cambridge.

Price, S. R. F. (1984) *Rituals and Power. The Roman Imperial Cult in Asia Minor*. Cambridge and New York.

Riccardi, L. A. (2007) 'The bust-crown, the Panhellenion, and Eleusis: a new portrait from the Athenian Agora', *Hesperia* 76.2: 365–90.

Rigsby, K. J. (1996) *Asylia. Territorial Inviolability in the Hellenistic World*. Berkeley, Los Angeles, and London.

Ritti, T. (1985) *Hierapolis Scavi e Richerche I. Fonti letterarie ed Epigrafiche*. Archaeologica 53. Rome.

Ritti, T. (2003) 'La neocoria di Hierapolis di Frigia', in *Epigraphica. Atti delle giornate di studio di Roma e di Atene in memoria di Margherita Guarducci (1902–1999)*. Opuscula epigraphica 10. Rome, 177–213.

Ritti, T. (2007) 'Iscrizioni pertinenti all'edificio teatrale di Hierapolis', in De Bernardi Ferrero, Ciotta, and Pensabene (2007), 389–439.

Ritti, T. (2008) 'La carriera di un cittadino di Hierapolis di Frigia: G. Memmios Eutychos', *Cahiers du Centre Gustave-Glotz* 19: 279–308.

Ritti, T. (2017). *Storia e istituzioni di Hierapolis*. Hierapolis di Frigia IX. Istanbul.

Ritti, T., Şimşek, C., and Yıldız, H. (2000) 'Dediche e καταγραφαί dal santuario frigio di Apollo Lairbenos', *Epigraphica Anatolica* 32: 1–88.

Robert, L. (1948) 'Deux textes inutilisés sur Perge et sur Side', *Hellenica* 5: 64–76.

Robert, L. (1982) 'Une vision de Perpétue martyre à Carthage en 203', *Comptes Rendus de l'Académie des Inscriptions e Belles Lettres* 126.2: 228–76.

Robert, L. (1984) 'Discours d'ouverture', in *Actes du VIIIe congrès international d'épigrafie grecque et latine à Athènes, 1982*. Athens, 35–45.

Rogers, G. M. (1991) *The Sacred Identity of Ephesos. Foundation Myths of a Roman City*. London and New York.

Roueché, C. (1981) 'Rome, Asia and Aphrodisias in the Third Century', *Journal of Roman Studies* 71: 103–20.

Rumscheid, J. (2000) *Kranz und Krone: zu Insignien, Siegespreisen und Ehrenzeichen der römischen Kaiserzeit*. Istanbuler Forschungen 43. Tübingen.

Rutherford, I. (2013). *State Pilgrims and Sacred Observers in Ancient Greece: A Study of Theoria and Theoroi*. Cambridge.

Ryberg, I. Scott (1955) *Rites of the State Religion in Roman Art*. Memorius of the American Academy in Rome 22. Rome.

Şahin, S. (1996) 'Studien zu den Inschriften von Perge III: Marcus Plancius Rutilius Varus und C. Iulius Plancius Varus Cornutus, Vater und Sohn der Plancia Magna', *Epigraphica Anatolica* 27: 115–26.

Şahin. S. (ed.) (1999) *Die Inschriften von Perge Teil I*. Inschriften griechischer Städte aus Kleinasien Band 54. Bonn.

Şahin, S. (ed.) (2004) *Die Inschriften von Perge Teil II*. Inschriften griechischer Städte aus Kleinasien Band 61. Bonn.

Scardozzi, G. (2012) 'New data on the North theatre in Hierapolis in Phrygia. Archaeological, topographical and geophysical surveys', in Masino, Mighetto, and Sobrà (2012), 218–35.

Scott, M. (2014) *Space and Society in the Greek and Roman Worlds*. Cambridge.

Shepherd, S. (2016) *The Cambridge Introduction to Performance Theory*. Cambridge.

Sherk, R. K. (1988) *The Roman Empire: Augustus to Hadrian*. New York.

Şimşek, C. and Sezgin, M. A. (2012) 'The west and north theatres in Laodicea', in Masino, Mighetto, and Sobrà (2012), 103–28.

Singer, M. (1972) *When a Great Tradition Modernizes: An Anthropological Approach to Indian Civilization*. London.

Skorupski, J. (1976) *Symbol and Theory. A Philosophical Study of Theories of Religion in Social Anthropology*. Cambridge and New York.

Slater, W. (2008) 'Hadrian's letters to the athletes and Dionysiac artists concerning arrangements for the "circuit" of games', *Journal of Roman Archaeology* 21: 610–20.

Slater, W. (2013) 'The victor's return and the categories of games', in P. Martzavou and N. Papazarkadas (eds), *Epigraphical Approaches to the Post-classical Polis, Fourth Century BC to Second Century AD*. Oxford, 139–63.

Smith, R. R. R. (1998) 'Cultural choice and political identity in honorific portrait statues in the Greek East in the second century AD', *Journal of Roman Studies* 88: 56–93.

Sobrà, G. (2012) 'The analysis of the fragments from the scaenae frons of the theatre at Hierapolis', in Masino, Mighetto, and Sobrà (2012), 183–204.

Sobrà, G. and Masino, F. (2010) 'La frontescena severiana del Teatro di Hierapolis di Frigia. Architettura decorazione e maestranze', in S. F. Ramallo Asensio and N. Röring (eds), *La scaenae frons en la arquitectura teatral romana*. Cartagena, 373–412.

Soja, E. W. (2009) 'Taking space personally', in Warf and Arias (2009), 11–35.

Squire, M. (2018) 'Embodying the dead on classical Attic grave-stelai', *Art History* 41.3: 518–45.

Strasser, J.-Y. (2010) '"Qu'on fouette les concurrents…".: à propos des lettres d'Hadrien retrouvées à Alexandrie de Troade', *Revue des Études Grecques* 123.2: 582–622.

Sturgeon, M. (1977) *Sculpture: The Reliefs from the Theater*. Corinth 9.2. Princeton.

Turner, V. (1975) *Dramas, Fields and Metaphors. Symbolic Action in Human Society*. Ithaca and London.

Turner, V. (1984) 'Liminality and the performative genres', in J. J. MacAloon (ed.), *Rite, Drama, Festival, Spectacle: Rehearsals towards a Theory of Cultural Performance*. Philadelphia, 19–41.

Turner, V. W. and Turner, E. L. B. (1982). 'Religious celebrations', in V. W. Turner (ed.), *Celebration. Studies in Festivity and Ritual*. Washington, DC, 201–19.

Warf, B. and Arias, S. (eds) (2009) *The Spatial Turn. Interdisciplinary Perspectives*. London and New York.

Weiss, P. (1991) 'Auxe Perge. Beobachtungen zu einem bemerkenswerten städtischen Dokument', *Chiron* 21: 353–92.

Wiemer, H.-U. (2011) 'Von der Bürgerschule zum aristokratischen Klub? Die athenische Ephebie in der römischen Kaiserzeit', *Chiron* 41: 487–537.

Woolf, G. (2010) 'Afterword: the local and the global in the Graeco-Roman East', in T. Whitmarsh (ed.), *Local Knowledge and Microidentities in the Imperial Greek World*. Cambridge, 189–200.

Wörrle, M. (1988) *Stadt und Fest im kaiserzeitlichen Kleinasien: Studien zu einer agonistischen Stiftung aus Oinoanda*. Munich.

Zuiderhoek, A. (2009) *The Politics of Munificence in the Roman Empire*. Cambridge.

7
An Epigraphic Stage

Inscriptions and the Moulding of
Festival Space at Aphrodisias

Naomi Carless Unwin

7.1. Introduction

Inscriptions were not viewed in isolation but were components of larger 'epigraphic landscapes.'[1] Individuals walking around ancient urban centres would be confronted with an accumulation of texts, both formal and informal; how they interacted with these texts was dependent on the material and spatial contexts in which they were displayed. The study of epigraphy has witnessed a 'material turn' in the last decades, as scholars seek to consider the practice of inscribing as a social and cultural phenomenon. The materiality of inscriptions should thus be considered central to how they were 'read', both in terms of interaction with the contents of the text, and in terms of how texts-as-monuments were interpreted.[2] The 'epigraphic habit' of the ancient world, the practice of inscribing in stone (among other media), flourished during the Roman imperial period and encompassed a wide variety of genres.[3] Studying the cultural and spatial contexts in which inscriptions were erected can reveal something about the mentality driving this habit, which awarded the epigraphic medium a social significance as a mode of communication.

This chapter seeks to advance a material approach by considering the aggregative force of epigraphic output within a defined urban context: that of the Roman-era theatre in the Karian city of Aphrodisias between the first century BC and the

---

[1] See the discussion of Bolle, Machado, and Witschel (2017b), 16–18. The research for this paper was conducted as part of the Leverhulme Trust Research Project Grant, 'Materiality and meaning in Greek festival culture of the Roman imperial period', based at the University of Warwick. I would like to extend my thanks to Zahra Newby, Alison Cooley, and the anonymous reviewers for offering useful comments on an earlier draft. I must also express my gratitude to Charlotte Roueché and the New York University Excavations at Aphrodisias for permission to reproduce their images.

[2] For example, see Cooley (2012); Berti et al. (2017); Petrovic, Petrovic, and Thomas (2019); Angliker and Bultrighini (2023).

[3] The phrase the 'epigraphic habit' was famously coined in MacMullen (1982). It has come to be widely adopted; see Beltrán Lloris (2014).

Fig. 7.1 Aerial view of theatre.
Photograph: New York University Excavations at Aphrodisias.

early fourth century AD (Fig. 7.1).[4] It is hoped that by reconstructing the epigraphic landscape of this structure in its entirety, we can interrogate the factors affecting the decision to engrave texts; how epigraphic activity was meant to interact with its civic setting, the extent to which it was generated in response to the display of other texts, and how inscriptions could be employed to reinforce a sense of (civic) tradition.

The practice of inscribing texts was not neutral; there was a consciousness to the public engraving of texts and the process could be utilized to curate a particular civic, communal, or familial image. A close study of the epigraphic landscape of the theatre at Aphrodisias has the potential to illuminate the dynamics of this process and different aspects of communal engagement with the environment, and how this developed over time. Aphrodisias is somewhat exceptional in this regard, due to the quality and quantity of the inscriptions, statuary, and architecture that have survived; however, it also offers the opportunity to separate the layers of intervention in the theatre across centuries, and consider how different texts could speak to different concerns and respond to each other within a single space. The volume and context of material from Aphrodisias may be unusual, but

---

[4] The theatre and its inscriptions have been well published; see de Chaisemartin and Theodorescu (1991); Theodorescu (1996); de Chaisemartin (2011) and (2012); Erim and Smith (1991); for the inscriptions, see Reynolds (1982) and (1991); Roueché (1991) and (1993). The inscriptions of Aphrodisias have also been published online, see *I.Aphrodisias 2007*.

observations about how such texts functioned in civic space, and how they were interacted with, are of wider relevance to our understanding of the epigraphic habit in the Graeco-Roman world.

In the Graeco-Roman *polis*, the theatre was a prominent meeting place, a venue for inhabitants (and visitors) to gather to be entertained during festivals and participate in rituals or civic assemblies.[5] As a focal point of communal expression, it offers a useful test case for exploring how inscriptions could be used in public places to help project an image of the city, or mould and respond to the experience of the space.[6] It is worth bearing in mind that an inscription's lifespan could exist long beyond the original circumstances of its display.[7] It could remain *in situ* for decades, or in some cases centuries, after its carving. The intention is to explore how different types of inscriptions served to project a particular civic image and shape reactions to the space, creating in effect an epigraphic stage where notable individuals were commemorated, euergetic behaviour was modelled, and the history and prestige of the city was celebrated. It will also consider the audience responses to this quintessential civic stage, exploring the 'informal' epigraphy found in this space, including the graffiti of the crowd and texts restricted to the performers' realm backstage. The moulding of festival space at Aphrodisias will be contextualized within the festival culture of the city, with parallels drawn with other cities in Asia Minor during the imperial period.

The history of the theatre, as with so much of the urban centre of Aphrodisias, can be traced to the second half of the first century BC, with the addition of different architectural features over the subsequent centuries.[8] A number of agonistic festivals are attested in the city during this period, from the Sebasta in the first century AD[9] to those named after local benefactors.[10] In the third century AD, contests remained prominent in the cultural life of the city, and evidence is found

---

[5] See Di Napoli (2017) on the symbolic and political significance of the theatre within the Graeco-Roman city.

[6] See the contribution of Newby, this volume, Chapter 6, which similarly explores the construction of civic imagery in the theatrical space of Hierapolis, both through sculpture and text.

[7] Cooley (2000).   [8] Ratté (2000).

[9] *I.Aphrodisias 2007*, 11.5 (= *I.Aphrodisias Performers* 48). The text is an honorific inscription for an individual (Papulos?) who had served as *agonothetes* of τῶν Σεβαστῶν ἀγῶνες; cf. Ebert (1994), 298, who suggests they were the contests of the Sebasta, rather than 'contests of the Augusti', as translated by Roueché (1993), 162. For an overview of the agonistic festivals of Aphrodisias, see Roueché (1993), appendix 1; Ebert (1994).

[10] The Lysimachea, for instance, was named after M. Flavius Antonius Lysimachos: *I.Aphrodisias 2007*, 12.538 (= *I.Aphrodisias Performers* 54). A letter from the curator M. Ulpius Appuleius Eurykles in the AD 180s discusses issues with funding for this contest (*I.Aphrodisias 2007*, 12.538 = *I.Aphrodisias Performers* 50); the endowment had reached 120,000 denarii so it was possible to hold the musical contest every four years, as Lysimachos had wished. A number of other such contests are named in a second letter from Eurykles (*I.Aphrodisias 2007*, 15.330 = *I.Aphrodisias Performers* 51), including those of Kallikrates, son of Dioteimos, Claudius Adrastos, Hossidios Ioulianos, and those of Philemon son of Philemon. On Hos(s)idios Ioulianos, see below.

for the Attalea Gordianea Kapetolia and the Valeriana Pythia.[11] Although beyond the scope of this paper, a different form of popular entertainment emerged from the fifth century AD, as demonstrated by the multiple graffiti for the different circus factions (the 'Greens' and the 'Blues') found in the theatre.[12] While chariot races, the primary spectacles associated with the factions, would have taken place elsewhere, the activities of the Greens and the Blues as supporters' groups were more extensive and the theatre remained an important meeting/performance space in the Christian city.[13]

The early fourth century AD has been chosen as the point at which to end the survey; this allows us to consider the cumulative impact of epigraphic monuments in the landscape, taken from the period at which the civic (and epigraphic) culture of the imperial age was experiencing a shift. A number of cities in Anatolia experienced a decline in the second half of the third century; Aphrodisias was in part resilient to this wider pattern. This can be connected with its continued regional significance as a provincial capital, first of the joint province of Karia and Phrygia from the mid-third to early fourth century AD, and subsequently of Karia alone.[14] Building and restoration activity continued at a healthy level in the city into the sixth century AD, and C. Roueché has ably documented the continued vitality of the city's epigraphic output.[15] However, a shift can be detected in the epigraphic landscape, with the development of different modes of commemoration and a reduced role awarded to festivals. Evidence for agonistic contests disappears in the second half of the fourth century AD; though, as S. Remijsen observes, this does not necessarily mean that athletic and other contests did not continue, only that their place in the public record diminishes.[16] In late antiquity, the theatre continued to serve as a stage for performances and spectacles, including mimes and pantomimes.[17] The epigraphic landscape of this civic venue in the fourth century AD thus offers a glimpse of the communal life of Aphrodisias as accumulated over three centuries and at the cusp of a shift away from the agonistic culture that typified civic society in the imperial period.[18]

---

[11] Attalea Gordianea Kapetolia: *I.Aphrodisias 2007*, 12.36; 15.281(= *I.Aphrodisias Performers* 56–7). Valeriana Pythia: attested on coins: ΟΥΑΛΕΡΙΑΝΑ (e.g. *SNG von Aulock* 8066); ΠΥΘΙΑ (e.g. *SNG von Aulock* 2470). Roueché (1993), 182, suggests they refer to the same contest, the Pythia, which, at least under Valerian, was also named the Valeriana.
[12] See Roueché (1993), 44–7, 55–60.
[13] Roueché (1993), 143–56, suggests that they took over from the earlier synods.
[14] Roueché (1981), 117–18. Cf. Dmitriev (2001).
[15] Roueché (1989) and (2007). On the theatre: Roueché (1991). See also the online resource: *I.Aphrodisias Late Ant.*² https://insaph.kcl.ac.uk/ala2004, last accessed 12 September 2022.
[16] Remijsen (2015), 81–4. In the mid-fourth century, agonistic monuments began to be reused in the city walls. The office of *agonothetes* still existed in the fifth century: Remijsen (2015), 83.
[17] See the detailed study of Roueché (1993), esp. 15–28. Cf. Pont (2014) on the late antique theatre more broadly.
[18] The rise in the number of festivals during this period was famously referred to as the 'explosion agonistique' by Robert (1984), 38.

7.2. Modelling benefaction

Theatres were constructed, renovated, or monumentalized in cities across Anatolia during the imperial period. Aphrodisias was no exception; between the first phase of construction in the late first century BC and the end of our survey in the fourth century AD, various restorations and adaptations can be traced (Fig. 7.2). The origins of the theatre are in the Augustan age, c.28 BC, when Gaius Iulius Zoilos, the Aphrodisian freedman of Octavian, contributed funds for the *logeion* and *proskenion*: this apparently referred to the Doric portico and platform that extended from the *scaenae frons*.[19] The benefaction itself was commemorated with two identical inscriptions that record the dedication of the structure to Aphrodite and the *demos*:

Γάϊος Ἰούλιος Ζωΐ|λος θεοῦ Ἰουλίου υἱ[ὶ]|οῦ Καίσαρος ἀπελε|ύθερος στεφανοφο|ρήσας τὸ δέκατον ἑξῆς | τὸ λογῆιον καὶ τὸ προ|σκήνιον σὺν τοῖς ἐν αὐ|τῶι προσκοσμήμασιν | πᾶσιν Ἀφρ[οδίτῃ] καὶ τῶι Δήμωι.[20]

Gaius Iulius Zoilos, freedman of the divine Iulius' son Caesar, after being *stephanephoros* for the tenth time in succession (gave) the stage and the proscenium with all the applied ornaments on it to Aphrodite and the Demos.

The first inscription (quoted above) was engraved on the architrave of the Doric half-columns that ran in front of the lower porch of the stage building (Fig. 7.3); the frieze above was carved on the same marble blocks as the architrave, which numbered ten in total.[21] The second inscription was originally displayed on the architectural moulding underneath the Ionic columns that constituted the second storey, divided between groups of two or four columns;[22] it was thus set above and behind the first, at the rear of the narrow platform that was originally supported by the Doric colonnade.[23]

The decision to inscribe the same text twice, in such close proximity, is unusual.[24] One explanation could have been to make the text visible to all quarters of the theatre; both texts were carefully inscribed, though it should be noted that the letters on the lower storey were slightly larger (0.11 m) than those above

---

[19] See the discussion of Reynolds (1991), 15–16; de Chaisemartin and Theodorescu (1991), 32–3. Cf. Sear (2006), 328–9.
[20] *I.Aphrodisias 2007*, 8.1.i (= *I.Aphrodisias and Rome* 36a).
[21] This inscription has now been restored *in situ*.
[22] *I.Aphrodisias 2007*, 8.5 (= *I.Aphrodisias and Rome* 36b): Γάϊος Ἰο[ύλιο]ς Ζωΐλος [θε]οῦ Ἰουλίου υἱ[ο]|ῦ Καίσαρος ἀ[πελεύθερο]ς στεφανοφορήσας τὸ | δέκατον ἑξῆς v. [τὸ] λογ[ῆι]ον καὶ τ|ὸ προσκήν[ι]ον σὺν τοῖς | ἐν αὐ[τῶι π]ροσκοσμή|μασιν πᾶσιν, v. Ἀφροδίτ]ηι καὶ τ[ῶι Δήμωι]. See the comments of Theodorescu (1996), 131, on the role of the inscription in reconstructing the second storey, with symmetrical groups of two and four columns.
[23] On the locations of both, see Reynolds (1991), 15–16. It is possible that this platform was originally used in performances; however, the subsequent display of statues in this area suggest that it was later used solely for such displays; Reynolds (1991), 18–19. See below.
[24] On epigraphic duplication at Aphrodisias, see Graham (2019).

Fig. 7.2 View of the theatre, facing east/south east.
Photograph: New York University Excavations at Aphrodisias (N. Carless Unwin).

Fig. 7.3 View of stage front, with Doric entablature and the dedication of Zoilos.
Photograph: New York University Excavations at Aphrodisias (N. Carless Unwin).

(0.07–0.075 m). Another interpretation could relate to the nature of the dedication itself: the two inscriptions could be meant to reinforce the duality of Zoilos' benefaction, which consisted of the stage and the *proscenium*. His gift also extended to the ornaments on the *proskenion*, apparently the sculptural decoration on the stage building, which was maintained in the centuries after its construction until the fourth century AD.[25]

A number of free-standing sculptures were discovered during the excavation of the theatre, many of which were originally displayed on the stage building. Some of these may have been part of the original decorative scheme; others were added in the subsequent centuries.[26] These include a group of Apollo and Muses (carrying theatrical masks), located in the central niche of the third storey; a number of figures of Nike also framed the stage building, which may have alluded to the recent victory of Octavian at Actium.[27] A base recording the dedication of a statue of the *demos* was discovered in the vicinity, and likely stood on the stage building, perhaps in one of the niches.[28] It was set up for Aphrodite, the *theoi Sebastoi*, and the People by Nikomachos, son of Menodotos the son of Menandros, and Menodotos son of Nikomachos the son of Menodotos, 'as they promised to contribute'.[29] Certainly, a personification of the people was an appropriate benefaction from civic-minded citizens; a marble bust statue of Aphrodite, with her familiar mural crown, was also dedicated by a certain Theodotos.[30]

On discovery, the base of *demos* was paired with a statue of a young man uncovered nearby, though it has since been ascertained that they do not belong together. This figure wears a himation and a crown, made of bands with the remains of two draped busts; the statue has been dated to the late first/early second century AD.[31] The figure likely represents a priest or another office holder, such as the *agonothetes*.[32]

---

[25] See Theodorescu (1996); de Chaisemartin (2011). The carved Ionic frieze consists of a number of motifs that were in circulation in the Augustan age, including bulls' heads, tritons, acanthus leaves, and pateras; the Corinthian frieze above depicted Egyptianizing themes (de Chaisemartin (2011), 81–6).

[26] For a full survey, see Erim and Smith (1991); de Chaisemartin (2011).

[27] As proposed by Erim and Smith (1991), 67; de Chaisemartin (2011), 87–9, offers a broader perspective on the significance of such motifs, which could also be interpreted to mark the advent of Augustus' reign.

[28] Erim and Smith (1991), 80–1. Cf. Di Napoli (2017), 416–21.

[29] *I.Aphrodisias 2007*, 8.52: Ἀφροδίτῃ θεοῖς Σεβαστοῖς | τῷ Δήμῳ τὸ ἄγαλμα τοῦ Δή|μου Νικόμαχος Μηνοδότου | τοῦ Μενάνδρου καὶ Μηνόδο|τος Νικομάχου τοῦ Μηνοδό|του καθὼς ἐπηνγίλαντο.

[30] *I.Aphrodisias 2007*, 8.228: Θεόδωρος | ἀνέθηκεν.   [31] Smith (2006), no. 50.

[32] Smith (2006), no. 51, was also discovered in the theatre, and again depicts a figure wearing a bust-crown; cf. no. 48, the statue of Domeiteinos from the Bouleuterion (third century AD), where he is shown wearing a high bust crown with ten busts. The association between the bust-crown and the *agonothetes* is attested in the foundation document for the Demostheneia at Oinoanda; it is specified that the *agonothetes* was to wear a crown with relief portraits of Hadrian and the ancestral god Apollo: Wörrle (1988), ll. 54–7. At Hierapolis, the *porta regia* frieze on the theatre depicts agonistic themes, including a figure identified as the *agonothetes*; he also wears a crown with four busts; see Ritti (2006),

Another statue base was discovered in the theatre, which records the honours voted to Gaius Iulius Zoilos by the demos.[33] Zoilos was the first and most prominent builder in the theatre, responsible for part or all of the stage building in the earliest phase of construction, and thus it is natural that he would be honoured with a statue in this space. The theatre became a prominent venue for displaying euergetism through highly visible donations that also had the advantage of prominently bearing the name of the donor.[34] In return, such benefactors appear to have been rewarded with honorific statues. The theatre had natural advantages as the location for such actions, and the accretion of epigraphic activity on and around the stage building reveals it as a magnet for individuals wishing to distinguish themselves.

There are no traces of what constituted the cavea in the late first century BC, and it is possible that it was constructed in wood. The next substantial building phase followed in the mid-first century AD, driven by the beneficence of a certain Aristokles Molossos, son of Artemidoros. A number of inscriptions from the theatre attest to his donations (see Table 7.1 below); the works listed include three (?) entrances, buttresses, roofing, stairways, and vaults; also seating and paving, likely in the orchestra.[35] In sum, the building work of Aristokles Molossos appears to consist of the majority of the cavea and surrounding passageways/entrances. The texts are not identical, though in many cases duplicate information. Three were inscribed on marble panels (see Fig. 7.4), while a fourth was engraved on moulded blocks, likely forming part of an architectural structure. Their original locations may have been in proximity to the works described, or perhaps the panels were distributed at different entrance points, where they were visible to the highest density of foot traffic.

Aristokles Molossos himself belonged to a prominent local family, and his benefactions were a family affair: two of the preserved inscriptions mention that the dedications were made by Molossos and his brother, Kaikos Papias.[36] Molossos appears to have died before the completion of his project, and three of the texts mention that the work was subsequently supervised by his foster-son Hermas, in accordance with his will;[37] Hermas is also said to have promised the third bank of seats (?) from the income of Molossos' estate.[38] It should be noted that there was a potential 'gap' between promises of benefactions and their fulfilment,

---

105; Newby (this volume, Chapter 6). On the iconography of the bust-crown more generally, see Rumscheid (2000); Riccardi (2007).

[33] Smith (2006) 103, no. 1 tentatively suggests that the statue head of an old man found in the theatre could be identified as Zoilos.

[34] See Di Napoli (2017) for other examples from Roman Greece of theatres being used for the display of honorific statues.

[35] See Reynolds (1991), 16–18 for discussion of terminology.

[36] *I.Aphrodisias 2007*, 8.108, 8.113.

[37] *I.Aphrodisias 2007*, 8.108 (= Reynolds (1991), A2); 8.112 (= Reynolds (1991), A4); 8.113 (= Reynolds (1991), A5).

[38] *I.Aphrodisias 2007*, 8.108 (= Reynolds (1991), A2), ll. 8–14; 8.113 (= Reynolds (1991), A5), ll. 2–3.

Fig. 7.4 Molossos dedication panel.
Photograph: C. Roueché.

and there is no later inscription recording Hermas' building work.[39] But the stature of the family is paramount in the records of their benefactions.[40] In an inscription to accompany a statue of the son of Aristokles, also named Aristokles Molossos, set up by his mother Ammia, he is described as a member 'of the foremost family and one which had shared in the foundation of his city'.[41] A permanent memorial to Molossos' generosity appears to have been established in the theatre to commemorate the family's generosity: a fallen lintel block records the name of a *Molosseon*.[42] The excavators have restored its original location over the door leading into a chamber in the north buttressing structure, entered from the north *parodos*; the function of the room is not known, though it may have housed a statue or shrine of Molossos.[43]

---

[39] See comments of Ng (2015), 106.   [40] See Pont (2008).
[41] *I.Aphrodisias 2007*, 12.706, ll. 7–9: γενόμενον γέ|νους τοῦ πρώτου καὶ συν|εκτικότος τὴν πατρίδα. The statue was set up after his death, which appears to indicate that he died young. The base was reused; its original location is unknown.
[42] *I.Aphrodisias 2007*, 8.14 (= Reynolds (1991), A3): v. Μολοσσῆον v.
[43] In this context, an honorary decree for Aristokles Molossos, referencing his service and liturgies to Aphrodisias, can be mentioned: *I.Aphrodisias 2007*, 12.803. It was discovered re-used in the walls of the city, though its original location remains unknown. The text was inscribed in columns on three or four blocks, suggesting a fairly large structure. A parallel for a shrine to a benefactor can be identified in the heroön to Diodoros Pasparos at Pergamon (first century BC); see below.

In a similar manner to Zoilos, Aristokles Molossos dedicated his donations to Aphrodite, the *theoi Sebastoi* and the people.⁴⁴ Molossos' gifts in the Julio-Claudian period were set alongside and in communication with those of Zoilos, separated by approximately three generations. For Molossos and his family, the theatre was the prime location to demonstrate their devotion to their native city, both due to its prominence in civic ritual and assembly, and because of the standing of the other great civic benefactor, Zoilos. They were awarded with the public and repeated recognition of this generosity, with texts displayed in locations around the theatre; following the pattern of Zoilos and the stage building, we can assume that the texts were positioned in relation to the structures mentioned.⁴⁵ Again in accordance with Zoilos' example, it is possible that the inscriptions also interacted with statues of the benefactors.

Over the subsequent centuries, the theatre continued to attract the attention of civic benefactors, as they sought to augment or restore the architectural space; the works that securely relate to the theatre are summarized in Table 7.1. In the mid-second century AD, Tiberius Claudius Zelos is said to have provided funds for the columns and entablature; also, the veneer for the walls and floor.⁴⁶ This inscription was inscribed along the front of the stage, mirroring the position of the two Zoilos dedications above, with letters of similar proportions (0.07 m). It appears to have been purposefully preserved after the renovations to the theatre, including the extension of the stage and lowering of the orchestra, in the Antonine period.⁴⁷ Again, the family of Zelos was prominent in Aphrodisias, and it is possible that he was related to Zoilos through marriage, which would make the choice of the theatre as the venue for his benefaction particularly appropriate.⁴⁸ Zelos fulfilled a number of civic offices, including as *archiereus* (chief priest) and as priest for life of Aphrodite, which were mentioned in his dedication; a number of his other offices were listed in the honorary decree that was also inscribed in the theatre, on the stage building itself, apparently in recognition of his gift (see below).⁴⁹

A certain Grypos, son of Artemidoros, was also responsible for repairs to two statues in the theatre in the second century AD, as recorded in an inscription on the *proskenion* frieze, above the dedication of Zoilos.⁵⁰ The letter heights were

---

⁴⁴ *I.Aphrodisias 2007*, 8.112, ll. 1–2; 8.113, l.1. The exception is *I.Aphrodisias 2007*, 8.108, which is only dedicated to Aphrodite and the *theoi Sebastoi*.
⁴⁵ Another fragmentary text may record the dedication of a building or a statue (of Nemesis?) by a member of the family: *I.Aphrodisias 2007*, 8.82 (= Reynolds (1991), A6): Νεμέ[σει] θεᾷ ἐπ[ηκόῳ ?ὁ ?δεῖνα ·· ? ·· Ἀρτεμιδ]ώρου Μολοσσοῦ [·· ? ··]. It was inscribed on an architrave fragment, with a relief of a theatrical mask.
⁴⁶ *I.Aphrodisias 2007*, 8.85.i (= Reynolds (1991), B1).
⁴⁷ Reynolds (1991), 19. On the alterations, see below.
⁴⁸ Reynolds (1991), 26.   ⁴⁹ *I.Aphrodisias 2007*, 8.84.
⁵⁰ *I.Aphrodisias 2007*, 8.86. Additional work in the theatre in the second century AD is attested in a text honouring M. Ulpius Carminius Klaudianos, which mentions his gift of seating: *I.Aphrodisias 2007*, 1111, ll. 19–20. No inscriptions commemorating this benefaction are known from the theatre itself; see Reynolds (1991), 20.

Table 7.1 Details of the benefactions epigraphically attested in the theatre.

Name of Benefactor	Date	Details of Benefaction	Reference	Location of Text
Gaius Iulius Zoilos	c.28 BC	Stage	IAph2007 8.1.i	Proskenion architrave
		Proskēnion	IAph2007 8.5	Stage building
Aristokles Molossos	1st c. AD	Entrances	IAph2007 8.108	Marble panel
		Buttresses	IAph2007 8.111	Marble panel
		Stairways	IAph2007 8.112	Marble panel
		Vaults	IAph1007 8.113	Unknown building
		Seats		
		Paving		
		Roofing		
		Akroteria		
Ti. Claudius Zelos	139–61 AD	Columns and entablature	IAph2007 8.85.i	Stage front—cornice
		Panelling of the walls and the floor		
[Gr]ypos son of Artemidoros	167–8 AD	Two statues	IAph2007 8.86	Proskenion frieze
M. Aurelius Menestheus Skopas	3rd c. AD	Veneer of the orchestra	IAph2007 8.115	Orchestra—surrounding wall
Androkles(?)	4th c. AD	Unknown benefaction	IAph2007 8.85.ii	Stage front—cornice

smaller than those of the earlier dedications (0.04 m), but would have been legible, particularly if painted. Later in the third century AD, a prominent text on the wall of the orchestra, roughly opposite the stage, honoured M. Aurelius Menestheus Skopas for the panelling of the said wall; this dated to after the lowering of the level of the orchestra, to permit gladiator and perhaps wild animal fights in the theatre.[51] Finally, a fragmentary text on the cornice of the stage, which was partly painted, records verse honours for a certain Androkles; he is mentioned in relation to a benefaction, which likely related to work in the theatre, though no more can be said.[52]

The visibility of such benefactions within the theatrical space appears to have been of greatest concern. There is no way of knowing whether people paused to read the texts in full, though they were legible to the attentive audience member and a cursory engagement would have quickly revealed the identity of the donor.

[51] I.Aphrodisias 2007, 8.115.   [52] I.Aphrodisias 2007, 8.85.ii.

But it is also important to appreciate the value derived from the physicality of these texts, forming part of a material and highly visible dialogue of benefactions. They functioned as markers and advertisements of the generosity of prominent individuals or families, traced back to the earliest benefactor in the theatre in the first century BC, Gaius Iulius Zoilos. The permanence of their names in the civic landscape, especially in such an important meeting space of the city, was considered an essential aspect of the euergetic transaction; as we have seen, the image conveyed was not static, as additional benefactions were bestowed throughout the imperial period.[53] We can also wonder whether such texts were interacted with in other ways, through recognition during festivals and/or assemblies held in the theatre. As Angelos Chaniotis has explored, a number of inscriptions specify the crowning of individuals during civic ceremonies, especially festivals; this would have involved the pronouncement of their benefactions and achievements that made them worthy of such an honour, whether through the reading out of the relevant decree in full or a summary.[54] The proximity of the results of such investment, and the inscriptions recording their details, would thus gain a particular significance through recognition of their donors in communal ritual.

In this context, the statue base recording honours voted by the *demos* for Gaius Iulius Zoilos gained a particular resonance when read in conjunction with the record of his benefactions.[55] It is probable that Zoilos was ceremonially crowned at important ceremonies during his lifetime, including during festivals and civic rituals. We can also wonder whether his statue itself was distinguished in this way after his death.[56] An inscription from Gerasa, for instance, honours the first *agonothetes* of games in honour of Trajan; it was resolved to erect his statue in the theatre, alongside the inscription of the guild, 'with the proviso that both contestants in the games and persons who perform in the theatre on other occasions must bring in wreaths for the statue'.[57] Among the numerous distinctions awarded to Diodoros Pasparos at Pergamon in the first century BC were stipulations that his statue be dressed with a headband or crown, when other statues were so distinguished; the implication is that this was a standard accompaniment to the erection of honorific statues.[58] In this way, the inscriptions related to the benefactions of Zoilos at Aphrodisias would have acquired a special significance during civic gatherings and festivals; it is possible that they were read out or referred to

---

[53] Ng (2015), 108–11. See also Ng (2016), on the potential limits of honorific statues as a mode of memorialization.
[54] Chaniotis (2007), 54–9.
[55] *I.Aphrodisias 2007*, 8.203: [v. ὁ] δῆμος vac. [?ἐτείμησεν] | Γάιον Ἰούλιον Ζωίλ[ον·· ? ··]
[56] See n. 33 for the possible identification of his statue.
[57] Welles (1938), no. 192 (*SEG* 7, 825), ll. 17–19: ἔδοξεν ἀναστῆσαι αὐτοῦ ἀνδριάντα ἐν ᾧ πρῶτος ἠγωνοθέτησε | θεάτρῳ ἐπιγραφὴν ἔχοντα τὴν ἐξ ἔθους τῆς συνόδου, ἐφ᾽ ᾧ οἵ τε ἀγων[ιζ]όμενοι πάντες καὶ οἱ κατὰ καιρὸν θεατρίζοντες | εἰσφέρωσιν ἐπάνανκες στεφάνους τῷ ἀνδριάντι.
[58] *I. Pergamon* 256 (*OGIS* 794 C), ll. 16–18.

as an accompaniment to any crowning ceremony, in order to reiterate the city's gratitude.

In the centuries after its construction, the theatre became a prominent venue for honouring individuals, relating their activities both there and elsewhere (Table 7.2).[59] A series of texts inscribed on the *proskenion* frieze, above the dedication of Zoilos, appear to indicate that the stage building itself was used to honour individuals (Fig. 7.5). As noted, one of these was an inscription in honour of Ti. Claudius Zelos; it mentions the civic offices he had held, and he is called founder and *euergetes*.[60] Another text honoured Ti. Claudius Diogenes, where he is named as a euergete alongside a list of his offices.[61] A further two honoured Hosidios Ioulianos (one voted by the *boule* and the *demos*, the second by the

Table 7.2 Details of individuals honoured in the stage area.

Name of Honorand	Date	Civic Offices/ Benefactions	Voting Body	Reference	Location of Text
Ti. Claudius Diogenes	Mid-to late 1st c. AD	Archierus Sebastophantes Agonothetes Euergetes Nomothetes Gymnasiarch (twice)	Boule and demos	IAph2007 8.23	Proskenion frieze
Hosidios Ioulianos	2nd c. AD	Money for *agones*. Offerings to Aphrodite of silver inlaid with gold.	Gerousia Boule and demos	IAph2007 8.38 IAph2007 8.39	Proskenion frieze Proskenion frieze
Ti. Claudius Zelos	139–61 AD	Archiereus Priest for life of Aphrodite Founder Euergetes	Boule, demos, gerousia, and the neoi	IAph2007 8.84	Proskenion frieze
Ti. Claudius. Apollonios Markianos	2nd/ 3rd c. AD	Archiereus	Patris	IAph2007 8.83	Stage front— cornice
Androkles(?)	4th c. AD			IAph2007 8.85.ii	Stage front— cornice

[59] It is also possible that certain of the emperors were recognized with statues in the same venue. See Erim and Smith (1991), 86–9: no. 25 is identified as a head of Claudius. No. 26 was originally identified as a head of 'Julius Caesar'; however, this is the same statue that Smith (2006), 102–4, suggests was of Gaius Iulius Zoilos (see n. 33).
[60] *I.Aphrodisias 2007*, 8.84.   [61] *I.Aphrodisias 2007*, 8.23.

Fig. 7.5 Doric entablature showing relative location of the Zoilos dedication and the honorific texts above.
Photograph: New York University Excavations at Aphrodisias (N. Carless Unwin).

gerousia), and it is noted that he had provided money for games.[62] In the same location is the record of the statues dedicated by Grypos; it can be envisaged that these statues stood directly above the inscriptions on the frieze. The texts were spaced out across the front of the porch, suggesting that the platform was clustered with statues; in this way, civic benefactors were constantly present in the theatrical space, overseeing proceedings.[63] It is not clear whether the inscriptions on the cornice of the stage front referred to nearby statues, which could indicate that they were erected on the stage itself.[64]

The theatre was the performance hub of the city, where both the community and visitors would convene during festivals and other rituals. It was thus a natural venue in which to demonstrate beneficence and be recognized for it. A survey of the epigraphic activity in the area of the stage and orchestra reveals that from the

---

[62] *I.Aphrodisias 2007*, 8.38; 8.39. These contests are attested elsewhere; see n. 10.
[63] Reynolds (1991), 18–19. Three of these inscriptions across the cornice remain unpublished; they also appear to be honorific in nature. Di Napoli (2017), 420, likens the arrangement of the statues to orators before an assembly, or priests officiating at games. Cf. the personification of the *agonothetes* on the theatre frieze at Hierapolis; Newby, Chapter 6, Section 6.2.1 above.
[64] See Table 7.2.

beginning of its construction it served as a prime location for leading individuals to advertise their generosity and to be rewarded for it. The theatre became a venue for modelling this euergetic transaction between community and benefactor, with individuals perhaps responding to previous activity;[65] by the early fourth century AD, a history of this relationship could be traced in the inscribed monuments that had amassed over the preceding centuries.

7.3. Modelling victory

The theatre would have played a central role during the festival calendar, whether for rituals or sacrifices, as a gathering point during processions, or as the venue for competitions.[66] In its early history, these were likely restricted to the musical and theatrical contests that were an important aspect of the agonistic circuit; alterations to the orchestra and auditorium, however, occurred during the second century AD, which adapted the space to accommodate gladiatorial fights and other contact sports.[67] Larger-scale contests and animal hunts (*venationes*) would have been better suited to the stadium, though smaller battles would have taken place in the theatre.[68]

This diversity of activities is not readily represented in the official epigraphic record of the theatre. The *agonothesia* was one of the offices for which Ti. Claudius Diogenes was honoured with his statue on the stage, while Hosidios Ioulianos was honoured (twice) for the money he provided for contests (*agones*). A statue of the Polykleitan 'Doryphoros' type was also discovered during the excavations of the theatre area, and may have been erected on the *scaenae frons*; it served to complement the other representations of culture and education from the stage.[69]

The primary (surviving) evidence for the competitive activities of the theatre is provided by two statues of boxers that were discovered with their associated bases. They have been reconstructed as either standing at the ends of the

---

[65] See Burrell (2009), 70, in relation to Ephesos, though the pattern can be traced more broadly; see also 88: 'Buildings attract further buildings, texts attract texts'.

[66] Inscriptions related to processions both at Ephesos, *I.Ephesos* 27; Rogers (1991), and Oinoanda, Wörrle (1988), reveal the crucial role of the theatre in ritual proceedings: those processing would travel to the venue, where rituals were enacted in front of a gathered crowd. For the variety of functions that the theatre had in civic life, consider St Paul and his acquaintances being judged, and almost provoking a riot, in the theatre at Ephesos (*Acts* 19:23–41).

[67] The level of the orchestra was lowered, and a podium built around it, with a balustrade: de Chaisemartin and Theodorescu (1991), 38–9. Cf. Sear (2006), 43–4.

[68] Reliefs depicting animal hunts have been discovered out of context at Aphrodisias; see Texier (1839–49), vol. 3, pl. 158. The imperial addition of friezes depicting (scenes of) animal hunts, often involving *erotes*, have also been discovered at Aizanoi, see Wörrle (2011), Ephesos, see Aurenhammer and Plattner (2018), and Miletos, see Altenhöfer and Bol (1989). The popularity of such themes reveal the penetration of more typically 'Roman' activities in the civic life of cities of the Greek East. The stadium at Aphrodisias was converted into an amphitheatre c. AD 400; see Welch (1998).

[69] Smith and Erim (1991), no. 5; cf. Newby (2005), 255–7.

analemma walls, or framing the stage.[70] In both instances, the accompanying inscriptions survive, identifying the figures as circuit-victors. The statue discovered in the northern area of the theatre (Fig. 7.6) also distinguished the honorand Kandidianos for his victory at the Aktian games, part of the 'new' *periodos* of the imperial age:

> Κανδιδιανὸν vac. Ἄ{τ}`κ´τεονίκην[71]
> περιοδονίκην vac. ἡ πατρίς
>
> The fatherland (honours) Kandidianos, victor at the Aktia, circuit-victor.[72]

The standing figure is shown bearded, facing left; he is nude except for the boxing gloves he wears. His body is weighted onto the right leg, and his forearms originally projected perpendicularly to his body. The profession of the victor is not specified in the text itself; it is only from the statue that Kandidianos can be identified as a boxer.

The inscription from the statue to the south of the orchestra is similar in content (Fig. 7.7). It is inscribed over three lines and employs leaf motifs to draw attention to the fatherland as granter of the honours. It also preserves the sculptor's signature, which remains on the base of the figure, separate from the statue base:

> ii.   Πολυνείκ[ης Ἀφρ]οδεισιεὺς
>   vac. ἐποί[ει] vac.
> i.   Πίσεαν Πισέου
>   περιοδονίκην
>   leaf ἡ πατρίς leaf
>
> Polyneikes, Aphrodisian, made (this).
> The fatherland (honours) Piseas, son of Piseas, circuit-victor.[73]

Piseas is again depicted nude and wearing boxing gloves; he is bearded and wears his hair in the typical hairstyle of athletes, *cirrus in vertice*, with hair gathered on the top of the head in a small 'ponytail'.[74]

The erection of the two statues and their bases served to model the type of victory that warranted public commemoration in the theatre: it was reserved for two individuals who were 'circuit-victors'. Traditionally, the *periodos* was constituted of the four major international games, the Olympia, the Pythia, the Nemeia, and

---

[70] Van Voorhis (2008), 233, discusses the different interpretations, and proposes that they stood directly on the stage, in front of the analemma walls and facing the cavea. See also the discussion of Newby (2005), 255–60.

[71] The cutter wrote ATT, before inserting a K in the middle.

[72] *I.Aphrodisias 2007*, 8.87; *I.Aphrodisias Performers* 74; Smith (2006), no. 40.

[73] *I.Aphrodisias 2007*, 8.88 ii, i; *I.Aphrodisias Performers* 75; Smith (2006), no. 39. I have represented the text here as the viewer would encounter it, with the sculptor's signature on the base of the statue itself and above the honorific inscription on the base below.

[74] On this hairstyle, see Thuillier (1998); Van Voorhis (2008), 243–5.

Fig. 7.6 Statue and base of the boxer Kandidianos. Inv. 1967-287, 1967-28.
Photograph: New York University Excavations at Aphrodisias (R. Wilkins).

the Isthmia; in the imperial period this was sometimes supplemented by other prestigious festivals that attracted competitors from across the Mediterranean (the Capetolia, the Aktia, and the Heraia).[75] The victory of Kandidianos at the Aktian games is noted, indicating the prestige attached to the event, though it is considered distinct from his *periodos* victory. The honours were voted by their

---

[75] See the comments of Ebert (1994), 302.

Fig. 7.7 Statue and base of the boxer Piseas. Inv. 1970-508-511.
Photograph: New York University Excavations at Aphrodisias (R. Wilkins).

patris Aphrodisias; the expense of paying for their erection may have fallen on the state or their family, but official permission would have been required to erect the statues in the theatre.

The base for Kandidianos had been reused and re-inscribed,[76] which was a fairly common practice in the crowded epigraphic landscape of the imperial and

---

[76] Van Voorhis (2008), 241, observes that the block displays 'footprints' on the top for a bronze statue.

late antique city.⁷⁷ On the basis of letter forms, both inscriptions have been dated to the second half of the third century / early fourth century AD.⁷⁸ This is later than the statues themselves, which have been dated to the early to mid-third century AD on stylistic grounds.⁷⁹ The statues were thus reused, and it can be supposed that they were chosen to reflect the occupations of the honorands.

It was a rare achievement to be victorious at all the main games on the international circuit; the only other known circuit-victor from Aphrodisias honoured with a statue is Kallimorphos the flautist, whose victories are dated between AD 117–38.⁸⁰ The abbreviated form of the texts themselves are typical of late antique honours; unlike with other (earlier) honorific inscriptions for victors, there are no details about their families and achievements, or their service more widely in Aphrodisian society.⁸¹ We can wonder whether both Kandidianos and Piseas accomplished such honours only in the late third / early fourth century AD. It is possible that their victories were contemporary with the erection of the statues, though the notion that earlier *periodos* victors were being recalled and commemorated in the late third century AD should also be considered.⁸²

The erection of the boxer statues reveals the endurance of Greek athletics as an important part of civic and elite culture, at least at the point of their erection. The two monuments were apparently set up to mirror each other, on either side of the stage, even though the texts were not inscribed by the same hand and may not have been precisely contemporary. While only two individuals were singled out for honour, the monuments served as a physical manifestation of the continued significance and prestige attached to traditional athletic contests in the city. Alongside the statues erected on the stage to recognize civic benefactors, the boxers Kandidianos and Piseas modelled the types of achievements that were deemed worthy of public honour in a late antique context.

7.4. Civic history on display

As we have seen, the concentration of gatherings in the theatre meant that it was an attractive location for individuals to display and be rewarded for their civic

---

⁷⁷ See Shear (2007); Bolle, Machado, and Witschel (2017b), 18–20; Witschel (2017) and Machado (2017), in relation to late antique Italy; Tantillo (2017), in relation to Roman Africa; the motivations behind such repurposing were varied.

⁷⁸ Van Voorhis (2008), 241–2.

⁷⁹ Van Voorhis (2008), 236–40, identifies two different workshops for the statues. The sculptor's signature on the statue of Piseas should be considered original.

⁸⁰ *I.Aphrodisias 2007*, 12.716. The stone was found re-used in the walls.

⁸¹ See Remijsen (2015), 82. The text for Kallimorphos (*I.Aphrodisias 2007*, 12.716), for instance, records his patrilineage (son of [Tiberius] Claudius Agathangelos), and his service as priest for life of the goddess Nike; it also lists all the sacred games at which he was victorious; cf. Ebert (1994), 302. See also the contribution of Scharff, Chapter 2 above.

⁸² Van Voorhis (2008), 242.

Fig. 7.8 Archive Wall.
Photograph: C. Roueché.

service and athletic achievements. Similar motivations appear to have prompted the choice of the theatre as the location in which to inscribe one of the most impressive epigraphic monuments at Aphrodisias, the so-called 'archive wall' (Fig. 7.8).[83] This extensive collection of documents was displayed as one entered the orchestra from the north parodos, and effectively traced the history of relations between Aphrodisias and Rome, in particular repeated Roman recognition of the city's independence (*eleutheria*). The documents were carefully selected, including copies of letters sent from different emperors to the city that demonstrated the consistent favour shown to the city; a copy of the *senatus consultum* of 39/38 BC, recording official confirmation of the privileges of the city and the *asylia* of the sanctuary of Aphrodite, was inscribed in full to the left of the wall.[84] The collection also extended onto the face of the pilaster and stage entablature, with the inscription of a letter of Quintus Oppius, dated *c*.85 BC, in which he thanked the Aphrodisians for their military support and assumed the role of patron;[85] the decree of Plarasa/Aphrodisias in which they voted to offer Oppius support was also inscribed.[86]

A number of the documents date to the Triumviral period, including a series of letters from Octavian in which he records his liberation of Aphrodisias;[87] he

---

[83] On the monumentalization of documents, see Davies (2003); Cooley (2012); Kokkinia (2015–16).
[84] *I.Aphrodisias 2007*, 8.27 (= *I.Aphrodisias and Rome* 8).
[85] *I.Aphrodisias 2007*, 8.2 (= *I.Aphrodisias and Rome* 3).
[86] *I.Aphrodisias 2007*, 8.3 (= *I.Aphrodisias and Rome* 2).
[87] *I.Aphrodisias 2007*, 8.25–8.32 (= *I.Aphrodisias and Rome* 6–13).

writes that 'this one city I have taken for my own out of all Asia'.[88] It is interesting to note that two of the missives dated to a similar period were not actually addressed to Aphrodisias: one was sent to Ephesos, relating to property and goods that had been seized from the community of Plarasa/Aphrodisias in the war against Labienus (including a gold statue of Eros).[89] The second was sent by Octavian/Augustus to Samos, in which he writes that 'I have given the privilege of freedom to no people except the Aphrodisians'.[90] We can only speculate how Aphrodisias came to acquire such documents, as it is unlikely that they were in the city's own civic archive.

The other documents confirm the impression of preferential treatment, recording imperial recognition of the freedom of Aphrodisias and other privileges by successive emperors. The relationship was reasserted in the second century under Trajan and Hadrian, while there is further correspondence from Commodus and joint letters from Severus and Caracalla.[91] It has been proposed that the collection was inscribed in the early stages of the third century AD; J. Reynolds has suggested that a letter of Severus Alexander, dated c. AD 224, originally served as the final item in the dossier.[92] There was then a second phase of inscription, with later correspondence added on the lower course;[93] texts dated to the reign of Gordian III were inscribed here and on the nearby analemma.[94]

Nothing is known of the circumstances surrounding the inscribing of the collection, though it is apparent that the Aphrodisians had made an effort to gather documents relevant to the overall scheme. The repurposing of older documents and their public display should be considered as political in motivation, as the city sought to curate a consistently favourable image of its relationship with Rome.[95] This may be related to the status of the city as provincial capital, first of the joint province of Karia and Phrygia, and subsequently of Karia alone.[96] During this period, Aphrodisias functioned as the seat of the governor, which may have influenced the epigraphic output of the city and the types of documents it chose to inscribe. The decision to inscribe Diocletian's Price Edict and Currency Reform on the façade of the Civil Basilica in the south *agora*, for instance, has

---

[88] *I.Aphrodisias 2007*, 8.29 (= *I.Aphrodisias and Rome* 10), ll. 3–4.

[89] *I.Aphrodisias 2007*, 8.31 (= *I.Aphrodisias and Rome* 12).

[90] *I.Aphrodisias 2007*, 8.32 (= *I.Aphrodisias and Rome* 13), ll. 2–3: τὸ φιλάνθρωπον τῆς ἐλευθερίας οὐδενὶ δέδωκα δήμῳ πλὴν τῷ τῶν | [Ἀφροδεισιέων].

[91] *I.Aphrodisias 2007*, 8.33–8.37 (= *I.Aphrodisias and Rome* 14–18).

[92] *I.Aphrodisias 2007*, 8.99 (= *I.Aphrodisias and Rome* 19). Reynolds (1982) and Kokkinia (2015–2016) both support a date c. AD 224 for the original phase; Bowersock (1984) preferred a date of c. AD 198.

[93] Reynolds (1982), 36–7: there is a difference in letter forms between the lower course, containing letters of Gordian III, and those above; see also 131. Kokkinia (2015–16), 19, suggests that the Triumviral decree (*I.Aphrodisias 2007*, 8.26), the Letter of Stephanos to Plarasa/Aphrodisias (*I.Aphrodisias 2007*, 8.30), and the letters of Gordian III (*I.Aphrodisias 2007*, 102–3) were inscribed as part of the second phase. Cf. Bowersock (1984).

[94] *I.Aphrodisias 2007*, 8.100–8.103 (= *I.Aphrodisias and Rome* 20–4).

[95] See Chaniotis (2003); see also Chaniotis (1988), 256–7; von Hesberg (2009).

[96] See above.

been linked to an official directive.⁹⁷ There is no reason to suggest that the 'archive wall' was engraved on instruction from the imperial authorities; however, it is possible that these carefully chosen texts were displayed to reflect the city's metropolitan status and advertise the historical context of its provincial importance.

The visibility of the collection was paramount in the planning. Its location at the northern entrance to the theatre meant that it was readily accessible to audiences travelling in and out of the venue. Whether the dossier was easily readable and/or read is another question; the texts were well carved, with regular letters; traces of red paint have been found, which may have been intended to aid accessibility/document division.⁹⁸ At the same time, the passageway was vaulted in antiquity, which might have restricted light.⁹⁹ But it would not have been necessary for an observer to read every text in detail in order to gain an overview of the relationship with Rome being commemorated. An awareness of the memorial function of the wall could also have been gained in other ways, through signposting in civic and/or individual discourse; its visibility was of equal value to its readability, though the two aspects were ultimately intertwined.

The way in which the collection was organized is not immediately discernible, with no strict chronological or thematic order.¹⁰⁰ It is possible, however, that they were not meant to be approached sequentially. As C. Kokkinia has noted, the audience's attention was immediately drawn to the centre of the collection, with the large title *ΑΓΑΘΗ ΤΥΧΗ*, 'to good fortune', at the top of Column 4.¹⁰¹ Kokkinia proposes that this central field was occupied by documents that traced the development of Roman interest in Aphrodisias, which were then elaborated in the surrounding texts.¹⁰²

In this context, it is interesting to note that an altar, dated on the basis of letter forms to the second century BC, was also discovered in the theatre.¹⁰³ It records an oath between Plarasa/Aphrodisias, Kibyra, and Tabai, in which they assert their *homonoia* and brotherhood (ἀδελφότης) with one another, and swear never to act in opposition to the Romans or each other. The original location of this inscription is not known (it was found reused in the north *parodos* wall); it can be speculated, however, that it was redeployed in proximity to the 'archive wall' as a physical memorial of the antiquity of Aphrodisian goodwill towards Rome.¹⁰⁴

---

⁹⁷ Erim et al. (1970); Erim, Reynolds, and Crawford (1971). Cf. Stinson (2012), 118–20.
⁹⁸ Reynolds (1982), 36: it appears that there was only colour in the initial letters of paragraphs in a fragment from the *SC*, *I.Aphrodisias 2007*, 8.27 (= *I.Aphrodisias and Rome* 8).
⁹⁹ Reynolds (1982), 33.
¹⁰⁰ Reynolds (1982), 37, does note that they were arranged to fill the space in a 'satisfactory way.'
¹⁰¹ Kokkinia (2015–16), 44–5.   ¹⁰² Kokkinia (2015–16), 45–6.
¹⁰³ *I.Aphrodisias 2007*, 8. 210 (= *I.Aphrodisias and Rome* 1).
¹⁰⁴ Reynolds (1982), 6–11; de Chaisemartin (2012), 80–1. On the continued value of (older) inscriptions in creating a sense of antiquity, see Carless Unwin (2023).

The 'archive wall' commemorated and memorialized the history of Aphrodisias, or at least its history in relation to Rome; it further promoted an image of continuity in this relationship, which sought to balance the city's proclaimed independence with the realities of Roman rule.[105] The selection of the theatre as the location for this display was intentional, as the documents were made widely visible to both inhabitants and visitors.[106] Whether the foot traffic that travelled in front of the wall stopped to read the texts in detail or merely skimmed the contents, the message was clear: the provincial metropolis of Aphrodisias had a long and esteemed past, which witnessed the repeated recognition of its liberty by successive emperors. It was a physical touchstone in the urban centre that was meant to be seen and referred to as a testament to the distinguished history of the city.

7.5. Inscribing the cavea

In *poleis* across the ancient world, the theatre was the venue where the city could meet and project an image of itself, both to internal and external audiences. Attempts to structure and control how this manifested in practical terms can be detected in the epigraphic record; at Hierapolis in Phrygia, for instance, the names of civic tribes were inscribed directly onto the seats in the theatre, allocating different areas for the different *phylai*; similar demarcations are found elsewhere.[107] The theatre was also an arena for elite performance, and the front rows were frequently reserved for specific offices, as in the theatre of Dionysos at Athens.[108] In the imperial period, this was further demonstrated by the frequent addition of special box seats in auditoria, often positioned centrally, and thus in pride of place in the cavea.[109]

Attempts to demarcate the theatrical space at Aphrodisias are more difficult to identify. A podium for a seat of honour for an important (imperial?) official formed part of the works conducted in the orchestra in the second or third century AD, which indicates some level of stratification among spectators.[110] A number of texts engraved on the seats in the cavea have also been discovered, but they defy easy interpretation and have no clear scheme. The situation is similar in the

---

[105] Chaniotis (2003).

[106] The choice of the theatre as the location for displaying important texts can be identified elsewhere; e.g. the texts related to the benefactions of C. Vibius Salutaris were engraved on the wall of the theatre at Ephesos: *I.Ephesos*, 27; see Rogers (1991).

[107] Hierapolis: Kolb (1974); see also Newby, Chapter 6, Section 6.2 above. See also tribal demarcations at Saittai (*SEG* 40, 1063), Philippopolis (*SEG* 34, 712) and Stobi (*SEG* 43, 454). At Ephesos, the different groups commemorated by statues (including the tribes and the civic bodies of the boule) in the procession of C. Vibius Salutaris were also mapped onto the theatre space; the bases on which these statues were placed were located adjacent to the seating area of each tribe/group; see *I.Ephesos*, 28–35.

[108] *IG* II² 5022–79.   [109] See Sear (2006), 5.

[110] Roueché (1991), 99–100. Similar seats of honour were distinguished in other imperial theatres: see Sear (2006), 5.

stadium, where a number of fragmentary texts have been found; it is possible that they were abbreviations for different civic divisions, though the names of the tribes of Aphrodisias remain unknown.[111] Sections of seating, however, were reserved for the sacred ephebes and for the *oikonomoi* of the *neoteroi*;[112] a *topos* inscription for the *neoteroi* is further found in the *odeion*.[113] As members of foremost civic institutions that served to publicly model the qualities and behaviours of elite youths, both the ephebes and *neoi* played a prominent role in communal ritual and performance.[114] It is possible that similar allocations were originally defined in the theatre as well. Certainly, the reservation of seating for different groups in the theatre is suggested by a series of benches inscribed with abbreviated texts, which may relate to the names of different associations.[115] Elsewhere, a *topos* inscription appears to reserve space for (an association or family of) butchers.[116] It is one of a number of texts that 'reserve' seats, though it is not always known who they were being reserved by or for, and it is possible that some were more 'informal' in nature.[117]

The international audiences attracted to Aphrodisias for festive occasions also left their mark in the epigraphic record. In the *tetrastoon* area behind the theatre, two *topos* inscriptions for the Hierapolitans have been discovered, which may have marked their incorporation into festivities in some capacity.[118] In the stadium, seats were also reserved for the people of Mastaura in Lydia and Antiocheia (on-the-Maeander?).[119] The circumstances in which the texts were engraved are not known, but we can envisage delegations sent from these cities to partake in ceremonies receiving official accommodation from Aphrodisias. In this context, a series of inscriptions recording honours for cities who had shared in the sacrifice (*synthusia*) to celebrate the grant (*dorea*) of the sacred contest may be of relevance.[120] The texts, the majority of which were statue bases, have been dated to the third century AD, and Roueché suggests that the unnamed games in question were provincial games to mark Aphrodisias' metropolitan status; she identifies them with either the Attalea Gordianea or the Valeriana Pythia, which are both attested in the city during this period.[121] The cities honoured were primarily

---

[111] Roueché (1993), 122–3.   [112] *I.Aphrodisias 2007*, 10.26. Row S; U; V.
[113] *I.Aphrodisias 2007*, 2.6. Row 5.i.
[114] On the institution of the *ephebeia* in the imperial period, see Kennell (2009). The ephebes, for instance, were tasked with carrying the statues from the Magnesia Gate to the theatre in the Salutaris procession: *I.Ephesos* 27, ll. 49–55, 423–5, 564–8. Seat inscriptions for the *epheboi* are also found on four rows in the theatre at Termessos: *TAM* III.1, 872, BIII. Two of the groups of ephebes were named after individuals, Automenes (BIII n. 39) and Heliophoros (BIII n. 37), which could relate to the source of funding for different groups; see Kennell (2009), 329. On ephebic festivals at Athens, see Gkikaki, Chapter 5 above.
[115] *I.Aphrodisias 2007*, 8.265: e.g. i. Θεοδ(ωριτῶν); ii. Εὐτ(υχιτῶν); iii. Ἡρακ(λειτῶν).
[116] *I.Aphrodisias 2007*, 8.61, Row 13 (=Roueché (1993), J. 13): τόπο τῶν μακελλίτων.
[117] e.g. *I.Aphrodisias 2007*, 8.54, Row 15, 19; 8.55, Row 21; 8.56, Row 12, 19; 8.57, Row 24; 8.60, Row 19, 20.
[118] *I.Aphrodisias 2007*, 12.402: τόπος Ἱερα|πολιτῶν;12.403.
[119] *I.Aphrodisias 2007*, 10.4, Row O: τό|πος | Μα|σταυρο|[πολίτων?]; 10.29, Row S: [Ἀ]|ν|τ|ι|ο|χ|ε|[ί]|ω|ν.
[120] On *synthusia*, see Newby, Chapter 6, Section 6.2.2 above.
[121] Roueché (1981), 118–19; Roueché (1993), 182–7.

located in the vicinity of Aphrodisias, concentrated in the region around the Morsynus and Lykos valleys, which may indicate something about the reach of the Aphrodisian festival network; the preserved monuments were erected to the people of Keretapa,[122] Hierapolis,[123] Kibyra,[124] Apollonia Salbake,[125] Herakleia Salbake,[126] and Tabai.[127] The original location of these texts is not known, though it can be speculated that they were erected in proximity to each other in order to memorialize this event, and thus in proximity to where the communal sacrifice took place.[128]

The majority of inscriptions discovered in the cavea can be classified as graffiti. While difficult to date,[129] such texts offer invaluable insights into the response of the audience to the space; notably, the longevity of the desire to mark one's presence, and the entrenched nature of the epigraphic mentality among the community. A number of *topos* inscriptions count among their number, recording the names of individuals; whether they were the scratchings of audience members[130] or the (temporary?) allocation of seats cannot be ascertained.[131] Others can more explicitly be linked to a festival context, in particular the engraved images of gladiators; they may have been another way of expressing support for a particular competitor, or a mode of commemoration. One graffito, inscribed with Θρᾷξ ('Thracian'), depicts a male figure holding a circular shield; it likely depicts one of the heavily armed Thracian gladiators that performed in the theatre.[132] Another graffito in the same block of seats also portrays a gladiator, holding a shield and spear (Fig. 7.9).[133] A figure of a boxer/wrestler, with his arms strapped, was also roughly incised into the surface of a seat. It is again possible that the image reflected a contest taking place in the theatre, though M. Langner has observed a crude similarity with the two statues of boxers that were erected on either side of the stage in the third century AD.[134] If we look further ahead into late antiquity, the persistence of the theatre's role as a place of spectacle is revealed by the number of texts tracing the fortunes of the circus factions of the Greens and the Blues.[135] The spatial distribution of the texts

---

[122] *I.Aphrodisias 2007*, 12.924 = *I.Aphrodisias Performers* 58).
[123] *I.Aphrodisias 2007*, 12.925 (= *I.Aphrodisias Performers* 59).
[124] *I.Aphrodisias 2007*, 12.926 (= *I.Aphrodisias Performers* 60).
[125] *I.Aphrodisias 2007*, 12.927 (= *I.Aphrodisias Performers* 61).
[126] *I.Aphrodisias 2007*, 12.928 (= *I.Aphrodisias Performers* 62).
[127] *I.Aphrodisias 2007*, 12.929 (= *I.Aphrodisias Performers* 63). Another text, *I.Aphrodisias 2007*, 12.930 (= *I.Aphrodisias Performers* 64), does not preserve the name of the city.
[128] The monuments were erected in different years, though they should still be viewed as a group; Marcus Aurelius Papias was named as first *archon* in the inscriptions honouring Keretapa, Hierapolis and Kibyra, while those honouring Apollonia Salbake and Herakleia Salbake name the first *archon* as Marcus Antonius Neikomachos Blastos.
[129] It should also be noted that the variety of texts and other graffiti in the theatre was likely much larger at the time of our snapshot in the fourth century AD, with others painted or rendered in a less durable medium.
[130] As can be suggested for *I.Aphrodisias 2007*, 8.62, Row 9: ἐγὼ πυγίστης | εἰμε 'I am a bugger.'
[131] e.g. *I.Aphrodisias 2007*, 8.53, Row 24; 8.55, Row 26; 8.58, Row 18, 23; 8.59, Row 12.
[132] *I.Aphrodisias 2007*, 8.60, Row 9. See Roueché (1993), 110.
[133] *I.Aphrodisias 2007*, 8.60, Row 4.
[134] *I.Aphrodisias 2007*, 8.61, Row 3; Langner (2001), 45.
[135] E.g. *I.Aphrodisias 2007*, 8.54, Row 1; 8.61, Row 13; 8.55, Row 18; 8.59, Row 12, i.

Fig. 7.9 Graffito of a gladiator.
Photograph: C. Rouaché.

suggests that the supporters of each faction were allocated different areas of the theatre, with those related to the Greens concentrated in the north of the auditorium, and those of the Blues in the south.[136]

The diversity of inscribed material on the seats of the theatre serves as a reminder that not all epigraphic output was officially sanctioned or planned; the carving of texts or images also took place as individuals responded to their environment and sought to record their participation as spectators. As much as monumental texts created an official image of the city, their production was driven by the civic authorities, which in turn would be dominated by the elites. The wealth of graffiti from the theatre reveals that members of the community also contributed to the epigraphic landscape as a means of asserting their sense of belonging or ownership. This also extended to those individuals called upon to perform on the stage in a number of capacities; the next section will focus on the mark they left in the theatrical space of Aphrodisias.

7.6. The backstage area

The backstage of the theatre at Aphrodisias offers fascinating glimpses of how performers interacted with, and functioned within, the theatrical space, again employing the epigraphic medium to record their presence. C. Rouaché has provided a comprehensive account of these sometimes difficult texts;[137] the

---

[136] Rouaché (1993), 99.   [137] Rouaché (1993), 15–60.

discussion here offers a summary of the evidence and considers what it can add to our understanding of how individuals engaged with the written word in antiquity. Beginning on the stage itself, the flat backs of the Doric half-columns that supported the architrave were adorned with texts of various degrees of formality. Notably, there are lists of the Muses on the reverse of three of the columns. Counting from the south, the first column is the best preserved, with well-cut letters; it is difficult to date, though the letter forms (lunate epsilon and omega) suggest a late imperial date (Fig. 7.10).[138] The depth of the carving and the general orderliness of the list indicate that it was engraved by a professional, and it can be supposed that it received official sanction.

A similar list adorned the second column, though with a less regular layout; the text has been partially erased, so it is difficult to judge the letter forms; they were also not engraved as deeply as on column 1.[139] The third list is preserved on the back of column 13. The letter forms are clearly different, with more angular types (rhomboid theta and omicron); again, they are carefully inscribed, with some issues of spacing.[140] On the same column, traces of red paint indicate that a similar list had also been painted above the engraved list; the implication is that at some point the carved text was no longer visible.[141]

Fig. 7.10 Muses list from the stage.
Photograph: C. Rouché.

---

[138] *I.Aphrodisias 2007*, 8.89 (= *I.Aphrodisias Performers* 6.1).
[139] *I.Aphrodisias 2007*, 8.98 (= *I.Aphrodisias Performers* 6.2).
[140] *I.Aphrodisias 2007*, 8.97, b (= *I.Aphrodisias Performers* 6.13, b). Rouché (1993), 7 notes that l. 5 was squeezed in after the text had been cut.
[141] *I.Aphrodisias 2007*, 8.97, a; (= *I.Aphrodisias Performers* 6.13, a).

The invocation of the Muses appears rational in a theatrical context. As noted, the functions of the theatre had expanded in the third century AD to include certain types of athletics (boxing), gladiatorial contests, and set-piece wild animal fights. However, other types of theatrical entertainment continued, notably mime and pantomime.[142] The date of the lists is relatively late, likely in the early third century AD; we can wonder whether earlier texts were painted, and thus not preserved. At this time, the presence of the lists appears to have been a persistent concern, as evidenced by the different phases and modes of presentation. It can be speculated that the physical citation or acknowledgement of the Muses had some incantatory force among performers or was incorporated into a ritual to the Muses enacted before performances; the texts may have served to reinforce the community of performers through repetition.

A variety of other texts were also discovered in the area of the stage, though they are more fragmentary in nature; however, their frequency reveals the widespread impetus to inscribe among the community. Some record the names of individuals, engraved to mark their presence or participation.[143] Other graffiti are sketches, including of a head in profile[144] and a long-necked bird;[145] an image of a tight-rope walker carved into the surface of the stage offers a hint of the variety of entertainments put on in the theatre.[146] A further, irregular, text, cut on a small space on the stage front, has been interpreted by Roueché as a reference to a performer of the Pyrrhiche, a war-dance, which could have formed part of the theatrical repertoire.[147]

Moving backstage, the six rooms to the rear of the stage preserve a number of texts; notable are those inscribed above the doorways, by which performers recorded the storage of their equipment. Some of these were carefully cut, and record something about the achievements of the individuals concerned; for instance, the text inscribed on the lintel of Room 4 (counting from the north):

$Καπυρᾶ$ stop $διασκευή$ stop $ἄμαχα$
$καὶ\ Φιλολόγου\ Ὀλυμπιονεί$ -
$κου$

Unbeatable equipment of Kapyras and of Philologos, Olympic victor.[148]

References to the equipment as 'unbeatable' are found in other of the texts; for instance, that carved on the block over the door to Room 3 records the victory of

---

[142] See n. 17.
[143] e.g. I.Aphrodisias 2007, 8.94: $Ζήνων\ ἔγρ|αφε$ ('Zenon wrote (this)'); 8.95: $Ἡλιώδρ[ρ](ος?)$. There are a number of other *topos* inscriptions (e.g. I.Aphrodisias 2007, 8.12, d, e).
[144] I.Aphrodisias 2007, 8.91; (= I.Aphrodisias Performers 6.4).
[145] I.Aphrodisias 2007, 8.97, c; (= I.Aphrodisias Performers 6.13).
[146] I.Aphrodisias 2007, 8.12, c (= I.Aphrodisias Performers 8, b. ii).
[147] I.Aphrodisias 2007, 8.11; (= I.Aphrodisias Performers 7, e): $πυρριχ(ιστής)\ ὁ\ α'\ |\ Αὐρ(ήλιος)Συμ[··?··]$ ('The first pyrrich(istes), Aur(elius) Sym[...]').
[148] I.Aphrodisias 2007, 8.17; (= I.Aphrodisias Performers 1. 4. i).

the performer Autolykos at the Nemean games; it is also decorated with a wreath and a palm leaf, common symbols of victory.[149] Roueché proposes that these performers were mimes; this appears to be confirmed by other texts in the backstage rooms, including references to a *mimologos*,[150] *homeristes*,[151] and *archaiologoi*.[152] The first could refer to actors or writers of mimes, while the *homeristes* performed battle scenes from Homer; the *archaiologoi* likely performed ancient tales.[153]

The process by which certain texts were inscribed does not appear to have been uniform: the inscription on the lintel of Room 4 is well executed, which may indicate a 'formal' planning process, as a means of recognizing prominent local personalities. Other evidence from this restricted area is more informal in nature, apparently carved or painted by the performers who used this area to dress, prepare, and store their equipment. With both forms of text, a similar desire to memorialize the presence and participation of performers in their domain can be recognized. In this way, performers stamped their mark on the theatrical space and used the backstage area as a venue for their own, less public, form of commemoration.

7.7. An epigraphic stage

The epigraphic record offers a wealth of information about the local intricacies of the organization and realization of civic festivals and rituals; however, the ways in which inscriptions were positioned within festival spaces, and how they were meant to interact with their civic settings, can also reveal a great deal about the epigraphic mentality of a community. In late antiquity, the theatre at Aphrodisias continued to function as a centre of activity, with citizens, residents, and visitors alike congregating in this space during festivals, whether for contests, performances, or the enactment of ritual. The concentration of inscriptions found in the theatre was in part a response to this activity; in this chapter, I have sought to trace how the space attracted persistent epigraphic attention over the course of its history because of its role as a stage for communal representation and commemoration.

The theatre was first of all a space in which to play out publicly the dialogue between benefactors and community and honour prominent individuals; this was initiated by the freedman Gaius Iulius Zoilos, before being consolidated by successive benefactors, who followed his example to create a layered epigraphic record. The

---

[149] *I.Aphrodisias 2007*, 8.16 (= *I.Aphrodisias Performers* 1. 3. Ii): Αὐτολύκου διασκευή ἄμαχα | Νεμεακοῦ ἄμαχα.
[150] *I.Aphrodisias 2007*, 8.9 (= *I.Aphrodisias Performers* 1. 1. ii) l.1: Παρδαλᾶ μειμολόγου.
[151] *I.Aphrodisias 2007*, 8.21. I (= *I.Aphrodisias Performers* 1. 6. i): Δημητρίου ὁμηριστοῦ | διασκευή.
[152] *I.Aphrodisias 2007*, 8.15 (= *I.Aphrodisias Performers* 1. 3. i): τόπος [ἀρ]χεολόγων.
[153] Roueché (1993), 21–2; cf. Robert (1936).

stage building itself also became a prominent location in which to erect statues of civic *euergetai*. In this way, the theatrical space was adapted to model civic-minded behaviour for the audience and to encourage the perpetuation of such activities. The significance of agonistic culture in civic discourse was further illustrated through the erection of the pair of statues of boxers; while this occurred relatively late, the statues reveal the continued importance of athletic ideals in the late antique city.

The choice of the theatre as the location in which to inscribe the 'archive wall' further reinforces its role as a civic hub; in this monument, the city authorities actively curated an image of Aphrodisias and its heritage, effectively creating a *lieu de mémoire*.[154] While not linked with a specific festival context, the theatre was considered the most appropriate place in which to communicate this image due to its role as a meeting space for multiple civic celebrations, attracting the widest possible audience. Such dynamics of self-presentation were also translated among the audience, which used inscriptions (broadly defined) to engage with the performances on show and commemorate their participation as spectators through informal engravings and exhortations.

The epigraphic landscape of the theatre thus functioned as more than a sum of its parts, and the impact would have been aggregative. An audience member in the theatre of Aphrodisias in the early fourth century AD would have been confronted with an accumulation of texts, which engaged multiple narratives and perspectives, and effectively spanned the urban history of the city. This in turn reflected the central role of the theatre as a locus of activity, with gatherings taking place during festivals or other civic celebrations. The epigraphic choices made in the theatre reflect its role as a space for communal display, creating a multifaceted image of the city and its history.

Works Cited

Altenhöfer, E. and Bol, R. (1989) 'Der Eroten-Jagdfries des Theaters von Milet', *Istanbuler Mitteilungen* 39: 17–47.

Angliker, E. and Bultrighini, I. (eds) (2023) *New Approaches to the Materiality of Text in the Ancient Mediterranean. From Monuments and Buildings to Small Portable Objects*. Turnhout.

Aurenhammer, M. and Plattner, G. (2018) 'The erotes and satyr frieze of the theatre at Ephesos—seen in the context of Ephesian, Asian and metropolitan sculpture', in M. Aurenhammer (ed.), *Sculpture in Roman Asia Minor: Proceedings of the International Conference at Selçuk, 1st–3rd October 2013*. Vienna, 161–73.

---

[154] Nora (1984–92) and (1989).

Beltrán Lloris, F. (2014) 'The "epigraphic habit" in the Roman world', in C. Bruun and J. Edmondson (eds), *The Oxford Handbook of Roman Epigraphy*. Oxford, 131–48.

Berti, I., Bolle K., Opdenhoff, F., and Stroth, F. (eds) (2017), *Writing Matters. Presenting and Perceiving Monumental Inscriptions in Antiquity and the Middle Ages*. Berlin and Boston.

Bolle, K., Machado, C., and Witschel, C. (eds) (2017a) *The Epigraphic Cultures of Late Antiquity*. Heidelberger Althistorische Beiträge und Epigraphische Studien 60. Stuttgart.

Bolle, K., Machado, C., and Witschel, C. (2017b) 'Introduction: defining the field', in Bolle, Machado, and Witschel (2017a) 15–30.

Bowersock, G. W. (1984) 'Reviewed work(s): *Aphrodisias and Rome. Documents from the Excavation of the Theatre at Aphrodisias* by Joyce Reynolds and Kenan T. Erim', *Gnomon* 56.1: 48–53.

Burrell, B. (2009) 'Reading, hearing, and looking at Ephesos', in W. A. Johnson and H. N. Parker (eds), *Ancient Literacies: The Culture of Reading in Greece and Rome*. Oxford, 69–95.

Carless Unwin, N. (2023) 'Epigraphy and the power of precedence in Asia Minor', in Angliker and Bultrighini (eds), *New Approaches to the Materiality of Text in the Ancient Mediterranean*. Turnhout, 127–140.

Chaniotis, A. (1988) *Historie und Historiker in den griechischen Inschriften*. Stuttgart.

Chaniotis, A. (2003) 'The perception of imperial power in Aphrodisias: the epigraphic evidence', in L. de Blois, P. Erdkamp, O. J. Hekster, G. de Kleijn, and S. Mols (eds), *The Representation and Perception of Roman Imperial Power. Proceedings of the Third Workshop of the International Network Impact of Empire (Roman Empire, 200 BC–AD 476), Rome, March 20–23, 2002*. Amsterdam, 250–60.

Chaniotis, A. (2007) 'Theatre rituals', in P. Wilson (ed.), *The Greek Theatre and Festivals. Documentary Studies*. Oxford, 48–66.

Cooley, A. (2000) 'The life-cycle of inscriptions', in A. Cooley (ed.), *The Afterlife of Inscriptions: Reusing, Reinventing and Revitalizing Ancient Inscriptions*. BICS Supplement 75. London, 1–5.

Cooley, A. (2012) 'From document to monument. Inscribing Roman official documents in the Greek East', in J. Davies and J. Wilkes (eds), *Epigraphy and the Historical Sciences*. Oxford, 159–82.

Davies, J. K. (2003) 'Greek archives: from record to monument', in M. Brosius (ed.), *Ancient Archives and Archival Traditions: Concepts of Record-Keeping in the Ancient World*. Oxford, 323–43.

de Chaisemartin, N. (2011) 'Remarques sur la syntaxe décorative de la frons scaenae d'Aphrodisias: le rôle des décors en bande', in F. D'Andria and I. Romeo (eds), *Roman Sculpture in Asia Minor*. Journal of Roman Archaeology Supplement 80. Portsmouth, RI, 77–90.

de Chaisemartin, N. (2012) 'Le théâtre d'Aphrodisias, espace civique et identitaire', in O. Henry (ed.), *Archéologies et espaces parcourus. Premières rencontres d'archéologie de l'IFEA Istanbul, 11–13 Novembre*. Istanbul, 73–84.

de Chaisemartin, N. and Theodorescu, D. (1991) 'Recherches préliminaires sur la *frons scaenae* du théâtre', in Smith and Erim (1991), 29–65.

Di Napoli, V. (2017) '"στᾶ[ν]αι δὲ αὐτοῦ καὶ κατὰ φυλὴν ἀνδριάντας ἐν τῷ προσκηνίῳ": honorary statues in the theatres of Roman Greece', in A. Heller and O. M. van Nijf (eds), *The Politics of Honour in the Greek Cities of the Roman Empire*. Leiden, 397–431.

Dmitriev, S. (2001) 'The end of "Provincia Asia"', *Historia* 50.4: 468–89.

Ebert, J. (1994) 'Rezensionen: Charlotte Roueché, performers and partisans at Aphrodisias in the Roman and late Roman periods: a study based on inscriptions from the current excavations at Aphrodisias in Caria', *Nikephoros* 7: 296–303.

Erim, K. T., Reynolds, J., Wild, J. P., and Balance, M. H. (1970) 'The copy of Diocletian's Edict on Maximum Prices from Aphrodisias in Caria', *Journal of Roman Studies* 60: 120–14.

Erim, K. T., Reynolds, J., and Crawford, M. (1971) 'Diocletian's currency reform: a new inscription', *Journal of Roman Studies* 61: 171–7.

Erim, K. T. and Smith, R. R. R. (1991) 'Sculpture from the theatre: a preliminary report', in Smith and Erim (1991), 67–97.

Graham, A. (2019) 'Re-appraising the value of same-text relationships; a study of "duplicate" inscriptions in the monumental landscape at Aphrodisias', in A. Petrovic, I. Petrovic, and E. Thomas (eds), *The Materiality of Text: Placement, Perception, and Presence of Inscribed Texts in Classical Antiquity*. Brill Studies in Greek and Roman Epigraphy 11. Leiden and Boston: 275–302.

von Hesberg, H. (2009) 'Archäologische Charakteristika der Inschriftenträger staatlicher Urkunden—einige Beispiele', in R. Haensch (ed.), *Selbstdarstellung und Kommunikation: die Veröffentlichung staatlicher Urkunden auf Stein und Bronze in der römischen Welt. Internationales Kolloquium an der Kommission für Alte Geschichte und Epigraphik in München (1. bis 3. Juli 2006)*. Munich, 19–56.

Kennell, N. M. (2009) 'The Greek ephebate in the Roman period', *International Journal of the History of Sport* 26.2: 323–42.

Kokkinia, C. (2015–16) 'The design of the "archive wall" at Aphrodisias', *Τεκμήρια* 13: 9–55.

Kolb, F. (1974) 'Zur Geschichte der Stadt Hierapolis in Phrygien: Die Phyleninschriften im Theater', *Zeitschrift für Papyrologie und Epigraphik* 15: 255–70.

Langner, M. (2001), *Antike Graffitizeichnungen: Motive, Gestaltung und Bedeutung*. Wiesbaden.

Machado, C. (2017) 'Dedicated to eternity? The reuse of statue bases in late antique Italy', in Bolle, Machado, and Witschel (2017a), 323–61.

MacMullen, R. (1982) 'The epigraphic habit in the Roman empire', *American Journal of Philology* 103: 233–46.

Newby, Z. (2005) *Greek Athletics in the Roman World: Victory and Virtue*. Oxford.

Ng, D. (2015) 'Commemoration and elite benefaction of buildings and spectacles in the Roman world', *Journal of Roman Studies* 105: 101–23.

Ng, D. (2016) 'Monuments, memory, and status recognition', in K. Galinsky (ed.), *Memory in Ancient Rome and Early Christianity*. Oxford, 235–60.

Nora, P. (1984–92) *Les lieux de mémoire*. 3 vols. (Paris). English translation by A. Goldhammer (1996–8) *Realms of Memory: Rethinking the French Past*. 3 vols. New York.

Nora, P. (1989) 'Between memory and history: les lieux de mémoire', *Representations* 26: 7–24.

Petrovic, A., Petrovic, I., and Thomas, E. (eds) (2019) *The Materiality of Text: Placement, Perception, and Presence of Inscribed Texts in Classical Antiquity*. Brill Studies in Greek and Roman Epigraphy 11. Leiden and Boston.

Pont, A.-V. (2008) 'Évergètes Bâtisseurs à Aphrodisias au Haut-Empire', in A. D. Rizakis and F. Camia (eds), *Pathways to Power. Civic Elites in the Eastern Part of the Roman Empire*. Athens, 181–208.

Pont, A.-V. (2014) 'The city at the theater in Anatolia from the 260s to the 320s AD: signs of a major transformation', *Center for Hellenic Studies Research Bulletin* 2.2. https://research-bulletin.chs.harvard.edu/2014/06/20/city-at-the-theater-in-anatolia, last accessed 12 September 2022.

Ratté, C. (2000) 'The urban development of Aphrodisias in the late Hellenistic and early imperial periods', in C. Berns et al. (eds), *Kontinuität und Diskontinuität in den Städten frühkaiserzeitlichen Kleinasiens*. Munich, 5–32.

Remijsen, S. (2015) *The End of Greek Athletics in Late Antiquity*. Cambridge.

Reynolds, J. M. (1982) *Aphrodisias and Rome: Documents from the Excavation of the Theatre at Aphrodisias Conducted by Professor Kenan T. Erim, Together with Some Related Texts*. London.

Reynolds, J. M. (1991) 'Epigraphic evidence for the construction of the theatre: 1st c. BC to mid 3rd c. AD', in Smith and Erim (1991), 15–28.

Riccardi, L. A. (2007) 'The bust-crown, the Panhellenion, and Eleusis: a new portrait from the Athenian Agora', *Hesperia* 76.2: 365–90.

Ritti, T. (2006) *An Epigraphic Guide to Hierapolis (Pamukkale)*. Istanbul.

Robert, L. (1936) 'Archaiologos', *Revue des Études Grecques* 49: 235–54. Reprinted in *Opera Minora Selecta* I, 654–70.

Robert, L. (1984) 'Discours d'ouverture', in *Actes du VIIIe Congrès international d'épigraphie grecque et latine*. I. Athens, 35–45. Reprinted in *Opera Minora Selecta* VI, 709–19.

Rogers, G. M. (1991) *The Sacred Identity of Ephesos: Foundation Myths of a Roman City*. London.

Roueché, C. (1981) 'Rome, Asia and Aphrodisias in the third century', *Journal of Roman Studies* 71: 103–20.

Roueché, C. (1989) *Aphrodisias in Late Antiquity*. Journal of Roman Studies Monograph 5. London.

Roueché, C. (1991) 'Inscriptions and the later history of the Theatre', in Smith and Erim (1991), 99-108.

Roueché, C. (1993) *Performers and Partisans at Aphrodisias in the Roman and Late Roman Periods: A Study Based on Inscriptions from the Current Excavations at Aphrodisias in Caria.* With appendix IV by Nathalie de Chaisemartin. London.

Roueché, C. (2007) 'From Aphrodisias to Stauropolis', in J. Drinkwater and R. S. Salway (eds), *Wolf Liebeschuetz Reflected*. London, 183-92.

Rumscheid, J. (2000) *Kranz und Krone. Zu Insignien, Siegespreisen und Ehrenzeichen der römischen Kaiserzeit*. Tübingen.

Sear, F. (2006) *Roman Theatres. An Architectural Study*. Oxford.

Shear, J. L. (2007) 'Reusing statues, rewriting inscriptions and bestowing honours in Roman Athens', in Z. Newby and R. Leader-Newby (eds), *Art and Inscriptions in the Ancient World*. Cambridge, 221-46.

Smith, R. R. R. (2006), *Roman Portrait Statuary from Aphrodisias. Aphrodisias II: Results of the Excavations at Aphrodisias in Caria*. Mainz am Rhein.

Smith, R. R. R. and Erim, K. T. (eds) (1991) *Aphrodisias Papers 2. The Theatre, a Sculptor's Workshop, Philosophers, and Coin-Types; Including the Papers Given at the Third International Aphrodisias Colloquium Held at New York University on 7 and 8 April, 1989*. Journal of Roman Archaeology Supplement 2. Ann Arbor.

Stinson, P. (2012) 'Local meanings of the Civil Basilica at Aphrodisias: image, text, and monument', in L. Cavalier, R. Descat, and J. des Courtils (eds), *Basiliques et agoras de Grèce et d'Asie mineure*. Bordeaux, 107-26.

Tantillo, I. (2017) 'La trasformazione del paesaggio epigrafico nelle città dell'Africa romana, con particolare riferimento al caso di Leptis Magna (Tripolitania)', in Bolle, Machado, and Witschel (2017a), 213-70.

Texier, C. (1839-49) *Description de l'Asie Mineure: faite par ordre du gouvernement français de 1833 à 1837, et publiée par le Ministère de l'instruction publique. Beaux-arts, monuments historiques, plans et topographie des cités antiques*. 3 vols. Paris.

Theodorescu, D. (1996) 'La frons scaenae du Théatre: innovations et particularités à l'époque de Zoilos', in C. Roueché and R. R. R. Smith (eds), *Aphrodisias Papers 3: The Setting and Quarries, Mythological and Other Sculptural Decoration, Architectural Development, Portico of Tiberius, and Tetrapylon*. Journal of Roman Archaeology Supplement 20. Ann Arbor, 127-48.

Thuillier, J.-P. (1998) 'Le cirrus et la barbe. Questions d'iconographie athlétique romaine', *Mélanges de l'École française de Rome. Antiquité* 110.1: 351-80.

Van Voorhis, J. (2008) 'Two portrait statues of boxers and the culture of athletics in the 3rd c. A.D.', in C. Ratté and R. R. R. Smith (eds), *Aphrodisias Papers 4. New Research on the City and its Monuments*. Journal of Roman Archaeology Supplement 70. Portsmouth, RI, 230-52.

Welch, K. (1998) 'The stadium at Aphrodisias', *American Journal of Archaeology* 102.3: 547–69.

Welles, C. B. (1938) *Gerasa, City of the Decapolis: The Inscriptions*. New Haven.

Witschel, C. (2017) 'Spätantike Inschriftenkulturen im Westen des Imperium Romanum—einige Anmerkungen', in Bolle, Machado and Witschel (2017a), 33–53.

Wörrle, M. (1988) *Stadt und Fest im kaiserzeitlichen Kleinasien: Studien zu einer agonistischen Stiftung aus Oinoanda*. Munich.

Wörrle, M. (2011) 'Aizanoi's theatre in use: an epigraphic approach', in A. N. Bilgen, R. von den Hoff, S. Sandalci, and S. Silek (eds), *Archaeological Research in Western Central Anatolia. Proceedings of the IIIrd International Symposium of Archaeology, Kütahya. 8th–9th March 2010*. Kütahya, 140–50.

8
The Artists of Dionysos and the Festivals of Boiotia

Paul Grigsby

8.1. Introduction

Elsewhere in this volume Scharff and Gordillo Hervás have examined the impact of the emperor on agonistic competition in the Roman period, with Gordillo Hervás in particular looking at the interactions between the emperor and the artistic guilds of Dionysos. These artistic guilds were one of the major players in Hellenistic and Roman festival culture, and this chapter will shift its gaze a little earlier to assess the role played by these guilds in the organization of the festivals in Hellenistic and Roman Boiotia as revealed through inscriptions. In particular, it will uncover the role of the guilds in the agonistic boom enjoyed by Boiotia in the third century BC and in creating a new artistic identity for the region and its games, before going on to examine how the role of the guilds gradually changed during the Roman period.

Why Boiotia? The epigraphic record of Boiotian *agones* is an area worthy of particular study, for while the festival culture of the Greek East (the Greek mainland and Asia Minor) gained momentum after Alexander the Great, seeing a spectacular rise especially of agonistic contests—with over 150 new festivals recorded in this period—from the middle of the third century BC Boiotia experienced an agonistic boom quite unlike any other mainland Greek region.[1] Inscriptions from Boiotia reveal evidence of festival re-organization and the inauguration of new festivals beyond anything seen elsewhere in the Greek world, while also giving clear evidence of the complex organization and interactions at many different levels in the creation and running of these festivals. The epigraphy linked to the festival of the Mouseia at Thespiai, for example, reveals the different interest groups involved in the festival (civic and regional powers, the artistic guilds and performers, and wider powers such as Hellenistic kings and Roman emperors), each with an integral interest in these games, each playing different though key roles in its organization, and each seeking prestige from the contests in a

---

[1] Chaniotis (1995), 164–9.

distinctive way. The inscriptions relating to the Mouseia and other festivals are a manifest testimony of these complex relationships, while the decisions behind their erection—by whom, where, and to what end—symbolizes and makes concrete the structures of power and relationships. Thus, the epigraphy reveals the power plays of the major agents at work in structuring festival culture in the Hellenistic and Roman period, something that would otherwise remain hidden.

The epigraphic record of Greek festivals and games offers a unique view into a world of complex interactions and relationships between different groups and individuals. But it was also a creation of the self-same relationships and power structures that the inscriptions themselves purport to record and display. Inscriptions allow us to reconstruct a whole social world while being products of that same world and thus permit us to interrogate the motives behind their creation and display.[2] As Zahra Newby shows in her introduction to this volume, in seeking the reality behind the epigraphic testimonies, we must not forget that these texts and images were not innocent documents, but the product of deliberate choices, of what to record and how and where to present it. 'Where?' is as important a consideration as 'why?' when considering each document's intended readership.[3] An example of the ways in which inscriptions can make manifest power relationships can be seen in the dedications of proxeny decrees at Oropos as observed by Alexandra Wilding. These decrees were a vital medium through which the community of Oropos articulated its identity, and their placement within the sanctuary of Amphiaraos commanded the widest public attention and interest while also affording them religious status.[4] The inscriptions examined in this chapter will be afforded similar considerations.

This chapter seeks to interrogate the part played by the Guilds of Artists or *Technitai* of Dionysos—especially the Guild of *Technitai* of Isthmos and Nemea—in the agonistic development of Boiotia from the Hellenistic period onwards. It will show how the interaction of the Guilds of *Technitai* with various groups and individuals allowed these *agones* to become the hub of a complex set of relationships between different levels of society. Specifically, it will examine the role played by the Guilds alongside the Boiotian *poleis* in the inauguration and revitalization of *agones* from the third century BC onwards through an examination of the inscriptions relating to those festivals with which the Guild were most intimately involved: the Trieterides of Dionysos Kadmeios at Thebes, the Mouseia at Thespiai, and the Ptoia at Akraiphia (Fig. 8.1).

Further, it will examine the pivotal role played by the artists of Dionysos during the Hellenistic period in creating a new artistic identity for Boiotia. Previously, the types of games typically favoured by the Boiotians down through

---

[2] Ma (2013), 3.   [3] Newby, this volume, Chapter 1.
[4] Wilding (2015), 55–8; see also Lambert (2011), 193–214.

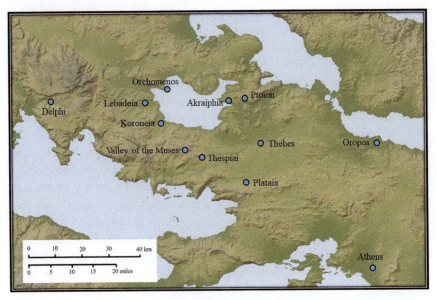

Fig. 8.1 Map of Central Greece, with sites mentioned in the chapter. Adapted from Corinth Archaeological Data and Basemaps by James Herbst [https://www.ascsa.edu.gr/excavations/ancient-corinth/digital-corinth/maps-gis-data-and-archaeological-data-for-corinth-and-greece] licensed under a Creative Commons Attribution-ShareAlike 4.0 International License.

the fifth and fourth centuries BC had been hippic and athletic.[5] And while the trend towards inclusion of a wider variety of events was characteristic of Hellenistic games more widely—seeking to imitate and gain the same status as the games of the *periodos*, especially the Olympics and Pythian games—the change in favour of thymelic competitions within Boiotia was particularly marked.[6] The earlier artistic reputation of Boiotia, home to Helikon and the Muses, birthplace of Hesiod in nearby Askra and of Pindar in Thebes, may have played a role in the success of this reinvention of tradition by the Guilds and Boiotian *poleis*. Thus, the Boiotians were able to firmly establish themselves on the Hellenistic agonistic map, to the Hellenistic agonistic pattern, through the memory of their illustrious artistic past. Finally, following the actions of the *Technitai* into the period of Roman domination, this chapter will end by discussing how the stage created by the *Technitai* for these interactions and relationships

---

[5] For example, the hippic (later militaristic) events of the fifth century Pamboiotia (see Pindar fr. 94b 1.46–7) and the athletic and hippic Herakleia at Thebes of the same century (Pindar, *Isthmian Odes* 1.55–6; 4.67–71b; Pindar, *Nemean Odes* 4.19). See Grigsby (2017), 95–102 for summary of pre-Hellenistic games in Boiotia.

[6] On the categories of games see Remijsen (2011), 97–109.

became the locus of prestige for a new group during the imperial period as the *Technitai* withdrew to the wings.

8.2. The Artists of Dionysos in the Hellenistic period in Boiotia

At the beginning of the Hellenistic period, a surge in the number of festivals and contests across the Greek world resulted in an increased demand for performers and athletes.[7] This demand was satisfied through the creation of a number of quasi-religious professional associations, the *Koina* or Synods of artists of Dionysos (οἱ περὶ τὸν Διόνυσον τεχνῖται) that operated beyond the local level, their members coming from different parts of the Greek world and working over a wide geographical area that extended from the Greek mainland to Asia Minor and Egypt.[8] Three associations dominated the agonistic landscape of Greece and Asia Minor, those of Athens, of Ionia and the Hellespont, and of the Isthmos and Nemea.[9]

The Athenian guild (the *Synodos* or *Koinon* of the Artists of Dionysos at Athens) was the earliest to be set up and is first attested in 279/8 or 278/7 BC.[10] In Asia Minor, evidence appears in the second half of the third century BC for the '*Koinon* of the Artists of Dionysos (who are active in) or (who travel to) Ionia and the Hellespontine region'. This association merged with *Technitai* from Pergamon, closely associated with the Attalid court, to form τὸ κοινὸν τῶν περὶ τὸν Διόνυσον τεχνιτῶν τῶν ἐπ' Ἰονίας καὶ Ἑλλεσπόντου καὶ τῶν περὶ τὸν Καθηγημόνα Διόνυσον—the '*Koinon* of the Artists of Dionysos in Ionia and the Hellespont and those around Dionysos *Kathegemon* ('leader')'.[11] Teos was the first known base of the Ionian and Hellespontine *Koinon*, followed by Ephesos and then Lebedos on the Aegean coast.[12]

The '*Koinon* of the Artists of Dionysos who travel together/contribute towards Isthmos and Nemea' (τὸ κοινὸν τῶν περὶ Διόνυσον τεχνιτῶν τῶν εἰς

---

[7] Aneziri (2014), 431. On the 'spectacular rise' of religious festivals from the Hellenistic period see Van Nijf and Williamson (2021).

[8] Aneziri (2014), 431; on these *Technitai*, see Aneziri (2003) and (2009), 217–36; Le Guen (2001). Similar professional associations for athletes do not appear until the end of the first century BC—Aneziri (2014), 431 n. 44. *Koina* is the most common term but Synod is used for example *IG* II² 1134, 1338, 1348, *I.Eleusis* 271 and Aneziri has argued for Synod being the more important term: see Aneziri (2003), 23–5.

[9] In addition to these three associations, we may also cite the *Synodos* of the Artists in Egypt, *OGIS* 50–1; a branch in Cyprus, and smaller associations in south Italy and Sicily—Aneziri (2003), 119–20.

[10] Aneziri (2009), 219 and n. 10. This is a decree through which the Delphic Amphictyony granted privileges to the Athenian Guild. See *IG* II² 1132, *CID* IV 116, and *CID* IV 12.

[11] Aneziri (2009), 220 and n. 13. Inscriptions are *F.Delphes* III, 3, 218B, ll. 5–8; Bringmann et al. (1995), no. 262; *SEG* 41, 1003, 1005; *IG* IX.1² 192; *CID* IV 97; Rigsby (1996), 295–6 no. 134; *I.Cos Segre* ED79; *I.Magnesia* 54.

[12] Kotlińska-Toma (2015), 277. See Aneziri (2003), 106 on foundation of the Pergamene branch.

Ἰσθμὸν καὶ Νεμέαν) was created as early as the first half of the third century BC to participate in the games held at the Isthmos and at Nemea.[13] This group had headquarters in the nearby *poleis* of Corinth and Argos—being responsible for organizing the association's two most important games at Isthmia and Nemea respectively—but also had branches elsewhere in the Peloponnese (possibly at Messene, Elis, and Sikyon), Macedonia (Dion?), and central Greece in Lokris (Opous), Euboea (Chalkis), and both Thebes and Thespiai in Boiotia.[14] The branch at Thespiai near the Sanctuary of the Muses below Mount Helikon (τῶν συντελούντων εἰς Ἑλικῶνα) was closely connected with the festival of the Mouseia.[15]

These guilds provided a ready-made assemblage of competitors from a wide-range of locales across the Hellenic world.[16] Evidence for the activities of the guilds are found in a range of epigraphic material including honorary decrees of cities, letters of Hellenistic kings and Roman officials, victory lists, and accounts of *agonothetai*.[17] In addition to delivering professional competitors, in several cases the guilds also helped to organize festivals and games, examples being the Soteria at Delphi, the Mouseia at Thespiai, and the Trieterides of Dionysos Kadmeios (Agrionia) at Thebes.[18]

It is not without significance that the cities where the Isthmian-Nemean *Technitai* were based also had their own theatres—all either built or rebuilt in the Hellenistic period—so we might be tempted to assume their construction or conversion was thanks to this active organization.[19] But the presence of the *Technitai* in Boiotia had an even wider if less tangible transformative effect on the *agones* within the region and upon the regional identity reflected through them.[20] In the first part of this chapter I will discuss how the strong association between various Boiotian *poleis* with the *Koinon* of *Technitai* of Isthmos and Nemea at Thebes transformed Boiotia's agonistic profile, introducing a distinctly artistic flavour of competition in place of a previously athletic and hippic focus, setting the scene for a later agonistic flourishing unlike anywhere else on the Greek mainland. I will also demonstrate how the *Technitai* became an important link in mediating

---

[13] *Syll.*³ 460 and *IG* XI.4, 1059. See Aneziri (2009), 219.

[14] See Aneziri (2009), 219–20 and n. 12. For a concordance of the texts gathered by Le Guen (2001) and Aneziri (2003) see *SEG* 51, 2279. For evidence of branches, see for example Argos: *IG* VI 558; Messene: Plutarch, *Cleomenes* 12.2—see Aneziri (2003), 60 and n. 232; Elis: *I.Olympia* 405; Sikyon: *F.Delphes* III, 2, 70 ll. 20–2; Dion: *IG* VII 2486 and Aneziri (2003), 57; Chalkis: *IG* XII⁹ 910; Opous: *IG* IX¹ 278; Thebes and Thespiai: below and *IG* VIII 1760, *IG* VII 2484–6. For the structure of the association, see Aneziri (2003), 56–65; Kotlińska-Toma (2015), 276.

[15] Roesch (1982), 444–5; Pickard-Cambridge (1988), 285; Aneziri (2003), 57; Kotlińska-Toma (2015), 276.

[16] See for example Aneziri (2009), 226.

[17] For inscriptional sources during the Hellenistic and Roman periods see Aneziri (2009), 219 and nn. 4–7, 220–1 nn. 20–1. See also Gordillo Hervás, Chapter 3 in this volume.

[18] Kotlińska-Toma (2015), 278.   [19] Kotlińska-Toma (2015), 276.

[20] For the expression of local identities through games see Grigsby (2017). Grigsby argues that the change from militaristic to artistic games suggests a change in how the Boiotians both viewed themselves and wanted to be seen by others.

relations between groups within Boiotia and abroad, revealing the ways inscriptions actively displayed the relationships between the different actors/agents involved. In the second part, I will argue that the presence of these *Technitai* was integral to the building of relations with the new power of Rome, much as it had been with earlier Hellenistic rulers. I will examine the inscriptional evidence for these Roman links: where and how these texts were displayed; how Boiotia maintained its reputation as an artistic hub through (and at times despite) Roman intervention; and how with the dispersal of the local *Technitai* into a central Synod of the *Oikoumene*, local Boiotian prestige with Rome was maintained through the actions of the local elites and their own promotion of local *agones*.

8.2.1. A Boiotian agonistic boom

From the middle of the third century BC, Boiotia experienced an agonistic boom quite unlike that seen anywhere else on the Greek mainland at this time. While the Greek East enjoyed an increase in festivals from the death of Alexander onwards, the Greek mainland was relatively unaffected save for the arena of Boiotian games where there was a marked increase in number from the classical period into the Hellenistic period and a steady growth thereafter: from four examples in the fifth century BC, five in the fourth, nine in the third, increasing to thirteen and fourteen in the second and first centuries BC respectively.[21] The latter third of the third century BC provides our first evidence for a number of Boiotian agonistic festivals, including the Eleutheria at Plataia, the Pamboiotia at Koroneia, the Trieterides of Dionysos Kadmeios (later Agrionia) at Thebes,[22] the Ptoia at Akraiphia, a festival at Orchomenos whose name is unknown, and—arguably the most important—the Mouseia at Thespiai. In addition, many, like the Basileia at Lebadeia, the Ptoia at Akraiphia, the Trieterides at Thebes, and the Mouseia at Thespiai, underwent further re-organization and revitalization during the decade of the 220s.

Changes in epigraphic habit across the Greek world may account for some of the perceived suddenness of this explosion, as increased prestige linked to Greek *agones* during the Hellenistic period resulted in an increased desire for involvement to be recorded—it is during this period that the accounts (*apologiai*) of *agonothetai*, the festival presidents responsible for the funding of the games, are first recorded, for example.[23] Yet a closer look at the inscriptions linked to the Boiotian *agones* reveals evidence of re-organization and inauguration rather

---

[21] See Grigsby (2017), 286–99 tables 1–2. For a list of new festivals see Chaniotis (1995), 164–9.
[22] The festival is named the Agrionia in *IG* VII 2447, *c*.100 BC.
[23] In Athens, for example, up to the late fourth century, individual citizens known as *choregoi* had assumed the cost, one for each separate chorus; after that a single *agonothetes* supervised all of the competitions in the name of the *demos*—see Tracy (2015), 554.

than simply better records of pre-existing festivals. So while it is important to understand this Boiotian expansion in the context of the general Hellenistic agonistic flourishing (of which it formed a prominent part) the Boiotian examples reveal a unique dynamic, a pattern which the idea of a shared and universal gradual increase masks.[24] Parker has singled out this Boiotian agonistic development as a unique example of an otherwise predominately east Greek phenomenon, attributing its existence to factors related to its own history rather than to the general trend.[25] Rigsby, too, has emphasized a unique dynamic within Boiotia, a self-involved celebration of festivals that underscored national unity and solidarity to a degree not paralleled in the rest of Greece.[26] In my PhD thesis I argued that *agones* could serve as markers of both regional and *polis* identity, with the choice of cults or events celebrated through games and festivals reflecting on one side what the holders themselves felt to be important, and on the other how they wished to be seen by the wider world.[27] In Boiotia, games were also used as a form of one-upmanship between the rival Boiotian *poleis*; as the games of each *polis* became more splendid, or received certain honours, others sought this for their own games and festivals. One such honour was that of *asylia*, whose bestowal may possibly be linked to the presence of the *Technitai* within Boiotia during the third century B C.

As religious organizations dedicated to Dionysos who performed sacred duties at festivals and competitions dedicated to gods or deified mortals, these Guilds of *Technitai* were able to seek recognition of their members' privileges by Greek cities and leagues. As resident artists associated with the games of the *periodos*, during their travels and competitions they were granted privileges like those of the events themselves, namely inviolability (*asylia*) and security (*asphaleia*).[28] Hellenistic kings and associations such as the Delphic Amphictyony and the Aitolian League recognized this *asylia*, both of sanctuaries and those artists performing there, and Rigsby has suggested that the presence of these artists in Boiotia, undertaking their own quest for personal inviolability, aided the bestowal of these privileges onto the Boiotian cults with which they became associated.[29]

In the history of *asylia*, as Rigsby points out, pride of place goes to Boiotia.[30] Plataia is the first recorded place outside the sanctuaries of the *periodos* to have been granted such a status, with Thucydides recording this bestowal of *asylia* in the direct aftermath of the victory over the Persians in 479 B C.[31] Boiotia also

---

[24] For this general agonistic upturn see Aneziri (2009), 223; Parker (2004), 9–23, esp. 19–20.
[25] Parker (2004),15. [26] Rigsby (1987), 240 and 729. [27] Grigsby (2017).
[28] Aneziri (2014), 432. Examples are preserved in *IG* II² 1132 = *CID* IV 12, 114–16 (recognition of the privileges of the Athenian *Synodos* by the Delphic Amphictyony) and *F.Delphes* III, 3, 218B, ll. 5–8 (acceptance of the privileges of the Isthmian *Koinon* by the Aitolian League). Aneziri (2009), 230.
[29] Aneziri (2009), 231. Links of Boiotian *asylia* and the presence of the *Technitai*, see Rigsby (1996), 54.
[30] Rigsby (1996), 54.
[31] Rigsby (1996), 54. On Plataia, see Thucydides, *History of the Peloponnesian War* 2.71. The games at Plataia, the Eleutheria, may date from the end of the fourth century B C—see Schachter (1994), 131.

boasts the first extant decree of the granting of *asylia* to one of its temples. According to an inscription set up close by the entrance to the Temple of Apollo at Delphi, just west of the tripod base of Gelon, in 266/5 BC or 262/1 BC, the Boiotians requested—and were granted—*asylia* for their sanctuary of Athena Itonia near Koroneia by an Amphictyonic decree.[32] The Itoneion, a key sanctuary for the Boiotian Federation, was the site where the quasi-militaristic team games of the Pamboiotia were held, a festival at which only members of the Boiotian Federation were able to take part.[33] The reason for the request for *asylia* is unknown. But while threat of military disruption may have played a role, this unprecedented seeking of an honour found up to that time only in the games of the *periodos* and at the all-important site of victory over the Persians at Plataia reveals a certain bravado on the part of the Boiotians, while demonstrating the importance in which they held their sanctuary and its *agon*.[34] The placement of this decree at the top of the Sacred Way in sight of the temple entrance allowed its display to all-comers to the shrine, a truly Panhellenic audience. But in addition, this granting of *asylia* seems to have opened other Boiotian sanctuaries and their respective *agones* to the possibility of claiming a similar honour.[35] Unique in mainland Greece, these grants of *asylia* gave to the Boiotian sanctuaries and their *agones* a status equal to the games of the *periodos* yet achieved in a distinctively Boiotian manner.[36] The inter-*polis* competitiveness of the Boiotians (which Perikles had likened to the self-destructive buffeting of closely packed holm-oaks) may have fuelled this process in characteristic one-upmanship.[37]

The presence of the *Technitai* within Boiotia from the middle of the third century BC may well have provided the impetus for these requests for *asylia*. As will be seen, far outstripping the simple answering of logistical needs and provision of manpower, the *Technitai* instead played a crucial role in the agonistic revitalisation of Boiotia. The epigraphy surrounding the Mouseia at Thespiai and Trieterides at Thebes, for example, clearly reveals how the *Technitai* were fundamental in the process of renaissance itself. While evidence exists for the Guilds as initiators of certain games outside Boiotia (thereby promoting the interests of their own

---

[32] *SEG* 18, 240. On the placement see Jardé (1902), 250–1 no. 6. The reading of Koroneia is tentative. Pouilloux (*F.Delphes* III, 4, 358) suggests instead the sanctuary in Achaea-Phthiotis, but Schachter is swayed by the evidence of Polybius, *Histories* 4.3.5 and 4.25.2, and Pausanias, *Description of Greece* 9.34.1—Schachter (1981), 123.

[33] During the Classical period the Itoneion became the focal point of Boiotia's *ethnos* religion—Beck and Ganter (2015), 135.

[34] The honour bestowed upon Plataia in 479 BC may have suggested to the Boiotians the possibility of gaining this honour for their most important joint sanctuary.

[35] It is probable that a copy of this inscription would have been set up at the Itoneion in Koroneia.

[36] These requests were not linked to gaining Panhellenic or stephanitic ('crown-games') status as was common for later games, but simply to the bestowal of honour. The normal procedure for attaining stephanitic status included a request recognition alongside the *periodos* with the sending of envoys throughout the Greek world, and recognition of the sanctuary and games as *asylos*, though not all of these steps were required—see Parker (2004), 10–11.

[37] Holm-oaks, see Aristotle, *Rhetoric* 3.4.

members and ensuring the success of the events) the Boiotian examples reveal a different dynamic, with the various *poleis* seizing the opportunity provided by these resident *Technitai* and their expertise (and status) to co-organize their agonistic festivals.[38] As such, it is likely that the presence of these resident artists inside Boiotia helped to extend *asylia* to the Boiotian *agones* to which they became aligned and helped organize, in something of a symbiotic relationship.[39] This symbiosis will be discussed for the Trieterides for Dionysos Kadmeios at Thebes and the Mouseia at Thespiai below.

8.2.2. Trieterides for Dionysos Kadmeios at Thebes

In line with a number of key Boiotian festivals, the Trieterides (later Agrionia) for Dionysos Kadmeios at Thebes was possibly established to commemorate an important historical event, namely the re-founding of Thebes by Kassandros in 315 BC.[40] From the third century BC these thymelic games were dedicated to Dionysos Kadmeios; they were trieteric—i.e. with a two year periodicity and thus held 'in the third year'—and were directed jointly by the city of Thebes and the *Koinon* of the Artists of Dionysos of the Isthmos and Nemea.[41] This co-organization is clearly demonstrated in the sending of both priest and *theoroi* from the Guild to announce the games, as well as in the administration of the Sanctuary of Dionysos Kadmeios itself by the *epimeletai* (officials) of the Guild.[42]

Like many of the Boiotian *agones*, the Trieterides seems to have undergone a change of status during the first half of the 220s BC as evidenced by the five remaining fragments of a dossier of three inscriptions concerning an Amphictyonic decree dated c.228–225 BC, once part of a wall of the Theban Treasury at Delphi.[43] This decree defined the privileges and responsibilities of the

---

[38] Examples of festivals inaugurated by the Guilds include that held by the Athenian *Synodos* of Dionysiac Artists in honour of the Cappadocian king Ariarathes V Eusebes Philopator *IG* II² 1330—Aneziri (2007), 68. Aneziri differentiates those contests directly instigated at the behest of the *Technitai* and those for which they were co-organizers—see Aneziri (2007), 67–9. See also Aneziri (2014), 432 and (2003), 269–87.

[39] The *Technitai* were linked to *asylia* at the Trieterides at Thebes (*F.Delphes* III, 1, 351), the Ptoia (*IG* VII 4135), and arguably at the Mouseia—see Knoepfler (1996), 161–2; Rigsby (1996), 56. See also Schachter (1986), 160.

[40] See *IG* IV 682. For timing see Schachter (1981), 191. Other examples include the Basileia set up at Lebadeia to commemorate the Theban/Boiotian victory over Sparta at Leuktra in 371 BC—see Diodorus Siculus, *The Library of History* 15.53; see also *SEG* 45, 434.

[41] As thymelic—see for example *SEG* 31, 539. See also *FD* III 1.351; *SEG* 19, 379; 28, 487; 31, 539. For Dionysos Kadmeios see Pausanias, *Description of Greece* 9.12.4. *SEG* 19, 379. A trieteric festival was typical of festivals of Dionysos—Rigsby (1996), 69. See also Aneziri (2007), 71.

[42] See Aneziri (2007), 71 and *CID* IV 70 ll. 13–14.

[43] *F.Delphes* III, 1, 351; *SEG* 31, 539. For full text see Rigsby (1996), 70–3. The Theban treasury was paid for with spoils taken either at the battle of Leuktra—Pausanias, *Description of Greece* 10.11.5—or perhaps during the Third Sacred War post-346 BC—Diodorus Siculus, *The Library of History* 17.10.5; see Jacquemin (1999), 60 n. 174. Scott prefers the former and sees the placement of the treasury as an attempt by Thebes to echo former expressions of Boiotian communal identity at Delphi—Scott (2016), 104.

Artists of Dionysos at the Trieterides, and declared the Theban temple of Dionysos Kadmeios inviolable (*asylos*) like the Sanctuary of Apollo at Delphi.[44] The first decree (ll. 11–29), rendered under the archonship of Nikarchos, ensured the participation of the Amphictyons in the protection of the sanctuary, festival and participating artists. The inscription reveals a joint role for both the *polis* and the *Technitai* in the organization of the festival, and records the granting of *asylia* for artists, contests, and sanctuary alike, along with the provision for recording these decisions in Delphi and in Thebes (ll. 26–9):

...ἀναγράψαι δὲ τὸν [γραμματέα τόδ]ε τὸ ψήφισμα ἐν στήλαις δυσὶν καὶ ἀναθεῖναι τὴν μὲν ἐν Δελφοῖς ἐν τῶ[ι ἱερῶι τοῦ Ἀπόλλωνο]ς ὅπου ἂν δοκῆι ἐν καλλίστωι εἶναι, τὴν δὲ ἐν Θήβαις παρὰ τὸν σηκό[ν τῆς Σεμέλης, ἀν]αθεῖναι δὲ καὶ τῶν ἄλλων ἱερῶν ὅπου ἂν δοκῆι ἐν καλλίστωι εἶναι.[45]

...And that the secretary inscribe this decree on two stelai, and set these up, one in Delphi in the sanctuary of Apollo, wherever it is deemed most favourable, the other in Thebes beside the precinct of Semele and also in other sanctuaries wherever it is deemed most favourable.

Thus the joint actions of the *Technitai* and the *polis* of Thebes were displayed in a prime location both at Delphi and in Thebes, which Pausanias described as part of the Sanctuary of Dionysos Kadmeios in the *agora* on the Theban acropolis.[46]

The second decree (ll. 30–9), also under Nikarchos, provided sanctions against artists failing without valid excuse.[47] The third, possibly dating from 214 BC and placed above the others (ll. 1–10), recorded the request by a single Theban envoy for the text of the previous decrees to be set up on the walls of the Theban Treasury at Delphi.[48] Perhaps the provision for display included in the first decree (l. 27) had not been carried out, or perhaps the place chosen had not been quite as good as the Thebans had hoped.[49] They may have been hoping for a placement close by the temple of Apollo where the decree of *asylia* for the Itoneion had been placed earlier in the century. Either way, the inscription now found itself gracing the wall of the most visible Theban/Boiotian monument at Delphi—the largest of all the treasuries—standing just off the first turn of the Sacred Way at the south-west corner of the sanctuary, facing the south-west entrance.[50] The exact location of the inscription on the Treasury walls is not known but a prominent position on

---

[44] Half a century later the artists stated that the oracles of Apollo had granted them inviolability because of their role in the contests of Dionysos at Thebes, amongst others (*IG* XI 4 1061. l.14–16 from Delos); see also Rigsby (1996), 68.
[45] Text from Bousquet (1961), 79.
[46] Pausanias, *Description of Greece* 9.12.3–6. Symeonoglou (2014), 127.
[47] Robert suggests that the Delphic oracle approved this agreement between Thebes, the *Technitai*, and the Amphictyons—see Robert (1977), 197–209.
[48] Bousquet (1961), 85. [49] Rigsby (1996), 73.
[50] Thus mirroring spatially the Spartan offerings for Aegospotamoi beside the south-east entrance.

the southwest facing front of the building where other inscriptions surrounded the entrance doorway is probable.⁵¹ These prominent locations for display at Delphi and within Thebes speak of the dual nature of this inscription and its intended audience. That in Thebes reminds us of the Oropos proxeny decrees described by Wilding.⁵² Here the placement at the sanctuary of Dionysos Kadmeios displayed the texts as religious documents to worshippers. That on the wall of the Theban treasury at Delphi revealed Theban pride in this grant of *asylia* to their *agon* and sanctuary, made visible to all in this Panhellenic setting. Rigsby has suggested a military motive for this request for *asylia*, but to my mind it is best understood as an honour (alongside those other Boiotian claims) for which the presence and input of the Dionysian *Technitai* (themselves already *asyloi* through their role in the *periodos*) no doubt played a convincing role.⁵³

In addition to this change of status, it is possible that the *Technitai* had been involved in the inauguration of the Trieterides, as they arguably were with the Delphic Soteria.⁵⁴ The Soteria seems to have been introduced to celebrate the victory over the Gauls at Delphi in 279/8 BC, and was reformed as a pentaeteric stephanitic festival in 246/5 BC by the Aitolians, as evidenced, for example, from a decree from Athens (*IG* II² 680).⁵⁵ On the basis of the geographical scope of the contestants (being from central Greece and the Peloponnese) and the presence in these earliest inscriptions of one Pythokles, son of Aristarchos of Hermione, who we know was priest for the *Technitai* amongst other roles, Manieri has suggested that in the initial stage of its existence, the Soteria was organized by the Isthmian and Nemean *Koinon* of *Technitai*.⁵⁶

Pythokles figures in a number of inscriptions at Delphi dated between 262 BC and 255 BC and is recorded on at least three occasions serving as priest of the *Technitai* at the Soteria, and once as victorious leader of the men's chorus at another celebration of the same festival.⁵⁷ This presence of Pythokles in these earliest recorded inscriptions for the Soteria suggests a role for the *Technitai* in the games' inauguration, so it is interesting that our first evidence of the Trieterides comes from an epigram for this same Pythokles (*IG* VI 682), set up by his brother in his hometown around the middle of the third century and which records (amongst many other victories, all in games associated with the *Koinon* of Isthmos and Nemea) the crown won from Dionysos Kadmeios at Thebes, possibly as rhapsode.⁵⁸ This latter is of some interest as the art of the rhapsode in competition fell out of favour elsewhere *except* in Boiotia where the event was championed by

---

⁵¹ Jacquemin and Laroche (2012), 109.   ⁵² Wilding (2015), 55–81.
⁵³ Rigsby (1996), 70.   ⁵⁴ See below.
⁵⁵ Champion (1995), 213. See n. 2 for related inscriptions.
⁵⁶ Manieri (2013), 140. Inscriptions of Pythokles as Priest of the *Technitai*—*CID* 4.31 = *F.Delphes* III, 4, 356; *CID* 4.42 = *F.Delphes* III, 1, 477; *CID* 4.45 = *BCH* 52 (1958) 259. On Pythokles as priest see Nachtergael (1977), 321; cf. Aneziri (2003), 276–7. See also Schachter (2016), 369.
⁵⁷ Men's chorus see *CID* 4.42 = *F.Delphes* III, 1, 477, c.260 BC.
⁵⁸ See Aneziri (2007), 72–3 and n. 34.

the Boiotians into the imperial period, with rhapsodic competition found *only* in Boiotia from this time.⁵⁹ Why so? Perhaps the figure of Hesiod is of interest here, for rhapsodes were known to perform the poems of Hesiod as well as Homer, and Hesiod's own assertion that he won a tripod as a prize with a song that he performed at the funeral games for Amphidamas of Chalcis (*Op.* 654–9) sets him up as the first rhapsode.⁶⁰ No wonder the Boiotians took this event for their own.

Returning to Pythokles and the Trieterides, that this epigram for a known member of the *Technitai* is our earliest evidence of the Theban festival supports (as with the Delphic Soteria) the theory of the central role played by the Guild in the festival's inauguration. Pythokles' epigram also records his victories at the Mouseia, another *agon* in whose development the *Technitai* were intimately bound and to which I will now turn.⁶¹

8.2.3. The Mouseia at Thespiai

The Valley of the Muses sits about 6 kilometres west of Thespiai, and 2 kilometres south-west of the probable site of Hesiod's Askra.⁶² Hesiod was honoured in Thespiai with a bronze statue in the *agora*, and in the temple of the Muses at Mount Helikon as the founder of the cult of the Muses.⁶³ This intimate association of the place and poet may well have played a role in the central position the Mouseia had amongst the Boiotian *agones*.

The few surviving architectural fragments at the Sanctuary of the Muses— two porticoes, a monumental altar, and a theatre built into the slope above the sanctuary—date from the latter half of the third century BC.⁶⁴ Although a number of literary sources hint at the possibility that the Mouseia was already an *agon* from as early as the fifth or fourth century BC, the first hard evidence comes from the middle of the third century BC, with the epigram mentioned above for the multi-talented Pythokles of Hermione, member of the Guild of Artists of Dionysos

---

⁵⁹ West (2013), 364. Like flute-playing, it might be possible that the art of the rhapsode was denigrated elsewhere as lacking creativity. But the Boiotians seem to have consciously excelled in this art, and the event with its epic links must have been a source of prestige. On the links to the Muses and Apollo, see Gangloff (2018), 143; on Boiotia's Hellenistic dominance in the event see Tsagalis (2018), 102. See Roesch (1989) 203–14 on Thebes' reputation with the aulos.

⁶⁰ For Hesiod as part of the rhapsode's art, see Gangloff (2018), 131 and 141. On Hesiod as first rhapsode see West (2013), 1.

⁶¹ *IG* IV 682, c.265–255 BC, ll. 13–14. Date from Schachter (2016), 369—see also Nachtergael (1977), 429–30, no. 15bis. Fossey (2014), 112 mistakenly dates this to the imperial period.

⁶² Schachter (1986), 150.

⁶³ Gangloff (2018), 141. Inscriptions from Thespiai to Hesiod include *IG* VII 4240 and 1785. Pausanias, *Description of Greece*, writes of Hesiod in the valley of the Muses at 9.27.5, 30.1–3, and 31.3–5.

⁶⁴ A statue by Strongylion mentioned by Pausanias, *History of Greece* 9.30.1 gives the *terminus post quem* of the start of the fourth century BC. See Schachter (1986), 157. For description of site see Roux (1954), 22–48.

(*IG* IV 682).⁶⁵ Once again his victory at the Mouseia at Thespiai suggests that the Isthmian and Nemean Dionysiac *Technitai* were involved in the festival from this period, at the very least as performers if not as organizers.⁶⁶

An impressive dossier of fragmentary inscriptions once displayed in the valley of the Muses (*I. Thespies* 152–8) gives an outline of the re-organization and change of status of the Mouseia c.230–208 BC in which the *Technitai* were involved. These must have been prominently displayed at a central location, although their remnants were discovered widely scattered across the valley. One fragment (*I. Thespies* 158), found in the walls of the ruined chapel of Hagia Trias that once stood upon the site of the monumental altar of the Muses (Fig. 8.2), suggests that the inscriptions may have been on show close to this central location around which, Roux has argued, many of the contests may have taken place.⁶⁷ Such a position would have afforded maximum visibility to suppliants and contestants alike, once again reiterating the sacredness of these decrees while allowing them greatest exposure at the most visited and holiest site within the valley.⁶⁸

Fig. 8.2 Altar to the Muses, once the site of Hagia Trias, looking west towards portico and theatre.
Photograph: Grigsby.

⁶⁵ Fifth century BC—Sophocles, *Oedipus Tyrannos* 1108; Schachter (1986), 156 n. 4; fourth century BC—*De genio Socratis* 7 (578E–579B); see Schachter (1986), 157.
⁶⁶ On role of the *Technitai* in the Mouseia, see Knoepfler (2004), 1273 and *I. Thespies* 156, 172.
⁶⁷ On the identification of the altar, see Roux (1954), 25–7; on competitions, Roux (1954), 42.
⁶⁸ Pausanias, *Description of Greece* 9.29.3–6 mentions no temple, and Roux has suggested this was characteristic of the cult of the Muses, see Roux (1954), 39. Votives were housed in the porticos and beneath the trees within the grove, and it is possible the inscriptions described here were on display at one of these spots instead.

Three of the inscriptions, carved onto the same stone (*I. Thespies* 152–4), record letters from foreign rulers concerning the re-organization of the games.[69] *I. Thespies* 152 is a letter of a queen, a sister of a king—usually taken to be Arsinoe III, sister of Ptolemy IV—accepting the introduction of a pentaeteric dramatic competition and dated *c*.210 BC; *I. Thespies* 153, possibly a letter of acceptance from Ptolemy IV, informs us that three Thespians were sent as ambassadors concerning the pentaeteric *agon*; and *I. Thespies* 154 is a letter from an unknown king *c*.215–208 BC.[70] A fourth inscription (*I. Thespies* 155), a decree of Thespiai *c*.225/220 BC or after 217 BC, speaks of previous letters from certain monarchs and a past request for recognition of the Mouseia as *stephanites* with iso-pythian status. These inscriptions may have been part of the same monument.[71]

A fifth inscription, dated *c*.225/220 BC or after 217 BC (*I. Thespies* 156), commemorates the first celebration of this stephanitic competition, and records a decree of the Guild of Artists of Dionysos of Isthmia and Nemea concerning the Mouseia, its new status as a Crown Games, and their decision to take part in it.[72] From this inscription we learn that the *agonothetes* Hierokles of Thespiai had been sent out to invite various Guilds and foreign states to accept the change in status. Along with this decree of acceptance, similar decrees exist from the Athenian Guild (*I. Thespies* 157 = *IG* VII 1735b), and possibly the *polis* of Oropos (*I. Thespies* 158).[73]

The dates of these inscriptions and precisely how they are related have been debated at length elsewhere.[74] Whatever the exact chain of events, the related inscriptions were displayed prominently, revealing to all-comers the complex network of relationships involved in the organization of these *agones*. The role played by the *Technitai* of Isthmos and Nemea as displayed in their own decree (*I. Thespies* 156 and 156bis) is of most interest to us in this present enquiry. This inscription reveals the very close collaboration (and mutual respect) between the *polis* of Thespiai, the Boiotian *koinon*, and the *Koinon* of *Technitai*, each of whom clearly played an important role in the games' organization in different ways. First, we read (ll. 11–13) of the Thespian envoy Hierokles' approach to the *Technitai* for

---

[69] These fragments were found in 1890 by Jamot in the pavement of the church Panagia Zoodochou Pigis between Néochori and (Palaio) Panagia near Thespiai—see Jamot (1895), 328.

[70] Roesch (2007), 4:16–18.

[71] See Schachter (2016), 346–7. The date reflects the unlikelihood of such undertakings during the Social War (220–217 BC). *I. Thespies* 155 as same monument—Knoepfler (1996), 162. He argues that the recipient monarchs were Ptolemy IV, his sister/wife Arsinoe, and arguably Antiochus III and Philip V. *I. Thespies* 155 is currently in the Museum at Thebes to where it was sent, so Jamot supposes, from Thespiai—Jamot (1895), 326.

[72] This inscription, now in Thebes, was found in the wall of Hagios Georgios in 1895—see Jamot (1895), 313.

[73] *I. Thespies* 157 was viewed by Jamot at the Museum of Erimocastro in Thespiai in 1888. The stone also contains *I. Thespies* 156bis, the end of the decree of the *Technitai* (*I. Thespies* 156). See Jamot (1895), 322. *I. Thespies* 158, possibly now in the Thebes Museum, was discovered in Hagia Trias by Jamot—see Jamot (1895), 331.

[74] See for example Knoepfler (1996), 141–67; Schachter (2016), 344–71.

their assistance, thus emphasizing the role of the *polis* in instigating the changes. Next (ll. 26-7), we read of how the *Technitai* had been involved in past celebrations of the festival—καθὼς καὶ ἐν τοῖς ἔμπροσ[θ]εν χρόνοις—'just as in previous times', while further on (ll. 45-61) we learn of the degree of this earlier involvement and of how the Mouseia had been considered a joint affair between the *Technitai* and the *polis* of Thespiai:

> ἀποκρίνασθαι δὲ αὐτοῖς
> ὅτε καὶ πρότερον οἱ τεχνῖται
> **κοινὸν ὑπολαμβάνοντες**
> **εἶναι τὸν ἀγῶνα τῶν Μουσῶν**
> **τῆι τε πόλει Θεσπιέων καὶ αὐ-**
> **τοῖς,** τὴν πᾶσαν προθυμίαν
> ἐνεδείξαντο καὶ συνθύοντες
> καὶ ἱερέα ἐξ αὐτῶν αἱρούμενοι
> καὶ θεωροὺς ἀποστέλλοντες
> καὶ ψηφίσματα γράφοντες καὶ
> συμπρεσβεύοντες περὶ τοῦ
> ἀγῶνος καὶ πρὸς τοὺς λοιποὺς
> Ἕλληνας καθὼς ἂν ἡ πολις παρ[α]-
> καλῆι τῶν Θεσπιέων· ἐμφανί-
> ζειν δὲ αὐτοῖς ὅτι καὶ νῦν πρῶτοι
> τὸν ἀγῶνα ταῖς Μούσαις στεφα-
> [νί]την ἀποδέχοντ[αι — —].

and to reply to them that previously also the artists, **considering that the contest of the Muses was a joint affair between the city of Thespiai and themselves,** had shown every eagerness concerning the contest by joining in the sacrifices; choosing a priest from amongst themselves; sending out *theoroi*; composing decrees; joining in embassies to promote the contest amongst the other Greeks, just as the city of Thespiai urged them to do; and to inform them that now also they would be the first to accept this contest, dedicated to the Muses with prizes of crowns....

Thus the *Technitai* praise the role of the *polis* of Thespiai and the Boiotian *koinon* for their involvement in the festival of the Muses, while mentioning their own role alongside the *polis* in the joint organization of the competition.[75] This complex interaction of different bodies reveals how games and festivals formed the hub of a complex set of relationships between various groups at different levels of society, with festivals such as the Mouseia a source of prestige and honour for all.

---

[75] Aneziri (2007), 71 states that the Mouseia was considered a joint contest of the Guild and the *polis* of Thespiai.

We know also that the Guild of Ionia and the Hellespont was involved in the festival at some point prior to 172–167 BC (*IG* XI 4.1061), so it is possible it too accepted these changes at this time.[76] A final inscription (*I.Thespies* 62) c.210 BC records a gift received from Ptolemy and Arsinoe with which lands were bought and rented out to provide funds for the games.[77] This association of foreign monarchs with the games (as with *I.Thespies* 152–5) reveals the prestige that games could bestow upon a *polis* and foreshadows the kind of relationships such games would foster with the foreign power of Rome during the following centuries, with the proviso of course that Rome became the preeminent power rather than being one of many.

The earliest third-century BC evidence for the Mouseia may once again be the epigraph of Pythokles (*IG* IV 682) which gave our first evidence for the Theban Trieterides (above, 8.2.1) and it is tempting, as with the Soteria and Trieterides, to suggest a central role of the *Technitai* in the inauguration of the games, with no other clear examples of a competition predating this inscription.[78] With a clear role in the third-century BC proliferation and increased status of a number of Boiotian *agones*, there is therefore convincing evidence that the presence of this particular group of artists with their thymelic specialities was changing the agonistic flavour of Boiotia, crafting for the region a different and prestigious artistic-agonistic identity which perhaps reflected Boiotia's earlier artistic reputation as best encapsulated in the figure of Hesiod. In this light it is interesting that Gangloff has suggested that the rhapsodes competing in the Mouseia recited excerpts from Hesiod's poems rather than Homer's, further cementing this link to the prestigious past.[79]

Of the three Boiotian *agones* for which the latter half of the third century BC provides our first evidence, all were thymelic.[80] It is possible, too, that the third century BC saw the introduction of thymelic events at the Basileia in Lebadeia.[81] While the inclusion of a wide variety of events was characteristic of Hellenistic games, as stated in the introduction, the break from the purely hippic and athletic events favoured by the Boiotians of the fifth and fourth centuries BC in favour of the thymelic is marked: no hippic events are recorded during the third century BC (save for those associated with the military team games of the Pamboiotia). While this may simply have been a local manifestation of the more widespread under-representation of hippic competition during the later Hellenistic period, the presence of the *Technitai*, with their ready-made thymelic competitors, clearly had an effect on the direction of the development of the Boiotian *agones*, and thereby on

---

[76] On the presence of this Guild in Thebes, see below.
[77] Presumably the same money asked for in *I.Thespies* 152 and 153—Schachter (2016), 351; see also *SEG* 15, 321.
[78] See Schachter (2016), 369–70 for the scant evidence for possible earlier dithyrambic competition.
[79] Gangloff (2018), 141.   [80] Trieterides of Dionysos Kadmeios, Ptoia, and Mouseia.
[81] Schachter suggests hippic events also occurred although there is no inscriptional evidence for the third century BC; Schachter (1994), 116 n. 5.

the identity that Boiotia was now projecting into the wider world.[82] This on-hand group of esteemed competitors allowed for the development of thymelic games, while the memory of Hesiod and Boiotia's artistic past provided the necessary model going forwards.

8.2.4. The Ptoia at Akraiphia

Another festival, the Ptoia to Apollo Ptoios near Akraiphia, is also unknown before the latter part of the third century BC, when the games seem to have been re-organized, if not inaugurated, during the same decade as the reorganization of the Mouseia. An incomplete inscription *IG* VII 4135 (*SEG* 25, 547) *c*.228–226 BC found at the Sanctuary of Apollo Ptoios (Fig. 8.3) records an Amphictyonic decree which granted personal inviolability to the participants of the Ptoia, and *asylia* to the sanctuary of Apollo Ptoios (ll. 1–4); a sacred truce and safe passage from the fifteenth of *Hippodromios* [the beginning of August] (ll. 10–11); and accorded full powers to the prophet and priest of Apollo Ptoios, the *polis* of Akraiphia and the Boiotian *koinon*, and the *agonothetes* of the Ptoia (ll. 12–16). Towards the end of the decree (ll. 16–18) we hear that Ptoiokles son of Potamodoros

Fig. 8.3 The sanctuary of Apollo Ptoios at modern Perdikovrysi, near Akraiphia.
Photograph: Grigsby.

---

[82] The underrepresentation of these races (at least in the later Hellenistic period onwards) suggests that hippic competition had become less attractive; presumably navigating the increasingly fraught agonistic circuit with horses was becoming a less attractive proposition—Remijsen (2015), 169. Equestrian events were still included in some *agones* and would return to Boiotia in the next century at the Theban Herakleia—see Heberdey et al. (1896), 81.

is to record the decision and set it up at Delphi and at the Ptoion.[83] So this decree was made visible both at Delphi—possibly in the SW corner where the Theban and Boiotian Treasuries stood and where the inscription recording the festival for Dionysos Kadmeios (*F.Delphes* III, 1, 351) was also displayed—and at the Sanctuary of Apollo Ptoios itself. With the beginning of the inscription lost, it is impossible to confirm or deny a direct involvement of the *Technitai* based at nearby Thebes, but the events recorded in later victory lists—as would be expected with the nature of the god honoured—reveal once again the introduction of games of an artistic nature.[84] Aneziri has suggested that the Ptoia were an example of games for which the Guild provided artists but had no active role in the organization, a situation more common than the direct organization found in the Mouseia and Trieterides.[85] But again we see a role, even if not organizational, in the presence of the *Technitai* within Boiotia in allowing new artistic games such as the Ptoia to flourish in the region.

The presence of these Guilds and their involvement with the games helped to create a very visible stage upon which prestige could be sought. By being part and parcel of the Boiotian sanctuaries' claims for *asylia* and helping to organize such widely respected games the *Technitai* were setting the stage upon which relations could be forged and prestige prominently displayed, relations writ large in the public inscriptions at local sanctuaries, *polis* centres, and Panhellenic sanctuaries such as Delphi. These inscriptions made clear the exact nature of the relations between these separate bodies, their networks and power structures, each group gaining prestige from association with the other and between them creating a new and innovative Boiotian agonistic and festival culture through which they were able to gain recognition from foreign monarchs—this recognition itself then being proudly displayed in the festival surrounds. Not only this, but in cementing a new artistic identity for Boiotia, the *Technitai* had created a means through which the Boiotian *poleis* would negotiate their relationship with the soon arriving power of Rome.

8.3. The Artists of Dionysos in Roman Boiotia

Boiotia is rarely at the centre of anyone's thoughts, and the literary accounts of the Roman occupation of Greece are no exception. Lacking sufficient detail to reconstruct the response of the various Boiotian *poleis* to these momentous events from literary sources, the epigraphy related to the Boiotian *agones* provides a unique window through which to view the Boiotian reaction to this externally imposed circumstance.

---

[83] Rigsby (1996), 59 and 65–6.
[84] See *IG* VII 4147 (late second/early first century BC); *BCH* 44 (1920) 249.10, 261.11, 262.12.
[85] Aneziri (2007), 80.

From 171 BC onwards, with the formal dissolution of the Boiotian *koinon*, the responses of individual *poleis* towards Rome (often expressed through *agones* and publicized through epithets for games or inscribed prominently in sanctuaries and *agorai*) would have serious consequences for their citizens.[86] From this time on, the various Boiotian *poleis* displayed their individual stance towards their new overseers through the medium of *agones*, be that through rebranding, re-organization, the introduction of new events, or the creation of completely new games (such as the Soteria at Akraiphia, possibly instituted to celebrate the beneficial actions of Rome under P. Cornelius Lentulus).[87] In this section I will look at the continuing role played by the *Technitai* in these negotiations with Rome, and how these changed and eventually fell away during the period of Roman occupation.

As shown in the chapters by Scharff, Gordillo Hervás, and Calomino elsewhere in this volume, games and festivals were a medium through which relations with the new power of Rome could be forged and displayed. Following the Roman subjugation of the mid-second century BC, there seems to have been a slight reduction in the scale and volume of agonistic festivals for Greece as a whole, and not until a century and a half later—with growing prosperity and growing imperial encouragement—do we see signs of revival.[88] Yet a closer analysis reveals that Boiotia initially bucked this trend, undergoing a small agonistic revival towards the end of the second century BC—as it had during the third—possibly in response to the Roman presence (with the inauguration of the Soteria at Akraiphia and Romaia in Thebes), with another upturn occurring directly following the Mithridatic War. The reasons for the latter may be found in the actions of Sulla on Boiotian soil, and once again in the presence in Thebes of the Guild of *Technitai* of Isthmos and Nemea and the renewed reputation of Boiotia as an artistic hub which their presence had done much to forge.

8.3.1. Boiotia as an artistic centre: the letter of Mummius to the *Technitai* at Thebes

The Romans early acknowledged the existing status and privileges of the various branches of *Technitai* in Greece, with the senate and the Roman generals (and later Hadrian, as explored above by Gordillo Hervás in Chapter 3) responding positively to the efforts of the Guilds and becoming willing guarantors of the

---

[86] Beck and Ganter (2015), 156. See also Roesch (1965), 69–71; Larsen (1968), 359–504; Buck (1993), 106; Müller (2007). Livy, *History of Rome* 42.47.4-9; Diodorus Siculus, *The Library of History* 30.1. A league of sorts operated under pro-Roman leadership from 167–146 BC, but this was then dissolved—Beck and Ganter (2015), 156.

[87] On the Soteria as a pro-Roman statement, see Schachter (1994), 94. For games as a means of easing tensions, especially through the revival of ancestral custom, see Graf (2015), 36–41.

[88] König (2005), 28.

artists' status and privileges.⁸⁹ The same was true of the Guilds in Boiotia. We know that Thebes had played host to a branch of the *Technitai* of the Isthmos and Nemea since the third century BC, with a subsidiary branch—the *Technitai* of Helikon—based at Thespiai. Previously centred in Argos and Corinth as well as the Boiotian *poleis*, with the destruction of Corinth in 146 BC Thebes became, almost by default, the administrative centre of the Guild of the Isthmos and Nemea, at the very least sharing this role with Argos.⁹⁰

A letter to the *Technitai* from Ionia and the Hellespont (*SEG* 32, 491; *IG* VII 2413–2414), inscribed and displayed at Thebes after 146 BC and possibly sent by L. Mummius, reassured (by the renewal of privileges essential to the conduct of their artistic activities) the Guild from Asia Minor, who were anxious over the new political situation in those regions. The name of the *Technitai* of the Isthmos and Nemea is missing on these incomplete fragments, but the *stele*'s prominent placement in Thebes suggests that the stone also displayed a second letter from L. Mummius to these Peloponnesian *Technitai* based in Thebes.⁹¹ Given the import of its contents, one ought to imagine these letters prominently and centrally displayed, for they guaranteed the *Technitai* the privileges which they had approached Mummius to confirm, his response thereby implicitly recognizing Thebes' right to remain one of the most important centres of musical and religious activity in Roman Greece.

Whether a branch of the Guild of Ionia and the Hellespont was housed in Thebes at this time is unclear, though their members had long taken part in games in Boiotia and continued to do so. From a decree by the *Koinon* of the Artists of Asia Minor passed in the second quarter of the second century BC, for example, it emerges clearly that their members participated in competitions organized by the *Koinon* of the Isthmos and Nemea, namely the Soteria, Mouseia, and the Trieterides, now called the Agrionia.⁹² Mummius' letter equally attests to the presence of the Guild within the usual sphere of the Peloponnesian branch, at the very least as interested competitors.⁹³ We know that artists from the Athenian Guild also competed in Boiotia at these Isthmian-run contests, with examples including Theodotos, son of Pythion, a victorious rhapsode at the Mouseia after 84 BC, and in the same competition in 146–95 BC Philotas, son of Theokles, a victorious herald, both hailing from Athens and being known artists from the Athenian *Koinon*.⁹⁴ What is more, a dispute between the Isthmian and Nemean *Technitai* and those from Athens, centred on Thebes and to which I shall turn

---

⁸⁹ Aneziri (2014), 432. See for example Sherk (1969), nos. 44, 49 = *I.Cos* Segre ED 7; *Corinth* VIII 3, 40.
⁹⁰ Knoepfler (2004), 1272.
⁹¹ Le Guen (2007), also suggests the existence of this second letter to the Peloponnesian Guild, 265 and n. 86; 267 and n. 93.
⁹² Daux (1935), 210–30.   ⁹³ See Aneziri (2014), 77.
⁹⁴ See Aneziri (2014), 76–7. Inscriptions: Jamot (1895), 339–40 no. 13, ll. 17–18 Museum Erimocastro (*I.Thespies* 172); Jamot (1895), 335–6 no. 10, ll. 11–12 (*I.Thespies* 167).

shortly, speaks of a strong presence and participation of members of the Athenian Guild in the city. Given this evidence, we begin to see Thebes as the artistic hub that the Romans must have come to view it.

8.3.2. A new festival at Thebes: the Romaia

The festival of the Theban Romaia was unknown until 2003, when the upper part of a limestone pedimental *stele* (Fig. 8.4) was unearthed near the west side of the Theban Kadmeia.[95] The Romaia was short-lived, our only evidence dating from the latter part of the second century BC.[96] The incomplete *stele*, possibly dating close to 100 BC, begins with the following inscription (*SEG* 54, 516) revealing an almost exclusively Theban clientele:

[Κ]λεοκρίτου ἄρχοντος·
ἀγωνοθετοῦντος τὰ Ῥωμαῖα
Ἰσμηνίου τοῦ Ἰσμηνοκλέους,
οἵδε ἐνίκων·
σαλπικτής·
Πολέμων Πολεμάρχου Δελφός·

Fig. 8.4 *Stele* recording Romaia c. second century BC—*SEG* 54.516. Archaeological Museum of Thebes.
Photograph: Grigsby, by permission of Museum of Thebes.

[95] *SEG* 54, 516. For a detailed assessment see Knoepfler (2004), 1241–79. See also *SEG* 54, 517.
[96] But not before c.140 BC. As Knoepfler has stated, the date of the victory lists, c.125–120 BC, merely provides a *terminus ante quem* for the games' inauguration, while the absence of any designation of the games as being the 'first' probably points to an earlier date of creation, though arguably not before 140 BC; see Knoepfler (2004), 1265–72, 1278.

κῆρυξ·
Νικίας Ἀγαθοκλέους Θηβαῖος·
ποιητὴς ἐπῶν·
Κλεώνδας Πυθέου Θηβαῖος·
ῥαψωιδός·
Ἄβρων Φιλοξένου Θηβαῖο[ς]·
αὐλητής·
Ἀριστοκλῆς Ἀμφικλέους Θηβαῖο[ς]·
κιθαριστής·
Μελίτων Ἀριστοβούλου Θηβα[ῖος]·
κιθαρωιδός·
Ἀθηναγόρας Δημητρίου Θηβαῖ[ος]·
ποιητὴς σατύρων·
[. . .]κλῆς [Ἀ]θ[ηνο(?)]δώρου Θηβαῖος·
[— — — — — — — — — — — —]

In the archonship of Kleokritos, when Ismenios son of Ismenokles was *agonothetes* of the Romaia, these were the victors: Trumpeter—Polemon son of Polemarchos, of Delphi; herald—Nikias son of Agathokles, of Thebes; epic poet—Kleondas son of Pytheos, of Thebes; rhapsode—Habron, son of Philoxenos, of Thebes; flute player—Aristokles son of Amphikles of Thebes; kitharist—Meliton son of Aristoboulos of Thebes; kitharode—Athenagoras son of Demetrios of Thebes; poet of satyr plays—[...]kles son of Athenodoros of Thebes....

Members of the Guild of Dionysian *Technitai* of the Isthmos and Nemea present in Thebes may have played a role in the inauguration of these musical and artistic contests, even if simply in the availability of a ready-made clientele on-hand to provide a fund of prestigious competitors.[97]

A second victory list (*IG* VII 2448) once linked to the Theban Trieterides for Dionysos Kadmeios by Schachter has now been identified by Knoepfler as belonging to the Romaia.[98] Dated to around the same time as the first—probably no later than 100 BC—once again all of the known artists are Thebans save for the victorious trumpeter, Asklepiades son of Theophrastos from Aigina (the first inscription boasts one solitary Phokian, the trumpeter Polemon son of Polemarchos, of Delphi).[99] Given the games' location and thymelic focus, the involvement of the *Technitai* is almost assured, especially if the would-be kitharist Philippos, whose patronymic is lost (*IG* VII 2448 l.12), is Philippos son of Herodes, a known Theban

---

[97] Knoepfler (2004), 1271. For *Technitai*, see *SEG* 32, 438; Le Guen (2001), nos. 27–9; see also *IG* VII 2484–5.
[98] *Agrionia*—Schachter (1981), 191; *Romaia*—Knoepfler (2004), 1262–4 and 1277. The list of contests is identical if one restores κιθαριστής (l.11) in the place of the original reading of αὐλωιδός for *IG* VII 2448. See also *SEG* 54, 517.
[99] Knoepfler (2004), 1263–4.

envoy of the Dionysian *Technitai* of Isthmos and Nemea to Rome in 112 BC.[100] While the presence of the *Technitai* might explain the form of the games, the reason for their creation—and epithet Romaia—remains unclear. Knoepfler has suggested that Mummius' actions to extend the privileges of the *Technitai* may have been encouragement enough.[101] If so, Thebes itself ought to be seen as the instigator rather than the *Technitai* themselves, for in the limited epigraphic record there is no direct evidence that the *Technitai* played any role in the organization of the games as they did at the Trieterides and Mouseia or that the chosen name represented the Guild's own particular gratitude to Rome.[102]

Agonistic epithets linked to Rome might be understood at attempts at flattery by the Greeks, but the motivation was doubtless more complex and different in each case.[103] As van Nijf and van Dijk have recently stated, Romaia were often organized by cities that had recently received Roman support or a major benefaction, while others will have set up the festival in the hope of future support or an alliance.[104] Examples of the former category exist in Boiotia, such as the Soteria at Akraiphia, the rebranding of the Amphiaraia at Oropos as the 'Amphiaraia and Romaia'—which seems to have been connected with clement acts on Sulla's behalf during and after the Mithridatic War—and possibly the 'Erotideia and Romaia' at Thespiai, whose inauguration may be linked to the recovery by Sulla of Praxiteles' statue of Eros.[105] If the *polis* of Thebes was the instigator of the Romaia, the recent Roman destruction of anti-Roman Haliartos, and the clemency shown to the equally disloyal Thebans by the proconsul of Macedonia, Q. Caecilius Metellus, may have inspired them to institute these games with a heady combination of flattery, gratitude, and relief at having escaped similar reprisals.[106]

No other victory lists exist for the Romaia, which seem to have been shortlived. One reason may have been the circumstances of its creation, having been inaugurated neither out of religious fervour, nor to celebrate a great Boiotian victory, but merely to signal the *polis*' good intentions towards the new power on

---

[100] *F.Delphes* III, 2, 70 (l.31). *SEG* 54, 517. See Knoepfler (2004), 1264.

[101] Knoepfler (2004), 1272.

[102] There is no mention of any involvement of a priest of the *Technitai*—see *IG* VII 2447; for Mouseia see *F.Delphes* III, 1, 351 and *SEG* 31, 539.

[103] Knoepfler has suggested these epithets were in later periods added almost without thought—Knoepfler (2004), 1270.

[104] van Nijf and van Dijk (2020), 5 n. 21.

[105] On the Erotideia see Knoepfler (2004), 1264. A festival of the Romaia was recorded at the Athenian colony of Delos from 167/6 BC, and another at Athens from 149 BC, and their foundation may be linked to the territorial and economic benefits following the Roman defeat of Perseus in 167 BC—Knoepfler (2004), 1265. See Mellor (1975) for other examples and van Nijf and van Dijk for a more recent overview (2020).

[106] Polybius (27.1.10–11): Thebes sends to Q. Marcius Philippus in Chalkis to ask forgiveness following their alliance with Perseus; Polybius, *The Histories* 28.3–170 BC: Thebans commended for dedication to Roman cause; Pausanias, *Description of Greece* 7.14.6: Thebans' enthusiastic support of Achaea against Rome; Knoepfler (2004), 1268–9.

the block.¹⁰⁷ That no evidence of the Romaia exists after the Mithridatic War suggests that Thebes, turning against Rome only to be humiliated once again—this time in its opposition to Sulla (see below)– was reluctant to resume a festival whose creation had been a celebration of Roman magnanimity.¹⁰⁸ But another reason for its brevity may be attributed to a dispute which occurred at this time between the Isthmian and Nemean *Technitai* and the Athenian Guild (*c.*128–112 BC) and which seems to have resulted in a schism of the Peloponnesian *Technitai* within Thebes in 118 BC.¹⁰⁹

From an inscription erected at Delphi and dated *c.*112 BC (*F.Delphes* III, 270), we know of the arbitration by the Roman senate of a dispute between the Athenian Guild and that of the Isthmian and Nemean *Technitai* that was centred in Thebes and finally resolved by the Roman senate in favour of Athens. With its extensive network effectively surrounding Attica, by the mid-second century the Isthmian-Nemean association's domination of the region was obviously beginning to grate with the Athenian Guild, and the expansionistic ambitions of the latter now led to open conflict.¹¹⁰ An arrangement between the two associations was made sometime *c.*138–128 BC creating a partial fusion with a common fund, sharing of income, and the Romans forcing both associations to cooperate in organizing *agones* on the territory of the Isthmian-Nemean association with joint meetings in Argos and Thebes (ll. 19–22). But the deal was cancelled a few years later, kicking off the dispute that was finally resolved by the Roman senate in 112 BC in favour of the Athenians.¹¹¹ The inscribed *senatus consultum* recording the Athenian victory was displayed at Delphi, engraved in four blocks on the lower part of the south wall of the Athenian Treasury, clearly visible to all passers on the Sacred Way.¹¹²

During the disagreement, a group of Theban *Technitai*, along with those of other unspecified Boiotian cities, defected from the Isthmian Guild to form their own splinter group, taking with them the archive (or at least part of it), money, dedications and sacred crowns.¹¹³ This new association of *Technitai* is thought to have entertained good relations with the Athenian Guild.¹¹⁴ Looking at the list of participants in the Theban Romaia, the heavy Theban-weighting (unique amongst any Boiotian *agon*) suggests one of two things: either, as Knoepfler has proposed, the inscriptions we possess come from this period of disruption, perhaps representing a group from whom certain elements had been excluded or the result of voluntarily

---

¹⁰⁷ Knoepfler (2004), 1275.
¹⁰⁸ Knoepfler suggests the Thebans now viewed them as a luxury, as expensive as they were useless—Knoepfler (2004), 1278.
¹⁰⁹ *F.Delphes* III, 2, 70, ll.50/51. See *SEG* 54, 516.   ¹¹⁰ Kotlińska-Toma (2015), 277.
¹¹¹ Kotlińska-Toma (2015), 277.   ¹¹² Sherk (1969), 86.   ¹¹³ Knoepfler (2004), 1276–7.
¹¹⁴ On the dispute: see Aneziri (2003), 306–16. The guild members of Isthmos and Nemea, either to gain favour or in recognition of the Roman decision, put up a statue at Delphi in 112 BC of the Roman P. Cornelius Lentulus—see Pomtow (1914), 302–3; Jacquemin (1999), 474; Scott (2014), 353 n. 39.

abstention of certain artists;[115] or that in celebrating the gratitude of Thebes towards their new overseers, the *polis* had consciously decided to field a fully Theban outfit (trumpeters notwithstanding). What is certain is that after this schism with the Athenian Guild, records for the Guild of the Isthmos and Nemea in Boiotia become much reduced, with examples restricted to a first century celebration of the Agrionia (formerly Trieterides) in Thebes (*IG* VII 2447) and two examples for the Mouseia after 84 BC (*I.Thespies* 172) with a final mention c. AD 20 (*I.Thespies* 175).

8.3.3. Sulla and the *Technitai*

To fund his campaign against Mithridates in Greece in 87 BC, Sulla had stolen treasures from the sanctuaries at Delphi, Epidauros, and Olympia.[116] Following his victory, Sulla imposed the repayment of these treasures on Thebes through the taking of land for taxation.[117] Although these lands were later returned, Pausanias dates the decline of Thebes—so apparent in his own days—to this action of Sulla's.[118] Sulla also celebrated victory games—the Epinikia—in Thebes following his victory at Chaironeia or that at Orchomenos the following year:[119]

> ταύτης τὰ ἐπινίκια τῆς μάχης ἦγεν ἐν Θήβαις, περὶ τὴν Οἰδιπόδειον κρήνην κατασκευάσας θυμέλην. Οἱ δὲ κρίνοντες ἦσαν Ἕλληνες ἐκ τῶν ἄλλων ἀνακεκλημένοι πόλεων, ἐπεὶ πρός γε Θηβαίους ἀδιαλλάκτως εἶχε, καὶ τῆς χώρας αὐτῶν ἀποτεμόμενος τὴν ἡμίσειαν τῷ Πυθίῳ καὶ τῷ Ὀλυμπίῳ καθιέρωσεν, ἐκ τῶν προσόδων κελεύσας ἀποδίδοσθαι τὰ χρήματα τοῖς θεοῖς ἅπερ αὐτὸς εἰλήφει.

> [Sulla] celebrated the festival in honour of this victory in Thebes, near the fountain of Oidipos, where an altar was prepared. The judges were Greeks invited from the other cities, since he remained un-reconciled towards the Thebans, taking away half of their territory and consecrating it to Pythian Apollo and Olympian Zeus, giving orders that from its revenues the money should be paid back to the gods which he himself had taken from them.

The choice of Thebes as the location of Sulla's victory games was dictated by a number of factors. It is possible that the games were put on at Theban expense as further punishment, Sulla inviting competitors from all over Greece, but allowing

---

[115] Knoepfler (2004), 1277.   [116] Pausanias, *Description of Greece* 9.7.5.
[117] See Santangelo (2007), 48.   [118] Pausanias, *Description of Greece* 9.7.6.
[119] Plutarch, *Sulla* 19.6. Appian does not mention these games, while Plutarch names them as following the victory of Chaironeia, and places them before the victory at Orchomenos in 85 BC. Knoepfler, however, states that these games celebrated both victories—Knoepfler (2004), 1265. They seem to have been typically 'Greek' games, not Roman. For the tradition of victorious Roman generals celebrating such Greek games, see Ferrary (1988), 554 and 565.

no Theban judges, and thus displaying his mastery over the errant city to all. Secondly, as headquarters of the *Technitai* of the Isthmos and Nemea, and as a *polis* with which the two other main Guilds had a close association, Thebes was a prestigious agonistic capital and artistic hub in its own right, with a ready-made abundance of competitors.[120] Knoepfler has even suggested that Sulla's Epinikia were musical, with the Theban *Technitai* forced to participate.[121]

Elsewhere in Boiotia, Sulla's involvement in the local *agones* was more beneficial, and following the Mithridatic Wars another agonistic revival occurred manifestly through the auspices of Roman intervention. Our best evidence comes from Oropos, where the Amphiaraia was re-invigorated post-86 BC after a possible hiatus of sixty years.[122] Evidence for the Amphiaraia is first found for the start of the second century BC (during which period the *agon* was known as the 'Amphiaraia Megala' and 'Amphiaraia') and then following the Mithridatic War, when the games were reorganized as the 'Amphiaraia and Romaia', the epithet Romaia signalling a direct relationship to the rising power of Rome and gratitude towards Sulla.[123] For following his victory (presumably his final victory at Orchomenos in 85 BC), the Roman consul had granted all of the taxes of wider Oropos to be paid to Amphiaraos in fulfilment of a vow—in response to a medical intervention by the healing god or a favourable oracle, we cannot be certain.[124] But it was doubtless this generous provision for the Amphiareion that gave its festival its great impetus and explains much of its strength during the first half of the first century BC.[125] Compared to its earlier incarnation, this renewed Amphiaraia Romaia offered a diverse range of competitors from widespread locations in huge numbers, the games also boasting the greatest assortment of competitions of any first century BC Boiotian *agon*.[126]

---

[120] On the close relations that Sulla maintained with various companies of *Technitai*, see Le Guen (2001), 237–8; Knoepfler (2004), 1265 n. 79.

[121] Knoepfler (2004), 1265—this must remain a supposition without literary or epigraphic grounding.

[122] Knoepfler (1997), 35–6. He dates *IG* VII 48 as post-Mithridatic War. Its previous late second- / early first-century BC dating would place it comfortably during the missing period. Kalliontzis has suggested an inauguration for the Amphiaraia Romaia during the empty second-century BC period, with the epithet Romaia linked to Roman actions surrounding disputes between Oropos and Athens c.156 BC, and the defeat of Andriskos by Rome in 148 BC, thus favouring a mid-second-century date for its celebration. Kalliontzis (2016), 92 and 105.

[123] Amphiaraia Megala—*IG* VII 411, 412; *SEG* 11, 338; Amphiaraia—*IG* VII 48; Didymos, in Schol. Pindar, *Olympian* 7.1 54a, compare Schol. Pindar, *Olympian* 7.154a—Schachter (1981), 25 n. 1. Epithet Romaia and Rome—van Nijf and Williamson (2015), 103.

[124] *IG* VII 413 (*I.Oropos* 308). Larsen has suggested that Sulla also made financial provision for Trophonios at Lebadeia—Larsen (1975), 365, no. 13; see also Feyel (1942), 86–7. Vow, see Dillon and Garland (2005), 535.

[125] Gossage (1975), 134. Sulla's moving of the Olympic Games to Rome in 80 BC led to a decline still evident years later: for example, a list of victors from 72 BC names seventeen Peloponnesians amongst the eighteen victors, seven of these being Eleans—a decidedly reduced and local competitive field.

[126] See Fossey (2014), 111. The average distance travelled by athletes and performers nearly doubled from what it was in the fourth century BC—van Nijf and Williamson (2016), 55.

That the *Technitai* may have played an important organizational role in the Amphiaraia Romaia is suggested by the tendency of individual victor lists—displayed in the sanctuary—to favour winners from single cities.[127] For example, during this post-war revival, all but three dramatic winners at the Amphiaraia Romaia on the lists *IG* VII 419 and *IG VII* 420 (*I.Oropos* 526 and 528) are Theban, while most on *IG* VII 416 (*I.Oropos* 523) are Athenian, suggesting that the *Technitai* of the Isthmos and Nemea had helped organize the former, the Athenian *Technitai* the latter.[128] So it appears once again that the presence of the *Technitai* proved crucial to the success of specific games. But this success was not limited to Oropos. The increased agonistic traffic occasioned by Sulla's provisions for Amphiaraos benefitted other Boiotian contests as well, such as the Thespian Mouseia and Erotideia. As is evidenced by the prosopography of the victors at each of the major games within Boiotia at this time, something akin to a Boiotian *periodos* was created in this post-war period, with each of the games benefitting from the success of the others.[129] Yet this boom was short-lived. A collapse c.50 BC seems to have swiftly followed the post-Mithridatic flourishing and is best understood as purely economic and linked to Greece becoming the theatre of the Roman Civil Wars, after which Boiotia never quite regained the agonistic heights of earlier times.[130]

8.3.4. The Boiotian *Technitai* in the imperial age

During the imperial period, perhaps as early as the reign of Claudius, the branches of the *Technitai* merged into one organization, the *Technitai* of the *Oikoumene* in place of the numerous artists' associations of the Hellenistic and early Roman periods, with another centrally organized synod also introduced for athletes.[131] Like their predecessors, these two associations systematically sought to secure the emperor's recognition and renewal of important privileges for their members.[132] While the regional branches did not cease to exist, they were subsumed as part of the central Synod of the *Oikoumene*.

What effect this had on the role of the *Technitai* in the Boiotian agonistic world is unclear, as at this time direct evidence for *Technitai* in the games in Boiotia falls away. Thebes had never revived as an artistic centre following the actions of Sulla,

---

[127] Kotlińska-Toma (2015), 269.
[128] Both post-date the Mithridatic Wars and pre-date the civil wars, but we cannot be more precise as to actual dating.
[129] See Grigsby (2017), 183 and n. 831 for competitors and their various victories across Boiotia; Gossage (1975), esp. 121–2.
[130] Müller (2014), 121. This pattern of collapse, shared by other regions of the Greek mainland, stands in direct contrast to the increase in agonistic expression found throughout the wider Greek world, and especially the Greek East at this time and in the coming centuries.
[131] Aneziri (2014), 432; cf. Aneziri (2009), esp. 220–3.   [132] Aneziri (2014), 432.

with no resumption of the Romaia, and only one further inscription recording the Trieteris, now named the Agrionia.[133] But the Theban branch of the Guild may well have remained, and Boiotia's artistic heritage—a legacy of the *Technitai*— was to continue at the Mouseia at Thespiai and Ptoia at Akraiphia. There is even evidence for a continuing Boiotian speciality which could be directly traced to the *Technitai*, that of the rhapsode.[134] To my mind the presence of the Guild of *Technitai* ought to have some bearing on this specialization: one recalls that Pythokles in the fourth century BC had been a rhapsode amongst other specialities.[135] Certainly given their later dominance, it is probable that the Boiotians felt this skill was characteristically theirs given the placement of Hesiod at the beginning of the tradition.[136]

Boiotian prestige with Rome continued to be negotiated through traditional festivals and games, none more so than in those games with an artistic reputation with which the *Technitai* had previously been linked as co-organizers and key participators, the Mouseia and the Ptoia. From the end of the first century BC into the first century AD and beyond, wealthy private individuals, who had no doubt done well under Rome, began to play a dominant role in the cultural concerns of the *koinon*, and were keen to promote Boiotia within the Roman world, and Rome within the Boiotian world.[137] Much has been written on the role played by one dominant family, that of Augustus' general T. Statilius Taurus, which retained connections (and probably estates) at Thespiai well into the first century AD and became patrons of the Mouseia and the Erotideia.[138] Their client Polykratides and his family built a gymnasium for the contests (*I. Thespies* 373), a stoa (*I. Thespies* 427), and played the role of *agonothetes*, while the events themselves were changed to include hymns of praise to the imperial family (*I. Thespies* 174).[139] With these inscriptions, once displayed in full view of visitors and competitors alike, we witness how private elite individuals were now visibly taking the initiative in the matter of the games, displaying this connection for their own prestige and usurping the position once the shared domain of the *polis* and the *Technitai*.[140]

---

[133] Although a flute player records a third-century AD victory at the Theban Herakleia (*F.Delphes* III, 1.550 l.13), and a pantomime is recorded for the same games in the second century AD—see *I.Ephesos* 2070/2071 and *F.Delphes* III, 1, 551. Agrionia, see *IG* VII 2518.
[134] West (2013), 364. See n. 59 above. [135] See *IG* IV 682 l.9.
[136] West notes Hesiod's winning the tripod at the funeral games of Amphidamas of Chalkis, which he had then dedicated to the Helikonian Muses who had first inspired him (*Works and Days* 654–9); West (2013), 347. Whether this performance of one's own work counts as rhapsody is not clear, but presumably it is the tradition of winning at poetic performance which West is highlighting.
[137] See Zuiderhoek (2009) on this elite giving as a political mechanism for deflecting social tensions away from open conflicts towards communal celebrations of shared citizenship and the legitimation of power in the cities.
[138] Schachter (2016), 137–8. [139] Marchand (2013), 159.
[140] Unfortunately, none of the inscriptions remains *in situ* to tell where they once stood. One would assume those related to buildings graced the monuments themselves; those dedicated by *agonothetes* were possibly located in the valley of Muses and or the *agora* of Thespiai.

Fig. 8.5 Church of Agios Georgios, Akraiphia.
Photograph: Grigsby.

We can see the same pattern repeated elsewhere. In AD 37 Epameinondas of Akraiphia, an ambassador to Rome on behalf of the Boiotian League at the accession of Caligula, reformed the *agon* of the Ptoia (for whose creation the *Technitai* had once proved integral). We read about his actions from an extensive dossier of inscriptions now part of the doorway and south wall of Agios Georgios in Akraiphia (Fig. 8.5) which records Epameinondas' honours and the recreation of the Ptoia festival (*IG* VII 2711–13). The recreation is related in *IG* VII 2712 (ll. 55–9):

...ἐγ[λε]λοιπό-
τος γὰρ ἤδη τριάκοντα ἔτη τοῦ τῶν Πτωΐων ἀγῶνος κατασταθὶς ἀγωνοθέ-
της προθυμότατα ἐπεδέξατο φιλοδοξήσας τὸ ἀνανεώσασθαι τὴν ἀρχα[ι]-
ότητα τοῦ ἀγῶνος, τῶν μεγάλων Πτωΐων καὶ Καισαρήων κτίστης ἄνωθε
γενόμενος·....

For when he was appointed *agonothetes*, after the contest of the Ptoia had been omitted for thirty years, he most eagerly took it upon himself in the hope of renewing creditably the ancient splendour of the contest, and he became all over again founder of the Great Ptoia and Kaisareia.[141]

This decree was set up both at the sanctuary of Apollo Ptoios (Fig. 8.3), in the hills a few kilometers east of Akraiphia, and in the *agora* of the *polis* itself,

---

[141] Adapted from Oliver (1971), 234.

the latter later plundered for the walls of the Agios Georgios. Once again, we see how through publicly accessible prominent inscriptions, relations between individuals, their *poleis*, and Rome were clearly displayed, and how festivals and games were an effective and visible medium for doing so. But the prominent role once played by the *Technitai* was no more, at least as publicly displayed in the epigraphy. In the almost 300-line corpus of Epameinondas, not one mention of the Guild occurs. Others had stepped up and taken their place on the stage these Artistic Associations had helped build.[142]

8.4. Conclusion

Around 260 BC, the Boiotians requested and were granted *asylia* for the sanctuary of Athena Itonia near Koroneia, this being the earliest such example of the granting of *asylia* in the Greek world outside the *periodos* except for Boiotian Plataia.[143] This bequest was prominently displayed near the Temple of Apollo at Delphi, just west of the tripod base of Gelon, visible to one and all visiting Apollo's shrine.

Buoyed no doubt by their characteristic competitiveness, by the end of the third century BC other Boiotia *poleis* had sought *asylia* and Panhellenic recognition for their own sanctuaries and re-organized *agones* as Boiotia underwent an agonistic boom. For this boom, as well as the bestowals of *asylia*, the presence in Thebes and Thespiai of branches of the Guild of *Technitai* of Dionysos of Isthmos and Nemea was integral, under whose influence Boiotia now developed a new artistic agonistic reputation harking back to the days of Hesiod.

The conspicuous role of the *Technitai*—working often as co-organizers of festivals and more often as participants—was prominently displayed at the various sites of the festivals and at other prominent locations across the Greek world. As with the granting of *asylia* to the Itoneion, the decree for Dionysos Kadmeios in Thebes was placed prominently at Delphi on the wall of the Treasury of the Thebans beside the SW entrance to the Sacred Way, displaying the role of the *Technitai* in the re-organization and recognition of *asylia* for the sanctuary and its games. Occupying a less prestigious site than the decree for the Itoneion, it would nevertheless have been visible to a Panhellenic audience of passing visitors, especially those entering the sanctuary from the south-west. We have no firm evidence that the decree for the Itoneion was set up at Koroneia (though one suspects it would

---

[142] That the Guilds were still involved is suggested by later victory lists from the second and third century AD which record victories in the usual thymelic subjects. One list (*IG* VII 4151) records three of the five artists as hailing from Argos, one of them a rhapsode; another (*IG* VII 4152) names one Laberius son of Perikles, of joint Corinthian and Thespian heritage. Such figures have a definite feel of *Technitai* about them.

[143] *F.Delphes* III, 4, 358; *SEG* 18, 240.

have been), but a copy of the Theban decree was also set up in Thebes, for a more interested local and visiting audience.

In a similar fashion, evidence from the valley of the Muses—doubtless once standing in prime viewing position at the heart of the sacred enclosure—recorded the role of the *Technitai* in attracting the interest (and money) of Hellenistic kings. And the inscriptions recording the bestowing of *asylia* to the Sanctuary of Apollo Ptoios and the Ptoia festival by the Delphic Amphictyony (*IG* VII 4135) c.228–226 BC were erected both at the Sanctuary of Apollo Ptoios and at Delphi itself, possibly again in the southwest corner where the Theban and Boiotian Treasuries stood and where the inscription recording the festival for Dionysos Kadmeios (*FD* III 1.351) was also displayed.

This new agonistic self-confidence seems to express a wider, more well-rounded and pointedly artistic picture of Boiotian identity closer to the Hellenistic ideal, where the new festivals mirrored the wider range of competitions of the games of the *periodos*. The previous athletic and hippic bias of the competitions in Boiotia broadened to embrace a different, more artistic form of competition, for which the presence of the *Technitai* in Thebes was pivotal. Through their joint collaboration in these new or revamped games, the self-interests of these two separate bodies—the overseeing *poleis* and the *Technitai*—coalesced to forge a new Boiotian festival cultural identity. And the inscriptions which celebrated and advertised these games displayed to all-comers the importance of these collaborations, revealing the power structures/networks within which the festivals operated and thus defined their social meaning.

In this very public way, games continued to develop as visible nodes of interaction and sources of prestige for the various interested groups and became a stage on which larger political affinities could also be displayed. During the second century BC, we first see evidence of the strong relations fostered between certain Boiotian *poleis* and Rome, with games such as the Soteria initiated at Akraiphia and the Romaia at Thebes, this latter possibly linked to the granting of continued privileges to the resident *Technitai* by Mummius which did much to cement Thebes as a continuing artistic centre. The importance of these Roman links become even more evident following the Mithridatic war, where the positive actions of Sulla towards a number of Boiotian *poleis* and their *agones* (such as the Amphiaraia and Romaia at Oropos) instigated a post-war agonistic boom, unique in the Greek world at this time, until the Roman civil wars, played out in part on Greek soil, led to a collapse of this circuit.

Boiotia never quite recovered its agonistic prowess after the civil wars, but the games with which the *Technitai* had been most closely associated now became the focus of ambition for a new group, the wealthy elite seeking prestige in their own *poleis* and a link to the power of Rome which was once again prominently displayed inscribed at key sites. The *Technitai*, who by now had been subsumed into the *Oikoumene* (although the regional branches no doubt continued to exist), continued to provide clientele, but their central organizational role had been usurped. It was individual ambition towards Rome that now drove and developed Boiotian agonistic identity, reflected in the merging of imperial cult and local tradition in the celebration of the Boiotian festivals and games such as the Ptoia Kaisareia and the Megala Kaisareia Sebasteia Mouseia. Thus, once again, the Boiotians proved themselves capable of re-invention and creative self-expression, a process for which the *agones* provide our best evidence, forging a positive and creative identity through their games, for which the presence of the *Technitai* in Thebes—along with the mutual corroboration between the groups—had been key.

Works Cited

Aneziri, S. (2003) *Die Vereine der dionysischen Techniten im Kontext der hellenistischen Gesellschaft. Untersuchungen zur Geschichte, Organisation und Wirkung der hellenistischen Technitenvereine*. Stuttgart.

Aneziri, S. (2007) 'Artists' participation and the organization of music contests in the Hellenistic period: an attempt at classification', in P. Wilson (ed.), *The Greek Theatre and Festivals: Documentary Studies*. Oxford, 67–84.

Aneziri, S. (2009) 'World travellers: the associations of Artists of Dionysos', in R. Hunter and I. Rutherford (eds), *Wandering Poets in Ancient Greek Culture: Travel, Locality and Pan-Hellenism*. Cambridge, 217–36.

Aneziri, S. (2014) 'Greek strategies of adaptation to the Roman world: the case of the contests', *Mnemosyne* 63.3: 423–42.

Beck, H. and Ganter, A. (2015) 'Boiotia and the Boiotian Leagues', in H. Beck and P. Funke (eds), *Federalism in Greek Antiquity*. Cambridge, 132–57.

Bousquet, J. (1961) 'Inscriptions de Delphes', *Bulletin de correspondance hellénique* 85: 69–97.

Bringmann, K., Ameling, W., and Schmidt-Dounas, B. (1995) *Schenkungen hellenistischer Herrscher an griechische Städte und Heiligtümer*, vol. I. Berlin.

Buck, R. J. (1993) 'The Hellenistic Boiotian League', *Ancient History Bulletin* 7: 100–6.

Champion, C. (1995) 'The Soteria at Delphi: Aetolian propaganda in the epigraphical record', *American Journal of Philology* 116.2: 213–20.

Chaniotis, A. (1995) 'Sich selbst feiern? Städtische Feste des Hellenismus im Spannungsfeld von Religion und Politik', in M. Wörrle and P. Zanker (eds), *Stadtbild und Bürgerbild im Hellenismus, Kolloquium*, München, 24.–26. Juni 1993. Munich, 147–72.

Daux, G. (1935) 'Craton, Eumène II et Attale II', *Bulletin de correspondance hellénique* 59: 210–30.

Dillon, M. and Garland, L. (2005) *Ancient Rome: From the Early Republic to the Assassination of Julius Caesar*. London.

Ferrary, J.-L. (1988) *Philhellénisme et impérialisme. Aspects idéologiques de la conquête romaine du monde hellénistique, de la seconde guerre de Macédoine à la guerre contre Mithridate.* Rome.

Feyel, M. (1942) *Contribution à l'épigraphie béotienne.* Le Puy.

Fossey, J. M. (2014) 'Foreigners at Boiotian festivals in Hellenistic-Roman times', in J. M. Fossey (ed.), *Epigraphica Boeotica II: Further Studies on Boiotian Inscriptions.* Leiden, 105–16.

Gangloff, A. (2018) 'Rhapsodes and rhapsodic contests in the imperial period', in J. L. Ready and C. C. Tsagalis (eds), *Homer in Performance: Rhapsodes, Narrators, and Characters.* Austin, 130–50.

Gossage, A. G. (1975) 'The comparative chronology of inscriptions relating to Boiotian festivals in the first half of the first century B.C.', *Annual of the British School at Athens* 70: 115–34.

Graf, F. (2015) *Roman Festivals in the Greek East: From the Early Empire to the Middle Byzantine Era.* Cambridge.

Grigsby, P. (2017) 'Boiotian Games: Festivals, Agones, and the Development of Boiotian Identity'. PhD Thesis, University of Warwick.

Heberdey, R., Wilhelm, A., and Kiepert, H. (1896) *Reisen in Kilikien, ausgeführt 1891 und 1892 im auftrage der Kaiserlichen akademie der wissenschaften (widmung seiner durchlaucht des regierenden fürsten Johann von und zu Liechtenstein).* Vienna.

Jacquemin, A. (1999) *Offrandes monumentales à Delphes.* Paris.

Jacquemin, A. and Laroche, D. (2012) 'Notes sur quatre édifices d'époque classique à Delphes', *Bulletin de correspondance hellénique* 136–7.1: 83–122.

Jamot, P. (1895) 'Fouilles de Thespies', *Bulletin de correspondance hellénique* 19: 311–85.

Jardé, A. (1902) 'Inscriptions de Delphes: actes amphictyoniques de la domination étolienne', *Bulletin de correspondance hellénique* 26: 246–86.

Kalliontzis, Y. (2016) 'La date de la première célébration des Amphiareia-Romaia d'Oropos', *Revue des Études Grecques* 129: 85–105.

Knoepfler, D. (1996) 'La réorganisation du concours des Mouseia à l'époque hellénistique: esquisse d'une solution nouvelle', in A. Hurst and A. Schachter (eds), *La Montagne des Muses: Recherches et Rencontres* 7. Geneva, 141–67.

Knoepfler, D. (1997). 'Cupido ille propter quem Thespiae visuntur. Une mésaventure insoupçonnée de l'Eros de Praxitèle et l'institution du concours des Erôtideia', in D. Knoepfler (ed.), *Nomen latinum. Mélanges de langue, littérature et de civilisation latines en l'honneur d'André Schneider à l'occasion de son départ à la retraite.* Neuchâtel and Geneva, 17–39.

Knoepfler, D. (2004) 'Les Rômaia de Thèbes: un nouveau concours musical (et athlétique?) en Béotie', *Comptes rendus des séances de l'Académie des Inscriptions et Belles-Lettres* 148: 1241–79.

König, J. (2005) *Athletics and Literature in the Roman Empire.* Cambridge.

Kotlińska-Toma, A. (2015) *Hellenistic Tragedy: Texts, Translations and a Critical Survey*. London.

Lambert, S. D. (2011) 'What was the point of inscribed honorific decrees in classical Athens?', in S. D. Lambert (ed.), *Sociable Man: Essays on Ancient Greek Social Behaviour in Honour of Nick Fisher*. Swansea and Oxford, 193–214.

Larsen, J. A. (1968) *Greek Federal States: Their Institutions and History*. Oxford.

Larsen, J. A. (1975) 'Roman Greece', in J. A. Larsen (ed.), *An Economic Survey of Ancient Rome*. Vol. IV. New York, 259–498.

Le Guen, B. (2001) *Les Associations de Technites Dionysiaques à 'époque Hellénistique*. Nancy.

Le Guen, B. (2007) 'Kraton, Son of Zotichos: Artists' associations and monarchic power in the Hellenistic period', in P. Wilson (ed.), *The Greek Theatre and Festivals. Documentary Studies*. Oxford Studies in Ancient Documents. Oxford, 246–78.

Ma, J. (2013) *Statues and Cities: Honorific Portraits and Civic Identity in the Hellenistic World*. Oxford.

Manieri, A. (2013) 'I Soteria anfizionici a Delfi: concorso o spettacolo musicale?', *Zeitschrift für Papyrologie und Epigraphik* 184: 139–46.

Marchand, F. (2013) 'The Statilii Tauri and the cult of the Theos Taurus at Thespiai', *Journal of Ancient History* 1.2: 145–69.

Mellor, R. (1975) ΘΕΑ ΡΩΜΗ: *The Worship of the Goddess Roma in the Greek World*. Göttingen.

Müller, C. (2007) 'La dissolution du koinon béotien en 171 av. J.-C. et ses consequences territoriales', in P. Rodriguez (ed.), *Pouvoir et territoire I. Antiquité et Moyen Âge*. Saint-Étienne, 31–46.

Müller, C. (2014) 'A Koinon after 146? Reflections on the political and institutional situation of Boiotia in the second half of the second century BC', in N. Papazarkadas (ed.), *The Epigraphy and History of Boiotia: New Finds, New Prospects*. Leiden, 119–46.

Nachtergael, G. (1977) *Les Galates en Grèce et les Sôtéria de Delphes*. Brussels.

van Nijf, O. M. and van Dijk, S. (2020) 'Experiencing Roman power at Greek contests: Romaia in the Greek festival network', in K. Berthelot (ed.), *Reconsidering Roman Power: Roman, Greek, Jewish and Christian Perceptions and Reactions*. Rome. doi.org/10.4000/books.efr.5704, last accessed 12 September 2022.

van Nijf, O. M. and Williamson, C. G. (2015) 'Re-inventing traditions: connecting contests in the Hellenistic and Roman world', in A. W. Busch and M. J. Versluys (eds), *Reinventing the 'Invention of Tradition'? Indigenous Pasts and the Roman Present*. Paderborn, 95–112.

van Nijf, O. M. and Williamson, C. G. (2016) 'Connecting the Greeks: festival networks in the Hellenistic world', in C. Mann, S. Remijsen, and S. Scharff (eds), *Athletics in the Hellenistic World*. Stuttgart, 43–71.

van Nijf, O. M. and Williamson, C. G. (2021) 'Connecting the Greeks Multi-Scalar Festival Networks in the Hellenistic World'. *Religion and Urbanity Online*, edited by

Susanne Rau and Jörg Rüpke. Berlin, Boston: De Gruyter, 2021. https://doi.org/10.1515/urbrel.11276379. Accessed 2023-05-30.

Oliver, J. H. (1971) 'Epaminondas of Acraephia', *Greek, Roman, and Byzantine Studies* 12: 221–37.

Parker, R. (2004) 'New "Panhellenic" festivals in Hellenistic Greece', in R. Schlesier and U. Zellmann (eds), *Mobility and Travel in the Mediterranean from Antiquity to the Middle Ages*. Münster, 9–23.

Pickard-Cambridge, A. (1988) *The Dramatic Festivals of Athens*. Oxford.

Pomtow, H. R. (1914) 'Zur delphischen Archontentafel des III Jhdts', *Klio* 14: 265–320.

Rau, S. and Rüpke, J. (2021) 'Connecting the Greeks: multi-scalar festival networks in the Hellenistic world', in S. Rau and J. Rüpke (eds), *Religion and Urbanity Online* edited by Susanne Rau and Jörg Rüpke. Berlin, Boston: De Gruyter, 2021.

Remijsen, S. (2011) 'The so-called "Crown-Games": terminology and historical context of the ancient categories for agones', *Zeitschrift für Papyrologie und Epigraphik* 177: 97–109.

Remijsen, S. (2015) *The End of Greek Athletics in Late Antiquity*. Cambridge.

Rigsby, K. J. (1987). 'A decree of Haliartus on cult', *American Journal of Philology* 108.4: 729–40.

Rigsby, K. J. (1996) *Asylia: Territorial Inviolability in the Hellenistic World*. London.

Robert, L. (1977) 'Les Fêtes de Dionysos à Thèbes et l'amphictionie', *Archaiologikēs Ephēmeris*: 195–210.

Roesch, P. (1965) *Thespies et la Confédération Béotienne*. Limoges.

Roesch, P. (1982) *Etudes Béotiennes*. Paris.

Roesch, P. (1989) 'L'Aulos et les aulètes en Béotie', in H. Beister and J. Buckler (eds), *Boiotika: Vorträge vom 5. Internationalen Böotien-Kolloquium zu Ehren von Professor Dr Siegfried Lauffer, Institut für Alte Geschichte, Ludwig-Maximilians-Universität München, 13.–17. Juni 1986*. Munich, 203–14.

Roesch, P. (2007) *Les Inscriptions de Thespies*. Lyon. Retrieved from https://www.hisoma.mom.fr/production-scientifique/les-inscriptions-de-thespies, accessed 13 July 2022.

Roux, G. (1954) 'Le Val des Muses, et les Muses Chez les Auteurs Anciens', *Bulletin de Correspondance Hellénique* 78: 22–48.

Santangelo, F (2007). *Sulla, the Elites, and the Empire: A Study of Roman Policies in Italy and the Greek East*. Leiden.

Schachter, A. (1981) *Cults of Boiotia: 1. Acheloos to Hera*. London.

Schachter, A. (1986) *Cults of Boiotia: 2. Herakles to Poseidon*. London.

Schachter, A. (1994) *Cults of Boiotia: 3. Potnia to Zeus; Cults of Deities Unspecified by Name*. London.

Schachter, A. (2016) *Boiotia in Antiquity: Selected Papers*. Cambridge.

Scott, M. (2014) *Delphi: A History of the Center of the Ancient World*. Princeton.

Scott, M. (2016) 'The performance of Boiotian identity at Delphi', in S. D. Gartland (ed.), *Boiotia in the Fourth Century B.C.* Philadelphia, 99–120.

Sherk, R. K. (1969) *Roman Documents from the Greek East. Senatus Consulta and Epistuale to the Age of Augustus.* Baltimore.

Symeonoglou, S. (2014) *The Topography of Thebes from the Bronze Age to Modern Times.* Princeton.

Tracy, S. (2015) 'The dramatic festival inscriptions of Athens: the inscribers and phases of inscribing', *Hesperia* 84.3: 553–81.

Tsagalis, C. C. (2018) 'Performance contexts for rhapsodic recitals in the Hellenistic period', in J. L. Ready and C. C. Tsagalis (eds), *Homer in Performance: Rhapsodes, Narrators, and Characters.* Austin, 98–129.

West, M. L. (2013) *Hellenica: Selected Papers on Greek Literature and Thought.* Vol. 3: *Philosophy, Music and Metre, Literary Byways, Varia.* Oxford.

Wilding, A. (2015) 'Aspirations and identities: proxenia at Oropos during the fourth to second centuries BC', *Bulletin of the Institute of Classical Studies* 58.2: 55–81.

Zuiderhoek, A. (2009) *The Politics of Munificence in the Roman Empire: Citizens, Elites and Benefactors in Asia Minor.* Cambridge.

9

Sacred Circles

Enclosed Sanctuaries and Their Festival Communities in the Hellenistic World

Christina G. Williamson

9.1. Introduction

Sanctuaries and festival culture in the Hellenistic world are increasingly seen as emanating from local urban strategies engaging with a widening horizon of religious practices and options. Yet their phenomena are largely analysed in isolation, corresponding to disciplinary lenses; rarely are they studied as belonging to the same dynamics. In this chapter I attempt a more holistic approach by examining the confluence of two fundamental characteristics of this period: the increase in catchment area of civic festivals and the increasing enclosure of space in their sanctuaries. In the Hellenistic period, several urban communities appealed to other cities and kings to acknowledge and join in their festivals, hosting games in honour of their main god as an echo of the great 'Panhellenic' festivals. Cities thus open up their sacred spaces to the Greek *oikoumene* through their festivals. At the same time, there was a growing tendency to enclose these sacred spaces within peristyle architecture. As the political borders of cities were temporarily suspended, so the edges of their great civic shrines were hardened, creating a paradox of simultaneous inclusion and exclusion.

Such sanctuaries were often situated either near the busy *agora* of their cities, or at strategic and often panoramic points in the landscape. At the same time they were surrounded by walls that visually isolated them, giving impetus to the meaning of *temenos* as an area cut off from its surroundings.[1] While in earlier periods

---

This article is part of a triad that includes Williamson (2022) and Williamson (forthcoming a) that stems from research done within the context of the project 'Connecting the Greeks' and 'Deep-mapping sanctuaries' at the University of Groningen and sponsored by the Netherlands Organization for Scientific Research (NWO) (see connectingthegreeks.com and deepmappingsanctuaries.org) and during a fellowship at the University of Erfurt within the DFG project 'Religion and Urbanity: Reciprocal Formations' (FOR 2779) (see urbrel.hypotheses.org). I would like to express my gratitude to the members of these different research groups for their comments and feedback on earlier drafts, and to the editor and anonymous reviewers of this volume for their helpful comments. Any remaining errors are entirely my own. All maps and plans were produced by myself unless otherwise stated.

[1] On the uses of the word τέμενος, see Ekroth (2023).

this delimitation was cognitive, or marked by boundary stones (*horoi*), the new corporeal partitioning signals a major shift in the conceptualization of landscape and ritual space, even at cult places that centre on 'natural' phenomena.[2] Moreover, this presents a clear departure from the perception of Greek temples as emblematic signposts in the landscape: many were now largely hidden behind walls. Finally, it requires a new reflection on Hellenistic terraced sanctuaries that seem designed to exploit their theatrical settings.[3] When such shrines were enclosed on at least three if not all four sides, one should consider whether the need for visual drama was counterbalanced by the need for an effective setting for the ritual events inside.

Grand architecture at sanctuaries typically corresponds with grand festivals. Innovations in ritual space often coincided with new, or revived, festivals.[4] The Hellenistic period not only witnessed an upscaling of spectacle but also of scope, with an outreach across the Greek world that until then had principally been the domain of great Panhellenic festivals as at Olympia or Delphi. Cities began hosting their own inter-urban, or 'local Panhellenic', festivals with games that attracted both citizens and foreign delegations, with participants from the region and sometimes far beyond. Sanctuaries were receptive spaces of diplomacy but also less formal exchanges, through which cities engaged with each other in a mutually acknowledged festival format. As Giovannini remarked, 'Panhellenic festivals were the *agora* of the Greek world'.[5] Festivals thus enabled cities to create new ties or reinforce old ones. Together this produced local and regional networks that became more and more interconnected, ultimately spanning much of the Mediterranean and parts beyond. As central hubs in this network, sanctuaries were critical portals to this extended world.

The question remains, then, why these spaces of external connectivity were internally separated and walled off from their surroundings. In what follows I will argue that the combination of collective ritual in concentrated space made these sanctuaries powerful amplifiers of common knowledge, promoting a shared value system through festival culture that engendered a new sense of community. In support of this I first examine 'sacred circles', in Frank Kolb's terminology, special places that create worlds within worlds, where different rules apply, as Johan Huizinga and Hannah Arendt have observed.[6] These are also concentrated spaces where collective ritual is most effective. Michael Suk-Young Chwe ascribes this to the generation of common knowledge via mutual eye contact, while Randall Collins denotes physical proximity and interaction as a source of interactive

---

[2] e.g. Lauter (1972); Mylonopoulos (2008); also Williamson (forthcoming a).
[3] On temples as territorial signposts, esp. de Polignac (1995). On terraced sanctuaries and the exploitation of panoramas Fehr (1969/70); Pollitt (1986), 230–49; Bek (2007), 208–9; also Pedersen (1991), 114–15 on terraced structures and the role of visibility as a Hekatomnid development in Karia.
[4] Mylonopoulos (2008); also Chaniotis (1995); Parker (2004). [5] Giovannini (1993), 282.
[6] Huizinga (1949); Kolb (1981); Arendt (1990).

emotional energy.⁷ Following this assessment, I proceed to the phenomenon of peristyle sanctuaries in the Greek world.⁸ In his comprehensive work, *Peristyl und Polis*, Burkhard Emme reckons sanctuaries among several types of enclosed urban space that, in his view, are indicative of increasing social complexity and the need for exclusion in the Hellenistic era.⁹ Regarding major peristyle sanctuaries, however, I follow a different tack. I re-examine the development of enclosed sanctuaries through the lens of their spatial contexts, corresponding festivals and their catchment area, in order to show how they are better understood on their own terms, as spaces of broad inclusion. Three case studies serve to highlight local strategies in effectuating the dynamics of ritual space in the context of festivals: Magnesia on the Maeander and Artemis Leukophryene, Stratonikeia and Hekate at Lagina, and Pisidian Antioch and Men Askaenos.

By examining architecture together with function and audience, this approach can lead us towards a new understanding of the rationale behind the enclosure of these civic sacred spaces, one that goes beyond the dialectic of inclusivity versus exclusivity. In fostering a new scale of community, peristyle sanctuaries and their festivals were highly powerful focal points in the expanding world of cities—they were critical mirrors for forging local identities through the eyes of the world, giving local communities every reason to heavily invest in them.

9.2. The sacred circle—ritual in enclosed space

While festivals, their rituals, games, competitions, and institutions created the collective experience, their effectiveness would have been determined, at least in part, by the shape of the sanctuary. Peristyle sanctuaries became more and more common across the Mediterranean, coinciding with great festivals. The question is whether their appearance was simply part of a wider trend in the compartmentalization of urban space or whether these sacred civic enclosures themselves shaped these ideas. Before turning to this question, however, it is important to understand the significance of ritual in enclosed space, and how this can foster a sense of community.

Enclosed public spaces have long been considered by historians as special places with a unique collective and hence political power. Hannah Arendt, for example, viewed the public space of the early *agora* as 'open' to political action and the 'freedom of appearance', as this is a space visible to all and where all are visible.¹⁰ Essential for the rise of democracy, the open *agora* was the starting point

---

⁷ Chwe (2001); Collins (2004).
⁸ As noted by Mylonopoulos (2008), with several examples.   ⁹ Emme (2013).
¹⁰ Arendt (1990), 31, 'The life of a free man needed the presence of others. Freedom itself needed therefore a place where people could come together—the agora, the market-place, or the polis, the political space, proper'.

for political discussion that ended in the *bouleuterion* and theatre; delimited, circumscribed spaces where debate took place and where real decisions were forged. Arendt's view has been challenged, as even the classical *agora* was subject to rules.[11] But the view of the open *agora* as an essential feature of Greek democracy is tenacious, and scholars have long assumed that the enclosure of *agorai* in the Hellenistic era corresponded with a decay of the democratic *polis*.[12]

Such inward-facing spaces are in themselves neither a sign of democracy or the opposite, but they are a sign of public attention. Most important is the concentricity of space in connection with performance and the ability of the audience to respond. Homer mentions the *hieros kyklos*, or 'sacred circle', where the elders sat on their seats of stone as they passed judgment (*Il.* 18.503–6). The term 'sacred circle' is also used for the ritual dance of Demeter in Aristophanes *Frogs*.[13] Kolb observed the early overlap of space for ritual, theatre, sport, council, and judgement.[14] As a term, 'sacred circle' can thus describe several functions that we separate today, and that eventually were separated spatially in Greek urban topographies, but much less so in the Greek mind in which the sacred, political, and the social were all part of the same tissue of life. Nonetheless, certain spaces were invested with their own code of behaviour, at least at particular times of the year, season, or day. Medieval scholar Johan Huizinga used the idea of the 'magic circle' among others to describe places set apart for ritual and play:

> All play moves and has its being within a play-ground marked off beforehand either materially or ideally, deliberately or as a matter of course. Just as there is no formal difference between play and ritual, so the 'consecrated spot' cannot be formally distinguished from the play-ground. The arena, the card-table, the magic circle, the temple, the stage, the screen, the tennis court, the court of justice, etc., are all in form and function play-grounds, i.e. forbidden spots, isolated, hedged round, hallowed, within which special rules obtain. All are temporary worlds within the ordinary world, dedicated to the performance of an act apart.[15]

Such spaces are distinguished by their 'special rules'. The word *temenos* already implies this distinction, as discussed in the beginning.[16] Sanctuaries are walled off and points of entry are accentuated because one should behave differently once inside. Awareness is key. In several cases the norms are even inscribed near the *propylon*.[17] These religious observances are part of the rules of the

---

[11] For critique of Arendt's assessment, see Chattopadhyay (2013) with references.
[12] Views of the supposed bankrupt democracy in the Hellenistic *polis* in relation to the *agora* are summarized in Dickenson (2016), 16–26 and (2019).
[13] Aristophanes, *Frogs* 445; these and other examples are discussed in Kolb (1981), 5–15.
[14] Kolb (1981).   [15] Huizinga (1949), 10.   [16] Ekroth (2023).
[17] e.g. *I.Pergamon Asklepieion* III 161, a list of regulations, was discovered in the sacred way before the *propylon* of the Asklepieion in Pergamon. This genre is called 'ritual norms' or 'sacred laws' in scholarly literature, see *CGRN*.

game, as with sport, drama, or law: they reinforce the link between form, function, and behaviour.

Game theorist Michael Suk-Young Chwe argues that such concentric spaces, in combination with public ceremony, have great potential as coordinating mechanisms.[18] Ritual has a unique capacity for structuring neural pathways and channels of memory, especially for the coordination of collective action.[19] Yet the configuration of space in which it takes place is critical to its effectiveness. In Chwe's analysis, 'inward-facing circles' generate common knowledge not only through their central focus, but also through their facilitation of inter-visibility. In other words, everyone observes the same event, but meanwhile, and most importantly, everyone also observes everyone else's reaction to the event, and everyone realizes this as well. 'Inward-facing circles' thus foster instantaneous reciprocal knowledge—the effect of 'you know that I know that you know', etc. Common knowledge resides in the awareness of shared knowledge, not just in the knowledge that is being shared. This is crucial for social cooperation.[20] Cooperation is moreover reinforced through the group experience in ritual space. In his analysis of the Telesterion at Eleusis, Michael Scott uses cognitive theory to delineate four ways that ritual space strengthens social cohesion, three of which are especially relevant here. First, passage through the high *temenos* walls affords a sense of importance (and exclusivity) for those participating in the ritual. Moreover, the high *temenos* walls block the view to the outside world and narrow the visual field, and hence attention, of the participants to each other. Finally, high *temenos* walls contributed to a different auditory experience, a different soundscape.[21]

Scott thus takes Chwe's rational rituals a step further in bringing in their cognitive and especially emotional dimension. Sociologist Randall Collins emphasizes the emotional energy that is uniquely transferred through ritual. Drawing on Émile Durkheim's 'collective effervescence' of rituals and Erving Goffmann's 'interaction rituals', Collins's *Interaction Ritual Chain* theory (IRC) stresses the importance of physical proximity—in assembly, people intuitively engage in a 'homogeneity of movement, synchrony'.[22] At festivals, bodies react to each other

---

[18] Chwe (2001). Also discussed in van Nijf and Williamson (2016) and Williamson (2022), among others.

[19] e.g. Connerton (1989); Assmann (1991); McCauley and Lawson (2007); Whitehouse and Laidlaw (2004), among many others.

[20] Chwe (2001), 30–3 on inward facing circles. He also discusses processions as generators of common knowledge in a similar vein.

[21] Scott (2022), 202–4; his second factor, of darkness, was particularly instrumental in the initiatory rituals of the Telesterion, but less central to the studies examined here. He moreover discusses how the centrality of the ritual event was frustrated at several turns, contributing in itself to the efficacy of the ritual. Darkness especially was a central factor in the 'echo-chamber' effect and resulting emotional contagion.

[22] Durkheim (1912); Goffman (1974); Collins (2004), 33–5. For a discussion of IRC regarding ancient social networks and festivals, see Williamson (2022). This aligns with Scott's consideration of emotional contagion through ritual, drawing on Hatfield et al. (1993).

both naturally and ritually in spontaneous organization. Today one might observe synchronous applause at the end of a crowd-pleasing performance. This is due in no small part to the emotional energy culminating in situational social interactions charged by ritual.[23]

Put together, then, these theories enable us to see the ways that enclosed, concentric spaces of festivals facilitated the kind of bodily interaction and mutual eye-contact needed to generate common knowledge, both rationally and at a more visceral, intuitive level. This is part of what makes these such powerful political spaces. The Greeks had visually and acoustically perfected the form of the theatre by the fourth century BC, amplifying the effect of bodily interaction. Theatres were increasingly a common feature in post-classical urban topographies and, besides theatrical contests, served as meeting places for the demos, where council proposals were voted on, honours handed out, etc.—the *proedria*, a seat of honour, was one of the highest privileges that a *polis* could bestow on individuals.[24] *Stadia* and later amphitheatres certainly fall in this category as well. We can observe this effect even in less architecturally defined spaces, such as the hilltop sanctuary of Zeus Stratios at Yassıçal near Amasya, where delegates gathered around the altar in a circle of crude stones with the names of their demes.[25] These 'magic circles', where special rules apply, were not only spaces of conformity, but were also potentially highly volatile, as spaces of rivalry and risk. They were the perfect place for assassination attempts or riots, as in the amphitheatre of Pompeii in AD 59, or the Nika revolt in the hippodrome at Constantinople under Emperor Justinian—all of these took place in such enclosed festival spaces. The Greeks were certainly not the first nor the last to be aware of the power of such inward-facing ceremonial circles; we see them from Göbekli Tepe in Anatolia, to Stonehenge, to the *pueblo kivas* in North America, and in the football arenas and council houses of most towns and parliaments today.[26]

9.3. When the circle is a square—festival culture and peristyle shrines

But not all enclosed public spaces are circles. The sanctuaries considered here had interior spaces that on the whole were framed by rectilinear porticoes, or stoas, that created formalized, rectangular-shaped spaces.[27] Although not round, these

---

[23] Chaniotis (2006) and (2010) address the emotional experience elicited by rituals in antiquity. See also Chapter 10 below.
[24] Among many others: van der Vliet (2011); von Hesberg (2015). See also Newby on performance theory and the theatre at Hierapolis, Chapter 6 above.
[25] French (1996).
[26] More examples of modern inward-facing circles as public spaces are discussed in Chwe (2001), 30–3.
[27] See von Hesberg (1990); Mylonopoulos (2008), 52.

spaces were nonetheless centripetal through their temples, altars, and monuments giving both iconic and performative *foci*.[28] Moreover, the surrounding stoas provided viewing platforms from which to observe the main events.[29] The general lack of seating implies that people stood and could move around, engage with each other, and perhaps gain an even better sense of the general mood of the crowd. In watching central events, such as the sacrifice, but also other performances such as dances and hymns, it is plausible that they would have organized themselves in some kind of encircling form that, whether a true circle, pi-shaped, or a looser form, would have enabled them to see each other as well as the main event.

Roland Martin uses the term '*peristyle-temenos*' to describe these enclosed sanctuaries, and they are central to Gottfried Gruben's category of *hellenistische Gesamtanlage* (Hellenistic complexes), focusing on the visual coherence of an ensemble that often extends across multiple terraces as at Lindos, Kos, and Pergamon.[30] This visual coherence through enclosure is part of a larger trend of urban spaces. Burkhard Emme notes the rapid rise of this phenomenon from the late classical period onwards, with archetypes being the *agorai* in Miletos, Pergamon, and Delos.[31] His query focuses on levels of access and restriction and their social implications in public space, observing how the rise of insulated spaces in the urban fabric coincides with the increasing stratification of urban society. Certain groups, especially associations, clearly felt the need to distinguish themselves through spaces reserved exclusively for them.[32]

While social exclusivity is certainly a valid interpretation for several types that Emme discusses, e.g. gymnasia, association halls, and some localized cult places, we must look elsewhere for the logic behind enclosed civic shrines. Especially in the Hellenistic period, these coincide with a new trend of cities promoting their tutelary gods and organizing grand festivals in their honour. This new surge in festivals eventually led to what Louis Robert called the 'explosion agonistique' in the imperial period.[33] Figure 9.1 shows 162 cities that hosted such festivals starting in the Hellenistic era and continuing in the early imperial period, and this is by

---

[28] Williamson (2021), 55–6, 82–3, on concentric ritual spaces at sanctuaries.

[29] Dickenson (2016), 86.

[30] Martin (1951); Gruben (1986), 401ff. and 409 on the Koan Asklepieion: 'Der moderne, im höchsten Grade avantgardistische Zug der Gesamtanlage liegt nicht in ihren einzelnen Bauten, sondern in der wirkungsvollen Komposition dieser Elemente, in einer neuen, das Auge fesselnden Ordnung'.

[31] Emme (2013), 8, further excludes *agorai* from his study as these have been extensively investigated by Martin (1951) and Coulton (1976) in connection with the increasing use of the grid or 'Hippodamic' system of urban planning; on the *agora*, see Dickenson (2016).

[32] Emme (2013), esp. 297–300, and building on Lauter's interpretation of such spaces, Lauter (1986), 45–6. In his classic work, Lauter largely conducts a more formal and aesthetic analysis of peristyle architecture among others, e.g. Lauter (1986), 112: 'Das peristyle antwortet dem peripteralen Motiv, mit dem außen um einen Bau gestellten Säulenkranz korrespondiert nunmehr der einwärts gewandte Säulenkring des umgebenden Hofes quasi als echohafte Umkehrung'. Ritual space could also be exclusive for initiates, as with the Eleusinian mysteries; Scott (2022).

[33] Robert (1984a), 38; Parker (2004).

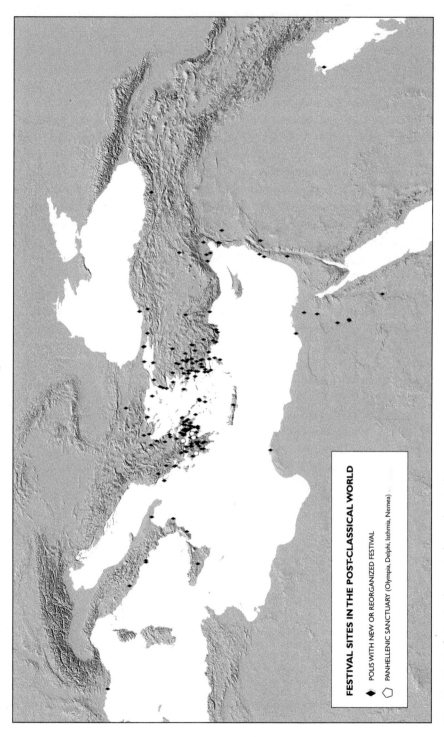

Fig. 9.1 Festival sites in the post-classical period.

no means complete.³⁴ Cities invited other cities to acknowledge and participate in their festivals through delegations (*theoroi*), performers, and competitors in their games.³⁵ Several of these were even crowned and were given the status of 'isolympic' or 'iso-pythic'.³⁶ While celebrating the hosting city, such festivals were designed to attract an inter-urban, regional, or even Panhellenic audience, often organizing a *panegyris*, usually a festival with a commercial fair including spectacles that increased their gravitational pull.³⁷ Cities took care to create an appropriate setting for these massive festivals, which generally took the form of enclosed civic-looking spaces.³⁸ Aimed exactly at drawing large populations from near and far, these peristyle sanctuaries were clearly inclusive in character.³⁹ Considering the development of enclosed sanctuaries as part of the increasing tendency towards compartmentalized space in the urban fabric is certainly valid regarding their form, yet in order to fully appreciate their function they need to be assessed within the context of a new emerging festival culture.

A brief sketch of the rise of enclosed shrines in context with their festivals and urban spaces will highlight characteristics regarding both their formal development and their capacity as social spaces (Fig. 9.2). An early example is the shrine to Apollo Delphinios in Miletos, a late archaic shrine at the north-east end of the *agora*, restored after the Persian destructions. The internal space of the shrine, c.27 × 50 m, was framed by stoas flanked with benches on the north and south sides; the southern stoa has been identified as the '*Molpon*', the centre of the *Molpoi*, the cult association also responsible for the social composition of Miletos.⁴⁰ The *Molpoi* watched over the male youth (*neoi*), and organized the Hamilliteria as an initiatory festival with games during which they became new citizens.⁴¹ Lists of *neoi* and new citizens were inscribed in the Delphinion, among proxeny and honorific decrees. Together they mark this space as the political heart of Miletos.⁴² Alexander Herda indeed considers the space of the Delphinion as a 'sacred

---

³⁴ Based on Chaniotis (1995), and the online databases of ancient competitors: *Database of Hellenistic Athletes* (Mannheim) athletes.geschichte.uni-mannheim.de, last accessed 12 September 2022 and *Connected Contests* (Groningen) connectedcontests.org, last accessed 12 September 2022.

³⁵ e.g. on theoroi, Rutherford (2013); performers, Aneziri (2011), Slater (2007); athletes, van Nijf and Williamson (2016); interurban connections, Britton et al. (forthcoming).

³⁶ e.g. Parker (2004); Remijsen (2011); Mann (2018), with references.

³⁷ e.g. Slater and Summa (2006); also Horster (2020); Kowalzig (2020); and Kristensen (2020).

³⁸ Hammerschmied (2018), 95, with references in n. 20.

³⁹ At some festivals, slaves and foreigners were explicitly invited and expected to participate alongside the citizen population; e.g. Stratonikeia and the festivals of Zeus and Hera at Panamara, *I.Stratonikeia* 256.

⁴⁰ Herda (2011) in discussing the '*Molpoi*' decree, a copy from c.200 BC of a decree from c.447 BC, with translation and references (see also *CGRN* 201). The interpretation of the South stoa as the *Molpon* is disputed by Emme (2013), 26–8.

⁴¹ Herda (2011), 63 n. 37, on the *Molpoi* decree containing the earliest use of the term *neoi*, but see also the commentary in *CGRN* 201. For the Hamilliteria, Herda (2011), 67.

⁴² Herda (2011), 67.

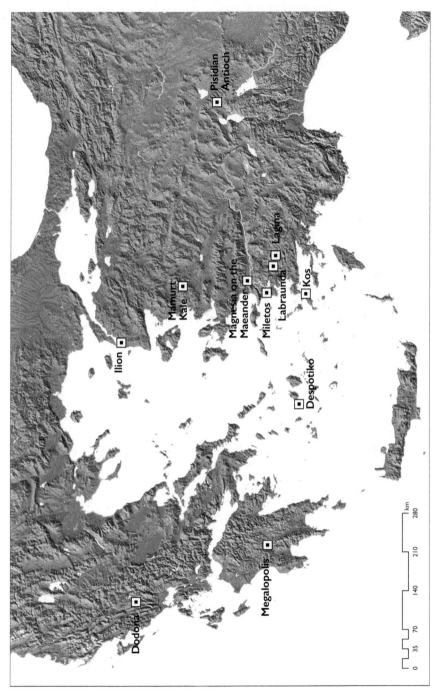

Fig. 9.2 Enclosed sanctuaries discussed in the text.

circle'.⁴³ The strikingly simple inward-facing stoa complex is further identified by Emme as a critical step towards the development of later enclosed sanctuaries.⁴⁴ But the Delphinion is not alone. The recent discoveries at the late archaic sanctuary of Apollo at Despotiko show an even more remarkable use of the concept with an architecturally formalized *temenos*, c.50 × 50 m, surrounding a central semicircular structure.⁴⁵

Not far from Miletos, the sanctuary of Zeus at Labraunda, on a mountainside overlooking Mylasa in Karia, included terracing as an innovation together with internalizing spaces. Possibly inspired by Achaemenid Persepolis, the Hekatomnid satraps drastically reshaped the archaic shrine in the mid-fourth century BC, expanding the area across three cascading terraces that encompassed an area of c.150 × 100 m (Fig. 9.3).⁴⁶ Each terrace had its own character, but they were all defined by stoas that left the south side open, framing the panorama across the plain of Mylasa below and beyond to the hills near Halikarnassos.⁴⁷ Coinciding with this engineering innovation was the new or expanded *panegyris*, the festival of Zeus Labraundos that addressed all of Karia, with a new focus on the dynasty.⁴⁸ Great crowds at the shrine are implied by monumental structures for public banqueting, including the *andrones* and the East Stoa, and for games at the *stadion* nearby, one of only two known to be directly linked to a sanctuary in late classical Asia Minor.⁴⁹ The *stadion* and elaborate complex are material echoes of the public spectacle and the intention of the Hekatomnids of establishing Labraunda as the sacred and political heart of their domain. Burkhard Fehr and Poul Pedersen both point to Labraunda as a crucial link towards the third century terraced sanctuaries of Asklepios on Kos and Athena at Lindos on Rhodes (rebuilt by civic conscription), but also towards the terraced complexes of the Attalids of Pergamon.⁵⁰

The mid-fourth century BC also saw the construction of the sanctuary of Zeus Soter in Megalopolis, in Arkadia, Emme's prime example of a peristyle sanctuary.⁵¹ Conceived with the foundation of Megalopolis, the *temenos* adjoins the *agora* but is simultaneously separated from it: a passer-by would see only the solid walls marked by pillars. Yet upon entry through one of the axial *propylaia*, the visitor would find themselves in an 'open' space of c.55 × 55m (not including the extension)

---

⁴³ Herda (2011), 73, also noting the proximity of *agora*, *prytaneion*, and shrine. On markets at sanctuaries, Iannaccone et al. (2011); Collar and Kristensen (2020); and Frejman (2020).
⁴⁴ Emme (2013), 28.   ⁴⁵ Kourayos (2012), the North Temenos.
⁴⁶ Hellström (2011); Hellström and Blid (2019).   ⁴⁷ Williamson (2014a), with references.
⁴⁸ The *panegyris* is mentioned in *I.Mylasa* 3, l. 5; and in the third century BC, *I.Labraunda* 5 and 8b; see Hellström (2011), 149–50, also Frejman (2020) on the market function of Labraunda. On the dynastic presence, see Henry (2017) with references.
⁴⁹ Roos (2011), with the other in Didyma. *I.Labraunda* 54, heavily fragmented, gives the events day by day. The incomplete lists of names in *I.Labraunda* 53–4 and 67 are interpreted as *theoroi* to the festival; see also the commentary of Crampa (1972) with these inscriptions.
⁵⁰ Fehr (1969/70); Pedersen (2004), with references. The examples of Lindos and Kos are well known and are not further discussed here, but see Pollitt (1986), 230–49; Melfi (2016), with references.
⁵¹ See Emme (2013), 16, 32–9 for an analysis of the sanctuary of Zeus Soter at Megalopolis (Kat. No. 47), and 39–49 for the Asklepieion in Messene (Kat. No. 49).

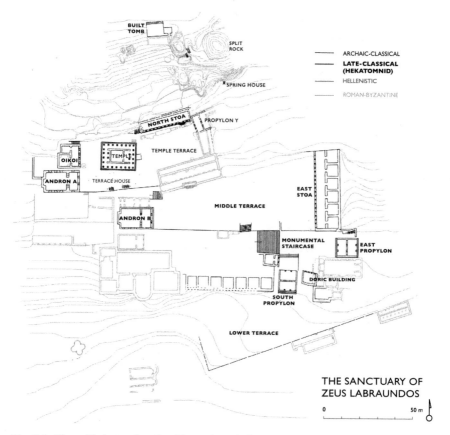

Fig. 9.3 Plan of Labraunda, after Henry (2017), figs 2, 15.

punctuated by the rhythm of columns, a porosity allowing people to pass through and behind them (Fig. 9.4, left). One could move from the *agora* into a similar and yet separate setting, with access filtered via the *propylaia*. The peristyle shrine was built near the altar of Zeus Lykaios on the *agora*, an urban 'doublet' of the Arkadian god's shrine on Mount Lykaion.[52] The Lykaia festival, reckoned among the oldest of Greek games,[53] was revived by Megalopolis and the Arkadian League. Two victor lists found at the mountain shrine reflect the Arkadian focus but also include athletes from as far away as Macedonia, Syracuse, and Miletos.[54]

---

[52] Jost (1994), 224; Lauter-Bufe (2009).

[53] According to Pliny, *Natural History* 7.57 gymnastic games were first instituted at the Lykaia. Aristotle identifies them as the fourth oldest Greek games behind the Eleusinia, the Panathenaia, and games founded at Argos by Danao (Frg. 637 Rose schol. Aristid. *Panathen.*). Pausanias, *Description of Greece* 8.2.1–2, however, states that the Lykaian games are also older than the Panathenaia; cf. the 'Parian Marble' (*FGrH* 239 A 17), which also claims the Lykaia were established after the Eleusinia.

[54] Two inscriptions found at the festival site on Mount Lykaios list the Lykaionikai, *IG* V.2 549 and 550. Of these, eighteen are simply listed as Arcadian, fourteen are from Argos, three from Sparta, three from Elis, and one from Helaia. Three victors are listed as Macedonian, and another from

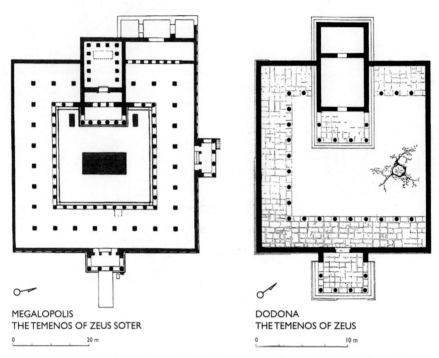

Fig. 9.4 Side-by-side comparison of the shrines of Zeus Soter at Megalopolis and Zeus at Dodona, after Emme (2013), 445 Taf. 57 (Megalopolis) and Gruben (1986), 113 Abb. 107 (Dodona).

The famous oracle shrine at Dodona underwent a similar architectural transformation, but over a greater time span. Here the ancient venerated source of the oracle, the oak tree, was accompanied by a simple *naos* in the late fifth or early fourth century BC. By the end of the fourth century, the ensemble was surrounded by a parapet. In the third century BC, this was replaced by stoa architecture (Fig. 9.4, right). The formal enclosure of the small space of the *temenos*, c.18 × 18 m, was thus made complete, with access provided by the *propylon* in axial alignment with the new prostyle temple.[55] All of this was situated within an expanding and highly complex array of structures that reflect the role of Dodona as the political and sacred, but also festival, epicentre of Epeiros.[56] The addition of tribunes, a *stadion*, and a great theatre coincide with epigraphic evidence of the

Kassandreia; other non-Arcadian athletes came from Athens and Acarnania, but also Miletos and Syracuse. These games were later expanded to include crowned and 'isolympic' events, and they appear to have drawn contestants from across the Greek world, especially in the later third and second century BC, *IG* II³.1 1184 and *IG* II² 993, two fragments of theoric inscriptions, from Megalopolis to Athens.

[55] Illustrated in Gruben (1986), 113–14; more recently re-evaluated in Dieterle (2007).
[56] Moustakis (2006).

organization of the pentaeteric Naia festival in the third century BC.⁵⁷ The games are presumed to have been aimed principally at the region of Epeiros, yet were also a link to the larger Greek world.⁵⁸

Although their settings could hardly be more different, these two sanctuaries of Zeus, one on the *agora* of Megalopolis and the other in the mountainous landscape at Dodona, show some striking similarities. Both shrines used stoa architecture to define a nearly perfect square of space with the temple at one end and a propylon at the other. As with Labraunda, both shrines also functioned as regional centres, each employing a similar strategy of festivals as a means of uniting populations across an expansive area.

In the Hellenistic era, enclosed sanctuaries became part of the *koine* of urban topography, as noted above. They were often combined with terracing on hills and mountains; the resulting ritual platforms with their boxed-in shrines created a paradox of external allure versus internal seclusion.⁵⁹ Labraunda under the Hekatomnids is an example of this and may well have served as a source of inspiration for Attalids of Pergamon, as Fehr and Pedersen suggest.⁶⁰ Philetairos, the first of the Attalids, deployed a somewhat similar transformation of the shrine of Meter Theon in the Aspordenon. Perched on Mamurt Kale, the highest summit in the region, the open cult place afforded a sweeping panorama until the early third century BC, when the *naiskos* and altar were enclosed with a pi-shaped stoa armature (Fig. 9.5). This created simultaneously a sightline with Pergamon and an internally focused area of roughly 63 × 67 m.⁶¹ Although little is known of the festivals and their rituals, the terracottas and range of Hellenistic coinage speak of a regional attraction.⁶² The epigraphic evidence indicates that the shrine was promoted as a state cult under the Attalids.⁶³ By the early imperial period, Strabo (13.2.6) could assume that his readers were well aware of the sanctuary of the Mother of the Gods on the bare hills of the Aspordenon.

---

⁵⁷ On the Naia: Robert (1984b), 34–45; Chaniotis (1995); Parker (2004). The earliest attestations are the decrees on bronze tablets, Carapanos (1878), pl. 29.3 and 31.3–4; Dieterle (2007), 43–4; further discussed in Cabanes (1988).

⁵⁸ Piccinini (2016) reinterprets several of the so-called *naoi* as *thesauroi*, treasuries from Epeirote communities. Dieterle (2007), 42–4, and 43 n. 193, with references on the foundation of the games under Pyrrhos.

⁵⁹ Discussed further in Williamson (forthcoming a).

⁶⁰ Fehr (1969/70); Pedersen (2004), with references.

⁶¹ The open spaces between the stoa and the temple have been interpreted as providing a sightline with Pergamon: Conze and Schatzmann (1911); Wulf (1999); further discussed in Williamson (2014b).

⁶² Terracottas: Töpperwein-Hoffmann (1978). Coinage: Conze and Schatzmann (1911), 41–3, identifiable origins of Hellenistic coins include: Adramyttion, Gambreion, Pergamon, Pitane, Aigai, Elaia, Apollonis, Sardis, Thyateira.

⁶³ Also Conze and Schatzmann (1911), 44. Philetairos inscribed his name on the architrave of the temple, and the two other inscriptions found at the shrine relate to the Attalids as well: a statue base by Philetairos' nephew Attalos (father of Attalos I) for his wife Antiochis, see Conze and Schatzmann (1911), 38–9 and also a dedication by the priestess to Attalos I, Conze and Schatzmann (1911), 6–7.

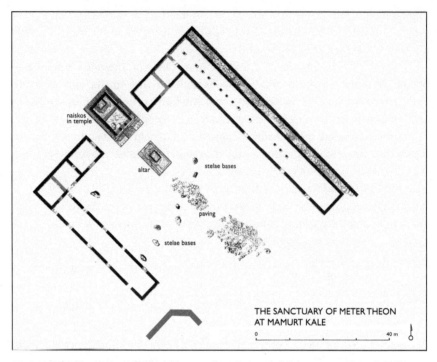

Fig. 9.5 The Sanctuary of Meter Theon, after Conze and Schatzmann (1911), Taf. I.

The Attalids became masters of the terraced complex with enclosed spaces and framed views, particularly under Eumenes II.[64] The many examples in Pergamon include the Asklepieion, a sanctuary open to all who sought healing, which appears to have acquired its form as an enclosed, internalizing space in the early second century BC as it transitioned into a state cult.[65] But the shrine of Athena Polias Nikephoros on the *acropolis* especially stands out for its play with visibility. The new two-storeyed pi-shaped stoa complex enhanced the view of the temple near the edge of the plateau, allowing for a symbolic connection with the Great Altar on the terrace below, while framing the view to the south-west, over the theatre and across the Kaikos valley towards the sea. Attalid influence extends throughout Asia Minor especially in the second century BC; it is inferred with the temple of Men Askaenos near Pisidian Antioch (discussed below) and with the Asklepieion at Kos.[66]

The transformation of the Asklepieion on Kos, however, began in the early third century BC and largely predates Attalid involvement. Probably influenced by Labraunda, and possibly prompted by benefactions from Ptolemy II Philadelphos,

---

[64] On the Attalids as textbook example, Gruben (1986), 421–45.
[65] Bauphase 9 in Ziegenhaus and de Luca (1968).
[66] On Attalid *Kulturpolitik*, Schalles (1985).

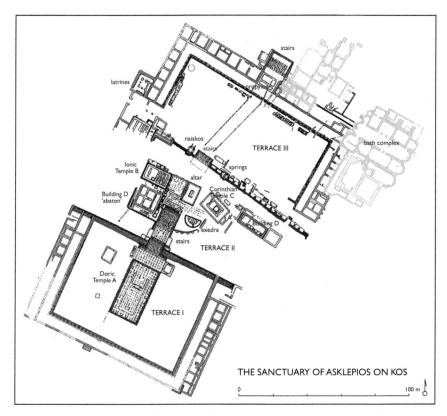

Fig. 9.6 The Sanctuary of Asklepios on Kos, after Interdonato (2016), 171 fig. 10.1.

the Koans undertook major earthworks at the Asklepieion, some three and a half kilometres uphill from the urban centre.[67] At least three terraces were constructed, focusing on the central, open terrace with the old temple and other ritual structures, including a pi-shaped altar (Fig. 9.6).[68] The upper and lower terraces were symmetrically framed on three sides by stoa architecture, with rooms at the back. The lower terrace, where those seeking healing may have gathered, was largely sealed off on the fourth side by the terrace wall, save for the *propylon* and the stairs leading up to the middle terrace. The second staircase, more monumental and leading to the upper terrace, may also have been used as a *theatron* for viewing the rituals on the middle terrace.[69] This staircase is part of the second phase of construction at the shrine, dated to 170–150 BC, when the stoas were rebuilt in marble, and the

---

[67] On the Asklepieion, Herzog and Schazmann (1932); Interdonato (2013) and (2016), with references; Gruben (1986), 409.
[68] This is an early example of a pi-shaped altar. Linfert (1995) relates their appearance to grants of *asylia* (except at Pergamon).
[69] Hollinshead (2015), 72–7.

upper terrace was crowned with Temple A, attributed to Eumenes II.⁷⁰ In contrast with the lower terrace, the upper portico framed a spectacular view towards the polis of Kos and across the bay to Halikarnassos. The innovations of the Asklepieion extended to its festival. Following a Delphic grant of *asylia* in 242 BC, the Koans organized the Asklepieia as a *panegyris* with crowned games, embarking on a large-scale theoric mission to gain recognition and participation from across the Greek world.⁷¹ This example would later be followed by other *poleis*, such as Magnesia and Stratonikeia, discussed below.

Another spectacular example is the transformation of the Athena sanctuary at Ilion in the Hellenistic era. As Charles Brian Rose has discussed, the famous shrine has multiple layers of meaning that were invested by different parties. At the end of the fourth century BC, Antigonos I initiated a federation of twelve cities in the Troad with the shrine of Athena Ilias at its heart, and the *panegyris* of the Panathenaia as unifying event.⁷² Rose argues that the festival and its games were intentionally modelled on the Athenian Panathenaia, one of the means of writing the mainland city into the prestigious history of the Trojan past.⁷³ Moreover, the temple of Athena Ilias, constructed in the later third century BC as one of the largest Doric temples in Asia Minor, bore *metopes* that echo those of the Parthenon. At this time, the temple terrace was also vastly expanded across the Bronze Age citadel and extended to the east, resting on the citadel wall.⁷⁴ Stoas on the east, south, and west sides defined an interior space of roughly 100 × 100 m, while framing the view across the plains of Troy and the Dardanelles, thereby affording a Trojan backdrop for the events of the Panathenaia.⁷⁵

The precinct of Athena Ilias and its incorporation of Trojan memory is in many ways exceptional, but the peristyle formalization of sanctuaries in tandem with the expansion of festivals is a concept that became increasingly common in the Hellenistic era, with many more examples than can adequately be addressed here. The combination of form, ritual performance, and social interaction with divine and civic authority made enclosed sanctuaries especially powerful places that kings and cities increasingly invested in. The dynamics between form, function, and setting are worth exploring in closer detail.

---

⁷⁰ Critically discussed in Hollinshead (2015), 76–7, with references.

⁷¹ The *asylia* grant: *SEG* 12, 371, with *IG* XII.4, 207–46, representing the responses of at least forty-three cities, see Rigsby (1996), 106–54; Buraselis (2004); also Williamson (forthcoming b) on the scope of the festival; the number of responses may increase with the new publications of the inscriptions, e.g. Bosnakis and Hallof (2020).

⁷² Rose (2012), 155–60; Aslan and Rose (2013), 23. The foundation of *koinon* and *panegyris* is stipulated in *I.Ilion* 1 and included: Parion, Lampsakos, Abydos, Dardanos, Rhoiteion, Ilion, Skepsis, Alexandria, Assos, and Gargara, and also Myrlea and Chalcedeon; see Pillot (2020), who emphasizes its amphictyonic character. On the *panegyris*: Ma (2007).

⁷³ Rose (2012), 160.

⁷⁴ Aslan and Rose (2013), 23 assign a date in the third quarter of the second century BC and credit this construction to Antiochos Hierax (r. 241–228 BC), who established Ilion as his power base.

⁷⁵ Rose (2012), 160.

9.4. Three case studies

Three sanctuaries in Asia Minor show different ways that cities shaped their prime religious centres into geo-political festival spaces, focused on mediation for communities at multiple levels. Magnesia on the Maeander used the shrine of their goddess Artemis Leukophryene as a fulcrum to draw the world to their doorstep. The shrine of Hekate at Lagina had a gravitational pull in the region that the nearby *polis* of Stratonikeia used first to coordinate the surrounding communities, and later to connect with Rome and the larger world. The shrine of Men Askaenos had a spectacular view over the territory of Antioch in Pisidia, and served as a prime centre of devotion for the local community, but also as a showcase for the games. Each case shows local strategies of human interaction in ritual space and the overall organization in relation to the (intended) scope, or catchment area, of the sanctuary and its festivals.

9.4.1. Magnesia and the festival of Artemis Leukophryene

A first example concerns the shrine of Artemis Leukophryene at Magnesia on the Maeander in the later third century BC. After an epiphany of Artemis, the Magnesians sent an embassy to Delphi in 221 BC.[76] The oracle bestowed the status of 'holy and inviolate' (*hieros kai asylos*) to the city and its territory (*chora*) and the Magnesians were instructed by the oracle to honour the goddess with a festival, including crowned games.[77] The Magnesians did so, discussed further below, but also responded by initiating a building programme centred on a temple and altar that reflected the epiphany of the goddess. The pediment above the entrance of the west-facing temple included three apertures. The largest one in the centre has been interpreted as a kind of *Erscheinungstur* for the epiphany of the goddess, who could then oversee the sacrifices taking place in the east-facing pi-shaped altar.[78] The temple was moreover pseudo-dipteral, functioning as a kind of stoa either for ritual performances, or from which they could be viewed. Vitruvius attributed the innovative design to Hermogenes of Priene.[79] Strabo discusses the tremendous scale of the temple, the third largest in Asia, after that of Artemis in Ephesos and Apollo in Didyma, noting:

---

[76] Thonemann (2007) on the date.
[77] *I.Magnesia* 16, esp. ll. 8–10. On *asylia*, Rigsby (1996); also Sosin (2009).
[78] On the visual link in connection with the epiphany, Humann et al. (1904) 64 n. 1. For *Erscheinungstur*, Gruben (1986 [1966]), 347; also Williamson (2020), 114. Linfert (1995), on such pi-shaped altars in the Hellenistic era. See Hammerschmied (2018), 104, fig. 6 for a reconstruction.
[79] Vitruvius, *De architectura* 3.2.6.

but in the fine proportion (*eurythmia*) and the skill exhibited in the structure of the enclosure (*peri ten kataskeuen tou sekou*), it greatly surpasses the Ephesian temple.[80]

The attention given to the 'structure of the enclosure' stresses the importance of this public space in the eyes of the Magnesians—it not only articulated the sacred precinct within the cityscape, but did so in a very beautiful way. In his detailed discussion of the Magnesian building programme following the epiphany of the goddess, Kristoph Hammerschmied attributes the design of these open spaces to Hermogenes as well, emphasizing the confluence of *temenos* and *agora* at the intersection of the main roads in the city (Fig. 9.7).[81] Not unlike some of the sanctuaries of the previous section—especially Labraunda, Mamurt Kale, and Ilion—the *agora/temenos* of Magnesia was enclosed on three sides: north, west, and south, with the entry to the *agora* through the street between the south and

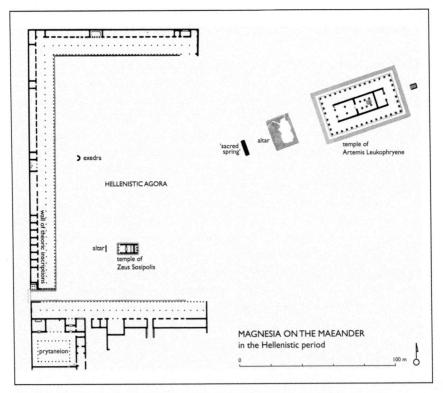

Fig. 9.7 The Sanctuary of Artemis Leukophryena and the Hellenistic *agora* of Magnesia on the Maeander, after Hammerschmied (2018), 99 fig. 2.

[80] Strabo, *Geography* 14.1.40, trans. Hamilton and Falconer (1903).
[81] Hammerschmied (2018), 96, 98–105.

west arms, and the *prytaneion* at the back of the southern stoa. The three-sided enclosure helped frame the view to the fourth side, in this case the temple itself, which is set at an angle. The unusual alignment has been linked to the cults on the slopes of Mount Thorax, clearly visible from the deep *pronaos* of the temple.[82] This vantage point, however, also drew the eye to the west and south-west stoas, where the Delphic oracle and associated epigraphic dossier were inscribed, opposite the small temple of Zeus Sosipolis, and illumined by the large windows in the short southern stretch of this end of the stoa.[83]

The oracle of Delphi is recorded in *I.Magnesia* 16, dated to 208 BC, in the context of a delayed attempt at organizing the festival commanded by Apollo some years before. The meaning of this time lag is debated among scholars, whether it represents a renewed effort after a failed first attempt, or whether there even was a first attempt.[84] According to Peter Thonemann, the main point of the inscription is to assert Magnesian pride of place as being the first in Asia to organize crowned games.[85] Kos had previously undertaken a similar approach for the Asklepieia, but the scale of Magnesian diplomacy was unprecedented. The scope of embassies for the Leukophryenea is highlighted in lines 24–35:

> …In Moeragoras' year, they established the crowned contest, equal to the Pythia, giving a crown worth fifty staters, with the approval of the kings and all the other Greeks to whom they sent ambassadors, voting by nations and cities to honour Artemis and to make inviolable the city and country of Magnesia, because of the god's urging.[86]

Magnesia thus embarked on a massive diplomatic mission in order to gain recognition for the *asylia*, or inviolability, of the city and sanctuary from across the known world, and to maximize participation in the festival.[87] Invitations were individually tailored and the delegates, or *theoroi*, were armed with historical dossiers that would underscore their claimed relations with the targeted addressees, emphasizing kinship, mythical bonds, or their own importance in the Greek world, in order to persuade their hosts to support and participate in the festival.[88] Their endeavour resulted in a positive response from over a hundred cities and kings across the Mediterranean and beyond (Fig. 9.8).

---

[82] Scully (1962), 91. Assessed by Saldaña (2020) in the spatial reconstruction on the website *Procedural Magnesia*, proceduralmagnesia.com/cave-and-city.html, last accessed 2 June 2023.

[83] Hammerschmied (2018), 100–1, fig. 3 gives a good reconstruction.

[84] Slater and Summa (2006); Thonemann (2007); Sosin (2009).

[85] Thonemann (2007) in the context of a rivalry with Miletos, that quickly organized crowned games; Knäpper (2019).

[86] *I.Magnesia* 16, ll. 27–35 (transl. Rigsby (1996), 187).

[87] Also van Nijf and Williamson (2015); van Nijf and Williamson (2016); Williamson (2022). See further Sumi (2004); Carless Unwin (2017), 169–88; Hammerschmied (2018).

[88] Also Rigsby (1996), 179–279. Further discussed in Williamson (2022) with references. On *theoric* missions in general, Rutherford (2013).

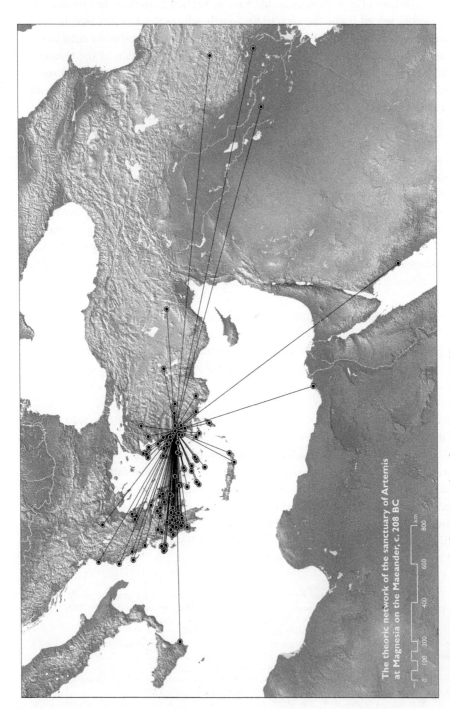

Fig. 9.8 The theoric network of Magnesia, based on *I.Magnesia* 17-87.

The letters from this emerging network were later collected and inscribed in the south section of the west wall of the *agora*, a carefully planned location in the prime space near the entry and the *prytaneion*.[89] This was surely the most conspicuous place, the *epiphanestatos topos*, for Magnesia.[90] The illumination of the inscriptions by the windows enhanced their legibility and helped turn this wall into a cognitive map of Magnesia's perception of the world and its own relevance in it.[91]

Whereas Miletos and Megalopolis positioned their prime civic sanctuaries near their urban centres, yet spatially segregated them from it, the Magnesians instead adjoined the *temenos* to the *agora*, creating thereby a concentric space that was both religiously and politically charged, aimed not only at their own community but also at their relations from across the *oikoumene*. This spatial consolidation lasted at least until the imperial era, when a divergent conceptualization of space led to the construction of a cross-wall on the east side of the *agora*, thus separating it from the *temenos* of Artemis while accentuating access in either direction.

9.4.2. Stratonikeia and the festival of Hekate at Lagina

A second example is the shrine of Hekate at Lagina, some 8 kilometres north of Stratonikeia in Karia, located on a gentle slope near the ancient settlement of Koranza (modern Turgut) and overlooking the Marsyas valley. By the later second century BC, Hekate's sanctuary had become one of the grand peristyle precincts, at roughly 110 × 110 m slightly larger than that of Athena at Ilion.[92] A monumental gateway brought the visitor down into the large open hectare, enclosed on all sides with porticoes (Fig. 9.9). The *propylaia*, main altar and probably most of the precinct walls were repaired under Augustus, but the perimeter of the *temenos* as such appears to have already been in place in the fourth century BC.[93]

The shrine was approached via the sacred way that led from Stratonikeia through several of the older communities that were eventually incorporated into

---

[89] Hammerschmied (2018), 101 observes how most of the honorific statues were found in this area.
[90] The term *epiphanestatos topos* is common in epigraphic clauses, stipulating the location of the inscription in the most conspicuous public place, usually a sanctuary or *agora*, e.g. *I.Magnesia* 59, the letter from Laodikeia, or *I.Magnesia* 79–80, the letter from city An[...], accepting the invitation to the festival of Leukophreyena.
[91] See above on the illumination of the wall. On lists of sacred lands inscribed on temple walls as a kind of 'cognitive map': Ma (2003); Horster (2010).
[92] On Lagina: Baumeister (2007); Gider (2012); Tırpan et al. (2012); Aydaş (2015); Büyüközer (2018); Söğüt (2019), 243–77; also Williamson (2012) and more extensively in Williamson (2021), 241–330, for the chronology, 254–9 and 268–84.
[93] Gider (2012); Büyüközer (2018).

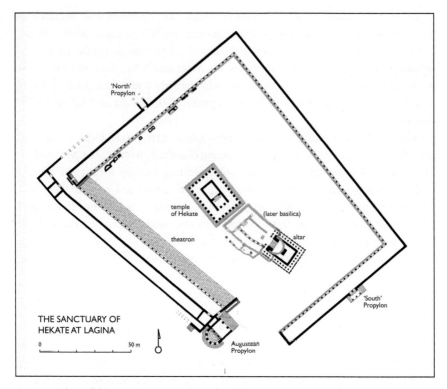

Fig. 9.9 Plan of the sanctuary complex of Hekate at Lagina by the first century BC, after Gider (2012), 274 fig. 1.

the new *polis*. On descending into the *temenos*, the visitor would have passed by the prestigious monuments that were clustered around the entryway, similar to the entry of the *agora* in Magnesia.[94] The enigmatic open area between the *propylon* and the south-east stoa may have been filled with temporary structures, or perhaps was the area of the sacred grove.[95] From here, the visitor faced the south-west side of the altar. As at Magnesia, this was also an enclosed pi-shaped structure and was linked to the temple by a paved walkway, as at Mamurt Kale.[96] The temple of Hekate is best known among scholars for the somewhat enigmatic 'north' frieze,[97] yet it is remarkable in several other respects as well. The shortened *cella* and deep *pronaos* were surrounded by a peristyle of 8 × 11 Corinthian columns that were set up on a pseudodipteral stylobate. Originating with the temple of

---

[94] *I.Stratonikeia* 1426 and 1427, the monument of the brothers Menekles and Epainetos, from the later first century BC, discussed in Williamson (2021), 273, 320–1. See Section 9.4.1 on Magnesia.

[95] Mentioned in *I.Stratonikeia* 513; Williamson (2021), 308–9.

[96] In his discussion of pi-shaped altars, Linfert (1995) notes how their connection to the temple and cult image is underscored by a paved surface.

[97] See Baumeister (2007), with references.

Artemis Leukophreyene at nearby Magnesia on the Maeander, this feature provides ample room to progress in the shade around the *naos* and a comfortable place to view events in the rest of the *temenos*.[98] North and east of the temple is a large open area; honorific monuments and *naiskoi* may have been clustered in this space, near the peristyle of the stoa complex. Yet the trapezoidal space between the temple and the south-west arm of the complex, which deviates from the temple but is parallel with the altar, seems to have been prime public space as it is lined with extended rows of seating along the entire length. This would have functioned as a *theatron*, turning the area and perhaps the south-west temple flank into a zone for ritual performances.[99]

The cult of Hekate was a critical instrument in remapping civic identity as the wider region was drawn into the orbit of the *polis*, especially in the second century BC.[100] The goddess of Lagina became the main poliad deity, along with Zeus of Panamara, and both are testified on civic coinage.[101] The festivals of Hekate first appear to have been directed towards the constitution of Stratonikeia, functioning as a coordinating mechanism that helped fold local polities into the sphere of the emerging *polis*. But after the Mithridatic wars in the first part of the first century BC, Hekate's cult at Lagina expanded again as a geo-political medium, used by the city to gain favour from Rome. Stratonikeia was one of the few cities that had remained loyal to Rome, despite their severe sufferings at the hand of Mithridates VI. After reminding Sulla and the senate of this, they received the *Senatus consultum de Stratonicensibus* of 81 BC, which included a territorial extension and a grant of *asylia*.[102] Stratonikeia responded by attaching the cult of Thea Roma to that of Hekate, who now received the epithet *Soteira Epiphaneia* (Epiphanous Savior), and installed a new pentaeteric festival, the Hekatesia-Romaia, to celebrate the divine partnership.[103] As with Kos and Magnesia, a *theoric* initiative was launched to assemble an audience from across the Greek world to sanction this joint festival. At least fifty-seven cities acknowledged the *asylia* of the sanctuary and the games, and were listed just below the *senatus consultum*, most likely on the south-west flank of the temple opposite the tribunes.[104] This dossier of decrees put Stratonikeia on the map of world affairs, commemorated for generations to come by these inscriptions (Fig. 9.10). This area between the temple

---

[98] Discussed in Tırpan et al. (2012); also Mitchell and Waelkens (1998), 63–8, on the Lagina temple as part of the legacy of Hermogenes' design at Magnesia, along with the temple of Men Askaenos.
[99] Nielsen (2002), 138; Mylonopoulos (2006); Hollinshead (2015).
[100] Williamson (2012); Şahin (1976) on the persistence of ethnic usage of the names of villages, later *demes*, in the onomastics of Stratonikeia.
[101] Meadows (2002).   [102] *I.Stratonikeia* 505; Williamson (2021), 318, with references.
[103] Laid out in *I.Stratonikeia* 507.
[104] *I.Stratonikeia* 508; van Bremen (2010). The network created in this process is further discussed in van Nijf and Williamson (2016). On temples and their archival wall: von Hesberg et al. (2007); and Roels (forthcoming). On the importance of place for epigraphy with the example of Aphrodisias, see Carless Unwin, Chapter 7 above.

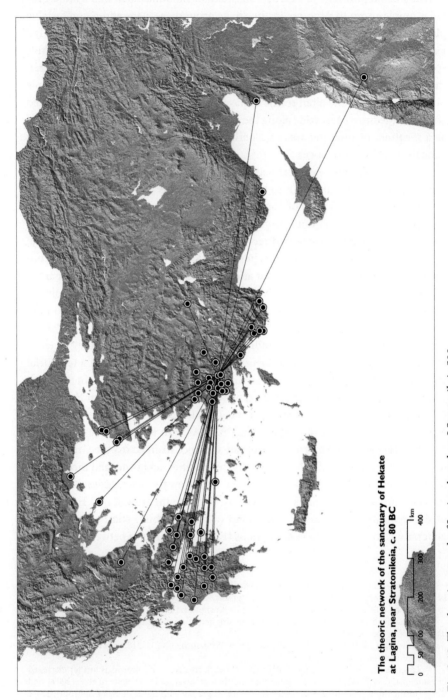

Fig. 9.10 The theoric network of Lagina, based on *I.Stratonikeia* 508.

and the *theatron* was prime space in the sanctuary, and the performance of rituals against this inscribed backdrop of global relevance surely amplified the sense of civic pride for Stratonikeians and respect from other spectators.

The capacious peristyle sanctuary thus comprised space that was both open and concentrated, filtering the crowd through the *propylaia*, directing their gaze to the central area where they engaged in a shared festival experience. But it was a collective experience in the broadest sense, one that the Greek world was meant to be aware of, as part of a religious-political strategy. The festivals of Hekate continued well into the imperial period, but seem to have returned to a more regional or local sphere. The shrine at this time is known as the *peripolion* and is vibrant, with a food market and a settlement known as the *katoikountes*, who increasingly appear alongside the *boule* and *demos* in bestowing honours in the shrine.[105]

9.4.3. Pisidian Antioch and the festival of Men Askaenos

Lagina is an example of a sanctuary complex that Mitchell and Waelkens used in their comparative analysis of the sanctuary of Men Askaenos near Pisidian Antioch.[106] Both shrines show a large sacred area with a wide variety of structures, yet the shrine of Men Askaenos also had a concentrated *temenos* area within the larger complex that arguably represents the most tightly enclosed peristyle shrine discussed so far. Little is known about the festivals or its exact scope, yet several features at the shrine allow us to infer a large and varied crowd.

Mitchell and Waelkens have suggested Attalid involvement in the monumentalization of the sanctuary of Men Askaenos in Pisidian Antioch, based in part on the dating of the complex to roughly the mid-second century BC, i.e. after the Peace of Apamea (188 BC), when Pisidia fell under the domain of the Attalids.[107] More compelling are the stylistic grounds, and the scholars cite similarities with Sagalassos and Termessos where Pergamene construction has been identified, as well as the shrine at Pessinous, known to be a recipient of Attalid benefactions.[108] In any case, the sanctuary on the Karakuyu hilltop, just a few kilometres southeast of Antioch, represents a clear case of formal enclosure (Fig. 9.11).

The walls of the shrine were fitted with buttresses as supports for the *temenos* terrace and would have stood three to five metres in height, or at least as high as

---

[105] *I.Stratonikeia* 524, 536, 539, and 540; discussed in Williamson (2021), 307–9, with references.
[106] Especially regarding banqueting facilities, but also provisional tents (*skenae*): Mitchell and Waelkens (1998), 84, also citing the sanctuary complex of Zeus at Panamara, the second and perhaps even larger shrine in the hinterland of Stratonikeia; see Williamson (2021), 331–410.
[107] Mitchell and Waelkens (1998), 37–90, esp. 68; Mitchell (2002).
[108] Mitchell and Waelkens (1998), 67–8.

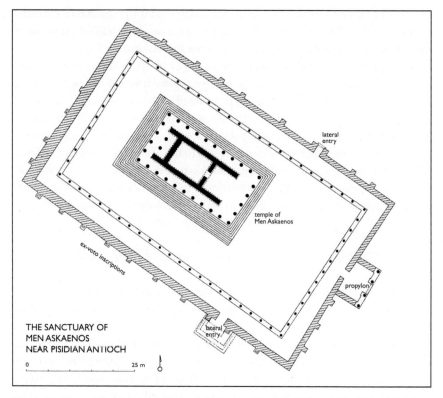

Fig. 9.11 Plan of the *temenos* of Men Askaenos, after Mitchell and Waelkens (1998), 40 fig. 6.

the columns of the interior portico.[109] The main entrance to the complex was the *propylon* in the shorter south-east wall, directly opposite the temple, and later enhanced with a prostyle porch. A stepped lateral entrance was built into the east end of the long south-west side with a smaller entry on the opposite north-east flank. The plan in Figure 9.11 shows narrow openings in the wall, roughly a metre wide, that gave access to the interior of roughly 36 × 69 m, surrounded by porticoes on all sides.[110] The temple is offset to the north in the interior of the complex, making room in the court for ritual space between its stylobate and the porticoes, as at Lagina. The space before the temple may have been used for an altar, although this has not been identified. The *temenos* terrace is set into a slope, so that the north-west and south-west ends of the *krepis* (stepped foundation) are four steps higher than the rest. The temple itself was a contrast of dark limestone with bright marble features used for the columns, steps, and door frames. Perched on the

---

[109] Mitchell and Waelkens (1998), 42.
[110] The dimensions of the *temenos* are discussed in Mitchell and Waelkens (1998), 38.

podium-like *krepis*, the striking bi-coloured temple near the top of this hill with a sweeping view across the plain below was clearly meant to be noticed, and yet the high *temenos* walls simultaneously curtained it off from its surroundings.[111] This play of access and restriction surely heightened the anticipation of the ritual experience within, although the exact nature of this remains unknown.

The cult of Men Askaenos is perhaps most famous for the *ex voto* relief inscriptions, largely dated to the imperial era.[112] These accumulated on surfaces of exposed rock lining the sacred way from the city to the sanctuary, with the highest concentrations on the south-west perimeter wall of the *temenos*.[113] Much has been written about these intriguing dedications,[114] but for the purposes here it is especially important to note the traces of the festival experience which they present, giving us a glimpse into the rituals performed by a broad cross-section of the urban population, including the elite as well as the lower ranks, entire households, also individual women and slaves.[115] The increasing intensity of clusters of these inscriptions along the south-west perimeter of the *temenos* wall show this area as a prime spot in the sanctuary.

The interior of the shrine shows a very different side. All of the official inscriptions at the site were either found within the *temenos* or are presumed to have originally been set up there, marking this inner space as the most representative place, at least in the imperial period.[116] These concern honorific monuments but also victor lists from the games that appear to have been initiated in this later phase, surely as part of the revival of the festival at the hands of the local elite in the Antonine period. This is when additional structures began to appear, such as the *stadion* and *thesauroi*, and the *oikoi* or *andrones* for banqueting.[117] The hilltop was thus transformed into a major festival space for Antioch, one which retained, or reinvented, local traditions such as the *ex votos* while embedding them in the larger Greek festival culture of contests. The central and internalizing space of the *temenos* near the top would have served as a showcase that both concentrated and commemorated the festival experience.

9.5. Conclusions: worlds within worlds

Even though some of the earliest examples of peristyle architecture in the Greek world are found in highly public sanctuaries, architectural historians have long

---

[111] The aspect of height and visual access is further discussed in Williamson (forthcoming a).
[112] Published in Levick (1970).   [113] Hardie (1912); Labarre (2002).
[114] Hardie (1912); Levick (1970); Labarre (2002).   [115] See especially Blanco Pérez (2016).
[116] Discussion of find spots in Mitchell and Waelkens (1998), 48–50; Anderson (1913), nos. 7 and 8 are victors' lists.
[117] C. Ulpius Baebanius was a prominent priest, *agonothetes*, and benefactor who provided endowments for the festivals: Anderson (1913), nos. 11, 12; Mitchell and Waelkens (1998), 72–86 for the *oikoi* and *andrones*; also Raff (2011), 149–52.

attributed their development to a breakdown of identity between the individual and the polis.[118] The great, sensational architectural complexes have often been seen as royal endowments imposed upon urban topographies, or as halls of fame for local elite benefactors, geared towards manipulating individual attitudes, rather than as part of a composite civic experience.[119] This view is no longer widely held, yet much remains to be done towards interpreting these spaces within the context of *polis*-driven strategies. In this regard, Emme advances a new view in assessing the social implications of peristyle sanctuaries within the larger trend of the compartmentalization of urban space. His general conclusion of the segregation of these spaces as a reflection of increasing societal stratification, as spaces of inclusion for some and exclusion for most, surely holds true in many and even most cases.[120] But it is also important to observe the capacity of these internalizing spaces to create a new focus by physically isolating the participants from the urban environment, a focus made all the more strong through ritual. The combination is a powerful tool for fostering a sense of community at several levels, however exclusive or inclusive that community may have been.

Ritual is another key factor, making sacred spaces that were enclosed even more charged than the everyday spaces of the *agora* and gymnasium. Ritual space carried with it the direct sanction of the gods, and civic sanctuaries were moreover imbued with the political authority of the state. A lot was at stake with these major places of cult, particularly when they were home to the 'Panhellenic' festivals that were on the rise in the Hellenistic era.[121] These festivals turned their sanctuaries and festival sites into geo-political arenas, and theoric missions ensured the presence of delegates from as far away as the *polis* could afford. The examples discussed above, especially the Asklepieia at Kos, the Leukophryenea at Magnesia, and the Hekatesia-Romaia at Stratonikeia, point to the heavy investments by civic councils in sending embassies to draw support from cities, kings, and leagues across the known world, thereby securing their future while putting their sanctuary and city on the map of places that mattered. Meanwhile, a network was being forged through such inter-urban connections and maintained by the recurring festivals and their contests. Athletes, musicians, dramatists, but also craftsmen and traders that travelled from festival to festival, whether locally, (inter)regionally, or across the Mediterranean, helped create or reinforce the ties that held this Panhellenic world together.[122] The prestige that these festivals held was steeped in

---

[118] Lauter (1986), 40–1 on the banquet hall of the Argive Heraion, and the *pompeion* in Athens. Lauter primarily focuses on formal aspects, but the alienation and soul-searching of the individual in the Hellenistic world, presumably reflected in sensational sacred architecture that highlights sensory experience, is a recurring theme in other reference works, e.g. Gruben (1986), 401–2 (on the Koan Asklepieion); Pollitt (1986), 230–49.

[119] e.g. Gruben (1986), 401–2; Pollitt (1986), 230–49; discussed further in Williamson (2020).

[120] Emme (2013), 297–300.   [121] Esp. Parker (2004), discussed above.

[122] Discussed further in van Nijf and Williamson (2016); Williamson (forthcoming b); see also the Groningen project websites connectedcontests.org and connectingthegreeks.com.

intersecting and overlapping layers of myth, tradition, and individual and political identity, buttressed by public ritual. The importance of not only getting the ritual right, but doing it better than the others, and especially being seen to do it better than the others in front of the others, cannot be underestimated in this 'regime of honour'.[123]

But the setting of the ritual also made a difference. All of this took place in the 'sacred circle'. The centripetal force of these major civic sanctuaries is crucial to their understanding. They naturally occupied an overlap of religious, social, and highly politicized spaces, much like the *agora*. Oftentimes they functioned as a kind of second *agora*, even with a festival market; it is hardly a coincidence that their enclosed spaces were very similar to the great market centres of the Hellenistic city—further research may even show which came first. But it is significant to observe that a number of them appeared at the edges of the *agora*, as in Miletos, Megalopolis, and Magnesia, which even blurred the boundaries. In Ilion, the shrine of Athena consciously straddled the old citadel, but also stood just above the *bouleuterion*. Sanctuaries in landscapes well removed from the urban core created a kind of alternate centre, for example in the sanctuaries of Zeus at Labraundos, near Mylasa, of Asklepios, near the polis of Kos, of Hekate at Lagina, near Stratonikeia, of Men Askaenos, near Antioch, but also of Meter at Mamurt Kale, in the region of Pergamon. The shrine of Zeus at Dodona is exceptional in this regard, as it was not connected to a city, but was both a regional sanctuary and political centre for Epeiros.[124] On the whole, these major enclosed shrines were situated at prime locations, and their porticoes were sometimes three-sided in order to frame a strategic view on the fourth—Labraunda, Mamurt Kale, Kos, and Ilion are good examples of this.

Wherever they were located, peristyle shrines shared a certain logic of space and ritual that made sense to their urbane participants. After their long travels, pilgrims (delegates, athletes, traders, etc.) from other cities would have found themselves in a familiar setting. Cut off from the outer physical world, they would have felt translocated to a cosmopolitan realm.[125] While not identical to those in their hometown, travellers would nonetheless have understood the general architectural grammar and the spatial intention with little effort, needing to know only the particulars of locale. Their focus would immediately have been directed towards the central events and towards the reactions of others around them. These pockets of concentric, cosmopolitan spaces and their rituals precipitated the kind of common knowledge and emotional energy that helps create and coordinate globalizing communities—a transcendent world within the existing world. The same dynamics would have worked for segregated groups within the city. Yet when

---

[123] For 'regime of honour', Quass (1993); Habicht (1995); Heller and van Nijf (2017); on correct ritual performance, McCauley and Lawson (2007).
[124] Moustakis (2006). [125] Also Kamphorst (2023) on cosmopolitan spaces.

applied to the major civic and geo-political sanctuaries, they surely fostered a profound sense of bonding, shared values and intense connectivity at several scales simultaneously, crossing borders while at the same time reifying the relevance of the local city within this expanding world.

Works Cited

Anderson, J. G. C. (1913) 'Festivals of Mên Askaênos in the Roman colonia at Antioch of Pisidia', *Journal of Roman Studies* 3: 267.

Aneziri, S. (2011) 'World travellers: the associations of Artists of Dionysus', in R. Hunter and I. Rutherford (eds), *Wandering Poets in Ancient Greek Culture. Travel, Locality and Pan-Hellenism*. Cambridge, 217–36.

Arendt, H. (1990) *On Revolution*. New York. First published 1963.

Aslan, C. C. and Rose, C. B. (2013) 'City and citadel at Troy from the Late Bronze Age through the Roman period', in S. Redford and N. Ergin (eds), *City and Citadels in Turkey. From the Iron Age to the Seljuks*. Leuven, 7–38.

Assmann, J. (1991) 'Der zweidimensionale Mensch. Das Fest als Medium des kollektiven Gedächtnis', in J. Assmann (ed.), *Das Fest und das Heilige. Religiöse Kontrapunkte zur Alltagswelt*. Studien zum Verstehen fremder Religionen 1. Gütersloh, 13–30.

Aydaş, M. (2015) 'Stratonikeia ve Lagina. Polis ve Peripolion', in B. Söğüt (ed.), *Stratonikeia ve Çevresi Araştırmaları*. Stratonikeia Çalışmaları 1. Istanbul, 71–7.

Baumeister, P. (2007) *Der Fries des Hekateions von Lagina. Neue Untersuchungen zu Monument und Kontext*. BYZAS 6. Istanbul.

Bek, L. (2007) 'Sight, object, space. The notion of landscape in antiquity as a functional or an aesthetic category', *Proceedings of the Danish Institute at Athens* 5: 199–212.

Blanco Pérez, A. (2016) 'Mên Askaenos and the native cults of Antioch by Pisidia', in M. Paz de Hoz Garcia-Bellido, J. P. Sánchez Hernández, and C. Molina Valero (eds), *Between Tarhuntas and Zeus Polieus. Cultural Crossroads in Temples and Cults of Graeco-Roman Anatolia*. Colloquia Antiqua 17. Leuven, 117–50.

Bosnakis, D. and Hallof, K. (2020) 'Alte und neue Inschriften aus Kos VI', *Chiron* 50: 287–326.

van Bremen, R. (2010) 'The inscribed documents on the temple of Hekate at Lagina and the date and meaning of the temple frieze', in R. van Bremen and J.-M. Carbon (eds), *Hellenistic Karia. Proceedings of the First International Conference on Hellenistic Karia—Oxford, 29 June–2 July 2006*. Bordeaux, 483–503.

Britton, T., A. Wiznura, C. G. Williamson, and O. M. van Nijf (eds) (forthcoming). *Rooted Cities, Wandering Gods. Interurban Religious Interactions in the Ancient World*. Leiden.

Buraselis, K. (2004) 'Some remarks on the Koan *asylia* (242 B.C.) against its international background', in K. Höghammar (ed.), *The Hellenistic Polis of Kos. State, Economy and Culture*. Acta Universitatis Upsaliensis. Boreas 28. Uppsala, 15–20.

Büyüközer, A. (2018) 'The sanctuary of Hekate at Lagina in the 4th century BC / MÖ 4. yy'da Lagina Hekate Kutsal Alanı', *Arkhaia Anatolika* 1: 15–30.

Cabanes, P. (1988) 'Les concours de Naia de Dodone', *Nikephoros* 1: 49–84.

Carapanos, C. (1878) *Dodone et ses ruines*. Paris.

Carless Unwin, N. (2017) *Caria and Crete in Antiquity. Cultural Interaction between Anatolia and the Aegean*. Cambridge.

Chaniotis, A. (1995) 'Sich selbst feiern? Städtische Feste des Hellenismus im Spannungsfeld von Religion und Politik', in M. Wörrle and P. Zanker (eds), *Stadtbild und Bürgerbild im Hellenismus. Kolloquium, München, 24. bis 26. Juni 1993*. Vestigia 47. Munich, 147–72.

Chaniotis, A. (2006) 'Rituals between norms and emotions. Rituals as shared experience and memory', in E. Stavrianopoulou (ed.), *Ritual and Communication in the Graeco-Roman World*. Kernos Supplément 16. Liège, 211–38.

Chaniotis, A. (2010) 'Dynamic of emotions and dynamic of rituals. Do emotions change ritual norms?', in C. Brosius and U. Hüsken (eds), *Ritual Matters. Dynamic Dimensions in Practice*. London, 208–33.

Chattopadhyay, S. (2013) 'Visualizing the body politic', in A. Sen (ed.), *Making Place. Space and Embodiment in the City*. Bloomington, 44–68.

Chwe, M. S.-Y. (2001) *Rational Ritual. Culture, Coordination, and Common Knowledge*. Princeton.

Collar, A. and Kristensen, T. M. (2020) *Pilgrimage and Economy in the Ancient Mediterranean*. Religions in the Graeco-Roman World 192. Leiden.

Collins, R. (2004) *Interaction Ritual Chains*. Princeton.

Connerton, P. (1989) *How Societies Remember*. Cambridge.

Conze, A. C. L. and Schatzmann, P. (1911) *Mamurt-Kaleh, ein Tempel der Göttermutter unweit Pergamon*. Jahrbuch des Kaiserlich Deutschen Archäologischen Instituts. Ergänzungsheft 9. Berlin.

Coulton, J. J. (1976) *The Architectural Development of the Greek Stoa*. Oxford.

Crampa, J. (1972) *Vol. III. Part 2. The Greek Inscriptions Part II. 13–133*, Acta Instituti Atheniensis regni Sueciae, Series in 4°, V, III, 2. Lund.

Dickenson, C. P. (2016) *On the Agora. The Evolution of a Public Space in Hellenistic and Roman Greece (c. 323 BC–267 AD)*. Mnemosyne Supplements 398. Leiden.

Dickenson, C. P. (2019) 'The myth of the Ionian agora. Investigating the enclosure of public space through archaeological and historical sources', *Hesperia* 88: 557–93.

Dieterle, M. (2007) *Dodona. Religionsgeschichtliche und historische Untersuchung zur Entstehung und Entwicklung des Zeus-Heiligtums*. Hildesheim.

Durkheim, É. (1912) *Les formes élémentaires de la vie religieuse. Le système totémique en Australie*. Paris.

Ekroth, G. (2023) '"A room of one's own?" Exploring the temenos concept as divine property', in M. Haysom, M. Mili, and J. Wallensten (eds), *Stuff of the Gods. The Material Aspects of Religion in Ancient Greece*. Stockholm.

Emme, B. (2013) *Peristyl und Polis. Entwicklung und Funktionen öffentlicher griechischer Hofanlagen*. Urban Spaces 1. Berlin.

Fehr, B. (1969) 'Plattform und Blickbasis', *Marburger Winckelmann-Programm* 1969: 31–67.

Frejman, A. (2020) 'With Gods as Neighbours. Extra-temenal Activity at Greek Rural Sanctuaries, 700–200 BCE'. PhD diss. Uppsala Universitet.

French, D. H. (1996) 'Amasian notes 5. The temenos of Zeus Stratios at Yassıçal', *Epigraphica Anatolica* 27: 75–92.

Gider, Z. (2012) 'Lagina kuzey stoanın ön cephe düzenlemesi / Façade Arrangement of North Stoa at Lagina', in B. Söğüt (ed.), *Stratonikeia'dan Laginaya Ahmet Adil Tırpan Armagani/From Stratonikeia to Lagina. Festschrift in Honour of Ahmet Adil Tırpan*. Istanbul, 263–80.

Giovannini, A. (1993) 'Greek cities and Greek commonwealth', in A. Bulloch (ed.), *Images and Ideologies. Self-Definition in the Hellenistic World*. Berkeley, 265–86.

Goffman, E. (1974) *Frame Analysis. An Essay on the Organization of Experience*. New York.

Gruben, G. (1986) *Die Tempel der Griechen*. 2nd edition. Munich.

Habicht, C. (1995) 'Ist ein "Honoratiorenregime" das Kennzeichen der Stadt im späteren Hellenismus?', in M. Wörrle and P. Zanker (eds), *Stadtbild und Burgerbild im Hellenismus. Kolloquium, München, 24. bis 26. Juni 1993*. Vestigia 47. Munich: 87–92.

Hamilton, H. C. and Falconer, W. (1903) *The Geography of Strabo. Literally Translated, with Notes, in Three Volumes*. London.

Hammerschmied, K. (2018) 'The Panhellenic festival of Artemis Leukophryene in Magnesia on the Meander. A spatial analysis of a Hellenistic procession', in U. Luig (ed.), *Approaching the Sacred. Pilgrimage in Historical and Intercultural Perspective*. Berlin, 91–127.

Hardie, M. M. (1912) 'The shrine of Men Askaenos at Pisidian Antioch', *Journal of Hellenic Studies* 32: 111–50.

Hatfield, E., Cacioppo, J. T., and Rapson, R. (1993) *Emotional Contagion*. Cambridge.

Heller, A. and van Nijf, O. M. (eds) (2017) *The Politics of Honour in the Greek Cities of the Roman Empire*. Leiden.

Hellström, P. (2011) 'Feasting at Labraunda and the chronology of the *Andrones*', in L. Karlsson and S. Carlsson (eds), *Labraunda and Karia. Proceedings of the international symposium commemorating sixty years of Swedish archaeological work in Labraunda. The Royal Swedish Academy of Letters, History and Antiquities, Stockholm, November 20–21, 2008*. Acta Universitatis Uppsaliensis. Boreas. Uppsala Studies in Ancient Mediterranean and Near Eastern Civilizations 32. Uppsala, 149–57.

Hellström, P. and Blid, J. (2019) *Labraunda 5. The Andrones*. Stockholm.

Henry, O. (2017) 'Sanctuaire et pouvoir. Nouvelles pistes de réflexion à partir des recherches archéologiques récentes sur le site de Labraunda en Carie (Turquie)', *Comptes rendus de l'Académie des Inscriptions et Belles-Lettres* 161.1: 545–79.

Herda, A. (2011) 'How to run a state cult. The organization of the cult of Apollo Delphinios in Miletos', in M. Haysom and J. Wallensten (eds), *Current Approaches to Religion in Ancient Greece*. Papers presented at a symposium at the Swedish Institute in Athens, 17–19 April, 2008. ActaAth-8°. Stockholm, 57–93.

Herzog, R. and Schazmann, P. (1932) *Kos. Ergebnisse der deutschen Ausgrabungen und Forschungen*. Band 1: *Asklepieion, Baubeschreibung und Baugeschichte von Paul Schazmann, mit einer Einleitung von Rudolf Herzog*. Berlin.

von Hesberg, H. (1990) 'Platzanlagen und Hallenbauten in der Zeit des frühen Hellenismus', in *Akten des XIII. Internationalen Kongresses für klassische Archäologie*. Mainz, 231–41.

von Hesberg, H. (2015) 'Theatergebäude und ihre Funktion in der Polis frühhellenistischer Zeit', in A. Matthaei and M. Zimmermann (eds), *Urbane Strukturen und bürgerliche Identität im Hellenismus*. Die hellenistische Polis als Lebensform Bd. 5. Heidelberg, 99–122.

von Hesberg, H., Eck, W., and Gronke, M. (2007) 'Die Stimme der Bauten. Schrift am Bau', in *Kosmos der Zeichen*. Schriftbild und Bildformel in Antike und Mittelalter. Ausstellung im Römisch-Germanischen Museum der Stadt Köln, 26. Juni bis 30. September 2007. Wiesbaden, 211–34.

Hollinshead, M. B. (2015) *Shaping Ceremony. Monumental Steps and Greek Architecture*. Wisconsin Studies in Classics. Madison.

Horster, M. (2010) 'Le concept de "paysage religieux" I. Religious landscape and sacred land. Connections of space and cult in the Greek world', *Revue de l'histoire des religions* 227: 435–59.

Horster, M. (2020) 'Hellenistic festivals. Aspects of the economic impact on cities and sanctuaries', in A. Collar and T. M. Kristensen (eds), *Pilgrimage and Economy in the Ancient Mediterranean*. Religions in the Graeco-Roman World 192. Leiden, 116–39.

Huizinga, J. (1949) *Homo Ludens. A Study of the Play-Element in Culture*. Oxon.

Humann, C., Kohte, J., and Watzinger, C. (1904) *Magnesia am Maeander. Bericht über die Ergebnisse der Ausgrabungen der Jahre 1891–1893*. Berlin.

Iannaccone, L. R., Haight, C. E., and Rubin, J. (2011) 'Lessons from Delphi. Religious markets and spiritual capitals', *Journal of Economic Behavior and Organization* 77: 326–38.

Interdonato, E. (2013) *L'Asklepieion di Kos. Archeologia del culto*. Supplementi e monografie della rivista 'Archeologia classica' 12 = n.s. 9. Rome.

Interdonato, E. (2016) 'Architecture and rituals in the Hellenistic Age. The case of the Asklepieion in Kos', in M. Melfi and O. Bobou (eds), *Hellenistic Sanctuaries. Between Greece and Rome*. Oxford, 170–81.

Jost, M. (1994) 'The distribution of sanctuaries in civic space in Arkadia', in S. E. Alcock and R. Osborne (eds), *Placing the Gods. Sanctuaries and Sacred Space in Ancient Greece*. Oxford, 217–30.

Kamphorst, S. (2023) 'Carving communities in stone. Inscriptions as a medium of Hellenistic globalisation'. PhD diss. University of Groningen.

Knäpper, K. (2019) '"With a little help from my friends" oder das Asyliederby zwischen Magnesia am Mäander und Milet', in K. Freitag and M. Haake (eds), *Griechische Heiligtümer als Handlungsorte. Zur Multifunktionalität supralokaler Heiligtümer von der frühen Archaik bis in die römische Kaiserzeit*. Stuttgart, 303-22.

Kolb, F. (1981) *Agora und Theater, Volks- und Festversammlung*. DAI Archäolog. Forsch. IX. Berlin.

Kourayos, Y. (2012) 'The sanctuary of Despotiko in the Cyclades. Excavations 2001-2012', *Archäologischer Anzeiger* 2012.2: 93-174.

Kowalzig, B. (2020) 'Festivals, fairs and foreigners. Towards an economics of religion in the Mediterranean "Longue Durée"', in A. Collar and T. M. Kristensen (eds), *Pilgrimage and Economy in the Ancient Mediterranean*. Religions in the Graeco-Roman World 192. Leiden, 287-328.

Kristensen, T. M. (2020) 'Space, exchange and the embedded economies of Greek sanctuaries', in A. Collar and T. M. Kristensen (eds), *Pilgrimage and Economy in the Ancient Mediterranean*. Religions in the Graeco-Roman World 192. Leiden, 204-27.

Labarre, G. (2002) 'La dévotion au dieu Men. Les reliefs rupestres de la Voie Sacrée', in T. Drew-Bear, M. Taşlialan, and C.M. Thomas (eds), *Actes du Ier Congrès International sur Antioche de Pisidie*. Paris, 257-312.

Lauter, H. (1972) 'Kunst und Landschaft. Ein Beitrag zum rhodische Hellenismus', *Antike Kunst* 15: 49-59.

Lauter, H. (1986) *Die Architektur des Hellenismus*. Darmstadt.

Lauter-Bufe, H. (2009) *Das Heiligtum des Zeus Soter in Megalopolis*. Mainz.

Levick, B. (1970) 'Dedications to Mên Askaenos', *Anatolian Studies* 20: 37-50.

Linfert, A. (1995) 'Prunkaltäre', in M. Wörrle and P. Zanker (eds), *Stadtbild und Bürgerbild im Hellenismus. Kolloquium, München, 24. bis 26. Juni 1993*. Vestigia 47. Munich, 131-46.

Ma, J. (2003) 'Peer polity and interaction in the Hellenistic age', *Past and Present* 180: 9-39.

Ma, J. (2007) 'Dating the new decree of the confederation of Athena Ilias', *Epigraphica Anatolica* 40: 55-7.

Mann, C. (2018) 'Cash and crowns. A network approach to Greek athletic prizes', in M. Canevaro, A. Erskine, B. Gray, and J. Ober (eds), *Ancient Greek History and Contemporary Social Science*. Edinburgh Leventis Studies 9. Edinburgh, 293-312.

Martin, R. (1951) *Recherches sur l'agora grecque. Études d'histoire et d'archéologie urbaines*. Bibliothecque des Écoles françaises d'Athènes et de Rome CLXXIV. Paris.

McCauley, R. N. and Lawson E. T. (2007) 'Cognition, religious ritual, and archaeology', in E. Kyriakidis (ed.), *The Archaeology of Ritual*. Los Angeles, 209-54.

Meadows, A. R. (2002) 'Stratonikeia in Caria. The Hellenistic city and its coinage', *Numismatic Chronicle* 162: 79-134.

Melfi, M. (2016) 'Introduction. On sanctuaries and poleis', in M. Melfi and O. Bobou (eds), *Hellenistic Sanctuaries. Between Greece and Rome*. Oxford, 1-17.

Mitchell, S. (2002) 'The temple of Men Askaenos at Antioch', in T. Drew-Bear, M. Taşlialan, and C. M. Thomas (eds), *Actes du Ier Congrès International sur Antioche de Pisidie*. Paris, 313–22.

Mitchell, S. and Waelkens, M. (1998) *Pisidian Antioch. The Site and its Monuments*. London.

Moustakis, N. (2006) *Heiligtümer als politische Zentren. Untersuchungen zu den multidimensionalen Wirkungsgebieten von polisübergreifenden Heiligtümern im antiken Epirus*. Quellen und Forschungen zur antiken Welt, Bd. 48. Munich.

Mylonopoulos, J. (2006) 'Greek sanctuaries as places of communication through rituals. An archaeological perspective', in E. Stavrianopoulou (ed.), *Ritual and Communication in the Graeco-Roman World*. Kernos Supplement. Liège, 69–110.

Mylonopoulos, J. (2008) 'The dynamics of ritual space in the Hellenistic and Roman East', *Kernos* 21: 9–39.

Nielsen, I. (2002) *Cultic Theatres and Ritual Drama. A Study in Regional Development and Religious Interchange between East and West in Antiquity*. Aarhus.

van Nijf, O. M. and Williamson, C. G. (2015) 'Re-inventing traditions. Connecting contests in the Hellenistic and Roman worlds', in D. Boschung, A. Busch, and M. J. Versluys (eds), *Reinventing 'The Invention of Tradition'? Indigenous Pasts and the Roman Present*. Morphomata 32. Paderborn, 95–111.

van Nijf, O. M. and Williamson, C. G. (2016) 'Connecting the Greeks. Festival networks in the Hellenistic world', in C. Mann, S. Remijsen, and S. Scharff (eds), *Athletics in the Hellenistic World*. Stuttgart, 43–71.

Parker, R. (2004) 'New "Panhellenic" festivals in Hellenistic Greece', in R. Schlesier and U. Zellmann (eds), *Mobility and Travel in the Mediterranean from Antiquity to the Middle Ages*. Münster, 9–22.

Pedersen, P. (1991) *The Maussolleion at Halikarnassos. Reports of the Danish archaeological expedition to Bodrum. 3. The Maussolleion terrace and accessory structures. 1. Texts and appendices, 2. Catalogue*. Jutland Archaeological Society Publications 15, 3, 1 & 2. Aarhus.

Pedersen, P. (2004) 'Pergamon and the Ionian renaissance', *Istanbuler Mitteilungen* 54, 409–34.

Piccinini, J. (2016) 'Renaissance or decline? The shrine of Dodona in the Hellenistic period', in M. Melfi and O. Bobou (eds), *Hellenistic Sanctuaries. Between Greece and Rome*. Oxford, 152–69.

Pillot, W. (2020) 'Making regional identity. The Koinon of Athena Ilias, A religious association of Greek cities, from Troad to the Bosporus', in V. Keleş (ed.), *Propontis ve çevre kültürleri/Propontis and Surrounding Cultures*. Parion Studies 3. Istanbul, 673–80.

de Polignac, F. (1995) *Cults, Territory, and the Origins of the Greek City-State*. Chicago.

Pollitt, J. J. (1986) *Art in the Hellenistic Age*. Cambridge.

Quass, F. (1993) *Die Honoratiorenschicht in den Städten des griechischen Ostens. Untersuchungen zur politischen und sozialen Entwicklung in hellenistischer und römischer Zeit*. Stuttgart.

Raff, K. A. (2011) 'The architecture of the sanctuary of Mên Askaênos. Exploration, reconstruction, and use', in E. K. Gazda and D. Y. Ng (eds), *Building a New Rome. The Roman Colony of Pisidian Antioch (25 BC–700 AD)*. Kelsey Museum Publications 5. Ann Arbor, 131–52.

Remijsen, S. (2011) 'The so-called crown games. Terminology and historical context of the ancient categories for agones', *Zeitschrift für Papyrologie und Epigraphik* 177: 97–109.

Rigsby, K. J. (1996) *Asylia. Territorial Inviolability in the Hellenistic World*. Hellenistic Culture and Society 22. Berkeley.

Robert, L. (1984a) 'Discours d'ouverture', in C. Pelekides, D. Peppa-Delmouzou, and B. C. Petrakos (eds), Πρακτικά του Η' Διεθνούς Συνεδρίου Ελληνικής και Λατινικής Επιγραφικής, Αθήνα, 3–9 Οκτωβρίου 1982, τόμος Α. Athens, 35–45.

Robert, L. (1984b) 'Documents d'Asie Mineure', *Bulletin de correspondance hellénique* 108: 457–532.

Roels, E. (forthcoming) *The Writing on the Wall. Aspects of Epigraphic Culture in Hellenistic Asia Minor*. Heidelberger althistorische Beiträge und epigraphische Studien. Stuttgart.

Roos, P. (2011) 'The stadion at Labraunda', in L. Karlsson and S. Carlsson (eds), *Labraunda and Karia. Proceedings of the International Symposium Commemorating Sixty Years of Swedish Archaeological Work in Labraunda. The Royal Swedish Academy of Letters, History and Antiquities, Stockholm, November 20-21, 2008*. Acta Universitatis Uppsaliensis. Boreas. Uppsala Studies in Ancient Mediterranean and Near Eastern Civilizations 32. Uppsala, 257–66.

Rose, C. B. (2012) 'Architecture and ritual in Ilion, Athens, and Rome', in B. D. Wescoat and R. G. Ousterhout (eds), *Architecture of the Sacred. Space, Ritual, and Experience from Classical Greece to Byzantium*. Cambridge, 152–74.

Rutherford, I. (2013) *State Pilgrims and Sacred Observers in Ancient Greece. A Study of Theōriā and Theōroi*. Cambridge.

Şahin, M. Ç. (1976) *The Political and Religious Structure in the Territory of Stratonikeia in Caria*. Ankara.

Saldaña, M. (2020) 'Procedural Magnesia. Reconstructing the Urban Topography of Magnesia on the Maeander in 3D', URL: http://proceduralmagnesia.com/index.html.

Schalles, H.-J. (1985) *Untersuchungen zur Kulturpolitik der pergamenischen Herrscher im dritten Jahrhundert vor Christus*. Istanbuler Forschungen 36. Tübingen.

Scott, M. (2022) 'Walls and the ancient Greek ritual experience. The sanctuary of Demeter and Kore at Eleusis', in E. Eidinow, A. W. Geertz, and J. North (eds), *Cognitive Approaches to Ancient Religious Experience*. Cambridge, 193–217.

Scully, V. J. (1962) *The Earth, the Temple, and the Gods. Greek Sacred Architecture*. New Haven.

Slater, W. J. (2007) 'Deconstructing festivals', in P. J. Wilson (ed.), *The Greek Theatre and Festivals. Documentary Studies*. Oxford, 21–47.

Slater, W. J. and Summa, D. (2006) 'Crowns at Magnesia', *Greek, Roman, and Byzantine Studies* 46: 275-99.

Söğüt, B. (ed.) (2019) *Stratonikeia (Eskihisar) ve kutsal alanları*. Stratonikeia çalışmaları 5. Istanbul.

Sosin, J. D. (2009) 'Magnesian inviolability', *Transactions of the American Philological Association* 139: 369-410.

Sumi, G. (2004) 'Civic self-representation in the Hellenistic world. The festival of Artemis Leukophryene', in S. Bell and G. Davies (eds), *Games and Festivals in Classical Antiquity*. Proceedings of the Conference Held in Edinburgh 10-12 July 2000. BAR International Series 1220. Oxford, 79-92.

Thonemann, P. J. (2007) 'Magnesia and the Greeks of Asia (*I.Magnesia* 16.16)', *Greek, Roman and Byzantine Studies* 47: 151-60.

Tırpan, A. A., Gider, Z., and Büyüközer, A. (2012) 'The Temple of Hekate at Lagina', in T. Schulz (ed.), *Dipteros und Pseudodipteros*. Bauhistorische und archäologische Forschungen. *BYZAS* 12. Istanbul, 181-202.

Töpperwein-Hoffmann, E. (1978) 'Die Terrakotten van Mamurt Kale', in K. Nohlen and W. Radt (eds), *Kapıkaya. Ein Felsheiligtum bei Pergamon. Altertümer von Pergamon XII*. Berlin, 77-89, Taf. 34-7.

van der Vliet, E. C. L. (2011) 'Pride and participation. Political practice, euergetism, and oligarchisation in the Hellenistic Polis', in O. M. van Nijf and R. Alston (eds), *Political Culture in the Greek City after the Classical Age*. Groningen-Royal Holloway Studies on the Greek City after the Classical Age 2. Leuven, 155-84.

Whitehouse, H. and Laidlaw J. (2004) *Ritual and Memory. Toward a Comparative Anthropology of Religion*. Cognitive Science of Religion Series. Walnut Creek, CA.

Williamson, C. G. (2012) 'Sanctuaries as turning points in territorial formation. Lagina, Panamara and the development of Stratonikeia', in F. Pirson (ed.), *Manifestationen von Macht und Hierarchien in Stadtraum und Landschaft*. BYZAS 13. Istanbul, 113-50.

Williamson, C. G. (2014a) 'A room with a view. Karian landscape on display through the Andrones at Labraunda', in L. Karlsson, S. Carlsson, and J. Blid Kullberg (eds), *LABRUS. Studies presented to Pontus Hellström*. Acta Universitatis Upsaliensis. Boreas. Uppsala Studies in Ancient Mediterranean and Near Eastern Civilizations 35. Uppsala, 123-38.

Williamson, C. G. (2014b) 'Power of place. Labraunda, Mamurt Kale and the transformation of landscape in Asia Minor', in C. Moser and C. Feldman (eds), *Locating the Sacred. Theoretical Approaches to the Emplacement of Religion*. Joukowsky Institute Publication 3. Oxford, 87-110.

Williamson, C. G. (2020) 'Constructing the sublime. Landscape, architecture and human encounter in Hellenistic sanctuaries', in A. Müller and A. Haug (eds), *Hellenistic Architecture and Human Action. A Case of Reciprocal Influence*. Scales of Transformation in Prehistoric and Archaic Societies 10. Leiden, 101-24.

Williamson, C. G. (2021) *Urban Rituals in Sacred Landscapes in Hellenistic Asia Minor* Religions of the Graeco-Roman World 196. Leiden.

Williamson, C. G. (2022) 'Ritual ties, "portable communities" and the transmission of common knowledge through festival networks in the Hellenistic world', in A. Collar (ed.), *Networks and the Spread of Ideas in the Past. Strong Ties, Innovation and Knowledge Exchange*. Digital Research in the Arts and Humanities. London.

Williamson, C. G. (forthcoming a) 'Crowned heights. Sacred mountains and developing political landscapes in Asia Minor', in B. Vergnaud and N. Carless Unwin (eds), *Anatolian Landscapes. Inhabiting Western Anatolia in Antiquity*. Istanbul.

Williamson, C. G. (forthcoming b) 'Webs of ritual ties. Festivals as multiscalar network strategies in the Hellenistic world', in S. Kravaritou and M. Stamatopoulou (eds), *Religious Interactions in the Hellenistic World*. Leiden.

Wulf, U. (1999) 'Vom Herrensitz zur Metropole. Zur Stadtentwicklung von Pergamon', in E.-L. Schwandner and K. Rheidt (eds), *Stadt und Umland. Neue Ergebnisse der archäologischen Bau- und Siedlungsforschung*. Diskussionen zur archäologischen Bauforschung 7. Mainz, 33–49.

Ziegenhaus, O. and de Luca, G. (1968) *Altertümer von Pergamon XI. Das Asklepieion. Teil 1. Der südliche Temenosbezirk in hellenistischer und frührömische*. Berlin.

10
The Materiality of Light in Religious Celebrations and Rituals in the Roman East

Angelos Chaniotis

10.1. Introduction: shedding light on nocturnal celebrations

Nocturnal rituals and celebrations were an integral part of religion in Greece since the Bronze Age, and presumably earlier.[1] In Athens, most festivals of which the exact date is known, took place around the middle of a month (between the eleventh and the twentieth day), and as C. Trümpy has argued, this may be because (at least originally) they coincided with the full moon.[2] In archaic Greece, one of the most important ritual activities performed by girls was their participation in nocturnal choral dances near or around an altar.[3] In Athens, choral performances during παννυχίδες are known to have taken place during the festival of the Chalkeia that honoured Athena Ergane and at the Panathenaia.[4] Nocturnal ceremonies of an orgiastic nature have traditionally been part of the worship of Dionysos.[5] Naturally, the worship of deities associated with the moon and the night (e.g. Hekate, Artemis Phosphoros, and Nyx) required nocturnal rites.[6]

Even festivals that were not exclusively nocturnal, included rites that took place after sunset or before sunrise. The Athenian Anthesteria are a good example—the rituals of *Pithoigia* (the opening of the jars with the new wine), and the silent drinking of wine on the *Choes*, and the sacred marriage of the *basilinna* and Dionysos took place during the night.[7] The Daidala of Boiotia started at dawn and ended after sunset, and the same applies to the great procession of the

---

[1] For examples see Parisinou (2000); Boutsikas (2017); Chaniotis (2018b), 196–202; Pirenne-Delforge (2018).
[2] Trümpy (1998).
[3] Parisinou (2000), 158–61; Anghelina (2017); Boutsikas (2017); Schlesier (2018).
[4] *Agora* XV, no. 253 (118/7 BC); Parker (2005), 464–5. *Pannychides* in Hellenistic and Roman Asia Minor: Chaniotis (2018c), 26–7.
[5] See Kerenyi (1976), 204–37; Parisinou (2000), 71–2, 118–23; Chaniotis (2018c), 24–5; Pirenne-Delforge (2018), 150–5.
[6] Chaniotis (2018b), 197; Pirenne-Delforge (2018).   [7] Deubner (1966), 93–123.

Ptolemaia in Alexandria (see below). In Athens, nocturnal rites were an important component of the Arrhephoria.[8] Since the fifth century BC, torch-races organized as nocturnal spectacles are attested in Athens and elsewhere.[9]

Nocturnal religious activities became more diffused from the Hellenistic period on, especially in urban centres. Four interrelated phenomena contributed to this development.[10] First, one observes a tremendous increase in the number of private associations, more specifically of Dionysiac associations, associations of worshippers of the Egyptian gods, and associations of worshippers of the so-called Oriental deities. These associations regularly organized gatherings that started after or lasted beyond sunset. Second, nocturnal rites played an important part in mysteries and other cults with a soteriological or initiatory aspect, already in the archaic and classical period.[11] Such cults experienced an unprecedented diffusion from the third century BC onwards. Thirdly, festivals organized by Hellenistic kings, such as the famous procession of the Ptolemaia in Alexandria (c. 275/274 BC?) that started before dawn and ended after sunset, with monumental, valuable torches providing artificial light,[12] served as trend-setters and influenced the nocturnal celebrations of cities and associations, including newly founded festivals endowed by benefactors. For instance, the Delian inventories of the third and second centuries BC regularly mention torches that were provided for choral performances, presumably in the evening or the night, in connection with nine festivals and also on the occasion of the visit of sacred envoys (*theoroi*); most of these festivals were founded in the course of the third century BC.[13] Finally, the direct communication between mortals and gods through incubation (*enkoimesis*) in sanctuaries, especially of Asclepius and Sarapis, in expectation of an epiphanic dream, became far more common than in earlier periods.[14]

These trends continued in the imperial period. Mystery cults—especially the Isiac mysteries, mysteries celebrated by the associations of Dionysiac *mystai*, and the mysteries of Mithras—spread throughout the Roman East and with them also rites that took place between dusk and dawn. According to Philo, the Jewish *therapeutai* in Egypt in the early first century AD also had nocturnal spiritual activities, connected with wine consumption, allegedly under the

---

[8] The sources in Deubner (1966), 9–17. Recent discussion: Parker (2005), 219–28.
[9] Parisinou (2000), 36–44; Chaniotis (2018c), 28–9.
[10] Chaniotis (2018c); cf. Chaniotis (2018b), 197–202. [11] See n. 77 below.
[12] On the procession see Rice (1983); (Kallixeinos, *FGrH* 627 F 2; Athenaios, *Deipnosophistai* 5.197c–203a). Torches (λαμπάδες, δᾷδες) are mentioned in connection with the procession's early and late part, i.e. before and after sunset: Athenaios, *Deipnosophistai* 5.197e, 202b.
[13] The standard expression is χορῶι τῶν γενομένωι + name of a festival. The following festivals are mentioned: Antigoneia, Aphrodisia, Apollonia, Artemisia, Britomartia, Demetrieia, Philokleia, Ptolemaia, Soteria, and celebrations on the occasion of the visits of *theoroi*. For the references see Chaniotis (2018c), 27 n. 97. The following festivals were founded in the course of the third century BC: Antigoneia, Aphrodisia, Demetrieia, Philokleia, Ptolemaia, and Soteria.
[14] For the limited early evidence see Renberg (2017), 100–6.

influence of Dionysiac worship.[15] The gatherings of early Christian communities and the prayers of the worshippers of Theos Hypsistos also took place before dawn.[16] Finally, consultation of certain oracular sites, e.g. the sanctuary of Apollo in Klaros, took place during the night in architectural settings that enhanced the feeling of secrecy and darkness,[17] and a particular type of divination used lamps as a medium (λυχνομαντεία).[18] Although some night-time celebrations are only attested in the imperial period, they may have existed earlier. For instance, in the whole of Asia Minor *pannychides* are epigraphically attested only in the Hellenistic and imperial periods.[19] It is very likely that the availability of evidence in this period is the result of changes in the epigraphic habit and not of the introduction of new practices. But in other cases, we are dealing with innovations; e.g., a nocturnal torch-race (ἱερὰ λαμπάς) in honour of Melikertes seems to have been added to the contests of the Isthmia in the imperial period.[20]

Nocturnal festivals confronted their organizers with challenges and offered them opportunities. The organizers had to provide artificial light and security, especially to women—the rape of a girl during a nocturnal religious festival was a *topos* in New Comedy.[21] But they could also exploit the opportunities offered by the emotional impact of darkness, the use of shadows and the manipulation of artificial light, and the association of the night with non-human agents, for instance with divine epiphanies, the invocation of chthonic demons, and epiphanic dreams.

The materiality of nocturnal religious activities was multifaceted. It concerns manufactured objects, foodstuff, structures (such as altars, shrines, and subterranean chambers), the physical setting of the celebrations (e.g. caves or wooded mountains), and, of course, the bodies of the participants (human and non-human). This materiality can be inferred from archaeological finds (dark underground buildings and lamps), iconography (representations of torchbearers) and references in literary sources and inscriptions. Sometimes, the textual and the archaeological evidence converge, providing us with some insights into the importance of the architectural setting and the cult paraphernalia in nocturnal celebrations. However, in other cases, the information given by texts is sufficient only to tickle our imagination about objects and devices that are no longer preserved. And often, we know nothing about the material paraphernalia of nocturnal rites. For instance, in the third century AD the citizens of Termessos in Lycia

---

[15] Philo, *On the Contemplative Life* 83–9: 'After the supper they hold the sacred vigil....They rise up all together and standing in the middle of the refectory (*symposion*) form themselves first into two choirs, one of men and one of women....Then they sing hymns to God....Having drunk as in the Bacchic rites of the strong wine of God's love they mix and both together become a single choir....Thus, they continue till dawn, drunk with this drunkenness in which there is no shame.'
[16] Christians: Pliny, *Epistles* 10.96. Theos Hypsistos: see below, n. 55.
[17] Boutsikas (2017), 16.   [18] Petropoulos (1999).
[19] The evidence in Chaniotis (2018c), 27 n. 95.   [20] Biers and Geagan (1970), 91–3.
[21] Bathrellou (2012).

regularly sent an embassy to the moon goddess.[22] We only know that the envoys were members of the elite. But how were they dressed? What did they carry during their procession? What gifts did they present to Selene?

Most of the material objects used during daytime rituals and celebrations did not differ from those used in nocturnal rites. The same banquet hall could be used for meals during daytime and after sunset. For a sacrifice, one needs an altar, a knife, a libation cup, a sacrificial basket, musical instruments, and dry and liquid offerings, regardless of whether the sacrifice takes place at dusk, in the darkest part of the night, or at dawn.[23] There are exceptions. The type of altar and victim may differ. We also know of particular types of sacrificial cakes only used for nocturnal rites. The ἀμφιφῶν was a sacrificial cake on which small torches were placed. It was offered to Artemis in her sanctuaries and at cross-roads at dawn, when the setting moon and the rising sun could be seen at the same time.[24] Particular magical rituals that were often performed during the night, and are not discussed in this study, had their own very distinctive material aspects: the use of lead tablets (*defixiones*), the manipulation of figurines made of lead or wax, and the use of lamps of specific forms and iconography.[25] Incubation in the sanctuaries of healing deities required special architectural settings, such as incubation rooms (ἐγκοιμητήρια, ἄβατα).[26] However, the main difference between day- and night-time rituals is the use, production, and manipulation of light, e.g. the use of lamps and torches, the illumination through celestial bodies,[27] and the selection of nights with or without moonlight.

For this reason, this contribution primarily addresses the manipulation of artificial light and its contribution to the emotional impact and the perceived efficacy of nocturnal celebrations. Can references to material objects provide information about the timing of cultic activities, i.e. their performance during the night? Can we recognize in the material evidence objects that are associated with nocturnal festivals? Can the material evidence for nocturnal festivals be associated with cognitive and emotional processes?

In an introductory section, I will address the emotional impact of nocturnal ritual performances and collect examples of the material evidence for the use of artificial light in temples and sanctuaries. Then I will approach the aforementioned

---

[22] SEG LVII 1482 (c. 212–30 AD): δωδεκάκ[ις σὺν τοῖσδε πρεσ]βευταῖς Θεᾷ Σελήνῃ συνεπρέσβευσεν ....

[23] On different types of darkness and the importance of distinguishing between nocturnal and dawn rites see Boutsikas (2017), 3–5.

[24] Athenaios, *Deipnosophistai* 645a–b. See Parisinou (2000), 153–4.

[25] See e.g. Bevilacqua et al. (2010), 67–8, for a bronze lamp in the shape of a mummy with the double Egyptian crown and the body wrapped in bandages forming a net-like pattern, interrupted by two holes for a hook and three cartouches filled with magic words (Canusium, second century AD). See also n. 32.

[26] Renberg (2017), 24–167.

[27] An overview of lighting devices in ancient Greece in Moullou and Topalis (2017). The importance of constellations in religious celebrations has been highlighted by Boutsikas in a series of studies: Boutsikas and Ruggles (2011); Boutsikas and Hannah (2012); Boutsikas (2014); Boutsikas (2017), 4 and 10.

questions through the study of four religious celebrations: the mystery cult of an Oriental deity in Larisa, the festival of Zeus' cult in the Idaean cave, the highpoint of the mystery cult in Abonou Teichos, and the festival of the Daidala in Boiotia. I have intentionally selected festivals from both the Hellenistic and the imperial period. In the Greek and Hellenized East, religion in these two periods should be studied as a unit; the battle of Actium certainly was a turning point in political history, but it was not a turning point in religious practices and religious mentality. With the exception of Christianity and the cult of the emperor, all major religious phenomena of the imperial period have their roots in the Hellenistic period.[28]

10.2. The emotional impact of nocturnal rituals

Theokritos' second idyll is one of the few detailed descriptions of a nocturnal ritual from Graeco-Roman antiquity.[29] Simaitha and her slave Thestylis are alone near the sea in the darkest hours of the night; only burning fire (l. 18) and the moon (ll. 10-11) provide some light. They perform a magical ritual that aims at bringing Delphis, Simaithas' unfaithful lover, back to her. The poem starts with a reference to the *material magica* necessary for the ritual:

> Where are my bay-leaves? Bring me them, Thestylis. And where are my magic stuffs? Wreathe the bowl with fine crimson wool that I may bind a spell upon my love, so hard to me.

Chanting the words 'My magic wheel, draw to my house the man I love', Simaitha handles a magical instrument called *iynx* and a bronze rhomb, melts wax, and pours a libation, while her slave throws barley groats, bay-leaves, and bran on the fire. The silence of the night is disturbed by the barking of dogs at a distance and the clashing of a bronze cymbal or bell. Taking a fringe from Delphis' cloak, Simaitha shreds it and casts it into the flames. She then instructs her slave to knead magic herbs over Delphis' threshold while it is still dark.

The materials applied by Simaitha hardly find exact parallels in the magical handbooks.[30] It was probably the intention of the poet to underscore Simaitha's despair by presenting her as an amateur and helpless practitioner of magic.[31] The efficacy of a magic ritual depends on words said, actions performed, and

---

[28] Chaniotis (2013) 188-9; Chaniotis (2018a) 345-9.
[29] I use the edition and translation of Gow (1952) I, 16-29; see also his commentary (II, 33-63) and the analysis by Petrovic (2007) 1-56.
[30] Graf (1996) 159-71.   [31] Petrovic (2007) 1-3, 14-40.

materials properly handled.³² Readers familiar with magic would have understood that Simaitha's ritual was doomed to fail.

It was believed, at least from the classical period on, that the efficacy of rituals requires more than automatisms; it requires justifications.³³ In the case of magic, a particular group of texts labelled 'prayers for justice' often use emotional language,³⁴ and Simaitha's prayer to Selene resembles a 'prayer for justice'. Left alone, only in the presence of the shinning moon, Simaitha remembers how it all started, mourns her lost love, and accuses Delphis for his betrayal. 'Mark, Lady moon, whence came my love', is the refrain of a narrative in which love is mixed with hatred.

The night is an enhancer of emotions, fear, erotic desire, and especially the pain of a broken heart. Ancient novelists did not fail to observe that. Achilles Tatius notes that all the emotions that are dormant during the day, as eyes and ears are distracted and absorbed in many activities, burst out during the night: 'the woes of the grieving, the cares of the troubled, the fears of the endangered, the fire of lovers'; similarly, Heliodoros commented on the feeling of his protagonists: 'in my opinion, the night aggravated their misery, for there was no sight or sound to distract them, and they could devote themselves solely to their grief'.³⁵

The night was an emotional enhancer for lovers. What was its emotional impact on the participants of nocturnal rites? Undoubtedly, the blurred vision due to the absence of natural and the manipulation of artificial light would have enhanced fear and anxiety but also facilitated the belief in divine epiphanies. Two narratives, by Pausanias and Apuleius, provide some clues. Based on personal experience, Pausanias describes the consultation of the cave-oracle of Trophonios.³⁶ The inquirer was taken during the night (τῇ νυκτί) to a river, where he was washed and anointed by two boys. After he had drunk the water of forgetfulness from a fountain, and seen and worshipped an ancient image, he was brought to an artificial chasm. As soon as he got his knees into the hole, his body was swiftly drawn into the chasm, where the future was revealed to him by sight or hearing. Then he was taken to the chair of memory to reveal all that he had learned. He was finally delivered to his relatives, paralyzed with terror and unconscious of himself and his surroundings (κάτοχόν τε ἔτι τῷ δείματι καὶ ἀγνῶτα ὁμοίως αὑτοῦ τε καὶ τῶν πέλας); only later he recovered his faculties and the ability to laugh (γέλως ἐπάνεισίν οἱ). In his *Metamorphoses*, Apuleius vividly describes the conflicting

---

³² See the contributions in Boschung and Bremmer (2015).
³³ On ancient implicit criticism on ritual automatism see Chaniotis (2018d) 43–7.
³⁴ See Versnel (2003); for 'prayers in justice' see Versnel (1991), (2010), and (2012).
³⁵ Achilles Tatius, *Leukippe and Kleitophon* 1.6.2–4; Heliodoros, *Aithiopika* 1.8.1; on these passages see De Temmerman (2018) 260–2.
³⁶ Pausanias, *Description of Greece* 1.39.1–1.40.2; on the consultation of the oracle see Bonnechere (2003), xxiii–xxx, 32–61, 139–202; Ustinova (2009), 91–2, 243; see also Plutarch, *Moralia* 590B–592F.

emotions of Lucius, transformed into an ass, when during the night he prays to Isis and the goddess responds to his prayer and appears in a vision:

> (11.1)...Now that fate, it seemed, had taken its fill of my many great misfortunes and was offering, though late, a hope of deliverance (*spem salutis*), I decided to address in prayer the sacred image of the goddess now present in person. So, shaking off at once my torpid slumber, I gladly and eagerly (*laetus et alacer*) arose and, anxious to purify myself, I went to bathe in the sea. Seven times I plunged my head under the waves, since the divine Pythagoras pronounced that number to be very specially suitable in sacred rites. Then with a tear-stained face (*lacrimoso vultu*) I prayed to the all-powerful goddess...
> (11.7)...steeped in fear, joy, and then a surge of sweat (*pavore et gaudio ac dein sudore nimio permixtus*), I arose full of rapt wonder at such a direct manifestation of the mighty goddess....Everything seemed to me to be throbbing with such a sense of joy (*hilaritudine*), quite apart from my personal happiness, that I felt that all kinds of animals too and all the houses and the very day itself were rejoicing (*gaudere*) with bright faces.

The initiation into mysteries associated with Isis and Sarapis, which I will not be discussing here, took place during the night. Describing Lucius' initiation, Apuleius mentions the time and the setting:[37]

> The sun was setting, bringing twilight on, when suddenly a crowd flowed towards me, to honour me with sundry gifts, in accord with the ancient and sacred rite. All the uninitiated were ordered to depart, I was dressed in a new-made robe of linen and the high-priest, taking me by the arm, led me into the sanctuary's innermost recess.

After the completion of the nocturnal ceremony, Lucius appeared in front of the crowd at dawn dressed like the Sun. A second initiation into the 'nocturnal mysteries of the Supreme God' followed.

Because of the impact of darkness on the senses, the cognitive abilities, and, consequently, the feelings of people, the night has played across cultures and times an important part in the multifaceted communication between the living and the dead, and the mortals and the gods: through dreams, incubation, magical and funerary rites, and nocturnal festivals.[38]

In Greek religion, the institutionalized communication between mortals and gods occurred in festivals, to which the gods were invited to come. Their attention was attracted by bright clothes, crowns, beautiful animals with gilded horns,

---

[37] Apuleius, *Metamorphoses* 11.20–1, 23–4.
[38] See the various contributions in Gonlin and Nowell (2018).

decorated altars, and tables. Acoustic signals—hymns, prayers, and acclamations—invited them, accompanied by signals that could be smelled, such as incense, wine, and thighs burning on the altar. Unclean or impure bodies were expelled from the sanctuary as potential obstacles to this communication.[39] Materiality mattered.

10.3. The materiality of artificial light: lamps, lamp-hangers, and torch-bearing statues

Lamps belong to the usual finds in excavations of temples and sanctuaries, and lamps and lamp-stands are often mentioned in temple inventories of the classical and Hellenistic periods.[40] Lamps was needed mainly for celebrations, sometimes also for the illumination of covered spaces; by contrast, torches were more suitable for outdoor lighting because of the smoke that they emit.[41] Although some temples opened their doors only on the days of festivals,[42] others were accessible on a daily basis or for longer periods of time.[43] In the Erechtheion, a golden lamp used to burn without interruption,[44] and there are occasional references to altars on which fire burned day and night.[45] An inscription that narrates the attack of Labienus and his Parthian troops against the sanctuary of Zeus in Panamara (39 BC) reports that 'the lamps of the god were observed burning and they remained burning until the end of the siege', but this incident is mentioned among the miracles that occurred during the attack.[46] However, light was usually provided during celebrations. For instance, the objects kept in the *Chalkotheke* on the Athenian Acropolis (369 BC) include a large bronze lamp (λυχνεῖον τὸ μέγα), probably with more than one nozzle, which shed light during reception rites for gods (τὸ [ε]ἰς θεοξένια), that is, only on certain occasions.[47]

From the Hellenistic period on, the illumination of interior spaces, both during festivals and on a daily basis, acquired a new dimension. The diffusion of Egyptian cults, in which the burning of lamps during celebrations (λυχνοκαΐα, λυχναψία) was particularly important, was a significant factor in this development.[48] The Isiac cult employed λυχνάπτριαι ('the women who light the lamps') and

---

[39] Chaniotis (2017a), 105–6.   [40] For examples see Parisinou (2000), 31–5 and 136–61.
[41] Moullou and Topallis (2017), 21.
[42] See *IG* V.2.265 l. 24; *IG* XII.4.346 l. 9; *I.Kalchedon* 12 ll. 23–4; *I.Magnesia* 73b ll. 14–15; *I.Milet* III.1.144B l. 8; *OGIS* 332 l. 28.
[43] See *IG* XII.4.295 B l. 12.
[44] Pausanias, *Description of Greece* 1.26.6–7; Parisinou (2000), 20–31.
[45] See Pausanias, *Description of Greece* 5.15.9 (altar of Pan in Olympia) and 8.37.11 (sanctuary of Pan in Megalopolis).
[46] *I.Stratonikeia* 10 l. 27: οἵ τε λύχνοι τοῦ θεοῦ καιόμενοι εὑρέθησαν καὶ διέμειναν μέχρι τῆς πολιορκίας. For μέχρι in the meaning 'until the end of, throughout'; cf. Herodotos, *Histories* 1.160.
[47] *IG* II² 1424a II l. 125 and 255: [ἐν] τῆι χαλκοθήκηι... λυχνεῖον τὸ μέγα τὸ [ε]ἰς θεοξένια.
[48] Podvin (2011) and 2014; see also Seidel (2012), 93 fig. 45 (representation of an Egyptian priest carrying a lamp).

λαμπτηροφόροι ('the women who carry lamps').⁴⁹ It is probably under the influence of the cult of Isis that this office was adopted by other cults as well for their festivals. A *lychnaptria* is attested for the cult of the Meter Theon at Leukopetra, near Beroia (AD 193/4); her service was limited only to certain festive days.⁵⁰ Among the functionaries of a Dionysiac cult association in Philippopolis (c. 241–4 AD) one finds Aurelia Artemidora, a λυχνοάπτρια,⁵¹ while a contemporary association in Thessalonike had an ἀρχιλαμπαδηφόρος ('chief torch-bearer'), who probably led a group of torch-bearers in nocturnal ceremonies.⁵² In Physkos (Lokris) in the second century AD, a Dionysiac association provided three lamps for its meetings.⁵³

Apart from the specialized personnel dedicated to the task of lighting the lamps, another innovation is the existence of a specialized lamp production for certain cults. Lamps with an iconography connected with the Isiac myths and rituals or with shapes associated with the worship of Isis and Sarapis were produced specifically for these cults (Fig. 10.1).⁵⁴ A similar phenomenon can be observed in the cult of Theos Hypsistos. An oracle of Apollo of Klaros (second century AD) recommended a daily prayer to the god at dawn: 'he said that *aether* is god who sees all, gazing upon whom you should pray at dawn, looking towards the sunrise.'⁵⁵ In Magnesia on Sipylos, a family dedicated to Theos Hypsistos an altar and τὰς λυχναψίας.⁵⁶ Λυχναψία literally means the process of lighting a lamp, but in this case, it refers to a material object, some sort of a lamp-stand. A particular lamp type, produced for the cult of Theos Hypsistos may give as a clue as to the identity of the λυχναψίαι. It consists of a bronze lamp hanging from an elaborate hanger device (Fig. 10.2). The hanger consists of a *tabula*, on which dedicatory inscriptions were engraved, with an eyelet on its top and two stylized dolphins on its bottom, from which the lamp hangs.⁵⁷ In three cases, the lamps were explicitly dedicated to Theos Hypsistos, in one case to Zeus. Only in one case is the origin known: Novae. As Norbert Franken has plausibly argued, the lamp hangers were produced by different workshops, probably in the third century AD.

Evidence for daily illumination of civic temples is scarce and it seems to be an innovation of the imperial period. It is attested for Teos and Epidauros in connection

---

⁴⁹ For λυχνάπτριαι see IG II² 4771 (Athens, 120 AD); for the service of λαμπτηροφόροι in the cult of Sarapis in Delos (early first century BC) see *I.Délos* 2619 b I ll. 7, 22, 27.
⁵⁰ *I.Leukopetra* 39; Chaniotis (2018c), 28.   ⁵¹ *IGBulg* III.1.1517 l. 30.
⁵² IG X.2.1s.1077 l. 25.   ⁵³ IG IX².1.670 ll. 6–7.
⁵⁴ For lamp rituals and the production of lamps see Podvin (2011), 37–104 (iconography), 107–22 (production), 123–46 (distribution), 157–60 (discovery in temples of Isis). On a building called λυχνάπτιον in Saqqâra see Renberg (2016).
⁵⁵ SEG XXVII 933: αἰ[θ]έ[ρ]α πανδερκ[ῆ θε]ὸν ἔννεπεν, εἰς ὃν ὁρῶντας | εὔχεσθ' ἠώους πρὸς ἀνατολίην ἐσορῶ[ν]τα[ς]. Busine (2005), 35–40, 203–8, 423, with further bibliography.
⁵⁶ *TAM* V.2.1400.
⁵⁷ These objects were studied by Franken (2002) who associated them with Theos Hypsistos; on p. 81, he mentions the inscription from Magnesia on Sipylos and its possible connection with these lamps. Norbert Franken has informed me that more relevant material has come to light since his study; I am very grateful to him for providing the image in Fig. 10.2.

Fig. 10.1 Clay lamp from Egypt (c. AD 150–250), decorated with a relief of Serapis with a staff in one hand and a wreath in the other; a lamb is at his feet. 3.9 × 9.4 × 6.7 cm.
Photograph: Artokolo/Alamy Stock Photo, Image ID: 2B0E2D0.

with daily service in the temples. A cult regulation from Teos (AD 14–37) stipulates that 'at the opening and closing of the temple [of Dionysos] by the priest of Tiberius Caesar, one should offer libations, burn incense, and light lamps, using the sacred funds of Dionysos'.[58] In Epidauros, a fragmentary cult regulation from the sanctuary of Asklepios in the second or third century AD refers to the services that the torchbearer had to perform daily in the shrines of the Mother of the Gods and Aphrodite, to duties involving lamps (*lychnoi*) and the 'sacred lamp' (*hiera lychnia*), and to rituals at dusk (ὅταν ἑσπέρας αἱ σπον[δαὶ γίνωνται]) and dawn ([ὁ ἔω]θεν ἀνατέλλωγ).[59]

A good example of the manipulation of artificial light in interior spaces during a festival is provided by a decree of Messene establishing the imperial cult after Tiberius' accession to the throne (AD 14).[60] The decree refers to the duties of the

---

[58] SEG XV 718 ll. 10–14: [ἐπὶ δὲ τῆ]ς ἀνοίξεως καὶ κλείσεως τοῦ νε[ὼ τοῦ θεοῦ ὑπὸ τ]οῦ ἱερέως Τιβερίου Καίσαρος σ[πένδεσθαι] καὶ θυμιᾶσθαι καὶ λυχναπτεῖσθαι ἐ[κ τῶν ἱερ]ῶν τοῦ Διονύσου πόρων; Robert (1937), 31–3.
[59] IG IV².1.742.
[60] SEG 41, 328. Recent discussion: Muñiz Grijalvo (forthcoming).

Fig. 10.2 Bronze lamp associated with the cult of Theos Hypsistos (imperial period). Of unknown provenance, in the antiquities marker. *Antike Kunst und Fossilien. Auktion 6.6.2000, Palais Dorotheum, Wien*, 105 no. 256.
Photograph: Norbert Franken (cf. Franken (2002), 380–1 fig. 9).

priest of Augustus during the annual celebration for the emperor. The relevant passages are very fragmentary, but one recognizes a reference to the priest of the imperial cult, who served as torchbearer (ll. 22–3: [ἱερεὺς] ὁ κατ' ἔτος τοῦ Σεβαστοῦ δαδουχείτω). He was to approach the sanctuary, walking solemnly (l. 24: εἰς τὸ ἱερὸν παρέρπων)[61] and to be the first to do something starting from the right side (l. 24: καὶ πρῶτος ἐκ δεξιῶν σ[- -]). After a lacuna, there is a reference to illumination (l. 25: φωτίσαι) followed by a list of members of the imperial family (ll. 26–9). Presumably, the priest illuminated the statues of the members of the imperial family in the Sebasteion. The service of torchbearers is mentioned in another fragmentary passage of the text, ll. 30–1: [—τοῦ Σεβα]στοῦ ἱερεὺ⟨ς⟩ καὶ δαδουχείτωσα[ν—].

---

[61] I take παρέρπω here to mean 'walk solemnly, walk with reverence', not 'to creep secretly'. This is the meaning of this verb in grave epigrams addressing the passer-by and asking him to read the text and continue his walk; e.g. *I.Cret.* II.v.49; *SEG* 58, 891; cf. *IG* V.2.514 l. 3: παρέρπην... ἐν τὸ ἱερόν (with luxurious items).

Illumination was also needed for the banquets that were an integral part of civic festivals in the imperial period. It is explicitly mentioned in inscriptions from Asia Minor that honour benefactors for their generosity. A *neopoios* in Ephesos (late second/early third century AD) was honoured for 'lighting up' lamps or torches for eleven days and offering a reception to the council, the boards of magistrates, and 1,040 citizens.[62] Bithynian inscriptions record the donations made by local benefactors for drinking parties (οἰνοπόσιον), concerts (συμφωνία), and the lighting of lamps (λυχναψία), which suggests nocturnal feasts.[63] However, the material evidence for the illumination by means of hanging lamps and torches is very limited—or difficult to recognize.

Andrew Wilson has recently observed that several of the columns of the north portico of the city park in Aphrodisias (previously known as the 'South Agora') have holes cut in them in late antiquity for iron hooks or brackets. They are located at heights 1.55–1.64 m above the stylobate—and, therefore, higher than the original ground level of the park (Fig. 10.3). He suggested that they may have been used for the hanging of lamps, a little above eye-level, that would illuminate the names of the stallholders and the portico.[64] Similar holes can be found on columns of porticos in other sites as well (e.g. in Hierapolis and Laodikeia; Fig. 10.4). They could have been used for other purposes, e.g. the hanging of wooden *tabulae* with the names of the owners of shops. I mention them as an example of the problems associated with the study of illumination of public spaces in the cities of the imperial period.

Fortunately, a short note in a poem, corroborated by both inscriptions and archaeological finds, may shed some light on the illumination of banquets during religious celebrations. Nonnus (c. mid-fifth century AD), writing on Kadmos' visit to Samothrace, mentions a gold statue holding a torch, with the light of the flame falling on those who dined in the evening.[65] There is good evidence for ritual eating and drinking in the mystery cult of the Great Gods,[66] whose popularity skyrocketed in the imperial period.[67] Nonnus had accurate knowledge of the topography of the sanctuary, and his reference to a banquet may well reflect actual practices. Epigraphic finds leave no doubt that torch-bearing statues were used in the Hellenistic and Roman East within public spaces.

An inscription of the late Hellenistic period refers to λαμπαδηφόροι ἀνδριάντες set up in the theatre of Miletos and in the temple of Apollo in Didyma by a

---

[62] *I.Ephesos* 951 ll. 4–9: ἀνάψαντα ἡμερῶν ἕνδεκα | καὶ ὑποδεξάμενον τήν τε | κρατίστην Ἐφεσίων βουλὴν | καὶ πάντα τὰ συνέδρια, καὶ | πολείτας χειλίους τεσσαρά|κοντα. Cf. Robert (1937), 33 n. 1.
[63] *TAM* IV.1.16 and 17.   [64] Wilson (2018), 71. On hanging lamps see Dossey (2018), 298–9.
[65] Nonnus, *Dionysiaca* 3.169–71: καὶ πολὺς εὐποίητος ἐρεισάμενος πόδα πέτρῳ | χρύσεος ἵστατο κοῦρος ἀναντία δαιτυμονήων | λαμπάδος ἑσπερίης τανύων ἐπιδόρπιον αἴγλην. On lighting at ritual meals in archaic and classical Greece see Parisinou (2000), 147–8.
[66] See Cole (1984), 36–7.   [67] Dimitrova (2008).

Fig. 10.3 Column with holes, possibly for the suspension of a lamp (imperial period). Aphrodisias, Place of Palms, north portico.
Photograph: Chaniotis.

prophetes (first century BC).[68] Unlike the other statues that he dedicated (Apollo and the statue of an Ethiopian), the inscription does not state what these (bronze)

---

[68] I.Didyma 346 ll. 10–17: προφητεύων ἀνέθηκε τοὺς λαμπαδηφόρους ἀνδρ[ι]άντας καὶ περιραντήρια δύο ἐν τῷ ναῷ τοῦ Ἀπόλλωνος τοῦ Διδυμέως, στεφανηφορῶν δὲ τὸν Ἀπόλλωνα τὸν Δελφείνιον καὶ τὸν αἰθίοπα τὸν χάλκηο[ν] καὶ ἐν τῷ θηάτρῳ λαμπαδηφόρους ἀνδριάντας δύο. As Zahra Newby points out to me, the torchbearers depicted flanking the statue of Apollo at Didyma on Milesian coins must be statues.

Fig. 10.4 Column with holes, possibly for the suspension of a lamp (imperial period). Laodikeia on the Lykos, colonnaded street.
Photograph: Chaniotis.

statues depicted; they are simply identified by the fact that they held torches. Such torch-bearing statues should be distinguished from statues of divinities for whom the torch was a common attribute (e.g. Hekate, Artemis Phosphoros, or Eros).[69] The λαμπαδηφόροι ἀνδριάντες of Miletos correspond to a *statua lucifera* mentioned in an inscription from Heliopolis-Baalbek[70] and to the λαμπαδηφόροι and δαδοῦχοι mentioned in inscriptions from Syria and Palaestina (Bostra, Hauran, Skythopolis, Eleutheropolis, and Gerasa).[71]

It is possible that two statues of Erotes, dedicated by a *strategos* in Aphrodisias in a palm grove in Aphrodisias—the city park previously known as the 'South Agora'

---

[69] Koßmann and Eck (2016), 285–6. For images of torch-bearing deities (Artemis, Hekate, Ennodia, Demeter and Kore, Dionysos, Zeus) see Parisinou (2000), 81–91.

[70] *IGLS* VI.2716 (Heliopolis-Baalbek, c. AD 238–44): *statuam luciferam*.

[71] *IGLS* XIII.1.908 and 909 (Bostra, early third century AD): τὸν δᾳδοῦχον; *CIG* 4555a (Hauran, imperial period): τέσσαρε[ς] λαμπαδηφόρου[ς]; Foerster and Tsafrir (1993), 12 (Skythopolis, AD 238/9): δᾳδοῦχος; Koßmann and Eck (2016) (Eleutheropolis, early third century AD): τὸν δᾳδοῦχον. Agusta-Bularot and Seigne (2017) 144–52 nos. 1–4 (Gerasa, mid-third century AD): τοὺς δᾳδούχους. On these torch-bearing statues see Koßmann and Eck (2016), 285, who reject the assumption that the δᾳδοῦχοι were simple supports for torches.

(late first century AD)—had a similar function. These two statues are explicitly designated as torch-bearing (*Ἔρωτας λαμπαδηφόρους*) and clearly distinguished from another statue of Eros (*καὶ τὸν πρὸ αὐτοῦ Ἔρωτα μαρμάρινον*).[72] Although it is possible that the dedicant simply refers to a well-known iconographic type of Eros represented with a torch in either hand, the use of the attribute *λαμπαδηφόρος* brings these statues close to the aforementioned torch-bearing statues in public spaces.

Such statues have left little material evidence, possibly because of the recycling of the material from which they were made. But we do know of life-size or nearly life-size statues of *ephebes* that held lamps (*λυχνοῦχοι*) for the illumination of interior spaces.[73] Instead of lamps, they held torches, similar to the smaller than life-size statues of torch-bearing Erotes.[74]

All these torch-bearing statues in the epigraphic sources were dedications by civic magistrates and set up in public spaces: the theatre in Miletos, the temple in Didyma, and the city park in Aphrodisias. They provided outdoor illumination, either on a daily basis or during celebrations. The gold statue of a youth holding a torch and described by Nonnus in connection with the Samothracian banquet is undoubtedly the literary equivalent of the *λαμπαδηφόροι* and *δᾳδοῦχοι* of the epigraphic sources. With this evidence on objects that provided artificial light during celebrations, we now turn to the examination of four festivals.

10.4. Oriental nights in Larisa

One of the most important new epigraphic finds concerning religious rituals in the late Hellenistic period is a cult regulation from Marmarini, near Larisa.[75] It is quite instructive as an example of nocturnal celebrations and their material background. The text dates to the second century BC and details rituals connected with the cult and the mysteries of an anonymous goddess of Oriental origin. The regulations most probably originate in a voluntary cult association, not the city. In addition to the anonymous goddess, the association worshipped a variety of gods (Artemis Phylake, Mes, Apollo, Helios, Moira, the Syrian equivalent of Pan, Mogga, Adara, and Lilla). The names of the goddess's festivals *Νισαναῖα* and *Ἀλουλαῖα* (or *Ἐλουλαῖα*) derive from the Semitic month names Nisan and Elul,[76]

---

[72] MAMA VIII 448 = I.Aphrodisias 2007, 12.204: ἀνέθηκε τὸν Ἑρμῆ καὶ τὴν ἐπίχ[ρυ]σον Ἀφροδείτην καὶ τοὺς παρ'ἑκάτερα Ἔρωτας λαμπαδηφόρους καὶ τὸν πρὸ αὐτοῦ Ἔρωτα μαρμάρινον.

[73] Discussed by Lenski (2013); cf. Koßmann and Eck (2016), 285–6. On human figures (slaves) as lamp stands see also Bielfeldt (2018); Grawehr (2019).

[74] Koßmann and Eck (2016), 286 fig. 5, with further bibliography.

[75] Decourt and Tziafalias (2015); improved edition by Bouchon and Decourt (2017); detailed discussion and translation by Parker and Scullion (2016). On the identity of the goddess: Parker (2016). The text I presented in SEG 65, 376, considers these studies as well as contributions by J. M. Carbon (2016).

[76] Carbon (2016).

and ritual influences from the Near East are abundantly evident: bird sacrifice, table offerings, tending of the goddess's statue, and the Mesopotamian 'washing of the mouth' ceremony. The text explicitly states that some rituals took place during the night; but the nocturnal rites may not have been limited to those explicitly mentioned. After all, one of the deities worshipped by the association was the moon-god Mes/Men.

The text informs us that during the main festivals of the Nisanaia and the Aloulaia processions took place in the morning: 'at the Nisanaia, if the goddess comes from the river, let the procession be on the next day; at the Aloulaia let it be on the 17th day (of the month), in the morning' (B ll. 61–2: ἔστω δὲ ἡ πομπὴ Νισαναίοις μὲν ἐὰν ἡ θεὸς ἀπὸ ποταμοῦ ἔλθηι, τῆι αὔριον, Ἀλουλαίοις δὲ τῆι ἑπτακαιδεκάτηι τὸ πρωΐ). These processions, connected with the goddess's arrival and epiphany, were followed by rites at night, under torchlight: εἰς νύκτα δὲ λαμπαδεύεσθαι (B l. 63). I take the expression εἰς νύκτα—with the use of εἰς, not νυκτί, νύκτωρ, or ἐν νυκτί—as an indication that the ritual, probably a procession of worshippers carrying torches, started at dusk and continued into the night. As twilight gave its place to darkness and the moon appeared in the sky, the torches must have created an atmosphere of awe, connected with the perceived presence of the goddess.

An important component of this cult was the initiation of *mystai*. The initiates had to contribute a series of objects for the performance of the vows (or prayers): 'half a *kotyle* of oil for the lamp, an *obolos*, torches, incense, a libation (B ll. 10–12: φέρειν δὲ [ἐ]|πὶ ταῖς εὐχαῖς ἐλαίου ἡμικοτύλιον ἐπὶ λύχνον, | ὀβολόν, δαΐδας, λιβανωτόν, σπονδήν). The reference to a lamp (λύχνος) and to torches (δαΐδας) implies a ceremony in the darkness, either during the night or in a dark space (or both). This would not be unusual, since darkness played an important part in the Eleusinian, Dionysiac, Egyptian, and other mysteries.[77]

On the fifteenth day of the festival Aloulaia (or Eloulaia), which included a sacrifice to the Syrian equivalent of Pan, a nocturnal rite took place. The relevant passage is ambiguous: ὑδρεύεσθαι δὲ καὶ τῆι χύτραι τὸ ὕδωρ τῆι νυκτερινῆι ἀπὸ κρήνης (A ll. 13–14). If νυκτερινῆι is an attribute of χύτραι, the text means 'also draw water (for the ritual) using the nocturnal pot, (having fetched water) from a spring'. But it may be an attribute of a word that is not mentioned but implied, e.g. τελετῆ ('draw water from the pot for the nocturnal rite, having fetched the water from a spring').[78] The nature of the rite is not explained; but since the source of the water was not a well but a spring that guaranteed continual flow, it may have been used for purifications.

---

[77] Eleusinian mysteries: Parisinou (2000), 67–71; Gatton (2017). Samothracian mysteries: Cole (1984), 36–7 and above nn. 64–5. Dionysiac celebrations: Parisinou (2000), 71–2, 118–23. Isis: Podvin (2011), 167–88. Idaean Cave: below n. 96. Mithras: Brashear (1992), 49.

[78] My translation differs from that of Parker and Scullion (2016), 213: 'fill the *chytra* with water at the night ceremony (?) from a spring'. But the text uses the medium ὑδρεύομαι (take water for one's self); it does not refer to the filling of the pot, but to drawing water from a pot.

Limited as this information may be, it reveals the importance of night-time rituals and celebrations in this cult. The specifically 'nocturnal' objects are those that we would expect: lamps and torches, but also a pot. The setting of the rituals is not mentioned, but the λαμπαδεύεσθαι must have been an outdoor activity. The initiation may have involved activities both outside (sacrifice, purification) and inside the temple, and lamps could have been used both indoors and outdoors.[79]

The lamps needed to be fed with olive oil, and the expression ἐλαίου ἡμικοτύλιον or κοτύλη ἐπὶ λύχνον ('half a *kotyle*' or 'one *kotyle* for the lamp') appears several times, in connection with the prayers or vows of the initiation (B ll. 10–11: φέρειν δὲ [ἐ]πὶ ταῖς εὐχαῖς ἐλαίου ἡμικοτύλιον ἐπὶ λύχνον) as well as with offerings to be made during sacrifices,[80] during the offering of a table of food (τραπεζοπλησία),[81] and during an all-day celebration for the goddess (πανημερίζειν).[82] Other contributions by the worshippers on these occasions include objects needed precisely for the performance of these rituals, e.g. 'an adequate amount of firewood' for the altar (ξύλα τὰ ἱκανά: B ll. 66–7 and 70), incense to be thrown on the altar (λιβανωτός: B l. 12), and torches (δᾴδες: B ll. 12, 70). Considering this evidence, one would be tempted to assume that the olive oil would be used to feed a lamp during the ritual attended by the worshipper who contributed it. However, the requested amount (c. 120 ml and c. 240 ml) would be sufficient to let a lamp burn for days.[83] A lamp consumes c. 3–6 ml per hour depending on the size and the material of the wick (flax or *lumini*), and one *kotyle* of oil would cover the lighting needs for five to ten days.[84] Additionally, one notes that for a 'one-day ritual' (πανημερίζειν) the regulation requests half a *kotyle*, while for the offering of a table of food, which did not last a whole day, double as much (one *kotyle*). Therefore, there is no relation between the requested amount of oil and the needs of the respective ritual. Finally, the text distinguishes between items to be placed on the altar or the offering table (e.g. B l. 36: ἐπὶ τὴν τράπεζαν τὰ ἐπιτιθέμενα) and other items, such as money. The requested money contributions were a due or tax to be delivered to the 'money box' (e.g. B l. 37: τριώβολον εἰς θησαυρόν; l. 47: εἰς τὸν θησαυρὸν δραχμήν; ll. 53–4: εἰς τὸν θησαυρὸν ὀβολόν, τοῦ δὲ χηνὸς τριημιωβέλια). Interestingly, the 'olive oil for a lamp' appears twice together with money payments (B ll. 37–8: καὶ τριώβολον εἰς θησαυρὸν καὶ ἐλαίου ἐπὶ λύχνον κοτύλην; ll. 47–8: εἰς τὸν θησαυρὸν δραχμήν, ἐλαίου κοτύλην ἐπὶ λύχνον). For this reason, it is more likely that the olive oil was not to be consumed during the ritual performed by the individual worshipper, but was a sort of due, like the money for

---

[79] On the architecture of the sanctuary as can be inferred from the text, see Parker and Scullion (2016), 218–20. For lamps in the cellas of temples see Parisinou (2000), 157.
[80] B ll. 35–8: ἐπὶ δὲ τῆ[ι] θυσίαι, φέρειν δεῖ…καὶ ἐλαίου ἐπὶ λύχνον κοτύλην; B l. 69: κοτύλην ἐπὶ λύχνον; ll. 69–71: ἐὰν δέ τις χῆνα ὁλοκαυτῆται…ἐλαίου ἐπὶ λύχνον ἡμικοτύλιον.
[81] B ll. 47–8: ἐλαίου κοτύλην ἐπὶ λύχνον.
[82] B ll. 48–50: ἐάν τις πανημερίσαι βούληται τῆι θεῶι,…ἐπὶ λύχνον ἐλ[αί]ου ἡμικοτύλιον.
[83] On the capacity of one *kotyle* of olive oil (c. 220–45 ml) see Viedebandt (1922), 1547–8.
[84] Moullou and Topalis (2017), 4–5.

the 'money box'. With such a due, the cult association would make sure that there was sufficient olive oil for lamps burning in the temple during nocturnal rituals, but perhaps also on a daily basis. We have already seen that the daily illumination of shrines and temples is a significant innovation of the imperial period.

10.5. Fire in the Cave of Zeus

One of the least known initiatory cults of the imperial period is that of the Idaean Cave. Believed by some to be the place where Zeus was brought after his birth and was protected by the Kouretes—other competitors included Dikte near Lyktos, Palaiakastro, the Trojan Ide, and Halikarnassos—the Idaean Cave was Crete's most important sacred place, associated by ancient authors with a mystery cult (Fig. 10.5).[85] The mysteries of Zeus Idaios are mentioned by Euripides in a fragment of his tragedy *Cretans*. An initiate, a βάκχος, explains how he leads a pure life as a Διὸς Ἰδαίου μύστης, having performed a Dionysiac rite involving the consumption of raw meat and having raised torches to Meter Oreia together with the Kouretes.[86] Thanks to the discovery in central Crete of gold *lamellae* with 'Bacchic-Orphic' texts, we now know that at least in the late Hellenistic period a connection existed between the so-called Orphic ideas and the cave.[87] The popularity of this cult increased in the imperial period, when the cult of Zeus Idaios was somehow connected with the Cretan Koinon and possibly the imperial cult.[88] In the mid-first century AD, the cave was allegedly visited by the 'holy man' Apollonios of Tyana. There, he had access to discourses about the gods.[89] Some knowledge of the mysteries of Zeus existed until late antiquity, when Porphyry (late third century AD) included the cave among the places allegedly visited by Pythagoras. According to the Neoplatonic philosopher, Pythagoras visited the cave after having been purified by 'the initiates of Morgos, one of the Idaean Daktyloi' by means of a 'thunder stone' (κεραυνία λίθος)—probably a neolithic axe-head.[90] At the cave, the sage stayed for twenty-seven days, offered a sacrifice, and inscribed an epigram on the grave of Zeus. This narrative vaguely associates the cave with purification rites and concepts of death and rebirth that typically

---

[85] Idaean Cave: Kallimachos, *Hymn of Zeus* 42–54; Aratos, *Phainomena* 30–5; Apollonios, *Argonautika* 2.1235–8; 3.13–136; the area of Lyktos: Hesiod, *Theogony* 481–4; Palaikastro: *I.Cret.* III. ii.2; Mount Ide near Troy: Demetrios of Skepsis, *FGrH* (2013) F 53; Halikarnassos: *SEG* XLVIII 1330.

[86] Fr. 472c, ed. Kannicht ll. 9–15. Recent edition and discussion: Bernabé Pajares (2016). I give his translation (192): 'Pure is the life I have led since I became an initiate of Idaean Zeus, and celebrated the thunderbolts of night-ranging Zagreus performing his feasts of raw flesh; and raising torches high to the Mother of the mountain, among the Curetes, I was consecrated and named a Bakchos.'

[87] Tzifopoulos (2010), 202–15 and 225–35.   [88] Chaniotis (2008), 95.

[89] Philostratos, *Live of Apollonius of Tyana* 4.34.2–3: προῄει δ' ἐπὶ Γόρτυναν πόθῳ τῆς Ἴδης. ἀνελθὼν οὖν καὶ τοῖς θεολογουμένοις ἐντυχὼν ἐπορεύθη καὶ εἰς τὸ ἱερὸν τὸ Λεβηναῖον.

[90] Porphyry, *Life of Pythagoras* 17: τοῖς Μόργου μύσταις προσῄει, ἑνὸς τῶν Ἰδαίων Δακτύλων, ὑφ' ὧν καὶ ἐκαθάρθη τῇ κεραυνίᾳ λίθῳ. On the meaning of κεραυνία λίθος and the use of thunderstones as amulets see Faraone (2014).

Fig. 10.5 The cult cave of Zeus on Mount Ida (Idaion Antron).
Photograph: Efi Sapouna-Sakellaraki.

accompany mystery cults.[91] As late as the reign of Julian, a provincial governor of the *provincia insularum* visited the cave and offered a sacrifice.[92]

---

[91] For a discussion of this passage in connection with mystery cults of Crete: Chaniotis (1992), 96–100.
[92] Chaniotis (1987); latest edition of the inscription in *IG* XII.6.584 II (with a different date that I do not find convincing).

The Idaean Cave may be famous for its early archaic bronze shields, but the largest group of finds excavated there in 1982–6 consists of clay lamps of the imperial period.[93] Only a dozen lamp fragments can be attributed to the pre-Roman period, as opposed to hundreds of fragments from the imperial period. This suggests a change in ritual practices. Can we associate this most characteristic find of the imperial period with the cult? The number of the lamps has not—and probably cannot—be estimated, because only seven are intact, only two of them found during the systematic excavations of 1982–6.[94] Because of their small dimensions, lamps can easily be preserved, only with the handle or the nozzle broken off. The fact that hundreds of lamps have been found broken into small pieces, mostly in the deepest parts of the cave,[95] cannot be attributed simply to destruction inflicted by time. The lamps were most likely broken on purpose during a ritual. It is possible that this occurred during a ritual of divination by means of lamps, that were destroyed after the divination was completed.[96] But there is an alternative explanation. According to Antoninus Liberalis (c. second century AD), a big light was seen during a celebration that commemorated Zeus' birth:[97]

> At a designated time, every year, one sees a great blaze glowing from inside the cave. According to the myth, this occurs when the blood from Zeus' birth boils out.

The author explicitly refers to fire or blaze ($\pi \hat{u} \rho$), not to light that could have been produced with the use of media such as torches. We can imagine that the lamps, brought by the worshippers—their iconography is rarely connected with the cult of Zeus[98]—or bought at the site, were filled with oil, set alight, and thrown into the cave during that ceremony.

In the case of a cult cave, the contrast of light and darkness is provided by nature itself. The entrance of the cave, viewed from the interior, resembles a huge observatory of the night sky, and it is very probable that the movement of the celestial bodies, the observation of constellations and the solstices played a part in the cult.[99] In a famous passage in his *Republic* (514a–520a), Plato uses the allegory of people chained in a cave who can only see the shadows of objects as they pass in front of light. Only the philosophers who free themselves from these chains can perceive the true form of the objects. This allegory is based on sensory

---

[93] See Sakellarakis and Sapouna-Sakellaraki (2013), II, 228–40; cf. Sapouna (1998), 18–19.

[94] *I.Cret.* I.xii.4–7 (from a private collection) and Sapouna (1998), 31 no. 82 (found in 1958), 42 no. 168, 44 no. 188. Sapouna's catalogue lists 350 fragments of lamps with figural decoration; a total of 734 fragments have been catalogued (Sapouna (1998), 17), but the number of the lamp fragments is much larger.

[95] Sapouna (1998), 18.

[96] Sapouna (1998), 172; cf. Sakellarakis and Sapouna-Sakellaraki (2013), II, 240.

[97] Antoninus Liberalis, *Metamorphoses* 19.2: ἐν δὲ χρόνῳ ἀφωρισμένῳ ὁρᾶται καθ' ἕκαστον ἔτος πλεῖστον ἐκλάμπον ἐκ τοῦ σπηλαίου πῦρ. Τοῦτο δὲ γίνεσθαι μυθολογοῦσιν, ὅταν ἐκζέῃ τὸ τοῦ Διὸς ἐκ τῆς γενέσεως αἷμα.

[98] There are some representations of Zeus, but the decorative themes vary and range from erotic images to gladiatorial themes; see Sapouna (1998), 119–71.

[99] Sakellarakis and Sapouna-Sakellaraki (2013), I, 223–5.

experiences in caves, such as the near-death experience of consultants of the oracle of Trophonios in his cave near Lebadeia.[100] The impact of the natural darkness can be enhanced with the use of artificial light provided by torches and lamps that illuminate particular objects of the cult, make stalagmites resemble divine figures, or generate shadows on the walls. In the case of the cult cave of Zeus on Mount Ida, a single literary testimony, the note of Antoninus Liberalis, suggests an association of the lamps with a particular ritual.

10.6. Torches and cranes in Abonou Teichos

The paraphernalia used in nocturnal celebrations that aimed at creating the illusion of divine epiphanies or presented 'sacred dramas' went beyond lamps, torches, and altars. Lucian's description of the cult of Glykon New Asklepios, introduced by Alexander in Abonou Teichos (c. AD 140), certainly has satirical overtones, but the information that he provides, e.g. about the god's appearance (a snake with long hair and big ears) is confirmed by archaeological finds. The cult included initiation into mysteries. After the representation of the birth of Apollo, his marriage to Koronis, the birth of Asklepios, and the epiphany of Glykon were represented in 'sacred dramas' during the first two days, the third day was dedicated to three more enactments of events connected with the cult and its founder. Although this is not explicitly stated by Lucian, at least part of the performances of the third day took place during the night:

> This day was called the Day of Torches, and torches were lighted. Finally, the love of the moon goddess and Alexander was represented, and the birth of Rutilianus' wife [Alexander's daughter]. Alexander, the new Endymion, served as torchbearer and mystical expounder. While he lay as if he were asleep, there came down to him from the roof, as if from heaven, not the moon goddess but a certain Rutilia, a most beautiful woman, wife of one of the emperor's stewards, who was truly in love with Alexander and he with her. And before the eyes of that rascal, her husband, they engaged in kisses and embraces in public. And if there had not been that many torches, very quickly copulation would have occurred.[101]

The references to torches and Selene suggest a nocturnal setting, as in the Eleusinian mysteries that were Alexander's model.[102] The venue of this spectacle is not stated, but it was a covered space, since Rutilia, who played the part of Selene, was lowered from the roof to Alexander/Endymion. Presumably, a device

---

[100] Pausanias, *Description of Greece* 9.39.9–11. On the emotional and cognitive impact of caves, see Ustinova (2009); on Trophonios, see n. 36.
[101] Lucian, *Alexander* 38–9.   [102] Sfameni Gasparro (1999), 299–302; Chaniotis (2002), 78–9.

similar to the crane (*mechane*) used in the theatre for the representation of divine epiphanies (*deus ex machina*) was used. We can only speculate about this machinery adducing parallels. Statues of Nikai were used twice in the early first century BC to honour Mithridates VI in Pergamon in 88 BC and Caecilius Metellus in Rome in *c.* 75 BC.[103] The golden Nikai held crowns in their hands and were lowered with the use of some machinery (ὄργανα) towards the honorand, in order to place the crown on his head. In Pergamon, this did not work out as planned; the statue broke into pieces just as Nike was about to touch Mithridates' head. Alexander's crane did work.

10.7. Statues that burn and statues in flames: the Daidala of Boiotia

Probably during the Antonine Plague (*c.* AD 165–80), a city in Lydia (Sardis?), asked an oracle what measures it should take in order to avert evil. The oracle, most likely that of Apollo Klarios, attributed the disease to a sorcerer, and recommended the city's inhabitants to bring a golden statue of Artemis represented as holding torches, to set it up in a temple, and worship her with hymns, sacrifices, and choral dances of boys and girls:[104]

> ...Her form bring in from Ephesos, brilliant with gold. Put her up in a temple, full of joy: she will provide deliverance from your affliction and will dissolve the magic of pestilence, which destroys men, and will melt down with her flame-bearing torches in nightly fire the kneaded works of wax, the signs of the evil art of sorcerer. But when you have performed for the goddess my decrees, worship with hymns the shooter of arrows, the irresistible, straight shooting one, and with sacrifices, the renowned and vigilant virgin; and during dancing and feasting, your girls together with the boys, above the salty lands of Maeonic Hermos, praising her in every respect wear crowns of large myrtle, having called from the Ephesian Land the pure Artemis, in order that she might always be to you an unfailing helper....

Apart from common forms of worship, the text recommends an unusual ritual: the burning and melting of waxen objects, presumably figurines, by the goddess with her torches in a nocturnal rite (ἥ κεν ἀλύξει πήματα καὶ λοίμοιο βροτοφθόρα φάρμακα λύσει λαμπάσι πυρσοφόροις νυχίᾳ φλογὶ μάγματα κηροῦ τηίξασα μάγου κακοτήια σύμβολα τέχνης). The interpretation of this passage is not easy. One

---

[103] Mithridates: Plutarch, *Sulla* 11. Metellus: Plutarch, *Sertorius* 22. See Hölscher (1967), 39 n. 202, 62, 143 n. 898; von Hesberg (1987), 61.
[104] *SEG* XLI 981; Graf (1992).

possibility is that waxen figurines had been discovered and interpreted as the work of a magician.¹⁰⁵ But this seems to me unlikely; if they had been found, the authorities would have not required the advice of an oracle to destroy them. This was standard practice.¹⁰⁶ Fritz Graf has pointed to an Assyrian ritual during which figurines, representing the sorcerer, were made and burned, noting, however, the fact that in Assyria the figurines were not the work of the magician but represented him; he assumes an Oriental influence in this ritual, but leaves the question open.¹⁰⁷ The waxen objects are not explicitly called the work of a sorcerer, but tokens (σύμβολα) of his evil art. It is, therefore, not inconceivable that the oracle prescribed the making of figures and then their destruction in the temple by Artemis, represented through her torch-bearing statue, in a nocturnal ceremony. A similar manipulation of statues was recommended by another oracle of Apollo Klarios.¹⁰⁸

Closer to our subject of the materiality of festivals, not rituals, is the making and burning of statues in Boiotia during the festival of the Daidala. The earliest literary references to this festival date from the imperial period and refer to the form that it had after a long period of development.¹⁰⁹ Plutarch, who wrote a treatise on this festival (*Peri ton en Plataiais Daidalon*), gives the aetiological myth of the rite.¹¹⁰ When Hera was hiding after a quarrel with Zeus, Alalkomenes advised Zeus to pretend that he would marry another woman. Zeus cut a big and beautiful oak, shaped it as a woman, decorated it as a bride, and called it Daidale. The nymphs of the river Triton gave her the nuptial bath and the wedding song was sung. Losing her patience, Hera came down from Mount Kithairon full of anger and jealousy, followed by the women of Plataia. When she realized that Daidale was a doll, she reconciled herself with Zeus and took the role of bridesmaid for herself. She honoured this wooden image and named the festival Daidala. Nonetheless, she burned the image because of her jealousy. A similar *aetion* and a description of how the festival was celebrated in the late second century AD is given by Pausanias:¹¹¹

> Not far from Alalkomenai is an oak grove. Here the trunks of the oaks are the largest in Boiotia. To this grove come the Plataians, and lay out portions of boiled flesh. They keep a strict watch on the crows, which flock to them, but they pay no attention to the other birds. They mark carefully the tree on which a crow settles with the meat he has seized. They cut down the trunk of the tree on which the crow has settled, and use it to make the *daidalon*; for this is the name that

---

¹⁰⁵ Gordon et al. (1993), 150.   ¹⁰⁶ Examples in Graf (1992), 277.
¹⁰⁷ Graf (1992), 277–8.   ¹⁰⁸ Merkelbach and Stauber (1996), 30–1, no. 15.
¹⁰⁹ For a review of the various views concerning the festival's origins, see Chaniotis (2002), 26–37. For recent discussions, Knoepfler (2001); Chaniotis (2002); Iversen (2007).
¹¹⁰ Plutarch, *FGrH* 388 F 1.
¹¹¹ Pausanias, *History of Greece* 9, 2, 7–9, 3, 8; Pirenne-Delforge (2008) 223–6.

they give to the wooden image. This festival the Plataians celebrate by themselves, calling it the Little Daidala, but the Great Daidala, which is celebrated with them by the Boiotians, is a festival held with intervals of fifty-nine years, for that is the period during which, they say, the festival could not be held, as the Plataians were in exile. There are fourteen wooden images ready, having been provided each year at the Little Daidala. Lots are cast for them by the Plataians, Koronaians, Thespians, Tanagraians, Chaironeis, Orchomenians, Lebadeis, and Thebans. For at the time when Kassandros, the son of Antipater, rebuilt Thebes, the Thebans wished to be reconciled with the Plataians, to share in the common assembly, and to send a sacrifice to the Daidala. The towns of less account pool their funds for images. Bringing the image to the Asopos, and setting it upon a wagon, they place a bridesmaid also on the wagon. They again cast lots for the position they are to hold the procession. After this they drive the wagons from the river to the summit of Kithairon. On the peak of the mountain an altar has been prepared, which they make in the following way. They fit together quadrangular pieces of wood, putting them together just as if they were making a stone building, and having raised it to a height they place brushwood upon the altar. The cities with their magistrates sacrifice a cow to Hera and a bull to Zeus, burning on the altar the victims, full of wine and incense, along with the *daidala*. Rich people as individuals sacrifice what they wish; but the less wealthy sacrifice the smaller cattle; all the victims alike are burned. The fire seizes the altar and the victims as well, and consumes them all together. I know of no blaze that is so high, or seen so far as this.

There is no doubt that the ritual of the imperial period was the result of amalgamations and artificial transformations under the influence of political factors, with the role of the Boiotian cities mirroring the structure of the Boiotian Federation.[112] There is no agreement on the different origins of the festival's components— mainly rituals promoting fertility—and this is not the place to discuss them. Although Pausanias does not explicitly mention this, the highlight of the celebration must have taken place after sunset. The rituals probably started in the morning at the river Asopos, and it would have taken at least four hours to bring the images in procession from there to the top of Mount Kithairon (height: 1,117 m). The sacrifices would have taken place in the afternoon, and Pausanias' comment that he knew 'of no blaze that is so high, or seen so far as this' makes sense if the fire was observed in darkness; finally, wedding processions—and this is what the festival imitated—took place at dusk, under the light of torches, when the bride was led to the nuptial chamber. Here, the nuptial chamber is replaced by an altar, on which the 'bride' is burned. The attention paid by Pausanias in the description

---

[112] See more recently Prandi (1983); Knoepfler (2001); Chaniotis (2002).

of the altar is striking, in particular his remark that the altar is constructed in the way one builds a stone building; the altar probably represented the *oikos* which one expects in a wedding.[113]

10.8. Conclusions

Nocturnal activities that range from celebrations and private dinning parties to visits to baths and gymnasia after sunset are a distinctive feature of culture in the imperial period. The material background of these activities is diverse, ranging from architectural settings[114] to objects. But an important shared feature of all types of activities—whether we are dealing with the imperial cult in Messene or with the mysteries of Glykon in Abonou Teichos, a banquet in the sanctuary of the Great Gods in Samothrace or the festival of the Daidala in Boiotia, the prayer to Theos Hypsistos at dawn or the annual festival of Zeus in the Idaean Cave—is the production and manipulation of artificial light. We cannot measure the consumption of artificial light in the imperial period and compare it with that of earlier periods. The impression that night-time activities increased from the Hellenistic period onward is up to a certain extent the result of the increased number of sources—especially inscriptions. But one should consider a series of socio-cultural developments as well that do support the assumption that more economic, social, and cultural activities took place during the night in the Hellenistic than in earlier periods and that this trend continued into the imperial period. These activities required artificial light. That the satirical author Lucian made lamps the inhabitants of a City of Lamps (*Lychnopolis*) in the skies, between the Pleiades and the Hyades,[115] reveals an awareness of the importance of illumination; this awareness was possible in the late second century AD and unthinkable in the past.

The production and consumption of artificial light in religious celebrations and rituals in the Roman East had an economic, a socio-political, and a cognitive dimension. The artificial light provided by lamps required olive oil, and the increased use of lamps in celebrations and rituals as well as the trend to keep lamps burning day and night caused significant expense.[116] The cult regulation from Larisa (see Section 10.4 above) reveals the effort to transfer the cost onto the worshippers, who were to contribute significant amounts of olive oil 'for the lamp', either for the ritual they attended or, as I argue, in order to keep lamps burning in the temple. Another economic aspect of the use of artificial light in festivals and

---

[113] Cf. Furley (1981), 207.
[114] On how temple architecture facilitated light effects, Boutsikas (2017), 5–6.
[115] Lucian, *True History* 29.
[116] On the financial burden carried by individuals for street illumination see Dossey (2018), 293–4; Wilson (2018).

rituals is the production of special types of lamps, notably in the cults of Isis and Theos Hypsistos, as well as the development of particular types of torch-bearing statues for the illuminations of public spaces, exactly as there were lamp-stands in the form of slaves for the illumination of private spaces.

The use of lamps and torches in celebrations, exactly as the use of other cult paraphernalia, expressed hierarchical distinctions. The bearer of the torch (*dadouchos*) in the imperial cult in Messene and the mysteries of Abonou Teichos was the most important person officiating in the celebration, while the chief torch-bearer in Thessalonike had a leading position in his association; by contrast, 'the women who light the lamps' and 'the women who carry lamps' belonged to the lower cult personnel. We can only assume that the play of light and darkness also marked the transition of status in mystery cults. A different symbolic dimension of artificial light can be recognized in the case of the Daidala. The distinctive feature of this festival was the great blaze created by the burning of a huge altar, wooden images, and sacrificial animals. The creation of this huge blaze was the result of the common effort of all Boiotian cities, and observed from afar, all over Boiotia, it expressed local unity and identity.

Except for Pausanias, who was impressed by the great blaze on top of Mount Kithairon, we do not have sources about the cognitive and emotional impact of the manipulation of light. In the case of the mysteries at Abonou Teichos, torches and a crane were used in a dark space to re-enacted important events connected with the cult, especially the 'sacred marriage' of the prophet Alexandros and the Moon. Here, the aim was illusion and awe. In the case of the mysteries, the play of darkness and light was connected with secrecy and revelation, death and rebirth; it enhanced emotional arousal, engendering feelings of exclusivity and a sense of identity.[117]

We can assume that all the senses—not only the vision—of the worshippers were stimulated. The Mithras mysteries, puzzling as they may be in many respects, are a case in point regarding sensory stimuli.[118] In the dark spaces of the Mithraea, dominated by the contrast between light and darkness, filled with multi-coloured frescoes and sculptures with bright colours, the senses of the worshippers would have been overwhelmed: they saw the images, whose significance must have been explained by exegetes of the higher grades and may have remained a puzzle to those of the lower grades; they were blindfolded for the initiation.[119] They

---

[117] Boutsikas (2017), 10–14. On possible optical illusions in the Eleusinian mysteries: Gatton (2017). On the importance of emotional arousal in mystery cults see Chaniotis (2011), 267–72; Martzavou (2012).

[118] Recent cognitive approaches to the cult of Mithras: Martin (2015); Beck and Panagiotidou (2017), esp. 141–64, on the creation of cohesion and identity through the rituals. A good summary of the state of the art is given by Gordon (2012). On night-time initiation see Brashear (1992), 49.

[119] On the architecture and decoration of the Mithraea: e.g. Clauss (2001) 42–61; apprehension of symbols: Beck and Panagiotidou (2017), 8–9; perception of space in the Mithraea: Beck and Panagiotidou (2017), 83–105. Blindfolding: Martin (2015), 33; Mastrocinque (2017), 13.

listened to narratives.[120] They said prayers and sacred words, and made inarticulate sounds—e.g. the initiates of the lowest grade, the *korakes*, imitated the cry of ravens. They shouted *nama* in approval of fellow initiates.[121] They smelled the blood of the sacrificial animal and the incense on the altar. They touched sacred objects and each other. They felt the cold floor on their skin as they kneeled naked on it for their initiation; they underwent an ordeal that probably culminated in a near-death experience.[122] Finally, they tasted the food that was shared among the worshippers in the common banquet with which the ceremony ended.[123]

The Greeks were aware of the impact of the night on cognition. The proverb ἐν νυκτὶ βουλή ('deciding during the night') highlighted the possibilities offered by the night for calm reflection on important matters.[124] It did not require the sensibility of novelists, such as Achilles Tatius and Heliodoros, for people in antiquity to recognize that the night affected the senses and enhanced emotions, not only erotic desire and grief but also fear. Exactly as pirates and generals exploited the night for attacks, authors of narratives mentioned the fact that an event—an earthquake, a crime, or an attack—took place during the night in order to increase the emotional impact of the narrative on the readers.[125] That this awareness of the cognitive, emotional, and sensory impact of the night did not influence the staging of nocturnal celebrations and rituals is inconceivable. 'Darkness possesses solemnity' (σεμνότητ' ἔχει σκότος), is Dionysos' answer to the question if he performs his rites in the night or during the day (*Bacchae* 486). With the exception of phenomena such as Maenadism[126] or the experience of the visitors of Trophonios' oracle, ancient authors do not often directly describe how a nocturnal rite affected individuals and groups. But both textual and archaeological sources attest to the importance of the manipulation of artificial light. Thus, the study of the materiality of artificial light in festivals and celebrations can offer a small contribution to the growing field of historical, archaeological, and philological research on the emotions and the senses in classical antiquity.[127]

---

[120] Cf. Clauss (2001), 62–101.
[121] Prayer: Clauss (2001), 105–8. The sound of the *korakes*: Ps.-Augustinus, *Quaestiones veteris et novi testamenti* 113.11 ed. Souter: *vocem coraci imitantes*. The acclamation *nama*: Mastrocinque (2017), 8–9.
[122] Vermaseren (1971), 24–42; Clauss (2001), 103; Martin (2015), 32–3.
[123] Mithraic meal: Clauss (2001), 108–13; Martin (2015), 47–51, 66; Beck and Panagiotidou (2017), 62–4.
[124] *Corpus Paroemiographorum Graecorum* I 82 edd. Leutsch/Schneidewin: ἐν νυκτὶ βουλή... ἐπειδὴ ἡσυχίαν ἔχει ἡ νὺξ καὶ δίδωσι κατὰ σχολὴν λογισμοὺς τοῖς τῶν περὶ τῶν ἀναγκαίων βουλευομένοις.
[125] Violence in the night: Chaniotis (2017b); the night as an emotional enhancer in narratives: e.g. Chaniotis (2017b), 101–6; (2018c), 8–9; in art: Mylonopoulos (2018).
[126] e.g. Parisinou (2000), 118–23.
[127] Recent research on the senses: Harvey (2006); Schettino and Pittia (2012);); Bradley and Butler (2014); Butler and Purves (2014); Hamilakis (2014); Bradley (2015); Emerit, Perrot, and Vincent (2015); Squire (2016); Betts (2017); Purves (2017); Butler and Nooter (2018); Rudolph (2018). Bibliography on recent research on emotions: Chaniotis (2020), 10.

Works Cited

Agusta-Bularot, S. and Seigne, J. (2017) 'Dédicaces de statues "portes-flambeaux" (δᾳδοῦχοι) à Gerasa (Jerash, Jordanie)', *Zeitschrift für Papyrologie und Epigraphik* 203: 144–56.

Anghelina, C. (2017) 'Athena's birth on the night of the dark moon', *Journal of Hellenic Studies* 137: 175–83.

Bathrellou, E. (2012) 'Menander's *Epitrepontes* and the festival of the Tauropolia', *Classical Antiquity* 31: 151–92.

Beck, R. and Panagiotidou, O. (2017) *The Roman Mithras Cult: A Cognitive Approach*. London.

Bernabé Pajares, A. (2016) 'Two Orphic images in Euripides' *Hippolytus* 952–957 and *Cretans* 472 Kannicht', in *New Trends in Classics* 8.2: 183–204.

Betts, E. (ed.) (2017) *Senses of the Empire. Multisensory Approaches to Roman Culture*. London and New York.

Bevilacqua, G. et al. (2010) *Scrittura e magia. Un repertorio di oggetti iscritti della magia greco-romana*. Rome.

Bielfeldt, R. (2018) '*Candelabrus* and Trimalchio: embodied histories of Roman lamp stands and their slaves', in M. Gaifman, V. Platt, and M. Squire (eds), *The Embodied Object, Art History Special Issue*. Oxford and Boston, 420–43.

Biers, W. R. and Geagan, D. J. (1970) 'A new list of victors in the Caesarea at Isthmia', *Hesperia* 39: 79–93.

Bonnechere, P. (2003) *Trophonios de Lébadée: cultes et mythes d'une cité béotienne au miroir de la mentalité antique*. Leiden.

Boschung, D. and Bremmer, J. N. (eds) (2015) *The Materiality of Magic*. Leiden.

Bouchon, R. and Decourt, J.-C. (2017) 'Le règlement de Marmarini (Thessalie): nouvelles lectures, nouvelles interprétations', *Kernos* 30: 159–86.

Boutsikas, E. (2014) 'Greek temples and rituals', in C. L. N. Ruggles (ed.), *Handbook of Archaeoastronomy and Ethnoastronomy*. New York, 1573–81.

Boutsikas, E. (2017) 'The role of darkness in ancient Greek religion and religious practice', in C. Papadopoulos and H. Moyes (eds), *The Oxford Handbook of Light in Archaeology*. Oxford [online resource. DOI: 10.1093/oxfordhb/9780198788218.013.22].

Boutsikas, E. and Hannah, R. (2012) 'Aitia, astronomy, and the timing of the Arrhephoria', *Annual of the British School at Athens* 107: 233–45.

Boutsikas, E. and Ruggles, C. (2011) 'Temples, stars, and ritual landscapes. The potential for archaeoastronomy in ancient Greece', *American Journal of Archaeology* 115: 55–68.

Bradley, M. (2015) *Smell and the Ancient Senses*. London.

Bradley, M. and Butler, S. (eds) (2014) *Synaesthesia and the Ancient Senses*. London and New York.

Brashear, W. M. (1992) *A Mithraic Catechism from Egypt (P. Berol. 21,196)*. Tyche Supplementband I. Vienna.

Busine, A. (2005) *Paroles d'Apollon. Pratiques et traditions oraculaires dans l'Antiquité tardive (IIe–VIe siècles)*. Leiden.

Butler, S. and Nooter, S. (eds) (2018) *Sound and the Ancient Senses*. London and New York.

Butler, S., and Purves, A. (eds) (2014) *Synaesthesia and the Ancient Senses*. London and New York.

Carbon, Jan-Mathieu (2016) 'The festival of the Aloulaia, and the association of the Alouliastai. Notes concerning the new inscription from Larisa/Marmarini', *Kernos* 29: 185–208.

Chaniotis, A. (1987) 'Plutarchos, praeses insularum', *Zeitschrift für Papyrologie und Epigraphik* 68: 227–31.

Chaniotis, A. (1992) 'Die Geschichte von Amnisos von Homer bis zur Eroberung Kretas durch die Türken', in J. Schäfer (ed.), *Amnisos nach den archäologischen, topographischen, historischen und epigraphischen Zeugnissen des Altertums und der Neuzeit*. Berlin, 73–127.

Chaniotis, A. (2002) 'Ritual dynamics. The Boiotian festival of the Daidala', in *Kykeon. Studies in Honour of H. S. Versnel*. Leiden, 23–48.

Chaniotis, A. (2008) 'What difference did Rome make? The Cretans and the Roman empire', in B. Forsén and G. Salmeri (eds), *The Province Strikes Back. Imperial Dynamics in the Eastern Mediterranean*. Helsinki, 83–105.

Chaniotis, A. (2011) 'Emotional community through ritual. Initiates, citizens, and pilgrims as emotional communities in the Greek World', in A. Chaniotis (ed.), *Ritual Dynamics in the Ancient Mediterranean: Agency, Emotion, Gender, Representation*. Stuttgart, 264–290.

Chaniotis, A. (2013) 'Staging and feeling the presence of God: emotion and theatricality in religious celebrations in the Roman East', in L. Bricault and C. Bonnet (eds), *Panthée: Religious Transformations in the Roman Empire*. Leiden, 169–89.

Chaniotis, A. (2017a) 'The life of statues of Gods in the Greek world', *Kernos* 30, 91–112.

Chaniotis, A. (2017b) 'Violence in the dark: emotional impact, representation, response', in M. Champion and L. O'Sullivan (eds), *Cultural Perceptions of Violence in the Hellenistic World*. London, 100–15.

Chaniotis, A. (2018a) *Age of Conquests: The Greek World from Alexander to Hadrian*. London.

Chaniotis, A. (2018b) 'The polis after sunset: what is Hellenistic in Hellenistic Nights?', in H. Börm and N. Luraghi (eds), *The Polis in the Hellenistic World*. Stuttgart, 181–208.

Chaniotis, A. (2018c) 'Nessun Dorma! Changing nightlife in the Hellenistic and Roman East', in A. Chaniotis (ed.), *La nuit. Imaginaire et réalités nocturnes dans le monde gréco-romain*. Entretiens Hardt 64. Geneva, 1–58.

Chaniotis, A. (2018d) 'Greek purity in context: the long life of a ritual concept', in J. M. Carbon and S. Peels-Matthey (eds), *Purity and Purification in the Ancient Greek World: Concepts and Practices*. Liège, 35–48.

Chaniotis, A. (2020) 'Display, arousal, and performance of emotions: introduction', in A. Chaniotis (ed.), *Unveiling Emotions III. Display, Arousal, and Performance of Emotions in the Greek World*. Stuttgart, 9–30.

Clauss, M. (2001) *The Roman Cult of Mithras: The God and His Mysteries*, translated by Richard Gordon. London.

Cole, S. G. (1984) *Theoi Megaloi. The Cult of the Great Gods at Samothrace*. Leiden.

De Temmerman, K. (2018) 'Novelistic nights', in A. Chaniotis (ed.), *La nuit. Imaginaire et réalités nocturnes dans le monde gréco-romain*. Entretiens Hardt 64. Geneva, 257–85.

Decourt, J.-C. and Tziafalias, A. (2015) 'Un règlement religieux de la région de Larissa: cultes et grecs et 'orientaux'', *Kernos* 28: 13–51.

Deubner, L. (1966) *Attische Feste*. 2nd edition. Berlin.

Dimitrova, N. M. (2008) *Theoroi and Initiates in Samothrace. The Epigraphical Evidence. Hesperia* Supplement 37. Princeton.

Dossey, L. (2018) 'Shedding light on the late antique night', in A. Chaniotis (ed.), *La nuit. Imaginaire et réalités nocturnes dans le monde gréco-romain*. Entretiens Hardt 64. Geneva, 293–322.

Emerit, S., Perrot, S., and Vincent, A. (ed.) (2015) *Le paysage sonore de l'Antiquité. Méthodologie, historiographie et perspectives. Actes de la journée d'études tenue a l'École française de Rome, le 7 janvier 2013*. Châtillon.

Faraone, C. A. (2014) 'Inscribed Greek thunderstones as house- and body-amulets in Roman imperial times', *Kernos* 27: 257–84.

Foerster, G. and Tsafrir, Y. (1993) 'The Bet-She'an excavation project (1989–1991): city center (north)', *Excavations and Surveys in Israel* 11: 3–32.

Franken, N. (2002) 'Lampen für die Götter. Beobachtungen zur Funktion der sogenannten Vexillumaufsätze', *Istanbuler Mitteilungen* 52: 369–81.

Furley, W. D. (1981) *Studies in the Use of Fire in Ancient Greek Religion*. New York.

Gatton, M. (2017) 'The Eleusinian projector: the Hierophant's optical method of conjuring the goddess', in C. Papadopoulos and H. Moyes (eds), *The Oxford Handbook of Light in Archaeology*. Oxford [online resource. DOI: 10.1093/oxfordhb/9780198788218.013.34].

Gonlin, N. and Nowell, A. (eds) (2018) *Archaeology of the Night: Life after Dark in the Ancient World*. Boulder.

Gordon, R. (2012) 'Mithras (Mithraskult)', *Reallexicon für Antike und Christentum* 24: 964–1009.

Gordon, R., Beard, M., Reynolds, J., and Roueché, C. (1993) 'Roman inscriptions, 1986–1990', *Journal of Roman Studies* 83: 131–58.

Gow, A. S. F. (1952) *Theocritus. Edited with a Translation and Commentary*, 2 volumes. 2nd edition. Cambridge.

Graf, F. (1992) 'An oracle against pestilence from a western Anatolian town', *Zeitschrift für Papyrologie und Epigraphik* 92: 267–79.

Graf, F. (1996) *Gottesnähe und Schadenzauber. Die Magie in der griechisch-römischen Antike*. Munich.

Grawehr, M. (2019) 'Of toddlers and donkeys: Roman lamps with slaves and self-representations of slaves', in A. Binsfeld and M. Ghetta (eds), *Ubi servi erant? Die Ikonographie von Sklaven und Freigelassenen in der römischen Kunst*. Stuttgart, 91–118.

Hamilakis, Y. (2014) *Archaeology of the Senses: Human Experience, Memory, and Affect*. Cambridge.

Harvey, S. A. (2006) *Scenting Salvation: Ancient Christianity and the Olfactory Imagination*. Berkeley.

Hölscher, T. (1967) *Victoria Romana. Archäologische Untersuchungen zur Geschichte und Wesensart der römischen Siegesgöttin von den Anfängen bis zum Ende des 3. Jh. n. Chr*. Mainz.

Iversen, P. (2007) 'The small and great Daidala in Boiotian history', *Historia* 56: 381–418.

Kerenyi, K. (1976) *Dionysos. Archetypal Image of Indestructible Life*. Translated by R. Mannheim. Princeton.

Knoepfler, D. (2001) 'Daidala de Platées chez Pausanias: une clef pour l'histoire de la Béotie hellénistique', in D. Knoepfler and M. Piérart (eds), *Éditer, traduire, commenter. Pausanias en l'année 2000*. Geneva, 343–74.

Koßmann, D. and Eck, W. (2016) 'Schmuck für die Polis. Die Basis für die Statue eines δᾳδοῦχος aus Eleutheropolis in Syria Palaestina', *Zeitschrift für Papyrologie und Epigraphik* 200: 282–6.

Lenski, N. (2013) 'Working models: functional art and Roman conceptions of slavery', in M. George (ed.), *Roman Slavery and Roman Material Culture*. Toronto, 129–57.

Martin, L. H. (2015) *The Mind of Mithraists: Historical and Cognitive Studies in the Roman Cult of Mithras*. London.

Martzavou, P. (2012) 'Isis Aretalogies, initiations, and emotions. The Isis aretalogies as a source for the study of emotions', in A. Chaniotis (ed.), *Unveiling Emotions: Sources and Methods for the Study of Emotions in the Greek World*. Stuttgart, 268–91.

Mastrocinque, A. (2017) *The Mysteries of Mithras: A Different Account*. Tübingen.

Merkelbach, R. and Stauber, J. (1996) 'Die Orakel des Apollon von Klaros', *Epigraphica Anatolica* 27: 1–54.

Moullou, D. and Topalis, F. V. (2017) 'Reconstructing artificial light in ancient Greece', in C. Papadopoulos and H. Moyes (eds), *The Oxford Handbook of Light in Archaeology*. Oxford [online resource. DOI: 10.1093/oxfordhb/9780198788218.013.33].

Muñiz Grijalvo, E. (forthcoming) 'Imperial mysteries and religious experience', in A. Alvar Nuño, J. Alvar Ezquerra, and G. Woolf (eds), *Sensorium. Sensory Perceptions in Roman Polytheism*. Leiden.

Mylonopoulos, I. (2018) '"Brutal are the children of the night"! Nocturnal violence in Greek art', in A. Chaniotis (ed.), *La nuit. Imaginaire et réalités nocturnes dans le monde gréco-romain*. Entretiens Hardt 64. Geneva, 173–200.

Parisinou, E. (2000) *The Light of the Gods. The Role of Light in Archaic and Classical Greek Cult*. London.

Parker, R. (2005) *Polytheism and Society at Athens*. Oxford.

Parker, R. (2016) 'The nameless goddess of Marmarini', *Zeitschrift für Papyrologie und Epigraphik* 199: 58–9.

Parker, R. and Scullion, S. (2016) 'The mysteries of the Goddess of Marmarini', *Kernos* 29: 209–66.

Petropoulos, M. (1999) *Τα εργαστήρια των ρωμαϊκών λυχναριών της Πάτρας και το λυχνομαντείο*. Athens.

Petrovic, I. (2007) *Von den Toren des Hades zu den Hallen des Olymp. Artemiskult bei Theokrit und Kallimachos*. Leiden.

Pirenne-Delforge, V. (2008) *Retour à la source. Pausanias et la religion grecque*. Liège.

Pirenne-Delforge, V. (2018) 'Nyx est, elle aussi, une divinité. La nuit dans les mythes et les cultes grecs', in A. Chaniotis (ed.), *La nuit. Imaginaire et réalités nocturnes dans le monde gréco-romain*. Entretiens Hardt 64. Geneva, 131–65.

Podvin, J.-L. (2011) *Luminaire et cultes isiaques*. Montagnac.

Podvin, J.-L. (2014) 'Illuminer le temple: la lumière dans les sanctuaires isiaques à l'époque gréco-romaine', *Revue des Etudes Anciennes* 116: 23–42.

Prandi, L. (1983) 'L'Heraion di Platea e la festa di Daidala', in M. Sordi (ed.), *Santuari e politica nel mondo antico*. Milan, 82–94.

Purves, A. C. (ed.) (2017) *Touch and the Ancient Senses*. London and New York.

Renberg, G. (2016) 'I.GrÉgLouvre 11 and the *Lychnaption*: a topographical problem at Saqqâra', *Zeitschrift für Papyrologie und Epigraphik* 200, 215–18.

Renberg, G. (2017) *Where Dreams May Come. Incubation Sanctuaries in the Greco-Roman World*. Leiden.

Rice, E. (1983) *The Grand Procession of Ptolemy Philadelphus*. Oxford.

Robert, L. (1937) *Études anatoliennes. Recherches sur les inscriptions grecques de l'Asie Mineure*. Paris.

Rudolph, K. C. (2018) *Taste and the Ancient Senses*. London and New York.

Sakellarakis, Y. and Sapouna-Sakellaraki, E. (2013) *Το Ιδαίο Άντρο: ιερό και μαντείο*. Athens.

Sapouna, P. (1998) *Die Bildlampen römischer Zeit aus der Idäischen Zeusgrotte auf Kreta*. Oxford.

Schettino, M. T. and Pittia, S. (eds) (2012) *Les sons du puvoir dans les mondes anciens. Actes du colloque international de l'Université de la Rochelle (25–27 novembre 2010)*. Besançon.

Schlesier, R. (2018) 'Sappho bei Nacht', in A. Chaniotis (ed.), *La nuit. Imaginaire et réalités nocturnes dans le monde gréco-romain*. Entretiens Hardt 64. Geneva, 91–121.

Seidel, Y. (2012) *Künstliches Licht im individuellen, familiären und öffentlichen Lebensbereich.* Vienna.

Sfameni Gasparro, G. (1999) 'Alessandro di Abonutico, lo "pseudo-profeta" ovvero come construirsi un'identità religiosa. II. L'oracolo e i misteri', in C. Bonnet and A. Motte (eds), *Les syncrétismes religieux dans le monde méditérranéen antique. Actes du colloque international en l'honneur de Franz Cumont.* Brussels and Rome, 275–305.

Squire, M. (ed.) (2016) *Sight and the Ancient Senses.* London and New York.

Trümpy, C. (1998) 'Feste zur Vollmondszeit. Die religiösen Feiern Attikas im Monatslauf und der vorgeschichtliche attische Kultkalender', *Zeitschrift für Papyrologie und Epigraphik* 121: 109–15.

Tzifopoulos, Y. (2010) *'Paradise' Earned. The Bacchic-Orphic Gold Lamellae of Crete.* Washington, DC.

Ustinova, Y. (2009) *Caves and the Ancient Greek Mind: Descending Underground in the Search of Ultimate Truth.* Oxford.

Vermaseren, M. J. (1971) *Mithraica I. The Mithraeum at S. Maria Capua Vetere.* Leiden.

Versnel, H. S. (1991) 'Beyond cursing: the appeal to justice in judicial prayers', in C. A. Faraone and D. Obbink (eds), *Magika Hiera. Ancient Greek Magic and Religion.* Oxford, 60–106.

Versnel, H. S. (2003) 'Sachliche Sprache und emotionale Sprache in griechischen und römischen Fluch-Texten', in A. Kneppe and D. Metzler (eds), *Die emotionale Dimension antiker Religiosität.* Münster, 87–116.

Versnel, H. S. (2010) 'Prayers for justice, east and west. New finds and publications since 1990', in R. L. Gordon and F. Marco Simón (eds), *Magical Practice in the Latin West. Papers from the International Conference held at the University of Zaragoza, 30 Sept.–1st Oct. 2005.* Leiden, 275–354.

Versnel, H. S. (2012) 'Response to a critique', in M. Piranomonte and F. Marco Simón (eds), *Contesti Magici—Contextos Magicos.* Rome, 33–45.

Viedebandt, O. (1922) 'Kotyle', in *Real-Encyclopädie der classischen Altertumswissenschaft* XI.1. Stuttgart, 1546–8.

von Hesberg, H. (1987) 'Mechanische Kunstwerke und ihre Bedeutung für die höfische Kunst des frühen Hellenismus', *Marburger Winckelmann-Programm*, 47–72.

Wilson, A. (2018) 'Roman nightlife', in A. Chaniotis (ed.), *La nuit. Imaginaire et réalités nocturnes dans le monde gréco-romain.* Entretiens Hardt 64. Geneva, 59–81.

11
Conclusions and Future Directions

Zahra Newby

11.1. The material expression of social networks, collaborations and hierarchies

The papers collected in this volume explore the material dynamics of festivals in a number of different ways, showing both how material evidence asserted and constructed social connections, hierarchies, and identities and how spatial and material frameworks gave meaning to the activities which took place within them. In this concluding chapter, I will draw together some of these threads, to suggest the ways in which they further our understanding of the social roles played by festivals in the Graeco-Roman East, illuminate the workings of material culture, and also offer a foundation for further research.

A key strand running through a number of the chapters in the volume is the idea that material culture represents, confirms, and creates the social meaning for festivals, identifying the roles played by particular groups or individuals and commemorating links between them. Inscriptions, in particular, place individuals or cities within a social network, underlining the connections between particular groups, or setting up dialogues of conversation or competition. Within the world of the Roman empire, the emperor was clearly at the top of the social pyramid, with overall responsibility for authorizing new festivals and confirming the rewards and benefits which accrued to victorious performers. Occasionally present in person, more often he was symbolically present through the images which decorated festival spaces or were carried in processions, and through his inscribed name which stamped his authority over individual festivals and the wider festival calendar.

Scharff shows the centrality of the emperor within imperial festival culture, as well as the ways in which victorious athletes responded to that centrality in their epigraphic self-representation, advertising their 'proximity to power'. Yet these athletic inscriptions do not only set up connections between the victor and the emperor; they also operated in competition with other victor inscriptions, placing their honorand as 'first' of a given area, or commemorating the numbers of cities in which they held citizenships or were members of the *boule*.[1] Thus athletic

---

[1] Scharff, Section 2.4 above.

inscriptions assert both vertical (athlete-emperor) and horizontal (athlete-athlete, or athlete-city) connections, in which the athlete takes on different levels of primacy. These assert the victorious athlete's place as a valued subject and member of a global community, but also as occupying a privileged position among his peers.

Gordillo Hervás's examination of the inscriptions from Alexandria Troas also reveals the preeminent place held by the emperor in imperial festival culture, but this time in relation to a different set of agents, the synods representing the interests of athletes and performers which played a crucial role in the organization of ancient festivals. Her analysis shows that while the emperor set out the legal and chronological frameworks in which festivals took place, the synods had an important role in the dissemination of these rules. The challenges of organizing an empire-wide system, with consistent rules and rewards, are clearly shown by these letters. But they also reveal the material means by which the emperor's authority was stamped onto the cities and sanctuaries of the empire and the opportunities that individual cities took to assert themselves and their local festivals.

The key role played by the Artists of Dionysos earlier in the Hellenistic period is also shown in Grigsby's chapter on Boiotia. Local branches of the guild played an active role in the creation of a distinctively musical agonistic culture in Boiotia during the Hellenistic period, and their role was made manifest through the prominent display of inscriptions celebrating the collaboration between cities and the guild in public spaces such as in the sanctuary at Delphi. Here too, as in Scharff's chapter, we see both how individual inscriptions celebrate social relationships and collaboration but also how they can be seen as players within a wider conversation of civic competition when considered within their original contexts.

The inscriptions set up at Delphi on the wall of the Theban treasury advertised Thebes' Trieterides festival to a wider Panhellenic audience, asserting Thebes' importance, in conversation with earlier inscriptions elsewhere in the sanctuary, such as that recording the grant of *asylia* to the Itoneion in the 260s BC, which was positioned near the entrance to the Temple of Apollo. The inscription includes details of an earlier Amphictyonic decree of c.228–225 BC which says that the text should be inscribed on *stelai* at Delphi and Thebes, as well as a later decree (c.214 BC), asking again for it to be inscribed, presumably specifying the particular location of the Theban treasury.[2] Another decree of c.228–226 BC records Amphictyonic recognition of the Ptoia festival at Akraiphia and includes the instruction that it should be inscribed both at the Ptoion and at Delphi.[3] Though the Delphic copy does not survive we can see how this Panhellenic

---

[2] Itoneion: *SEG* 18, 240; Trieterides festival: *F.Delphes* III.1, 351. The reference to the Treasury is restored, but plausible given the findspot. See Section 8.2.1–2 above.
[3] *IG* VII 4135. The surviving copy comes from the Ptoion but states that it is also to be inscribed at Delphi (ll. 18–19). See Section 8.2.4 above.

sanctuary acted as a stage for display of the recognition granted to Boiotian sanctuaries and festivals. The additional request for the Trieterides degree to be inscribed specifically on the Theban Treasury suggests that individual players were aware of a sense of competition, and keen to draw attention to their particular claims to prominence. The duplication of texts in local sanctuaries and the Panhellenic centre at Delphi also creates a network of connections, commemorating Amphictyonic approval of specific festivals and cults. Christina Williamson shows how similar networks were celebrated in the decrees inscribed in the sanctuaries at Magnesia and Stratonikeia. Here, however, it is the individual city and the festival whose recognition through the Mediterranean world they are proud to assert which lies at the heart of the network created.[4]

Inscriptions speak of social relationships, connections, and hierarchies, but in their wider spatial contexts they also speak to one another, collectively creating networks of collaboration and competition.[5] Similar conversations of rivalry or emulation can be seen in the inscriptions of the theatre at Aphrodisias, as discussed by Naomi Carless Unwin. As her analysis shows, the inscriptions set up to commemorate benefactors of the city seem to engage consciously with the deeds and records of the first benefactor, C. Julius Zoilos. Thus the theatre offers a collection vision of the euergetic culture of Aphrodisias, which could have been specifically reinvigorated at times of festival by ceremonies such as the crowning of statues.[6]

Similar assertions of social roles and hierarchies, and networks of connection and competition can also be seen in visual media, sometimes in combination with inscribed texts. As Newby's chapter shows, the decoration of the theatres at Hierapolis and Perge offers different visions of their festival cultures. Hierapolis celebrates both the authority of the imperial family and the importance of the city, as well as the parts played by performers, officials and sacred envoys; Perge offers a more targeted vision, drawing attention to the inclusion of all age groups of the male citizen body in the honour of their patron goddess. Calomino's chapter offers yet another view on civic festivals, showing how Nikaia used her festivals in honour of the imperial family to create links with the imperial authority and gain prestige in relation to her neighbour. In both these chapters, specific iconography is chosen to assert a particular message, and identify the individual aspects of civic festivals which have significance for their communities. Both also set their cities into their regional contexts, drawing in participants from outside at Hierapolis, but asserting primacy in opposition to their rival Nikomedia, at Nikaia.

---

[4] See above Section 9.4.1–2 and Figs 9.8 and 9.10.
[5] For a fuller discussion of the patterns and dynamics in the epigraphy relating to festivals, see Carless Unwin (forthcoming).
[6] Carless Unwin, Section 7.2 above.

11.2. Forging memories and identities through material culture

A number of the chapters collected here have explored the ways in which material culture can mediate between the experience of ephemeral events and the creation of longer-term memories or expectations. Representations of aspects of festivals in either visual or written form can help to set expectations about the normative workings of festivals, or to solidify a particular authorized record into the visual landscape. This might comprise particular expressions of religious festivals, as shown in Newby's chapter, or of wider civic concerns, presented to the civic body on occasions when they gathered together, as at festivals.

Carless Unwin's chapter shows how the inscribing of the archive wall of the theatre at Aphrodisias presented a particular view of Aphrodisias' history and relationship with Rome to its citizens. This gave a sense of prestige to the city, and created a cumulative view of imperial recognition over a series of centuries.[7] At Lagina, the festival of the Hekatesia-Romaia accommodated the new power of Rome into Stratonikeia's religious identity.[8] Earlier than at Aphrodisias, Rome's recognition of the loyalty of the city (here during the Mithradatic wars) was inscribed on the temple at Lagina in close proximity to the records of the cities which recognised the new festival.[9] Festival activities in the precinct worked together with the inscriptions and imagery to celebrate Lagina's connections with Rome, and the importance and prestige of her patron goddess.[10] The records of civic history inscribed at both Lagina and Aphrodisias show how the spaces frequented during festivals—sanctuaries and theatres—were charged with particular memories, which could be reinvigorated and recalled by individuals visiting during times of festival.

In other cases, imagery could evoke particular aspects of the religious, mythological, and historical past to create new meanings and identities in the present. Mairi Gkikaki's chapter shows how the images portrayed on tokens appealed to Athens' religious traditions and important gods, as well as to key moments in its mythological and historical past, through the figures of Theseus and Themistokles. These suggest use in particular festivals, but also created a shared cultural memory of the city which bound together those using the tokens, while also celebrating particular notable elite families. Grigsby's analysis of the festivals at Boiotia also shows how cities and synods worked in combination to promote a particularly musical flavour to the festivals celebrated here. Drawing on the longstanding connection of the poet Hesiod with Boiotia, the celebration of festivals with a

---

[7] Carless Unwin, Section 7.4 above.   [8] Williamson, Section 9.4.2 above
[9] *I.Stratonikeia* 505, 507–8; see van Bremen (2010) and Williamson, Section 9.4.2 above.
[10] For discussion of the interpretations of the Temple's north frieze see Baumeister (2007) and van Bremen (2010).

focus on musical performance, including that of the rhapsode, suggests an archaizing element to festival culture here, which sought, in both the Hellenistic and Roman periods, to maximize the prestige which could be gained from their musical past.[11]

Indeed, some of the patterns shown in the chapters here map well onto the wider picture of the importance of the past in the construction of civic memories and identities in the Roman present.[12] It is notable that reference to and revival of past traditions seems to be especially common in the area of mainland Greece, with the cities of Asia Minor often more content to draw prestige from their contemporary links. This emerges well from the comparison of Chapters 4 and 5: while on the civic coinage of Nikaia and Nikomedia the key reference is to the favour of and loyalty to the imperial family, on the tokens from Athens it is to the city's past and traditions.[13]

Indeed, in his forthcoming monograph on civic coinages associated with festivals, Calomino notes similar patterns in the material as a whole. While some cities chose to focus on assertions of the continuity of their festivals, with references to the long-established iconography of the festival wreath, as in the distinctive spiked crown which appears on coins minted at Nikopolis,[14] others adopted novel forms of representation suited to the particular political moment. Calomino also notes a tendency of the civic coinages of mainland Greece to stress long-standing civic festivals as opposed to those celebrating the imperial family, which appear much more commonly on the coins of Asia Minor.[15]

11.3. Static and portable monuments: capturing the ephemeral and creating communities

Fixed images and texts required their audience to move past them, engaging with the text or imagery presented in a particular space. The activities in which viewers were engaged would have affected how this imagery was understood, with individual texts or images being activated in particular ways when specific activities were taking place. Thus when processions carrying the cult statuettes of Apollo, Artemis, or Aphrodite entered the theatres at Hierapolis, Perge, and Aphrodisias, as they would have done during times of religious festivals, the images and texts

---

[11] Section 8.2 above.

[12] The bibliography on this is extensive; for some useful discussions see Alcock (2002); Spawforth (2012); and Dijkstra et al. (2017). On the idea of 'invented traditions', see Hobsbawm and Ranger (1983); Boschung, Busch, and Versluys (2015). For further discussion of athletic festivals and activity, with relation to the Second Sophistic, see Newby (2005), 7–14 and 143–271.

[13] Note, though, that Gkikaki, Section 5.5 above, suggests that images of Theseus and Herakles could also be seen as references to festivals honouring the emperors Hadrian and Commodus.

[14] e.g. https://rpc.ashmus.ox.ac.uk/coins/4/4177, last accessed 5 June 2023.

[15] Calomino (forthcoming), ch. 5.

within the theatre would take on additional significance. At Aphrodisias, a himation bust of a priest carrying the statuette of the goddess was found in the Atrium House.[16] We can imagine its flesh-and-blood equivalent carrying the image of Aphrodite into the theatre, and setting up a direct connection with the bust statue of the goddess dedicated there by one Theodotos.[17] Other replications of the cult image across the cityscape also acted to set up connections with one another, linked together during times of ritual procession.[18]

Portable and replicated objects, such as coins or tokens, could work differently, helping to bring together separate members of a community through common ownership of the same visual imagery. The tokens studied by Gkikaki helped to create communities engaged in the same ritual actions, while the coins discussed by Calomino also asserted difference, pitching Nikaia against her neighbour Nikomedia. In both cases the imagery shown could have helped to activate memories or expectations of personal involvement in festivals either as a participant or a spectator. However, while those issued with tokens were likely given them for a particular use within this context, those handling civic coinage might be doing so for other reasons entirely. The relationship between user and imagery thus varies, from a very tight connection to a particular activity, to a looser one, in which the handler of a coin might be an outsider, to be persuaded by the view of Nikaia's festival culture and closeness to the imperial family presented by the coins, or even a citizen from the rival community of Nikomedia. The response of the user to the imagery of the coin would vary depending on whether they were a citizen of Nikaia, a resident from another regional community, or a complete outsider, visiting the city or region for a specific reason. While most civic coinages seem to have circulated within a fairly limited geographical range, further research into coins found in excavations might help to unpick some of this variety of response.[19]

Gkikaki's analysis of the senses of community created by the tokens of Athens prompts us to consider how distinctive or not this case study might be. While work has been done on the clay tesserae from Palmyra which also seem to have functioned like tokens, a vast amount of other evidence from the Greek East still remains to be catalogued and analysed.[20] Rubina Raja's analysis of the Palmyra tesserae has shown that they were closely linked with priestly euergetism and the granting of access to sacred banquets, but Rowan's analysis of the tokens from

---

[16] Smith (2006), 238–40, no. 127, pl. 95.   [17] *I.Aphrodisias 2007*, 8.228.
[18] See, in reference to Perge, Newby in Newby and Calomino (2022), 41–8. For discussions of the ways the interaction between movement and monuments helped to create memories in Rome, see Östenberg, Malmberg, and Bjørnebye (2015); Latham (2016); Popkin (2016).
[19] See Section 1.1, n. 35 above, and Calomino (forthcoming), ch. 3.
[20] On Palmyra see Raja (2020) with earlier bibliography. These objects take a different form to other tokens, but seem to have functioned in similar ways. A project to investigate the tokens from Greece and Asia Minor is planned by Rowan and Gkikaki. On the tokens from Athens see Gkikaki (forthcoming); for other work on ancient tokens see Crisà, Gkikaki, and Rowan (2019); on the tokens from Ephesos see Kuhn (2014).

Roman Italy shows a much wider array of potential associations between the imagery on tokens and festivals and spectacles, including legends such as 'IO SAT IO', an abbreviated version of the chant from the Saturnalia festival.[21] Here the tokens invite their users to vocalize their participation in the festival, and later recall the raucous shouting which accompanied its festivities. Coins from the Greek east also sometimes include legends which may evoke the acclamations given at festivals. Peter Weiss has suggested that the legend ΕΙΣ ΑΓΩΝ which appears on some third-century coins from Perge should be understood as an acclamation, chanted by the crowd during the festivities.[22] Such coins may have been issued as part of the public distributions which took place during festivals, prompting their recipients to join in particular chants and later prompting memory of this emotional moment of unity in civic pride. They could help to create a moment of, and later a memory of, emotional community, where different members of society joined together in celebration of their festival, city, and goddess.[23]

Other forms of material culture could have acted as souvenirs to recall an individual's participation in a particular festival. Creating replicas of cult images was an important part of a city's economic prosperity, as is memorably shown in the episode recounted in the Acts of the Apostles, where the silversmith Demetrius of Ephesos rails against the threat to the prominence of the patron goddess Artemis, and the craftsmen's livelihoods, posed by the visiting Christians.[24] Mould fragments and medallions found in the Agora at Athens show that detailed miniature replicas of both the head of Athena Parthenos and her shield were manufactured here, probably to be sold as souvenirs to those attending the goddess' festival or visiting her temple.[25] Lamps found at Nikopolis in mainland Greece show a prize table with the distinctive wreath of bulrushes awarded to victors at the Aktian games, echoing the imagery shown on civic coins; while the coins were minted by the city, the lamps may have been produced by local workshops to satisfy a demand from those attending the games, and wanting to take a souvenir home.[26]

Such souvenirs of past experience may have evoked memories of one's participation in ritual activities, or spectatorship of contests, after the fact. As Popkin

---

[21] Raja (2020); Rowan (2023), ch. 4. Examples include Rostovtzeff (1903), nos. 504, 506–7. See https://coins.warwick.ac.uk/token-types/id/TURS504; https://coins.warwick.ac.uk/token-types/id/TURS506; https://coins.warwick.ac.uk/token-types/id/TURS507, last accessed 5 June 2023.

[22] Weiss (1991), 362, n. 26; 375, nos. 6–7 linking them with the legends on the graffiti found in Tacitus street, as well as the acclamation inscription found there: *I.Perge* nos. 313, 331, 333–7.

[23] On rituals as times of shared emotion see Chaniotis (2006); on the link between festivals and memories see Beck and Wiemer (2009); also Popkin (2016), 116–25 in the context of the Roman triumph. On acclamations and emotions see Kuhn (2012). On emotional communities, see Rosenwein (2006).

[24] *Acts of the Apostles* 19:23–7. For discussions see Elsner (1997); Popkin (2022), 25

[25] Athenian Agora Excavations inv. nos. 1,3703; T 2367; T 3577. See Popkin (2022), 35, 38, figs 14, 19, 20.

[26] Pliakou (2007), 559, no. 106. Similar images on coins: *RPC* III, 501, 566.

notes, souvenirs could make a place present even when it was absent, 'acting as proxies for that which had been experienced'.[27] She presents them as the mirror of graffiti recording the past presence of an individual at a particular site.[28] While Popkin's study is focused on touristic visits, tourism and pilgrimage were closely linked in the ancient world.[29] We can see records of participation, such as those at Aphrodisias discussed by Carless Unwin (Section 7.5-6) as the mirror of the material mementoes which visitors might have acquired during their participation in a festival, which could then evoke that experience later in time. However, they can also act vicariously, allowing someone who had not actually visited or experienced a particular place or event to acquire a sense of shared experience and memory of it, thus creating or projecting senses of community.[30]

There is scope here for further study to explore the common patterns as well as regional or local variations which can be determined in this material, and to explore the ways that small or disposable objects might have helped to disseminate particular visions or memories of festival activities across participating groups. Images of gladiators, charioteers, and theatrical performances were all common on portable objects, sometimes bearing inscriptions echoing the chants of spectators urging on their favourites, imaginatively bringing their users into the experience of spectatorship.[31] Greek athletes seem less common on this material, while gladiators and wild beast hunts are generally missing from imagery on civic coinages even though we know that they were an important part of festivals in honour of the imperial cult. References to gladiators and *venationes* appear in architectural reliefs, monumental tombs (probably commemorating those who funded such spectacles), as well as in gladiator tombstones from across the Greek East, so their omission from civic coinages is a deliberate choice and may reflect the desire to assert traditional Greek aspects of festivals and spectacle in this particular medium.[32] While this volume has focussed specifically on Greek-style festivals and on public uses of festival iconography, there is room for further research to examine the interplays between Greek and Roman-style festivals and spectacles and their representation in material culture and to interrogate the choices made by different groups. The normative picture of festivals which emerges from elite-authored texts and images could be very different from the passions revealed by objects prized by others within the same society.[33]

---

[27] Popkin (2022), 8.   [28] Popkin (2022), 8.
[29] On pilgrimage see e.g. Elsner and Rutherford (2007); Friese and Kristensen (2017).
[30] Popkin (2022), 18.   [31] See Popkin (2022), 152-5.
[32] Dunbabin (2016), 181-6; on scenes of Erotes fighting beasts in theatre reliefs see Di Napoli (2015) 262-7, 274-5. On the omission from coinages see Calomino (forthcoming) ch. 4. On the ways gladiators aligned themselves with athletes in their self-representation in the East, see Mann (2009), 284-8.
[33] For a discussion of the ways material evidence from Rome reveals a different picture of attitudes to athletics from that given in the literary sources, see Newby (2005), 21-87.

11.4. Material framings of the ritual experience

A further aim of this volume was to assert the active role played by material culture in creating and framing the festival experience. As already shown, the chapters by Newby and Carless Unwin show how the visual display of the important space of the theatre helped to create an elite-authored view of what particular festivals meant, and how the city's history should be remembered. In the preceding two chapters of the book we explore instead how the spatial and material framing of ritual activities helps to activate particularly charged emotions and experiences.

Williamson's examination of the architectural development of sanctuaries as enclosed spaces from the Hellenistic into the Roman periods demonstrates the emotional effects that this created for participants. These enclosed inward-facing space fostered a heightened awareness of the communal rituals in which all were involved, intensifying the ritual experience. Taken together with the increased catchment of Hellenistic festivals, it helped to create a shared ritual community. Common architectural forms would have fostered a sense of familiarity even among those visiting from far away, linking the participants together and creating a communal emotionally-charged experience.

Angelos Chaniotis likewise explores the ways that material frameworks created a particular emotional character by focusing on nocturnal festivals. Material culture such as lamps and torches helped to create the atmosphere of these rituals, fostering a closeness and sense of community between worshippers, while rituals themselves often involved conspicuous destruction of material objects, as in the fires which characterized the rituals of Zeus in the Idaean Cave on Crete and the Great Daidala in Boiotia. In focusing on the emotional and ritual experience engendered by material frameworks, these chapters link in with a wider interest in recreating ancient religious experiences, and the roles played by the senses in their creation.[34]

Throughout the papers collected here we can see a number of common themes—the important roles played by the emperor, performers, and civic elites, the ways in which the past can be used to assert prestige in the present, and the importance of positioning oneself upon a wider international stage. Yet there is also much variability in the ways individuals and communities chose to represent themselves and their festivals. A number of different types of festivals are represented here, ranging from local ephebic festivals to those given international status, or which celebrated a city's *neokoria*. We have seen both continuity with the Hellenistic period, and also change, as the emperor comes to take centre stage. The focus here has been on the areas of mainland Greece and Asia Minor;

---

[34] e.g. Eidinow et al. (2022), especially Scott (2022). For other work on the sensory aspects of festivals see e.g. Weddle (2017); Power (2019); Roberts (2019).

further research could extend this by comparison with other areas of the empire, and with discussion of the self-representation of other individual groups. Taken as a whole, however, we hope that this volume shows the importance of considering material culture as an active agent in the experience of ancient festivals, guiding participants in their different roles, setting up expectations and authorized memories, and framing and constructing particular emotional and ritual experiences.

Works Cited

Alcock, S. E. (2002) *Archaeologies of the Greek Past: Landscape, Monuments and Memories*. Cambridge.

Baumeister, P. (2007) *Der Fries des Hekateions von Lagina. Neue Untersuchungen zu Monument und Kontext*. BYZAS 6. Istanbul.

Beck, H. and Wiemer, H.-U. (eds) (2009) *Feiern und Erinnern. Geschichtsbilder im Spiegel antiker Feste*. Studien zur Alten Geschichte 12. Berlin.

Boschung, D., Busch, A., and Versluys, M. J. (eds) (2015) *Reinventing 'The Invention of Tradition'? Indigenous Pasts and the Roman Present*. Morphomata 32. Paderborn.

van Bremen, R. (2010) 'The inscribed documents on the Temple of Hekate at Lagina and the date and meaning of the Temple frieze', in R. van Bremen and J.-M. Carbon (eds), *Hellenistic Karia. Proceedings of the First International Conference on Hellenistic Karia—Oxford, 29 June–2 July 2006*. Bordeaux, 483–503.

Calomino, D. (forthcoming) *Pride, Profit and Prestige. Civic Coinage and Greek Festival Culture in the Roman East*.

Carless Unwin, N. (forthcoming) *Inscribing Festival Culture in the Graeco-Roman East*.

Chaniotis, A. (2006) 'Rituals between norms and emotions: rituals as shared experience and memory', in E. Stavrianopoulou (ed.), *Ritual and Communication in the Graeco-Roman World*. Kernos Suppl. 16. Liège, 211–38.

Crisà, N., Gkikaki, M., and Rowan, C. (eds) (2019) *Tokens: Culture, Connections, Communities*. London.

Dijkstra, T. M., Kuin, I. N., Moser, M., and Weidgenannt, D. (eds) (2017) *Strategies of Remembering in Greece under Rome (100 BC–100 AD)*. Leiden.

Di Napoli, V. (2015) 'Figured reliefs from the theatres of Roman Asia Minor', *Logeion. A Journal of Ancient Theatre* 5: 260–93.

Dunbabin, K. M. D. (2016) *Theatre and Spectacle in the Art of the Roman Empire*. Ithaca.

Eidinow, E., Geertz, A., and North, J. (eds) (2022) *Cognitive Approaches to Ancient Religious Experience*. Ancient Religion and Cognition. Cambridge.

Elsner, J. (1997) 'The origins of the icon: pilgrimage, religion and visual culture in the Roman east as "resistance" to the centre', in S. E. Alcock (ed.), *The Early Roman Empire in the East*. Oxford, 178–99.

Elsner, J. and Rutherford, J. (eds) (2007) *Pilgrimage in Graeco-Roman and Early Christian Antiquity: Seeing the Gods*. Oxford.

Friese, W. and Kristensen, T. M. (eds) (2017) *Excavating Pilgrimage. Archaeological Approaches to Sacred Travel and Movement in the Ancient World*. Abingdon and New York.

Gkikaki, M. (forthcoming) *Symbola: Athenian Tokens from Classical to Roman Times*. Liverpool.

Hobsbawm, E. and Ranger, T. (eds) (1983) *The Invention of Tradition*. Cambridge.

Kuhn, C. T. (2012) 'Emotionality in the political culture of the Graeco-Roman East. The role of acclamations', in A. Chaniotis (ed.), *Unveiling Emotions: Sources and Methods for the Study of Emotions in the Greek World*. Stuttgart, 295–316.

Kuhn, C. T. (2014) 'Prosopographical notes on four lead tesserae from Roman Ephesos', *Zeitschrift für Papyrologie und Epigraphik* 190: 137–40.

Latham, J. A. (2016) *Performance, Memory, and Processions in Ancient Rome. The Pompa Circensis from the Late Republic to Late Antiquity*. New York.

Mann. C. (2009) 'Gladiators in the Greek East: a case study in Romanization', *International Journal of the History of Sport* 26.2: 272–97.

Newby, Z. (2005) *Greek Athletics in the Roman World: Victory and Virtue*. Oxford.

Newby, Z. and Calomino, D. (2022) 'The materiality of Greek festivals in the Roman East. The view from Perge', *Asia Minor* 2: 41–54.

Östenberg, I., Malmberg, S., and Bjørnebye, J. (eds) (2015) *The Moving City: Processions, Passages and Promenades in Ancient Rome*. London.

Pliakou, G. (2007) 'Lychnaria apo tis nekropoleis tes romaikes Nikopoles', in K. L. Zachos (ed.), *Nikopolis 2: praktika tou Deuterou Diethnous Symposiou gia te Nikopole, 11–15 Septemvriou 2002*. Preveza, I. 533–62.

Popkin, M. (2016) *The Architecture of the Roman Triumph. Monuments, Memory and Identity*. New York.

Popkin, M. (2022). *Souvenirs and the Experience of Empire in Ancient Rome*. Cambridge.

Power, T. (2019) 'The sound of the sacred', in S. Butler and S. Nooter (eds), *Sound and the Ancient Senses*. London and New York, 15–30.

Raja, R. (2020) 'Come and dine with us: invitations to ritual dining as part of social strategies in sacred spaces in Palmyra', in V. Gasparini et al. (eds), *Lived Religion in the Ancient Mediterranean World: Approaching Religious Transformations from Archaeology, History and Classics*. Berlin: 385–404.

Roberts, E. M. (2019) 'Weaving for Athena: the Arrhephoroi and mundane acts of religious devotion', *Journal of Hellenic Religion* 12: 61–84.

Rosenwein, B. H. (2006) *Emotional Communities in the Early Middle Ages*. Ithaca.

Rostovtzeff, M. (1903) *Tesserarum urbis Romae et suburbi plumbearum sylloge*. St. Petersburg.

Rowan, C. (2023) *Tokens and Social Life in Roman Imperial Italy*. Cambridge.

Scott, M. (2022) 'Walls and the ancient Greek ritual experience: the sanctuary of Demeter and Kore at Eleusis', in E. Eidinow, A. Geertz, and J. North (eds), *Cognitive Approaches to Ancient Religious Experience. Ancient Religion and Cognition*. Cambridge: 193–217.

Smith, R. R. R. (2006) *Aphrodisias II. Roman Portrait Statuary from Aphrodisias*. Mainz.

Spawforth, A. J. (2012) *Greece and the Augustan Cultural Revolution*. Cambridge.

Weddle, C. (2017) 'Blood, fire and feasting: the role of touch and taste in Graeco-Roman animal sacrifice', in E. Betts (ed.), *Senses of the Empire: Multisensory Approaches to Roman Culture*. London, 104–19.

Weiss, P. (1991) 'Auxe Perge. Beobachtungen zu einem bemerkenswerten städtischen Dokument des späten 3. Jahrhunderts n. Chr.', *Chiron* 21: 353–92.

Index

For the benefit of digital users, indexed terms that span two pages (e.g., 52–53) may, on occasion, appear on only one of those pages.

age categories 149, 162, 169
agonothesia 142–4, 193
agonothetes 10–11, 52–3, 148–9, 185, 190–1, 218–20, 227, 230–1, 234, 241–2, 241n.140
agora 250–3, 258–61, 263, 268–9, 271–5, 278–9
Agoraios Kolonos 97, 100–1, 119
Agrionia, *see* Trieterides of Dionysos Kadmeios
Aitolia 224
Aitolian League 220
Akraiphia 10–11, 215–16, 219, 230–2, 236, 240–4, 323–4, *see also* Ptoia, Soteria
Aktian games 61, 84, 86–7, 193–6, 328
Alexander of Abonou Teichos 309–10, 314
Alexander the Great 105, 123–4, 214–15, 219
Alexandria Troas 2, 13, 32–4, 51–9, 64
altar 86, 88–9, 292, 296
Amphiaraia at Oropos 239–40, 244
Ankara 56
Antinoeia 110
Antioch in Pisidia 251–2, 259, 264, 267, 275–7, 279
  sanctuary of Men Askaenos 251–2, 259, 264, 267, 275–7, 279
Antiparos, sanctuary at Despotiko 259
Antoninus Pius 11–12
Aphrodisias 11, 15, 26, 61, 63–4, 153–4, 179–208, 300, 302–3, 324, 326–9
  Archive Wall 197–201, 208, 325, *see also* Aphrodite of Aphrodisias
Aphrodite of Aphrodisias 185, 326–7
Apollo 10–11, 14, 146–7, 151–2, 159–60
  Apollo Ptoios (Sanctuary of Akraiphia) 230–1, 242–4
  Apollo Smintheus 57–8
  Pythian Apollo 238
Apolloneia Pythia (Hierapolis) 144–5
aqueduct 11, 58
Arendt, Hannah 251–3
Argos 217–18, 218n.14, 232–3, 237, 243n.142
Aristokles Molossos 186–8
Arsinoe III 227–9, 227n.71
Artemis Ephesia 97–8, 146–7, 154–9
  mysteries of 121

Artemis Pergaia 14, 161–2, 165
Artists of Dionysos 2, 11, 13, 15–16, 33, 52, 151, 215–17, 323
  Artists of Dionysos (Athens) 217, 217n.10, 220n.28, 222n.38, 227, 233–4, 236–8, 240
  Artists of Dionysos (Helikon) 217–18, 232–3
  Artists of Dionysos (Ionia and the Hellespont) 217, 228–9, 233–4
  Artists of Dionysos (Isthmos and Nemea) 215, 217–19, 220n.28, 222–43
Asklepeia 78–9, 110
Asklepios 104–6, 110, 124, 297–8
Askra 215–17, 225
Asphaleia 220
asylia 165, 197–8, 219–24, 220n.29, 222n.39, 230–1, 243–4, 264–7, 269, 273–5, 323–4
Athena 101–2, 104–5, 110–11, 124
  Athena's rivalry with Poseidon 113n.70
  Athena Parthenos (Pheidias' cult statue of) 114–15, 117, 123
Athenaia 110
Athens 14, 16, 33, 53–5, 59–60, 76–7, 95, 328
  Odeion of Agrippa 115–16, 123
  Stoa of Attalos 102–3, 106–7, *see also* tokens
athletes 10, 13, 16, 36–42, 75–6, 84–5, 88–9, 149–50, 322–3, *see also* boxers, circuit-victors
Attalids 217, 263–6, 275
Augustus 100
Aurelian 105

Balbilleia/Barbilleia 63
banquet 10–11, 53, 300, 327–8
Basileia at Lebadeia 219, 222n.40, 229–30
benefactions, *see* euergetism
Bithynia 70–4
Boiotia 15, 214–17, 314, 323
  agonistic boom (1st century BC) 240, 244
  agonistic boom (3rd century BC) 214–15, 219–22, 243
  'artistic' identity 214–19, 229–31, 244–5
bouleuterion 11–12
boxers 193–7

INDEX

calendar, festival 13, 35, 51–3, 59–63
Caligula 242
Capitoline games 29–30, 59–61, 63
Caracalla 81–90, 105, 144–5, 199, *see also* Severans
cave 306–9
Chaironeia 238, 238n.119
chariot races 181–2, 203–4, 329
christians 181–2, 328
Chwe, Michael Suk-Young 251–2, 254–5
circle
  'inward-facing' 253–5, 258–60
  sacred 251–5, 279, *see also* circles 'inward-facing'
circuit, agonistic 32–5, 51, 53, 193–7, 240
circuit-victors 193–7
circus, *see* chariot races
cities 16, 42, 69–70
cities, rivalries of 70–4, 169, 219–20, 324
citizenry 96, 113, 119–20
citizenship, Roman 119
citizenships, multiple 38, 43
civic elite, *see* elite
Claudii
  of Marathon 112–13
  of Melite 112–13, 119
Claudius 240
Claudius Atticus, Tiberius 120–1
coinage
  circulation of 6, 327
  civic 4–6, 13–14, 69, 167–8, 326
  festival 5–6
  iconography 4–6, 13–14, 70, 72–81, 84–5, 326
Collins, Randall 254–5
Commodeia 75–6, 110–12
Commodus 75, 107–9, 199
  in the guise of Herakles 105, 110–12
common knowledge 251–2, 254–5, 279–80
community 14–16, 153–4, 251–2, *see also* citizenry, elite, ephebes, *gerousia*
  festival 95–6, 117–18, 122–3, 159–60, 327–8, 330
concord, see *homonoia*
Corinth 217–18, 232–3
Cornelius Sulla, L. 232, 236–41, 244
council membership 38, 43

Daidala 311, 314
Damas of Miletos 10–11
damnatio memoriae 89–90, 145
dances 10–11, 167
Delphi 51, 56–7, 60, 218, 220–5, 230–1, 234–8, 237n.114, 243–4, 323–4
  Delphic Amphictyony 217n.10, 220–3, 223n.47, 230–1, 244
  Theban Treasury 222–4, 222n.43

Demostheneia, *see* Oinoanda
Didyma 10–11
Diocletian's price edict 199–200
Diodoros Pasparos 190–1
Dionysia
  at Nikaia 79–81
  the Greater or City Dionysia at Athens 97–8, 114
Dionysiac Artists, *see* Artists of Dionysos
Dionysos 10, 104–6, 106n.39, 109, 113–14, 124, 290–1, 296–8
  Dionysos Eleuthereus 113–14
    Alkamenes' cult statue of 113–14, 117, 123
distribution 11, 97, 100, 109, 118–22, 327–8, *see also* euergetism
Dodona 262–3, 279
  Naia festival 262–3
  sanctuary of Zeus 259, 262–3
Domitian 30

egyptian cult 296–7, 313–14, *see also* Isis
Eleusinian mysteries 120–1
  priest of the Eleusinian Mysteries 120–1
Eleusis 111–12
Eleutheria at Plataia 219, 220n.31
Elis 217–18, 218n.14
elites 6, 9–10, 14, 16, 39–40, 96, 112–13, 118–20, 122, 139, 169–70, 201, 241–2, 329–30, *see also* euergetism
emotion 15–16, 254–5, 279–80, 291–6, 308–9, 314–15, 327–8, 330
emperor
  as *agonothetes* 30–1
  as competitor 28–9
  as spectator 31
  image of 75–7, 88–9.
  proximity to 26–7, 40–2, 197–9
  role in festivals 2, 10–13, 16, 29, 73–4, 100, 145–6, 322–3
  symbolic presence of 8, 13–14, 31–2, 84–5
enclosed space 252–5, 279–80
Epameinondas of Akraiphia 10–11, 242–3
ephebes 96, 107–8, 117–18, 121, 163–4, 201–2, *see also* processions
  festivals, *see* festivals, ephebic and *Theseia*
  games 104, 110
  naval contests 111n.62
  peri alkes contest 111–12
  ephebic decrees 110n.55, 112nn.66, 67, 116n.86, 122n.117
ephemeral 8, 139–40, 150–1, 159
Ephesos 8, 11, 31–2, 56, 76–7, 121, 153–6, 163–5, 217, 300, 310, *see also* Artemis Ephesia *and* tokens of Ephesos
Epidauros 238

epigram, agonistic 36
epigraphic habit 3, 179–81
epigraphy, see inscriptions
　as source on festivals 3
Epinikia
　at Athens 110
　at Thebes 238–9
epiphany 267–9, 273–5
eponymos archon 119–20
Erotideia at Thespiai 236, 240–1
Euboea 217–18
euergetism 10–12, 118–21, 139, 183–93, 207–8, 324
Eumolpids 120–1
Eusebeia 61, 64

Fabius Maximus, Paullus 57–9
feast, see banquet
festivals
　connected with imperial cult 74–5, 99, 110–11, 145–6, see also tokens of the imperial cult
　ephebic 14, 104, 110–12, 114, 330–1
　roman imperial Athens 95–8, 107–8, 122
　increase in number 1–2, 15, 51, 214–15, 250–1, 256–8, see also Boiotia, agonistic boom.
　nocturnal 15, 289–93, 304
　panhellenic 15, 250–1, 256–8, 278–9
　tokens 95–100, 107–8, 110–11, 119–20
fire ritual 308, 310–14
Flavius Xenion of Gortyn 120–1

Gallienus 78–9, 102–3
Gerasa 190–1
Germanikeia 110
gerousia
　archon of the 108–9, 121
　sacred 96, 108–10, 112n.69, 113, 117–20
　tokens of 113–14, 116–18
Geta 81–90, 145–6, see also Severans
gladiatorial contests 193, 203–4, 206, 329
Gordian III 199
graffiti 165–7, 181–2, 203–4, 206, 328–9
guilds, see Artists of Dionysos and Synod
gymnasium 10–12, 36
Gytheion 5, 163–4

Hadrian 2, 5, 11, 13, 32–5, 52–63, 97–8, 109, 122, 199, 232–3
　as New Dionysos 56
　associated with Theseus 108n.49
Hadrianeia 110
Haliartos 236
Handelmann, Don 168–9

Hekatomnids 260, 263
Helikon 215–18, 225, 232–3, 241n.136
Helios 104–5, 124
Hellenistic period 11, 15–16, 36–7, 153–4, 219–22, 256–8, 263, 292–3
Hephaistos 104–5, 124
Hera 311–13
Herakleia (Thebes) 216n.5, 230n.82, 241n.133
Herakleidae 111–12
Herakles 10–11, 14, 56, 101–2, 104–6, 110–12, 117, 124
　as model for the ephebes 111–12
　Farnese 111–12
Hermes/Mercury 10–11, 97–8, 100
Herodes Atticus 58–9, 113n.71, 120–1
　Odeion of 114
Heruli 95–6
　sack of Athens 95–7, 100, 102n.23, 111
Hesiod 215–17, 224–5, 225nn.60, 63, 229–30, 240–1, 241n.136, 243
Hierapolis 14, 140–60, 201–3, 324
Hierokles of Thespiai 227–8
hippic games 215–19, 216n.5, 229–30, 244
homonoia 82–4, 158–9, 200
Huizinga, Johan 251–4
Hygieia 104–6, 124

Idaean Cave 306–9
identity 4–8, 14, 16, 325–6
　Athenian 96, 114
　Boiotian 218–20, 229, 244, 325–6
　of token holders 115
Ilion 259, 266, 271, 279
　Panathenaia festival 266
　sanctuary of Athena Ilias 259, 266, 271
imperial cult 75–6, 298–9, see also neokorate status
incubation 292
inscriptions
　materiality of 3–4, 179, 189–90
　monumentality of 3–4, 15–16, 33–4
　victory 13, 26–7, 36–42
　visibility of 33–4, 54, 146, 189–90, 200, 220–1, 223–4, 226, 230–1, 237, 271, 323–4
Isis 294–5
Isthmian games 51, 53
Italy 29
Itoneion (Sanctuary of Athena Itonia, Koroneia) 220–1, 223–4, 243–4

Julia Domna 145

Kallicrateia 63
Kandidianos of Aphrodisias, boxer 193–4, 197
Karia 182, 199–200
Kibyra 200, 202–3

Kleanax of Kyme 10
Koinon of Asia 60, 63
Koinon/koina of Artists, *see* Artists of Dionysos
Kolb, Frank 251–4
Koroneia 219–21, 221nn.32, 35, 243–4
Kos 256, 259–60, 264, 278–9
　Asklepieia 264–6, 278–9
　sanctuary of Asklepios 256, 259–60, 264–6, 278–9
Kyme 10

Labienus 198–9
Labraunda 259–61, 263, 279
　sanctuary of Zeus Labraundos 259–60, 263
Lagina 251–2, 259, 267, 271–5, 278–9, 325
　Hekatesia-Romaia festival 278–9, 325
　sanctuary of Hekate 251–2, 259, 267, 271–5, 278–9
lamps 6–7, 15, 292, 296–300, 303–6, 308, 313–14
landmark monuments 115–16
Larisa 303–6
Lebadeia 219, 222n.40, 229–30, 239n.124
Lebedos 217
Lentulus, P. Cornelius 232, 237n.114
letters 13, 33–5, 52–9, 197–9, 218, 227
lieux de mémoire 208
light, artificial 15, 291–2, 294–304, 313–15, *see also* lamps, torches
Lindos (Rhodes) 256, 260
　sanctuary of Athena 256, 260
local tradition 156–8
Lokris 217–18, 218n.14
Lysimacheia games 61, 63

Macedonia 217–18, 218n.14, 236
magic 293–4
Magnesia on the Maeander 251–2, 259, 264–71, 278–9
　Leukophryenea festival 278–9
　sanctuary of Artemis Leukophryene 251–2, 259, 267–71, 278–9
Marathonian bull 110
Marcus Aurelius 109
material culture
　agency of 1–2, 9
material turn 6–7, 179
materiality, *see* inscriptions, materiality of
Megalopolis 259–63, 279
　Lykaia festival 260–1
　sanctuary of Zeus Lykaios 260–1
　sanctuary of Zeus Soter 259–61, 263
Melankomas 30–1, 41–2
memory 1–2, 6–7, 14–15, 96, 325–6, *see also* past

Messene 217–18, 218n.14, 298–9, 314
Miletos 10–11, 256, 259–61, 279, 300–3
　Hamilliteria festival 258–60
　sanctuary of Apollo Delphinios 258–60
Miltiades 112–13, 123
Mimes/pantomimes 182, 206–7
Minotaur 105–6, 110, 124
Mithras 290–1, 314–15
Mithridatic Wars 232, 236–7, 239–40, 244
molpoi 258–60
monumentality, *see* inscriptions, monumentality of
Mouseia 214–15, 217–19, 221–2, 225–31, 233–8, 240–1, 244–5
Mummius, L. 232–4
Muses 151, 204–6, 215–17, 225
Mylasa 260, 279, *see also* Labraunda, sanctuary of Zeus Labraundos
mystery cult 290–1, 295, 300, 303–10, 314–15
mystikos agon 56

Naples 59–61
Nemausus 56–7
Nemean games 51, 53
neoi 164, 201–2, 258–60
neokorate status 13–14, 70–1, 73–4, 79, 145–6, 145n.36, 153–4, 158n.98, 165n.127, 330–1
Nikaia 13–14, 70–4, 324, 327
Nike 104–5, 110, 124, 167–8
Nikomedia 13–14, 70–4, 324
Nikopolis 61
numismatics, *see* coinage
nymphaeum 58
Nysa 55–6

Octavian 183, 185, 198–9
oikoumene 15–16, 37–8, 154–6, 250, 271
Oinoanda 2–3, 5, 10–11, 76–7, 145–6, 149, 153–4, 159
Olympian Zeus 238
Olympic Games 51, 53, 59, 215–17, 239n.125
Oppius, Quintus 197–8
Orchomenos (Boiotia) 219, 238–9, 238n.119
Oropos 215, 223–4, 227, 236, 239–40, 244

Palmyra 327–8
Pamboiotia at Koroneia 216n.5, 219–21, 229–30
Panathenaia 60, 97–9, 109–11
panegyris 256–8, 260, 264–6
Panhellenia at Athens 53, 59, 97–8
Panhellenion 59, 122
　archon of the 120–1
pankratiast 56

past
    memories of the Athenian 101, 112–17, 123
    use of 8, 14–16, 146–7, 201, 325–6
pentedrachmia (money distribution) 98n.13
performance theory 138
performers 138–53, 204–7, *see also*
    athletes, Artists of Dionysos, Synod.
Pergamon 190–1, 217, 217n.12, 256, 279
    sanctuary of Asklepios 264
    sanctuary of Athena Polias 264
    sanctuary of Meter Theon at Mamurt
        Kale 259, 263–4, 279
Perge 14, 160–8, 324, 327–8
Perikles 123
Perinthos 84, 86–7
periodos 215–17, 220–1, 221n.36, 223–4, 243–4,
    see also circuit
    Boiotian 240
peristyle, *see* sanctuaries, peristyle *and* temenos,
    peristyle
Persephone 147
Pindar 215–17, 239n.123
Piseas of Aphrodisias, boxer 194, 197
Plancii, of Perge 162
Plarasa 197–200
Plataia 219–21, 243, 311–13
Poseidon 115–16
    Poseidon-Erechtheus, priesthood
        of 112–13, 119
power 7–8, 14
priesthoods 10
prize crowns 79–81, 142–4, 154–6, 165–7
prizes 52–3
Probus 105
processions 8–9, 14, 89–90, 159, 162–7, 169,
    304, 312–13, 326–7
    ephebes 114, 163–4
propylon, propylaea 253–4, 260–3, 271–3, 275–7
prytany 120–1
Ptoia at Akraiphia 10–11, 215, 219, 222n.39,
    229n.80, 230–1, 240–2, 244–5, 323–4
Ptolemy IV 227–9
Puteoli 61, 64
Pylae 60
Pythian Games 51, 53, 56–7, 60, 78–81, 84,
    86–7, 215–17, 227, *see also*
    Apolloneia Pythia
Pythokles of Hermione 224–6, 224n.56,
    229, 240–1

Rhapsodes 224–5, 233–4, 240–1,
    243n.142, 325–6
ritual 7–8, 14–15, 76–7, 206, 278–9
    'interaction rituals' 254–5

ritual space 252–5, 263, 266–7, 271–3,
    275–80
Romaia at Thebes 232, 234–8, 240–1, 244
Rome
    as centre of power 53, 55–6, 59–61, 63, 145,
        197–200, 218–19, 231–43, 325

sacred circles, *see* circles, sacred
sacrifices 10, 157–8, 162–3, 165–7, 292, see also
    synthusia
Salutaris, Gaius Vibius 8, 31–2, 120n.104, 121,
    see also Ephesos
Samothrace 300, 303, 313
sanctuaries 7–8, 15–16
    in the landscape 250–1
    peristyle 251–3, 255–66, 277–80
Sardis 54–6
Saturnalia 327–8
Sebasta
    at Aphrodisias 181–2
    at Naples 29–32, 61
Selene 104–5, 124
senatus consultum 197–8, 237, 273–5
senses 314–15
Septimius Severus 142–6
Serapis 101–2, 104–6, 124
Severans 81–90, 144–6, 167–8
Severus Alexander 199
Sikyon 217–18
Smintheia Pauleia 57–9
social advancement 30–1, 41–2
social meaning 14, 138, 168–9, 244, 322
Soteria
    at Akraiphia 232–4, 232n.87, 236, 244
    at Delphi 218, 224–5, 229
souvenirs 328–9
spatial dynamics 3–4, 6–8, 15–16, 139–40
spatial turn 6–7, 139
spectacles, Roman 11–12, 193, 329
spectators 7–8, 328–9
stadium 255, 260, 262–3, 277
staircases 7–8
Statilius Taurus, T. 241
statues 8, 146–7, 153, 193–7, 203–4, 207–8,
    326–7, *see also* emperor, image of
    crowning of 190–1
    torch-bearing 300–3
Stratonikeia (Karia) 251–2, 264–7, 271–5,
    see also Lagina, sanctuary of Hekate
symbolon 97n.3
Synod
    of Artists, *see* Artists of Dionysos
    of athletes 42, 51–2, 56, 58–9, 64
    of musicians of Dionysos Choreios 54–5

Synod (*cont.*)
   of *technitai* 52–9, 64, *see also* Artists of Dionysos
   of the *oikoumene* 218–19, 240, 244–5
   of victors 152
synthusia 153–60, 202–3, see also *theoroi*

Tabai 200, 202–3
Tarentum 59–61
Tarsos 31–2
technitai, *see* Artists of Dionysos
Telesphoros 104–6, 124
temenos 250–1, 253–4, 256, 258–63, 268–9, 271–3, 275–7
   peristyle-temenos 256
Teos 217
Termessos 10
theatre 14, 16, 137–70, 179–81, 218–19, 255, 262–4, 324, 330
theatron 264–6, 271–5
Thebes 215–17, 222–5, 229n.76, 230–41, 243–5, 323–4, *see also* Delphi, Theban treasury
Themistokles 14, 117, 325–6
   type on tokens and coins 105, 107–8, 111–13, 123–4
Theoi Sebastoi 185, 188
Theophoroumene 103–4, 116, 124
theorikon 97–100, *see also* tokens for the *theorikon*
theoroi 256–8, 264–6, 270, 273–5, 278–9, 290, see also *synthusia*
Theos Hypsistos 290–1, 297, 313–14
Theseia 107–8, 110, 122
Theseus 14, 112, 117, 325–6
   and the Minotaur (type on coins and tokens) 105, 107, 107n.43, 110–13, 122, 124
   as a model for ephebes 107–8
Thesiadae 107–8, 111–12
Thespiai 214–15, 217–18, 221–2, 225–9, 232–3, 236, 240–1, 243
Tiberius 5
titles 70–1
Titus 30–1, 41–2

tokens 6–7, 14, 16, 95–124, 327
   as entrance tickets to festivals 100, *see also* festival tokens
   as entrance tickets to sanctuaries 115
   assimilated to coins 106–8, 111, 114
   countermarks on 100–1, 104, 106, 109–10, 119
   distribution 109–10, 119–20
   for the *theorikon* 99–100
   imagery 101–6, 110, 114–15, 117–18, 122–3
   issuing authority of 106–9, 119
   of Roman Ephesos 118–19
   personal names inscribed on 116–19, 121, see also *gerousia*
   from the Stoa of Attalos 95–7, 100–6, 108–9, 122, *see also* Athens, Stoa of Attalos
torches 15, 290, 292, 296–307, 309–14
   torchbearer 149–50, 291–2, 297–9, 314
   torch-bearing statue 300–3, 310–11, 313–14
   torch-race 290–1
Trajan 31–2, 190–1, 199
Trebius Sergianus 56
Trebonianus Gallus 58
Trieterides of Dionysos Kadmeios 215, 218–19, 221–5, 229–31, 229n.80, 233–8
Triton 101–2, 116–17, 123–4
Trophonios 294–5, 315
trumpeter 149
Turner, Victor 138
Tyche 101–2, 104–5, 124, 145, 154–6, 161, 167–8

Ulpius Appuleius Eurykles, M. 61, 63

Valerian 78–9, 102–3
Vedius Antoninus, P. 11–12
victors 10, 13, 16, 149–53, 156–7

women 296–7, 314

xystarch 52–3

Zeus 104–5, 110, 124, 306–9, 311–13
Zoilos, Gaius Iulius 183–5, 189–91, 207–8